BIRNBAUM'S

2015

Walt Disney World®

Expert Advice From the Inside Source

THE OFFICIAL GUIDE

Wendy Lefkon   EDITORIAL DIRECTOR

Jill Safro   EDITOR

Jessica Ward   CONTRIBUTING EDITOR

Pam Brandon   CONTRIBUTING EDITOR

Clark Wakabayashi   DESIGNER

Alexandra Mayes Birnbaum   CONSULTING EDITOR

Stephen Birnbaum   FOUNDING EDITOR

Disney
EDITIONS

NEW YORK • LOS ANGELES

Contents

7 **Getting Ready to Go**

Here is all the practical information you need to organize a Walt Disney World visit down to the smallest detail: when to go, how to get there, how to save money and work within a budget, and how to book Fastpass+ assignments for favorite attractions; plus sample schedules and hints for parents, travelers with disabilities, singles, and older visitors.

61 **Transportation & Accommodations**

Two big questions about Walt Disney World are where to stay and how to get around. Accommodations range from concierge suites to modest campsites, with thousands of rooms and villas in between. Our guide describes every Disney resort, with details presented in a handy chart. And we explain the World's vast transportation system, to boot.

111 **Magic Kingdom**

The enchantment of Walt Disney World is most apparent in the wealth of attractions and amusements that fill this, the most famous entertainment zone of all. Our land-by-land guide describes all there is to see and do, where to shop, and how to avoid the crowds, plus plenty of other insider tips and the scoop on the "new" Fantasyland.

141 **Epcot**

A gleaming silver geosphere introduces Disney's wonderland of discovery— an ambitious exploration of the world of the future as well as the present. Future World and World Showcase offer every visitor the opportunity to be a global and cerebral voyager, without setting foot outside Florida. Here's how to make the most of this uniquely fascinating destination.

173 **Disney's Hollywood Studios**

Now's your chance to be part of Hollywood's golden years. Everything from the magic of animation to the excitement of daring stunts and special effects is waiting to be enjoyed. There are also opportunities to go behind the scenes, bond with Disney characters, and even experience a thrill ride or two. We've developed strategies for seeing this Tinseltown, ensuring the most fun and the least time standing around.

191 **Disney's Animal Kingdom**

The most sprawling member of Walt Disney World's theme park lineup celebrates the circle of life and all the wonders of the animal world. Amid nature's soothing majesty, you'll experience a stirring African safari, dodge dastardly dinosaurs, and ride raging rapids. Our detailed coverage guarantees a fun-filled trip to a place where humans are humbly reminded of their tenuous position in the food chain.

209 Everything Else in the World

Beyond the theme park boundaries lie countless acres full of just the sorts of wonders for which Disney is famous: state-of-the-art water parks and an entertainment, shopping, and dining district among them. So if you want to ride down watery slides, dance the night away, shop at elegant boutiques, pamper yourself at a spa, or even learn a few tricks of the trade by slipping behind the scenes, this chapter will help you find your way.

235 Sports

Walt Disney World has more tennis courts and golf greens than most posh resorts, plus plenty of places for boating, biking, horseback riding, swimming, and fishing. Here's how to combine these options with the rest of the WDW fun.

243 Good Meals, Great Times

Restaurants around Disney World property run the gamut from simple snack shops to bastions of haute cuisine. Choices are nearly endless, so we've organized them in an area-by-area directory that lets you know where each restaurant is located and what specialties it offers, and a roundup of the dining spots we consider Birnbaum's Bests. We also tell you about dinner shows, the best family fare, where to dine with Disney characters, and where to enjoy an after-dinner drink.

309 Disney Cruise Line

Many guests choose to make a Walt Disney World visit more magical by pairing it with a cruise to the Caribbean or the Bahamas—the ultimate Land and Sea vacation, Disney-style. This "bonus" chapter tells you how to plan it.

344 Trip Tracker

Organize the details of your Walt Disney World vacation in the soon-to-be personalized Trip Tracker. Be sure to jot down all your Fastpass+ assignments!

357 Coupons

We've stuffed the final pages of this book with valuable coupons to help you save hundreds of dollars on Walt Disney World food, merchandise, and more.

What's New?

To spotlight attractions making their debut, listings are marked with the stamp shown below. Look for it throughout the book. Here are a few highlights:

- ❤ **Celebrate the Magic castle show** (page 135)
- ❤ **Food Trucks at Downtown Disney** (page 266)
- ❤ **Four Seasons Orlando (at Walt Disney World)** (page 104)
- ❤ **House of Blues Smokehouse** (page 267)
- ❤ **Kabuki Cafe** (page 258)
- ❤ **Marketplace Co-op** (page 213)
- ❤ **Piston Cup: Richard Petty—Junior Ride-Along Program** (page 242)
- ❤ **Seven Dwarfs Mine Train** (page 127)
- ❤ **Spice Road Table** (page 256)
- ❤ **Winged Encounters—The Kingdom Takes Flight** (page 197)

For Steve, who merely made all this possible.

ISBN 978-1-4231-9410-1
G942-9090-6-14220

Printed in the United States of America

Other 2015 Birnbaum's Official Disney Guides:

Disneyland
Walt Disney World for Kids

A Word from the Editor

For some of us, our first Walt Disney World experience dates back to 1971, the year this new "Disneyland in Florida" made its debut. At that time, the Magic Kingdom was the only theme park to explore. Nonetheless, for those who came, it was love at first sight, and we've returned again and again. Fast-forward four decades and Disney World boasts four theme parks, two water parks, dozens of hotels, hundreds of restaurants, and much more.

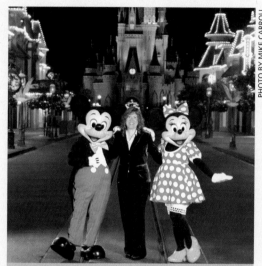

Editor Jill Safro consults with Mickey and Minnie, the ultimate Disney insiders.

Never before has there been so much incentive to visit (and revisit) the memory-making capital of the world. Last year Magic Kingdom completed the final stage of its unprecedented expansion with the addition of the Seven Dwarfs Mine Train coaster. It joined park newcomers such as the Festival of Fantasy parade and Celebrate the Magic—a merry mix of music and animation that uses Cinderella Castle as its canvas. Over at Disney's Hollywood Studios, Tower of Terror remains atop most thrill-seekers' must-do lists and Toy Story Mania! continues to dazzle guests of all ages. At Epcot, a revamped Test Track attraction is wowing a new generation, while Soarin' still sends scads of giddy guests to happy heights. The Epcot International Food & Wine Festival gets bigger and better each year. Of course, that's just the tip of the iceberg, as so much of Walt Disney World has grown and evolved since our last edition. We are privileged and proud to provide readers with our extensively researched, insider look at some of the most cherished attractions, resorts, and eateries on Earth.

When Steve Birnbaum launched this guide back in 1981, he made it clear what was expected of anyone who worked on it. The book would be meticulously revised each year, leaving no attraction untested, no snack or meal untasted, no hotel untried. First-hand experiences like these, accumulated over the years, make this book the most authoritative guide to the World. Our expertise, however, is not achieved by being escorted through back doors of attractions (although we would enjoy that). Instead, we wait in lines with everyone else, always hoping to have a Disney experience like that of any other guest. This year, in addition to investigating all of the nooks and crannies of Walt's vast World, we bonded with fellow park-goers while learning to navigate the ambitious new Fastpass+ attraction reservation system. And we'll continue to keep a close eye on it and other additions to the Walt Disney World vacation-planning universe—homework we're happy to do for readers like you.

After more than 43 fun-filled years, the World has vastly expanded—and so has our knowledge of the most popular vacation destination on the planet. On some occasions we've encountered sweltering weather and swelling crowds—times when even the happiest of travelers can turn into Grumpy for a moment or two. Had we known then what we know now, we could have spared ourselves some trying experiences. In one case, a staffer waited more than an hour to take a tour at the Studios. Standing in line with a notebook, she was asked by another guest if there was a quiz at the end. When she explained what she was doing, he expressed surprise to learn that she was waiting with the masses. But that's always been our strategy. We believe the best way to gather useful advice for a Walt Disney World guest is to be one. Over and over again!

Take Our Advice

We've done our best to keep you from making any tactical mistakes. We realize that even the most meticulous vacation planner needs detailed, accurate, and objective information to prepare a successful itinerary. To achieve that goal, we encourage the sharing of insight and information from Walt Disney World staffers—but the decision of whether or not to include such information is entirely up to the discretion of this book's editor.

To that end, we have packaged handy bits of advice in the form of sample itineraries and "hot tips" throughout the book. This advice comes directly from the copious notes we've taken during our thousands of days spent in Walt Disney World. We've also used our "Birnbaum's Best" stamp of approval wherever we deemed it appropriate, highlighting our favorite attractions and restaurants—the crowd-pleasers we believe stand head, shoulders, and ears above the rest.

You, the reader, benefit from the combination of our many years of experience that, together with our access to current insider information, makes this guide unique. We like to think it's indispensable, but we'll let you be the judge of that a few hundred pages from now.

Credit Where Credit Is Due

Enormous thanks to the teams of dedicated, detail-conscious Walt Disney World cast members from Guest Communications, the Disney Reservation Center, Food & Beverage, Merchandise, Resort Operations, Sports & Recreation, Attractions Operations, Disney Cruise Line, Disney Vacation Club, Marketing, and Disney Parks Synergy.

Kudos to Michelle Olveira for her skilled fact-checking, and to Tracey Randinelli for her meticulous proofreading. Thanks also to copy editor extraordinaire Diane Hodges, and to Jerry Gonzalez, Marybeth Tregarthen, Jennifer Eastwood, and Dushawn Ward for their editorial support and production panache.

Heartfelt thanks to our photography team: Mike Carroll, Stacey Cook, Irene Ferdinand, Ana Rivera, and Lori Loftis—and, of course, Mickey Mouse and Minnie Mouse.

Hats off to those for whom doing Walt Disney World research is truly a labor of love. The "volunteer" class of 2015 includes the Safro family (Roy, Irene, Joy, Hayden Fullerton, and Delaney Irene), the Henning family (Amy, Chris, Avery, Elle, and Reid), the Lagano family (Judy, Chris, Jessica, Max, and Kyle), Linda Verdon, Margaret Verdon, Trace Schielzo, Heidi Munyer, Susan Kiernan, Denise Kiernan, Joe D'Agnese, and Christina Fontana.

Of course, no list of acknowledgments would be complete without mentioning our founding editor, Steve Birnbaum, whose spirit, wisdom, and humor still infuse these pages, as well as Alexandra Mayes Birnbaum, who continues to be a guiding light—to say nothing of being a careful reader of every word.

The Last Word

Finally, it's important to remember that every worthwhile travel guide is a living enterprise; the book you hold in your hands is our best effort at explaining how to enjoy Walt Disney World at this moment, but its text is in no way etched in stone. Disney is constantly changing and growing, and in each annual edition we refine and expand our material to serve your needs even better. For this year's edition, though, this must be the final word.

Have a great visit!

— Jill Safro, Editor

DON'T FORGET TO WRITE!

No contribution is of greater value to us in preparing the next edition of this book than your comments on what we have written and on your own experiences at Walt Disney World. Please share your insights with us by writing to:

Jill Safro, Editor
Birnbaum's Walt Disney World 2015
Disney Editions
125 West End Ave., 3rd Fl.
New York, NY 10023

Getting Ready to Go

8   **When to Go**

14   **How to Get There**

17   **Planning Ahead**

21   **Theme Park Tickets**

28   **Money-Saving Tips**

32   **Sample Schedules**

46   **Customized Travel Tips**

The key to a fabulous vacation at Walt Disney World is advance planning. This remarkably varied complex is too vast and diverse to allow a spontaneous visit to be undertaken with much success—especially when you consider the rapid rate at which the World has expanded. That does not mean that even the most casual visitors can't have some significant fun, but they are bound to have regrets about things they missed because of time pressures or a simple lack of information. The purpose of this guide is to eliminate potential frustration while getting the biggest bang for your vacation buck.

What follows, then, is meant to provide a sensible scheme for planning a satisfying visit to Walt Disney World, one that will offer the most fun and the least amount of disappointment. But how do you know which of the countless activities will be the most enjoyable for you and your family? Do your homework. The best strategy is to make sure you have a clear idea of all that is available long before you arrive in the Orlando area.

When to Go

When talk finally turns to the best time to make a trip to Walt Disney World, Christmas and Easter are often mentioned, as well as the traditional summer vacation period—especially if there are children in the family. But there is also good reason to avoid these periods, namely the tremendous crowds they attract. And when Disney World is crowded, it can be very crowded, indeed. On the busiest days, visitors may wait more than two hours to experience the most popular attractions when waiting in lines. That's at least twice as long as during less busy times of the year. Weekends, in general, are quite popular with locals. Monday through Wednesday are generally quieter.

Considering seasonal hours, weather, crowd patterns, and Disney resort rates, optimal times to visit Disney are usually mid-January through early February, late April through late May, and September through December (except Martin Luther King Day/weekend, Thanksgiving and Christmas weeks).

Note that during some of the less crowded times of the year—particularly during the winter—some attractions are closed for renovations. In addition, water parks are often closed for refurbishment during cooler months. Call 407-824-4321, or check *www.disneyworld.com* for a current schedule, updated each season.

Mid-November through December is a festive time of year the world over, and Disney World is no exception. The theme parks are decorated to the nines for the holiday season. Epcot holds stirring Christmas concerts, and the Magic Kingdom drapes Cinderella Castle in thousands of sparkling lights. Many other special events are held during this period, including Mickey's Very Merry Christmas Party in the

Magic Kingdom (a separate admission ticket is required). The party brings a dusting of "snow" to Main Street from about 7 P.M. to midnight for several days between mid-November and the first three weeks of December. It also features holiday shows around the park, including Mickey's Once Upon a Christmastime Parade, plus a unique fireworks show: Holiday Wishes. Select performances from Mickey's Very Merry Christmas Party are also staged in the park during regular hours on the days leading up to,

including, and following Christmas. Note that this event is popular and usually sells out way ahead of time. Get tickets in advance by calling 407-W-DISNEY (934-7639). It's usually easier to snag tickets for dates earlier in the season.

Epcot celebrates with Holidays Around the World, including the nightly Candlelight Processional, complete with a mass choir, 50-piece orchestra, and a reading of the story of Christmas by a celebrity narrator. Dinner packages are available for some World Showcase restaurants. (We recommend the dinner package: It guarantees seating for dinner as well as preferred seating at the Candlelight Processional. Without a package, you should arrive at least two hours before showtime or risk being shut out of your preferred performance.) Disney's Hollywood Studios features the Osborne Family Spectacle of Dancing Lights, a grand display of lights depicting holiday scenes. For updated information regarding the dates and location of this perennially popular, sparkly spectacular, visit *www.disneyworld.com*.

Downtown Disney gets into the spirit with "Festival of the Seasons," featuring twinkling lights and jolly entertainment. There are holiday decorations at each WDW hotel, too, including a Victorian Christmas at the Grand Floridian, a seaside party at the Yacht and Beach Club, and a Cajun holiday at Port Orleans Riverside.

For reservations, call 407-W-DISNEY (934-7639), a travel agent, or the Walt Disney Travel Company at 407-828-8101. Visit *www.disneyworld.com*, or call 407-939-7630 for additional information. Special-event tickets are sold separately.

HOT TIP!

The period of time between the end of Thanksgiving weekend and the week before Christmas is one of the less crowded and most festive times of the year. It's a wonderful time to visit.

Crowd Patterns

Day-to-Day Trends

In general, the weekends tend to be among the most crowded days at Walt Disney World theme parks, followed by Thursdays and Fridays. Morning through early afternoon is a bustling time for the theme parks and their respective "E-ticket" attractions. Days that offer Extra Magic Hours tend to be more crowded at their respective theme parks (see page 22). When the weather's steamy, the water parks tend to pack them in—so be sure to get an early start if you're headed to Blizzard Beach or Typhoon Lagoon.

When the time comes to plot an itinerary, it's helpful to know about crowd patterns beyond the four theme parks as well. As a rule, Downtown Disney and Disney's water parks host their largest throngs on weekends. Of course, in these circles, a bigger crowd could possibly mean a better time. Golfers should note that weekend tee times are typically in the highest demand, while Monday and Tuesday tee times tend to be the easiest to come by.

Seasonal Shifts

The chart below indicates the density of crowds in the theme parks throughout the year. Though it's tough to generalize about a property as vast and ever-changing as Walt Disney World—special events (such as the Disney Marathon and Epcot's Food & Wine Festival) and package deals can swell park attendance during a period typically marked by smaller crowds—the chart highlights historic trends.

Least Crowded means that there will be lines, but most shows and attractions can be visited with a bit less waiting than during busier times of the year.

Average Attendance refers to times when there are lots of people around, but lines are relatively manageable.

Most Crowded reflects times when lines at popular attractions can mean a wait of as much as two to three hours (or more). As a rule, when school is out, the crowds are most definitely in at Walt Disney World.

Least Crowded

- 2nd week of January through 1st week of February (excluding Marathon Weekend)
- Week before Labor Day until the start of Epcot's Food & Wine Festival
- Period after Food & Wine Festival ends until Thanksgiving week
- Week after Thanksgiving through week before Christmas

Average Attendance

- 1st week of January
- 2nd week of February until Presidents' week
- End of February through 2nd week of March
- Last week of April through May
- Thanksgiving week (excluding Thanksgiving Day, which is "most crowded")

Most Crowded

- All major holidays
- Presidents' week
- Marathon Weekend
- 3rd week of March through 3rd week of April
- June through the 3rd week of August
- Epcot Food & Wine Festival
- Christmas through New Year's Day
- Any time school's out for vacation

Holidays & Special Events

Special events are staged at Walt Disney World throughout the year, not only to mark holidays but also to celebrate other interests. The dates and details below are subject to change without notice; call 407-824-4321 to confirm, or check out *www.disneyworld.com* for up-to-the-minute information about specific events.

JANUARY

Walt Disney World Marathon Weekend

(January 8–12): Some 20,000 entrants run through several theme parks and many other areas of the World during this 26.2-mile race (January 12). Characters and cast members are on hand to inspire runners. Similar hoopla surrounds the half marathon (January 11). There is a 10K run (January 10) and a 5K family run on January 9. (It's okay to walk the 5K, but you must maintain a 16-minute mile.) Hard-core runners may take the "Dopey Challenge"— all of the aforementioned events within the pacing requirements—and earn a Dopey Challenge finisher medal. Packages are available. Call 407-939-4786 for package details or to book. For additional marathon weekend event information and schedules, call 407-938-3398, or visit *www.rundisney.com* for details. Note that hotel rooms are in high demand for this event. Reserve yours as early as possible. For additional details on other Walt Disney World running events, visit *www.rundisney.com*.

MARCH–JUNE

Atlanta Braves Spring Training (Late February–March): Play ball! Having weathered a long winter, giddy baseball fans flock to the ESPN Wide World of Sports complex to enjoy a dose of America's favorite pastime. For information, visit *www.espnwwos.com/atlantabraves*.

Saint Patrick's Day (March 17): Everyone is Irish on Saint Patrick's Day—especially at the Mighty St. Patrick's Festival at Downtown Disney. The family-friendly festivities include music, dancing, dining, and more. Of course, every day is St. Patrick's Day at Raglan Road, the neighborhood's Irish pub. Epcot's United Kingdom pavilion marks the day with Irish dining, dancing, and green beer.

Easter (April 20): Most of the Disney parks stay open late during the two weeks straddling the Easter holiday. The Easter Bunny greets guests in the Magic Kingdom. Epcot hosts a park-wide "Egg-stravaganza" hunt—cost is about $5 for a map with stickers (find all the eggs and win a prize). And many of the WDW resorts offer special Easter-themed fun. Catholic and Protestant services may be offered at the Contemporary resort. Call 407-W-DISNEY for specifics. Keep in mind that this is an extremely busy time to visit.

Epcot International Flower & Garden Festival (March 4–May 17): Epcot is blooming with elaborate gardens (including more than 30 million fragrant blossoms) and topiary displays, behind-the-scenes tours, gardening workshops, concerts, and guest speakers. Learn from the experts how to create a gorgeous garden. Be sure to pick up a Garden Passport and get it stamped as you explore the Outdoor Kitchens throughout the day. Passports are free and may be found at the Festival Center, all Disney Vacation Club kiosks, all Outdoor Kitchen stations, and many merchandise locations. Each Outdoor Kitchen has its own unique stamp.

Another popular element of the Flower and Garden Festival is the Flower Power Concert Series, presented at the America Gardens

Theater by the American Adventure pavilion. Past performers have included The Village People, The Loving Spoonful, Paul Revere & the Raiders, and Herman's Hermits starring Peter Noone. Shows are included with Epcot admission and seats are first-come, first-served.

Mother's Day (May 10): Celebrate Mom by treating her to a special Mother's Day buffet. Several WDW restaurants, such as Animal Kingdom Lodge's Boma—Flavors of Africa, Chef Mickey's and The Wave at the Contemporary, Yachtsman Grille at Yacht Club (brunch), and the Swan's Garden Grove (dinner), have been known to offer Mother's Day meals. For details on the 2015 options, call 407-WDW-DINE (939-3463).

Star Wars Weekends (weekends mid-May to mid-June): The Force is strong this time of year, when Disney's Hollywood Studios salutes the beloved film franchise Star Wars. Weekend fanfests feature appearances by actors and iconic characters from the movies, plus photo opportunities, trivia contests, and more. Actor meet-and-greets are extremely popular. Get there as early as possible! And visit *www.disneytheforce.com* for additional details.

Sounds Like Summer Concert Series (June –July): An Epcot annual tradition, rock 'n' roll tribute bands have guests dancing to the likes of the Bee Gees, Bon Jovi, the Eagles, U2, and more. Nightly shows are presented at the America Gardens Theater at the American Adventure Pavilion. There are usually three shows a night, weather permitting. Seats are on a first-come, first-served basis, so get there early.

JULY

Fourth of July Celebration: Double-size fireworks presentations over the Magic Kingdom, Epcot, and Disney's Hollywood Studios make for a very colorful night. Ben Franklin, Betsy Ross, and Disney characters greet guests at Epcot's American Adventure pavilion throughout the day. That pavilion's America Gardens Theater hosts a patriotic show featuring the Spirit of America Fife and Drum Core and an expanded cast of the Voices of Liberty. The evening's presentation of IllumiNations (Epcot's nightly lagoon show) may feature a patriotic finale. This is an exceptionally busy time to visit Walt Disney World—possibly the busiest.

SEPTEMBER–NOVEMBER

Night of Joy (September): Two nights of celebration highlight contemporary Christian music presented live in the Magic Kingdom.

For dates and tickets, call 407-827-7200. This popular event attracts a bit of a rowdy crowd (of mostly teens and young adults).

Epcot International Food & Wine Festival (September 25–November 16): Epcot's World Showcase celebrates the flavors of different countries (even those not usually represented around the lagoon) through tastings (about $2 to $8 per sample), demos from top chefs, and wine and cooking seminars. It's a satisfying way in which to wander World Showcase. For additional details or to make a reservation for a special event, visit *www.epcotfoodfestival.com*.

A Tisket, A Tasket ...

. . . a "Welcome to Walt Disney World Basket." The Disney Florist can deliver this and a striking array of themed surprises to any room on Disney property (and many that aren't). There's no occasion they can't rise to—from a birthday to Earth Day, from engagements to golden wedding anniversaries. A call to the Disney Florist (the only one serving Walt Disney World) can yield custom-tailored bouquets, baskets, and even Christmas trees. (They also have a division dedicated exclusively to Walt Disney World engagements.)

Not satisfied with a simple delivery to a resort room? The Florist folks encourage creativity. Got a favorite Disney character? Into the basket he or she goes! One package known as "Create a Fairy Tale" (complete with slipper and tiara) can actually be delivered to guests enjoying a romantic carriage ride.

For more information or to place an order, call 407-939-4438 (daily from 8 A.M. to 6 P.M.), or visit *www.disneyflorist.com*.

Halloween (late September–October): The festivities vary a bit from year to year. Here's a sampling of what to expect:

Fort Wilderness Resort and Campground usually hosts a pumpkin-carving contest and a kids' costume contest, followed by a screening of a scary movie. It also offers Halloween-themed wagon rides with storytelling and surprises along the way. Animal Kingdom may also invite guests to trick-or-treat.

The Magic Kingdom will play host to its Halloween spectacular, **Mickey's Not-So-Scary Halloween Party**, September through October. The special-ticket activities include a costume parade, dancing, appearances by Disney villains, trick-or-treating, and Halloween fireworks. This is an extremely popular Magic Kingdom event. Purchase tickets as far in advance as possible. And don't forget to wear a costume. Note that guests with tickets to the Halloween Party may be able to enter the park at 4 P.M. (Ask when you buy your ticket.) As a spooky bonus, **Mickey's Boo-to-You Halloween Parade** makes its way through the Kingdom during the Halloween party. For information about dates on which the not-so-scary party takes place, call 407-827-7200. The Magic Kingdom may offer a holiday version of the Jungle Cruise, aka the Jingle Cruise.

Festival of the Masters (early November): This three-day fine arts show draws more than 150 of the world's top artists to Downtown Disney. The outdoor festival features unique and limited-edition paintings, photographs, sculpture, jewelry, and more. There are activities for guests of all ages, plus live music. For details, visit *www.disneyworld.com/art*.

Thanksgiving (November 27): All WDW restaurants are open on Turkey Day, many of them offering Thanksgiving specialties. For details, call 407-WDW-DINE (939-3463).

Old Spice Classic (November 27–30): This early-season college basketball tournament features 8 NCAA teams and 12 games. Each team competes in one game a day and advances through a bracket-tournament format. Book your hotel early if you want to stay at a WDW resort for this popular weekend. For details and ticket information, visit *www.oldspiceclassic.com*.

NOVEMBER–DECEMBER

Disney's Magical Holidays: Decorations and festivities abound in WDWs parks and resorts. The Magic Kingdom park hosts **Mickey's Very Merry Christmas Party** on several nights from mid-November through the first three weeks of December, complete with snow flurries on Main Street and hot cocoa. Entertainment for the special-ticket party includes **Mickey's Once Upon a Christmastime Parade** and a special edition of the Wishes fireworks show; select performances are staged during regular hours just before Christmas. (Guests with tickets to the Christmas Party may be able to enter the Magic Kingdom as early as 4 P.M.) Epcot's **Holidays Around the World** (November 29–December 30) features the Christmas Candlelight Processional, including a choral concert, plus a celebrity narrator who reads the story of Christmas. The event is included with park admission, but seating is limited and it is extremely popular. Arrive at least an hour before showtime, or book a dinner package (which combines dinner at a World Showcase eatery with guaranteed Processional seating). For details, call 407-939-3463.

Downtown Disney gets into the spirit with **Festival of the Seasons**, a cheery mix of twinkling lights, seasonal music, a towering tree, and visits from the North Pole's most famous resident. Past years have brought carolers, stilt-walkers, and a lively holiday dance party.

The Osborne Family Spectacle of Dancing Lights (November–January) is a big crowd-pleaser. This dazzling light display brightens Disney's Hollywood Studios with millions of lights "performing" in synchronized motion with music. It's presented in the Streets of America backlot area. *Note that at press time there was a possibility that the Osborne Lights would not be presented in 2015.*

BIRNBAUM'S ★BEST★

New Year's Eve Celebration (December 31): There are extra-large fireworks displays over the Magic Kingdom, Epcot, and Disney's Hollywood Studios (though there are no fireworks at all at Animal Kingdom—imagine the stampede!). These parks stay open until approximately 1 A.M. (It varies from year to year.) Many of the resort restaurants, as well as the nightspots at Downtown Disney, also welcome the new year Disney style. La Nouba by Cirque du Soleil features a festive finale to ring in the new year (Downtown Disney, West Side).

Keeping WDW Hours

Since operating hours fluctuate quite a bit, call 407-824-4321 or visit *www.disneyworld.com* for current schedules.

THEME PARKS: Disney theme park hours vary seasonally. In May, September, October, parts of November and December, and all of January, the Magic Kingdom is usually open from 9 A.M. to 8 P.M.; Epcot is typically open from 9 A.M. to 9 P.M. (some Future World attractions close at 7 P.M.), later during peak seasons; Disney's Hollywood Studios is open from 9 A.M. until about an hour after sunset; and Animal Kingdom is usually open from 9 A.M. until about 5 P.M. The parks take turns offering Extra Magic Hours throughout the week. That is, on any given day, one of the parks may allow Disney World resort guests to enter an hour early or stay in the park for two hours after it closes to the public. Participating Walt Disney World resorts have schedules at the front desk. (Note that while Extra Magic Hours are—by far—the best time to visit for guests craving shorter lines, some attractions do not operate during EMH.)

The Magic Kingdom keeps later hours through summer and other busy periods, including Christmas and Easter weeks. The parks may be open until 1 A.M. on New Year's Eve. Disney's Hollywood Studios often stays open until 10 or 11 P.M. in the summer, too.

DOWNTOWN DISNEY MARKETPLACE: Shops are open from about 9:30 A.M. until 11 P.M. Sunday through Thursday; 11:30 P.M. on Friday and Saturday. Restaurant hours vary.

DOWNTOWN DISNEY WEST SIDE: At the AMC cineplex, movies begin as early as 10 A.M. Restaurants are open from about 11:30 A.M. to midnight. Shops are open from about 10:30 A.M. to 11 P.M. (midnight on Friday and Saturday).

WATER PARKS: Water parks are usually open from about 10 A.M. to 5 P.M., but extend hours during the hot summer months. Check for morning Extra Magic Hour on select "peak" days.

WDW PARK TRANSPORTATION: Bus, boat, and monorail transportation service begin one hour prior to park opening time and continues until about one hour after the parks close. Boats and monorails do not operate for Extra Magic Hours. For specifics, check with the lobby concierge at any WDW resort.

WDW Weather

	TEMPERATURE AVERAGE		RAINFALL AVERAGE
	HIGH	LOW	INCHES
JANUARY	71	49	2.4
FEBRUARY	74	52	2.5
MARCH	78	56	3.8
APRIL	83	60	2.7
MAY	88	66	3.4
JUNE	91	72	7.6
JULY	92	74	7.2
AUGUST	92	74	7.1
SEPTEMBER	90	72	6.1
OCTOBER	85	66	3.3
NOVEMBER	79	59	2.2
DECEMBER	73	52	2.6

How to Get There

By Car

While most visitors to the Orlando area fly in, some prefer to drive. If you opt for a road trip, figure on logging no more than 350 to 400 miles a day—a distance that won't wear you down so much that you can't enjoy your trip.

Contact state tourist boards to inquire about the availability of free maps; for a Florida map and guide, call 888-735-2872, or pick up a copy of *Rand McNally Road Atlas* or the *AAA North*

American Road Atlas; both are sold in bookstores. If you plan to navigate with GPS, note Walt Disney World's address in the Hot Tip on the top of page 15.

From Orlando International Airport*

By car: During rush hour, take the airport's South Exit to the Central Florida Greeneway (Route 417) to Route 536, which leads to Walt Disney World. The tolls run about $4.

For the shortest route, take the North Exit to Route 528, going west toward Tampa. Pick up I-4 west, and go to a WDW exit. Tolls are about $4. The route is usually heavily trafficked, but manageable during non-rush periods of the day. It's busiest on weekday mornings and evenings and any time when a theme park is scheduled to open or close.

By Disney's Magical Express: This tailor-made, complimentary transportation program is available to guests staying at select Disney resorts. For more information, turn to page 16.

By car service: Florida Towncar offers efficient, direct service to Disney area resorts. And they offer our readers a special rate, too! Simply mention the Birnbaum Guide when you book your ride and expect a round-trip rate (to and from *Orlando International Airport only*) of about $85 for up to five passengers (that's $15 off). Call 407-277-5466 (from Florida) or 800-525-7246 (from out of state) up to 24 hours ahead, or visit *www.floridatowncar.com*. Online reservations should be made at least 24 hours in advance.

Reliable towncar service is also available from Noris Limousines. Drivers take guests directly to their resort. The company also offers a special round-trip rate for Birnbaum readers—mention this book and expect to pay about $120 for up to four passengers for a towncar, or about $225 for a limo for up to 8 passengers. Reservations are required and cancellations must be made at least 48 hours ahead. Call 407-240-4533, or visit *www.norislimousines.com*. Prices may increase if there is a significant jump in prices at the pump.

By shuttle: At Orlando International Airport, Mears Motor Shuttle offers vans and buses 24 hours a day. It serves the Swan and Dolphin, Hotel Plaza Blvd. properties, and other non-Disney area hotels. Shuttles make multiple stops; a trip can take an hour or more. On the return trip, Mears requires guests be picked up at least 3–4 hours prior to flight times. Reservations should be made 24 hours ahead. There is often a long wait at the airport (even with a reservation), and employee attitudes fluctuate wildly. This is not our preferred mode of transit.

The shuttle cost to most hotels is $22 one way, $36 round-trip per adult; $17 one way, $27 round-trip per child ages 4 through 11; free for children under 4. Fares to International Drive properties are a little lower. There may be a long wait to get on a shuttle at the airport, and service is not direct. Call 407-423-5566 for information, or visit *www.mearstransportation.com*.

By taxi: Metered cabs may cost between $60 and $70 each way, depending on the destination—and the integrity of the driver. Some taxis can accommodate up to 9 people (for the price of one). Bell services can call for a cab at any WDW resort. Note that many drivers do not have SunPass, so it'll cost you at least 45 cents a minute while waiting to pay each toll. What's more, many drivers do not know the area streets (or pretend not to)—resulting in bigger fares than necessary. Until cabs offer a flat rate to and from the airport, we are sticking with Magical Express or towncars.

Gratuities are not included in any of the transfer rates. It is customary to tip for good service.

Reputable automobile clubs offer help with breakdowns; towing; insurance that covers personal injury, accidents, arrest, bail bond, and lawyers' fees for defense of contested traffic cases; and travel-planning services, including free maps and route mapping. Services vary from one club to the next, and membership fees range widely, from about $50 to $120 a year.

By Air

When it comes to airfares, there is no real trick to unearthing the most economical ones: Simply shop around. Call a travel agent, browse the Internet, and keep these tips in mind:

- Take advantage of advance-purchase fares (lower rates that apply if a ticket is bought up to several weeks prior to departure).

- Fly when most people don't: For vacation destinations, that usually means leaving the ground on Tuesday or Wednesday.

Resources for Road Trippers

There are a variety of reputable national automobile associations to choose from. Among the leading clubs:

- **Allstate Motor Club Customer Service Center**
  P.O. Box 3094
  Arlington Heights, IL 60006
  800-998-8697
  www.allstatemotorclub.com

- **American Automobile Association** (AAA)
  1000 AAA Dr. #28
  Heathrow, FL 32746
  407-444-7000 or 800-564-6222
  www.aaa.com

- **Auto Club of America**
  P.O. Box 21443
  Oklahoma City, OK 73156
  800-411-2007
  www.autoclubofamerica.com

- **Ford Customer Relationship Center**
  P.O. Box 6248
  Dearborn, MI 48126
  800-392-3673

- **GeicoNow**
  800-841-0728
  www.geiconow.com

- **Signature's Nationwide Auto Club**
  Attention: Customer Service
  P.O. Box 968008
  Schaumburg, IL 60173
  800-323-2002
  www.autoclub.com

Travelers may also check with state tourist boards for free maps. Other map sources are the *AAA North American Road Atlas* and the *Rand McNally Road Atlas*; they are sold in many bookstores.

- Keep in mind that the lowest airfares usually carry a penalty if you have to revise your ticket, and that most discounted tickets are nonrefundable.

- When you call to make a reservation, ask about any fare restrictions, including an obligatory Saturday night stay-over.

- Visit airline websites. They may e-mail details about discounted fares. Some offer a discount for purchasing tickets online.

By Train

Amtrak serves the Orlando, Florida, area twice daily to and from New York City, with stops made along the way. The trip takes approximately 22 hours and costs from about $250 to $400 round-trip, coach. (Book early for lower fares; discounts are often available, so be sure to ask. Passengers over the age of 18 must present valid government-issued photo ID upon request.) If you're staying at Walt Disney World, plan to take a cab or shuttle to the area hotels. Rental cars are also available. They are not on-site, but are easily reached by shuttle.

For reservations and additional train information, call 800-USA-RAIL (872-7245), visit the Amtrak Website at *www.amtrak.com*, or contact a travel agent.

By Bus

Greyhound provides frequent direct service to Orlando and Kissimmee (the latter is closer to Walt Disney World). From either destination, you can take a taxi to your hotel, but first check if your hotel offers shuttle service. For more information, contact Greyhound at 800-231-2222, or visit *www.greyhound.com*.

Disney's Magical Express Service

Disney's Magical Express service is for guests planning a stay at a Walt Disney World-owned-and-operated resort and arriving at Orlando International Airport. Meant as a money-saver as well as a convenience, the service lets guests check luggage at their airport of origin, bypass baggage claim, and board a bus to their WDW resort. The luggage, which guests affix with special tags before leaving home, is usually delivered to the resort room within several hours of arrival. On the final day of a trip, prior to boarding the bus back to the airport, guests who fly domestically with participating airlines (at press time, that included AirTran, Alaska, American, Delta, JetBlue, Southwest, US Airways, and United) check their luggage at their resort and receive a boarding pass for their airline. (Luggage fees may apply.) Once at the airport, guests can skip the airline check-in counter and proceed directly to the line for security. If you'd prefer to schlep your own bags, you can still hitch a free ride on the bus. Here are some specifics:

- Magical Express service is booked when you book your resort and must be done at least 10 days prior to arrival. (Have flight information handy when you make the call.) We recommend making the reservation as early as possible—preferably five to six weeks ahead. Be sure to confirm.

- Reservations may be made via *www.disneyworld.com*, 407-W-DISNEY, or a travel agent.

- Tip the driver as you would had you paid for the trip: $1–$2 per bag is appropriate.

- Special luggage tags will be sent to the party that makes the reservation. These tags must be put on all bags that will be checked at the airport.

- Upon landing at Orlando International Airport, skip baggage claim (if you tagged your bags) and proceed to the Disney Welcome Center, located in the Main Terminal Building on the B side, Level 1. Don't forget to have your transfer vouchers and a photo ID handy. Check in at the desk. Note that one person may check in the whole party, so there's no need for everyone to stand in the check-in line.

- On the return trip, expect to be picked up at least three hours before your scheduled flight departure time. Consider that when you make your air arrangements.

- Guests who require wheelchair-accessible transportation should make their needs known when making the reservation. Confirm reservations before you leave home.

- Guests flying on "non-participating" airlines are entitled to the free shuttle service, too.

The good news? It is a money-saver. In fact, a family of four can shave at least $130 off their total vacation cost by taking the Magical Express shuttle as opposed to other forms of transportation. It's also handy to bypass check-in at the airport on the return trip. The downside? Well, to call any service "magical" is to elevate expectations. It's not really "express," either—as most buses make multiple stops at Disney resorts. So if time is of the essence, it might not be the best choice. Same goes for the transportation of luggage. It may take an hour to arrive at your resort room, but it may also take three to six. So if you'll need anything right away—swimsuits, pajamas, medication, snacks, etc.—pack it in a day bag, carry it onto the plane, and transport it to the resort yourself. We could do without the noisy promotional video that's played throughout the journey, but the bus is comfy and the price is right!

Planning Ahead
Logistics

Organizing a trip properly takes time, but most travelers find the increased enjoyment well worth the effort. The fact is, planning can be a pleasant sort of "armchair" exercise, and kids will enjoy their visit to Disney all the more if they, too, are involved in the process. Take it from us, the more information you can gather, the better.

To assist in that effort, we immodestly recommend *Birnbaum's Walt Disney World For Kids*, a colorful look at the World, written for readers ages 7 through 14. For those planning to pair a Disney cruise with a Walt Disney World visit, cruise information beginning on page 309 is a good place to start.

HOT TIP!

So you've used this book to plan your trip to Walt Disney World. What are you going to do now? Go to *www.disneyworld.com*! Here you can get WDW news and park hours, purchase tickets, and more.

Information Sources

For additional information about Walt Disney World, call 407-W-DISNEY (407-934-7639) or visit *www.disneyworld.com*. Specifics such as park hours, ticket prices, refurbishment schedules, and directions are available through an automated system 24 hours a day. For information by mail, write to: Walt Disney World, P.O. Box 10000, Lake Buena Vista, FL 32830-1000.

Internet and smartphone users can tap into updates about happenings in the World, get information on trip planning, reserve a room, order tickets, book dining reservations, and get park hours and special-events listings by visiting *www.disney world.com* or *mydisneyexperience.com*. Disney Cruise Line vacation packages may be booked at *www.disneycruise.com*.

For info and discounts on (non-Disney) area attractions, restaurants, and hotels, contact the Official Visitor Information Center, 8723 International Drive, Suite 101, Orlando, FL

32819 (it's a satellite office of the Orlando Convention & Visitors Bureau); 407-363-5872, or 800-551-0181; *www.visitorlando.com*.

For details about other Central Florida attractions, contact Visit Florida; 888-735-2872 (to request a complimentary visitors guide and map) or 850-488-5607; *www.visitflorida.com*.

On-site Resources: Those staying at a WDW resort should consider their lobby concierge desk a primary resource. Resort guests also receive information via their room's TV. Fort Wilderness campers are advised to stop at the Pioneer Hall Info and Ticket Window, call extension 2788, or touch 11 on a phone near any restroom. Tablet and smartphone users can access *mydisneyexperience.com* via the free app.

What to Pack

While there is hardly a formal dress code at Walt Disney World, neat, casual clothing is the rule, with few exceptions. Most notably, jackets are required for men at Victoria & Albert's restaurant in the Grand Floridian resort. More generally, T-shirts and shorts are perfectly acceptable during the day. For evening, slacks, jeans, or Bermuda-length shorts are appropriate. Bathing suits are a must, along with the appropriate attire for any sport you want to pursue.

Lightweight sweaters are necessary even in summer—to wear indoors when the air-conditioning gets chilly. From November through March, warmer clothing is a must for evening. Pack for weather extremes so you'll be comfy should it become unseasonably warm or cool. Always bring plenty of sunscreen, and don't forget the bug spray. If possible, pack lightweight rain gear (a poncho is best). The most important item of all? Comfortable walking shoes (two pairs).

Guests at the resorts on Hotel Plaza Boulevard may access a tourist-information television station of their own. Some other area hotels also show a version of the programming, usually aiming to provide an overview of all Central Florida attractions.

For Day Visitors: When purchasing one-day admission to a given theme park, guests receive a complimentary guidemap and entertainment Times Guide for that park. Ticket holders may receive all four park guides upon request. Extra guidemaps are available at City Hall (in the Magic Kingdom) and at Guest Relations (in Epcot, Disney's Hollywood Studios, and Animal Kingdom), as well as in many shops and restaurants throughout the park.

Package Pointers

The sheer number and diversity of packages offering vacations in Central Florida are enough to bewilder even the savviest traveler. Still, such plans are worth exploring. Most offer the convenience of a vacation that's completely organized in advance, and one that will generally cost less than the sum of the same transportation, accommodations, and admission elements purchased separately. In addition, since most package providers purchase blocks of Disney resort rooms, they are an excellent source for securing a room on Walt Disney World property when the hotel of your choice is booked.

Southwest Vacations (800-243-8372), American Airlines Vacations (800-321-2121), *www.expedia.com, www.travelocity.com*, and the Walt Disney Travel Company (407-939-6244 or *www.disneyworld.com*) all offer packages that feature WDW on-site hotels, as well as choice off-property accommodations. Many packages include the added attraction of low-cost air transportation. The American Automobile

Association (visit *www.aaa.com*, or call 407-444-7000) offers AAA Vacations and other travel packages, which include certain perks and discounts. For other possibilities, check the travel section of your local newspaper or consult a travel agent.

Walt Disney Travel Company offers six vacation plans: Magic Your Way base package, Magic Your Way Plus Dining package, Magic Your Way Plus Quick Service Dining package, Magic Your Way Plus Deluxe Dining package, Magic Your Way Premium package, and the Magic Your Way Platinum package. (Visit *www.disneyworld.com/dvd* to order a complimentary vacation planning DVD.)

Travel agents may design packages around a specific type of vacation: say, a golf getaway, honeymoon, or family reunion. They may include extra elements such as unlimited tee times or a carriage ride. Still others are tied to an annual event, such as the Walt Disney World Marathon (see Holidays & Special Events on page 10 of this chapter). Finally, Disney's Sand and Castle package combines a Disney World vacation with a stay at Disney's Vero Beach Resort or other Florida beach resorts. (See page 93 in *Transportation & Accommodations* for details on the Disney Vacation Club.) Air transportation, rental car, or airport transfers can be added to most packages.

The value of a package depends on your needs. Before considering options, use this book to help determine which of the accommodations, activities, and attractions most appeal to you. There's real value in some package elements, such as airport transfers and meal discounts. Several packages also include meals with the Disney characters, tennis lessons, golf greens fees, spa treatments, boat rentals, and the like.

Never choose a package that includes elements you don't want or won't have time to enjoy. While extras such as welcoming snacks may sound appealing, their cash value is negligible. Also beware of any packages that tout certain services as selling points that are actually available to every Disney guest.

HOT TIP!

When purchasing a Walt Disney World package, pay attention to the type of WDW ticket that's included—and make sure you are able to customize the ticket to meet your needs. See page 21.

"Magic Your Way" Packages

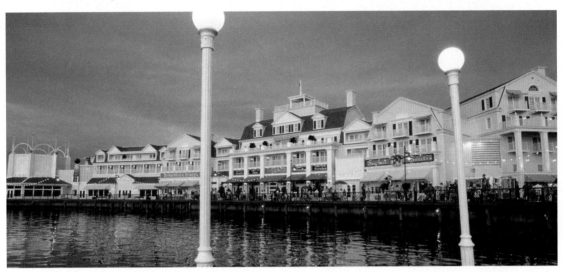

"Magic Your Way" is the name of the game when it comes to Disney World vacation planning. The phrase, meant to reflect each individual's freedom to customize a vacation, covers quite the gamut of options. Most of all, it covers six vacation packages: Magic Your Way, Magic Your Way Plus Dining, Magic Your Way Plus Quick Service Dining, Magic Your Way Plus Deluxe Dining, Magic Your Way Premium, and Magic Your Way Platinum. They can be booked through the Walt Disney Travel Company (407-939-7675), travel agents, and *www.disneyworld.com*.

The packages have some elements in common. For starters, they're all intended to be flexible and include a Walt Disney World resort stay and a theme park ticket of some kind. They must be paid for in full. All packages must be canceled at least 45 days before the trip to avoid a penalty. Everyone staying in the room must have the same package and ticket options. Finally, they all come with the following:

- Extra Magic Hours benefit: WDW resort guests may enjoy exclusive access to theme parks select mornings and evenings. (For details on Extra Magic Hours, see page 22.)
- Disney's Magical Express service: complimentary transportation to and from Orlando International Airport, plus baggage delivery to your resort room. (See page 16 for details.)
- Complimentary use of the Walt Disney World transportation system (buses, boats, and the ever-popular monorail).

Magic Your Way Base Package: This "package" is, quite simply, a stay at any Walt Disney World-owned-and-operated resort paired with a theme park ticket. The big decisions to be made here are (1) which resort to reserve, and (2) the number of days and add-ons you want on your park ticket. (For more on Walt Disney World theme park ticket structures and pricing, turn to pages 21–24.)

Magic Your Way Plus Dining Package: Take the above description of the Magic Your Way package, throw in a Disney Dining Plan, and you've got a vacation plan with the freedom to dine at more than 100 different eateries—not to mention the potential to shave a few bucks off your dining budget. The basic package includes one quick-service meal, a snack, plus one meal at a table-service restaurant per person, per night of your vacation. (For more on the Dining Plan, see the box on page 20.) The package also includes a Magic Your Way base ticket and a "RapidFill" refillable mug (see page 270).

Magic Your Way Plus Quick Service Dining Package: This plan includes two meals and one snack per day, per guest—but all meals are of the quick-service variety. It includes a refillable mug for each member of the party participating in this package.

Magic Your Way Plus Deluxe Dining Package: Similar to the two aforementioned packages, but this plan comes with three meals a day, all of which can be cashed in at any eatery that is a Dining Plan participant (regardless of whether it is quick service or table service).

Magic Your Way Premium Package: It's called "premium" because it includes many of the World's most popular features:

- A stay at a Disney-owned-and-operated resort.
- Magic Your Way ticket with "add-ons" (see page 21 for details).
- Premium Dining Plan: breakfast, lunch, and dinner per person, per night. For details on the Disney Dining Plan, see sidebar and visit *www.disneyworld.com*, or call 407-WDW-DINE (939-3463).
- Unlimited access to select recreation opportunities, including golf, guided fishing excursions, water sports, and more. (Restrictions apply, and advance reservations may be required.)
- Admission to Cirque du Soleil's La Nouba show (one admission per person).
- Admission to a Disney Children's Activity Center at a select Walt Disney World resort (ages 4–12).
- Unlimited admission to select Theme Park tours: Magic Kingdom's Family Magic Tour, The Magic Behind Our Steam Trains, and Keys to the Kingdom; Epcot's Behind the Seeds and The Undiscovered Future World; and Animal Kingdom's Backstage Safari and Wild By Design. (See pages 232–234 for tour details.)

- Special dining experiences, including meals with assorted Disney characters, "Signature" dining experiences, and dinner shows.
- One resort refillable soft drink mug per person (good for the length of your stay).

Magic Your Way Platinum Package: An upgrade from the Premium Package, the Platinum version features a stay at a deluxe Walt Disney World resort, plus options such as spa treatments and high-end dining opportunities.

Disney Dining Plan

The Disney Dining Plan is popular for a reason: Forget the flexibility of dining at more than 100 different eateries for a moment, and ponder the possibility of saving up to 20–30 percent on rations for your trip. (We're salivating at the prospect.) For details on Dining Plan options, visit *disneyworld.com*. Here's a summary of the basic Disney Dining Plan (details are subject to change):

Each day of the plan—which starts at about $56 a day for adults ($18 for kids) and is offered as part of the Magic Your Way Plus Dining package—includes:

- One table-service meal, including entrée, dessert (lunch or dinner), and soft drink.
- One quick-service meal, including entrée, dessert, and non-alcoholic beverage.
- One snack, such as ice cream, popcorn, or a medium soft drink at select quick-service spots or snack carts.
- The option of exchanging two table-service meals for one meal at a high-end "Signature" restaurant or a dinner show, such as the Hoop-Dee-Doo Musical Revue.

To sum up: Say your family of four was to purchase a five-night package. Together you'd be entitled to 20 quick-service meals, 20 table-service meals, and 20 snacks. And you are free to use them in any way you want. That is, if you want to skip a meal one day or have five meals in a single day, by all means go for it. (Just remember that you have a finite number of meals allotted.) Usage is tracked electronically via your room key or MagicBand bracelet (see page 24 for details). Taxes are included, gratuities are not. Be sure to tip your servers. Hold on to your receipts, as they show your remaining meal balance.

In addition to the traditional table-service establishments, certain "character dining" experiences are available to Dining Plan participants, as are select Downtown Disney locations. Note that kids ages 3–9 are required to order from the children's menu where available.

To find out which restaurants are participating, turn to our *Good Meals, Great Times* chapter. For updates, call 407-939-3463 or go to *www.disneyworld.com*.

The Dining Plan must be purchased at the same time you book your WDW resort stay. Finally, if you get the Dining Plan, you still need to make reservations. We recommend doing so as far ahead as possible (180 days).

All About Theme Park Tickets

Buying a park ticket can be very simple. Do you plan on visiting one park on one day? Just pick up a One-Day Base Ticket. Perhaps you are a frequent visitor and expect to pass through theme park gates dozens of times over the next year. In that case, an Annual Pass is what you're looking for. Now, if your park-going plans lie somewhere in between (and most do), you will have to be a little more strategic.

When it comes to selecting the perfect type of admission ticket, it pays to do some homework. Study the options, evaluate your priorities, and make no hasty decisions. For starters, there are four major factors to consider: (1) total number of days you'd like to visit theme parks, (2) to park-hop or not to park-hop, (3) whether you want to pre-pay (and save some time) for "extras" such as admission to the water parks, DisneyQuest, etc., and (4) whether you should invest in the No Expiration option for your ticket.

HOT TIP!

At the end of your visit, note the number of unused days on a multi-day ticket. Write it on the ticket itself. (Make sure you purchase the No Expiration add-on within 14 days of first use.) If your ticket is linked to a MagicBand, be sure to manage your account at *www.mydisneyexperience.com*.

The following information was correct at press time and is meant to help you make wise choices. Keep in mind that Disney ticket prices are likely to change in 2015 (they always do!), so call 407-824-4321 for updates.

Magic Your Way Tickets

Base Tickets: Available for 1 to 10 days. Valid for admission to one park per day—the Magic Kingdom (one-day Magic Kingdom base tickets are priced higher than the other parks), Epcot, Disney's Hollywood Studios, or Disney's Animal Kingdom. (The base ticket does not allow for park-hopping.) Unused days expire 14 days after the ticket is activated, which is the first day a park is visited. (For pricing, see page 26.) The ticket is called a base ticket because, with the exception of Annual Passes, all other tickets begin as such. Guests may customize base tickets to fit their own vacation needs. Note that you can't use a second day's admission to enter a

DID YOU KNOW?

The phrase "E-ticket ride" is American slang for "the ultimate in thrills." It comes from the early days of Disney parks, back when tickets were used for each attraction. E-tickets were reserved for the most elaborate and exciting rides of all.

second park on the same day you visited another park. To do that, you must purchase the Park Hopper Option for the Magic Your Way pass.

Park Hopper Option: This option lets guests visit more than one theme park on a single day. The privilege extends through the length of the ticket. It costs $34 to add to a one-day Magic Kingdom base ticket, $39 to add to a one-day ticket to all other theme parks, and $59 to add to all other base tickets (regardless of the number of days on the ticket).

Water Park Fun & More Option: This option covers entry to Blizzard Beach and Typhoon Lagoon water parks, DisneyQuest (arcade), Disney's sports complex, mini golf, or a round of golf at Disney's Oak Trail golf course. For $59, you'll get between two and ten visits to these spots. The number of visits depends on the number of days on your base ticket—the more days, the more visits.

HOT TIP!

Want to maximize your theme-park-ticket dollar? Buy more days than you plan to use and get the No Expiration option. You can save unused days for a future trip and save a lot on your per-day admission price.

No Expiration Option: Unused days on multi-day base tickets expire 14 days after the first day is used. The good news? You can add the No Expiration peace of mind for a fee: $35 for 2-day tickets; $45 for 3-day tickets; $95 for 4 days; $145 for 5 days; $190 for 6 days; $220 for 7 days; $245 for 8 days; $280 for 9 days; and $325 for 10 days. The No Expiration Option must be purchased at Walt Disney World (at any theme park entrance) or through an authorized ticket agent.

Theme Park Annual Pass: This pass offers admission to the four theme parks for a year. It can be used in more than one park on the same day (also known as park-hopping), and includes use of Disney transportation, as well as free parking at the theme parks. Annual passes can be purchased at the entrance to any of the theme parks (they can be renewed there or by mail). A valid, government-issued photo ID must be presented for purchase by adults and may be required for future use of the pass. Passes are non-transferable. At press time, the cost was about $609 for adults and kids.

Annual pass-bearers qualify for many Walt Disney World discounts and benefits, such as reduced rates at select Disney resorts at certain times of year. A newsletter called the *Mickey Monitor* keeps passholders up to date regarding discount offers. The pass expires one year after it is first used. A discounted renewal rate applies if the pass is renewed before expiration. (The old pass must be presented in order to receive the discounted renewal rate.) A pass may be renewed by mail or at any Disney theme park.

Premium Annual Pass: This pass has everything the Theme Park Annual Pass offers and more—namely, admission to the water parks, ESPN Wide World of Sports complex (non-premium events only), and DisneyQuest for a year, plus one round of golf at the Oak Trail golf course. Premium Annual Passholders are eligible for the same discounts and benefits as Theme Park Annual Passholders. Premium Annual Passes

Extra Magic Hours

How'd you like to visit a Disney theme park before it opens to the public? Or stick around for hours after it's officially closed for the day—at no extra cost? Well, if you're a guest staying at a Walt Disney World-owned-and-operated resort, the Swan, Dolphin, Shades of Green, or the Hilton on Hotel Plaza Boulevard, you can. It is one of the major perks that comes with staying on Disney property.

Here's how it works: One park opens its doors an hour early or stays open two hours late on any given day. Basically, the park becomes something of a members-only private playground for Walt Disney World resort guests. So, provided that you have a WDW resort ID and valid admission media, you're in! No secret password necessary. Keep in mind that you will need park-hopping privileges if you plan to visit a park other than the one offering extra hours on any given day. If you don't plan to park-hop, you must visit the theme park offering Extra Magic Hours on that particular day. Typhoon Lagoon and Blizzard Beach water parks may offer Extra Magic Hours on select "peak" days.

When a theme park opens early in the morning, guests are admitted starting one hour prior to the official opening time. Transportation to the park starts about 30 minutes before that. Be sure to have your WDW resort ID or MagicBand bracelet handy. Flash it and you'll be allowed to visit some (but not all) attractions and mingle with Disney characters.

Ask your resort's lobby concierge for a schedule, or visit *www.disneyworld.com*.

can be purchased at the entrance to any of the four theme parks (they can be renewed there or by mail). A photo ID must be presented for purchase by adults and may be required for future use. Premium Annual Passes are non-transferable. These passes expire one year after first use. The cost is about $729 for adults and kids.

Premier Annual Pass: This pass provides admission to all Disney theme parks and water parks on both U.S. coasts (including Disneyland Park and Disney California Adventure) for one year. It also includes admission to WDW's DisneyQuest, ESPN Wide World of Sports complex (non-premium events only), and the Oak Trail golf course. Unlimited park-hopping and parking are included, as are the same discounts offered with Disney's other annual passes (select merchandise, food, and resort discounts).

The Premier Pass costs about $1,029, plus tax. Guests already bearing Walt Disney World or Disneyland Resort Annual Passes may upgrade to the Premier Pass at any time. For details, visit *www.disneyparks.com/Premier*, or call 407-824-4321.

Deciding Factors

Choosing the Right Ticket: Before you make your decision, it helps to map out your vacation. Remember, all tickets start as Base Tickets. They are a bare-bones, admission-to-one-theme-park-at-a-time deal. That's perfect for many folks—especially those planning a relatively short stay. Still, the first step for every potential guest is to decide just how many days they plan to spend in the theme parks. Keep in mind that as days are added, the average price per day drops a little. Any unused days expire 14 days after the ticket is activated, unless the No Expiration option is purchased (in person at WDW or at an official Disney ticket wholesaler). Once the length of stay is determined, it's time to customize the ticket. Do you want to park-hop? Add $59. Want to add the Water Park Fun and More package? For an extra $59, you can do so. Finally, if you're not certain that you'll use all the days on your pass, you can add on the No Expiration option. That starts at $35. It's a lot to think about, but it makes for a very organized Disney vacation. And it can save you a chunk of change, too.

If you are planning a longer visit, or two trips in a year, we recommend a 10-day Park Hopper with No Expiration or an Annual Pass. In addition to unlimited admission to the parks, an Annual Pass entitles bearers to discounts on everything from dinner shows to room rates.

Note: Only one person per party needs to have an Annual Pass to net a resort discount. This option is great for travelers with flexible schedules, as discounts vary and are often announced shortly before they go into effect.

Tickets with Unused Days: Prior to 2005, WDW tickets never expired. That is no longer the case. Remaining days on any multi-day admission ticket now expire 14 days after the ticket is first activated unless the No Expiration option is purchased.

Attractions Outside the Theme Parks: For Typhoon Lagoon or Blizzard Beach, prices are about $53 for one day and about $104 for an annual pass for adults; $45 for one day and about $85 for an annual pass for kids (ages 3–9). At DisneyQuest, adults pay $45 per day or $90 for an annual pass, while the price for kids is $39 per day or $72 for an annual pass. There is also a DisneyQuest/Water Parks annual pass. Cost is about $132 for adults, $102 for kids. The ESPN Wide World of Sports complex runs about $15 for adults, about $11 for kids. Cirque du Soleil's La Nouba is $61–$144 for adults, $49–$117 for kids. Prices are likely to rise in 2015.

MyMagic+

"MyMagic+" is the all-encompassing moniker attached to all vacation-planning tools managed via the My Disney Experience planning page or smartphone app. It links cards and MagicBands (bracelets that are connected to various vacation features) and includes the Fastpass+ attraction reservation system (see page 25).

My Disney Experience: An app that can be downloaded for free and is compatible with most smartphones and tablets, My Disney Experience is a tool for reserving tables at Walt Disney World restaurants and dinner shows, booking, revising, and keeping track of Fastpass+ assignments at WDW theme park shows and attractions, viewing attraction wait times, and more. For those without smartphones or tablets, *www.MyDisneyExperience.com* can be accessed by personal computer. It allows for all of the same advance planning. The service is free and requires guests to create an account (to which all members of the traveling party should be linked). Note that children under age 13 are not permitted to have live, individual accounts. Instead, parents create and manage a profile for each child (kids' profiles are attached to their parents'). There is a bit of a learning curve, so get started as soon as you can.

After linking a Disney World resort reservation or vacation package and tickets to your account, guests then link MagicBands (see details at right), make and monitor WDW dining reservations, book and track Fastpass+ times, and load the Memory Maker Photo Package (see page 27). It is important to link the accounts of up to 10 members of your traveling party (parties larger than 10 should call 407-939-5277).

All guests may use this service, whether they stay on WDW property or not, provided they can access the Website or utilize the app.

HOT TIP!
Adults should always carry a government-issued photo ID. You will need it should you have any issues with your MagicBand while visiting WDW.

MagicBands: This colorful accessory is something of a technological wonder—it can serve as a resort room key and be loaded with theme park and water park admission tickets. Guests can also use it to make purchases throughout Walt Disney World (provided it is backed up with a credit card and a personal PIN code has been selected); use it for Disney's PhotoPass (see page 133), Fastpass+ (in conjunction with *MyDisneyExperience.com* or the associated app); and more. To use it to make a purchase in a shop or restaurant, just tap the not-so-hidden-Mickey on the band to the Mickey on the console. MagicBands may be purchased when you book your Disney World vacation. The standard version comes in gray but may be customized in one of 7 different colors. (We recommend using different colors for each member of a party.) Bands customized within 10 days of arrival will be sent to your home. Bands ordered within 5 to 9 days will be sent to your WDW resort. (Bands picked up at a Walt Disney World resort may be linked with My Disney Experience accounts at the resort's front desk or by smartphone or tablet.) When your bands arrive in the mail, remember to link them to your party's My Disney Experience accounts. (Be sure to link each band to the right account!) Note that MagicBands cannot be shipped to all countries.

How Do You Book a Room? Let Us Count the Ways

You're ready to reserve a room at a resort on Walt Disney World property. How nice for you! But before you dial 407-W-DISNEY (934-7639) or a travel agent, know this: There are three different ways to book your WDW stay. It's best to know what you want in advance. It will save you time and spare confusion while on the phone. Here's the scoop:

• Room-Only Reservation—What you hear is what you get: a hotel room only. It requires an advance deposit and allows you to cancel up to 5 days prior to the start of the reservation (penalty-free). It comes with a 12-digit confirmation number.

• Walt Disney World Travel Company Basic Plan—A package that includes room, luggage tags, and a round of mini-golf for the entire party. Must be paid in full up front and must be canceled at least 45 days prior to check-in to avoid a penalty. (The confirmation number has 8 digits.) We recommend adding trip insurance to the package (at an additional cost), just in case.

• Magic Your Way Base Package—Includes room and theme park tickets. It may be customized in many ways, such as adding the Disney Dining Plan, Water Park admission, and more (see page 21). Must be paid in full upon reserving and may be canceled up to 45 days ahead (any later and there will be hefty penalties). Once reserved, expect to get an 8-digit confirmation number.

Save Time in Line with Fastpass+

Walt Disney World's Fastpass+ is a service that was designed to allow guests to bypass the traditional standby line and enjoy a number of theme park shows and attractions with little or no wait. It's a virtual queue—one you join by visiting "My Disney Experience" via the Internet (with a computer, tablet, or smartphone). Once you've established an account, you can link your ticket (and those in your party) and access Fastpass+ to book times to visit attractions during a pending visit to the park.

To WDW veterans, the term Fastpass conjures happy memories of bypassing lines after securing assignments while visiting the parks. That concept is still the same, but the procedure has changed quite a bit. In fact, we wish they had called the new system something other than Fastpass+, because it really is a bold departure from the original. Think of Fastpass+ as an *advance reservation system*—one that is completely free to all guests bearing a valid park ticket.

The most popular WDW attractions and shows (aka E-Ticket experiences), like the hottest restaurants in town, are often very crowded, with long waits and no guarantee you'll get in. By using Fastpass+, you can reserve a time to enjoy at least one popular ride (and several other attractions) during each day of your WDW visit. In most cases, you won't walk right in, but you will have an expedited wait time and guaranteed admission to some crowd-pleasers such as Toy Story Mania, Soarin', Expedition Everest, or Enchanted Tales with Belle. Ideally, Fastpass+ aims to spread guests throughout the parks, making traditionally congested areas less so. For folks who prefer to do things on the fly or who find the new system a bit daunting or difficult to navigate, traditional standby lines will always be available. That said, tech-savvy, detail-minded guests may relax a bit, knowing each day of their vacation is pre-planned.

Begin by paying a visit to My Disney Experience via the Internet or smartphone app. Set up an account and link it with your park ticket. Then, if it's within 30 days of your visit (60 if you are staying in a WDW–owned-and-operated resort or the Swan and Dolphin), you can start booking Fastpass+ assignments. When the one-hour Fastpass+ window kicks in, go to the attraction and touch your MagicBand or ticket card to the Fastpass+ redemption console, wait for the light, and head inside.

We recommend using Fastpass+ assignment for your must-sees. We've placed a Fastpass+ symbol (FP+) beside the listing for all shows and attractions that were included at press time. However, since experiences may be added or dropped, visit *www.mydisneyexperience.com* for updates. And remember, all WDW attractions continue to offer the option of standing in a traditional queue. Fastpass+ is just a bonus option for folks who like to plan ahead. By using it, we have gleaned the following (specifics may change, as the program was still in a testing phase as this book went to press):

• To make advance Fastpass+ reservations, you must have access to the Internet.
• It's possible to reserve a same-day Fastpass+ assignment at a park kiosk (which actually offers more options and better flexibility). But using them can be time-consuming, and the chances of getting convenient, same-day access to the most popular attractions are slim. Get there early!
• Fastpass+ lets you experience at least 3 attractions or shows per day without waiting in the (usually) longer standby line. You may be able to get more same-day assigments at in-park kiosks once the times for your first 3 have been used or the times have expired.
• Fastpass+ allows for park-hopping after the first Fastpass+ assignment has been used or expired. (Although you are required to book 3 Fastpass+ assignments in one park, you can make changes at an in-park kiosk after you use your first Fastpass+ assignment of the day and "hop" to another park.)
• Fastpass+ times are linked to your MagicBand (see page 24) or park ticket card and can be viewed, modified, or canceled via smartphone, tablet, computer, or in-park Fastpass+ kiosk.
• You generally can't ride the same attraction via Fastpass+ twice in one day. If you want to ride a major attraction twice, we recommend getting a Fastpass+ assignment and going to your attraction as soon as the park opens for your first ride. You can ride again when your Fastpass+ window kicks in.
• Fastpass+ assignments are non-transferable.
• Coordinating Fastpass+ assignments for large groups is possible, but it can be challenging.
• If you make Fastpass+ arrangements via park kiosk, write down the assignment times in case your smartphone battery dies. You can check times at a park kiosk, but there is often a wait to do so.
• Parades, fireworks, and Disney character meet-and-greets are included in the Fastpass+ system.
• You don't have to use Fastpass+ to have fun in the parks. All shows and attractions continue to offer traditional standby lines.
• If you experience a glitch, visit the park's Guest Relations window or Fastpass+ kiosk for help.
• Fastpass+ is a work in progress. There will be bumps along the way to perfection. There always are.

TICKET PRICES

		10-Day	9-Day	8-Day	7-Day	6-Day	5-Day	4-Day	3-Day	2-Day	1-Day
Base Ticket*	Ages 10 & UP	$339 ($33.90/ day)	$329 ($36.65/ day)	$319 ($39.88/ day)	$309 ($44.15/ day)	$299 ($49.84/ day)	$289 ($57.80/ day)	$279 ($69.75/ day)	$262 ($87.34/ day)	$184 ($92.00/ day)	$90–$95
	Ages 3–9	$320 ($32.00/ day)	$310 ($34.45/ day)	$300 ($37.50/ day)	$290 ($41.43/ day)	$280 ($46.67/ day)	$270 ($54.00/ day)	$260 ($65.00/ day)	$244 ($81.34/ day)	$172 ($86.00/ day)	$84–$89
ADD: Park Hopper**		$59	$59	$59	$59	$59	$59	$59	$59	$59	$34–39
ADD: Water Park Fun & More***		$59 10 visits	$59 9 visits	$59 8 visits	$59 7 visits	$59 6 visits	$59 5 visits	$59 4 visits	$59 3 visits	$59 2 visits	$59 1 visit
ADD: No Expiration****		$325	$280	$245	$220	$190	$145	$95	$45	$35	Not available

* Base Ticket admits guest to one theme park each day of use. Park choices are Magic Kingdom, Epcot, Disney's Hollywood Studios, and Disney's Animal Kingdom.

** Park Hopper option entitles guest to visit more than one theme park on each day of use. Park choices are any combination of theme parks on each day of use.

*** Water Park Fun & More option entitles guest to a specified number of visits to a choice of entertainment and recreation venues. Choices include Disney's Blizzard Beach water park, Disney's Typhoon Lagoon water park, DisneyQuest, and ESPN Wide World of Sports complex.

**** No Expiration means unused admissions on a ticket have no expiration date. All multi-day tickets expire 14 days after first use unless No Expiration is purchased. Available at Walt Disney World and select official Disney wholesalers only. Cannot be purchased online, by phone, or by mail.

If you book a Fastpass+ assignment for a child to meet a Disney character (or experience an attraction), remember to book one for yourself!

The MagicBand is waterproof (but does not float), hypoallergenic, and can be adjusted to fit most wrists. If a MagicBand is lost it can be disabled via the My Disney Experience app (and the Website) or with the help of a cast member. MagicBands are non-transferable. No personal information is stored on the band—it only links to entitlements that were prepurchased.

Fastpass+: WDW's new reservation system for select attractions, shows, and character meet-and-greets at its four theme parks is a free service, available to all guests with valid theme park tickets. It may be accessed up to 30 days in advance via the My Disney Experience app or Website. Guests with a reservation at a Walt Disney World-owned-and-operated resort may book Fastpass+ assignments up to 60 days prior to checking in. It's possible to make same-day Fastpass+ reservations, too—by using the aforementioned ways and by visiting a Fastpass+ kiosk in any of the WDW theme parks. Note that it is not possible to get Fastpass+ assignments at the attractions themselves. For details on Fastpass+, turn to page 25.

Memory Maker Photo Package: Previously known as PhotoPass+, Memory Maker includes the standard Photopass CD, plus photos snapped on select WDW attractions and character meal locations. You can review the photos at sites in the park or when you get home via the Web. It's possible to customize photos with banners and Disney art, too. At press time, the price was about $200; about $149 if pre-ordered. (We think this is one of Walt Disney World's better values.) Note that it is still possible to buy and customize photos via the traditional PhotoPass system (see page 133).

Purchasing Tickets

Admission tickets are sold at park entrances, WDW resorts, Four Seasons, the resorts on Hotel Plaza Boulevard, Orlando International Airport, the Transportation and Ticket Center (TTC), and Downtown Disney Guest Relations. Cash, traveler's checks, American Express, Visa, MasterCard, Diner's Club, Discover, JCB Card, Disney Dollars, and Disney gift cards are accepted. Not all tickets are available at each location, so call 407-934-7639 to confirm.

We recommend buying tickets in advance (it can save time when you arrive at the parks) from a travel agent, or in one of these ways:

Tickets by Phone: All tickets can be purchased by phone; call 407-W-DISNEY (934-7639). There is a $5 handling fee for standard home delivery (allow 15 days); $15 for express delivery (allow 7 days); and $25 for international delivery (allow 12 days). There is no fee for pick-up at a WDW Will Call window.

Tickets Online: Tickets can be bought through *www.disneyworld.com*. The fees for delivery are the same as those listed above.

Tickets at a Disney Store: Select multi-day theme park tickets are available for purchase at any local Disney Store.

Tickets by Mail (3- to 7-day Magic Your Way tickets only): Allow at least three to four weeks for processing, and include a return address. Send a money order (for the exact amount, plus $4 for handling), payable to Walt Disney World Company, to: Walt Disney World, Box 10140, Lake Buena Vista, FL 32830-0030. Attention: Ticket Mail Order.

Ticket Tag System

As a means of enforcing the non-transferability aspect of all Walt Disney World tickets, Disney has devised a system to trace each ticket to its rightful owner. The procedure is as follows: Touch your MagicBand or ticket to the brass orb at any park entrance. While the machine is crunching the data encrypted on your MagicBand or ticket, gently press the tip of your forefinger onto the glowing gizmo perched beside the orb. Remove your finger and presto! Your MagicBand or ticket will link to your forefinger, giving you the bright green light to enter. Grown-ups have to do this every time they use the ticket. Remember to use the same finger every time you enter a park. (Kids ages 10 and under are spared the hassle.)

Money-Saving Tips

A Walt Disney World vacation can be an exceptionally expensive undertaking, but it is possible to keep costs down a bit. When budgeting for your trip, keep in mind that WDW prices are comparable to those in a big city. Here are a few tips to help you conserve cash.

Lodging

- When it comes to saving money on hotel accommodations, timing is truly the key. While off-season dates tend to vary, depending on the hotel, value season for most Walt Disney World resorts generally means January through mid-February, late August through late September, and early November through late December.

- The Swan and Dolphin resorts often have rate specials when other WDW resorts have peak rates. Check *www.swandolphin.com*.

- Consider how much time you will actually spend at your hotel, and don't pay for a place with perks you won't have time to enjoy. Hotels often allow kids to stay free in parents' rooms, but the cutoff age varies.

- When considering the cost-effectiveness of off-property lodging, factor in the time, money, and inconvenience of commuting to and from attractions.

- Realize, too, that the advantages of staying on-property (tops among them the Extra Magic Hours perk, Disney's Magical Express, and access to Walt Disney World's transportation system) also apply to those staying in the least expensive rooms in Disney's hotels. The most important addresses for budget-watching Disney fans, the All-Star and Pop Century resorts, offer the lowest rates on Disney property. Rooms at Caribbean Beach, Port Orleans French Quarter and Riverside,

HOT TIP!
To save money on Walt Disney World golf, merchandise, food, behind-the-scenes tours and more, use the coupons at the back of this book!

Disney's Art of Animation, and Coronado Springs are slightly higher priced. Also, note that the only difference between the least and most expensive rooms in a hotel is often the view. Consider how often you'll be looking out that window.

Food

- Visit costlier establishments at lunchtime (if you so desire) rather than at dinner; entrées often cost a bit less at the midday meal.

- While Club Level accommodations can absorb the cost of some meals and snacks, a better way to stretch your dining dollar is a Disney Dining Plan (especially the Quick-Service option).

- Carry snacks and sandwich fixings and enjoy them picnic style wherever possible.

- Look for lodging with kitchen facilities. The savings on food may be more than the extra accommodations expense.

- Small refrigerators are available in guestrooms at all Walt Disney World-owned-and-operated resorts (no charge).

- A souvenir mug can be purchased at most resorts, good for refills during your stay at participating resorts. (Similar mugs are sold in the parks, but don't come with free refills.)

- Buy bottled water, snacks, and other supplies at a local supermarket or have them delivered to your room. (See page 59 for shopping details.)

- Pack kid-friendly snacks, such as fruit, cereal, or even a lollipop. (Snack stands are plentiful, but not always handy or cost-efficient.)

- Don't plan on eating three big table-service meals a day. It gets expensive—and filling!

- The Magic Your Way vacation package with the basic Dining Plan can control meal costs. It provides two meals and a snack per day. The fixed price (starting at about $56 a day for guests ages 10 and up and $18 for kids between 3 and 9) includes tax, but not gratuity. It is customary to tip for good service.

Satisfying Substitutes

Fewer frills rarely mean less fun at Walt Disney World. Here are money-saving alternatives to two of Disney's higher-priced treats.

If you'd rather not spring for admission to Downtown Disney West Side venues, consider taking a trip to the BoardWalk resort. Among other diversions, you will find Jellyrolls (a sing-along piano bar with a cover of about $12), Atlantic Dance (a nightclub with no cover charge), and ESPN Club (a cover-free sports bar). A short walk will take you to the Swan hotel, home to the karaoke-friendly Kimonos Lounge.

If the Grand Floridian ($517–$1,405 a night) doesn't quite fit into your budget, consider staying in a Mansion room at Port Orleans Riverside ($162–$318 a night). Southern hospitality replaces Victorian splendor, and though the guestrooms aren't quite as spacious, the air of sophistication makes for a most satisfying stay. And for a sweet deal on a suite, consider the vibrant new resort called Disney's Art of Animation.

Discounts

- Theme Park Annual and Premium Annual Passholders receive so many discounts on meals, dinner shows, tours, room rates, and more that it may be worth purchasing an Annual Pass for longer visits or if you plan to take more than one trip within a year.

- WDW resorts that offer Annual Passholder discounts vary from month to month, and discounted rooms aren't always available for booking very far in advance. It's best to be flexible with travel dates. For more information, call 407-560-7277 or 407-W-DISNEY (939-7639). Passholders can save 20 percent at many WDW eateries by joining the Tables in Wonderland program. For details, call 407-WDW-DINE (939-3463).

- Discounts on Disney World resort rates and theme park tickets are available to Florida residents, and seasonal promotions occur. Call 407-W-DISNEY (939-7639) for specifics.

- The Swan, as well as some off-property hotels, offers discounts to seniors and AAA or AARP members as well. Some AAA branches offer discounts on some park passes, as well as discounts on rooms and select packages with the AAA Disney Magic Moments Savings Program. Contact your local branch for additional information.

HOT TIP!

Bring inexpensive, light rain gear from home. You'll need it—especially in the stormy months of summer.

HOT TIP!

It may be cheaper to spread out over two rooms in a "value" or "moderate" resort than to have everyone stay in one room at "deluxe" Disney digs.

- Web-based *travelocity.com* offers a variety of Disney vacation packages. Vacation Outlet sometimes offers packages at a reduced rate; visit *www.vacationoutlet.com*, or call 800-825-3633 for details.

- To request your free Orlando Magicard, visit *www.orlandoinfo.com/magicard*. Cardholders may net discounts at area hotels, restaurants, shops, and more.

- Disney Rewards Visa members earn reward dollars when they use the card. These dollars can be redeemed at Disney World, the Disney Cruise Line, and Disneyland. If you'd like to become a Disney Rewards Visa cardholder, flip to the back of this book. Our coupon can help you get a $50 Birnbaum bonus. You can use the Disney Visa Card wherever Visa is accepted. Visit *disneyrewards.com* for details.

- Okay, so it's not exactly a discount, but we think the 10-day Magic Your Way ticket with the No Expiration add-on is a great value. It brings down the daily cost of visiting a theme park. Plus, the tickets "don't expire until you do," so unused days can be saved for another trip.

- Visit *disneyworld.disney.go.com/special-offers/* to see if any discounts apply for your WDW visit.

Making a Budget

A stay at Disney's kingdom need not cost a king's ransom (though it easily can). In fact, with a well-planned budget, money at Disney World can stretch relatively far.

Vacation expenses tend to fall into five major categories: (1) transportation (which may include any combination of costs for airfare, airport transfers, train tickets, car rental, gas, parking, and taxi service); (2) lodging; (3) theme park tickets; (4) meals; and (5) miscellaneous (recreational activities, cover charges, tips, souvenirs, postcards, forgotten items, and home expenses such as pet boarding, etc.).

When planning your budget, first consider what level of service suits your needs. Some people prefer to spend fewer days at Disney but stay at a deluxe hotel or dine at pricier restaurants, while others would rather make their money cover a longer vacation that includes a value-priced resort and less-expensive meals. The choice is up to you. Once you've established your spending priorities, determine your price limit. Then make sure you don't exceed it when approximating your expenses—without a ballpark figure to work around, it's easy to get carried away.

Sample Budget

The following is an example of a low- to moderately priced budget designed for a family of four (two adults and two kids planning to stay at WDW for five nights and six days). Totals do not include tax.

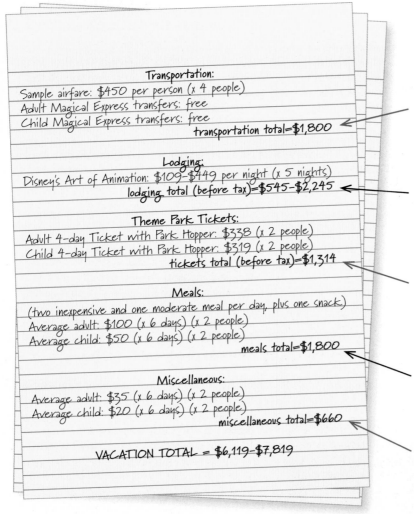

Transportation:
Sample airfare: $450 per person (x 4 people)
Adult Magical Express transfers: free
Child Magical Express transfers: free
transportation total=$1,800

Lodging:
Disney's Art of Animation: $109-$449 per night (x 5 nights)
lodging total (before tax)=$545-$2,245

Theme Park Tickets:
Adult 4-day Ticket with Park Hopper: $338 (x 2 people)
Child 4-day Ticket with Park Hopper: $319 (x 2 people)
tickets total (before tax)=$1,314

Meals:
(two inexpensive and one moderate meal per day, plus one snack)
Average adult: $100 (x 6 days) (x 2 people)
Average child: $50 (x 6 days) (x 2 people)
meals total=$1,800

Miscellaneous:
Average adult: $35 (x 6 days) (x 2 people)
Average child: $20 (x 6 days) (x 2 people)
miscellaneous total=$660

VACATION TOTAL = $6,119-$7,819

Magical Express service is cost-efficient (hey, it's free!), but it can be time-consuming. If you'd like to get from point A to B quickly (and quietly), take a towncar or taxi.

Extend your vacation by splitting nights between a more and less expensive resort (end with the fancier one).

If you don't plan to use all of the days on your park ticket, be sure to purchase the No Expiration option when you arrive—that way you can use extra days on a future trip.

Even if you stick to fast food, expect to spend at least $40 (adult) and $25 (child) per day.

Careful packing should cut down on miscellaneous expenses, which often include forgotten toiletries like toothpaste or the all-important sunscreen.

Planning Your Itinerary

A TIMELINE

First Things First

- Make hotel and transportation arrangements as far ahead as possible. Note that many WDW hotels fill up more than six months ahead. Call 407-W-DISNEY (934-7639) to book a room; your confirmation should arrive within two weeks. Log it and other pertinent information in your Birnbaum Trip Tracker that starts on page 344.

- Check park hours for your planned visit. (Hours are available up to 7 months ahead; call 407-824-4321, or visit *www.disneyworld.com*.) Closing times will be particularly helpful when making evening plans. Create a day-by-day schedule, deciding which area of WDW to visit on each day of your trip. Use the Trip Tracker at the end of this book!

6 Months

- Choose dining spots from those listed in the *Good Meals, Great Times* chapter. Call 407-WDW-DINE (939-3463) to make restaurant reservations. Guests with a confirmed reservation at a WDW-owned-and-operated resort may call 180 days before scheduled check-in date and book dining reservations for up to 10 days of their planned stay.

- Popular meals such as those at Cinderella's Royal Table, Le Cellier, and Be Our Guest Restaurant (dinner) should be booked 180 days ahead. Call 407-WDW-DINE (939-3463) and have a credit card handy.

- Dinner-show reservations may be secured up to 180 days in advance. Consult page 300 for details, and call 407-WDW-DINE (939-3463) for reservations.

- Unless you purchased a package that includes theme park admission, it's time to order tickets. Refer to pages 21–24 for details, and call 407-824-4321; tickets should arrive within four weeks. Keep in mind that you will save money by purchasing select tickets in advance.

- Specialty cruises (see page 231) may be booked by calling 407-WDW-PLAY (939-7529).

- If you have purchased a Magic Your Way Premium or Platinum package and plan to play golf, or will be staying at a WDW resort or a resort on Hotel Plaza Boulevard, you may book a tee time on one of WDW's golf courses now (see pages 236–237 for details on the courses). Golf lessons may also be reserved at this time. Call 407-WDW-GOLF (939-4653) for reservations. Those not staying on WDW property may make reservations 60 days ahead.

- Fishing excursions (see page 239) may be booked by calling 407-WDW-BASS (939–2277).

- Tennis lessons may be reserved by calling 407-621-1991. Turn to page 237 for information.

- Parasailing and waterskiing excursions (for details, see pages 238–239) may be booked by calling 407-WDW-PLAY (939-7529) or 407-939-0754 or by visiting *www.sammyduvall.com*.

- Trail-ride reservations may be made up to 180 days in advance. Call 407-WDW-PLAY (939-7529).

- If you'd like to add a behind-the-scenes tour to your vacation, now is the time to make a reservation.

3 Months

- Double-check park hours for your stay, as they may have changed. Take note of Extra Magic Hours (extended park hours for guests registered at a Walt Disney World-owned-and-operated resort).

60 Days

- If you have valid park tickets linked to a reservation at a participating WDW resort, you may book Fastpass+ assignments up to 60 days in advance of your visit to the parks, via the My Disney Experience Website or app.

30 Days

- If you have valid park tickets and are not staying in a WDW resort, you may book Fastpass+ assignments up to 30 days ahead.

10 Days

- Airline confirmation and travel-package vouchers should have arrived by now.

- Will you be staying at a WDW-owned-and-operated resort? If so, check in online! (See page 66.)

- If you haven't already customized your MagicBand color, today is the last day to do it and have it shipped to your home. If customized between 9 and 5 days before arrival, your band will be sent to your WDW resort.

1 Week

- Reconfirm all reservations. Finalize your schedule, including all confirmation numbers and Fastpass+ times.

Many visitors have a deep desire to cover each and every inch of Walt Disney World in the span of a few short days. While we hesitate to discourage these most ambitious of travelers, we feel the need to enlighten them: Walt Disney World is a staggeringly large place. In fact, it's nearly as big as San Francisco and jam-packed with about as many diversions as you might expect from a city that size. You could spend two full weeks on Walt Disney World property and still not have time to do it all. The theme parks alone require every bit of four days just to see the major attractions.

What's the best strategy for organizing a Walt Disney World visit? Make a list of the parks, attractions, and activities you most want to see and use it to create an itinerary. Don't forget to allow time for swimming, boating, or relaxing in a hammock.

Assuming you've narrowed your "must-do" list to the barely manageable, we recommend a stay of at least four to five days. This allows for a visit to each of the theme parks and some time to enjoy many of the recreational activities at your resort, not to mention relaxing a bit. You are on vacation, after all. Longer stays can include water parks, Downtown Disney, a dinner show, and more. When planning your days (which you should do before leaving home), be sure to take into account theme park hours and seasonal temperatures in Central Florida.

The following sample schedules assume that you eat breakfast at your resort (unless otherwise stated) and arrive up to 20 minutes before the official opening time. These schedules, though tirelessly tested and proven successful by Birnbaum's editors, are not carved in stone. Use them as a guide, tailoring the itineraries to suit your family's individual tastes. And use them in conjunction with complimentary theme park Times Guides (available at park entrances).

Note that we have not included specific instructions with regard to Fastpass+ in our sample itineraries. It's not because we don't use the service. In fact, we highly recommend using Fastpass+, even if working it into a daily schedule is an inexact science. Without it, there's always the risk of a long line or missing out on a "must-see." By all means, take advantage of the Fastpass+ opportunity every chance you get—especially first thing in the morning for the über-popular attractions. Not only might it make you feel like a VIP, but it will free up time in your schedule for things you otherwise might not have gotten to. (If you didn't pre-book Fastpass+, head to an in-park kiosk to see what's available.)

ONE-DAY SCHEDULE

❦ Begin the day with a brisk stroll down Main Street, U.S.A. If you haven't pre-booked Fastpass+ assignments, stop at an in-park kiosk and do so. Check a park map for kiosk locations. Then head to Splash Mountain and Big Thunder Mountain Railroad. Finish up Adventureland with Pirates of the Caribbean, Jungle Cruise, The Magic Carpets of Aladdin, or Walt Disney's Enchanted Tiki Room.

❦ Access Frontierland via the path near the Enchanted Tiki Room. Consider lunching at Pecos Bill Cafe or Columbia Harbour House. Be sure to check out the Hall of Presidents in Liberty Square.

❦ If time allows, squeeze in The Haunted Mansion before the Festival of Fantasy parade. Watch the parade and move on to Fantasyland.

❦ See as much of Fantasyland as possible, including Dumbo, It's a Small World, Peter Pan's Flight, Seven Dwarfs Mine Train, and Under the Sea—Journey of The Little Mermaid.

❦ If the timing's right, head to the front of the Castle for a live stage show, or take a relaxing ride on Tomorrowland's PeopleMover.

❦ Haven't seen Tom Sawyer Island, the Haunted Mansion, or the Country Bear Jamboree? Go for it!

❦ If the Main Street Electrical Parade is scheduled to run twice, explore Tomorrowland during the earlier showing. Visit Space Mountain, Buzz Lightyear's Space Ranger Spin, Monsters, Inc. Laugh Floor, Stitch's Great Escape, and the Tomorrowland Speedway.

❦ View Wishes, an impressive nightly fireworks display, from the middle of Main Street, U.S.A.

❦ Watch the Main Street Electrical Parade from Frontierland. And if there's time, revisit a favorite attraction (guests are usually admitted right up until closing time).

Continued on page 34

ONE-DAY SCHEDULE

Continued from page 33

MAGIC KINDGOM MUSTS:

Here's a list of the attractions that put the magic in the Magic Kingdom. (Note that these are all Fastpass+ attractions):

Splash Mountain

Big Thunder Mountain Railroad

The Haunted Mansion

Festival of Fantasy (afternoon parade)

Pirates of the Caribbean

Peter Pan's Flight

It's a Small World

Space Mountain

Buzz Lightyear's Space Ranger Spin

The Many Adventures of Winnie the Pooh

Seven Dwarfs Mine Train

Under the Sea—Journey of The Little Mermaid

The Main Street Electrical Parade

Wishes (fireworks)

More FASTPASS+ ATTRACTIONS:

Ariel's Grotto

The Barnstormer

Dumbo the Flying Elephant

Enchanted Tales with Belle

Jungle Cruise

Mad Tea Party

The Magic Carpets of Aladdin

Mickey's PhilharMagic

Monsters, Inc. Laugh Floor

Princess Fairytale Hall

Tomorrowland Speedway

Town Square Theater

LINE BUSTERS:
Even when the park is packed, there are some attractions with shorter or faster-moving lines. Among them are: Tomorrowland Transit Authority PeopleMover, Walt Disney World Railroad, The Enchanted Tiki Room, Carousel of Progress, Country Bear Jamboree, It's a Small World, and Tom Sawyer Island.

IF YOU HAVE YOUNG CHILDREN:

• Head directly to Fantasyland (walk right through the Castle) and visit Dumbo, Peter Pan, Under the Sea—Journey of The Little Mermaid, and The Many Adventures of Winnie the Pooh. Cool off at Casey Jr. Splash 'N' Soak Station.

• Stop for a spin in a teacup on the way to Frontierland. Sing along with Big Al and the gang at the Country Bear Jamboree.

• Check the schedule for the Castle stage show before riding the carousel and It's a Small World.

• Line up for the afternoon parade about 30 minutes early. Or skip the parade, finish up Fantasyland, and take a magic carpet ride in Adventureland. If it's hot (and your tot has swim diapers), head to the tiki statues near Jungle Cruise. They spit water!

• Most little ones enjoy Tom Sawyer Island and the Walt Disney World Railroad, too.

ONE-DAY SCHEDULE

❤ If you haven't booked Fastpass+ assignments, you can do so at a park kiosk. Check a guidemap for locations. Then start the day by making a beeline for Future World's Soarin' and Test Track. (If the Test Track line is long, consider jumping on the "single riders" line. It moves a bit faster.) If you have no health issues and no susceptibility to motion sickness *whatsoever*, experience the out-of-this-world adventure known as "highly intense" Mission: SPACE Orange Team. (Otherwise, ride Mission: SPACE-Green Team—the less intense, non-spinning version.) Follow it up with The Seas with Nemo & Friends. Keep in mind that World Showcase opens at 11 A.M.

❤ Stop for lunch at The Land's Sunshine Seasons, The Electric Umbrella, or Coral Reef in The Seas.

❤ After exploring The Land, view *Captain EO* in the Imagination pavilion. Be sure to enjoy ImageWorks, a small, high-tech playground. Little kids love it.

❤ If you're up for some serious pin trading (or shopping), stop by Pin Central in Innoventions Plaza. (Workers wearing pins are always willing to swap Disney pins.)

❤ Check out Spaceship Earth before heading to Innoventions. If the Universe of Energy is open for business, pay it a visit.

❤ Make your way to World Showcase by early evening and start your circular tour of the world at Canada. Proceed counterclockwise around the lagoon. Don't miss the *Impressions de France* movie in the France pavilion, the American Adventure show, and Maelstrom in Norway. Take in as much live entertainment as you can—World Showcase has a lot to offer!

❤ After dinner, scope out a spot to watch IllumiNations—Reflections of Earth. (We enjoy the areas near Italy and Japan, but there are excellent viewing locations all around World Showcase Lagoon.) Return to your viewing spot about 30 to 40 minutes before the show.

TIMING TIP: If you have a restaurant reservation at World Showcase, allow 30 to 40 minutes to get there from the front gate. Taking a FriendShip water taxi can shave a few minutes off your trip, but it isn't much faster than brisk walking.

EPCOT

Continued on page 36

ONE-DAY SCHEDULE

Continued from page 35

EPCOT ESSENTIALS:

There is a lot to see and do at Disney's discovery park. Don't leave without investigating these outstanding attractions:

- Soarin'
- Test Track
- Spaceship Earth
- Turtle Talk with Crush
- Universe of Energy
- Living with the Land
- IllumiNations—Reflections of Earth
- The Seas with Nemo & Friends
- The American Adventure show
- Mission: SPACE ("non-spinning" version)

FASTPASS+ ATTRACTIONS*:

Group A:
- *Test Track*
- *Living with the Land*
- *Soarin'*
- *IllumiNations— Reflections of Earth*

Group B:
- *Mission: SPACE*
- *Captain EO*
- *Maelstrom*
- *Spaceship Earth*
- *Turtle Talk*
- *Epcot Character Spot*

LINE BUSTERS:

Tired of long lines? Go to: The Circle of Life movie in The Land, Journey into Imagination with Figment in Imagination!, Universe of Energy, *Impressions de France* in the France pavilion, or The American Adventure. The Spaceship Earth line thins out in the afternoon, as does the line for the attractions inside The Seas with Nemo & Friends.

IF YOU HAVE YOUNG CHILDREN:

- Begin the day by visiting the Epcot Character Spot, then thoroughly exploring The Seas with Nemo & Friends. After that, head over to Imagination! to experience Journey Into Imagination with Figment and the Image-Works interactive playground.

- At World Showcase, head to Mexico's boat ride and, for braver tots, Norway's Maelstrom.

- Visit the Kidcot Fun Stop in each country. Don't miss the koi pond in Japan and Germany's tiny village.

- If the weather is warm, let little ones splash in the inter-active fountain on the pathway joining Future World with World Showcase or the spray zone in front of Test Track.

* At press time, guests could reserve a Fastpass+ time for 1 attraction from Group A and 2 from Group B. That may change in 2015. Visit *www.MyDisneyExperience.com* for updates.

ONE-DAY SCHEDULE

❤ Some attractions open later in the morning; consult a park Times Guide for exact times. Also, many shows here run on a schedule (e.g., Indiana Jones Epic Stunt Spectacular and Beauty and the Beast—Live on Stage); check for times throughout the day. Stop at a park kiosk to get Fastpass+ assignments if you haven't booked them in advance.

❤ Toy Story Mania! is wildly popular. Arrive as early as possible and pre-book a Fastpass+ assignment if you can.

❤ Daredevils should begin the day with Rock 'n' Roller Coaster, followed by some eye-opening drops at The Twilight Zone™ Tower of Terror.

❤ If Beauty and the Beast is playing soon, grab a seat. Otherwise, plan to come back later and go to The Magic of Disney Animation, Voyage of The Little Mermaid, and Walt Disney: One Man's Dream.

❤ Pause for lunch at the 50's Prime Time Cafe, Sci-Fi Dine-In Theater, Backlot Express, or Starring Rolls Cafe.

❤ Post-lunch is a great time to visit Voyage of The Little Mermaid or The Great Movie Ride. If a parade is offered, be sure to catch it.

❤ Be sure to see Muppet★Vision 3-D, followed by the Studio Backlot Tour; Star Tours—The Adventures Continue; Lights, Motors, Action—Extreme Stunt Show; and the Indiana Jones Epic Stunt Spectacular.

❤ Take tots to the Honey, I Shrunk the Kids Movie Set Adventure and Disney Junior—Live on Stage.

❤ If you missed Beauty and the Beast—Live on Stage, go now and, if you haven't hit it yet, be sure to experience The Great Movie Ride.

❤ If Fantasmic is being presented today, you want to get a spot in line at least 50 minutes before showtime. Note that if you choose to skip Fantasmic, plan to exit the park before the last performance breaks. If you do stay for the show, know that you can meander through select shops while the throngs file through the exit.

Continued on page 38

ONE-DAY SCHEDULE

Continued from page 37

STUDIO STANDOUTS*:

If you're short on time, be sure to catch as many of the following four-star attractions at Disney's Hollywood Studios as possible. Note that they are all included in Fastpass+:

Group A:
Toy Story Mania!
Rock 'n' Roller Coaster—starring Aerosmith
Beauty and the Beast—Live on Stage
The Great Movie Ride
Fantasmic!

Group B:
The Twilight Zone™ Tower of Terror
Muppet★Vision 3-D
Star Tours—The Adventures Continue

More FASTPASS+ ATTRACTIONS*:

In addition to those listed on the left, these attractions are classified by Disney as Group B:

Disney Junior—Live on Stage!

Indiana Jones Epic Stunt Spectacular!

Voyage of The Little Mermaid

Lights, Motors, Action— Extreme Stunt Show

LINE BUSTERS:
When lines abound at Disney's Hollywood Studios, we suggest the following: Indiana Jones Epic Stunt Spectacular (the theater fits about 2,000 guests at a time); The Magic of Disney Animation; Honey, I Shrunk the Kids Movie Set Adventure; Studio Backlot Tour; Lights, Motors, Action—Extreme Stunt Show (this theater also has enormous seating capacity); American Film Institute Showcase; and Walt Disney: One Man's Dream.

IF YOU HAVE YOUNG CHILDREN:

• Begin with Toy Story Mania, followed by the Voyage of The Little Mermaid attraction (but warn kids about moments of darkness and a thunderstorm), and Muppet★Vision 3-D. (If kids won't wear 3-D glasses, skip the movies and head directly to Disney Junior—Live on Stage.)

• Have lunch at Pizza Planet, then watch the parade (if it is offered). Romp in the Honey, I Shrunk the Kids Movie Set Adventure; catch Disney Junior—Live on Stage, and see Beauty and the Beast—Live on Stage. Skip Fantasmic—it tends to terrify tots.

• Catch up with Disney characters at Animation Courtyard and on Pixar Place.

* At press time, guests could reserve a Fastpass+ time for 1 attraction from Group A and 2 from Group B. That may change in 2015. Visit *www.MyDisneyExperience.com* for updates.

ONE-DAY SCHEDULE

❤ Guests who arrive at park opening may enjoy a good-morning greeting from Disney characters. Many shows here run on a schedule, so check for times throughout the day. If you want to experience Expedition Everest (and you should), book Fastpass+ or arrive as early as you can. Make a point of perusing the schedules for Festival of the Lion King and Finding Nemo— The Musical. Note that if you haven't pre-booked Fastpass+ assignments, you can make same-day arrangements at a Fastpass+ kiosk in the park.

❤ As you enter the park, pass through the Oasis and head toward DinoLand. After riding Expedition Everest, catch Finding Nemo—The Musical (arrive early). Take young children to the Boneyard before leaving the area.

❤ In Asia, tackle Dinosaur, ride Kali River Rapids, then visit the tigers at the Maharajah Jungle Trek, and see the delightful Flights of Wonder bird show at the Caravan Stage.

❤ Check a park Times Guide for the Festival of the Lion King schedule. Plan to arrive at the theater at least 45 minutes prior to your preferred showtime (it's a very popular production). If possible, mingle with Mickey and Minnie (at the Adventurers Outpost) before seeing Festival of the Lion King.

❤ Stop at Yak & Yeti or Tusker House for lunch. Then jump aboard the Wildlife Express train to Rafiki's Planet Watch. Don't miss the Song of the Rainforest and the Affection Section petting farm.

❤ After experiencing Africa's Kilimanjaro Safaris, take a relaxing hike on the animal-laden Pangani Forest Exploration Trail.

❤ Wander the Discovery Island Trails around the Tree of Life, taking time to search for animals carved into the tree and its roots.

❤ Finish off the day with a viewing of It's Tough to be a Bug and revisiting your favorite attractions.

Continued on page 40

ONE-DAY SCHEDULE

Continued from page 39

ANIMAL KINGDOM ACES:

An abbreviated visit to Disney's Animal Kingdom is enough to make anybody growl. The following attractions should help soothe the savage beast, er, guest:

- Dinosaur
- Kali River Rapids
- Kilimanjaro Safaris
- Pangani Forest Exploration Trail
- Expedition Everest
- Finding Nemo—The Musical
- Maharajah Jungle Trek
- Flights of Wonder
- Festival of the Lion King
- It's Tough to be a Bug!
- Winged Encounters—
    The Kingdom Takes Flight

FASTPASS+ ATTRACTIONS:

Dinosaur
Expediton Everest
Festival of the Lion King
Finding Nemo—The Musical
It's Tough to Be a Bug!
Kali River Rapids
Primeval Whirl
Winged Encounters

LINE BUSTERS:

When herds of guests mob Disney's Animal Kingdom attractions, there are a few places to escape the stampede: The Oasis, Pangani Forest Exploration Trail, Maharajah Jungle Trek, Discovery Island Trails, The Boneyard playground, and Rafiki's Planet Watch. (You have to take the Wildlife Express train to reach Rafiki's Planet Watch.)

IF YOU HAVE YOUNG CHILDREN:

- We recommend lingering a bit in the Oasis on your way into the park. As you cross the bridge to Discovery Island, stop at the Wilderness Explorer Headquarters and get started collecting badges. Then go to the Adventurers Outpost to meet Mickey and Minnie.

- Stop by the Tree of Life to notice all of the animal carvings in its trunk. (Note that the show inside the tree, It's Tough to be a Bug, is very intense and may frighten young children.) Take in a performance of Winged Encounters—The Kingdom Takes Flight (a high-flying show featuring colorful macaws).

- Eat lunch at Pizzafari or head to DinoLand's Restaurantosaurus. Be sure to see The Boneyard playground, Flights of Wonder, and Chester and Hester's Dino-Rama.

- In Asia, go to the Maharajah Jungle Trek. Ride Africa's bumpy Kilimanjaro Safaris. See the Pangani Forest Exploration Trail. Then take the train to Rafiki's Planet Watch.

HALF-DAY SCHEDULE

Morning at the Magic Kingdom*

❦ Where to begin? It's a big decision. Know that the area you postpone may have long lines by the time you get there. We like to start in Adventureland.

❦ Visit Pirates of the Caribbean, then head over to Splash Mountain (if you don't mind getting a little soggy) and Big Thunder Mountain Railroad.

❦ Visit The Haunted Mansion, and then grab a spot for the afternoon parade, Festival of Fantasy.

❦ Watch the Festival of Fantasy parade (and wave hello to Anna and Elsa!) in Frontierland. Or skip the parade and go to Peter Pan's Flight, Winnie the Pooh, It's a Small World, Under the Sea—Journey of The Little Mermaid, and the Seven Dwarfs Mine Train.

❦ Head to Tomorrowland to experience Space Mountain. Follow it up with Buzz Lightyear's Space Ranger Spin. Take youngsters for a relaxing trip on the PeopleMover (but warn them that there will be moments of total darkness).

The Magic Kingdom* After Lunch

❦ Check a Times Guide and choose a time to take in the Castle stage show. And don't miss the Festival of Fantasy parade!

❦ Explore Town Square Theater. If the wait to meet Mickey Mouse is more than 45 minutes, consider coming back in the evening—or get a Fastpass+ assignment.

❦ Start in Adventureland. Ride the Jungle Cruise and Pirates of the Caribbean.

❦ Head to Frontierland. Do Splash Mountain and Big Thunder Mountain Railroad. Then see the Country Bears or Tom Sawyer Island (the latter closes at dusk).

❦ Take a spin at the Mad Tea Party, and see the highlights of Fantasyland, including It's a Small World, Seven Dwarfs Mine Train, Peter Pan, Under the Sea—Journey of The Little Mermaid, and The Many Adventures of Winnie the Pooh.

❦ Join the afternoon street party known as Move it, Shake it, Celebrate it! if it is offered.

❦ Pop in at The Haunted Mansion and The Hall of Presidents before dinner.

❦ Now it's time for Tomorrowland. (If you have the energy and the evening parade is running twice, stay in Tomorrowland during the early run. Watch the parade later.) Go to Space Mountain or Buzz Lightyear's Space Ranger Spin.

❦ If it's scheduled, catch the Main Street Electrical Parade. And don't miss the fireworks. (They are presented rain or shine.)

❦ Shop on Main Street, U.S.A., while the exiting masses file out.

* For details on where to meet Disney characters, see page 136.

Half Day with Young Children

Start at Town Square Theater. Meet Mickey inside. If it's close to parade time, grab a spot on the curb. After exploring Fantasyland (do not miss It's a Small World), consider the Country Bear Jamboree. Soar on a magic carpet in Adventureland, then head to Tomorrowland. Cap off the day with Buzz Lightyear, followed by the Main Street Electrical Parade and the fireworks.

Magic Kingdom

HALF-DAY SCHEDULE

Morning at Epcot

❦ Head directly to Soarin', then Test Track. If you're up for the "intense" Mission: SPACE, go for it. (We prefer the "less intense," non-spinning version of the attraction.) Then move on to The Seas with Nemo & Friends, followed by Captain EO in the Imagination pavilion.

❦ See Universe of Energy and check out Innoventions before moving on to World Showcase—it opens at 11 A.M. Save Spaceship Earth for later, when the line dies down a bit. When hunger calls, stop for lunch. See the countries that interest you most, making sure to see the show inside the American Adventure and the boat rides in Norway (Maelstrom) and Mexico (Gran Fiesta Tour Starring the Three Caballeros).

Epcot After Lunch

❦ If you don't have restaurant reservations and would like to have dinner at a table-service restaurant, stop by Guest Relations to make them. If not, consider dining at the nearby BoardWalk resort (it's a short stroll or FriendShip ride away).

❦ See as much of Future World as possible before heading to World Showcase. (Future World usually closes at 7 P.M., while World Showcase stays open until 9 P.M.)

❦ Spend the evening touring World Showcase. Keep an eye on the clock so you can secure a good spot around the lagoon to watch the evening's presentation of IllumiNations—Reflections of Earth.

❦ Avoid the crush of exiting crowds by browsing the wares in the Mouse Gear shop in Future World or relaxing by the Fountain of Nations.

Half Day with Young Children

Begin with a visit to the Epcot Character Spot, followed by The Seas with Nemo & Friends (take a ride in a "clam-mobile," see Turtle Talk with Crush, and romp in Bruce's Shark World). Follow it up with a visit to Spaceship Earth. Check out the Kidcot Fun Stops throughout the park and stop by the miniature village in Germany. If there's time, check out Journey Into Imagination with Figment and ImageWorks in the Imagination pavilion.

WHERE TO MEET THE CHARACTERS*

Epcot Character Spot (Mickey, Minnie, Pluto, and Goofy); **Mexico** (Donald Duck); **Germany** (Snow White); **France** (Beast, Belle, and Marie from *The Aristocats*); **United Kingdom** (Mary Poppins and Alice in Wonderland); **China** (Mulan); **Morocco** (Jasmine and Aladdin); **Showcase Plaza** (Duffy the Disney Bear)

* Characters subject to change.

HALF-DAY SCHEDULE

Morning at Disney's Hollywood Studios

❦ Kick-start the day with a visit to Toy Story Mania!, followed by trips to Rock 'n' Roller Coaster and Tower of Terror (just don't do the thrill rides on a full stomach). From there, move on to Muppet★Vision 3-D and Star Tours—The Adventures Continue.

❦ Before lining up for the parade (if one is scheduled), see The Magic of Disney Animation; Beauty and the Beast—Live on Stage; Lights, Motors, Action—Extreme Stunt Show; and The Great Movie Ride.

❦ For a quick bite, stop at The Backlot Express or Starring Rolls Cafe.

❦ If time permits, take in Voyage of The Little Mermaid and Walt Disney: One Man's Dream.

Disney's Hollywood Studios After Lunch

❦ Begin with Tower of Terror, Rock 'n' Roller Coaster, and Beauty and the Beast—Live on Stage.

❦ See Voyage of The Little Mermaid; Star Tours; Muppet★Vision 3-D; The Great Movie Ride; Lights, Motors, Action—Extreme Stunt Show; Toy Story Mania! (expect a wait of at least an hour at all times); the Indiana Jones Epic Stunt Spectacular; and the Studio Backlot Tour.

❦ If there's time, see Walt Disney: One Man's Dream and the Magic of Disney Animation before grabbing a spot in line for Fantasmic (if the nighttime spectacular is being presented today). Or skip Fantasmic and revisit favorite attractions.

Half Day with Young Children

Start with Disney Junior—Live on Stage (it's a can't-miss), followed by Voyage of The Little Mermaid, the Honey, I Shrunk the Kids Movie Set Adventure, and Beauty and the Beast—Live on Stage. Youngsters ages 4 to 12 can harness The Force at the Jedi Training Academy. If the weather is warm, take tots to play in the spray from the giant bottle near the the Studios Backlot Tour. Plan to skip Fantasmic—it is just too intense (and a bit long) for most tykes.

WHERE TO MEET THE CHARACTERS*

Hollywood Boulevard at park opening time (Mickey, Donald, Chip, Dale, and more); **Animation Courtyard** (Disney Junior friends such as Sofia the First and Jake from *Jake and the Never Land Pirates*, plus Mickey Mouse); **Pixar Place** (Woody, Jessie, Bullseye, or other *Toy Story* characters); **Streets of America** (friends from *Phineas and Ferb*, *Monsters, Inc.*, and *Cars*)

* Characters subject to change.

Morning at Disney's Animal Kingdom

❦ Go to Asia to ride the thrilling Expedition Everest and the soaking Kali River Rapids, and hike the Maharajah Jungle Trek.

❦ Experience Flights of Wonder bird show on the way to Kilimanjaro Safaris and the Pangani Forest Exploration Trail.

❦ Check a Times Guide to see when the Festival of the Lion King show is playing today. Plan to arrive at least 45 minutes before showtime.

❦ Finish up with Finding Nemo—The Musical; Dinosaur; and It's Tough to be a Bug— though the last two are too intense for tots. Take little ones to The Boneyard playground instead.

Disney's Animal Kingdom After Lunch

❦ Check a Times Guide for Festival of the Lion King and Finding Nemo—The Musical schedules. Arrive 30 to 45 minutes before showtime. Then visit Mickey and Minnie at the Adventurers Outpost on Discovery Island.

❦ If there is entertainment, such as Winged Wonders—The Kingdom Takes Flight, stick around Discovery Island to enjoy it. Otherwise, head to the Kilimanjaro Safaris ride. Do the Pangani Forest Exploration Trail, and take the train to Rafiki's Planet Watch.

❦ Ride Expedition Everest and Kali River Rapids, and experience the Maharajah Jungle Trek. Try to catch Flights of Wonder and Winged Encounters, too.

❦ Wander the Discovery Island Trails and see It's Tough to be a Bug.

❦ Before dinner, dodge dastardly dinos on Dinosaur.

Half Day with Young Children

Scope out animal life in The Oasis before stopping at the Wilderness Explorer Headquarters on the bridge to Discovery Island. Then go to the Adventurers Outpost to meet Mickey and Minnie, followed by a visit to DinoLand U.S.A. Explore The Boneyard and ride TriceraTop Spin. If time allows, take the train to Rafiki's Planet Watch, where kids can bond with live animals (mostly goats) in the Affection Section. The Flights of Wonder and Winged Encounters bird shows captivate guests of all ages.

WHERE TO MEET THE CHARACTERS*

Park Entrance at park opening (characters vary); **Cretaceous Trail** (Donald Duck); **Discovery Island Trails** (Pocahontas); **Discovery Island Character Landing** (Winnie the Pooh and Tigger); **Adventurers Outpost on Discovery Island** (Mickey and Minnie); **Rafiki's Planet Watch** (Rafiki, Chip 'n' Dale); **Upcountry Landing** between Asia and Africa (Baloo and Louie); **DinoLand Service Station** (Pluto and Goofy); **It's Tough to be a Bug** entrance (Russel and Dug).

* Characters subject to change.

Disney's Animal Kingdom

Making the Most of Longer Visits

Longer stays allow the chance to sample some of the World's myriad offerings. Spend another day in the one park you most enjoyed. Lounge by the pool, go biking, or play tennis or golf. Go shopping at Downtown Disney. Cool off at one of Disney's innovative water parks. Have lunch at a WDW resort, and try a special dinner at Victoria & Albert's in the Grand Floridian or at Flying Fish Cafe at the BoardWalk resort. Check out the restaurants at Downtown Disney or spend the evening at the BoardWalk. Take golf, tennis, or surf lessons. Go fishing, waterskiing, or horseback riding. Visit a relaxing day spa. Participate in a behind-the-scenes program. Play a round or two of miniature golf. See a game at the ESPN Wide World of Sports complex. For even more ideas, see our *Sports*; *Everything Else in the World*; and *Good Meals, Great Times* chapters.

How to Save a Rainy Day

Florida rain showers come and go with such regularity that you could set your watch by them, especially during summer months. They're usually brief, though torrential. Of course, there are times when gray clouds linger longer. Here are some ways to make the most of a soggy day:

- Head for DisneyQuest, a huge interactive play zone at Downtown Disney West Side. It'll keep the whole family entertained (and dry) for hours.

- See a movie on one of AMC Theatres' many screens at Downtown Disney.

- Check out Cirque du Soleil's La Nouba.

- Consider taking in an indoor event at the ESPN Wide World of Sports complex. For information, call 407-939-1500.

- Don your rain gear and go to Epcot. The pavilions in Future World house a bounty of sheltered diversions. (Ponchos are sold throughout WDW for about $8 each.)

Customized Travel Tips:
Traveling with Children

Tell kids that a Walt Disney World vacation is in the works and the response is apt to be overwhelming! Our guide *Birnbaum's Walt Disney World For Kids 2015*, written for children ages 7 through 14, can be a useful resource for getting them involved in the planning from the outset. Filled with information about the World from a kid's perspective, it can be used as a reference before and during the trip, a place to collect character autographs, and kept as a souvenir.

Walt Disney World ranks among the easier spots on Earth for families with children. Keep in mind, however, that kids under 7 must be accompanied by a guest age 14 or older to enter the theme parks; kids under 10 must be accompanied by an adult at the water parks. With most teens, however, it is enough to establish a meeting place and time inside the parks.

Child Care: In-room child-care service can be summoned to all Disney-owned resorts. The service is available 24/7, though it is not run by Disney. For pricing and to make a reservation with Kid's Nite Out, visit *www.kidsniteout.com*, call 407-828-0920 or 800-696-8105, or inquire at your resort's lobby concierge. Another company, Super Sitters, offers this child-care service as well. In addition to resort babysitting, they can accompany a party during theme park visits. This allows parents to take older kids on attractions while the sitter keeps an eye on the younger ones. To reach them, call 407-382-2558, or visit *www.super-sitters.com*.

Children's Activity Centers: The Polynesian Village, Animal Kingdom Lodge, Wilderness Lodge, Yacht and Beach Club, and Dolphin resorts each have an on-site children's activity center. The cheery centers accept (potty-trained) kids ages 4 through 12. For

details and availability, phone 407-939-3463 for all but the Dolphin. "Camp Dolphin" operates daily from 5:30 P.M. to midnight and accepts children ages 3 through 12. Camp Dolphin costs $10 per hour, per child. For information, call 407-934-4241.

Baby Care Centers: Located in all theme parks, these centers are for parents with young children. They are not meant as day care. All kids must be accompanied by a parent or guardian. There are rooms with rocking chairs and couches in feeding rooms for nursing mothers and screenings of Disney films for kids. Centers have facilities for changing diapers, preparing formula, warming bottles, and washing bottles. Diapers, bottles, formula, pacifiers, and baby food are among the supplies for sale. Baby Care Center locations are listed on theme park guidemaps. There are changing areas in most women's and in many men's restrooms.

Lost Children: Disney employees (also known as "cast members") will know what to do if a child starts to call for his or her parents. If your child wanders off, stop in at the Baby Care Center or City Hall in the Magic Kingdom; at Guest Relations or the Baby Care Center in Epcot; at Guest Relations in Disney's Hollywood Studios; or at Guest Relations in Animal Kingdom. A computerized system allows for a detailed description of the child and his or her status, helping to reunite families quickly. It helps if your child has your mobile phone number, too. There are no paging systems, but in emergencies an all-points bulletin can be put out among cast members. The Guest Relations staff at each Disney park can help, too.

Parental Perk

Families with babies or small children should know about the "rider switch" policy (aka "baby swap") at the theme parks. At attractions with age or height restrictions, a parent who waits nearby with a young child while the other parent rides the attraction can go right on soon after the first parent comes off. Be sure to ask the attendant at the attraction's entrance. They'll tell you how to proceed.

It's smart to prepare youngsters for the possibility of an accidental separation. Direct him or her to contact a park worker (anybody wearing a name tag) and ask for help.

Refrigerators: For parents of young children, an in-room fridge is not a mere luxury, it's a necessity. Accommodations at all Walt Disney World–owned-and-operated resorts generally come equipped with a small refrigerator. (If your room doesn't have one, request it—you won't be charged.)

Baby Food: Many parents choose to ship a box of food and baby supplies to their resort before they leave home. It is possible to purchase jars of baby food at most Disney resorts, but the selection isn't huge. For a wider variety of foodstuffs to choose from, make a trip to the Winn-Dixie at 11957 Apopka-Vineland Road (just beyond the Crossroads shopping center) or Gooding's at the Crossroads, near Hotel Plaza Boulevard. For driving directions, inquire at your resort's front desk.

Winn-Dixie and Gooding's, as well as nearby convenience stores, are also within a reasonable cabbing distance. Be sure to hire an authorized cab for the trip. Your resort staff can make the arrangements and give you an estimate of the cost. Another option is to order groceries from *gardengrocer.com*. They are authorized to deliver to most Disney-area hotels and stock a wide variety of items, including many organic, gluten-free, and kosher selections.

If you have a milk (or other food) need after hours, know that these Disney resorts have 24-hour snack bars: Grand Floridian, Polynesian Village, Dolphin, and Buena Vista Palace.

Cribs: Most Walt Disney World resort rooms come with a small, playpen-like crib. (Look for it in the closet. If it's not there, call to request one.) They're free, but somewhat flimsy. If you'd like something a little bigger or sturdier,

consider renting a crib from Orlando Crib Rental (407-433-7770).

Diapers: Each Disney resort has at least one shop in which to pick up diapers. If you're brand loyal, pack your own. (Consider shipping diapers to your resort so you don't have to pack them.) Be sure to throw a few swim diapers into your bag each morning. You never know when you'll run into an interactive fountain on Disney property. They're necessary for pool use, too.

Resort Fun: Most WDW resorts have at least one arcade. Most of the hotels have little playgrounds as well as toddler-friendly pools.

Tips for Tots

Walt Disney World is as toddler-friendly as it gets. Here are a few pointers to make it even more so:

- Familiarize your child with Disney characters before your trip. That way they'll be more likely to enjoy meeting them and less likely to be frightened by them.

- Fireworks can scare little ones silly. If your tot is spooked by loud noises, be prepared to make a hasty exit once the booms begin. That said, most babies are enchanted by the Main Street Electrical Parade, the Magic Kingdom's nighttime processional.

- Be sure to bring snacks when you head out for the day. It's tough to find toddler-friendly nibbles once you leave your resort.

- You will be asked to collapse your stroller before boarding a WDW resort bus or boat—but not on the monorail. This makes the monorail resorts even more appealing to the stroller set.

- Don't forget sunscreen that's sensitive to toddler skin. Pack a hat for an infant.

- Pack a small but treasured toy from home and keep it with you at all times.

- Don't underestimate the play value of a good splash. Take time to relax and enjoy the invaluable amenity that is the Walt Disney World resort pool. Of course, swim diapers are a must.

- Remember that your child may enter the parks for free until his or her third birthday.

HOT TIP!

Small children may become a bit anxious when dropped off at one of Disney's child activity centers. If that's the case, plan to stick around until the trepidation passes. And prepare your child ahead of time. Let him or her know they'll be playing with other kids—coloring, playing games, watching movies, and the like. Reassure kids that you'll be nearby, and tell them what time you'll be coming back. That way, little minds can relax and have fun.

Tips for Teens

When it comes to teens at Disney World, The Little Mermaid's Ariel has plenty of company. Of course, be they of the fish or human variety, teenage guests have special needs all their own. Here are some tips from our WDW teen experts:

- Bring your own music. It's perfect for the trip to Walt Disney World and for sitting poolside at your resort. But don't wear your earphones for your whole trip.

- Have some of your own money on hand. If it's your hard-earned cash, you probably won't spend it as quickly as you would Mom and Dad's!

- Pack a hat. Why? It's much easier to throw a hat on than waste time doing your hair.

- Try to get along with your brothers and sisters—even if it isn't always easy. Don't bug them to do the things you want to do all the time. Try to do things they want to do, too.

- One of the coolest things for teens to do is an Extra Magic Hours evening at a theme park. They let you stay in a park after hours and ride all the best rides with basically no wait! Another good thing to do at night is to go shopping, especially at Downtown Disney Marketplace.

- Attention, parents! Try to include your teens in planning the trip. If they get a say during planning, they'll be much happier when they arrive at Disney World. Also, don't make them get up every morning at 6 A.M. Try to give them a day or two to wake up late and lounge around the pool or a water park.

For information on special children's activities at Disney resorts, turn to page 230.

Strollers: Available for $15 for one day and $13 per day of a multi-day rental at stroller rental areas at each of the theme parks. (Strollers are not available for rent at the water parks.) Double strollers cost $31 for one day and $27 per day of a multi-day rental. Deposits are no longer required for stroller rentals at the Walt Disney World theme parks.

Keep in mind that strollers are not permitted inside the attractions (they can be parked near each attraction entrance). If a stroller disappears while you're in an attraction, a replacement may be obtained. Ask a park worker for the nearest replacement location. Guests have to pay only

HOT TIP!

If you have a baby, you'll need a stroller during your Walt Disney World visit. Although they may be rented at the theme parks, consider bringing one from home. It'll save you money and the hassle of getting one each time you visit a park. Plus, there's the convenience of using it all over WDW property. (Disney rents strollers at the parks and Downtown Disney, but they are made of uncomfortable hard plastic and can't leave the place from which they are rented.)

When we do choose to rent a stroller, we call Magic Strollers (866-866-6177). For details, turn to page 67.

once a day for a stroller. If you rent one in the morning and plan to spend the afternoon at another park, just present your receipt for a stroller there.

If you'll need a stroller for several days, consider purchasing the Length of Stay rental ticket. It'll save you two dollars off the daily price, and it should cut down on time spent in the rental line. Simply buy the ticket on your first visit to a theme park and put your receipt in a safe place—that's what you'll need to show to get a stroller on the remaining days of your stay.

Downtown Disney Marketplace and West Side rent single strollers for $15 a day, plus a refundable deposit (there are no doubles available here). You may also bring your own stroller into the parks.

Note: You will be asked to remove the child and fold your stroller before boarding Disney World buses and boats. There's no folding necessary when boarding the monorail.

Traveling Without Children

Walt Disney World has become an extremely popular destination for adults without children, appealing to singles, couples, and empty nesters alike. Disney has responded to the demand with an entertainment and dining selection for grown-ups without kids in tow.

Couples

There is a place for lovebirds at Walt Disney World. Actually, there are many spots in the World perfectly suited to those with romantic intentions.

- Grown-ups love to roam the parks unencumbered by little ones and strollers. The Magic Kingdom's carousel-and-castle combo invokes the enchantment in true fairy-tale tradition. Epcot's World Showcase has the aura of a whirlwind tour (and the inspiration for a future trip?), with countries as exotic and far-reaching as Japan and Morocco. Disney's Hollywood Studios recaptures an era of starry-eyed elegance. And what could be more enjoyable than sharing a safari through Africa at Disney's Animal Kingdom?

  By day, there is romance in the theme parks for couples who are already inclined to hold hands; by night, the parks sparkle with an intensity that inspires sudden mushiness in those who never considered themselves the type, and that's before the fireworks.

- As Disney's themed resorts go about transporting guests to various times and places, they make quite a few passes through settings straight out of everyone's fantasy escape textbook—from the Victorian charms of the Grand Floridian to the exotic island getaway that is the Polynesian Village resort. You won't find a more inspirational backdrop than that at the rustic Wilderness Lodge, marked by geysers, waterfalls, steamy hot springs, and a grand stone fireplace. At the nostalgic Board-Walk resort, surrey bikes are available for

The Most Romantic Places in the World

WDW RESORTS

- Animal Kingdom Lodge
- Coronado Springs
- Grand Floridian
- Polynesian Village
- Port Orleans Riverside
- Wilderness Lodge
- Yacht and Beach Club

WDW RESTAURANTS

- Artist Point
- Cinderella's Royal Table
- Citricos
- Jiko—The Cooking Place
- Le Cellier Steakhouse
- Monsieur Paul
- Narcoossee's
- Sanaa
- Victoria & Albert's
- Yachtsman Steakhouse

WDW LOUNGES

- Belle Vue Lounge at BoardWalk
- Bongos' Pineapple Bar at Downtown Disney West Side
- Citricos Lounge at Grand Floridian
- Il Mulino New York Trattoria Lounge at the Swan hotel
- Rix Lounge at Coronado Springs
- The Lounge at The Wave . . . of American Flavors at Contemporary resort
- Portobello at Disney Springs

WDW THEME PARK SPOTS

- All of Epcot's World Showcase
- Castle rose garden in the Magic Kingdom

romantic rides along the waterfront. And a peaceful stroll around Crescent Lake is a lovely way to cap off the day.

- The myriad of recreational activities that couples may enjoy at Walt Disney World includes tennis, golf, water-skiing, sailing, horseback riding, couples' treatments at one of four on-property spas, and more.

Older Travelers

Disney World can sometimes be challenging for older travelers. And the heat, particularly in summer, can be hard to take. But with the proper planning and precautions, it's just as delightful for older visitors as for kids.

- For slower times, visit the parks Monday through Wednesday. (Thursdays through Sundays tend to attract lots of locals.)

- The Florida sun tends to be brutal year-round. Always wear sunscreen (don't forget your hands) and a hat.

- Try to eat early or late to avoid the mealtime crowds. In the Magic Kingdom, select restaurants such as Tony's Town Square Restaurant and Columbia Harbour House. Or take the monorail to the peaceful Polynesian Village, Contemporary, or Grand Floridian resorts, where pleasant dining options abound (check ahead to find out which restaurants serve lunch). In Epcot, the Coral Reef restaurant and La Hacienda are pleasant spots. At

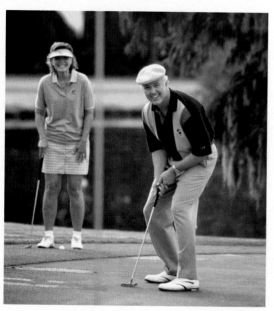

Vacation Insurance

No one books a vacation expecting to cancel it at the last minute—yet sometimes life intervenes and it's simply unavoidable. So it may be worth working travel insurance into your vacation budget (we do). It may include coverage for trip cancellation and interruption, travel delay, loss of baggage, medical expenses, and more. Be sure to ask about travel insurance when you reserve your trip.

Disney's Hollywood Studios, the Hollywood Brown Derby offers a relaxing meal, as does Mama Melrose's Ristorante Italiano.

- If you need to refrigerate medicine, know that small refrigerators are included with the room rate at all Walt Disney World-owned-and-operated resorts. They can be provided at most other resorts for a fee. Park First Aid Stations will store medicine, too.

- Don't underestimate distances at Epcot or Animal Kingdom; you may need to walk more than three miles in a day. Wear comfortable shoes and remember to take breaks.

- Pace yourself. It's smart to head back to your hotel for a swim or a nap in the afternoon and then return to the parks later on. The hotels connected by monorail are particularly convenient for this.

- Many Orlando-area hotels and attractions offer discounts to seniors and AARP members. Contact the Official Visitor Information Center (407-363-5872) for details.

HOT TIP!

Even the fittest of seniors may want to avoid some of Walt Disney World's more physically challenging attractions. Do heed all warning signs at attraction entrances to thrill rides and consider steering clear of high-activity-level experiences such as the Magic Kingdom's Swiss Family Treehouse (seemingly endless stairs!), the Maharajah Jungle Trek, and Pangani Forest Exploration Trail at Animal Kingdom (lots of walking and few places to rest).

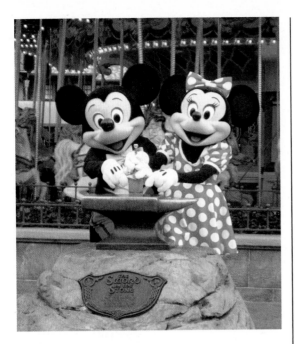

Solo Travelers

Those who travel alone (be it for business or just for fun) can have as memorable a time here as they would anywhere else.

- Solo travelers with extra time should consider taking a behind-the-scenes tour.

- Many of the finer restaurants now have counters at which to eat—perfect for chatting with other diners.

- Sometimes, being a solo traveler can mean shorter wait times at attractions. Test Track is among those with "single rider" lines.

- Other opportunities for unencumbered travelers include parasailing and waterskiing (at the Contemporary), horseback riding (at Fort Wilderness), taking a spin in a race car (at the Richard Petty Driving Experience), bass fishing (407-WDW-BASS; 939-2277), surfing lessons (407-939-7873), and watching a pro baseball game (at ESPN Wide World of Sports). Call 407-939-7529.

- Downtown Disney's lounges and restaurants can prove to be fertile meeting places. The BoardWalk is another lively destination. Sports fans find its ESPN Club most inviting. And suds fans appreciate the home-brewed libations at Big River Grille & Brewing Works. Sushi lovers fit right in at the California Grill sushi bar (in the lounge section of the eatery).

- The lounges at Walt Disney World hotels are relaxed and welcoming. The same atmosphere prevails at the Tune-In Lounge in the 50's Prime Time Cafe at Disney's Hollywood Studios, at the Rose & Crown Pub (in the United Kingdom pavilion), and the lovely lounge at Contemporary resort's The Wave . . . of American Flavors.

Important WDW Telephone Numbers

AMC Theatres (Downtown Disney):
888-262-4386

Behind-the-Scenes Tours:
407-WDW-TOUR (939-8687)

Central Reservations:
407-W-DISNEY (934-7639)

Dining Reservations:
407-WDW-DINE (939-3463)

Dr. P. Phillips Hospital:
407-351-8500

ESPN Wide World of Sports Complex:
407-939-1500

Florida Hospital Celebration Health:
407-303-4000

Golf Reservations:
407-WDW-GOLF (939-4653)

Recreation:
407-WDW-PLAY (939-7529)

Theme Park Lost and Found:
407-824-4245

Walt Disney Travel Company:
407-828-8101

Walt Disney World Information:
407-824-4321

Weather: 407-824-4104

Tips for International Travelers

Visitors from outside the U.S. need not feel like strangers in a strange land when they arrive at Walt Disney World—even if they speak a language other than English. Information is readily available in many different languages. These tips may also be helpful:

- Free park maps can be found in Spanish, French, German, Portuguese, and Japanese at the entrance to all Disney parks, as well as at Guest Relations.

- Free translation services are available at all four theme parks and include a specially designed translation device called Ears to the World, Disney's Show Translator. The units are lightweight headsets that use wireless technology to provide synchronized narration at several popular theme park attractions. They are available in French, German, Japanese, Portuguese, and Spanish. There is no charge to use the service, but a $100 refundable deposit is required to borrow one.

- Several Disney resorts offer services for their international guests. Ask about them when you inquire about reservations.

- When making your reservations through 407-WDW-DINE or WDW-PLAY, ask to speak with a foreign-language host or hostess.

- Most WDW restaurants offer menus in various languages. Some have picture menus.

- Foreign currency exchange is available at Guest Relations in each of the theme parks. Traveler's checks may be purchased at the SunTrust bank by Downtown Disney.

- Most Disney resort room keys can act as a charge card. Purchases made at Walt Disney World will be billed to a credit card that is presented at resort check-in.

- Many Disney employees are fluent in more than one language. Languages spoken are noted on employee name tags.

- Guests traveling long distances and through time zones should conserve their energy. It might be wise to relax by the pool on the day of arrival, instead of trying to fit in a full day at a theme park—it's never beneficial to start a vacation exhausted!

- Phone cards good for international calls can be purchased at several Disney World shops and in many resorts. Inquire at Guest Relations. Resist the urge to direct dial calls from resort rooms (see below).

Telephone Dos and Don'ts

It's a common practice for hotels to assess a surcharge for phone calls, and Disney is no exception. To avoid whopping bills, use your mobile phone, and keep these tips in mind for the hotel phone:

- A direct-dialed, long-distance call will set you back the cost of the call at the AT&T operator-assisted day rate, plus a 65 percent surcharge. The rate applies to both domestic and international long distance. Applicable taxes are included.

- Prepaid phone cards are available for purchase in most WDW resort lobbies.

- There is no extra fee for guests making credit card, prepaid phone card, or any type of operator-assisted calls from a resort-room telephone.

- There is no charge to call an 800 number from a WDW resort room.

- Landline directory assistance 411 phone calls cost $1.99 each; a 555-1212 call costs $1.40.

- There's no charge to call from room to room within a resort—but there may be a charge to call one Disney resort from another.

- Cell-phone users, check with your carriers to avoid tallying up "roaming" charges. And switch your mobile phone from roaming to Wi-Fi whenever possible.

- All Walt Disney World-owned-and-operated resorts support mobile computing via laptop and tablet. Hi-speed Wi-Fi service is free.

Travelers with Disabilities

Disney tends to get high marks from travelers with disabilities because of attention paid to special needs. Here is an overview:

GETTING AROUND: Special parking is available for guests at the theme parks; ask for directions at the Auto Plaza upon entering. From the Transportation and Ticket Center (TTC), the Magic Kingdom is accessible by ferry or by monorail. All monorail stations are accessible to wheelchairs. The ramps are lengthy and a bit steep, but manageable.

Wheelchairs: Guests are permitted to bring their own wheelchairs or Electric Conveyance Vehicles (ECVs). They also have the option of renting them at a theme park, BoardWalk resort, or from a local vendor. Wheelchairs may be rented in theme parks for $12 per day ($10 per day with a Length of Stay rental). In the Magic Kingdom, they are available at the Stroller and Wheelchair Rental. Epcot's rental areas are at the main entrance and at the International Gateway entrance. Oscar's Super Service rents wheelchairs at the Studios. At Animal Kingdom, wheelchairs may be rented at Garden Gate Gifts–Stroller Rental area.

If you plan to visit the parks for several days, consider getting a multi-day wheelchair rental. Called a Length of Stay ticket, it comes at a $2-per-day discount. Pay for the entire stay when you first visit a theme park. Simply show your receipt the next time you visit a rental location.

The water parks have a small number of wheelchairs to borrow. There's no charge, but the supply is limited. Guests must leave a valid ID as deposit. Downtown Disney Marketplace Strollers & Wheelchairs and DisneyQuest rent wheelchairs for $12 a day, plus a $100 deposit. ECVs are available at Marketplace Strollers & Wheelchairs for $50 per day with a $100 deposit. Wheelchairs at ESPN Wide World of Sports may be borrowed for free.

Resorts with zero-depth-entry pools may have a small number of wheelchairs available to assist guests entering the pools.

Electric Conveyance Vehicles (ECVs) are available for rent in every theme park. They cost $50 for one day, plus a $20 refundable deposit. They usually sell out early. A word of advice for first-time users: Practice makes perfect. So, before you head into a thicket of park guests, take it for a test drive.

HOT TIP!

For more information on the various services available to WDW guests with disabilities, call 407-824-4321, or visit: https://disneyworld.disney.go.com/faq/ guests-with-disabilities/attraction-access/

Equipment rented at a park cannot leave that park. If you'd like to hold on to yours for the whole trip, call a company that rents standard and electric wheelchairs, as well as scooters. Keep in mind that you will have to transport the wheelchair or scooter. (Monorails and buses are equipped to accommodate, but some boats are not.) Three companies from which to rent are LifeAire (800-417-9496), ScootAround (888-441-7575), and Walker Mobility (888-726-6837). Pickup and delivery (often for free or with a small surcharge) are available at all hotels in the WDW area (not just those on-property). In our opinion, guests are better off renting from a local vendor or bringing their own equipment. The quality is generally better, and you don't have to worry about availability. The Walt Disney Company is not affiliated with, nor does it endorse, these companies.

Buena Vista Scooters has an on-property presence at Disney's BoardWalk resort. They have a few first-come, first-served ECVs. The cost is about $30 a day. It's possible to reserve in advance; visit *www.buenavistascooters.com*, or call 407-938-0349 or 866-484-4797. These scooters have a two-day minimum rental period. The company provides free pickup and delivery to all WDW area resorts.

There are designated areas for guests using wheelchairs to view the fireworks at Epcot and to view the parades in each of the theme parks. Check a park guidemap for locations.

HOT TIP!

The theme park disability parking areas can be quite a distance from the wheelchair rental areas. If you require assistance, seek out a courtesy wheelchair to get you to the park's front entrance. The courtesy chairs are easily identified by their blue flags.

HOT TIP!

First aid locations (in the theme parks, water parks, and resorts) let guests store and use their own portable medical equipment, such as nebulizers, at their facilities.

Accessibility: It's relatively easy to get around the parks by wheelchair. Most attractions are accessible to guests who can be lifted from chairs with assistance from a member of their party, and some can accommodate guests who must remain in wheelchairs. Consult the park's *Guide for Guests with Disabilities* (for a free set, write to Walt Disney World Guest Correspondence, P.O. Box 10000, Lake Buena Vista, FL 32830) for details about access, or check with the ride host or hostess. At the water parks, life jackets are available for travelers with disabilities.

All Walt Disney World hotels have accommodations equipped for guests with disabilities, including roll-in showers. Other features—which vary, depending on the resort—include wheelchair-accessible bathrooms, bed accessories, strobe-light smoke detectors, in-room Text Typewriters (TTYs), and more. The following resorts have zero-depth-entry pools: Art of Animation, Animal Kingdom Lodge, Caribbean Beach, the Contemporary's Bay Lake Tower, Grand Floridian, Polynesian Village, and Saratoga Springs. For assistance in choosing a hotel that best fits your requirements, ask for the Special Reservations Department when you call Central Reservations (Voice: 407-939-7807; TTY: 407-939-7670).

RESOURCES: Visual Disabilities: Guests can get a handheld device that verbally describes each park as well as many attractions. Each requires a $25 refundable deposit. Braille guides, Braille menus at most restaurants, and Braille maps are also available.

Hearing Disabilities: Pay phones with Text Typewriters (TTYs) are available throughout Disney World. For more information, call 407-824-4321 or 407-827-5141. Sign language is available for some shows. Call at least two weeks ahead for arrangements.

Assistive-listening devices that amplify attraction audio are available at City Hall in the Magic Kingdom and at Guest Relations in Epcot, Animal Kingdom, and Disney's Hollywood Studios. A $25 refundable deposit is required. Sites with assistive-listening systems are listed on park guidemaps.

Attraction Access

Most park attractions are accessible to guests who are able to get out of their wheelchairs (with or without assistance). And a growing number have queues that can be navigated in a wheelchair. When that's the case, guests are urged to do so. If a wheelchair cannot be accommodated in the queue area, ask an attendant to direct you to an auxiliary entrance. Such entrances are intended for guests using wheelchairs or with service animals. For specifics on this policy, guests should visit a Guest Relations location.

Captioning systems, including reflective and handheld devices, are available at theme park Guest Relations windows. The former project show dialogue onto panels; the latter provide captioning on personal devices at certain attractions. A $25 deposit is required.

Note: Trained service animals are welcome in all Disney parks.

Booking the Trip: These organizations specialize in assisting disabled travelers:
- The Society for Accessible Travel & Hospitality (347 Fifth Ave., Suite 605, New York, NY 10016; 212-447-7284; *www.sath.org*)
- Accessible Journeys (35 W. Sellers Ave., Ridley Park, PA 19078; 610-521-0339 or 800-846-4537; *www.accessiblejourneys.com*)
- Flying Wheels Travel (143 W. Bridge St., Owatonna, MN 55060; 507-451-5005 or 877-451-5006; *www.flyingwheelstravel.com*)

Vehicles: Both Wheelchair Getaways (*www.wheelchairgetaways.com*; 800-642-2042) and Wheelchair Vans of America (800-910-8267; *www.wheelchairvansofamerica.com*) rent wheelchair-accessible vans and offer pickup and delivery for most area hotels.

HOT TIP!

What happens if your Electric Conveyance Vehicle breaks down? If you rented it at a Disney park, notify a nearby employee and a replacement will be delivered to you. If it's your own scooter, contact Guest Relations for information on assistance and rental or repair options. For units rented from outside companies, contact the rental provider—but know it's possible to rent a Disney replacement at the park. Ask an employee where you can plug it in to charge it safely.

WDW Weddings & Honeymoons

PHOTO BY JILL SAFRO

Believe it or not, Walt Disney World is one of the most popular honeymoon destinations in the United States. Why the appeal? The resorts offer romantic stretches of white-sand beaches for evening strolls, fine restaurants, and a host of activities to rival almost any other destination. Add to that the fantasy of the Magic Kingdom, the wonder of Epcot, the glamour of Disney's Hollywood Studios, and the majesty of Animal Kingdom—plus Downtown Disney and BoardWalk nightlife, water parks, and the nearby Disney Cruise Line—and it's not hard to see why Disney is tops with newlyweds.

After years of fending for themselves, folks looking to honeymoon here now have help at hand. A variety of packages cater specifically to newly married couples. For information, call toll-free: 877-566-0969.

The folks at Walt Disney World have also received oodles of requests from couples who wanted to actually get married at one of the theme parks. They responded by creating a program known as Disney's Fairy Tale Weddings. Today, couples can tie the knot in evening ceremonies at some parks during seasons when they close early.

The Yacht and Beach Club, BoardWalk, Polynesian Village, and Wilderness Lodge resorts also host their share of weddings. The Wedding Pavilion, on the grounds of the Grand

Honeymoon Registry

Launched, appropriately, on Valentine's Day, the gift registry lets happy couples plan their honeymoon. Gifts include theme park tickets, resort accommodations, spa treatments, and more. For more information or to sign up for the free Disney Honeymoon Registry, visit *www.disneyhoneymoonregistry.com*, or call 877-699-5884 during regular business hours.

Floridian Resort and Spa, offers a Victorian-style indoor setting with a prime view of Cinderella Castle and the Seven Seas Lagoon. A mix of stained glass, sage green and soft pink florals, and benches with heart-shaped cutouts (seating around 250 guests) creates the romantic ambience. Couples can fill their wedding albums with photos taken at Picture Point, under a trellis of climbing white roses, with the faraway castle in the background.

Weddings range from elegant affairs, without a hint of Disneyana, to ceremonies in which the bride arrives in Cinderella's Crystal Coach and Mickey and Minnie Mouse are among the guests at the reception.

At Franck's Bridal Studio, Walt Disney World specialists work with couples to customize each wedding. Among the services offered are cakes, photography, flower arranging, and musical entertainment. Franck's specialists can help secure accommodations, rehearsal dinners, bachelor parties, and more.

For details about planning a Walt Disney World wedding and honeymoon packages, call 321-939-4160, or visit *www.disneyweddings.com*.

My Disney Experience

The folks at Disney have unveiled My Disney Experience—"a whole new way to plan and share your Walt Disney World vacation." All potential guests are invited to visit *MyDisneyExperience.com* or download the free app. After setting up a profile, guests can ostensibly use the site to book most elements of a Disney vacation, including hotel, restaurant reservations, and even Fastpass+ assignments for select theme park attractions. For details on this work-in-progress, see page 24.

Fingertip Reference Guide

BARBERS AND SALONS

One of the most amusing places to get a haircut is the Magic Kingdom's old-fashioned Harmony Barber Shop. It's located beside the Car Barn in the Town Square section of Main Street. Cost is about $19 for adults and $15 for kids. Colored hair gel is $5 (kids love it). Treat tots to a very special "my first haircut" experience for $8. Hours are 9 A.M. to 5 P.M. daily. WDW resort guests may make reservations by calling 407-939-7529. Walk-ins are accommodated on a first-come, first-served basis.

Haircuts, coloring, manicures, and other services are available at Ship Shape at the Yacht and Beach Club (407-934-3260), Ivy Trellis at the Grand Floridian (407-824-3000, ext. 2581), the Mandara Spa at the Dolphin (407-934-4772), the Kay Casperson Spa at the Buena Vista Palace (407-827-3200), and the Casa de Belleza at Coronado Springs (407-939-7727).

BUSINESS SERVICES

Disney provides a range of services for those who simply must mix business with pleasure. Copiers, fax machines (also found at Guest Relations in the theme parks), and FedEx materials may be available at the lobby concierge or Business Center at many Walt Disney World resorts.

In addition, the Contemporary, Grand Floridian, Animal Kingdom Lodge, Yacht and Beach Club, Swan, Dolphin, and Coronado Springs resorts provide computers, printers, and Internet access for a fee. A video-conferencing center is located near Downtown Disney. For information, call 407-827-2000.

CAMERA NEEDS

Disney's PhotoPass photographers will happily snap a shot of your family with their camera (see page 133) or snap a picture using your camera or mobile phone.

Flash photography is not permitted inside any Disney attraction. Note that when capturing moments with Disney characters as video, refrain from using camera lights. (The lights are too bright for the characters' sensitive eyes.)

Camera Supplies: If you need a battery or a memory card, head to the Magic Kingdom's Town Square Theater; the Camera Center near Spaceship Earth or World Traveler at International Gateway in Epcot; The Darkroom on Hollywood Boulevard in Disney's Hollywood Studios; or Garden Gate Gifts in Disney's Animal Kingdom. One-time-use cameras are available at many shops throughout the World. The best selection can be found at the aforementioned camera shops.

CAR CARE

Three gas stations with well-stocked convenience stores are on the property, all of which are open 24 hours a day. One is on Buena Vista Drive across from Downtown Disney; another is on Floridian Way near the Magic Kingdom Auto Plaza. The third, near the BoardWalk resort on Buena Vista Drive, also has a car wash.

Breakdowns happen, but they don't spell disaster. All Disney roads are patrolled by police and security officers who can call for help. If you need a tow or other services, call the AAA Car Care Center (407-824-0976). This service is available to all WDW resort guests. Located in the Magic Kingdom Auto Plaza, the AAA Car Care Center offers full mechanical services and free towing on-property, Monday through Friday, 7 A.M. to 6 P.M.; Saturdays 7 A.M. to 4 P.M. After hours, call 407-827-4777. For off-property car care, rely on Riker's Wreckers (407-855-7776) for towing; Riker's Automotive (407-238-9800) for repairs; or AAA (if you're a member).

DRINKING LAWS

In Florida, the legal drinking age is 21. Minors are permitted to accompany their parents to WDW lounges and bars, but may not be allowed to sit at the bar. In the Magic Kingdom, liquor is served exclusively at dinner in the Be Our Guest Restaurant. Alcohol is available throughout the other theme parks and Downtown Disney.

Spirits are sold in at least one shop at most Disney resorts. Liquor may be purchased from room service at the Polynesian Village, Animal Kingdom Lodge, Contemporary, Grand Floridian, Yacht and Beach Club, BoardWalk, Swan, and Dolphin resorts; beer and wine are usually available for delivery at other resorts.

LOCKERS

Lockers can be found in the following theme park locations: to the right, just inside the Magic Kingdom entrance, beside Spaceship Earth in Epcot, near Oscar's Super Service at the Studios, and just inside the entrance (to the left) at Animal Kingdom. Lockers are also available at the Transportation and Ticket Center (TTC). Some spots offer "charging lockers" for phones and tablets.

Items too big to fit can be checked with the locker attendant at the Magic Kingdom, at Package Pickup in Epcot, and at Guest Relations at Disney's Hollywood Studios and Animal Kingdom. Cost is about $7 per day for small lockers and $9 for large ones (plus a $5 refundable deposit). Items may not be stored overnight. Lockers are cleaned out after the park closes.

Note: Be sure to save your rental receipt; it can be used again that day to secure a locker in any of the four theme parks.

LOST & FOUND

The extensive indexing system maintained by Walt Disney World's Lost and Found department is impressive, especially when a prized possession turns up missing, whether it's false teeth or a camera. (Both have been lost in the past; the dentures were never claimed.)

If you lose (or find) something, report it at any one of these Lost and Found locations: the Transportation and Ticket Center (TTC), City Hall in the Magic Kingdom, the Guest Relations lobby in Innoventions East at Epcot, at Guest Relations in Disney's Hollywood Studios, Guest Relations near the Animal Kingdom entrance, or the Concierge at any Walt Disney World resort. At Fort Wilderness, dial 7-2726 from a comfort station telephone; from outside the campground, phone 407-824-2726.

Items lost in a theme park may be claimed on the day of the loss at the park's Lost and Found, and thereafter at the Transportation and Ticket Center (TTC) Lost and Found station. To report lost items after your visit, call 407-824-4245. Hats, strollers, sunglasses, and Walt Disney World merchandise purchases are kept for one month; everything else is kept three months.

HOT TIP!

Nobody starts the day expecting to lose something. But trust us, it pays to plan ahead. Put your name and contact number on your valuables, especially cameras. Disney does a good job of tracking lost items, but it's a whole lot easier to pick a labeled camera out of the heap of look-alikes than it is to find your "little silver" one. (Yes, it happened to us. Doh!)

We highly recommend attaching contact information to all camera equipment. It makes it a whole lot easier for the folks at Lost and Found to pick your camera out of the giant, silver haystack!

MAIL

Postage stamps are sold at all WDW resorts; World of Disney at Downtown Disney; at the Newsstand shop in the Magic Kingdom; at shops near the lockers in Epcot, Disney's Hollywood Studios, and Animal Kingdom.

The old-fashioned mailboxes in the theme parks are not official U.S. mailboxes, but postcards and letters (with postage) can be mailed from them. Postmarks read "Lake Buena Vista," not "Walt Disney World."

Mail may be addressed to guests in care of their hotel. The address for all WDW resorts is Walt Disney World, P.O. Box 10000, Lake Buena Vista, FL 32830.

MEDICAL MATTERS

Travelers with chronic health problems should carry copies of all prescriptions and get names of local doctors from hometown physicians. However, Walt Disney World is equipped to deal with many types of medical emergencies. In the Magic Kingdom, next to the Crystal Palace, there is a First Aid Center staffed by a registered nurse; there is another such facility at Epcot in the Odyssey Center complex. At Disney's Hollywood Studios, the First Aid Center is inside the Guest Relations building at the main entrance. The Animal Kingdom First Aid Center is located on Discovery Island near the back side of the Creature Comforts shop.

Walt Disney World resort guests and theme park day guests staying at other area hotels have access to services providing non-emergency medical care. Centra Care Walk-In Urgent Care (*www.centracare.org*), owned and operated by Florida Hospital, has 23 area locations, most near pharmacies and with X-ray facilities.

The main facility is at 12500 South Apopka Vineland Road (407-934-2273; close to Downtown Disney) and is open 8 A.M. to midnight weekdays and 8 A.M. to 8 P.M. weekends. It is across from the Crossroads shopping center. The facility at 8014 Conroy-Windermere Road (407-291-8975; near the resorts at Universal Studios Orlando) is open 8 A.M. to 8 P.M. weekdays and 8 A.M. to 5 P.M. on weekends. One location in Kissimmee is at 8201 W. Irlo Bronson Highway (407-465-0846). It's open 8 A.M. to 8 P.M. weekdays and 8 A.M. to 5 P.M. weekends. There is also a 24-hour in-room physician service (407-238-2000).

Courtesy transportation is available from most area hotels to Centra Care clinics, and there is a no-tipping policy. Waits in walk-in clinics can be lengthy, but Centra Care drivers call ahead to learn which has the shorter wait. The most common maladies reported by Disney guests? Sunburn, blisters, colds, fevers, earaches, and injuries from falls. For emergencies, dial 911, or call nearby Florida Hospital Celebration Health (407-303-4000) or Dr. P. Phillips Hospital (407-351-8500).

For Diabetics: All Walt Disney World parks and resorts can provide refrigeration services for insulin. All WDW–owned-and-operated resort accommodations have refrigerators, and small refrigerators may be rented at most other resorts for a small fee. The fee may be waived for folks who need the fridge to store medicine, but a doctor's note may be required.

Prescriptions: Turner Drugs (407-828-8125) delivers medications to many area resorts, including those on Disney property.

MONEY

Cash, traveler's checks, American Express, MasterCard, Visa, Discover Card, Disney Visa, Diner's Club, JCB Card, Disney Dollars, and Disney gift cards are accepted as payment for most WDW charges. (Personal checks are accepted for park tickets and resort stays when presented with a credit card and valid ID.)

A Disney resort guest perk: Leave a credit card imprint at check-in, and the hotel IDs may be used to cover shop purchases, lounge and restaurant charges, and recreational fees incurred inside Walt Disney World. A bill will be sent to your home for all charges made past check-out time.

ATMs: Automated teller machines (operated by Chase) are scattered throughout Walt Disney World. Theme park locations include the Magic Kingdom (near the locker rental, in City Hall on Main Street, U.S.A., in Frontierland near the Shootin' Arcade, and in the Tomorrowland arcade); Epcot (near the main entrance, on the path between Future World and World Showcase, and in Germany), and at International Gateway; Disney's Hollywood Studios (at the entrance, inside Pizza Planet, and near Keystone Clothiers); and Animal Kingdom (near the entrance and near Chester & Hester's); plus the Transportation and Ticket Center (TTC). Most resorts have ATMs; the Fort Wilderness ATM is at Pioneer Hall. There are three at Downtown Disney: next to Tren-D in the Marketplace, and near the West Side's House of Blues and Starbucks. Most bank cards and credit cards are accepted; the fees range from about $2 to $3 (free for Chase customers).

Banking: SunTrust, across from Downtown Disney, offers a variety of services. Guests can get cash advances up to $5,000 on MasterCard, Discover, and Visa credit cards; receive incoming wire transfers up to $3,000 (for a $50 fee); and cash, replace, or purchase American Express traveler's checks. Fees may apply. This branch is open from 9 A.M. to 4 P.M. Monday through Thursday and until 6 P.M. Fridays (407-828-6103 or 800-786-8787).

Disney Dollars: Money bearing the image of Disney characters is available for purchase at Guest Relations at the theme parks, Walt Disney World resorts (at the Lobby Concierge), and at the World of Disney in $1, $5, and $10 denominations. (The exchange rate is always a buck for a buck.) Purchases are limited to $50 per person, per day. Disney Dollars are accepted as cash in most of the World.

Traveler's Checks: Even the most careful vacationer occasionally loses a wallet. Traveler's checks can take the sting out of that loss. Look for promotions by banks at home in the months preceding a vacation to see if one of the major brands—American Express, MasterCard, Visa, Citibank, and Bank of America—is available free. Stash the receipt bearing the check numbers in a place separate from the checks themselves, along with a piece of identification such as a duplicate driver's license or a spare credit card to speed the refund process should your checks get lost.

To purchase, cash, or replace American Express traveler's checks, go to the SunTrust bank across from the Downtown Disney Marketplace. (If you do not have a record of the check numbers, first contact the place where you purchased the traveler's checks. Then, an American Express referral number is required; call 800-221-7282.)

Foreign Currency Exchange: Up to $50 per person in foreign currency may be exchanged daily at Guest Relations in the theme parks, and up to $500 at the Concierge desk at Walt Disney World resorts.

PETS

No pets (other than trained service animals) are allowed in the theme parks, Downtown Disney, or the resorts, except at certain Fort Wilderness campsites. Of course, that's no reason to leave Fifi or Fido at home—especially when you can treat them to a pampered getaway at the new Best Friends Pet Resort, a sprawling luxury facility (don't call it a kennel!) complete with cat condos, doggy suites, and special acccommodations for "pocket pets," including birds and hamsters. Cats or dogs from shared households may share quarters, but cats and dogs are not permitted to cohabitate.

The facility, which is now the only place to board animals at Walt Disney World, provides a full range of hospitality services, including day care (boarding in suites), grooming services, and doggy day camp (group sessions where pups play games and frolic with other dogs under the supervision of a trained animal counselor).

Best Friends Pet Resort is located at 2510 Bonnet Creek Parkway, across from Disney's Port Orleans. Its services are available to everyone, but guests staying at Walt Disney World resorts net discounts. Indoor boarding (which includes two walks) costs $44 per day for Walt Disney World resort guests; indoor/ outdoor boarding (with one walk) runs $48 a day; vacation villas (one walk, play group, flat-screen TV, and a turndown biscuit) cost $72, and VIP luxury suites (two walks, two playgroups, flat-screen TV, webcam, and bedtime story) cost $89 a day (and, with a 3-day minimum, they throw in a "Go Home Fresh Bath").

To prevent separation anxiety, guests are encouraged to visit their pets during regular operating hours. Though hours vary, Best Friends is usually open from about one hour before the earliest theme park opening to about one hour after the latest park closing. The center is not open to the public 24 hours, but it is staffed round the clock (a handy service for guests experiencing travel delays or other emergencies). There are several certified veterinary technicians on staff, and all associates are trained in animal first aid. For directions, details on services, or to make reservations, call 877-4-WDW-PETS (493-9738), or visit *www.wdw.bestfriendspetcare.com.*

Be sure to bring along your pet's certificate of vaccinations, since Florida law requires proof of immunization for animals involved in biting incidents. Elderly pets must be in good health with bladder and bowel control, and be mobile. Pack your pet's favorite blanket or toy, too. And *never* leave your pet in the car—it is extremely dangerous and it's against the law.

Outside Walt Disney World: A few hotels in the Orlando area, including the Rosen Inn at Pointe Orlando (for $15 pet fee, plus tax per night; 407-996-8585), let pets stay with guests. Call Visit Orlando (407-363-5872 or 800-551-0181; the latter is a recording).

RELIGIOUS SERVICES

Though religious services are occasionally offered on Disney property, regular services are available at local houses of worship.

Protestant: Sundays at 8:15 A.M., 9:30 A.M., and 11 A.M. at the Community Presbyterian Church, 511 Celebration Ave., Celebration, FL; 407-566-1633.

Muslim: Prayer takes place five times a day at the Islamic Center of Orlando, 11543 Ruby Lake Rd. Call 407-238-2700 for more details.

Catholic: The closest Catholic church is Mary, Queen of the Universe Shrine, 2½ miles southeast of Lake Buena Vista, at 8300 Vineland Ave. This church seats 2,000 people. Call 407-239-6600 for mass times.

Jewish: Reform services are held at the Congregation of Reform Judaism (928 Malone Dr., Orlando; 407-645-0444), near Winter Park, about 20 miles from Walt Disney World. Conservative services are held at Temple Ohalei Rivka, also known as the Southwest Orlando Jewish Congregation (11200 South Apopka Vineland Rd.; 407-239-5444), about two miles from Downtown Disney.

SHOPPING FOR NECESSITIES

Almost any everyday item can be purchased right on Disney property. At least one shop in every WDW resort stocks a small selection of toiletries. In addition, over-the-counter health aids, plus many other useful items, can be purchased at the Emporium on Main Street in the Magic Kingdom; they're kept behind the counter, so ask for what you want.

Aspirin, sunscreen, and sundries are also available at Island Supply in Adventureland and

Mickey's Star Traders in Tomorrowland. In Epcot, sundries are sold in at least one shop in each World Showcase pavilion and at all Future World stores. At Disney's Hollywood Studios, stop by the Crossroads of the World and Movieland Memorabilia shops. At Animal Kingdom, you can pick up "the bare necessities" at Island Mercantile.

Local supermarkets include Winn-Dixie (11957 Apopka-Vineland Road) and Gooding's (at Crossroads shopping complex across S.R. 535 near Hotel Plaza Boulevard). Gooding's is slightly closer to WDW, but rather pricey.

Now that all Disney owned-and-operated resorts rooms come with mini fridges, it's a nice treat to have groceries delivered directly to the hotel. Our go-to source for grocery delivery is *www.gardengrocer.com*. Note that Winn-Dixie, Goodings, and Garden Grocer are not affiliated with nor endorsed by the Walt Disney Company.

SMOKING

Disney's strict nonsmoking policy became even stricter with the adoption of the Florida Clean Air Act. Smoking (including e-cigarettes) is prohibited in all indoor and outdoor spaces, unless specifically designated as "smoking areas." These areas are marked on park guidemaps. All eateries are smoke-free, as are clubs and lounges. Tobacco products are not sold in the theme parks. Guests may purchase tobacco products at some Walt Disney World resorts and Downtown Disney (with government-issued photo ID). Designated outdoor areas are available for those who choose to smoke. Remember, this is a statewide smoking policy, so if you venture off Disney property, the same rules apply.

Guests using e-cigarettes may do so in resort guestrooms, but not on balconies or patios.

TELEPHONE CALLS

Every time a local call is placed from a Central Florida landline, callers must dial the area code and seven-digit number. The rule applies to calls

Lost Adults

Occasionally, traveling companions get separated in the crush of the crowds, or someone may fail to show up at a meeting spot. When this happens, it's good to know that messages can be left for phone-free fellow travelers at Guest Relations in any of the theme parks.

HOT TIP!

The point is to escape the real world, so turn off that mobile phone—or at least stick to texting. That way the magic—for you and those around you—will be uninterrupted. If you have to make a call, do so by the nearest public phone station. And *PLEASE* do not use a phone while experiencing any Walt Disney World attraction. That's just plain rude.

made within the same area code as well as for those that connect with other area codes. For local calls, it is not necessary to dial 1 before the ten-digit number.

Local calls made from pay phones cost about 50 cents each. Rates charged by non-Disney resorts can vary quite a bit (for all calls). Ask about rates and fees before making calls beyond your resort. See page 52 for more phone tips.

TIPPING

Tips are no less valued at Disney resorts than at any other hotel—$1 per bag is appropriate for lugging luggage; $1 to $3 per person, per night for housekeeping services (include a note to avoid confusion). Gratuities of 15 to 20 percent (excluding tax) are customary at full-service restaurants. (If service is exceptional or otherwise, adjust accordingly.) Gratuity is included in the room-service bill at WDW resorts and some off-property hotels. Note that a 10 percent gratuity is added for dining at the Pepper Market at Coronado Springs (despite the self-serve setup).

Give cab drivers about 15 percent tip for good service. Baggage handlers at the train station and airport expect about $1 per bag. The same goes for Magical Express drivers. The ride may be free, but it's customary to tip when bags are handled. (See page 16 for details about Disney's Magical Express bus service to and from Orlando International Airport.)

WEATHER

Call Walt Disney World Weather Information (407-824-4104), or check The Weather Channel Website (*www.weather.com*).

Transportation & Accommodations

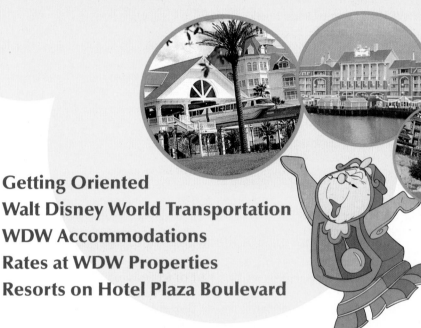

62 Getting Oriented

63 Walt Disney World Transportation

65 WDW Accommodations

72 Rates at WDW Properties

106 Resorts on Hotel Plaza Boulevard

The popularity of Walt Disney World has made the region around Orlando one of the world's major tourism and commercial centers and transportation sources—from a state-of-the-art airport to an efficient network of highways—bring visitors to the area by the millions.

There's no doubt that getting to and around the Walt Disney World region can be confusing. The only more perplexing dilemma may be choosing the best accommodations for your group from the huge assortment of resort hotels and motels.

The accommodations owned and operated by Disney itself range from futuristic towers to cabins buried deep in piney woods. In between are resorts that evoke striking images of Africa, the South Pacific, historic Florida, the Pacific Northwest, the Caribbean, New England, early Atlantic City, New Orleans, the Southwest, Mexico, and the sports, movie, and music worlds, plus a sprawling, well-maintained campground. And that list doesn't include the many villas or the studios and homes with one, two, and three bedrooms that can be "purchased" through a special vacation-ownership system (aka Disney Vacation Club). What follows should help travelers sort out the broad range of lodging options within the borders of Walt Disney World. Regardless of where you plan to stay, we offer this important piece of advice: Book your room as far in advance as possible. You won't regret it.

Getting Oriented

The Central Florida city of Orlando is the municipality with which Walt Disney World is most closely associated. Walt Disney World, however, is in a far smaller community called Lake Buena Vista, 15 miles from Orlando's business center. All Walt Disney World hotels and restaurants are located in Lake Buena Vista.

HOT TIP!

Parking lots are cleverly labeled through-out Walt Disney World. Yet, many drivers still misplace their vehicles. Avoid being dopey: Always snap a photo or jot down your parking location!

ORLANDO-AREA HIGHWAYS: The most important Orlando traffic artery is I-4, which runs diagonally through the area from south-west to northeast, cutting through the southern half of Walt Disney World. It then angles on toward Orlando and Winter Park, ending near Daytona Beach at I-95, which runs north and south along the Atlantic coast.

All the city's other important highways intersect I-4, and each has a name as well as a number. From south to north, they include U.S. 192 (aka Irlo Bronson Memorial Highway), which takes an east-west course that crosses the Walt Disney World entrance road and leads into downtown Kissimmee on the east; S.R. 528, aka the Beachline Expressway (formerly the Beeline), which shoots eastward from I-4; S.R. 435 (aka Kirkman Road), which runs north and south and intersects International Drive, where many motels catering to WDW visitors are located; U.S. 17-92-441 (aka Orange Blossom Trail), which runs north and south, paralleling Kirkman Road on the east; and S.R. 50 (aka Colonial Drive), which runs east and west.

WALT DISNEY WORLD EXITS: The 40-square-mile tract that is Walt Disney World is roughly rectangular. I-4 runs through its southern half from southwest to northeast. The major Disney destinations are most efficiently reached by taking the I-4 exits suggested in the paragraphs that follow; off the highway, clear signage makes it easy for visitors to get anywhere in the World. This road is congested more often

DID YOU KNOW?

When it comes to fashion, Walt Disney World is the biggest clotheshorse of them all. There are more than 2.5 million garments in its corporate costume closet, making it the largest working wardrobe in the world.

than not. Keep in mind that construction work and special events will often require rerouting of traffic patterns on I-4, so it's best to follow signs as directed:

- **Exit 64A**, marked "192/Magic Kingdom," leads to the Magic Kingdom, Disney's Hollywood Studios, Fort Wilderness, Palm and Magnolia golf courses, as well as the Contemporary, Polynesian Village, Grand Floridian, and Wilderness Lodge resorts.

- **Exit 65** leads to the ESPN Wide World of Sports complex, Disney's Animal Kingdom, Blizzard Beach, Art of Animation, Coronado Springs, All-Star Music, Sports, and Movies, Pop Century, and Disney's Animal Kingdom Lodge. It is also a good alternate route to Disney's Hollywood Studios park.

- **Exit 67**, marked "Epcot/Downtown Disney," leads to Epcot, Typhoon Lagoon, Downtown Disney, Lake Buena Vista golf course, Disney's Saratoga Springs Resort & Spa, the BoardWalk, Caribbean Beach, Swan, Dolphin, Yacht and Beach Club, Port Orleans Riverside and French Quarter, and Old Key West resorts.

- **Exit 68**, marked "S.R. 535/Lake Buena Vista," is the best route to the resorts on Hotel Plaza Blvd. and the Crossroads of Lake Buena Vista shopping center. It can serve as an alternate route to Epcot.

HOT TIP!

The cost to valet park a vehicle at any Walt Disney World-owned-and-operated resort is $15 per day (not including gratu-ity). There is no charge for self-parking for guests at any of the resorts.

TRANSPORTATION & ACCOMMODATIONS

WDW Transportation

Walt Disney World transportation is extensive, with boats, buses, and the monorail all doing their part to shuttle guests around. Visitors staying at WDW hotels should receive details about transportation options at check-in. (If you don't, just ask.) For transportation information, call 407-824-4321.

One of the system's hubs is called the Transportation and Ticket Center (TTC), located near the Magic Kingdom. Monorail, bus, and ferry service connect the TTC to points throughout the World. Day visitors must park here before taking a monorail or ferry to the Magic Kingdom. (Most Disney resort guests can bypass the TTC via direct buses.)

The monorail runs along a circular route near the Magic Kingdom, stopping at the TTC, Polynesian Village, Grand Floridian, Magic Kingdom, and Contemporary resorts. A separate extension of the monorail system connects the TTC to Epcot. Bus service is the cornerstone of the WDW transportation system. It is efficient, if a bit confusing. With occasional exceptions, buses arrive every 20 to 25 minutes, from one hour before park opening until about an hour after closing; bus stops are clearly marked. Travel times vary, depending on the route.

Although Disney resort guests are provided with complimentary transportation to all sites on-property, that transportation is not always direct. Build in extra time for travel, especially if you have made reservations at a restaurant. Also, know that traveling between resorts usually requires at least one transfer.

From several Walt Disney World locales, water launches usher guests to the Magic Kingdom,

Should You Rent a Car?

If you plan to spend all of your time on WDW turf, you can probably spare yourself the expense. Towncar and shuttle service from the airport to all area hotels is available around the clock, and taxis are another option. Within the World, an exhaustive network of transportation brings guests from point to point (if not always immediately or directly). Most area hotels offer their own bus service to and from Disney theme parks (inquire in advance about schedules and costs, if any). Note that strollers must be collapsed before boarding Disney bus transportation. (Some folks rent cars to spare themselves this hassle.)

For those planning to resort-hop within WDW or visit Orlando-area restaurants and any attractions outside Walt's world, a rental car is a must. (Just know that area traffic is often rather brutal—always allow extra time, especially if you have a reservation.) It is easy to rent a car at the airport: National (800-227-7368), Alamo (800-327-9633), Avis (800-331-1212), Budget (800-527-0700), or Dollar (800-800-4000). For day (or multi-day) trips, consider Alamo or National at the Disney Car Care Center (407-824-3470; free shuttle service is available) or one of the rental agencies that have desks at the resorts on Hotel Plaza Boulevard, or simply inquire about car rental at the front desk of your resort. It is also possible (and convenient) to rent a car from National or Alamo at the WDW Dolphin resort.

Epcot, Disney's Hollywood Studios, Downtown Disney, or between resorts. Boats generally depart every 20 to 25 minutes.

TRANSPORTATION ID REQUIREMENTS:

Guests who wish to use the Disney transportation system may be asked for proof of riding privileges. Accepted IDs afford different degrees of access. Valid Walt Disney World resort IDs and MagicBands, Magic Your Way tickets with Park Hopper options or Water Park Fun & More options, and Annual Passes let guests use all Disney buses, monorails, and boats. Valid one-day theme park tickets permit guests to use monorails and the ferries running between the TTC and the Magic Kingdom, and all buses.

TAXI SERVICE: Taxicabs are available for about $4.20 for the first mile, $2.40 per extra mile. Stick with authorized cab services. Many unauthorized services charge outrageous rates. When we travel between resorts that aren't joined by boat or monorail and find ourselves pressed for time, we may splurge and take a cab. Inquire at the bell services desk at your resort's front entrance. They'll direct you to the nearest authorized taxi or order one on your behalf. (Pay attention to the route the driver takes—we've been driven in circles on many occasions.)

THE MONORAIL: The Walt Disney World monorail system is usually an easy (and to many, downright exciting) way to travel. There are two main loops, which converge at the Transportation and Ticket Center (TTC) stop. One loop connects the TTC with the Magic Kingdom (and the Polynesian Village, Grand Floridian, and Contemporary resorts). The other loop links Epcot with the TTC. Guests staying in the aforementioned resorts have a private track on the Magic Kingdom loop, making for a quicker exit at closing time. Monorails run from about 7 A.M. until about one hour after park closing. Strollers don't have to be collapsed to ride.

Timing Tip: It can take 5 to 10 minutes to get from stop to stop on the Magic Kingdom's resort monorail loop, making for a grand circle total of about 20 to 30 minutes. The monorail does not run during Extra Magic Hours.

Transportation Tips

- If you are staying at a Disney resort, be sure you get a transportation guide at check-in.

- Most buses are equipped with wheelchair lifts. Such buses have a blue emblem on the windshield and rear door.

- When using the Walt Disney World transportation system to travel between your resort and a theme park, or from one park to another, allow an extra 45 minutes to get to your destination.

- The interval between the arrivals of most Disney buses is about 20 to 25 minutes.

- Be forewarned: It takes a long time to travel by bus from resort to resort. Plan on a trip of up to 90 minutes and at least one transfer (at a park or at Downtown Disney).

- Monorails usually run until one hour after the Magic Kingdom closing time (and they don't run during Extra Magic Hours).

- Note that there is no direct transportation between Disney's BoardWalk and most other resorts. You must first travel to Downtown Disney or a park and transfer to the appropriate bus (or take a cab).

- Try to avoid vacating a theme park just as it closes. Instead, plan to linger a bit in a shopping area, or grab a seat and watch the crowds crawl toward their respective buses, boats, cars, and monorails.

- It is not uncommon, especially at park opening and closing times, for guests to be asked to stand on the bus or monorail.

- Keep in mind that the most obvious mode of transportation may not be the quickest. For example, it is often faster to walk to the Magic Kingdom from the Contemporary resort than it is to take the monorail.

- It's possible to rent a car from any Disney resort. For details, inquire at the lobby concierge desk, or contact the front desk.

- Walt Disney World resort guests who arrive with a car receive a complimentary parking permit upon check-in. The permit, good for the length of your stay, allows you to park at all parks and most other places on WDW property for free.

DID YOU KNOW?

The Walt Disney World monorail system—a 14.7-mile highway in the sky—has carried more than a billion passengers since 1971.

WDW Accommodations

With hundreds of resorts in the Orlando area to choose from, it's definitely a challenge to select a hotel. Here's our advice.

Weigh the Options: First decide whether to stay on or off Disney property. Many opt for a Disney resort because the conveniences and perks offered to resort guests are appealing (see page 66). Given that, there are still two major factors that tend to lure guests off property: vacation budget and itinerary.

Travelers on a tight budget may find off-property options that are quite reasonable. However, Disney offers rooms as low as about $85–$202 per night (depending on hotel and season), so choose off-property digs only if the price difference is substantial. WDW room rates are based on double occupancy. Additional guests will result in an increase in the rate. There is no charge for kids age 17 or younger.

Guests who will spend only part of their trip exploring Disney may also prefer an off-property hotel—one that's closer to the other attractions on their itinerary.

There's also the issue of what one considers deluxe. Disney-owned-and-operated "deluxe" resorts do tend to provide more amenities and services than their "moderate" and "value" counterparts, but do not always rival comparably priced accommodations in the real world.

Deciding Factors: Once the on- or off-property decision has been made, it's time to look at hotels. The big differences among on-property accommodations are in the size of the rooms and bathrooms, attention to decor, level of service, dining options, transportation options, recreational facilities, landscaping, location, and, of course, cost.

Consider how much time you'll spend in the room, whether you'd like to return to the hotel during the day, and if you'll have time to use all the amenities that are included. Parties with five or more members have an additional concern: how best to accommodate their group. It may be less expensive to reserve adjoining, value-priced rooms instead of one luxe room or villa.

Ask the Right Questions: Once a hotel that meets all basic criteria is selected, it's best to do one last round of research, so there will be no surprises at check-in.

For example, ask about any possible hidden costs, like shuttle service to and from Walt Disney World (which can be more than $20 per person, round-trip) or taxes that may not be included in the quoted price. Though most off-property hotels offer transportation to WDW, the frequency and number of buses vary significantly. Find out the exact schedule and the number of stops made. Ask where the bus picks up and drops off, too. Try to avoid those that stop in busy parking lots.

Some hotels advertise a misleading proximity to Disney. While a hotel may be a short distance from the border, the commute to the parks may be considerable. Get specifics. (Distance from your favorite park is also a factor to consider when staying on-property.)

Last but not least, do not underestimate the value of Extra Magic Hours—a perk offered exclusively to guests staying at most resorts situated on Walt Disney World property (see page 22 for details).

Reserve a Room: Found the perfect hotel? Book it before someone else does, and don't forget to ask about any special discounts, seasonal promotions, and cancellation policies.

A Room with a View

There's a lot to be said for throwing back the curtains and gazing at a breathtaking view, provided you have the time to appreciate it and your view is within your price range. The following is a breakdown of different "views" you may select from at the various WDW resorts. It will help you determine the best view for your budget.

Although the categories vary, depending on the resort type, the "standard view" is always the lowest rate available:

Value Resorts
Standard View = Parking lot, pool, garden, and everything else

Moderate Resorts
Standard View = Parking lot or landscaping
Water View = Pool, marina, lake, river

Deluxe Resorts
Standard View = Parking lot
Garden View = Landscaping
Water View = Pool, lake, or other water
Lagoon View = Seven Seas Lagoon
Savanna View = Animal pastures
(at Animal Kingdom Lodge)

Walt Disney World Resorts

Walt Disney World hotels fall into two categories: Disney-owned-and-operated and non-Disney-owned resorts. Of all the WDW properties, the Swan and Dolphin, Four Seasons, and the resorts on Hotel Plaza Boulevard don't belong to Disney. Services and benefits in these resorts are slightly modified (see pages 89, 104, and 106).

On-Property Perks: Walt Disney World resorts offer guaranteed admission (with ticket) to the parks in most instances (though there are times, especially during holidays, when a park hits capacity and no further admissions are allowed by law); use of the WDW transportation system; the convenience of charging most purchases to the hotel bill; and the Extra Magic Hours benefit, which allows extra time in a select park on select days. Guests who stay at a Disney-owned-and-operated resort and arrive via air at Orlando International Airport are entitled to Disney's Magical Express service (see page 16).

Room Amenities: Disney rooms come with an alarm clock, a small safe, shampoo, phone with voice mail, a flat-panel TV, and free high-speed Wi-Fi. There are hair dryers, irons, small refrigerators (in all Disney-owned-and-operated resorts regardless of their category), and coffeemakers (with coffee, sugar, and non-dairy creamer) in many rooms. Laundry facilities, dry cleaning, and room service are offered in most resorts (for a fee).

Resort Primer

Payment Methods: Hotel bills and room deposits may be paid by credit card, Disney Dollars and gift cards, traveler's check, money order, cash, or personal check. Checks must bear the guest's name and address, be drawn on a U.S. bank, and be accompanied by proper photo ID (a valid driver's license or government-issued passport will do the trick).

Room Deposit Requirements: When booked through Central Reservations, a deposit equal to one night's lodging (or campsite rental) is required within 14 days of the time that a reservation is made. Reservations are automatically canceled if deposits are not received by the 14-day deadline. (Reservations booked less than 30 days prior to arrival will receive special instructions for deposits.) Reservations booked through the Walt Disney World Travel Company are subject to a substantial cancellation fee. Ask about the

Online Check-in

Are you planning a stay at a Disney-owned-and-operated resort? If so, you can take advantage of Disney's online check-in service. Meant to streamline the actual check-in experience, the virtual service is available 60 days in advance of and up through arrival day.

Online check-in expedites the arrival experience by getting the pesky paperwork out of the way prior to arrival. Before you log on, know that you'll be asked to provide the following: the credit card that will be used for room charges, mobile number, address, arrival and departure times, the names of all guests, and room requests (but know that special requests are subject to availability).

With all that info already in the system, guests just need to show up at the resort and present a valid government-issued photo ID. In return, they get a welcome packet including MagicBands (if they didn't have them shipped home) and WDW info. There should be clear signs indicating the spot for packet pickup.

How does one check in via the Internet? Simply visit *www.disneyworld.com* and click on the checking-in section under My Disney Experience. Checking in online does not mean you can check in early. (Unless, of course, there is a room available—a happy surprise that has been known to happen.)

cancellation policy when you book your room.

When booking by phone, guests may pay the deposit with a major credit card. Those who wish to use another payment method may do so by mailing it with the payment stub that comes with the reservation confirmation. Call to confirm that your payment was received.

Cancellation Policy: With the exception of Magic Your Way packages, deposits for resort stays will be fully refunded if the reservation is canceled at least five days before the scheduled arrival. Magic Your Way packages must be canceled at least 45 days ahead.

Additional Charges: Note that in some resorts, an extra bed may be required to sleep an extra adult. If so, beds cost $15 per night. If you need a crib that is sturdier than the provided Pack 'n' Play, you'll have to rent one from an outside company. For a recommendation, see page 47.

HOT TIP!

The following WDW resorts can accommodate up to 5 guests in a standard room: Grand Floridian, Yacht and Beach Club, Contemporary, Polynesian Village, BoardWalk, Port Orleans Riverside, and Fort Wilderness Cabins.

Check-in and Check-out: The relatively early check-out time (11 A.M. at all Walt Disney World-owned-and-operated lodgings) and the late check-in times (1 P.M. at the campsites, 3 P.M. in most hotels, 4 P.M. at Disney Vacation Club accommodations) often come as a bit of a surprise. Guests who arrive before check-in time can pre-register, store luggage at Bell Services (without a fee), and head to the parks or relax by the pool.

Walt Disney World MagicBands: Issued upon check-in at Disney resorts (if not pre-ordered; see page 24), the bands (which double as room keys) entitle guests to use of all WDW transportation (through the last day of your stay)

Magic Strollers

Brought to you by the folks behind Owner's Locker (above, right), this stroller-rental program is truly magical to the parenting populace. For starters, the strollers are all from the popular Baby Jogger City Mini series; they're delivered directly to any WDW resort (and many other area hotels) by 10 A.M. on the day guests check in and picked up before 2 P.M. on the day guests head home; and the convenience of using the strollers anywhere and everywhere is a major plus.

Cost is $25 for the first day and $6.50 for each additional day for a single stroller. The rate for doubles is $40 for the first day and $7.50 for each extra day. We recommend getting the insurance, too. For a flat $25, it covers you for any damage or theft that may occur during the time you have the stroller. For more information or to reserve a Magic Stroller, call 866-866-6177 or visit *www.magicstrollers.com*. To save ten percent off a stroller rental, use the coupon at the back of this book.

Stash Your Stuff

If you count yourself among the merry multitudes who travel to Walt Disney World at least once a year, a system called "Owner's Locker" was devised with you in mind. Simply put, it lets you stash your vacation gear in a private purple locker in the WDW area and have it delivered to you each time you visit the Mouse. That means you'll have less to check at the airport (the locker's great for storing liquids and "must-check" items) and lighten your load overall. Say good-bye to lugging items such as rain gear, sunscreen, baby supplies, cooking items, non-perishable snacks, toys, DVDs, rainy-day activities, first aid supplies, and more.

It's called Owner's Locker because customers actually buy an industrial-strength, secure storage bin when they join the program (extra lockers are an option). After a one-time $75 membership fee, expect to pay about $99 a year for the Standard Annual Plan (including one visit a year; $25 for each additional visit), or about $179 a year for the Premium Plan, which allows for unlimited visits at no additional charge.

How does it work? As soon as you plan a WDW trip, schedule a round-trip delivery via *www.ownerslocker.com*. Your locker will make its way from a climate-controlled storage facility to your resort before check-in time. Call the Bell Services desk and expect the purple chest to arrive in minutes (don't forget to tip accordingly). Owner's Locker service is available at all Disney resorts and many other area hotels (though the business is not owned or operated by the Walt Disney Company). For more details or to join, call 800-431-6588 or visit *www.ownerslocker.com*. The coupon at the end of this book will net you a discount on the initial membership fee.

and charge privileges (provided a credit card number is registered at check-in) to cover most purchases at Walt Disney World. You will be asked to program a personal pin code at check-in. Should you make a purchase on Walt Disney property, you will use that pin code to activate your MagicBand.

Note: Charges that are incurred on a Magic-Band or hotel ID after check-out will be reflected in a revised bill, which may be requested at the resort's front desk or e-mailed upon request. Swan and Dolphin guests may use their resort IDs to charge meals inside the two hotels only.

Walt Disney World Resort Finder

Name & Location	Setting/ Theme	Favored By	Romantic Hideaways
Animal Kingdom Lodge* Animal Kingdom Area (page 99)	African wildlife preserve	Animal lovers—nearly every room affords a view of wandering wildlife Art aficionados—authentic African artwork abounds Disney Vacation Club members	Private balconies by moonlight Sunset lounge overlooking the savanna
BoardWalk Inn* Epcot Area (page 91)	Turn-of-the-20th-century Atlantic City	Night owls—the entertainment options are numerous and right in the backyard Epcot lovers, who will appreciate the short commute Disney Vacation Club members	Moonlight strolls along the boardwalk A special fireworks cruise
Contemporary* Magic Kingdom Area (page 76)	Retro-futuristic exterior, thoroughly modern interior	Families—the monorail whisks through it, and the Magic Kingdom is a short walk away Professionals, who can take advantage of the hotel's many business services Disney Vacation Club members	The rooftop lookout (available only to California Grill patrons), which helps make up for the resort's otherwise less-than-romantic atmosphere
Grand Floridian* Magic Kingdom Area (page 80)	Victorian seaside resort	Honeymooners—who will love spending much of their vacation basking in the resort's unebbing romantic atmosphere Magic Kingdom and monorail fans Disney Vacation Club members	Manicured rose gardens Honeymoon suites The Grand Lobby for a cocktail while an orchestra performs on the balcony
Polynesian Village Magic Kingdom Area (page 78)	South Pacific	Romantics—the white-sand beaches and lush, tropical setting may make you swoon Vacationers looking for a hotel with a real resort feel Magic Kingdom and monorail fans Disney Vacation Club members	Beach swings for two Strolls on the white-sand beaches
Swan & Dolphin Epcot Area (page 89)	Beachfront whimsy	Guests who want many of the Disney perks but not necessarily the Disney hotel Bargain hunters—when WDW resorts are "peak," these resorts may offer discounts	A secluded area behind the grotto pool waterfall
Wilderness Lodge* Magic Kingdom Area (page 82)	America's grandest national parks	Sweethearts—love is always in the air at this resort Winter visitors—the warm, cozy atmosphere is even more inviting when the many fireplaces are roaring Disney Vacation Club members	Steamy, bubbling "hot springs" whirlpools The cozy alcoves hidden on each floor of the main building
Yacht & Beach Club* Epcot Area (page 86)	Martha's Vineyard and Nantucket Island	Ambitious guests—those who plan to see and do everything Disney has to offer will like the central location Everyone—deluxe atmosphere and amenities appeal to all Disney Vacation Club members	The Yacht Club's peaceful gazebo Secluded whirlpools The beach—perfect for twilight strolls

❤ These resorts host character meals.   * Animal Kingdom Lodge, Beach Club, BoardWalk, Contemporary,

Kids Adore	Dining Tip	Resort Category & Amenities
The kopje, a rocky outcropping from which to spy on critters Story time beside the lobby fireplace Rustic bunk beds (on request)	Sample the exotic eats and atmosphere of Boma while savoring the sights of the savanna.	
The Keister Coaster, a 200-foot waterslide at the main pool The face-painting booth on the boardwalk at night	Snack on saltwater taffy, cotton candy, or fresh-baked sticky buns while strolling along the boards.	
The "party" held every 45 minutes at Chef Mickey's fabulously fun character meals Watching the monorail whoosh through the resort	Reserve California Grill for a time that's likely to coincide with the Magic Kingdom's Wishes fireworks show. The view is amazing. ❦	Full-service restaurants, fast-food spots, room service Luggage service
Nightly marshmallow roasts and alfresco Disney films Having dinner with Cinderella and her friends at 1900 Park Fare Zero-depth-entry pool	Have a spot of traditional afternoon tea, accompanied by a scone, at the Garden View Lounge. ❦	Valet parking Swimming pools Beach access ‡
The Tuesday–Saturday torch-lighting ceremony in the Great Ceremonial Hall (offered on select evenings) The slide- and waterfall-endowed volcano pool	The sushi served at Kona Island is second to none. Enjoy it at the table-service counter, or get it to go and have a poolside picnic. ❦	On-site recreation, such as boat rentals ‡ On-site kids' activities Most rooms sleep five guests
The swan-shaped pedal boats The giant swan and dolphin statues perched atop their respective resorts	The Swan's Kimonos Lounge serves sushi with a side of karaoke. ❦	Monorail, bus, or boat transport to all parks
Totem poles, an erupting geyser, and countless Hidden Mickeys— there's even a free tour to help guests find them	Sample berry cobbler or the cedar plank salmon—Artist Point signature dishes. Savor morning coffee from a fireside rocking chair. ❦	‡ Except Disney's Animal Kingdom Lodge
Stormalong Bay—the sand-bottomed, three-acre pool, with a waterslide and a neat shipwreck to play on	Cape May Cafe's bountiful nighttime clambake has many a surf-and-turf fan lining up for more. ❦	

DELUXE

Grand Floridian, and Wilderness Lodge also have Vacation Club accommodations.

69

Name & Location	Setting/ Theme	Favored By	Romantic Hideaways
Disney's Old Key West Downtown Disney area (page 97)	Key West	Guests looking for a homey, village atmosphere Disney Vacation Club members Those who appreciate roomy rooms	Private whirlpool tubs— they come with all accommodations but the studios
Disney's Saratoga Springs Resort & Spa Downtown Disney area (page 96)	Historic Saratoga Springs, New York	Peace seekers—the atmosphere is meant to soothe Disney Vacation Club members Space seekers. The accommodations are generally more spacious than at other resorts.	Pretty gardens and meandering pathways Private whirlpool tubs— they come with all accommodations but the studios
Caribbean Beach Epcot area (page 85)	Tropical islands	Families—the colorful design, themed pool, and beach setting make this hotel ideal for families Pirate fans! The main pool and about 400 rooms have a buccaneer theme.	Aruba beach—the hotel's longest, most secluded strip of sand
Coronado Springs Animal Kingdom area (page 101)	Mexico and Southwest USA	Conventioneers—which means more business services (and a health club), higher food prices, and slightly less family entertainment than at the other moderate resorts at WDW	The waterfront in the peaceful Casitas area The gazebo-style boat-rental dock at twilight
Port Orleans French Quarter & Riverside Downtown Disney area (pages 94–96)	New Orleans French Quarter and Antebellum South, respectively	Lovebirds on a budget—the Riverside decor is like many of Disney's deluxe hotels, as is the romance factor, but the price is considerably less The French Quarter, which provides a peaceful, urban alternative	Any room in Magnolia Bend's stately mansions The peaceful gardens scattered about the Riverside quarters
All-Star Movies, Music, & Sports Animal Kingdom area (page 98)	Larger-than-life fun	Penny savers of all ages—these resorts offer fun, colorful theming, plus all the WDW perks, at a much lower price than at most other Disney resorts Space cravers—who adore the family suites at All-Star Music	All-Star Music's Jazz and Broadway areas (note that Music tends to attract more couples without kids than the other two themes)
Art of Animation Animal Kingdom area (page 103)	Classic and colorful Disney animation	Extended families and families with babies—it's great to have the extra sleeping area that comes with the family suites	The Drop Off pool bar is a sweet spot for a (quasi) quiet interlude
Pop Century Animal Kingdom area (page 102)	American pop culture	Budget watchers and nostalgia buffs—this sprawling resort celebrates pop history with bright colors and big icons Young athletes and their families—ESPN Wide World of Sports is located nearby	Sipping specialty cocktails poolside
Fort Wilderness Cabins and Campground** Magic Kingdom area (page 83)	Rustic woods	Seasoned RV enthusiasts—Disney's hookups are considered top-notch Families—who appreciate the modern amenities of the cabins, which fit six and fall into Disney's "moderate" category	The Fort Wilderness beach at night—perfect for viewing the Electrical Water Pageant on Bay Lake

♥ These resorts host character meals. † Known as "Disney Deluxe Villa Resorts" on *www.disneyworld.com*. Animal Kingdom Lodge, Beach

Kids Adore	Dining Tip	Resort Category & Amenities	
The weekly Tiny Tot Tea Parties and Un-Birthday Parties with snacks, games, and treats, held at Community Hall One super pool slide	Olivia's pleases all palates with a nice mix of pastas and fresh fish. The conch chowder is a yummy way to start a meal. ♥	Kitchens, restaurants, pizza delivery Luggage service Swimming pools On-site recreation, such as boat rentals Front-door parking Villas sleep 4–12 Bus or boat transport to all parks Washers and dryers Boat to Downtown Disney	DISNEY VACATION CLUB+
The kids-only water-spray area near the pool Kid-oriented activities offered at Community Hall	Turf Club is a low-key, local dining room. Downtown Disney's tempting array of eateries is a mere stone's throw away.		
The fortress pool and Caribbean Cay Island The coconut postcards sold at the Calypso shop (real coconuts!)	Try a food court kids' meal— it's served in a sand bucket with a shovel.	Restaurant, food court, limited room service Luggage service Swimming pools with slides On-site recreation, such as bikes and boat rentals	MODERATE
The Dig Site—which encompasses the resort's playground and main pool with its Mayan temple waterslide	Carry-out items at the Pepper Market food court are spared the 10 percent gratuity charge.		
The pool, fishing hole, and play area at the Riverside's Ol' Man Island. And the "Royal Rooms" rock! The French Quarter's Doubloon Lagoon—a sea-serpent-themed family pool	Sample the fresh beignets from the food court. You'll think you're in the Big Easy.	Rooms sleep four guests Bus transport to all parks	
Awe-inspiring, super-size icons— the movie and sports themes score the highest points Extra-large arcades	Pick up a pizza at the pickup window in the food court and have a pizza party by the pool.	Food court, pizza delivery Luggage service Swimming pools Bus transport to all parks	VALUE
The Righteous Reef soft-surface squirt zone Super-size icons from Finding Nemo, Cars, The Lion King, and The Little Mermaid	Dine in what is easily one of the loveliest food courts ever designed: Landscape of Flavors. Indulge in made-to-order smoothies, hand-scooped gelato, and Mongolian barbecue.		
The state-of-the-art arcade Wildly oversize cell phones, yo-yos, bowling pins, and more The interactive water fountain near the playground	The refillable mug, good for use at the resort throughout your stay, definitely scores points as far as bargains go.		
Pony rides, wagon rides, a blacksmith's shop, and campfire marshmallow roasts with Chip and Dale	Join the nightly campfire circle and roast marshmallows (for a fee) with Disney's famous chipmunk duo	Recipient of perfect ratings from Trailer Life and Woodall's magazines Bus transport to all parks	FT. WILDERNESS

Club, BoardWalk, Contemporary, and Wilderness Lodge also have Vacation Club accommodations. **Wilderness Cabins are "moderate."

Rates* at WDW Properties

	Value	Regular	Peak*
DELUXE‡			
Animal Kingdom Lodge			
Rooms (sleep 4 to 5)**	$284 – $574	$341 – $619	$414 – $652
Rooms–Club Level (5)	$457 – $569	$526 – $615	$598 – $696
BoardWalk Inn			
Rooms (5)	$381– $600	$449 – $645	$506 – $690
Rooms–Club Level (5 to 6)	$573 – $858	$655 – $923	$734 – $1,039
Contemporary			
Rooms–Garden Building (5)	$356 – $579	$379 – $600	$421 – $651
Rooms–Tower (5)	$507 – $644	$521 – $671	$596 – $752
Rooms–Club Level (4)	$655 – $861	$710 – $921	$803 – $1,002
Grand Floridian Resort & Spa			
Rooms (5)	$517– $746	$531 – $903	$635 – $970
Rooms–Club Level (5)	$636 – $1,071	$706 – $1,239	$854– $1,405
Polynesian Village			
Rooms (5)	$429 – $716	$480 – $805	$567 – $906
Rooms–Club Level (5)	$616 – $888	$622 – $1,053	$769– $1,162
Swan & Dolphin (Rates were accurate at press time but are likely to change. Call 800-227-1500 for updates.)			
Rooms–Standard View (4)	$169 – $449	$219 – $479	starting at $319
Rooms–Upgraded View (4)	$189 – $529	$239 – $519	starting at $339
Suites (5 to 10)	$209 – $509	$259 – $559	starting at $359
Wilderness Lodge			
Rooms (4)	$289 – $450	$346 – $527	$419 – $570
Rooms–Club Level (4)	$495 – $805	$552 – $884	$644 – $969
Yacht & Beach Club			
Rooms (5)	$356 – $533	$413 – $584	$493 – $637
Rooms–Club Level (5)	$536 – $929	$616 – $933	$694 – $1,053

* Rates for Friday and Saturday night stays are generally higher than other days. Call 407-934-7639 for specifics.

** Room Capacity: Numbers in parentheses reflect maximum occupancy based on existing beds. A trundle bed (for one) can be rented at some properties for $15 a day. Playpen-like cribs can be requested for free in most resorts. Rates include up to two adults. There is an additional charge for each extra adult in a room.

TRANSPORTATION & ACCOMMODATIONS

Rates* at WDW Properties

	Value	Regular	Peak*
DISNEY VACATION CLUB			
Animal Kingdom Lodge Villas			
Studios (4)	$318 – $570	$356 – $620	$435 – $702
Villas (4–12)	$474 – $1,809	$539 – $2,129	$631 – $2,299
Bay Lake Tower (at the Contemporary resort)			
Studios (4)	$444 – $559	$509 – $639	$588 – $708
Villas (4–12)	$562 – $2,073	$648 – $2,515	$756 – $2,602
Beach Club Villas			
Studios (4)	$369– $412	$429 – $452	$513
Villas (4–8)	$535– $803	$610 – $1,056	$720 – $1,245
BoardWalk Villas			
Studios (5)	$369– $412	$429 – $452	$513
Villas (4–12)	$535 – $1,931	$610 – $2,178	$720 – $2,363
Disney Old Key West			
Studios (4)	$327 – $362	$368 – $387	$431
Vacation Homes (4–12)	$452 – $1,416	$507 – $1,613	$586 – $1,739
Disney's Saratoga Springs Resort & Spa			
Studios (4)	$327 – $362	$368 – $387	$431
Villas (4–12)	$452 – $1,416	$507 – $1,613	$586 – $1,739
The Villas at Wilderness Lodge			
Studios (4)	$374 – $410	$427 – $449	$517
Villas (4–8)	$512 – $859	$586 – $1,094	$718 – $1,252

CALL 407-934-7639 FOR RESERVATIONS

‡ For information about suites, call 407-934-7639.

Note: The prices provided here were correct at press time, but rates are likely to change. Charge is for one day, single or double occupancy.

(continued on next page)

TRANSPORTATION & ACCOMMODATIONS

Rates* at WDW Properties

	Value	Regular	Peak*
MODERATE			
Caribbean Beach			
Rooms (4)**	$162 – $270	$188 – $312	$211 – $307
Coronado Springs‡			
Rooms (4)	$167 – $289	$193 – $326	$216 – $348
Port Orleans French Quarter and Riverside			
Rooms (4)	$162 – $259	$188 – $299	$211 – $318
Fort Wilderness Cabins			
Cabins (5)	$299 – $368	$359 – $404	$406 – $445
VALUE			
All-Star Movies, All-Star Music‡, and All-Star Sports			
Rooms (4)	$85 – $138	$109 – $168	$135 – $186
Family Suites (6)	$212 – $270	$272 – $320	$313 – $374
Art of Animation			
Rooms (4)	$109 – $144	$140 – $175	$164 – $197
Family Suites (6)	$269 – $329	$332 – $399	$379 – $449
Pop Century			
Rooms (4)	$95 – $157	$121 – $185	$145 – $202
FORT WILDERNESS CAMPGROUND			
Fort Wilderness Campsites			
Sites with partial hookup (10)	$50 – $62	$75 – $90	$83 – $100
Sites will full hookup (10)	$69 – $79	$91 – $112	$118 – $128
Preferred/Premium sites (10)	$79 – $98	$109 – $130	$129 – $143

CALL 407-934-7639 FOR RESERVATIONS

* Rates for Friday and Saturday night stays are generally higher than other days. Call 407-934-7639 for specifics.

** Room Capacity: Numbers in parentheses reflect maximum occupancy based on existing beds. A trundle bed (for one) can be rented at some properties for $15 a day. Playpen-like cribs can be requested for free in most resorts. Rates include up to two adults. There is an additional charge for each extra adult in a room.

‡ For information about suites, call 407-934-7639.

Note: The prices provided here were correct at press time, but rates are likely to change. Charge is for one day, single or double occupancy. Certain holidays and special events (such as WDW Marathon weekend) bring higher resort rates. Call 407-934-7639 for specifics.

Seasonal Dates

VALUE RATES APPLY: January 4 through February 11 and August 16 through September 10 for all Value and Moderate resorts; January 4 through February 11 and August 2 through October 3 for Campsites; January 4 through February 11, July 12 through September 24 for all other WDW properties (except Four Seasons, Swan, and Dolphin).

> ## HOT TIP!
> On weekends and when peak rates are in effect at Walt Disney World–owned-and-operated resort hotels, rates at Swan and Dolphin are often much lower. Conversely, Swan and Dolphin tend to have their highest rates on business days and during traditional convention times of year.

REGULAR RATES APPLY: February 22 through March 5, April 12 through May 28, and December 11 through December 17 for all Value and Moderate resorts; April 12 through August 1 for Campsites; February 22 through March 5, April 12 through May 28, and December 11 through 17 for all other WDW properties (except Four Seasons, Swan, and Dolphin).

PEAK RATES APPLY: February 12 through February 21 and March 6 through April 11 for Value and Moderate resorts; February 12 through April 11 and December 11 through 17 for Campsites; February 12 through February 21, March 6 through April 11, and December 18 through 24 for all other WDW properties (except Four Seasons, Swan, and Dolphin).

PRE-HOLIDAY RATES APPLY: October 4 through December 10 (Campsites only).

HOLIDAY SEASON (HIGHER THAN PEAK) RATES APPLY: December 25 through December 31 for Deluxe resorts; December 18 through December 31 for all other WDW properties (except Four Seasons, Swan, and Dolphin).

SUMMER RATES APPLY: May 29 through August 15 for Value and Moderate resorts; May 29 through July 11 for all other WDW properties (except Four Seasons, Swan, and Dolphin).

Category Conundrum

Value vs. Moderate vs. Deluxe—which resort category is best for you? Categories reflect the price of a room, the style of the accommodation, and the level of service.

- Deluxe properties (the most expensive) are defined by their larger, practically appointed rooms, several restaurants, and such amenities as extended room service hours. This category generally includes Disney Vacation Club properties.

- Moderate properties (in the middle range, price-wise) feature comfortably sized rooms, full-service restaurants and food courts, and bellhop luggage service.

- Fort Wilderness Camping covers campsites, but not Wilderness Cabins (which fall into the Moderate resort category).

- Value properties (the least expensive resort category) offer fewer frills and smaller quarters. Meals are provided at food courts. Recreation and transportation options at these resorts are limited.

FALL RATES APPLY: September 11 through December 10 for Value and Moderate resorts; October 18 through December 10 for Deluxe resorts and Fort Wilderness Cabins. Note that Campsites do not have Fall Rates.

NEW YEAR'S RATES APPLY: January 1 through 3 for all WDW resorts (except Four Seasons, Swan, and Dolphin).

> ## HOT TIP!
> For rates at the new Four Seasons resort at Walt Disney World, call 800-267-3046 or visit *www.fourseasons.com/orlando/*.

Magic Kingdom Area

Contemporary & Bay Lake Tower

Watching the monorail trains disappear into the Contemporary's 15-story A-frame tower never fails to impress. The sleek trains look like long spaceships docking as they glide inside the resort.

Passengers, for their part, are impressed by the cavernous lobby, with its tiers of balconies and, at its center, the soaring 90-foot-high, floor-to-ceiling tile mural depicting scenes from the Southwest. (Look carefully and you may spot the five-legged goat.)

This imposing structure has 655 rooms in its main tower and garden building, plus those in Bay Lake Tower—one of the newest additions to the Disney Vacation Club. There are shops, restaurants, snack bars, lounges, a marina, beach, health club, and more. The pool area incorporates two whirlpools and a waterslide. The convention center offers business services. One of the resort's most notable features is its 15th-floor observation deck. From here, guests dining at the resort's California Grill can enjoy a bird's-eye view of the Magic Kingdom. Another huge bonus: a walking path to the Magic Kingdom (it's a 5- to 10-minute stroll away).

A club-level package is available for guests who stay in the hotel's 14th-floor suites. Amenities include express check-in and check-out, complimentary (light) continental breakfast, evening refreshments, and nightly turndown service. The 12th floor also provides guests with special club-level privileges. To contact the Contemporary, call 407-824-1000.

ROOMS: Boasting a sleek and truly contemporary design, the standard rooms here are evenly apportioned among the main tower and garden building. All rooms located in the tower have private balconies and views of Bay Lake or the Magic Kingdom. Most rooms can accommodate five guests (plus a child under 3). Typical units have a daybed and two queen-size beds; some rooms have a king-size bed and a daybed. The bedding is a cut above most Disney resorts. And every room has a flat-screen TV.

Business-minded folks rejoice over the desk space and high-speed Internet connection (free of charge). While the ceiling fans have gone away, room temperature may be set as low as 65

PHOTO BY JILL SAFRO

degrees. Note that the bathrooms here, though elegant in design, are a bit baffling. There's not much shelf or counter space, the flat sinks tend to stay damp, and the sliding doors don't lock.

Connecting rooms may be requested, though not guaranteed. Suites, consisting of a living room and one or two bedrooms, can accommodate 4 to 12 people. Weekday newspapers may be picked up in the lobby (free of charge). Other amenities include hair dryers and coffeemakers.

Warning: The monorail can be heard from lower rooms in the main tower. For maximum quiet, request a park view on a higher floor or stay in the garden wing. Of course, all rooms get serenaded by the nightly fireworks at the nearby Magic Kingdom park.

The 15-story Bay Lake Tower, a Disney Vacation Club property that sits next to the Contemporary and is connected by a covered walkway, mimics the colors and strong horizontal lines of its neighbor (one of the original resorts on Walt Disney World property). The tower's crescent shape hugs a lakeside pool.

Studios sleep up to four and offer a kitchenette, queen-size bed, and double sleeper sofa. Sleeping up to five, the one-bedroom villas have full kitchens, two bathrooms, a king-size bed in the master bedroom and queen sleeper sofa, and a sleeper chair in the living room. Two-bedroom villas sleep up to nine, and the two-story grand villas sleep up to 12. All configurations feature a flat-screen TV and free Wi-Fi.

WHERE TO EAT: In addition to the many restaurants and snack spots, 24-hour room service provides a wide range of offerings.

California Grill: On the 15th floor. The specialty is California fare—flatbreads, grilled meats, seafood, and market vegetables. An added treat: the spectacular view of the Magic Kingdom fireworks for dining guests.

Chef Mickey's: Located on the fourth floor. Mickey and his friends host daily buffets. Breakfast features Mickey Mouse waffles as well as traditional items. Dinner offers carved meats, nightly specials, and a variety of entrées, plus a sundae and dessert bar.

Contempo Cafe: A quick-service spot with freshly prepared fare (there's a "grab and go" selection, too), this snack bar is on the fourth floor, next to Chef Mickey's.

The Wave . . . of American Flavors: A snazzy spot on the first floor, this eatery offers healthy, creative, locally sourced fare all day.

WHERE TO DRINK: The Contemporary resort is home to several of the World's most inviting lounges.

California Grill Lounge: On the resort's 15th floor, adjoining the California Grill. Picture windows provide a dramatic backdrop for sipping California wines and other drinks, and nibbling on appetizers. Seating is limited. The lounge opens at 4:30 P.M.

Contemporary Grounds: This lobby coffee bar serves cappuccino, espresso, latte, and other gourmet coffees, plus pastries and snacks.

Outer Rim: On the fourth-floor concourse, overlooking Bay Lake, the Outer Rim serves beer, wine, cocktails, and specialty drinks.

Sand Bar and Cove Bar: These poolside spots offer drinks, fruit plates, and light snacks.

The Wave ...of American Flavors Lounge: Inside The Wave restaurant, this bar features wine flights, locally crafted beer, specialty drinks, cocktails, and The Wave's full menu. It's a great destination if you find yourself caught without a dinner reservation.

WHAT TO DO: Volleyball nets may be set up on the beach. Waterskiing, wakeboarding, parasailing, and fishing excursions may be arranged (see *Sports* for details).

Arcade: Game Station, a spacious arcade, can be found on the resort's fourth floor.

Bass Fishing: See page 239.

Boating: Sea Raycer motorboats, Boston Whaler Montauks, and other boats may be rented at the resort's marina.

Health Club: The Olympiad Fitness Center has strength machines, bicycles, sauna, treadmills, lockers, and massage (by appointment). Equipment use is free to Contemporary guests.

Parasailing: Supervised excursions are offered at the marina. Cost is about $95 per person, or $170 for two to ride tandem. Reservations are necessary; call 407-939-0754.

Shopping: The fourth-floor concourse is home to several shops. Fantasia sells character merchandise, including plush animals and clothing for kids. Fantasia Market has newspapers, magazines, books, snacks, and liquor. Bay View Gifts (BVG) carries character merchandise and apparel for all ages, items with the Contemporary resort logo, jewelry, souvenirs, home decor items, kitchenware, and candy.

Swimming: In addition to a round, lakeside pool, the free-form pool features a 17-foot-high curving slide, interactive squirt zone for little ones, and a whirlpool or two. Life jackets may be borrowed at no cost. Cabanas can be rented at Bay Lake pool. Call 407-W-DISNEY for pricing and to make reservations.

PHOTO BY MIKE CARROLL

Tennis: Two tennis courts are available to guests of the Contemporary resort and Bay Lake Tower. No charge.

Watercraft Excursions: Guided excursions on personal Jet Ski-like watercraft are offered for $80 per half hour or $135 per hour. Call 407-939-0754.

Waterskiing, Wakeboarding, Tubing: Ski boats with instructors may be rented for $85 per half hour or $165 per hour at the marina. Call 407-939-0754 for reservations and pricing.

TRANSPORTATION: The Contemporary resort is connected to the Transportation and Ticket Center (TTC) and the Magic Kingdom by monorail. From the TTC, Epcot can be reached by transferring to another monorail. Buses take guests to Disney's Hollywood Studios, Animal Kingdom, Blizzard Beach, Typhoon Lagoon, and Downtown Disney. Watercraft travel from the marina to Magic Kingdom, Fort Wilderness, and Wilderness Lodge. Guests may walk to the Magic Kingdom (it takes 10–15 minutes).

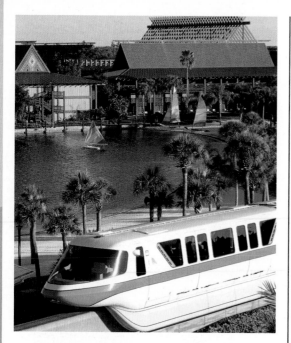

Polynesian Village

The newly re-imagined Polynesian Village resort is as close an approximation of the real thing as Walt Disney World's designers could create. The vegetation is lush, and the architecture summons the tropics. The mood is set by a completely renovated lobby that features bright open areas and sweeping vistas of Seven Seas Lagoon. The structure that contains this mass of greenery, the Great Ceremonial House, is the central building in the Polynesian Village. The front desk, shops, and most of the restaurants are located here. Flanking the Ceremonial House on either side are 11 two- and three-story village longhouses named for various Pacific islands. The Balinese-style huts on the beach are part of the new Disney Vacation Club accommodations at the resort. The monorail stops at this hotel, making it a convenient place to stay; in fact, it's just a short ride to the Magic Kingdom.

Club-level service offers such amenities as express check-in, continental breakfast, cookies and soft drinks every afternoon, hors d'oeuvres and desserts in the evening, and a lounge with a prime view of the Seven Seas Lagoon and Cinderella Castle (not to mention the nightly fireworks displays in the Magic Kingdom). Club-level rooms and suites are located in the Tonga and Hawaii buildings. The telephone number for the Polynesian is 407-824-2000.

ROOMS: Many of the recently refurbished rooms have balconies, and most have a view of the gardens, Seven Seas Lagoon, or one of the resort's swimming pools; rooms in the Tokelau and Rapa Nui buildings are the largest. Many rooms have two queen-size beds and a daybed, and can accommodate five guests (plus a child under age 3). Adjoining rooms may be requested (but are not guaranteed). The Polynesian's suites —located in the Tonga building—can accommodate four to nine guests. Some have a king-size bed in the bedroom and one queen-size bed in the parlor. Amenities include a flat-screen TV, free Wi-Fi, coffeemaker (with coffee), hair dryer, and a small refrigerator. This is one of a few WDW resorts to offer snacks and soft drinks via vending machines. Details are subject to change.

WHERE TO EAT: A variety of specialties are available from room service between 6:30 A.M. and midnight. Also, some interesting eating spots are located here.

Capt. Cook's: On the lobby level of the Great Ceremonial House. This is a good spot for light fare 24 hours a day. In addition to packaged salads and sandwiches, look for items such as sushi and fresh fruit. There is a made-to-order section, too. This is the place to head when you wish to fill your Resort Mug. (For a one-time purchase fee, you're entitled to unlimited soft-drink refills at all "RapidFill" locations for the length of your stay.)

Kona Cafe: On the second floor of the Great Ceremonial House. This family restaurant serves lunch and dinner with an Asian flair (including sumptuous sushi), while the breakfast menu is filled with traditional American selections.

Kona Island: A coffee bar by day, this spot delivers one of the best cups of coffee you'll get in all of Walt Disney World. The coffee bar is usually open until about noon. Come 5 P.M., this casual corner morphs into an extension of the Kona Cafe dining room (featuring stupendous sushi). Kona coffee is proffered in the evenings, too—as are bags of freshly ground coffee beans.

'Ohana: On the second floor of the Great Ceremonial House, 'Ohana serves family-style

PHOTO BY JILL SAFRO

dinners roasted in a large fire pit. Disney characters host a breakfast every morning.

Pineapple Lanai: The Polynesian Village is now an even happier place for fans of that chilly, tropical treat known as the Dole Whip (a frozen pineapple delight). It, along with other snacks and beverages, is served at this kiosk near the Nanea Volcano pool.

WHERE TO DRINK: As might be expected, both the drink offerings and the settings in which they are served are as tropical as they come. In addition to a new pool bar and grill, guests may sip a drink at the following:

Tambu Lounge: There's a tropical air about this lounge near 'Ohana. There's a full bar, but we go straight for the frozen piña coladas (available with or without alcohol).

Trader Sam's Grog Grotto: The spirited new first-floor lounge (opening in 2015) is next to Captain Cook's snack bar. Sam's is a welcome addition to the Disney bar scene, offering tropical drinks and small plates in a richly themed locale. FYI: Trader Sam is the "head salesman" in the Magic Kingdom's Jungle Cruise attraction. He'll gladly trade you two of his heads for one of yours. Either way, you'll come out a-*head*.

WHAT TO DO: A wide range of activities is available at the Polynesian, including a jogging path. Fishing excursions can also be arranged.

Bass Fishing: See page 239 or call 407-WDW-BASS (939-2277).

Boating: Several types of sailboats, Sea Raycer boats, Boston Whaler Montauks, and pontoon boats may be rented at the marina. Specialty cruises are available.

Shopping: BouTiki is the place for swimwear, resort-wear, souvenirs, and more. Trader Jack's sells Disney souvenirs, toys, newspapers, magazines, and fashions. It's also stocked with food, spirits, soft drinks, snacks, and other fixings for an impromptu room party.

Club Disney: The new supervised activity program for (potty-trained) kids ages 3 through 12 is offered between 4 P.M. and midnight. The cost is about $12 per hour. Reservations are necessary; call 407-939-3463.

Swimming: There are two pools here: the unguarded East Pool, in the shadow of the Tokelau, Hawaii, Tuvalu, Rapa Nui, and Tahiti buildings; and the larger free-form Nanea Volcano pool, near the marina. The latter is complete with slide and zero-depth entry. At press time, there were plans for a new aquatic playground for little ones, a new hot tub with views of the Magic Kingdom, and an enlarged poolside deck. A limited number of wheelchairs are available to borrow for use in the pool. The beaches are strictly for sunbathing, sand-castle-building, afternoon snoozing, and evening fireworks viewing (no swimming allowed). *Note that the pools may be under construction for parts of 2015. Guests may enjoy the pools at the nearby Grand Floridian and Contemporary resorts until the Poly's pools reopen.*

TRANSPORTATION: The Polynesian Village is on the monorail line to the Magic Kingdom and the Transportation and Ticket Center (TTC). From the TTC, Epcot can be reached by transferring to another monorail. Buses take guests to Disney's Hollywood Studios, Animal Kingdom, Blizzard Beach, Typhoon Lagoon, and Downtown Disney. Watercraft travel from the marina to Magic Kingdom.

Polynesian Village Villas & Bungalows

This year, Disney Vacation Club proudly unveils its newest "home away from home" right here at WDW's beloved Polynesian Village resort. The new DVC villas and waterside bungalows were under construction at press time and expected to open in 2015. For details on the Disney Vacation Club and the Polynesian Village Villas & Bungalows, call 800-500-3990, or visit *www.disneyworld.com*, and refer to page 93.

Grand Floridian Resort & Spa and Villas

At the turn of the 20th century, Standard Oil magnate Henry M. Flagler saw the realization of his dream: The railroad he had built to "civilize" Florida had spawned along its right-of-way an empire of grand hotels, lavish estates, prominent families, and opulent lifestyles. High society blossomed in winter, as the likes of John D. Rockefeller and Teddy Roosevelt checked into the Royal Poinciana in Palm Beach, enjoying the sea breezes from the oceanside suites.

The hotel later burned to the ground, and Florida's golden era faded with the Depression. But nearly a century after Flagler first made Florida a fashionable resort destination, Walt Disney World opened a grand hotel—an 867-room Victorian structure with gabled roofs and carved moldings—on 40 acres of Seven Seas Lagoon shorefront, between the Magic Kingdom and the Polynesian Village.

Like its late-19th-century predecessors, the Grand Floridian resort boasts abundant verandahs, ceiling fans, intricate latticework and balustrades, turrets, towers, and red-shingle roofs. And yet, it offers all the advantages of modern living, including monorail service. With five restaurants, multiple lounges, five shops, an arcade, convention center, two pools, a kids' splash zone, a marina, and full-service health club and spa, the Grand Floridian is not only a grand hotel but a complete resort.

The main building houses the Grand Lobby, a palatial space soaring five stories to a ceiling of stained-glass domes and glittering chandeliers. Palms and an aviary decorate the sitting area; an open-cage elevator carries guests to the shops and restaurants on the second floor. The turn-of-the-20th-century theme is everywhere,

from the costumes worn by the employees to the shop displays, restaurants, and room decor. The telephone number for the Grand Floridian resort is 407-824-3000.

ROOMS: The rooms are filled with charm, decorated as they might have been a century ago—with printed wall coverings, marble-topped sinks, ceiling fans, and Victorian woodwork. Amenities include hair dryer, bathrobes, mini fridge, flat-panel TV, clock radio with iPod dock, nightly turndown service, coffeemaker, free weekday newspaper (available in the lobby), and Wi-Fi Internet service (free of charge).

The main building houses club-level rooms and suites; lodge buildings, each four and five stories high, contain standard rooms, slightly smaller "attic" chambers, and suites. Most rooms measure about 400 square feet and include two queen-size beds, plus a daybed, to accommodate up to five people. Many rooms have terraces. Suites include a parlor, plus one, two, or three bedrooms; there are queen-size beds in the bedrooms. Most of the 15 Deluxe King Rooms, located on the second, third, fourth, and fifth floors, enjoy wonderful views.

On the third floor, the club-level desks offer such services as reservations and information. The fourth floor features a quiet seating area where continental breakfast and evening refreshments are served. Club-level service is also available in the Sugarloaf building.

WHERE TO EAT: Most restaurants and lounges are located on the first two floors of the main building. Room service is available 24/7.

Citricos: The largest of the hotel's restaurants is also the newest. It features market-fresh cuisine from southern Europe. Open for dinner only. All menu items are available in the lounge, too. Ask the bartender for service.

Gasparilla Island Grill: This 24-hour snack bar offers fresh-made selections such as sandwiches, salads, and flatbreads.

PHOTO BY JILL SAFRO

Grand Floridian Cafe: Its peaches-and-cream color scheme and verandah-like feel make this a great place for a simple sit-down meal. All meals are served.

Narcoossee's: This sophisticated restaurant and bar has a romantic shoreline location. The seasonal menu includes items such as sustainable seafood paired with award-winning wines. Guests may sip cocktails on the verandah.

1900 Park Fare: A buffet restaurant decorated with carousel horses, plants, and Big Bertha, the carnival organ. Characters host breakfast and dinner daily. This character experience is an excellent alternative to Cinderella's Royal Table in the Magic Kingdom and much easier to reserve.

Victoria & Albert's: The eatery is named after the former queen and prince consort of England. Meals are served to no more than 60 guests (age 10 and up) per seating. Jackets are required for men, and reservations are a must.

WHERE TO DRINK: Guests will find the refined lounges here to be lovely escapes. Citricos and Narcoossee's both have bars, complete with a full menu for dining. Drinks (bought in Mizner's Lounge) may also be enjoyed in the majestic lobby.

Citricos: Proof that good things come in small packages (eight bar stools and four tables), this lounge has an extensive wine list, specialty coffees, and full menu.

Garden View Tea Room: This pretty spot offers a view of the hotel's lush, landscaped garden and pool area. Afternoon tea is served (as are finger sandwiches and small desserts).

Mizner's Lounge: Named after the eccentric, wildly prolific architect who defined much of the flavor of Florida's Palm Beach County, this bar is on the second floor.

Narcoossee's: Located in the heart of the restaurant, this lounge offers an extensive wine list and craft beer selection, plus a full bar and menu.

Pool Bars: These spots (known as Courtyard and Beaches) both feature a variety of beverages, while the Beaches also serves lunch and dinner.

WHAT TO DO: The Grand Floridian offers all the recreational facilities of a beach resort. Fishing excursions can be arranged (refer to the *Sports* chapter for details).

Arcade: Arcadia Games is adjacent to the Gasparilla Island Grill (near the marina).

Bass Fishing: See page 239.

Boating: Sailboats, Boston Whaler Montauks, pontoon boats, and Sea Raycer speedboats are available for rent (by the hour or half hour) at Captain's Shipyard Marina. The *Grand 1* yacht (including a captain and first mate) can be rented for about $700 an hour and accommodates up to 18 guests.

Campfire: Guests are invited to gather round the campfire on a nightly basis and roast marshmallows on the shores of Seven Seas Lagoon. (Marshmallows and s'mores kits may be purchased.) Afterward, everyone is treated to a screening of a Disney film.

Golf: The resort is conveniently close to Disney's Magnolia, Palm, and Oak Trail golf courses. Call 407-WDW-GOLF (939-4653), or visit *www.disneyworldgolf.com* for information or to reserve tee times.

Health Club: The full-service exercise facility, adjacent to the Senses spa, is outfitted with fitness equipment. (Oddly enough, there is no restroom. Health Club patrons may use the facilities at the nearby restroom at the pool.)

Salon: The Ivy Trellis salon offers a full line of hair-care services.

Shopping: On the first floor of the main building is Summer Lace, specializing in women's resort-wear and swimwear, and Sandy Cove, for gifts, sundries, and home decor. One level up is the cheerful M. Mouse Mercantile character shop, Basin for bath supplies, and Commander Porter's, a men's shop.

Spa: The spa at Disney's Grand Floridian resort is an elegant pampering palace called Senses. In addition to the treatments offered at its sister spa at the Saratoga Springs resort (see page 229), this spot also offers a selection of soothing packages.

Treatment hours are usually 8 A.M. to 8 P.M. daily. Prices start at about $135 for a 50-minute massage and about $145 for a facial. To book an appointment, call 407-WDW-SPAS (939-7727). For info, visit *http://disneyworld.com/spas/*.

Swimming: There are two large pools for guests to cool off in. Both pools have zero-depth-entry and the Beach Pool also has waterfalls and a 181-foot slide. There's an Alice in Wonderland–themed splash zone for kids up to 48 inches tall (and their guardians).

TRANSPORTATION: The Grand Floridian is connected to the Transportation and Ticket Center (TTC) and Magic Kingdom by monorail. From the TTC, Epcot can be reached by transferring to another monorail. Buses take guests to Disney's Hollywood Studios, Animal Kingdom, Blizzard Beach, Typhoon Lagoon, and Downtown Disney. Watercraft travel from the marina to Magic Kingdom.

Wilderness Lodge & Villas

This resort recalls the spirit of the early American West and the feeling of the National Park Service lodges built during the early 1900s. These grand structures architecturally unified the elements of the unspoiled wilderness parks, kept harmony with nature, and incorporated the culture of Native Americans. The Wilderness Lodge artfully recaptures this rustic charm.

The resort is located between the Contemporary resort and Fort Wilderness on Bay Lake. The lobby, which is shared by the lodge and villas, is in an eight-story, log-structured building. Massive bundled log columns support a series of trusses, while two Pacific Northwest totem poles soar 55 feet into the air. Four levels of corridors surround the lobby, providing access to guestrooms, sitting nooks, and terraces. The monorail does not stop here. Club-level service is available on the top floor. The telephone number for the Wilderness Lodge and Villas is 407-824-3200.

ROOMS: Most of the 727 guestrooms have two queen-size beds and a balcony. Some have a queen-size bed and bunk beds. The bathrooms have separate vanity areas with double sinks. The wallpaper has a Native American–motif border, and the colorful bedspreads and plaid curtains add to the decor. Images of wildlife complete the theme. Rooms include an iron (with board), hair dryer, coffeemaker (with coffee), mini fridge, free Wi-Fi, flat-screen TV, and weekday newspaper (available in the hall or the lobby).

The 114 two-bedroom equivalents (villas) are housed in a five-story building adjoining Disney's Wilderness Lodge. This tribute to turn-of-the-20th-century design is also one of the Disney Vacation Club properties. The style of the villas building was inspired by the grandeur of Rocky Mountain geyser country. Villas are available to all guests when not occupied by Disney Vacation Club members.

Each studio has a queen-size bed and a double sleeper sofa, plus a kitchenette with microwave, coffeemaker, and mini refrigerator. Larger (one- and two-bedroom) villas sleep four to eight and have dining areas, kitchens, laundry facilities, master baths with whirlpool tubs, and DVD players. They include a king-size bed in the master bedroom, a living room with a queen sleeper sofa, and either two queen-size beds or a queen-size bed and a double sleeper sofa in the extra bedrooms.

WHERE TO EAT: The Northwest theme is carried out with flair in the hotel's eateries. Room service runs from 7 A.M. to 11 A.M. and 4 P.M. to midnight.

Artist Point: Decorated with art representing painters who first chronicled the Northwest landscape, this fine-dining spot features salmon, game, steak, and other seafood, as well as wines from the Pacific Northwest.

Roaring Fork: Fast food and light snacks are available at this snack bar. This is also the site of the resort's "refillable mug" station. (For details about the "Rapid Fill" mug program, see page 270.) Roaring Fork hours are generally about 6 A.M. until midnight.

Whispering Canyon Cafe: A boisterous, family-style restaurant with all-day dining.

WHERE TO DRINK: Two spots are available for a relaxing break.

Territory Lounge: This lounge honors the survey parties who led the move westward. In addition to specialty drinks, microbrewed beer, espresso, and snacks are served.

Trout Pass: The poolside bar features a variety of specialty drinks and snacks.

WHAT TO DO: The resort offers many recreational activities. Teton Boat & Bike Rental is in the Colonel's Cabin by the lake. Fishing clothing with the Wilderness Lodge logo and Disney character merchandise. There is a small selection of grocery items, too. The shop is usually open until about 11 P.M. There's also a pin-trading cart in the lobby.

Swimming: The main pool looks as if it were carved from the rockscape. A beach, a kiddie pool, two whirlpools, and a geyser complete the design. Fire Rock Geyser erupts on the hour from early morning until 10 P.M. The Hidden Springs pool and whirlpool spa near the Villas provide a quieter alternative.

TRANSPORTATION: Boats go to the Magic Kingdom, Contemporary, and Fort Wilderness. Buses go to Magic Kingdom, Epcot, Disney's Hollywood Studios, Animal Kingdom, Blizzard Beach, and the Transportation and Ticket Center (TTC). Buses go directly to Typhoon Lagoon and Downtown Disney. (The Fort Wilderness bus does not stop here.)

excursions may be arranged (refer to the *Sports* chapter for details).

Arcade: The Buttons and Bells Arcade has about 30 different games to keep kids (as well as grown-ups) busy.

Bass Fishing: See page 239.

Biking: Bikes may be rented for scenic rides around the resort. A three-quarter-mile path leads to Fort Wilderness.

Boating: A variety of watercraft may be rented for trips around Bay Lake and the Seven Seas Lagoon.

Carolwood Pacific Room: A fireplace and railroad memorabilia add atmosphere to this relaxing room, equipped with comfy seating, tables, and games. It is located in the Wilderness Lodge Villas building.

Children's Program: The Cub's Den is a supervised dining and entertainment club for (potty-trained) kids ages 3 through 12. Supervised activities, including classic Disney movies and Western-themed arts and crafts, keep kids entertained from 4:30 P.M. to midnight. The cost is about $12 per hour, per child. Dinner and a snack are included. Call 407-939-3463 for reservations.

Health Club: The only thing rustic about the Sturdy Branches health club is the structure it's housed in. Open 24 hours, it features modern cardio and strength equipment, bicycles, sauna, and more. Massage therapy is available.

Shopping: Wilderness Lodge Mercantile stocks necessities and sundries, as well as a line of

Fort Wilderness Resort & Campground

The very existence of this canal-crossed expanse—with more than 750 acres of cypress and pine—always surprises visitors who come to Walt Disney World expecting to find nothing more than theme parks.

Tucked among the campsites are hundreds of Wilderness Cabins for rent, complete with housekeeping service. The cost is comparable to that of some of the more expensive rooms at Disney resorts, but each sleeps up to 6 guests and offers about 500 square feet of space. The phone number for the Fort Wilderness resort and campground is 407-824-2900.

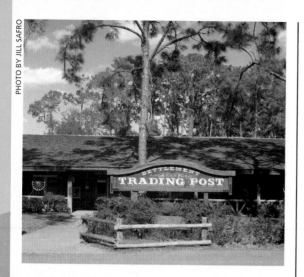
PHOTO BY JILL SAFRO

CAMPSITES: Fort Wilderness has 799 traditional sites. They feature electricity hookups (30/50-amp), water, sanitary disposal, free Wi-Fi, and cable television. Partial-hookup campsites supply electricity and water hookups only. All campsites feature a paved driveway pad, picnic table, and charcoal grill. Most loops have at least one air-conditioned comfort station with restrooms, private showers, an ice machine, phones, free Wi-Fi, and a laundry room. A site allows for occupancy by up to ten. Each site has room for one car (in addition to the camping vehicle). Other cars may be parked in the main lot at Fort Wilderness.

The various campground areas are designated by numbers. The 100–500 loops are closest to the beach, the Settlement Trading Post, and Pioneer Hall. The 1500–2000 loops are farthest away from the beach and many other Fort Wilderness activities, but they are quieter and more private. Premium campsites are big-rig friendly and are wider and deeper to accommodate large vehicles. Pets are welcome at certain campsites for a nightly charge of $5. They can frolic at Waggin' Tails Dog Park, the "off leash" pet play area.

WILDERNESS CABINS: These woodland dwellings offer a rustic escape (with all the comforts of home, plus housekeeping). Falling into WDW's "moderate" resort category, the interiors of the six-person, log cabin-like buildings are decorated with wilderness accents. Each one is shaded by a pine canopy. Cabins include air-conditioning, a full kitchen, two TVs, a DVD player, full bath, hair dryer, iron, a deck, picnic table, and charcoal grill.

Note: No extra camping equipment allowed; all guests must be accommodated in a cabin.

WHERE TO EAT: There are a couple of dining options, but many people cook their own meals here. A small selection of supplies is sold at the Meadow Trading Post and the Settlement Trading Post. Ask about nearby grocery stores when you check in.

Trail's End: This log-walled spot in Pioneer Hall serves home-style fare three times a day. Pizza is an option from 4:30 P.M. to 10 P.M. Spirits are available. The breakfast buffet delivers a hefty bang for the buck.

WHERE TO DRINK: Cocktails are served at Crockett's Tavern in Pioneer Hall.

FAMILY ENTERTAINMENT AFTER DARK: The Hoop-Dee-Doo Musical Revue is quite popular. It's offered year-round. Another crowd-pleasing dinner show, Mickey's Backyard Barbecue, is offered seasonally. Reservations are recommended; call 407-939-3463. There's a free nightly campfire program held near the Meadow Trading Post. (For details, see the *Everything Else in the World* and *Good Meals, Great Times* chapters.)

WHAT TO DO: There's a plethora of free activities to choose from, including two pools (the Meadow Swimmin' pool has an aquatic play zone for tots and a slide), tennis courts, and campfire sing-alongs. For a fee, guests can enjoy wagon rides, pony rides, carriage rides, guided fishing trips, Segway tours, archery, boats, bikes, and more. Activities are described in *Everything Else in the World* and *Sports*.

TRANSPORTATION: Buses circulating at 15- to 30-minute intervals provide transportation within the campground, while buses and boats connect Fort Wilderness to the rest of the World. The Magic Kingdom, Contemporary, and Wilderness Lodge are best reached via watercraft that depart from the marina. Buses to Wilderness Lodge and the TTC depart from the Settlement stop only. Buses to Epcot, Animal Kingdom, Disney's Hollywood Studios, Blizzard Beach, Typhoon Lagoon, and Downtown Disney leave from the Outpost stop.

Electric golf carts and bikes may be rented outside the Reception Outpost as an alternative means of getting around within the campground. Call 407-824-2742 for golf cart reservations. Available to Fort Wilderness guests only, golf carts cost about $59 per day, $378 per week. To drive a golf cart guests must have a valid license and be at least 18 years old.

Epcot Area

Caribbean Beach

This vibrant hotel is set on 200 acres southeast of Epcot and near Disney's Hollywood Studios. It is composed of five brightly colored "villages" surrounding a 45-acre lake called Barefoot Bay. Each village is identified with a different Caribbean island—Martinique, Barbados, Trinidad, Aruba, and Jamaica—and features pastel walls, white railings, and vividly colored metal roofs. There are 2,112 rooms in all, making Caribbean Beach one of the largest hotels in the United States.

The villages consist of a cluster of two-story buildings, a swimming pool, a guest laundry, and a lakefront stretch of white-sand beach. Guests check in at the Custom House, a reception building that projects the feeling of a tropical resort. Decor, furnishings, and staff costumes all reflect the Caribbean theme. Old Port Royale, a complex located near the center of the property, evokes images of an island market. Stone walls, pirates' cannons, and tropical birds and flowers add to the atmosphere. The area houses the resort's food court, restaurant and lounge, arcade, and two shops.

The lakeside recreation area includes a pool with waterfalls and a slide; the main beach; the Barefoot Bay Boat Yard and Bike Works, where boats and bicycles may be rented; and a 1.4-mile promenade around the lake that's perfect for

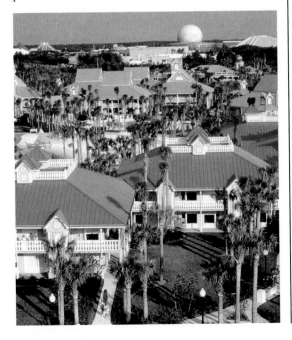

HOT TIP!

Avast, ye hearties! About 400 rooms at Caribbean Beach resort were redesigned to appeal to the swashbuckler in all of us. The pirate-pleasing parlors are perfect for swapping sea stories. Kids love them.

biking, walking, or jogging. Kids love it here. The telephone number for the Caribbean Beach resort is 407-934-3400.

ROOMS: Rooms are located in two-story buildings in each island village. A typical 340-square-foot room has two double beds and can sleep up to four. The rooms here are a bit larger than standard rooms at Disney's other moderate resorts. Rooms are decorated in tones softer than the colors found on the exterior. Many have a super-kid-friendly pirate motif. Each room has a small refrigerator, coffeemaker (with coffee), and high-speed Internet service (free of charge). A note for the budget-conscious: All rooms here are identical in terms of size and comfort, and the only difference between the most and least expensive is the view. To minimize time spent walking, request a room nearest the lobby or bus stop when you check in.

WHERE TO EAT: A full-service eatery called Shutters and the Old Port Royale food court are located in Old Port Royale. Limited room service is available from 4 P.M. to 11:30 P.M.

Bridgetown Broiler: Omelets, biscuits, and French toast are offered for breakfast. Dinner brings rotisserie chicken and other items.

Grab-N-Go Market: Open from early morning until about 11 P.M., this spot sells sandwiches and salads, plus an assortment of pastries, bagels, cheesecake, pies, and more.

Montego's Deli: Breakfast items such as pancakes, sausage, and oatmeal are served in the morning. Salads and deli sandwiches are offered for dinner.

Old Port Royale Hamburger Shop: Sandwiches, cheeseburgers, and fries are served for lunch and dinner. Mickey waffles are offered for breakfast.

Royale Pizza & Pasta Shop: Pizza is available in individual portions, along with pasta dishes and salads.

Shutters at Old Port Royale: This full-service Old Port Royale restaurant features items such as prime rib and a catch of the day. Cocktails and soft drinks are served, too.

WHERE TO DRINK: The tropical theme is carried out in the specialty drinks found at Banana Cabana. Light snacks are also available at this poolside spot.

WHAT TO DO: There are many recreational opportunities here. The promenade around the lake is ideal for walking, biking, or a jog.

Arcade: Goombay Games at Old Port Royale offers a selection of amusements.

Biking: Bikes may be rented at the Barefoot Bay Boat Yard and Bike Works.

Boating: Sailboats, Sea Raycer boats, Boston Whaler Montauks, canoes, pedal boats, and pontoon boats are available for rent at the Barefoot Bay Boat Yard and Bike Works for use on the resort's scenic 45-acre lake.

Fishing: Guided fishing excursions are offered on Barefoot Bay. Call 407-WDW-BASS for updates.

Playgrounds: Playgrounds are located on the Barbados, Jamaica, and Trinidad beaches.

Shopping: Calypso Straw Market carries swimwear and items featuring the resort's logo. Calypso Trading Post has Disney character merchandise and sundries.

Swimming: Each village has its own pool, and one of the pools has a waterfall and a slide in a Caribbean-themed setting, conjuring up images of high-seas pirate adventures. Youngsters simply adore it.

PHOTO BY MIKE CARROLL

TRANSPORTATION: Buses go to the Magic Kingdom, Epcot, Disney's Hollywood Studios, Animal Kingdom, and Blizzard Beach. Other bus routes lead to Downtown Disney and Typhoon Lagoon. Getting around within the resort is done via buses bearing an "Internal Resort Shuttle" sign.

Yacht & Beach Club and Beach Club Villas

The New England seaside exists at Disney World in the form of the Yacht and Beach Club, and the Beach Club Villas. Situated beside Epcot, the resorts, designed by noted architect Robert A. M. Stern, are set around a 25-acre lake. The adjacent properties share most facilities—including a convention center offering business services—and transportation options.

The Yacht Club's design evokes images of the New England seashore hotels of the 1880s. Guests enter the five-story beige clapboard building along a wooden-planked bridge. Hardwood floors and brass enhance the nautical theme. A lighthouse on the pier serves as a beacon to welcome guests back to the hotel from WDW attractions. To reach the Yacht Club by telephone, call 407-934-7000.

Distance from the ocean is irrelevant over at the sand-and-surf-focused Beach Club resort, approached along an entrance drive flanked by oak trees. A walkway leads past a croquet court to beachside cabanas on the white-sand shore. Guests are met by hosts and hostesses dressed in colorful beach resort costumes of the 1870s. The telephone number for the Beach Club resort is 407-934-8000.

ROOMS: Yacht Club rooms are decorated in a nautical motif. The Beach Club's rooms are also amply sized and, naturally, reflect a beach motif. In each room, the furniture is white, and (at the Yacht Club) the headboard design on the one king-size bed or two queen-size beds incorporates small ships' wheels. Some rooms have daybeds. Most of the suites have a king-size bed as well as two sleeper sofas. In the bathrooms, there is a separate vanity with double sinks. Each room has a ceiling fan, iron (with board), hair dryer, weekday newspaper (pick up a free copy in the lobby), free Wi-Fi, mini fridge, coffeemaker (with coffee, sugar, and non-dairy creamer), and a small safe. Club-level rooms (with exclusive access to a room with a private concierge, snacks, and drinks) are available.

A five-story building beside the Beach Club is home to 177 two-bedroom equivalents. The villas are available to Disney Vacation Club members. (They are available to all guests when not occupied by Vacation Club members.) Each studio has a queen-size bed and a double sleeper sofa, plus a kitchenette with a microwave, coffeemaker, and mini fridge, as well as a flat-screen TV and DVD player. Larger villas sleep four to eight, and all have a dining area, kitchen, laundry room, and a master bath with whirlpool tub. They include a king-size bed in the master bedroom, living room with queen sleeper sofa, and either two queen-size beds or a queen-size bed and a double sleeper sofa.

WHERE TO EAT: The themes of yachting and the sea play an important role in the restaurants that are found at their respective resorts. A wide variety of menu items is available from room service 24 hours a day.

Beach Club Marketplace: Stop here for hot and cold breakfast items such as scrambled eggs, croissants, pastries, as well as soup, salads, sandwiches, and snack selections.

Beaches and Cream Soda Shop: A small, classic soda fountain where shakes, malts, and sundaes are the prime lure. Burgers and sandwiches are served as well. The shop is located between the two resorts.

Cape May Cafe: An indoor clambake is held here at the Beach Club each night. The varied and bountiful buffet features several types of clams and mussels, plus beef ribs and chicken. A character breakfast is presented daily.

Captain's Grille: There is a breakfast buffet, as well as an à la carte menu for breakfast, lunch, and dinner. Located at Yacht Club.

Hurricane Hanna's Waterside Bar & Grill: Sandwiches, salads, burgers, and other snacks are served here. A full bar is also located here, and poolside beverage service is available. If you purchase a refillable resort mug, this is a spot to top it off during your stay.

Special Room Requests

Central Reservations accepts requests for rooms with particular views or in certain locations. Agents will do their best to accommodate such requests, but cannot guarantee they will be able to fulfill every wish. Call 407-W-DISNEY (934-7639).

Yachtsman Steakhouse: Select cuts of aged beef are the specialty of the house. Fresh seafood and poultry are also offered.

WHERE TO DRINK: The lounges in both resorts offer a variety of specialty drinks in relaxing seaside settings.

Ale and Compass: This Yacht Club lobby lounge, featuring specialty coffees and drinks, provides a nice respite after a long day. Mornings bring a selection of continental breakfast items.

Crew's Cup: The place to try beer shipped in from the world's seaports before dining at Yachtsman Steakhouse next door.

Martha's Vineyard: This quiet lounge at the Beach Club offers selections from American and international vineyards, served by the glass or bottle, as well as a full bar and appetizers.

WHAT TO DO: There is enough to do here to fill an entire vacation. A sand volleyball court may be found near the Beach Club. Equipment is available at no cost at the Ship Shape health club. Bikes and boats may be rented.

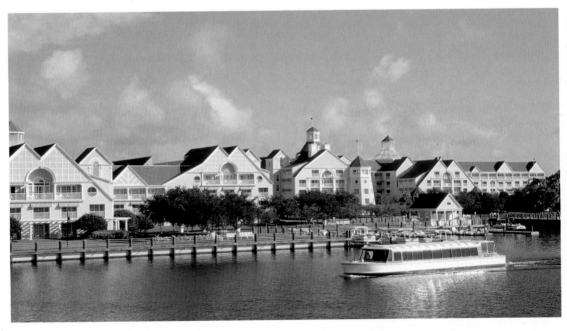

The Fantasia Gardens Miniature Golf complex is close by, and guided fishing excursions may be arranged (see *Sports*). And last but not least, the BoardWalk entertainment district is a short walk around the lake.

Arcade: Lafferty Place Arcade has about 60 video games and pinball machines.

Boating: Pontoons, Boston Whaler Montauks, Sea Raycers, and other boats are available for rent at the Bayside Marina.

Children's Program: The Sandcastle Club, for potty-trained kids ages 3 through 12, is available from 4:30 P.M. to midnight. Cost is about $12 per hour for each child. Reservations are required; call 407-939-3463. Toys, videos, games, and computers help keep children entertained. Dinner and a snack are included.

Health Club: The Ship Shape health club has strength and cardio machines, sauna, whirlpool, steam room, and massage. It's open 24/7 to resort guests age 14 and older. (Request an "after hours" keycard during operating hours.)

Salon: The Ship Shape salon sits between Yacht and Beach Club, poolside.

Shopping: At the Yacht Club, Fittings & Fairings Clothes and Notions is an all-purpose shop stocked with character merchandise and sundries. At the Beach Club, the Beach Club Marketplace has a similar selection of goods.

Swimming: Between the marina and the beach is the centerpiece of the dual resort—Stormalong Bay, a three-acre pool that's like a mini water park. There is a lagoon expressly for relaxed bathing, and another with currents, jets, and sand-bottomed areas. Several whirlpools are scattered throughout the area. Adjacent to the main pool is a shipwreck, where guests can enjoy a waterslide. There is one unguarded pool and whirlpool at the far end of each hotel. There is also an unguarded pool by the Beach Club Villas. Guests may sunbathe on the beach, though swimming is not permitted.

Tennis: There is one lighted tennis court on the Yacht Club side of the property. Rental equipment is available at the Bayside Marina.

TRANSPORTATION: Guests travel to Epcot and Disney's Hollywood Studios via FriendShip water taxis or walkways. Buses go to the Magic Kingdom, Animal Kingdom, Downtown Disney, Typhoon Lagoon, and Blizzard Beach.

Meetings & Conventions

Convention centers at Walt Disney World range in size from 20,000 to 200,000 square feet. The Dolphin's center, featuring an exhibit hall and an executive boardroom, is the largest; the Swan provides additional space. The Contemporary has three ballrooms and a spacious pre-function area with lots of natural light. The convention center at the Yacht and Beach Club is reminiscent of a grand turn-of-the-century New England town-meeting hall. The Grand Floridian Resort and Spa has a lavish center with silk brocade walls. The BoardWalk offers a smaller conference area with a lakeside gazebo for outdoor events. And Coronado Springs, the first moderately priced Disney resort to offer convention facilities, boasts one of the largest hotel ballrooms in the U.S.

Among the unique services available to Disney conventioneers is the use of Disney characters and performers for events. Special events can even be held in the parks. Resort business centers have clerical staffs and computers, in addition to faxing and photocopying equipment. (These services are available to all resort guests.)

Those interested in scheduling a convention should call 321-939-7221. Organizers are advised to book their events six months in advance, especially for large groups.

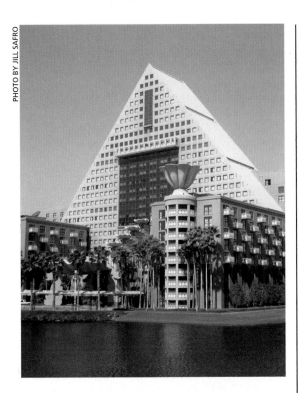

Swan & Dolphin

These sister resorts, situated on the shores of Crescent Lake, can easily be distinguished by the 47-foot swan and 56-foot dolphin statues that top them. The waterfalls, rows of palm trees, and beachfront location all reflect the tropical Florida landscape that was their inspiration. Both hotels were designed by noted architect Michael Graves as examples of "entertainment architecture." The turquoise waves on the colored facade of the Swan's 12-story main building and two 7-story wings are clearly evidence of this design, as is the Dolphin's exterior mural, which features a banana-leaf pattern. The soaring 27-story triangular tower at the center of the Dolphin is flanked by four 9-story guestroom wings.

The resorts share extensive convention facilities, many recreational options, and a host of restaurants. The Swan and Dolphin are operated by Westin and Sheraton, respectively, but are treated as Walt Disney World resorts; guests here enjoy most WDW resort benefits. One notable difference involves room-key-charging privileges: Guests cannot use their room keys to charge purchases on Disney property, with the exception of within the Swan and Dolphin resorts themselves. The direct line for the Swan and Dolphin is 407-934-3000. Reservations for either resort may be made by calling 888-828-8850 or by visiting *www.swandolphin.com.*

ROOMS: The rooms at both resorts have a fresh, contemporary look. Amenities include free weekday newspaper delivery, safes, mini bars, irons and boards, two dual-line telephones, and high-speed, wireless Internet access. Rooms equipped for guests with disabilities are available. Valet parking is $18 per day.

There are 756 rooms and 55 suites at the Swan, each of which comes with one king-size or two queen-size beds. At the Dolphin, the 1,509 rooms and 112 suites feature two double beds or one king-size bed. Dolphin rooms also include a separate vanity and dressing area.

WHERE TO EAT: In addition to many restaurant choices, 24-hour room service provides an extensive all-day dining menu. (The room service here is considered among the best at Walt Disney World.)

Cabana Bar & Beach Club: This full-service poolside spot near the Dolphin serves burgers, grilled chicken sandwiches, flatbreads, and more. The full bar serves specialty drinks.

The Fountain: Homemade ice cream is the specialty at this Dolphin eatery. Huge sundaes, shakes, malts, and burgers are also offered.

Fresh: Designed to resemble a cheerful marketplace, this Dolphin spot serves breakfast and lunch only. The menu features "healthy, sustainable, and organic" fare.

Garden Grove Cafe: This Swan eatery, which features a park-like atmosphere, serves breakfast, lunch, and dinner daily. A buffet breakfast with Disney characters is held on Saturdays and Sundays, while a character dinner takes place nightly.

Il Mulino New York Trattoria: The highly acclaimed Italian restaurant is located on the first floor of the Swan. The setting, which is reminiscent of an old-world trattoria, is relaxed yet vibrant. Features such as *Piatti per il Tavolo* (family-style dining) and wood-fired pizzas complement Il Mulino New York's family-friendly Walt Disney World locale.

Picabu: A cafeteria with a bit of flair. The 24-hour convenience store here sells snacks and sundries. It has Starbucks coffee, too.

HOT TIP!

The Swan and Dolphin resorts run seasonal promotions throughout the year. For information, call 888-828-8850, or visit *www.swandolphin.com.*

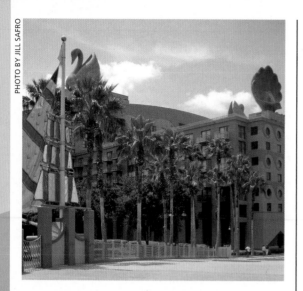

PHOTO BY JILL SAFRO

Shula's: An upscale celebration of two American favorites: steak and professional football. It's a bit pricey, but the steaks are superb and the side orders are big enough to share. Note that there is no children's menu. The dress code is business casual.

Splash: A poolside cafe near the Swan serving specialty sandwiches, pizza, and snacks. A full-service bar is also located here.

Todd English's bluezoo: This eatery features coastal cuisine, beef, and chicken dishes with international and domestic influences.

WHERE TO DRINK: It's easy to find a nice cocktail spot in this neck of the woods.

Java Bar: This spot at the Swan offers a quick bite for early birds on the go. Enjoy specialty coffees, light breakfast items, and fresh pastries until 11 A.M. each morning.

Kimonos: The Asian decor makes this Swan lounge an inviting place for sake, sushi, and other Japanese selections. Karaoke is a house specialty. This place is generally hopping a bit later than most other Walt Disney World resort lounges.

Lobby Lounge: A cozy Dolphin area featuring wine and specialty drinks.

Shula's Steak House Lounge: Settle into a comfy chair and sip a drink in this lounge adjacent to Shula's dining room.

WHAT TO DO: The Swan and Dolphin share many recreation options. Volleyball nets and hammocks are set up on the beach. The Fantasia Gardens Miniature Golf complex and Board-Walk are nearby (the proximity to BoardWalk and Epcot is a big plus). Disney's Hollywood Studios is a FriendShip water taxi ride (or about a 20-minute walk) away.

Arcades: A room full of cutting-edge video games is located near Picabu at the Dolphin. Another game room can be found near the Splash cafe at the Swan.

Boating: Watercraft are available for rent on the beach between the Swan and Dolphin.

Children's Program: Camp Dolphin welcomes children (potty-trained) ages 4 through 12 and has supervised activities from 5:30 P.M. to midnight. The cost is $10 per child, per hour.

Health Clubs: There is a fitness center near the pool area at the Dolphin. State-of-the-art equipment is available, as are personal trainers. There's also a smaller health club with basic exercise equipment near Splash at the Swan.

Playground: A sandy play area with swings and jungle gyms is located on the beach near the grotto pool.

Shopping: Disney Cabanas, located in the lobby of the Swan, features character merchandise and sundries. Four shops are located at the Dolphin. Sugar3 allows chocolate lovers the chance to sample some tasty concoctions. Lamont's offers resort-wear for men and women. Daisy's Garden is the place to find character goods at the Dolphin. Galleria Sottil is the Dolphin's art gallery. Expect to find paintings, sculptures, and other assorted works of art. The Cabana Beach Hut, by the Dolphin pool, specializes in "pool-fun" essentials, while the 24-hour convenience store within Picabu sells grocery items and sundries.

Spa and Salon: The Mandara Spa features full-service body treatments, plus hairstyling, manicures, pedicures, and more.

Swimming: In addition to a shared kids' wading pool, there are two lap pools, and a themed grotto pool with slides between the Swan and Dolphin. Several whirlpools are scattered around the area.

Tennis: Four hard-surface tennis courts are located behind the pool area closest to the Swan resort. They are open 8 A.M. to 10 P.M. and fully lighted. Racquet rentals and lessons may be coordinated at the resort's health club.

TRANSPORTATION: Guests travel to Epcot and Disney's Hollywood Studios via ferryboats or walkway. (It takes about 10 minutes to walk to Epcot's back entrance and about 20 minutes to reach Disney's Hollywood Studios on foot. Water taxis don't move much faster—and they make multiple stops—so allow plenty of time to reach either destination.) Buses go directly to the Magic Kingdom, Animal Kingdom, Downtown Disney, Typhoon Lagoon, and Blizzard Beach.

BoardWalk Inn & Villas

The enchantment of a bygone era is recaptured at the BoardWalk. The resort combines a waterside entertainment complex with deluxe hotel accommodations and vacation villas. Dining, recreation, shopping, and entertainment venues line the boardwalk, and twinkling lights trim the buildings. The ambience continues throughout, with detailed architecture featuring sherbet-colored facades, flagged turrets, and striped awnings, all reminiscent of the turn of the 20th century. The BoardWalk resort is adjacent to Epcot's International Gateway and connected to it via walkway. The telephone number for BoardWalk is 407-939-5100.

ROOMS: Accommodations here evoke the charm of early Eastern-seaboard inns. Most have private balconies or patios. The BoardWalk Inn has 372 deluxe hotel rooms decorated with cherrywood furniture, boardwalk postcard-print curtains, and light green accents. Guestrooms at the Inn sleep up to five, and feature two queen-size beds (or one king-size bed) and a child's daybed. Romantic two-story garden suites each have a private garden enclosed by a white picket fence. They sleep four, and have a living room on the first floor and a king-size bed in the unenclosed, bedroom loft. The Inn also has club-level rooms and suites.

The 282 two-bedroom equivalents are collectively called BoardWalk Villas. These are Disney Vacation Club villas, available when not occupied by members. Each studio has a queen-size bed and double sleeper sofa, plus a kitchenette with microwave, coffeemaker, and small refrigerator. Larger (one-, two-, and three-bedroom) villas sleep 4 to 12 people, and feature dining areas, fully-equipped kitchens, laundry facilities, master baths with whirlpool tubs, and flat-screen TV with DVD player. They also include a king-size bed in the master bedroom, living room with a queen sleeper sofa, and a queen-size bed, plus a double sleeper sofa in any additional bedrooms.

Rooms at the BoardWalk Inn include week-day newspapers (available near the elevators and in the lobby). All rooms have an iron and board, hair dryer, and free Wi-Fi.

WHERE TO EAT: This resort has a wealth of dining and snacking options. A variety of vendors along the boardwalk tempt with hot dogs, crêpes on a stick, gourmet coffee, and more. For those looking to eat in, room service is available.

Big River Grille & Brewing Works: This working brewpub features a full menu, complemented by fresh specialty ales. View the on-site brewmaster through floor-to-ceiling glass walls.

BoardWalk Bakery: A popular stop that offers fresh baked goods, sandwiches, soups, and salads. A display area allows customers to watch bakers at work. This is also the place to refill a Rapid Fill resort mug. It's one of our favorite spots for a light meal or a sweet snack.

Resort Roundup

What's the best place to stay at Walt Disney World? It's a tough question—and one that Birnbaum editors are asked all the time. The answer? Well, it depends. Do you have a favorite park? What's your price range? Will a clown's tongue that doubles as a pool slide make your day? All factors to consider. That said, here are our favorites in each of Disney's price categories:

BIRNBAUM'S ★BEST

DELUXE
Yacht Club: In addition to a picturesque setting, this resort is all about location. For starters, you can walk to Epcot (and the Studios if you're feeling ambitious). Of course, you can always take a water taxi. You're a stone's throw from the excitement of the bustling BoardWalk entertainment district, but get to enjoy the relative peace of life on the quieter side of Crescent Lake. Excellent dining options abound. And the Stormalong Bay pool area is tops. We enjoy the Beach Club, too, but Yacht Club is a bit quieter and there are more rooms with full balconies.
Honorable mentions: Contemporary and Polynesian Village

BIRNBAUM'S ★BEST

MODERATE
Port Orleans Riverside: One need not be a Southern aristocrat to live like one. Many of the guest buildings at this resort, formerly known as Dixie Landings, were designed to look like historic mansions. Even the food court has a certain Southern ambience. There's a table-service restaurant and a cozy lounge (which may offer entertainment). Kids enjoy dropping their hooks in the fishing hole (strictly catch-and-release) and splashing in the free-form pool on Ol' Man Island. Pretty gardens and a relatively reasonable price add to the appeal.
Honorable mention: Caribbean Beach

BIRNBAUM'S ★BEST

VALUE
Art of Animation: This colorful "value" property has some of the boldest and brightest theming around and a top-notch food court—but what sets it apart is the stunning Big Blue Pool and the adjacent splash zone. The family suites are a true value—we're particularly fond of the *Cars*-themed accommodations, but all areas get a thumbs-up.
Honorable mention: Pop Century

BoardWalk Pizza Window: This walk-up window sells pizza by the slice and the pie. It's open for lunch and dinner.
BoardWalk Carts: Stands along the boardwalk offer snacks such as corn dogs, pretzels, hot dogs, and frozen margaritas.
ESPN Club: A serious sports bar for serious sports fans, it provides sports video entertainment and all-day dining. Get there early if there is a big game scheduled.
Flying Fish Cafe: This restaurant has a show kitchen, and its dinner menu emphasizes seafood, steak, and fresh seasonal items.
Seashore Sweets': An old-fashioned sweet shop that serves candies, saltwater taffy, ice cream, frozen yogurt, and specialty coffees.

WHERE TO DRINK: Guests have a multitude of options right in their backyard.
Atlantic Dance: This waterfront club is an elegantly designed dance spot. You must be at least 21 to enter. There's usually no charge, but there are exceptions for special events.
Belle Vue Lounge: Listen to old-time tunes on antique radios and play board games in this cocktail lounge near the lobby. The room is available all day, but the bartender doesn't arrive until 5 P.M.
Jellyrolls: Dueling pianos provide live entertainment in a casual warehouse atmosphere. The cover charge is generally about $12 nightly. You must be at least 21 to enter Jellyrolls and able to prove it.
Leaping Horse Libations: The carousel-themed pool bar at Luna Park serves a variety of cocktails, as well as sandwiches and snacks.

WHAT TO DO: The three-quarter-mile pathway encircling Crescent Lake provides a ready venue for walkers and joggers. Guests may rent boats from Yacht and Beach Club's Bayside Marina. The Fantasia Gardens Miniature Golf complex is nearby. At the resort itself, Ferris W. Eahlers Community Hall rents equipment for many recreational pursuits, including croquet, table tennis, badminton—even books and DVDs. Fishing excursions can be arranged.
Arcade: Side Show Games Arcade has a selection of video games.
Biking: Ferris W. Eahlers Community Hall offers a variety of bicycles for rental. Surreys (canopied quadra-cycles for four) may also be rented there.
Health Club: Muscles & Bustles health club has steam rooms, modern exercise machines, and circuit-training equipment, as well as massages.

The health club is open 24 hours a day for BoardWalk guests.

Midway Games: This area on the Board-Walk's WildWood Landing features games of luck and skill similar to those found along traditional boardwalks. There is a charge to play.

Shopping: Dundy's Sundries in the lobby is the source for basic necessities. Character Carnival on the boardwalk has children's apparel as well as character merchandise. Screen Door General Store stocks groceries, dry goods, snacks, and beverages. Thimbles & Threads, also on the boardwalk, carries apparel for men and women. Wyland Galleries features marine and environmental art.

Surrey Bike Ride: A trip around the lake in a pedal-powered surrey is available for a fee.

Swimming: The BoardWalk's swimming area, Luna Park, has a pool with a 200-foot waterslide, "Keister Coaster," patterned after a wooden roller coaster. (The slide, shown at right, is a clown's tongue. Kids get a big kick out of it.) A family of elephants is found posed throughout the area; their trunks act as a shower for adults on the pool deck or children in the wading pool. The resort has two unguarded pools. There are three whirlpools, one in each pool area.

Tennis: Two lighted tennis courts are available for play. Equipment may be rented at Community Hall.

TRANSPORTATION: Guests may travel to Epcot and Disney's Hollywood Studios via ferryboats or walkways. (It takes about 10 minutes to walk to International Gateway, aka

Epcot's back door. The stroll to Disney's Hollywood Studios takes about 20 minutes.) Buses transport guests to the Magic Kingdom, Animal Kingdom, Typhoon Lagoon, Blizzard Beach, and Downtown Disney.

Disney Vacation Club

Disney Vacation Club grants members the convenience of flexible vacations from year to year, with the ability to choose when and where to visit, how long to stay, and the type of accommodations. It starts with the purchase of a real estate interest in a Disney Vacation Club property. For a one-time purchase price and annual dues, members can enjoy vacation stays at Aulani Resort & Spa (in Oahu, Hawaii); Bay Lake Tower (at Contemporary resort), Animal Kingdom Villas, The Villas at Disney's Grand Floridian Resort & Spa, Old Key West Resort, Beach Club Villas, BoardWalk Villas, the Villas at Disney's Wilderness Lodge, Saratoga Springs Resort & Spa, and (soon) the Polynesian Village Villas & Bungalows at WDW; Disney's Vero Beach Resort in Florida; Disney's Hilton Head Island Resort in South Carolina; and the Villas at Disney's Grand Californian Resort & Spa in Anaheim, California; plus access to additional destinations around the globe. Through Member Getaways, members may also elect to stay at their choice of more than 500 resorts worldwide, including most Disney resorts and the Disney Cruise Line.

Disney's Vero Beach Resort is a two-hour drive from Walt Disney World. It has villa-type accommodations comparable to those at Disney's Old Key West Resort—with lush surroundings, the beach, and local sights. The proximity makes it easy to tack a beach vacation onto a WDW visit.

Disney Vacation Club information centers may be found at each of the Walt Disney World hotels and theme parks. For more information, call 800-800-9100, or visit *www.disneyvacationclub.com*.

Downtown Disney Area

Port Orleans French Quarter

This 1,008-room resort invites comparisons to the historic French Quarter of New Orleans. (Although Port Orleans French Quarter and Port Orleans Riverside [formerly known as Dixie Landings] technically function as one resort, we give them individual attention to provide guests with the information necessary to select the area that works best for them.)

Starting at the entrance gate, with its wrought-iron portal and overgrown landscape, the appeal of the Delta City surrounds arriving guests. The entry drive leads to the heart of the "city," which is Port Orleans Square. The central building was based on a turn-of-the-20th-century mint. The Mint houses check-in facilities (for Port Orleans French Quarter only), a shop, food court, and an arcade. It has a vaulted ceiling, and the check-in desks are designed as bank-teller windows. The musical notes in the mural are the notes to "When the Saints Go Marching In."

The phone number for Port Orleans French Quarter is 407-934-5000.

ROOMS: The guestrooms are located in seven 3-story buildings (with elevators). Each room has two queen beds; some king-size beds are available. The rooms are a bit smaller than the standard rooms at the more expensive Disney hotels, but they are comfortable for a family of four. The buildings are painted cream, pink, blue, purple, and yellow, and feature wrought-iron railings of varying designs. Connecting rooms may be requested but can't be guaranteed. The least expensive rooms overlook gardens or parking areas, and the most expensive rooms offer water views. All rooms have coffeemakers (with coffee), mini refrigerators, and high-speed Internet service (free of charge).

WHERE TO EAT: A counter-service food court has a variety of dining options.

Sassagoula Floatworks & Food Factory: A variety of specialty foods is available in this food court, including gumbo, chicken with red beans and rice, freshly made beignets, and other traditional Creole dishes. Burgers, pizza, ice cream, and baked goods are also on the menu.

PHOTO BY JILL SAFRO

WHERE TO DRINK: A pool bar operates seasonally, and guests on a quest for a cocktail may head to Port Orleans Riverside—it's a short bus ride away. Of course, there's always Downtown Disney or any theme park other than the Magic Kingdom.

WHAT TO DO: A themed pool is the highlight of the recreational opportunities here.

Arcade: South Quarter Games is located at Port Orleans Square. It has a selection of state-of-the art, interactive games.

Biking: Bicycles and surrey bikes are available for rent at Port Orleans Riverside.

Boating: Pedal boats, kayaks, canoes, Sea Raycers, Boston Whaler Montauks, and pontoon boats may be rented at Port Orleans Riverside.

Carriage Rides: Refer to page 226 for details on carriage rides.

Fishing: Two-hour guided fishing excursions are available (see *Sports*).

Shopping: Jackson Square Gifts & Desires, located at Port Orleans Square, features Disney character merchandise, clothing bearing the Port Orleans resort logo, and sundries.

Swimming: Doubloon Lagoon is a free-form pool built around a bright blue sea serpent. The waterslide is actually the creature's tongue —kids love it. A shower at the pool features an alligator's head, and there is a large clamshell where an all-gator band serves as the centerpiece of a fountain. There is a large whirlpool nearby. Port Orleans French Quarter guests are also invited to swim in the pool at Ol' Man Island at Port Orleans Riverside.

TRANSPORTATION: Buses go to the Magic Kingdom, Epcot, Disney's Hollywood Studios, Animal Kingdom, Typhoon Lagoon, Blizzard Beach, and Downtown Disney. Small water taxis transport guests to Downtown Disney, too.

Port Orleans Riverside

Here, the city feel of the French Quarter gives way to the rural South. The resort is divided into "parishes." Closest to the "city," guestrooms are found in Mansion homes; farther upriver are the Bayou guestrooms, with a more rustic feel. The phone number for the Port Orleans Riverside resort is 407-934-6000.

ROOMS: The 2,048 Mansion and Bayou rooms are of the same size, and each has two queen beds (some king-size beds are available); 963 of the Bayou rooms have a bunk-size bed (recommended for kids under age 9) as well. There is a fee of $15 per night for a trundle bed. The Magnolia Bend Mansion rooms are situated in elegant manor homes with stately columns and grand staircases. The Alligator Bayou rooms are in rustic, weathered-wood buildings that are tucked among flora native to the area. Although all buildings have two to three floors, only the Magnolia Bend Mansions have elevators.

The Bayou rooms surround Ol' Man Island, a 3½-acre recreational area with a pool, playground, and fishing hole. Decorative touches include wood and tin armoires and pedestal sinks with brass fittings. The closet space is not enclosed. The rooms are a bit small, but they can accommodate four guests. Rooms have a coffeemaker (with coffee), fridge, and Wi-Fi (no charge).

More than 500 Riverside rooms invite guests to live like royalty. These "Royal Guest Rooms" feature special touches inspired by Disney's animated classics (all featuring royalty of some sort), ornately decorated beds with fiber-optic special effects, custom bed coverings and drapes, artwork featuring Princess Tiana and other regals, and more. If you want the royal treatment while residing at Port Orleans Riverside, make your wishes known when you book the room. Note that the rates for these rooms run higher than for standard rooms.

WHERE TO EAT: In addition to a restaurant and food court, the hotel offers limited pizza delivery from 4 P.M. until midnight.

Boatwright's Dining Hall: This 200-seat table-service eatery, next to Riverside Mill, serves Cajun specialties and American fare for dinner. Reservations are recommended.

Riverside Mill: This food court resembles an old-fashioned cotton mill with a working waterwheel that powers the cotton press inside. The five counter-service stands here offer all sorts of choices. The basic selections are available for breakfast. **Pizza 'n' Pasta** has pasta dishes, pizza, and bread sticks; **Grill Shop** offers fried fish, chicken nuggets, and burgers; **Carving Station** serves freshly sliced turkey; **Specialty Shop** offers soup and sandwiches; and the **Bakery** serves pastries, ice cream, yogurt parfait, and more. If you buy a resort refillable mug, Riverside Mill is where you fill it.

WHERE TO DRINK: Two lounges possess an enticing degree of charm.

Muddy Rivers: The poolside bar serves beer, wine, cocktails, and soft drinks. Seasonal.

River Roost: Situated in a room designed as a cotton exchange, this lounge features specialty drinks and light hors d'oeuvres.

WHAT TO DO: Many of the resort activities are at Ol' Man Island, a recreation center featuring a pool, whirlpool, wading pool, interactive fountains, and a playground.

Arcade: The Medicine Show Arcade features a small selection of games.

Biking: Bicycles of all types can be rented.

Boating: Pedal boats, canoes, kayaks, Sea Raycers, Boston Whaler Montauks, and pontoon boats are available for rent.

Carriage Rides: Horse-drawn carriages take guests for 25-minute rides throughout the resort grounds. Carriages hold up to 4 adults or 2 adults and 3 small kids. Each trip departs from the marina. Call 407-939-7529 for reservations.

Fishing: Two-hour guided fishing excursions are available (see *Sports*). It's also possible to drop a line at the Fishin' Hole on Ol' Man Island. Catch-and-release only.

Playground: An elaborate play area is located on Ol' Man Island next to the pool.

Shopping: Fulton's General Store in the Riverside building stocks Disney character merchandise, clothing, and sundries.

Swimming: In addition to the main pool and kiddie pool at Ol' Man Island, there are five unguarded pools at the resort. Guests may also swim in the French Quarter pool.

PHOTO BY JILL SAFRO

TRANSPORTATION: Buses go from Port Orleans Riverside to the Magic Kingdom, Epcot, Disney's Hollywood Studios, Animal Kingdom, Typhoon Lagoon, Blizzard Beach, and Downtown Disney. Small water taxis also ferry guests to and from Downtown Disney.

Disney's Saratoga Springs Resort & Spa

Just across the lake from the hustle and bustle of Downtown Disney, this Disney Vacation Club resort is a peaceful complement to its nearest neighbor. Disney's Saratoga Springs Resort & Spa aspires to recapture the heyday of upstate New York country retreats of the late 1800s. The resort covers 65 acres. To contact Saratoga Springs, call 407-827-1100.

ROOMS: There are studios and villas with one, two, and three bedrooms. A studio consists of a room with a queen-size bed and a double sleeper sofa, bathroom, kitchenette, microwave, and coffeemaker. All units have a porch or a balcony, access to complimentary laundry facilities, and high-speed Internet access (no charge).

One-bedroom villas have a king-size bed in the master suite and a queen-size sleeper sofa in the living room. The one bathroom has a whirlpool tub. The full kitchen has a fridge, stove, microwave, toaster, coffeemaker, dinnerware, and dishwasher. Each unit has a washer and dryer.

Two-bedroom villas have an additional bathroom and bedroom, with either one queen-size bed and a double sleeper sofa or two queen-size beds. The three-bedroom Grand Villa has similar features as the two-bedroom models, but is about twice the size and has four bathrooms.

The resort's Treehouse Villas, elevated on pedestals and designed to blend into the woodsy environment, offer serene views of the surrounding treetops. Each "cabin-casual" villa has a full kitchen, flat-panel TVs, three bedrooms, two bathrooms, and sleeps up to nine.

WHERE TO EAT: There are two eateries here and dozens across the lake. Several barbecue areas are available to resort guests.

The Artist's Palette: Set in a converted artist's loft, this spot offers all meals. Among the selections are fresh tossed salads, sandwiches, pizza, baked goods, and more.

Turf Club Bar & Grill: A cozy environment for dinner, Turf Club has a horse-racing motif.

Groceries: In these parts, in-room grocery delivery is available from Artist's Palette, and many guests cook their own meals. If you've got a car, ask for directions to a grocery store.

WHERE TO DRINK: In addition to local bars, guests imbibe at nearby Downtown Disney.

Backstretch Bar: A poolside watering hole.

On the Rocks: A pool bar serving the usual battery of cocktails.

Turf Club Bar & Grill: This spot serves a variety of drinks, plus it has a pool table.

WHAT TO DO: Besides enjoying spa treatments, guests may rent bikes, play basketball, swim, walk, swat tennis balls, and more.

Arcade: Expect to find the usual bells and whistles at "Win, Place, or Show."

Biking: Bicycles may be rented from Horsin' Around Rentals.

Boating: Boats may be rented at Captain Jack's Marina at nearby Downtown Disney.

Golf: The resort is adjacent to the Lake Buena Vista golf course.

Health Club: This spot features strength and cardio machines and weightlifting equipment.

Playground: There is a small kids' play area near an unguarded pool. (Be sure to supervise youngsters at all times.)

Shopping: The Artist's Palette stocks a variety of souvenirs and sundries.

Spa: The award-winning spa has treatment rooms for massage, manicures, facials, aromatherapy, and more.

Swimming: High Rock Spring cascades down rugged rockwork and feeds into a free-form, heated zero-depth-entry pool. The splash zone features a waterslide, two whirlpools, and an interactive play area for kids. There are four unguarded pools, too.

Tennis: Two courts are at the ready.

TRANSPORTATION: Buses go from Saratoga Springs to all theme and water parks. Small boats ferry guests to Downtown Disney.

Disney's Old Key West Resort

Escape to the spirit of the Florida Keys. Disney's Old Key West Resort is the original Disney Vacation Club property, but villas not occupied by members are available for nightly rental. It has the laid-back feel of a resort community and all the amenities that go with resort life. The homey accommodations have lots of space and the convenience of kitchen facilities, making the resort nice for longer stays. The villas, designed in a Key West theme, were completely refurbished in 2011. The telephone number for Disney's Old Key West is 407-827-7700.

VILLAS: A studio consists of a large room with two queen-size beds, a table and chairs, a small fridge, free Wi-Fi, microwave, and sink. Bathrooms are spacious. Each of the one-bedroom villas has a king-size bed in the master bedroom and a queen-size sleeper sofa and a sleeper chair in the living room; the master bath has a whirlpool tub, sink, and shower.

The two-bedroom villa features a king-size bed in the master bedroom, two queen-size beds in the second bedroom, living room with queen-size sleeper sofa and TV with DVD player, dining room, and a kitchen with a refrigerator, dishwasher, toaster, and coffeemaker, plus plates, flatware, cooking utensils, and more.

The master bathroom is divided into two rooms with an extra-large whirlpool tub and a sink in one and an oversize shower, sink and vanity, and toilet in the other. There's a porch or balcony off the living room and bedroom, and ceiling fans in each room. The configuration of the two-story, three-bedroom Grand Villas is similar to that of the two-bedroom models, but adds a third bedroom with two double beds. As for capacity, studios and one-bedroom villas sleep 5 people, the two-bedroom villas sleep 9 guests, and the two-story, three-bedroom villas accommodate 12.

WHERE TO EAT: In addition to the restaurant, there are grills and picnic tables. Pizza delivery is available from 4 P.M. to midnight.

Good's Food to Go: The perfect place to pick up fixin's for a continental breakfast, this place also offers burgers, soups, salads, sandwiches, and simple snacks.

Olivia's Cafe: This full-service restaurant serves Key West favorites, plus more traditional items, for breakfast, lunch, and dinner. Menus change seasonally.

WHERE TO DRINK: The watering holes at Old Key West are as laid-back as they come.

Gurgling Suitcase: This tiny bar serves specialty drinks, wine, beer, and soft drinks.

Turtle Shack: This poolside spot serves pizza, salads, sandwiches, and light snacks. Open seasonally.

WHAT TO DO: At Conch Flats Community Hall, table tennis, board games, a large-screen TV, DVD rentals, and planned activities are offered. There are basketball, shuffleboard, and volleyball courts, and equipment is available at Hank's Rent 'N Return.

Arcade: The Electric Eel Game Room is in the Hospitality House; the Flying Fish Game Room is by the Turtle Shack snack bar.

Biking: Bikes and surrey bikes may be rented from Hank's.

Boating: Pedal boats, Sea Raycers, Boston Whaler Montauks, and pontoon boats are available for rent at Hank's.

Health Club: The Fitness Center at R.E.S.T. Beach has a variety of exercise equipment.

Playground: A kids' play area is located by each of the resort's swimming pools.

Shopping: Conch Flats General Store has groceries, books, sundries, and more.

Swimming: The sprawling main pool, with a large whirlpool nearby, is located behind the Hospitality House. The children's pool and play area looks like a big sand castle and features a 125-foot slide. Additional pools are found around the resort.

Tennis: There are three courts.

TRANSPORTATION: Buses go to the theme parks, water parks, and Downtown Disney. Water taxis also make the trip between the resort and Downtown Disney.

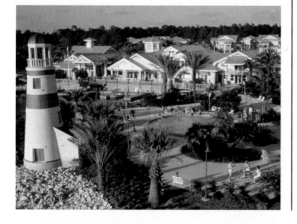

Animal Kingdom Area

All-Star Movies, Music, & Sports

The All-Star resorts are among the most brightly and boldly themed at Walt Disney World. Each resort has 1,500 to 1,920 rooms housed in ten buildings devoted to five Disney movies, types of music, and sports.

The All-Star Movies resort celebrates five classic Disney films: *Toy Story*, *The Mighty Ducks*, *Fantasia*, *101 Dalmatians*, and *The Love Bug*. Buildings are adorned with such icons as 40-foot Dalmatians and wildly oversize versions of Buzz Lightyear and Woody.

At the All-Star Music resort, Broadway, country, jazz, rock, and calypso are the themes. A walk-through, neon-lit jukebox; a three-story pair of cowboy boots; and a Broadway theater marquee are among the giant icons.

Sports fans will find themselves in a world of baseball, football, tennis, surfing, or basketball at the All-Star Sports resort. Brightly colored, larger-than-life football helmets, surfboards, tennis balls, basketball hoops, and baseball bats adorn the buildings.

As value resorts, the All-Star properties offer few frills, but the service and whimsical atmosphere are pure Disney.

Guests check in at Cinema Hall for All-Star Movies, Melody Hall for All-Star Music, or Stadium Hall for All-Star Sports. To reach All-Star Movies, call 407-939-7000; to phone All-Star Music, call 407-939-6000; to contact All-Star Sports, call 407-939-5000.

ROOMS: The guestrooms, measuring 260 square feet, are rather small compared with those at Port Orleans, which are 314 square feet. Each room has two double beds, a vanity area with a sink, a bathroom, free Wi-Fi, a small dresser, and a small table with chairs.

All-Star Music boasts 192 Family Suites. Each one sleeps up to six guests and has two bathrooms, a "master" bedroom with its own flat-screen TV, Wi-Fi (free of charge), and a kitchenette with counter space, mini fridge, sink, microwave, and coffeemaker.

WHERE TO EAT: Three food courts—World Premiere in Cinema Hall, Intermission in Melody Hall, and End Zone in Stadium Hall. Each features a bakery, convenience market, and several stands geared to pizza, pasta, salads, and burgers. Each food court has a seating area with a beverage bar. The All-Star resorts all deliver pizza and salads to rooms from 5 P.M. to 1 A.M.

WHERE TO DRINK: There are no traditional lounges at the All-Star resorts; however, the Silver Screen Spirits, Singing Spirits, and Grandstand Spirits pool bars serve drinks throughout the day and evening.

WHAT TO DO: Guests may swim in any of the resort pools. All-Star guests may rent boating equipment at any WDW resort marina.

Arcades: Each of the All-Star resorts has its own arcade.

Playground: A playground is located in each hotel's courtyard area.

Shopping: Maestro Mickey's in Melody Hall, Sport Goofy's Gifts and Sundries in Stadium Hall, and Donald's Double Feature in Cinema Hall all have magazines, books, character merchandise, and sundries.

Swimming: Each hotel has two pools and one kiddie pool. The main pool at All-Star Movies has a *Fantasia* theme (look for Sorcerer Mickey). The smaller Duck Pond Pool is based on *The Mighty Ducks*. At the All-Star Music resort, the Calypso Pool is in the form of a giant guitar, while the Piano Pool bears a striking resemblance to a grand piano. At All-Star Sports, Surfboard Bay has an ocean motif. The smaller Grand Slam Pool pays tribute to our national pastime.

TRANSPORTATION: Buses make pickups at All-Star's Cinema Hall, Melody Hall, and Stadium Hall for trips to each of the theme parks, water parks, and Downtown Disney. Each resort has its own bus stops.

A word about All-Star resort transportation: The bus service at these "value" resorts tends to be slightly more efficient than at other locations. The combination of fewer stops and connections is a bonus for guests staying here.

Disney's Animal Kingdom Lodge & Villas

At first glance, Disney's Animal Kingdom Lodge evokes images of a sleepy, little thatched-roof game lodge in the wilds of southern Africa. Upon closer examination, however, it's clear that the only things sleepy or little about this place are the small creatures that live in its shadow. Those animals, along with their more sizable cousins, inhabit acres of meticulously re-created African savanna that practically surround the resort. Exotic birds and all manner of hoofed animals, including giraffes, zebras, and Thomson's gazelles, call the wildlife reserve home. With the freedom to wander within a dozen or so yards of the lodge itself, these critters allow guests to go on safari without leaving their balconies.

The resort is located about a mile from Disney's Animal Kingdom park. The lobby is a huge, high-ceilinged room, richly appointed with colorful African artwork and artifacts. The biggest draw here is the four-story observation window overlooking the savanna. It's one of many portals through which to gaze upon meandering wildlife.

Like the African game lodges on which it is based, Disney's Animal Kingdom Lodge was

constructed using a semicircular design. From overhead, it looks a bit like a horseshoe. This allows for maximum animal-viewing potential. Indeed, many of the resort's guestrooms have direct views of the savanna areas. Be sure to specify your viewing preference when you book a room. The telephone number for Disney's Animal Kingdom Lodge is 407-938-3000.

ROOMS: The 972 rooms, all finished in tapestries and vibrant colors, feature hand-crafted dark-wood furniture, sand-colored walls, and earth-tone-patterned carpets. Deluxe rooms are a bit more spacious than their standard counterparts. Most rooms have two queen beds (some king-size beds are available), plus a daybed to accommodate up to five people; bunk beds are available in many rooms. All rooms have balconies. Suites include a parlor, plus one or two bedrooms; there are king-size or queen-size beds in the bedrooms. Bathrooms have a separate vanity area with double sink. All rooms include an iron (with board), hair dryer, free Wi-Fi, and refrigerator. Complimentary weekday newspapers may be picked up in the lobby. Club-level service is available.

As for the Villas, the first phase, located in Jambo House, opened in 2008. The second phase, Kidani Village, began hosting guests in its thatched-roof, hewn-timber homes in early 2009. Also included in this village are a pool, fitness center, shop, table-service restaurant, and more. As with all DVC resorts, the homes are available to guests when not being used by members. For information on this member of the Disney Vacation Club family, call 800-800-9100, or visit *www.disneyvacationclub.com*.

WHERE TO EAT: In addition to its restaurants, the hotel offers round-the-clock room service.

Boma—Flavors of Africa: Boma is modeled after a bustling African marketplace. The restaurant boasts many types of cuisine in what chefs describe as a "global fusion" style. Served buffet style, the fare is a mix of French, Malaysian, Indian, Chinese, and English.

Jiko—The Cooking Place: The colors of sunset are the backdrop for this sublime eatery with an African flair. Wines from South Africa are featured.

The Mara: A spacious fast-food restaurant serving such kid-pleasers as pizza, burgers, and chicken fingers.

Sanaa: This colorful, table-service eatery at Kidani Village features African- and Indian-inspired cuisine.

WHERE TO DRINK: The lounges here are rustic and inviting. Some even offer the opportunity to sip cocktails while observing wildlife.

Cape Town Lounge and Wine Bar: Located inside Jiko—The Cooking Place, this spot features wines from South Africa.

Maji and Uzima Springs: These poolside bars serve specialty and traditional drinks.

Sanaa: A 24-seat lounge located within the restaurant of the same name.

Victoria Falls: Set alongside a soothing waterfall, this mezzanine-level lounge features coffee, tea, domestic and South African wines, and assorted cocktails.

WHAT TO DO: Spying on African wildlife is the main event in these parts. However, if you can manage to pry yourself away from those hoofed exhibitionists for a bit, there are plenty

PHOTO BY MIKE CARROLL

of other diversions available—including tennis, basketball, shuffleboard, and a barbecue pavilion. Note that guests are welcome to partake in activities offered at other Walt Disney World resort hotels.

Arcades: Pumbaa's Fun & Games and Safari So Good are both stocked with the latest games.

Children's Program: The Simba's Cubhouse play area, for (potty-trained) kids ages 3 through 12, is open in the evenings, starting at 4 P.M. It costs about $12 per hour, per child. Reservations are required; call 407-939-3463. Kids can learn about the wildlife at the resort through nature-themed activities.

Health Club: Zahanati Massage and (24-hour) Fitness Center has exercise equipment, sauna, and spa services, including massage. Kidani Village's Survival of the Fittest also offers exercise equipment.

Playground: The Hakuna Matata playground is located near the pool.

Shopping: Zawadi Marketplace stocks Africa-themed gifts, Disney character-themed merchandise, clothing with the Animal Kingdom Lodge logo, and sundries. Johari Treasures tempts shoppers at Kidani Village.

Swimming: The resort's huge main pool, Uzima, looks like a natural watering hole. More impressive than the size of the zero-depth-entry pool, however, is the view from the pool deck. In addition to a kiddie pool, there are two whirlpools nearby. Kidani Village is home to another pool (Samawati Springs) and to Uwanja Camp, a watery playground.

Tennis: There are two clay courts available to all Animal Kingdom Lodge guests.

TRANSPORTATION: Buses go to the Magic Kingdom, Epcot, Disney's Hollywood Studios, Animal Kingdom, Typhoon Lagoon, Blizzard Beach, and Downtown Disney.

Coronado Springs

This resort reveals its Southwestern U.S.–Mexican theme in such elements as a tiled and stucco lobby with a fountain and a pyramid with water tumbling down from it that appears to have created the Mayan ruin-themed pool. The 1,921 rooms are found in three guest areas that stretch around Lago Dorado, a 22-acre lake. (It can take five minutes or more to walk to the farthest rooms.) The food court and restaurant are near the lobby. A convention center offers access to business services. The phone number for Coronado Springs is 407-939-1000.

ROOMS: Standard rooms are smaller than those at Disney's deluxe hotels, but adequate for up to four; each has two queen beds (some king-size beds are available). In-room amenities include a coffeemaker, refrigerator, hair dryer, and free Wi-Fi. Decor varies in each section but is characterized by yellow, blue, and scarlet accents. In the Casitas area, where most suites are located, terra-cotta guest buildings occupy a citylike landscape. In the pueblo-style Ranchos, scattered along a dry streambed, rooms have a rustic feel. Cabanas, located along the rocky palm-lined beach, reflect the casual feel of their namesake.

WHERE TO EAT: In addition to a full-service restaurant and food court, limited room service is available for breakfast and dinner.
    Cafe Rix: A quick-service eatery, Rix has offerings for breakfast, lunch, and dinner.
    Maya Grill: Open for breakfast and dinner, this spot offers seafood, steak, lamb, and pork cooked over an open-pit, wood-fired grill.
    Pepper Market: High ceilings make this nontraditional food court feel like an open-air market. The fare includes tacos, tostadas, pizza, pasta, and omelets made to order. Note that

there is an automatic ten-percent gratuity for dining in the Pepper Market.

WHERE TO DRINK: There are three places to wet your whistle at Coronado Springs.
    Laguna Bar: A lagoonside lounge outside the lobby, this spot serves drinks during pool hours.
    Rix Lounge: This colorful lounge provides cocktails, appetizers, and evening entertainment, and is located in the main building.

HOT TIP!

Coronado Springs' La Marina operates on a seasonal basis. If it isn't open during your stay, know that Coronado guests may rent boats, bikes, and enjoy other recreational experiences offered at any Walt Disney World resort.

    Siestas: In the Dig Site area, this poolside bar lets swimmers and archaeologists enjoy a variety of cocktails and light snacks.

WHAT TO DO: There is an array of water sports in which to participate, as well as volleyball and a short nature trail.
    Arcade: Iguana Arcade is in the Dig Site area.
    Biking: Bikes and surrey bikes may be rented at La Marina.
    Boating: A selection of equipment, including pedal boats and motorboats, is available for rent at La Marina.
    Fishing: Two-hour, guided fishing excursions are offered on the 22-acre Lago Dorado. Call 407-WDW-BASS. Fishing excursions are offered seasonally.

PHOTO BY JILL SAFRO

Health Club: La Vida fitness center offers a full range of strength and cardio equipment 24/7, plus spa services (by day).

Playground: The Explorer's Playground is part of the Dig Site play area and includes a huge sandbox, complete with Mayan carvings waiting to be excavated.

Salon: The Casa de Belleza salon is located near La Vida Fitness Center. A full-service facility, Casa de Belleza offers haircuts, sets, coloring, beard and mustache trim, manicures, pedicures, facials, and more. Operating hours are generally from 9 A.M. until 6 P.M. daily. To make an appointment, call 407-939-3965.

Shopping: Panchito's Gifts & Sundries is where you will find souvenir items with a Southwestern flavor, Disney merchandise, film, and necessities.

Swimming: The main pool is in the Dig Site area. It surrounds a Mayan pyramid and features a towering 123-foot waterslide. There is a whirlpool and a kiddie pool. Each guestroom area features an unguarded pool.

TRANSPORTATION: Buses go to the Magic Kingdom, Epcot, Disney's Hollywood Studios, Animal Kingdom, Typhoon Lagoon, Blizzard Beach, and Downtown Disney.

Pop Century

What do you get when you mix decades of American pop culture with a Disney resort? Pop Century! Like the All-Star resorts, Pop Century is a vivid celebration of Americana. The 2,880-room resort represents the second half of the twentieth century. The resort's larger-than-life "time capsules" commemorate the toys, fads, dance crazes, and catchphrases that swept the nation from the 1950s through the 1990s. It's groovy . . . you dig?

As a WDW value resort, the Pop Century property offers few frills, but the service is good, the atmosphere's colorful, and the transportation is efficient. Guests check in at Classic Hall, which also features a food and merchandise location, arcade, and guest services desk. To reach Disney's Pop Century resort, call 407-938-4000.

ROOMS: The guestrooms measure 260 square feet (a bit smaller than Port Orleans' rooms, which are 314 square feet). Each room has two double beds, a vanity area with a sink, a bathroom, a small dresser, a table with chairs, a fridge, and free Wi-Fi.

WHERE TO EAT: The food court features a bakery and a convenience market, plus several stands geared to pizza, pasta, and burgers. The Pop Century resort delivers pizza to guestrooms from about 4 P.M. to midnight.

WHERE TO DRINK: Petals is a bar located near the Hippy Dippy pool.

WHAT TO DO: Guests may swim in any of the Pop Century resort pools. They may rent boating equipment at any WDW resort.

Arcade: Revisit classic video games or discover some new ones at Fast Forward arcade.

Playground: There is a soft-surface playground with, among other compelling features, an interactive water fountain.

Shopping: The Everything Pop shop has a selection of books, character merchandise, sundries, and snacks.

Swimming: The hotel has three pools (in the shapes of a bowling pin, computer, and a flower), plus a kiddie pool.

TRANSPORTATION: Buses stop at Classic Hall for trips to each of the four theme parks, Blizzard Beach, Typhoon Lagoon, and Downtown Disney.

PHOTO BY JILL SAFRO

Art of Animation

The Walt Disney World resort landscape has gotten a serious burst of color with the addition of this vivid celebration of Disney animation. A "value" resort, Disney's Art of Animation made its debut in 2012.

Pop Century's next-door neighbor (the resorts share access to Hourglass Lake and the nearly 1.4-mile jogging path that surrounds it), Art of Animation boasts colossal figures from classic animated films. It also has three themed pools, playgrounds, festive courtyards, an arcade, and a splash zone featuring everyone's favorite clownfish, Nemo. The resort also offers free Wi-Fi, babysitting and child-care services, laundry, and dry cleaning (fees apply for the last three services).

ROOMS: The 864 standard rooms, which are housed in *The Little Mermaid*–themed buildings, sleep up to 4 and come with the usual amenities afforded to Walt Disney World's "value" resorts (see page 75 for details). Each measures 277 square feet and has two double beds, a vanity area with a sink, a bathroom, a small dresser, a table with chairs, and free Wi-Fi. The 1,120 festive family suites, which are themed to *Cars*, *Finding Nemo*, and *The Lion King*, feature

3 separate sleeping areas, accommodate up to 6 guests, and come with 2 LCD TVs, a queen-size bed, double-size pull-down bed, and sleeper sofa. Each 565-square-foot suite has a living room, 2 bathrooms, and a kitchenette (with a refrigerator, microwave, and coffeemaker).

WHERE TO EAT: The brilliantly hued Landscape of Flavors food court features four unique cooking stations serving international favorites, Mongolian barbecue, burgers, pizza, pasta, sandwiches, fresh smoothies, and hand-scooped gelato. It's open for breakfast, lunch, and dinner. There is a "grab and go" selection, too. In-room pizza delivery is also an option.

WHERE TO DRINK: The Drop Off is a full-service bar located near the Big Blue Pool.

WHAT TO DO: Guests may swim in any of the Art of Animation resort pools. They may rent boating equipment at any WDW resort.

Arcade: Pixel Play Arcade is in Animation Hall, across from Landscape of Flavors.

Jogging and Walking: The resort is encircled by a trail that's almost 1.4 miles long.

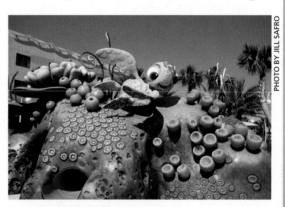

PHOTO BY JILL SAFRO

Playground: The Righteous Reef playground can be found in the middle of the Finding Nemo courtyard.

Shopping: The Ink and Paint Shop has a selection of books, character merchandise, Art of Animation Resort–themed souvenirs, sundries, and snacks.

Swimming: The hotel has three pools: Flippin' Fins, Cozy Cone, and The Big Blue Pool, plus a *Finding Nemo*–themed splash zone known as The Schoolyard.

TRANSPORTATION: Buses stop at Animation Hall for trips to each of the four theme parks, Blizzard Beach, Typhoon Lagoon, and Downtown Disney.

PHOTO BY JILL SAFRO

Resort on Dream Tree Blvd.

Four Seasons Orlando

Walt Disney World welcomed a Four Seasons resort into its happy hotel fold in August 2014. The 443-room luxury property boasts more than 26 lakeside acres of elegant design, as well as a multitude of recreational diversions, and high convenience for Disney guests. Spanish Revival architecture reflects Florida's Golden Age mansions and is surrounded by a vibrant array of 72,000 plants and nearly 1,000 palm trees. Check-in begins at 4 P.M. daily. Check-out time is 12 P.M. There is a 24-hour business center, plus ample meeting space suitable for conferences and social functions. For more information or to make reservations, call 800-267-3046, or visit *www.fourseasons.com/orlando*.

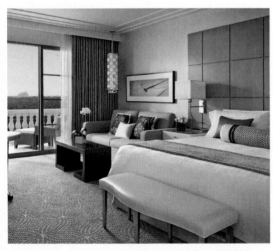

ROOMS: All rooms have furnished balconies, one king or two double beds, twice-daily housekeeping service, newspaper delivery, 24-hour room-service, and high-speed Internet and Wi-Fi. Rooms also come with a safe, coffeemaker (with coffee), DVD player, iPod docking station, flat-screen TV, and minibar. There are terrycloth bathrobes to use throughout your stay (kids' robes are available upon request). Accommodations feature luxurious marble bathrooms with double sinks and soaking tub, hair dryer, lighted makeup mirrors, and a TV in the mirror (yes, *in* the mirror!). Hypoallergenic bedding is available upon request. Cribs may be requested (no charge), as can high chairs, bottles, and toddler toys. Babysitting services may be arranged for an hourly fee (reservations must be made at least 24 hours in advance).

The resort has many rooms that are accessible for guests with disabilities. Make your needs known when you book the room. Four Seasons is a non-smoking resort.

Room categories include Park View, Lake View, Golden Oak View, and Four Seasons Rooms. Park View rooms offer a view of the Magic Kingdom and Wishes, the park's nightly fireworks presentation. Lake View rooms have views of a lake, golf course, or pool area. Golden Oak rooms offer "residential views" of privately owned homes, while Four Seasons rooms have limited views.

Suites have king beds, two bathrooms, and living area with queen sleeper sofa. To book a room, call 800-267-3046. For suites (including the 9-bedroom Royal Suite or Presidential Suite), call 407-313-6734.

The lobby's Disney Planning Center assists with the purchase of park tickets, making Disney dining reservations, reserving special events, and more. When it comes to Walt Disney World privileges, the resort fits somewhere between Swan and Dolphin and the resorts on Hotel Plaza Boulevard. Among them:

• Complimentary transportation to all Disney World destinations is provided by a Four Seasons shuttle. (There are on-site vehicles available for rent, too.)

• Guests may use the theme parks Package Express delivery service. Merchandise can be delivered directly to the resort from any WDW theme park and many shops (no charge).

• Fastpass+ assignments may be booked starting 30 days before arrival. (Refer to page 25 for details on this system that allows guests to book advance reservation times for theme park shows and attractions.)

• Disney characters visit the resort's Ravello restaurant for the "Good Morning Breakfast" on Thursdays and Saturdays year-round (and on Tuesdays during school breaks and major holidays). Expect the likes of Goofy and his pals.

WHERE TO EAT: There are four full-service eateries and a coffee bar, plus 24-hour in-room dining. Reservations are recommended for Capa and Ravello (call 800-267-3046).

Capa: This contemporary, Spanish-style steakhouse specializes in prime cuts, tapas (appetizer portions), and local seafood such as freshly shucked oysters. There is indoor and outdoor seating at this rooftop hot spot. Capa is open for dinner only, 6 P.M. to 10 P.M. The dress code here is "resort casual."

Lickety-Split: Located in the lobby, this is the perfect place for gourmet coffees and quick bites. Selections include breakfast pastries, grab-and-go items, gelato, and more. There is indoor and outdoor seating.

PB&G: Think pulled pork, smoked brisket, house-made hot dogs and burgers, and creative salads at this southern-style smokehouse and rotisserie, located poolside (all seating is alfresco). There is also an extensive children's menu. Open 11 A.M. to 6 P.M.

Plancha: A relaxed Cuban-American eatery, Plancha is located at the Tranquilo Golf Club. It offers empanadas, the classic Cubano sandwich, and chorizo burgers. The cocktail menu includes mojitos and Hemingway daiquiris. The hours are 10 A.M. till 6 P.M.

Ravello: Guests are invited to watch the action in this modern Italian eatery's open kitchen. In addition to regionally influenced specialties, fresh bread and pizza come straight from a wood-burning oven and a bountiful pasta bar beckons. Two private dining rooms are also available. Ravello is open for breakfast (6:30 A.M. to 11 A.M.) and dinner (5:30 P.M. to 10 P.M.). The dress code here is "smart casual."

WHERE TO DRINK: Guests may quench their thirst and enjoy creatively prepared nibbles at a duo of lovely lounges.

Ravello Bar: Drinks mix well with the imaginative appetizers and pastries at this lounge.

Capa Lounge: As you sip a beverage on the patio, you may also enjoy the Magic Kingdom's fireworks. Capa is open from 6 P.M. to 10 P.M.

WHAT TO DO: There's no getting bored in these parts. The Explorer Island play province could be enjoyed for days on end. In addition to a swimmer's paradise, the amusing island boasts a rock-climbing wall, volleyball, basketball, pool, Ping-Pong, and more. Outdoor movies are presented on select nights.

Children's Program: The resort's complimentary "Kids for All Seasons" program is open to youngsters ages 4 to 12. Trained staffers supervise and entertain kids throughout the day. Little ones under ages 4 are welcome to participate if accompanied by a guardian.

Fun and Games: The Mansion on the resort's Explorer Island is a family-focused hangout with outdoor activities such as table tennis, bocce ball, and pool (the kind you play with a cue stick). The Hideout has video games, basketball hoops, and beach volleyball.

Golf: Golfers may argue that the resort's crowning glory is the secluded course at the Tranquilo Golf Club. The Tom Fazio–designed, 18-hole, 6,968-yard, par 71 course is a certified Audubon sanctuary with abundant opportunities to view local wildlife between swings. Amenities include a pro shop, instruction, driving range, putting green, club rental and a restaurant (Plancha). The course is open to both guests of the hotel and daytime visitors (fees apply). To reserve tee times, call 800-267-3046.

Health Club: The 24-hour Fitness Centre has cardiovascular equipment, weights, and yoga, plus a steam room, sauna, and whirlpool spa. Certified trainers are on hand, too (for a fee).

Movies: The resort presents alfresco films on select nights at the Star Struck "dive-in" movie screen (near the pools on Explorer Island).

Spa: The Spa at Four Seasons evokes the peace and natural beauty of Florida's Everglades. The Zen zone features 18 treatment rooms, as well as two bungalows for private retreats. There are also outdoor lounges and a whirlpool. The Salon provides hairstyling, manicures, pedicures, and other services.

Swimming: The resort's swimming areas are part of an enormous playground known as Explorer Island: The Oasis, a lakeside adults-only pool; a zero-depth-entry family pool; Splash Zone, a soft-surface interactive fountain area that sprays water up to 30 feet in the air; a 1,203-foot-long lazy river, complete with a waterfall and bubbling rapids; and two winding, 242-foot water slides.

Tennis: The resort sports Three Har-Tru tennis courts for play and instruction (fees apply to both activities).

Weddings: From the rehearsal dinner, to the ceremony, reception, and even the honeymoon, Four Seasons can accommodate the wishes for most fairy tale occasions. Wedding specialists may be contacted by calling 800-267-3046 or visiting *www.fourseasons.com*.

TRANSPORTATION: A complimentary motor coach goes to Magic Kingdom every 30 minutes and to Epcot, Disney's Hollywood Studios, and Animal Kingdom once every hour. Airport and individual transfers throughout Walt Disney World are available for a fee.

Resorts on Hotel Plaza Blvd.

These seven hotels—Best Western Lake Buena Vista, DoubleTree Suites by Hilton, Wyndham Lake Buena Vista, Hilton, B in the Walt Disney World Resort, Buena Vista Palace Hotel & Spa, and Holiday Inn—though inside Walt Disney World boundaries, are neither owned nor operated by Disney. However, a few have been here since the park opened in 1971 or soon thereafter (sometimes under different names), accommodating Mickey enthusiasts from the beginning. The hotels are not Disney-themed, but the three largest (the Hilton, Buena Vista Palace, and Wyndham) do have meals hosted by Disney characters and Disney-themed shops.

Often referred to as the Downtown Disney Resort Area Hotels, they line the mile-long Hotel Plaza Boulevard. The Hilton, Buena Vista Palace, and Wyndham are across from the Marketplace, with its shops, restaurants, and nightlife. The other four properties are a 10- to 25-minute stroll away. They are also relatively close to the Crossroads at Lake Buena Vista shopping center, home to many eateries and a 24-hour grocery. The privileges of staying in one of these hotels include:

• Car rental desk on the premises (at all Hotel Plaza Boulevard resorts).

• Free bus service to the four theme parks, with limited service to Downtown Disney, Typhoon Lagoon, and Blizzard Beach. The buses, which are not part of the Disney transportation network, make two trips every hour; be sure to allow extra time for bus travel. One bus serves the Hilton, DoubleTree, and B in the Walt Disney World Resort; another serves the other hotels (it takes at least ten minutes to stop at all resorts on the loop). Note that buses load and unload in the middle of the parking lot at some of the parks.

• Flexibility to book tickets for both on- and, in most cases, off-WDW-property attractions.

• Preferred access to Disney golf courses.

• A "Passport to Savings" coupon book with exclusive discounts and specials on dining, shopping, and entertainment.

• Reservations for Disney dinner shows and theme park restaurants.

Note that guests staying in the resorts on Hotel Plaza Boulevard do have to pay for parking at Disney parks and other Walt Disney World attractions, and they cannot charge purchases made at Disney World shops and restaurants with a resort ID.

To book a room at a Hotel Plaza Boulevard resort, call the resort's toll-free number or WDW Central Reservations at 407-W-DISNEY (934-7639). The resorts on Hotel Plaza Boulevard are included in several Walt Disney Travel Company packages. Internet users can get information via *www.downtowndisneyhotels.com*.

All of the hotels offer nonsmoking rooms and accommodations for travelers with disabilities. To get to the hotels from the airport, take Exit 68 off I-4.

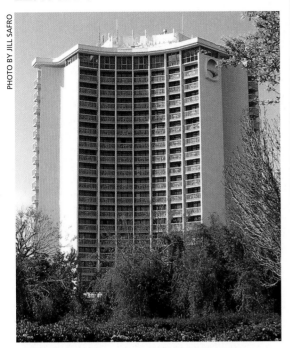

BEST WESTERN LAKE BUENA VISTA RESORT: This mostly leisure-oriented, 18-story hotel is surrounded by pines and has an entry lined with oaks draped in Spanish moss. Each of the 325 spacious, smoke-free rooms and suites has either one king-size bed and a queen sofa bed or two queen-size beds, as well as a balcony. Rooms also come with complimentary Wi-Fi, voice mail, coffeemaker, safe, hair dryer, and iron with board. Baths have one sink and plenty of counter space. Small refrigerators rent for $10 a day.

Each of the four suites occupies a corner of the 18th floor and features a wet bar, two phones, two TVs, a refrigerator, whirlpool tub, and an impressive glassed-in porch with skylights and a ceiling fan. Rooms on the seventh floor and higher offer fine views of the other resorts on Hotel Plaza Boulevard.

The hotel also has a fitness center, business center, a game room, a heated pool, small kiddie pool, shop, guest laundry facilities (for a fee), and room service. There is an Enterprise car rental desk in the lobby.

The hotel's lobby and restaurant area features Marketplace Café, and the new Trader's Tex Mex Restaurant & Grille, both open three meals a day. The Flamingo Cove offers poolside or inside seating and serves lunch, dinner, drinks, and snacks. For a pizza fix, try Pizza Hut Express.

Rates for this hotel range from about $99 to $239 for rooms; about $299 to $399 for suites. Self-parking is free, with optional valet parking for a fee. Best Western Lake Buena Vista Resort, 2000 Hotel Plaza Blvd., Lake Buena Vista, FL 32830; 407-828-2424 or 800-348-3765; *www.lakebuenavistaresorthotel.com.*

DOUBLETREE SUITES BY HILTON: This 229-unit property has a stellar staff, homey atmosphere, low-slung facade reminiscent of WDW's Contemporary hotel, bright colors, and whimsical patterns throughout. In the lobby, a child's check-in desk adjoins the one for grown-ups. Kids get a bag of goodies, and everyone gets a chocolate chip cookie. The only all-suite hotel in the Downtown Disney area, it has roomy (625 square feet) units, each with a living room and sleeper sofa, dressing area, and separate bedroom. The one-bedroom suites sleep up to six; there are five two-bedroom suites. Most of the bedrooms have two double beds; a few king beds are available.

The renovated decor features cheerful blues and oranges offset by contrasting neutrals. Room amenities include two TVs, pay-per-view movies, refrigerator, coffeemaker, microwave, hair dryer, high-speed Internet (for a fee), a desk, and safe.

Recreational facilities include a heated pool, splash pool for kids, and a whirlpool in a landscaped area, plus a fitness room, two lighted tennis courts, jogging trail, and small playground. Evergreen, a full-service restaurant with a pool bar, offers a breakfast buffet, lunch, and dinner as well as snacks and sandwiches throughout the day. Cocktails are available at the lobby bar. A market/deli provides snacks and groceries, including more of those famous chocolate chip cookies (though you'll have to pay for these!). There is a Budget Rental Car desk by the lobby.

Room rates range from $99 to $399. Parking charges apply. DoubleTree Suites by Hilton, 2305 Hotel Plaza Blvd., Lake Buena Vista, FL 32830; 407-934-1000 or 800-222-8733; *www.doubletreeguestsuites.com.*

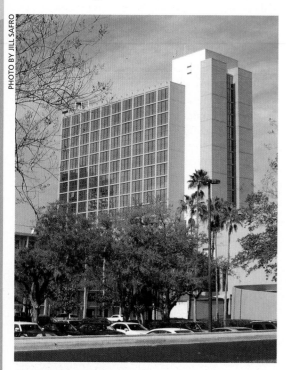

PHOTO BY JILL SAFRO

WYNDHAM LAKE BUENA VISTA
RESORT: The Wyndham sports a spiffy look, obvious upon stepping into the cheerful Bermuda-themed lobby. The 626 refurbished rooms are in a 19-story tower and two wings framing two large courtyards. Most rooms have two double beds, though 77 king-bed rooms are available. There are 7 spacious suites. All accommodations include a refrigerator, coffee-maker, Wi-Fi (free of charge), flat-screen TV, plush bedding, safe, hair dryer, iron, and daily newspaper (by request). Guests receive a discount at many shops and restaurants at nearby Downtown Disney.

Extensive recreational facilities—the hotel's major appeal—include an exercise room, two lighted tennis courts, a sand volleyball court, and a basketball court. The impressive Oasis Aquatic Playground features a heated pool with zero-depth entry, interactive features such as water cannons, and a relaxing hot tub with a lovely view of the lake. Special, kids-only activities are scheduled throughout the day. There's a health club, arcade, and business center, too.

Lake View Restaurant (on the mezzanine level) serves breakfast and dinner. Breakfast is hosted by Disney characters on Tuesday, Thursday, and Saturday. Sundial (in the lobby), open 24 hours, has snacks and light fare. For cocktails, there's Horizons Bar (next to Lake View), the Eclipse lobby bar, and Oasis pool bar.

A lobby merchandise shop sells assorted sundries and Disney-themed souvenirs. Room rates range from about $79 to $159 year-round; suites range from $150 to $350. There is an additional (daily) resort fee that includes self-parking, and other amenities. Wyndham Lake Buena Vista Resort, 1850 Hotel Plaza Blvd., Lake Buena Vista, FL 32830; 407-828-4444 or 800-624-4109; *www.wyndhamlakebuenavista.com.*

HILTON: This hotel gets high marks for its 23 well-groomed acres, laid-back ambience, pool area, and upscale shops. The 814 rooms, all of which recently underwent extensive refurbishment, have minibars, voice mail, safes, and high-speed Internet access.

Among the resort's restaurants and lounges, Andiamo Italian Bistro & Grille offers American and Italian fare, while Benihana Steakhouse and Sushi serves Japanese favorites and entertainment (both eateries serve dinner only); Covington Mill serves breakfast and lunch (with Disney characters attending Sunday breakfast); Rum Largo Poolside Cafe serves burgers, sandwiches, salads, and tropical drinks alfresco; Mainstreet Market, open 24 hours, is part deli, part country store (serving Starbucks coffee). For light meals, snacks, or drinks, drop by John T's lounge; specialty coffees and ice cream are served at Mugs. There is an Avis car rental on the premises.

PHOTO BY JILL SAFRO

Recreational facilities include a tropical whirlpool, two heated swimming pools, a kiddie pool, fitness room, and large game room. Rates range from $99 to $299; suites are $149 to $1,500. Parking charges apply for self-parking and valet. Hilton in the Walt Disney World Resort, 1751 Hotel Plaza Blvd., Lake Buena Vista, FL 32830; 407-827-4000 or 800-782-4414; *www.hiltonorlandoresort.com*.

Note: This is the only hotel on Hotel Plaza Boulevard to offer Extra Magic Hours. For details about this program (which, on select days, lets guests enter a theme park an hour before it officially opens or stay up to two hours after it closes), ask at the front desk.

HOLIDAY INN IN THE WALT DISNEY WORLD RESORT: This family-friendly hotel has reopened after being rebuilt for $35 million. All 323 rooms are nonsmoking and have either one king or two queen beds. Some are available with views of nearby Downtown Disney. Guestrooms are decorated in earth tones and include a flat-screen TV with DirecTV, coffee-maker, microwave, mini fridge, safe, and hair dryer. Bathrooms have granite countertops. Free high-speed Wi-Fi is available in all guestrooms, restaurants, and the lobby.

The Palm Breezes Restaurant, located in the atrium, serves three meals a day (kids through age 12 eat free). Palm Breezes has a "grab and go" section, a bar, and provides room service. There is a zero-depth-entry heated pool, a

whirlpool, arcade, Disney store, and 24-hour fitness center. Parking charges apply.

Room rates range from about $99 to $239 and suites about $299 to $399. Holiday Inn in the Walt Disney World Resort; 1805 Hotel Plaza Blvd., Lake Buena Vista, FL 32830; 407-828-8888 or 888-465-4329; *www.hiorlando.com*.

B RESORT: This glitzy new addition to Hotel Plaza Boulevard, which opened in late fall 2013, occupies the space formerly filled by the Hotel Royal Plaza. B pulls out all the modern stops in its 394 guestrooms and suites. Amenities include large HD televisions, bunk beds, in-room safe and mini-fridge, and iPad/iPod docking stations. Complimentary loaner iPads and gaming consoles are available upon request. B Resort at Walt Disney World is a non-smoking hotel.

Resort guests may enjoy the outdoor, heated infinity-edge pool, the 5,000-square-foot "B Indulged" full-service spa and wellness center, and the "B Active" fitness center. Free, high-speed wireless Internet service is available. American Q, the resort's signature restaurant, serves gourmet barbecue cuisine on a buffet on the back of a 1950 cherry-red Ford pickup truck. A quick-service option, Pick-Up, offers breakfast items, snacks, and sundries.

B Resort at the Walt Disney World Resort, 1905 Hotel Plaza Blvd., Lake Buena Vista, FL 32830. For additional information about B Resort, visit *www.bresortlbv.com* or call 888-662-4683.

PHOTO BY JILL SAFRO

TRANSPORTATION & ACCOMMODATIONS

BUENA VISTA PALACE HOTEL & SPA:

The tallest hotel in the Downtown Disney area and the largest of the resorts on Hotel Plaza Boulevard (it's actually at the intersection of Hotel Plaza Boulevard and Buena Vista Drive) is a cluster of towers set on 27 acres beside Lake Buena Vista. Each of the 1,014 rooms has a ceiling fan, two phones (one cordless; both with voice mail and speakerphone), high-speed Internet access (wired and wireless), two queen beds or one king, a coffeemaker, 32-inch flat-panel TV, and weekday newspaper in the lobby. Most rooms have a balcony or patio. In addition, there are 122 one- and two-bedroom suites and two-story penthouses with micro-waves. Twin/queen sofa beds are in suites and rooms with king beds. All guestrooms have a safe and refrigerator.

The resort's 10,000-square-foot Kay Casperson Lifestyle Spa features myriad treat-ments and services, a full-service salon, fitness center, and a private lap pool. Recreation Island accommodates two swimming pools, a kiddie pool, whirlpool, lighted tennis court, basketball court, sand volleyball court, children's play-ground, and arcade.

The hotel also provides room service, and it has boutiques and a guest laundry room. Dining spots include the lakeside Watercress Cafe, which serves breakfast and lunch only (Disney characters are in attendance Sunday mornings); the Watercress Mini Market, open from 6 A.M. to

PHOTO BY JILL SAFRO

Shades of Green

Shades of Green is a recreational retreat for active and retired military personnel and their families, members of the reserves and the National Guard, and U.S. Department of Defense employees. This 586-room resort is near the Grand Floridian but is not linked with the monorail system.

The resort features two tennis courts, two pools, a small health club, restaurant, bar and lounge, gift shop, arcade, laundry facilities, and free transportation around WDW.

Room rates are based on military or civilian grade. Select multi-day tickets are offered at a discount. The property's three golf courses—the Palm, the Magnolia, and Oak Trail—are open to all WDW guests (see *Sports* for details). All other activities are for hotel guests and their families only.

Magical Express motor coach service is not available to guests staying at this resort. The number for Shades of Green is 407-824-3400; *www.shadesofgreen.org*.

midnight for house-baked pastries, salads, sandwiches, and snacks; and the new Polynesian-style eatery, Avu-Avu Island Grill (family-style dinner). For light meals and cocktails, try the Lobby Lounge, the Kook Sports Bar, or the Castaway Grill.

Rates for rooms are generally about $99 and up per night (no charge for kids under 18); suites, which sleep four to eight, are $149 and up. Rollaways cost $30 per night; cribs are free. There is an Alamo/National car rental desk here, too. Buena Vista Palace Hotel & Spa, 1900 Buena Vista Dr., Lake Buena Vista, FL 32830; *www.buenavistapalace.com*; 407-827-2727 or 866-397-6516.

HOT TIP!

The Buena Vista Palace Hotel & Spa is just a 5-minute walk from the Marketplace at Downtown Disney. It is directly across the (busy) street.

110

Magic Kingdom

113 Getting Oriented

114 Park Primer

116 Attractions

131 Shopping

135 Entertainment

138 Hot Tips

The Magic Kingdom is the most enchanting part of the World. Few who visit it are disappointed, and even the most blasé travelers manage a smile. The sight of the soaring spires of Cinderella Castle, the gleaming woodwork of the Main Street shops, and the crescendo of music that follows the parades never fail to have an effect. Even when the crowds are large and the weather is hot, a visitor who has toured this wonderland dozens of times can still look around and think how satisfying this place is for the spirit.

What makes the Magic Kingdom timeless is its combination of the classic and the futuristic. Both childhood favorites and space-age creatures have a home here. Every "land" has a theme, carried through from the costumes worn by the hosts and hostesses and the food served in the restaurants to the merchandise sold in the shops, and even the design of the trash cans. Thousands of details contribute to the overall effect, and recognizing these touches makes any visit more enjoyable.

But the delight most guests experience upon first glimpse of the Magic Kingdom can disappear when disorientation sets in. There are so many bends to every path-way, so many sights and sounds clamoring for attention, it's too easy to wander aimlessly and miss the best the Magic Kingdom has to offer. So we earnestly suggest that you study this chapter before your visit.

MAIN STREET, U.S.A.
1 Main Street Vehicles
2 Walt Disney World Railroad
3 Town Square Theater

LIBERTY SQUARE
15 The Hall of Presidents
16 The Haunted Mansion
17 Liberty Belle Riverboat

FANTASYLAND
18 Prince Charming Regal
      Carrousel
19 It's a Small World
20 Mad Tea Party
21 The Many Adventures of
      Winnie the Pooh
22 Peter Pan's Flight
23 Mickey's PhilharMagic
24 Under the Sea—
      Journey of The Little Mermaid
25 Dumbo the Flying Elephant
26 The Barnstormer
27 Walt Disney World Railroad
28 Seven Dwarfs Mine Train
29 Enchanted Tales with Belle
30 Princess Fairytale Hall

ADVENTURELAND
4 Jungle Cruise
5 Pirates of the Caribbean
6 Swiss Family Treehouse
7 The Enchanted Tiki Room
8 The Magic Carpets
     of Aladdin

FRONTIERLAND
9 Big Thunder Mountain
     Railroad
10 Country Bear Jamboree
11 Frontierland Shootin'
      Arcade
12 Splash Mountain
13 Tom Sawyer Island
14 Walt Disney World
      Railroad Station

TOMORROWLAND
31 Astro Orbiter
32 Buzz Lightyear's Space
      Ranger Spin
33 Stitch's Great Escape!
34 Tomorrowland Speedway
35 Space Mountain
36 Tomorrowland Transit Authority
      PeopleMover
37 Monsters Inc. Laugh Floor
38 Carousel of Progress

·········· Parade Route

112

Getting Oriented

When you visit Walt Disney World's original theme park, it's vital to know the lay of the "lands." The Magic Kingdom has six lands — Main Street, U.S.A.; Adventureland; Frontierland; Liberty Square; Fantasyland; and Tomorrowland (Mickey's Toontown Fair has left town). Main Street begins at Town Square, located just inside the park gates, and runs directly to Cinderella Castle. The area in front of the castle is known as the Central Plaza or the Hub. Bridges over the waterways here serve as passages to each of the lands.

As you enter the Hub, the first bridge on your left goes to Adventureland; the next, to Liberty Square and Frontierland. On your right, the first bridge heads to Tomorrowland; the second, to Fantasyland. The end points of the pathways leading to the lands are linked by a street that is roughly circular, so that the layout of the Magic Kingdom resembles a wheel. All attractions, restaurants, and shops are found along the wheel's rim and spokes.

Guidemaps and Times Guides are available at the park entrance, at City Hall in Town Square, and at many shops. Be sure to pick them up as soon as possible. You'll find them to be valuable navigational and scheduling resources.

HOW TO GET THERE

Take Exit 64B off I-4. Continue about four miles to the Auto Plaza and park; walk or take a tram to the main entrance complex, known as the Transportation and Ticket Center (TTC). Choose a seven-minute ferry ride or a slightly shorter trip by monorail for the last leg of an anticipation-filled journey.

By WDW Transportation: From the Grand Floridian and Polynesian Village: monorail or boat. From the Contemporary: monorail or walkway. (It's roughly a 7- to 15-minute stroll, depending on the pace.) From Epcot: monorail to the Transportation and Ticket Center (TTC), then transfer to the Magic Kingdom monorail or ferry. From Disney's Hollywood Studios and Animal Kingdom: bus. From the resorts on Hotel Plaza Boulevard: bus to the TTC, then transfer to ferry or monorail. From Fort Wilderness: boat or bus. From Wilderness Lodge: boat or bus. From Downtown Disney: bus to any Walt Disney World resort and transfer to the Magic Kingdom bus (or monorail). From all other Walt Disney World resorts: buses.

PARKING

All-day car parking at the Magic Kingdom is $17 for day visitors (free to WDW resort guests with a valid resort ID, MagicBand, or an annual pass; trucks, trailers, and RVs cost more). Bear left after passing through the Auto Plaza; attendants will direct you into the nearest available lot. Several lots are within walking distance of the TTC; all others are served by trams.

Note the section and aisle in which you park. (Even better: take a photo with your phone.) The parking ticket allows for re-entry to the parking area throughout the day.

HOURS

The Magic Kingdom is generally open from 9 A.M. to 8 P.M. However, during busy seasons, it's open later. It's best to reach the park entrance about a half hour before the opening time. To avoid the morning crush, consider postponing your visit until 1 P.M. or later.

Note that on select days, the Magic Kingdom opens early or stays open late for Walt Disney World resort guests only (this is known as Extra Magic Hours). For details and current schedules, visit *www.disneyworld.com*, or call 407-824-4321. The park tends to be more crowded on such days, so consider starting here and "hopping" elsewhere later in the day.

GETTING AROUND

Walt Disney World Railroad steam trains make a 20-minute loop of the park, stopping to pick up and drop off passengers at stations on Main Street, Frontierland, and Fantasyland. (It's an efficient way to travel when parades are being run or there's a lot of foot traffic.) Horseless carriages, a fire engine, and horse-drawn trolleys take turns offering one-way trips down Main Street (during non-peak hours).

Park Primer

BABY FACILITIES

The best place in the Magic Kingdom to take care of little ones' needs is the Baby Care Center. This cheery site, equipped with changing tables and facilities for nursing mothers, is located next to the Crystal Palace restaurant. Disposable diapers are for sale at the Baby Care Center (if possible, bring your own—the packages are small and a tad pricey). All park restrooms are equipped with changing facilities.

CAMERA NEEDS

Box Office Gifts in the Town Square Theater proffers memory cards and batteries, plus photo albums, camera straps and cases, and disposable cameras.

DISABILITY INFORMATION

Most Magic Kingdom shops and restaurants, and many attractions, are accessible to guests using wheelchairs. Additional services are available for guests with visual or hearing disabilities. The *Guide for Guests with Disabilities* provides an overview of all services available, including transportation, parking, and attraction access. You can pick one up at the park entrance or at City Hall. For more information, see the "Travelers with Disabilities" section of the *Getting Ready to Go* chapter.

FERRY VERSUS MONORAIL

For guests arriving by car or bus, it's necessary to decide whether to travel to the Magic Kingdom by ferry or monorail. The monorail makes the trip from the Transportation and Ticket Center (TTC) in about five minutes, while the ferry takes about seven. During busy seasons, the ferry will often get you there faster (long lines can form at the monorail, and most people don't make the short walk to the ferry landing). Guests who use wheelchairs should note that while the monorail platforms are accessible, the ramp

leading to the boarding area is a bit on the steep side, prompting many guests to opt for the ferry.

FIRST AID

A registered nurse tends to minor medical problems at the First Aid Center, located near the Crystal Palace restaurant.

INFORMATION

City Hall, just inside the park entrance, serves as the Magic Kingdom's information headquarters. Guest Relations representatives can answer questions. Guidemaps and Times Guides, updated weekly (including details about entertainment, as well as character greeting times and locations), are available here, and all kinds of arrangements can be made, including reservations for restaurants. Should you have problems with your ticket or a question about the number of unused days remaining on a ticket, City Hall is the place to go.

LOCKERS

Attended lockers are located just inside the park entrance, all the way to the right. Lockers are also available at the Transportation and Ticket Center (TTC). Cost is $7–$9 per day (plus a $5 refundable deposit) for unlimited use. If you "hop" to another park on the same day, you don't have to pay to get another locker. Simply present your receipt to the attendant and you're all set.

LOST & FOUND

On the day of your visit, report lost articles at City Hall or at the TTC. Recovered items can also be claimed at these locations. After your visit, call 407-824-4245.

LOST CHILDREN

Report lost children at City Hall or the Baby Care Center, and alert the nearest Disney employee to the problem.

HOT TIP!

Certain attractions keep shorter hours than the Magic Kingdom itself (e.g., The Hall of Presidents, The Country Bear Jamboree, and Tom Sawyer Island). To make sure you catch all your favorites, check a Times Guide when you enter the park.

MONEY MATTERS

The Magic Kingdom has five Automated Teller Machines (ATMs): near the locker rental site just inside the entrance; inside City Hall on Main Street, U.S.A.; near the Frontier Shootin' Arcade; near Pinocchio Village Haus; and at the Tomorrowland Light & Power Co. arcade (next to Space Mountain). Most foreign currency can be exchanged at City Hall.

Credit cards (American Express, Visa, Master-Card, JCB, Discover Card, Diner's Club, and the Disney Visa card) are accepted as payment for admission, merchandise, and meals at all full-service restaurants and fast-food locations. Traveler's checks, Disney gift cards, MagicBand bracelets and WDW resort ID cards are also accepted in most places. Some food and souvenir carts accept cash only.

Disney Dollars are available at City Hall (as well as all Disney Stores) in $1, $5, and $10 denominations. They are accepted for dining and merchandise throughout Walt Disney World and can be exchanged at any time for U.S. currency.

PACKAGE PICKUP

Individual shops can arrange for purchases to be transported to the Package Pickup at the Main Street Chamber of Commerce, next to City Hall, for pickup between noon and park closing time (at least three hours after purchase). Packages may be sent to Disney resorts, too. The delivery service is free.

SAME-DAY RE-ENTRY

Be sure to wear your MagicBand bracelet if you used it for admission or retain your ticket if you plan to return later the same day.

SECURITY CHECK

All guests entering Disney theme parks are subject to a security check. Backpacks, parcels, purses, etc., will be searched by Disney security personnel before guests are permitted to pass through the entrance.

STROLLERS & WHEELCHAIRS

Wheelchair Rental, located just inside the entrance, all the way to the right, offers wheelchairs (some oversized) and Electric Conveyance Vehicles (ECVs). Strollers are available under the Main Street Train Station. The cost for strollers is $15 per day ($13 per day with a multi-day rental); double strollers cost $31 per day ($27 a day with a multi-day rental); wheelchairs are $12 per day, $10 with multi-day rental; $50 per day for ECVs, with a $20 refundable deposit.

HOT TIP!

Will you need a stroller during your visit? Consider bringing one from home. It will save you money, and it can be used all over WDW (Disney rentals may not be removed from the parks). Chances are your baby buggy is more comfortable than the ones in the parks, too. If yours is too cumbersome for travel, consider buying an "umbrella" stroller or renting a user-friendly carriage from a company such as Magic Strollers (see page 67).

Quantities are limited. Hold on to your receipt; it can be used on the same day to get a replacement stroller or wheelchair at any of the theme parks. Multi-day rentals, called Length of Stay tickets, save you two dollars off the daily price. Keep your receipt handy.

Note that during busy times, the park may offer "stroller express" service. Guests pre-pay for a stroller before passing through the turnstiles and bypass the line once inside.

To prevent your stroller from getting lost in a sea of stroller clones, consider personalizing it with an item such as a ribbon or a sign.

TIP BOARD

Located at the end of Main Street, U.S.A., closest to Cinderella Castle, the Tip Board is an excellent source of information on waiting times for attractions, as well as showtimes and other entertainment information. The board is often overseen by a park-savvy employee, ready and willing to answer guest questions. At press time, there was a possibility that the Tip Board would be removed. If that happens, head to City Hall for in-person park information or use the My Disney Experience app on your smartphone.

Admission Prices

ONE-DAY BASE TICKET
(Restricted to use only in the Magic Kingdom. **Prices do not include sales tax and are expected to rise in 2015.**)

Adult	$99
Child*	$94

*3 through 9 years of age; children under age 3 free

Main Street, U.S.A.

The street represents an ideal American town. Although such a town never really existed, many claim to have served as the inspiration for it. Chances are Walt Disney got the idea from Marceline, Missouri, the tiny rural town that was his boyhood home.

HOT TIP!

Plan to do your shopping in the early afternoon, rather than at day's end when the Main Street shops are normally jammed.

Most of the structures along the thoroughfare are given over to shops, and each one is different. Some emporiums are big and bustling, others are relatively quiet and orderly; some are spacious and airy, others are cozy and dark. Inside and out, maintenance and housekeeping are superb.

White-suited sanitation workers patrol the street to pick up litter and quickly shovel up any evidence of the horses that pull the trolley cars from Town Square to the Hub. As in the rest of the Magic Kingdom, the pavement here is washed down every night with hoses. There's one crew of maintenance workers whose sole job is to change the little white lights around the roofs; another crew devotes itself to keeping the woodwork painted. As soon as these people have worked their way as far as the Hub, they start all over again at Town Square. The greenish, horse-shaped, cast-iron hitching posts are repainted 20 times a year on average—and totally scraped down each time.

The "attractions" along Main Street, U.S.A., are relatively minor compared to the really big deals such as Tomorrowland's Space Mountain, Frontierland's Splash Mountain, or The Haunted Mansion in Liberty Square. But each and every shop has its own quota of merchandise that is meant as much for show as for sale. It's almost as entertaining to watch the cooks stir up gooey batches of fudge or peanut brittle at the Main Street Confectionery as it is to actually savor a sample. The shop windows, particularly at the Emporium, are also worth a look.

Once you start to meander along Main Street, be sure to notice the names on the second-story windows. Above the Uptown Jewelers store (near the Confectionery) is that of Walt's nephew, Roy E. Disney. And you will see Walt's name above the ice-cream parlor.

Stepping onto Main Street, U.S.A., is like jumping through a time portal. Welcome to turn-of-the-twentieth-century America! Horse-drawn trolleys are the transportation of choice, peppy patriotic music underscores the bustle of merry, moving masses, and the tantalizing aroma of fresh-baked cookies constantly perfumes the air.

A rose-colored retrospective? Maybe. But this is Disney's version of a small-town Main Street—and the charm of this nostalgic land is lost on no one. Anchored by an old-fashioned train station at one end and a fairy-tale castle at the other, Main Street, U.S.A., whisks you from reality to fantasy in a few short blocks.

All of the addresses here feature just-dried coats of paint, curlicued gingerbread moldings, and pretty details. Add to that the baskets of hanging plants and genuine-looking gaslights, and Main Street, U.S.A., becomes a true showplace—both in the bright light of high noon and after nightfall, when the tiny lights edging all of the rooflines are flicked on.

Other names are those of people closely connected with The Walt Disney Company.

Note: Attractions in Main Street, U.S.A., are described in the order in which they are encountered upon entering the park.

WALT DISNEY WORLD RAILROAD:
The best introduction to the Magic Kingdom, the 1½-mile journey on this rail line is as much a must for the first-time visitor as it is for railroad buffs. It offers an excellent orientation as it passes by most of the park's major lands.

Walt Disney himself was a railroad aficionado. During the early years of television, viewers watched films of him circling his own backyard in a one-eighth-scale train, the Lilly Belle (named for his wife). The 1928 steam engine is the same age as Mickey Mouse.

> ## HOT TIP!
> Kids under age 14 must be accompanied by someone age 14 or older when visiting any WDW theme park.

The Walt Disney World Railroad also has a Lilly Belle among its quartet of locomotives. The others are named Roy O. Disney, Walter E. Disney, and Roger E. Broggie (a Disney Imagineer who shared Walt Disney's enthusiasm for antique trains). All of them were built in the U.S. around the turn of the century and later taken to Mexico to haul freight and passengers in the Yucatán, where Disney scouts found them in 1969. The United Railways of Yucatán was using them to carry sugarcane. Brought north once again, they were completely overhauled, and even the smallest of parts were reworked or replaced.

PHOTO BY JILL SAFRO

> ## HOT TIP!
> Guests staying at the Contemporary resort can walk to and from the Magic Kingdom's front gate. The trip takes about 10 to 15 minutes. It's handy when there's a long line for the monorail.

The train circles the park in about 20 minutes, making stops in Fantasyland, Frontierland, and Main Street, U.S.A. Trains arrive every 5 to 10 minutes. The line is usually shorter in Frontierland, but there's rarely a long wait at any station. The train is the best way to reach the exit when parades take over Main Street, U.S.A.

Note: The Walt Disney World Railroad does not run during fireworks presentations.

MAIN STREET VEHICLES: A number of these can be seen traveling up and down Main Street—horseless carriages and jitneys patterned after turn-of-the-century vehicles; a spiffy scarlet fire engine; and a troop of trolleys drawn by Belgians and Percherons, two strong breeds of horse that once pulled plows in Europe. These animals—weighing in at about a ton each and shod with plastic (easier on their hooves)—pull the trolley the length of Main Street about two dozen times during each of their working days. Between shifts, they can be seen resting inside Main Street's Car Barn. Feel free to stop by and say hello. At day's end, they go home to their barn at Fort Wilderness.

Note: Main Street Vehicles generally operate during daytime hours on off-peak days.

TOWN SQUARE THEATER: FP+ Themed as a Victorian-era theater, this is an ideal spot to meet and mingle with Mickey Mouse. Of course, this being a magic kingdom, Mickey has a few tricks up his sleeve. Yep, in addition to all his other skills, the Mouse is a master magician. Who knew? Note that this is strictly a "backstage" experience, as Mickey's magic show is still in the rehearsal stage. The wait here can be quite long—get a Fastpass+ if you can.

Note: Guests who'd like to meet Minnie Mouse can do so at Pete's Silly Sideshow in the Storybook Circus section of Fantasyland.

> ## HOT TIP!
> Tuesday and Wednesday tend to be the least crowded days at the Magic Kingdom.

MAGIC KINGDOM

Adventureland

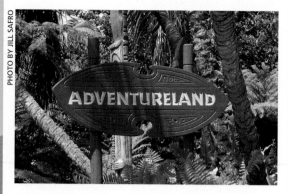
PHOTO BY JILL SAFRO

Adventureland seems to have even more atmosphere than the other lands. That may be due to its neat separation from the rest of the Magic Kingdom by the bridge over Main Street on one end and by a gallery-like structure (where it merges with Frontierland) on the other, or, possibly, it's because of the abundance of landscaping.

The centrally located attraction, The Magic Carpets of Aladdin, sets the tone for this corner of the Kingdom. Still surrounded by tropical splendor, the area has the look and feel of a bustling marketplace—the likes of which one might stumble upon in Agrabah. Shops here offer imports from around the globe.

As guests stroll away from Main Street, U.S.A., they just may hear the sound of beating drums, the squawks of parrots, and the regular boom of a cannon. Paces quicken. And the wonders that are soon to be encountered do not disappoint.

Calling All Pirates!

Captain Jack Sparrow needs your help. He knows there's treasure to be found and enemies to fight in Adventureland (yeah, that means you, Captain Barbossa!), but Jack can't do it alone. So he's recruiting Magic Kingdom guests to join his pirate posse.

The interactive quest, "A Pirate's Adventure . . . Treasure of the Seven Seas," begins at The Crow's Nest, near the Pirates of the Caribbean attraction. That's where potential pirates receive a talisman (which activates magical effects throughout the land) and a mission map. There are five missions in all, some of which involve dodging blow darts and cannon fire. It's free to play (how's that for a little hidden treasure?!) and the maps and talisman are yours to keep. Arrrrr!

SWISS FAMILY TREEHOUSE: This is everybody's idea of the perfect treehouse, with its many levels and comforts—patchwork quilts, mahogany furniture, candles stuck in abalone shells, even running water in every room. (The system is rather ingenious.) Based on the wondrous banyan-tree home in Disney's 1960 rendition of the classic story *Swiss Family Robinson*, it rarely fails to intrigue. It's easy to understand why, when given the chance to leave the island (several adventures later), all but one member of the Robinson family chose to stay on. The only modern convenience the Robinsons could use? An elevator! Expect to burn off a few calories climbing up and down the stairs. Be sure to enjoy the view of the park from the tree-top.

The Spanish moss draping the branches is real; the tree itself—unofficially christened *Disneyodendron eximus*, a genus that is translated roughly as "out-of-the-ordinary Disney tree" —was constructed entirely by the props department. Some statistics: The roots, which are made of concrete, poke 42 feet into the ground, and about 300,000 lifelike polyethylene leaves "grow" on the tree's 1,400 individual branches.

HOT TIP!

During non-peak seasons, the Jungle Cruise may open one hour after the rest of the Magic Kingdom opens for the day.

JUNGLE CRUISE: FP+ Inspired in part by the 1955 documentary film *The African Lion*, this ten-minute adventure is one of the crowning achievements of Magic Kingdom landscape artists for the way it takes guests through surroundings as diverse as a Southeast Asian jungle, the Nile Valley, and an Amazon rainforest. Along the way, passengers encounter zebras, giraffes, lions, headhunters, and more (all of the Audio-Animatronics variety); they also see elephants bathing and tour a temple— while listening to an amusing, though corny, spiel delivered by the skipper. (Bet you didn't know that Schweitzer Falls was named after the famous doctor Albert . . . Falls.)

This classic adventure, which is best enjoyed by daylight, is one of the park's slower-moving attractions. It's popular with guests of all ages.

WALT DISNEY'S ENCHANTED TIKI ROOM:

The Tiki Room is back under its original management. That's right, Iago is out and José, Michael, Pierre, and Fritz have once again taken center stage—as they did when the attraction first opened in 1963. Cherished for its historical significance (the Tiki Birds starred in the first Audio-Animatronics attraction ever), the Tiki show has evolved a bit over the years.

The show features the aforementioned fine-feathered friends, plus some 200 birds, flowers, and tiki statues singing up a tropical storm. Let's all sing like the birdies sing!

THE MAGIC CARPETS OF ALADDIN: FP+

Welcome to Agrabah! Adventureland's high-flying attraction is conveniently situated in the center of the action. It features not one, but 16 carpets that soar through the air in a fashion similar to those airborne elephants over in Fantasyland. Each flying carpet accommodates four guests at a time. Depending on where you sit, you'll have control of the carpet's movement (vertical controls are in the front row; side-to-side are in the back row). Be prepared to dodge the occasional stream of liquid, courtesy of an expectorating camel.

BIRNBAUM'S ★BEST★ PIRATES OF THE CARIBBEAN: FP+ Quite simply, this is one of the very best of the Magic Kingdom's classic adventures. The beloved ten-minute cruise is a Disneyland original, added to Walt Disney World's Magic Kingdom (in slightly revised form) due to popular demand. Here, guests board a small boat and set sail for a series of scenes showing a pirate raid on a Caribbean island town, dodging cannon fire and weathering one small, though legitimate, watery dip along the way. There are singing marauders, plastered pigs, and wily wenches; the observant may note a couple of new rapscallion residents. Yep, that beloved scallywag Captain Jack Sparrow has dropped anchor here, as has his nefarious nemesis, Captain Barbossa.

While it's by no means the most politically correct attraction on-property (far from it, actually), the rendition of "Yo Ho, Yo Ho, a Pirate's Life for Me"—the catchy theme song—makes what is actually a rather brutal scenario into something that comes across as good fun.

And, yes, this is the attraction that inspired the *Pirates of the Caribbean* movies—which, in turn, inspired the attraction.

Frontierland

With the Rivers of America lapping at its borders and Big Thunder Mountain rising up in the rear, this re-creation of the American Frontier encompasses the area from the Mississippi River to the Southwest, from the 1770s to the 1880s. In these parts, shops, restaurants, and attractions have unpainted barn siding or stone or clapboard walls, and there are several wooden sidewalks of the sort Marshal Matt Dillon used to stride along. The Walt Disney World Railroad makes a stop here.

FRONTIERLAND SHOOTIN' ARCADE:

This modest arcade is set in an 1850s town in the Southwest Territory. Positions overlook Boothill, a town complete with bank, jail, hotel, and cemetery.

Genuine Hawkins .54-caliber buffalo rifles have been refitted, and when the infrared beam strikes any of the targets, an interesting result is triggered. Struck tombstones rise, sink, spin, or change their epitaphs; hit a cloud and a ghost rider gallops across the sky; a bull's-eye on a grave digger's shovel causes a skull to pop out of the grave.

There is an additional charge to play here (usually about a buck).

COUNTRY BEAR JAMBOREE: The Country
Bears may never make it to the Grand Ole Opry, but they don't seem to mind. Disney's brood of banjo-strummin' bruins has been playing to packed houses in Grizzly Hall for more than a quarter century. Judging by all the toe tappin' and hand clappin' that accompany each performance, the show remains a countrified crowd-pleaser. As for the few folks who aren't charmed by the backwoods ballads and down-home humor, well, they just have to grin and bear it.

As guests are settling into their seats (all of which provide a decent view), Buff, Max, and Melvin are beginning to grumble. Despite their status as permanent fixtures in the theater, the mounted animal heads would rather not "hang around all day" waiting for the show to get going. The 16-minute revue opens with a rousing ditty by the Five Bear Rugs. The wheels set in motion, the remaining songs come fast and furious. Together, they capture the spirit of a genre that has a tendency to celebrate and lampoon itself simultaneously.

For example, Bunny, Bubbles, and Beulah bemoan "All the Guys That Turn Me On Turn Me Down"; Henry, the easygoing emcee who sports a coonskin cap (still attached to the 'coon), belts out "The Ballad of Davy Crockett"; and Big Al, the oversize tone-deaf fan favorite, woefully croons "Blood on the Saddle," much to the delight of the giggle-prone audience.

Timing Tip: This attraction opens at 10 A.M. each day, even when the rest of the park opens earlier in the morning.

TOM SAWYER ISLAND: This patch of land in
the middle of the Rivers of America has hills to scramble up; a working windmill, Harper's Mill, with an owl in the rafters and a perpetually creaky waterwheel; and a few pitch-black caves. To reach the island, guests take a raft across the river. (It's the only way to get there and back.)

Paths wind this way and that, and it's easy to get disoriented. Keep an eye out for mounted maps scattered about the island.

There are two bridges here—a suspension bridge and a barrel bridge, which floats atop some lashed-together wooden barrels. When one person bounces, everybody lurches—and all but the most chickenhearted laugh. Both of the bridges are easy to miss, so be sure to keep your eyes peeled.

Across the suspension bridge is Fort Langhorn. Poke around and you'll discover a twisting and slightly scary escape tunnel. Walk along the pathway on the banks of the Rivers of America and you'll find your way back to the bridges.

The whole island seems as rugged as backwoods Missouri and, probably as a result, it actually feels a lot more remote than it is—enough to be able to provide some welcome respite from the bustle.

One particularly pleasant way to relax here is at a waterside table. It's sometimes possible to buy a snack—and you are always welcome to bring your own. Restrooms are beside the main raft landing and inside Fort Langhorn.

Timing Tip: This attraction closes at dusk.

BIRNBAUM'S BEST SPLASH MOUNTAIN: FP+

On the day this attraction made its official 1992 Walt Disney World debut, everyone got soaked—thanks in part to a particularly potent Florida rain cloud. But the rain wasn't entirely responsible for the sea of soggy Magic Kingdom guests. The five-story drop into an aqueous briar patch was. And a steady stream of thrill seekers has been taking the plunge ever since.

HOT TIP!

If you'd like to get soaked on Splash Mountain, sit on the right side of the log.

In this guaranteed smile-inducer, guests enjoy a waterborne journey through brightly colored swamps and bayous, and down waterfalls, and are finally hurtled from the peak of the mountain to a briar-laced pond five stories below.

Splash Mountain is based on the animated sequences in Walt Disney's 1946 film *Song of the South*. The scenery entertains as the story line follows Br'er Rabbit as he tries to reach his "laughin' place." It's tough for a first-time rider to take in all the details, since the tension of waiting for the big drop is all-consuming.

It is a bit terrifying at the top, but once back on the ground, it seems most riders can't wait for another trip—even though they may get drenched. (Water-wary guests are often seen wearing rain ponchos on this attraction. On the other hand, if you want to get wet, try to sit up front or on the right; seats in the back receive a smaller splash.)

By the second or third time around, it's possible to relax a bit, enjoy the interior scenes, and take in the spectacular views of the Magic Kingdom from the top of the mountain. At this point, you may even manage to keep your eyes open for the duration of the final fall—or at least part of it.

Splash Mountain's designers not only borrowed characters and color-saturated settings from *Song of the South*, but also used quite a bit of the film's Academy Award–winning music in this attraction. As a matter of fact, the song in Splash Mountain's final scene, "Zip-a-Dee-Doo-Dah," has become something of a Disney anthem over the years.

Note: You must be at least 40 inches tall to ride Splash Mountain. (There is a small play area nearby to keep little ones occupied while older kids ride.) If you'd like to absorb as little precipitation as possible, sit on the left side of the log.

BIRNBAUM'S ★BEST★

BIG THUNDER MOUNTAIN RAILROAD: FP+

It's certainly not hard to spot Big Thunder, the lone red rock formation this side of the Mississippi. Even newcomers to the Magic Kingdom will be able to distinguish the land-mark from its famed counterparts—Splash and Space mountains—because it's the only one that actually looks like a real mountain range. The designers took Utah's Monument Valley as inspiration, and the resemblance is actually quite remarkable.

According to Disney legend, the 2.5-acre mountain is chock-full of gold. Unfortunately for the residents of Tumbleweed, the local mining town, a flood has ruined any chance of uncover-ing the remaining gold. Before the prospectors find drier land, they are having one last party at the saloon to celebrate their riches. Even though in danger of washing away, they don't seem too worried—and guests who decide to take a trip on the Big Thunder Mountain Railroad have nothing to worry about either.

After passing through the new interactive queue area, guests are advised to "hang on to your hats and glasses 'cause this here's the wildest ride in the wilderness." Do heed the warning, but don't despair. The ride, though thrilling, is relatively tame, so relax and enjoy the sights. (Passengers seated nearest the caboose experience more turbulence than those seated closer to the front.)

A bleating billy goat atop a peak, a family of possums hanging overhead, and a dark cavern full of bats, not to mention chickens, donkeys, and washed-up miners, can be spotted along the way. Be sure to keep an eye out for the not-yet-sunken saloon—it's easy to miss the first time around.

A continuous string of curves and dips around Big Thunder's pinnacles and caverns is sure to please thrill seekers of all ages, but the adrenaline surge is caused by more than just the speed of the trip. The added sound of a rickety track, a steam whistle that blows right before the train accelerates into a curve, and an unexpected earthquake all compound the passengers' anticipation, making this attraction one of the Magic Kingdom's most popular.

Note: You must be at least 40 inches tall and immune to motion sickness to experience the Big Thunder Mountain Railroad attraction.

Timing Tip: Plan to visit early in the morning, during a parade, or just before closing time. Of course, you can always plan ahead and get a Fastpass+. If you will be visiting during a parade, consider taking the Walt Disney World Railroad to the Frontierland station. The train circumvents much of the parade congestion.

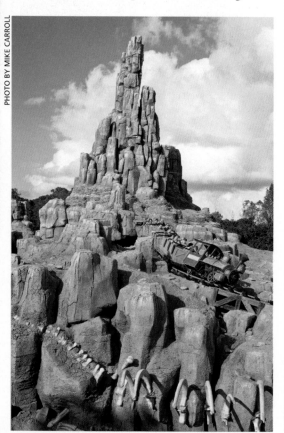

PHOTO BY MIKE CARROLL

Sorcerers of the Magic Kingdom

Uh-oh—Disney villains are trying to take over the Magic Kingdom and *you* can help defeat them. How? First, Merlin the magician will make you (and everyone with you) an appren-tice sorcerer. Then you'll use magic spell cards to beat the bad guys and save the park.

The interactive game starts at the Firehouse on Main Street, U.S.A. Simply present your valid park ticket or MagicBand and you'll receive a special key card, five magic spell cards, and a map. (The folks behind the counter can answer questions, too.) As you follow the clues, you will try to prevent villains from stealing Merlin's crystal ball and keep the Magic Kingdom safe.

There is no extra charge to play, and the magic spell cards are yours to keep. You may get a new set of cards each day you visit the park. Having trouble getting a complete set? Know that other guests are often eager to trade. Many guests—of all ages—enjoy collecting the cards as much as they do playing the game.

Liberty Square

The transition between Frontierland on one side and Fantasyland on the other is so smooth that it's hard to say just when you arrive at Liberty Square, yet ultimately, there's no mistaking the location. The small buildings are clapboard or brick and topped with weather vanes; the decorative moldings are Federal or Georgian in style; the glass is sometimes wavy; and there are flower boxes in shop windows. There's a bounty of shops, plus two of the park's most famous attractions—The Haunted Mansion and The Hall of Presidents—and the Liberty Tree Tavern, one of the few table-service restaurants in the Magic Kingdom park.

THE HALL OF PRESIDENTS: The Hall of Presidents attraction made its debut with the park way back in 1971. Though revered for its status as a classic Magic Kingdom attraction, it was starting to lose some of its luster. It was time for a change. And change it did. The revamped and revitalized show boasts cutting-edge technology and a new story line—not to mention a new president. (Barack Obama, the most advanced Audio-Animatronics figure to date, is the seventh commander-in-chief to be added to the attraction since it opened.)

The 25-minute celebration of U.S. leaders begins with a stirring, original film. It covers the country's origins, the framing of the Constitution, and national triumphs and struggles from the Civil War (which leads Abraham Lincoln to deliver the Gettysburg Address) to the present day. Throughout, it focuses on the role of U.S. presidents in the shaping of American history and applauds the ordinary people who rose to the nation's highest office and led us through extraordinary circumstances.

Following the film, the curtain rises and all 44 U.S. presidents are represented. (The observant may note that there are only 43 Audio-Animatronics figures on the stage. No, the Disney Imagineers did not misplace a president. Grover Cleveland served two non-consecutive terms, so he is the 22nd and 24th president of the United States.) After all the Commanders in Chief are introduced, both George Washington and Barack Obama deliver patriotic speeches (and, yes, that's really Mr. Obama's voice).

Displays in the pre-show area give guests a chance to gaze upon bits of Americana, such as painted eggs from a White House Easter egg hunt and dresses from former first ladies (exhibit items will change from time to time).

LIBERTY BELLE RIVERBOAT: Based in Liberty Square and built in dry dock at Walt Disney World, this is a genuine steamboat. Its boiler turns water into steam, which is then piped to the engine, which drives the paddle wheel that propels the boat. It is not the real article in one key respect, however: It moves

PHOTO BY JILL SAFRO

through the nine-foot-deep Rivers of America on an underwater rail.

The pleasant ride, with narration by an actor playing Mark Twain, is a good way to beat the heat on steamy afternoons. En route, a variety of props create a sort of Wild West effect: moose, deer, a burning cabin, and the like. The tour is completed within 17 minutes. Note that this attraction usually opens an hour or so after the park itself and shuts down before other park attractions do.

BIRNBAUM'S ★BEST★ THE HAUNTED MANSION:

FP+ This eerie, eight-minute experience is among the Magic Kingdom's most enjoyable. However, guests who expect to be scared silly when they enter the big old house, modeled after those built in New York's Hudson River Valley in the eighteenth century, will be just a tad unfulfilled. This haunted house steers clear of anything too terrifying, and a good-spirited voice-over keeps the mood light. Still, some of the scenes, as well as the darkness, may be too much for some tykes.

Once you're inside the portrait hall, entered after passing through the front doors, it's amusing to speculate: Is the ceiling moving up, or is the floor dropping? It's also where you will meet your "Ghost Host" and learn how he met his untimely demise.

The spooky journey through the mansion takes place in a "Doom Buggy." The attraction

is full of tricks and treats for the eyes; just when you think you've seen it all, there's something new: staircases to nowhere, bats' eyes on the wallpaper, a suit of armor that comes alive, a terrified cemetery watchman and his mangy mutt, and the image of a creepy lady in a floating crystal ball.

One of the biggest jobs of the maintenance crews here is not cleaning up, but keeping things dirty. The mansion is littered with some 200 trunks, chairs, dress forms, harps, rugs, and assorted knickknacks and requires a lot of dust. Cobwebs are bought in liquid form and strung up by a secret process.

When waiting to enter, take time to enjoy the interactive queue area. And on the way out, take a moment to pay your respects at the pet cemetery. Mr. Toad, we hardly knew you. *Sniff, sniff.*

Fantasyland

Walt Disney called this a "timeless land of enchantment," and his successors termed it "the happiest land of all"—and it is, for many. It is also the home of a number of rides that are particularly well liked by children of all ages. Fantasyland recently completed a merry metamorphosis and nearly doubled in size.

CINDERELLA CASTLE: Just as Mickey stands for all the merriment in Walt Disney World, this storybook castle represents the hopes and dreams of childhood—a time in life when anything is possible and dreams really do come true.

At a height of about 190 feet, Cinderella Castle is nearly twice the height of Disneyland's Sleeping Beauty Castle. For inspiration, Disney Imagineers looked to the palaces of Charles Perrault's France, still showplaces of Europe. Their design took the form of a romanticized composite of such courts as Fontainebleu, Versailles, and famed chateaux of the Loire Valley. Of course, they also turned to the original designs for the fairy-tale castle in Disney's 1950 classic, *Cinderella*.

Unlike real European castles, this one is made of steel and fiberglass; in lieu of dungeons, it has service tunnels. Its upper reaches contain security rooms; there's even a special Cinderella Castle Suite. (Future plans for this spectacular space were not determined at press time. Though we will happily volunteer to move in!) From any vantage point, Cinderella Castle looks as if it came straight from the land of make-believe.

PHOTO BY JILL SAFRO

Mosaic Murals: The elaborate murals beneath the castle's archway rank among the true wonders of the World. They tell the story of the little cinder girl and one of childhood's happiest happily-ever-afters, using a million bits of glass in some 500 different colors, plus real silver and 14-karat gold.

Cinderella Wishing Well: This pleasant alcove, nestled along a path to Tomorrowland, is a nice spot from which to gaze at the castle. Any coins tossed into the water are donated to children's charities. Don't forget to make a wish as you part with your penny.

PRINCE CHARMING REGAL CARROUSEL: Not everything in the Magic Kingdom is a Disney version of the real article. This carrousel, discovered at the now-defunct Olympic Park in Maplewood, New Jersey, was built back in 1917 (technically making it the oldest attraction in the park). That was the end of the golden century of carrousel building, which began around 1825. During the Disney refurbishment, many of the original horses were replaced with horses made of fiberglass. No two of the 90 horses are exactly alike. Can you spot Cinderella's horse? Hint: It's the only one with a golden bow on its tail.

FAIRYTALE GARDEN: This special spot is tucked beside Cinderella Castle. Several times a day, Merida (the heroine from *Brave*) stops by to visit with guests. Check a park Times Guide for appearance schedule. Character subject to change.

MICKEY'S PHILHARMAGIC: Mickey Mouse and a panoply of his pals (including Donald, Simba, and Ariel) strut their musical stuff in this 3-D production.

The show is an amalgam of music, effects, and animation. Of course, this being Fantasyland, the film is by no means ordinary. It's colorful, crisp, and to the delight of many a goggle-wearing guest, three-dimensional. The experience unfolds on a 150-foot-wide canvas. Special effects and surprises take place off-screen, too.

As with many attractions, there are moments of darkness. If you're unsure as to whether your child might find this (or any attraction) unsettling, express your concern to an attendant. They will help you make the right decision. Note that all guests need to wear 3-D glasses to enjoy the show.

BIRNBAUM'S ★BEST★

PETER PAN'S FLIGHT: FP+ "Come on, everybody, here we go!" So says Peter Pan at the start of this nonstop flight to Never Land. The 3-minute adventure, which takes you soaring in a pirate ship, fancifully retells the story of Peter Pan—a boy with a knack for flying and an immunity to maturity. The effects in this classic Fantasyland attraction are simple, but enchanting.

The journey starts in the Darling family nursery—which siblings Wendy, Michael, and John quickly abandon to follow Peter Pan on a trip to his homeland. As in Disney's animated feature, one of the most beautiful scenes—and one that makes this attraction a treat for grown-ups as well as smaller folk—is the sight of nighttime London, dark blue and speckled with twinkling lights. Keep your eyes peeled for Big Ben and Tower Bridge.

By the time you spot your first mermaid, you're deep in the heart of Never Land. Alas, something is terribly wrong—Captain Hook and his buccaneer buddies have taken the Darling kids captive. It's all really a trap for Peter (Hook is still peeved at Pan for serving his hand to a hungry crocodile). Does everyone live happily ever after? We'll never tell.

PHOTO BY JILL SAFRO

Originally created for New York's 1964–65 World's Fair, the attraction is an oldie-but-goodie (and is quite popular with young children). The ride moves at slightly swifter than snail's pace, drifting past hundreds of colorfully costumed dolls from around the world—all of whom know all the words to the ride's infectious theme song (written by the Sherman brothers).

A showcase of diversity, the attraction is a simple celebration of human similarities. It's also a relaxing alternative to many of the park's higher-tech, longer-line attractions.

HOT TIP!

Many Fantasyland attractions are dark, and, in some cases, special effects may be too intense for tots and small children. However, they all tend to *love* It's a Small World. Nothing scary about that!

PRINCESS FAIRYTALE HALL: FP+ Practice your curtsey as you approach this hall—once inside you'll meet regals such as Cinderella, Aurora, Rapunzel, and Snow White. Characters vary. This royal residence occupies the space formerly occupied by the Snow White's Scary Adventures attraction. The line is always frightening—get a Fastpass+ if you can.

IT'S A SMALL WORLD: FP+ *Hola! Guten Tag!* Hello! No matter what language you speak, what you look like, or where you live, you still have a lot in common with folks the world over (including an especially high tolerance for a singsong melody that repeatedly reminds us that it's a small world, after all). That's the message driving this ten-minute boat ride around the world.

PHOTO BY JILL SAFRO

DUMBO THE FLYING ELEPHANT: FP+ This is purely and simply a kiddie ride, though children of all ages have admitted to loving it.

A beloved symbol of Fantasyland, the ride moved to the Storybook Circus area and doubled in size—but rest assured, the Dumbo experience remains the same. Consider stopping here early in the morning, or during a parade, when the line—which is often prohibitively long—thins a bit. Inspired by the 1941 film classic *Dumbo*, the ride lasts a memorable two minutes.

Note: Guests in Dumbo's standby line receive a pager and are free to frolic in the interactive play zone while they wait to ride.

THE BARNSTORMER: FP+ At this mini roller coaster attraction, guests of most sizes follow the same fluky flight path taken by the daredevil pilot known as the Great Goofini. Don't let the size fool you: This 1-minute ride proves that big thrills do indeed come in small packages. Although guests as young as 3 may ride, they must be at least 35 inches tall. It may be too turbulent for some.

CASEY JR. SPLASH 'N' SOAK STATION: The famous locomotive Casey Jr. invites Magic Kingdom guests to cool off in this colorful, interactive splash zone, conveniently located beside Fantasyland's train station. Be sure to dress tykes in swim diapers.

MAD TEA PARTY: FP+ The theme of this two-minute ride—in a group of oversize teacups that whirl and spin wildly—was inspired by a scene in the Disney Studios' 1951 movie production of *Alice in Wonderland*. During the sequence in question, the Mad Hatter hosts a tea party for his un-birthday.

Unlike many rides in Fantasyland, this is not just for younger kids; the 5-to-20-something crowd seems to like it best. Keep in mind that when the cups stop spinning, your head may continue to do so. Skip this ride if you suffer from motion sickness or if you've recently enjoyed a snack. Don't miss the woozy mouse that pops out of the teapot at the center of the platform—he ignored our advice.

BIRNBAUM'S BEST **THE MANY ADVENTURES OF WINNIE THE POOH:** FP+ Everyone's favorite honey-lovin' cub treats Magic Kingdom guests to continuous, wild and whimsical 3½-minute tours of his home turf—the Hundred Acre Wood.

The attraction features a most unlikely form of transportation: honey pots! They whisk (and bounce) guests through the pages of a giant storybook and into the Hundred Acre Wood, where the weather's most blustery. The wind is

really ruffling the feathers of one of the locals. Sight gags abound, from a bubble-blowing Heffalump (hey, this is Fantasyland) to a treacherous flood that threatens to sweep Tigger, Piglet, and the rest of the gang away. When Pooh saves the day, it's time to celebrate— and everyone is invited to the party.

Like other Fantasyland attractions, some parts of this one take place in the dark. Some children may find it a bit unsettling. That said, little ones dig Pooh's new, interactive queue area. While waiting to ride or for others to do so, youngsters can bang on giant vegetable "drums," play tug-of-war with a gopher, and scrawl their names in a flowing wall of honey.

UNDER THE SEA—JOURNEY OF THE LITTLE MERMAID: FP+ In the Magic Kingdom's first attraction to feature everyone's favorite Disney mermaid, guests are invited to board continuously moving clam-mobiles and embark on a jolly journey above and below sea level. Along the way, they join Ariel, Flounder, and all of their aquatic acquaintances, and enjoy major musical movements and pivotal plot points from the classic animated feature. It's fun for the whole family.

BIRNBAUM'S BEST **SEVEN DWARFS MINE TRAIN:** FP+ Heigh-ho, heigh- ho! A brand-new roller coaster is whimsically transporting guests on a musical journey through the workplace of the Seven Dwarfs—the mine where a million diamonds shine. The ride vehicles swing back and forth as they zoom along the track, so folks with motion sickness or other health issues should sit this one out. Intensity-wise, the smooth, family-friendly attraction fits between the Barnstormer coaster and Big Thunder Mountain Railroad. The queue has a few interactive surprises, too. Guests must be at least 38 inches tall to ride. This 2½-minute attraction is very popular— get a Fastpass+ assignment if you can.

ENCHANTED TALES WITH BELLE: FP+ This clever mix of show and character meet-and-greet is one of those "you have to see it to believe it" experiences. Located in Maurice's exquisitely detailed cottage, the 30-minute experience includes interaction with lifelike Audio-Animatronics versions of Lumiere and Madame Wardrobe, plus an audience-participation performance by Belle in Beast's library.

Tomorrowland

The original Tomorrowland attempted a serious look at the future. But as Disney planners discovered, it isn't easy to portray a future that persists in becoming the present. So the old Tomorrowland has given way to a friendlier, space-age town whose neighborhood atmosphere is more in keeping with the other lands in the Magic Kingdom. This is the future that never was, the fantasy world imagined by the science-fiction writers and moviemakers of the 1920s and '30s. It's a land of sky-piercing beacons and glistening metal, where shiny robots do the work, whisper-quiet cars glide along an elevated highway, and even time travel is possible.

Note: Tomorrowland attractions are described in the order in which they are encountered upon entering the land from the Hub and heading away from Cinderella Castle.

STITCH'S GREAT ESCAPE!: Like its predecessor, the ExtraTERRORestrial Alien Encounter, this attraction features the adventures of a renegade alien. In this case, however, said extraterrestrial is more of a menace than a threat—not so much scary as ill-mannered and mischievous. The 20-minute show is a prequel to *Lilo & Stitch*, but one need not be familiar with the drooling, intergalactic imp to follow the attraction's story line.

HOT TIP!

Parents take note: This attraction is much less scary than The ExtraTERRORestrial Alien Encounter. Still, there are moments of darkness, and Stitch's madcap shenanigans may be daunting to little ones.

The action begins with a short pre-show, followed by the crowd spilling into a circular theater-type room. All chairs face center, where there's a mysterious tube. (Sit up straight when the shoulder harness is lowered—this will enhance the effects and make for a slightly less restraining experience.)

What's all the fuss about? Bad-boy Stitch, aka Experiment 626, is being moved to a prison processing center and you have been recruited to keep an eye on him. Up to the task? Chances are you're not: The little blue rascal manages to escape every time. And when he does, chaos ensues. This attraction tends to be best appreciated by younger park-goers and Stitch groupies.

Note: Some youngsters may be frightened by dark moments and loud noises. Also, the shoulder restraints may spook claustrophobes. You must be at least 40 inches tall to enter.

BIRNBAUM'S BEST **BUZZ LIGHTYEAR'S SPACE RANGER SPIN:** FP+ The Evil Emperor Zurg is up to no good. As soon as he swipes enough batteries to power his ultimate weapon of destruction—KERPLOOEY!—it's curtains for the toy universe as we know it. It's up to that Space Ranger extraordinaire Buzz Lightyear and his Junior Space Rangers (that means you) to save the day.

So goes the story line of Tomorrowland's video-game-inspired spin through toyland. The adventure is experienced from a toy's point of view. Guests begin their 4½-minute tour of duty as Space Rangers at Star Command Action Center. This is where Buzz gives his team a briefing on the mission that lies ahead. Then it's off to the Launch Bay to board the ride vehicles. The ships feature dual laser cannons, glowing lights, and a piloting joystick.

Once Junior Space Rangers blast off, they find themselves surrounded by Zurg's robots, who are mercilessly ripping batteries from toys. As Rangers fire at targets, beams of light fill the air. For every target hit, you will be rewarded with sight gags, sound effects, and points. The points, which are tallied automatically, are accumulated throughout the journey. Although the vehicles follow a rigid "flight" path (they're on a track), the joystick allows riders to maneuver the ships, arcing from side to side or spinning in circles while taking aim at their surroundings.

When the star cruiser arrives at Zurg's spaceship, it's showdown time. Will good prevail over evil? Or has time run out for the toy universe? And will you score enough points to be a Galactic Hero? Most people improve their scores with a little practice.

MONSTERS, INC. LAUGH FLOOR: FP+ That Mike Wazowski is one enterprising eyeball. It seems the fuzzy fellow from *Monsters, Inc.* has opened something of a comedy club. Why? Well, it turns out his hometown is experiencing a bit of an energy crisis. Mike's clever plan is to tap into a decidedly alternative (not to mention free) fuel source to provide power for Monstropolis . . . laughter. But where can he gather enough giggles to fuel a whole city?

In a 400-seat theater in Tomorrowland, that's where. To accomplish his goal, monster of ceremonies Mike has recruited a couple of cornball comedians. Their job is to make you laugh yourself silly. And they are not too proud to resort to slapstick while doing so. Guests are encouraged to text their favorite joke while waiting in the queue. (Standard text messaging rates apply.)

PHOTO BY JILL SAFRO

TOMORROWLAND TRANSIT AUTHORITY PEOPLEMOVER: Boarded near Astro Orbiter, these trains (known to Disney purists as the WEDway) move at a speed of about seven miles per hour along almost a mile of track, beside or through most of the attractions in Tomorrowland. They are operated by a linear induction motor that has no moving parts, uses little power, and emits no pollution.

The peaceful, breezy excursion through Tomorrowland takes about ten minutes. There's rarely a wait to board. It's one of our favorites. However, moments of darkness (as the train passes through Space Mountain) may be unsettling for little ones.

ASTRO ORBITER: Here, passengers fly for two minutes in machine-age rockets designed to look more like oversize Buck Rogers toys than twenty-first-century space shuttles. Riders are surrounded by vibrantly colored, whirling planets as they get an astronaut's-eye view of Tomorrowland.

TOMORROWLAND SPEEDWAY: FP+

Little cars that burn up the tracks at this attraction provide quite a bit of the background noise in Tomorrowland. Kids especially enjoy the not-so-speedy, herky-jerky driving experience.

The vehicles have rack-and-pinion steering and disc brakes, but unlike most cars, they run along a track. Yet even expert drivers have trouble keeping them going in a straight line. (Don't panic when you notice the lack of a brake pedal—when you take your foot off the gas, the car comes to a quick, if not screeching, halt.) The one-lap tour of Tomorrowland takes about five minutes.

Note: You must be at least 54 inches tall to drive the car by yourself. Guests must be at least 32 inches tall to ride shotgun. Babies younger than 12 months may not ride.

BIRNBAUM'S ▸BEST◂ SPACE MOUNTAIN: FP+

This attraction, which blasted onto the Magic Kingdom scene in 1975 (and was completely refurbished in 2009), is a can't-miss crowd-pleaser for throngs of thrill seekers. Rising to a height of more than 180 feet, this gleaming steel-and-concrete cone houses an attraction that most people call a roller coaster. The ride takes place in an outer-space-like darkness that gets inkier and scarier as the journey progresses. The rockets that roar through this blackness attain a maximum speed of just over 28 miles per hour—but somehow it feels a whole lot faster.

The Space Mountain experience is wild enough to send glasses, purses, wallets, and even an occasional set of false teeth plummeting to the bottom of the track, so be sure to find a safe place for your possessions before the ride starts. It's also turbulent enough to upset the stomachs of those so unwise as to ride it immediately after eating. (Those who chicken out at the last minute have access to an exit.)

Note: Guests who are under 44 inches are not permitted to ride, and you must be in good health and free from heart conditions, motion sickness, back or neck problems, or other physical limitations to ride. Expectant mothers should skip the trip. Children under age 7 must be accompanied by an adult.

WALT DISNEY'S CAROUSEL OF PROGRESS:

First seen at New York's 1964–65 World's Fair and moved here in 1975, this 20-minute experience showcases the evolution of the American family and how life changed— and ostensibly progressed—with the advent of electricity. The hook here is that as a scene ends, the audience moves to the next one—not unlike being on a carousel (hence the name of the attraction). This is a great place to escape the crowds and heat, not to mention take a much-needed load off weary feet.

Shopping

No one travels to the Magic Kingdom just to shop. But as many a visitor has learned, shopping is one of the most enjoyable pastimes here.

The Magic Kingdom's boutiques and stores stock much more than just Disneyana. Along with the more predictable items in Main Street shops, it's possible to find cookbooks and dishes, pirate hats and toy frontier rifles, 14-karat gold charms, and filigreed costume jewelry. In Adventureland, shops boast many items imported from the exotic regions the area represents. Throughout the park, stores generally have merchandise that complements the themes of the various lands.

HOT TIP!

Your WDW shopping spree doesn't have to end when your vacation does. Simply log on to *www.DisneyParks.com/store* and you'll have access to some souvenir items previously available only at WDW.

In some shops, you can watch people at work —a candy maker hand-dipping caramel apples in the Main Street Confectionery, a glassblower crafting wares in Main Street's Crystal Arts, etc.

We recommend shopping in the early afternoon, rather than at the end of the day, when the shops are more crowded. However, keep in mind that Main Street shops do stay open about a half hour after park closing, in case you need any last-minute gifts on the way out.

Main Street

THE ART OF DISNEY: Nestled inside the Main Street Cinema, the shop showcases Disney-inspired fine art and collectibles, books, CDs, DVDs, clocks, Vinylmation, and more. And, yes, you can still catch classic Mickey cartoons here, too. An artist may even be on hand to sketch your favorite character.

BOX OFFICE GIFTS: Found inside Town Square Theater, this shop has camera supplies such as memory cards, batteries, and disposable cameras. It's also the place to view and pick up PhotoPass photos.

THE CHAPEAU: This Town Square shop is the place to buy Mouse ears and have them monogrammed, and to shop for straw hats, baseball caps, and assorted other headgear.

CURTAIN CALL COLLECTIBLES: After visiting Mickey Mouse at the Town Square Theater, guests may shop for souvenir items featuring the Big Cheese himself.

CRYSTAL ARTS: Cut-glass bowls, vases, glasses, and plates glitter in the cases of this crystal-chandeliered emporium. They have a lovely selection of miniature Disney characters meticulously crafted from glass. An engraver or a glassblower is often at work. There's a fireplace, too. Stop here to watch craftspeople mold shields and carve metal—impressive!

Where to Eat in the Magic Kingdom

A complete listing of all eateries—full-service restaurants, fast-food emporiums, and snack shops—can be found in the *Good Meals, Great Times* chapter. See the Magic Kingdom section, beginning on page 244.

DISNEY CLOTHIERS: This shop offers clothing for young girls, including shirts and sleepwear, all of which incorporate Disney characters. Look for bags and accessories, too.

EMPORIUM: Framed by a two-story-high portico, the Magic Kingdom's largest gift shop stocks stuffed animals and toys, sundries, kitchen items, hats, T-shirts, and more.

The cash registers always seem to be busy, especially toward the end of the afternoon and before park closing. Nearby lockers make for convenient storage of purchases.

Don't forget to peer into the windows, which usually feature elaborate displays ranging from seasonal themes to character tableaux. Shop early to avoid the crowds, and remember to take advantage of package pickup or delivery to your Walt Disney World resort.

HARMONY BARBER SHOP: Situated next door to the Main Street Car Barn, the quaint, old-fashioned setting for this working shop (complete with occasional appearances by a harmonizing quartet) merits a peek even if you have no need for a trim. It's open from 9 A.M. to about 5 P.M. daily. This is a popular spot for a child's first haircut, but they serve grown-ups, too (haircuts and beard/mustache trims). Kids can get colored gel hair treatments, too. For an appointment, call 407-WDW-PLAY (939-7529). Walk-ins are accepted, too.

Let It Rain

The show doesn't stop just because of a storm. Instead, shops throughout the Magic Kingdom sell plastic Disney Parks–branded ponchos and umbrellas to outfit guests who have left their own rain gear back home, at their hotel, or in the car.

MAIN STREET ATHLETIC CLUB: Character-related gifts and apparel are the hallmarks of this shop. Some merchandise features images of Disney characters pursuing their favorite sports. The shop also stocks golf shirts with a small Mickey embroidered on the pocket. You'll find the shop next to Casey's Corner.

MAIN STREET CHAMBER OF COMMERCE: This is the place to go if you have any Magic Kingdom purchases "sent to the front of the park" (aka Package Pickup). Allow at least three hours for the package to get here. It's located near City Hall.

MAIN STREET CONFECTIONERY: Tasty chocolates are sold in this old-fashioned pink-and-white paradise. A delight at any time of day, but more so when the cooks in the shop's glass-walled kitchen dip apples in gooey caramel. Then the candy sends up clouds of aroma that you could swear were being fanned out onto the street. There is a selection of fresh-made fudge, along with jelly beans, marshmallow crispy treats, and dozens of other confections that will satisfy any sweet tooth.

NEWSSTAND: No newspapers are sold in the Magic Kingdom—even at its newsstand, which is near the park entrance. (It's to the left, just inside the turnstiles.) The stand sells character merchandise and souvenirs.

THE SHADOW BOX: Watching Rubio Artist Co. silhouette cutters snip black paper into the likenesses of children is one of Main Street's more fascinating diversions. The Shadow Box is at the corner of Main and Center streets.

UPTOWN JEWELERS: Designed to resemble a turn-of-the-twentieth-century collectibles shop, this spiffy store specializes in jewelry and other gift items. Look for colorful items celebrating Ms. Minnie Mouse: scarves, purses, wallets, shoes, phone cases and more. The shop also boasts what may be Walt Disney World's largest selection of footware. Other wares include cosmetics, tote bags, luggage, watches, sunglasses, and more.

WHEELCHAIR AND ECV RENTAL: Inside the turnstiles and under the Train Station, this rental concession offers a limited number of wheelchairs and Electric Conveyance Vehicles (ECVs). They are available on a first-come, first-served basis. (Hold on to your receipt—

Disney's PhotoPass

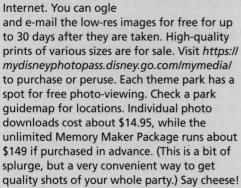

As you wander the theme parks, chances are Disney cast members will offer to snap your picture. After mugging for the camera (be sure to ask about "magic" shots), you'll be asked to scan your MagicBand (see page 24) or card. It'll link all such photos together for viewing on the Internet. You can ogle and e-mail the low-res images for free for up to 30 days after they are taken. High-quality prints of various sizes are for sale. Visit *https://mydisneyphotopass.disney.go.com/mymedia/* to purchase or peruse. Each theme park has a spot for free photo-viewing. Check a park guidemap for locations. Individual photo downloads cost about $14.95, while the unlimited Memory Maker Package runs about $149 if purchased in advance. (This is a bit of splurge, but a very convenient way to get quality shots of your whole party.) Say cheese!

it'll get you a replacement wheelchair or ECV should yours mysteriously disappear during the day.) Keep in mind that wheelchairs and ECVs rented here cannot be taken outside the Magic Kingdom. (Save your receipt and you may get a same-day replacement at another theme park.)

Adventureland

AGRABAH BAZAAR: Clothing and accessories with a safari theme are featured at this shop. In addition, look for souvenirs of the *Aladdin* ilk—toys, costumes, etc.

BWANA BOB'S: Stop here for tropical-themed jewelry, bags, pins, and hats, plus sunglasses, disposable cameras, and more.

ISLAND SUPPLY: This small tropical surf shop features a large selection of surfing attire and accessories, plus jewelry and dresses.

THE PIRATES LEAGUE: More than just a crew of plank-walkers, this group of savvy pirates transforms guests into one of their own—in exchange for booty, of course! Once you're swashbuckled up, they'll snap your photo in the "secret" treasure room. Call 407-WDW-CREW (939-2739) for pricing or to make a reservation.

You will find the Pirates League in the Plaza del Sol Caribe Bazaar by the Pirates of the Caribbean attraction.

PLAZA DEL SOL CARIBE BAZAAR: Ahoy there, mateys! A swashbuckler's delight, the joint adjoining the Pirates of the Caribbean sells stuff celebrating both the attraction and the feature films of the same name. It also stocks other pirate booty, including Jolly Roger flags, rings, dolls, pirate costumes, themed hats, and eye patches. If that's not enough treasure for you, check out the candy and snacks. The pièce de résistance for pirate fans? Pirate makeovers! (See The Pirates League at the bottom left of this page.) This is one of our favorite shops.

ZANZIBAR TRADING COMPANY: Across from Adventureland's famed Egg Roll Wagon, this corner shop stocks jungle collectibles, including hand-crafted wood items imported from Kenya: giraffes, and letter openers. Also found here are straw and woven items, drums, and animal-print apparel.

Frontierland

BIG AL'S: Named for the most popular (and least talented) member of the Country Bears, this riverfront shop is known for its selection of headwear, including Davy Crockett caps.

BRIAR PATCH: Toys and cuddly character items, plus kids' apparel and hats for the whole family, are featured wares at this shop, located near the Splash Mountain exit. There's also a pair of rocking chairs for those who need to take a load off.

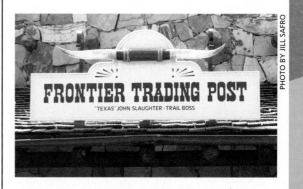

FRONTIER TRADING POST: This is the place to shop for collector pins and the associated accoutrements. Since it's got the largest selection of pins in the park, they might want to rename this the Pin Trading Post.

PRAIRIE OUTPOST & SUPPLY: Stop by this turn-of-the-twentieth-century general store for candy, coffee, and cookies.

Liberty Square

LIBERTY SQUARE PORTRAIT GALLERY: In the midst of Liberty Square, guests may have their portraits drawn in this open-air studio.

YANKEE TRADER: On your way to The Haunted Mansion? This quaint spot gives a taste of things to come, with Haunted Mansion–themed items and ghoulish goodies. There are souvenirs inspired by scenes and characters from the classic attraction, too. The rest of the shop is filled with housewares, mugs, magnets, picture frames, and blankets. They have a nice selection of snack items, too.

YE OLDE CHRISTMAS SHOPPE: A wide variety of festive Yuletide items, including decorative Disney-themed gifts and trinkets (many of which can be personalized) and ornaments, is available year-round. Look for items such as stockings, tree-toppers, and more.

Fantasyland

BIBBIDI BOBBIDI BOUTIQUE: Housed inside Cinderella Castle, this shop offers young guests the opportunity to be transformed into princesses and knights. Magical makeovers are available from 8 A.M. to 7 P.M. Prices vary. Magic Kingdom admission is required to enter this location. (There is an additional Bibbidi Bobbidi Boutique inside the World of Disney shop at Downtown Disney. While there is no admission fee, there is a charge for services at both locations.) For pricing information or to book a reservation, call 407-WDW-STYLE (939-7895). Photo packages are offered, too. Reservations are strongly recommended.

BIG TOP SOUVENIRS: Step inside the big tent for Disney merchandise and snacks galore. It's in the Storybook Circus part of Fantasyland.

BONJOUR VILLAGE GIFTS: Visit this charming addition to Fantasyland for items inspired by Disney's *Beauty and the Beast*. Expect to find apparel (we dig the Gaston's Tavern T-shirts), plush toys, royal dinnerware, glowing goblets, tapestries, castle artwork, and more.

CASTLE COUTURE: Can't get enough Disney princess merchandise? Stop here for royal toys, costumes, dolls, and kids' "princess apparel," plus jewelry, and accessories.

HUNDRED ACRE GOODS: Located at the exit of The Many Adventures of Winnie the Pooh, this shop has wares featuring the folks from the Hundred Acre Wood (among other places). Among the items the Pooh bear proffers are toys, hats, shirts, toddler clothing, and more.

SIR MICKEY'S: Expect to find all sorts of Disney-princess-themed clothing and souvenir items in this shop with a theme based on *The Brave Little Tailor*—the cartoon in which Mickey defeats a giant to win the hand of Princess Minnie. (It was one of the most elaborate and expensive Mickey Mouse cartoons ever made.) Mouse ears may be monogrammed here, too.

Tomorrowland

MERCHANT OF VENUS: The place for anything and everything Stitch to *Star Wars*, plus *Monsters University* merch, plush toys, games, and Vinylmation collectibles. It is located near Stitch's Great Escape.

MICKEY'S STAR TRADERS: This is one of the better places to go in the Magic Kingdom for Disney-themed items: plush toys, hats, shirts, candy, etc. Sunglasses and sun-care products are also available. The Tomorrowland Transit Authority passes through here, too. (To catch a glimpse of the TTA, look up!)

SPACE MOUNTAIN SHOP: After zipping through space, stop here to peruse Space Mountain–themed shirts and merchandise, plus accessories for cell phones and tablet computers.

Entertainment

In this most magical corner of the World, a slate of live performances ranks among the more serendipitous discoveries. The Magic Kingdom's entertainment mix includes dazzling high-tech shows and old-fashioned numbers alike. To keep apprised of the offerings on any given day, stop at City Hall upon arrival at the park to pick up a current guidemap and Times Guide.

While details may change in 2015, what follows is a good indication of the park's entertainment repertoire. Visit *www.disneyworld.com* to confirm specifics and schedules.

CAPTAIN JACK SPARROW'S PIRATE TUTORIAL: So you wanna be a pirate? Captain Jack and his mate Mack are looking for new recruits near the Pirates of the Caribbean in Adventureland. They'd like to test your pirate skills (swordplay, menacing looks, etc.) and decide whether you're worthy of the Pirate's Oath and the title of honorary buccaneer.

CASEY'S CORNER PIANO: A peppy pianist tickles the ivories of a snow-white upright, just outside Casey's Corner on Main Street.

CELEBRATE THE MAGIC: A relatively new nighttime spectacular (it premiered in late 2012), this 10-minute animated, musical celebration of Disney storytelling takes place on Cinderella Castle. Yes, *on* the castle. (The beloved WDW icon has evolved into a high-tech canvas for Disney artists without losing any of its classic charm.) The action starts with a sprinkling of pixie dust, courtesy of Tinker Bell. Then, a montage of memorable movie moments lights up the night. In addition to the regular show, expect Celebrate the Magic to include seasonal updates throughout the year. Note that the front and sides of the Castle offer slightly different viewing experiences—so if you've already enjoyed it from one vantage point, you might want to try another.

DREAM ALONG WITH MICKEY: There's a dream-inspired party being thrown in front of Cinderella Castle—and just about everyone is invited. Mickey, Minnie, Donald, and oodles of other Disney characters join the festivities as their dreams of adventure and "happily ever after" come to life through music and dance. That is, until evil party crasher Maleficent shows

up to wreak a little havoc. Collectively, however, party guests prove that believing in your dreams is more powerful than Maleficent's sorcery. The 20-minute show is presented several times a day.

DAPPER DANS: You just might encounter a barbershop quartet while strolling down Main Street. Conspicuously clad in straw hats and striped vests, the ever-so-jovial Dapper Dans tap-dance and let one-liners fly during their short, four-part-harmony performances.

FAIRYTALE GARDEN: Merida from *Brave* greets guests in this nook beside Cinderella Castle each day. Check a Times Guide for specifics. Character is subject to change.

BIRNBAUM'S BEST **FIREWORKS:** FP+ "Wishes," a dynamite, pyrotechnic extravaganza, is presented most nights when the Magic Kingdom stays open after dark. Narrated by Jiminy Cricket, this is one of the biggest, boldest, and truly eye-popping fireworks shows ever presented in the park. Showtimes vary—check a park Times Guide for specifics. Wishes is ideally viewed from Main Street, U.S.A., but can be seen from many vantage points. It is presented rain or shine.

FLAG RETREAT: At about 5 P.M. each day (check a current Times Guide), patriotic music fills the air as a color guard marches to Town Square, in Main Street, U.S.A., and takes down the American flag that flies from the flagpole.

BIRNBAUM'S ★BEST★ **FESTIVAL OF FANTASY PARADE:** FP+ A musical celebration of Disney Animation, this parade wends its way down Main Street once a day. The festival focuses on Disney friends who frequent Fantasyland. Kids love to wave to favorite characters—especially Anna and Elsa.

Festival of Fantasy highlights the stories of *Frozen*, *The Little Mermaid*, *Sleeping Beauty*, *Pinocchio*, *Tangled*, *Dumbo*, and more.

MOVE IT, SHAKE IT, CELEBRATE IT—STREET PARTY!: Whether you are celebrating a special occasion or just the fact that you are in the Magic Kingdom, this dance party is a special treat. An energetic spectacle of music and dance, the 35-minute jubilee invites guests to join in the fun as dancers and Disney characters take over the street in front of Cinderella Castle.

Holiday Happenings

It's a rare holiday that passes quietly in the Magic Kingdom. During certain holidays, such as Christmas, New Year's Eve, and the Fourth of July, this Kingdom usually breaks curfew, staying open extra late and stepping up its nighttime entertainment. On these occasions, special performances of the SpectroMagic parade and the fireworks are often in store. Of course, entertainment plans are subject to change, so it's important to call 407-934-7639 for information and performance schedules.

EASTER: Easter is a delightful, if a bit crowded, time to visit the Magic Kingdom. Mr. and Mrs. Easter Bunny have been known to appear in the park to help guests celebrate the occasion.

FOURTH OF JULY: The busiest day of the summer—and with good reason: There's a double-size fireworks extravaganza that lights up the skies above Cinderella Castle and the Seven Seas Lagoon. It's a thrilling display.

HALLOWEEN: This most spooky of holidays is celebrated on select nights from September through October with a special-ticket event: Mickey's Not-So-Scary Halloween Party. The park closes a bit early on nights when the party takes place. (Guests bearing tickets to the party can stay in the park.) Expect characters in costume, creepy music and fog effects, and trick-or-treating throughout the park. It's a hoot! Mickey's Boo-to-You Halloween Parade takes place, as does a special edition of the fireworks show. Visit *www.disneyworld.com/halloween*, or call 407-824-4321, to order tickets to the party.

CHRISTMAS: A towering Christmas tree goes up on Main Street, and the Magic Kingdom is decked out as only Disney can do it. (Cinderella Castle is draped in 250,000 sparkling lights!)

On select nights in November and December, the park hosts a special-admission celebration known as Mickey's Very Merry Christmas Party. The festivities, complete with hot chocolate,

Where to Find the Characters

Mickey and his pals make appearances throughout the day. Alice and her Wonderland friends may be found near the Mad Tea Party. Pooh and Tigger frequent Fantasyland. Woody, Jessie, and Bullseye appear in Frontierland. Tinker Bell and her fairy friends are in Adventureland's Pixie Hollow. Disney regals also greet guests in Princess Fairytale Hall. Mickey greets guests at the Main Street Theater. You'll find Goofy, Donald, Daisy, and Minnie at Pete's Silly Sideshow in Fantasyland. And various characters greet guests in Town Square at park opening time. Check a Times Guide for updated information. Eateries such as Cinderella's Royal Table and Crystal Palace offer opportunities to meet with characters, too. For details on dining with Disney characters, turn to page 282.

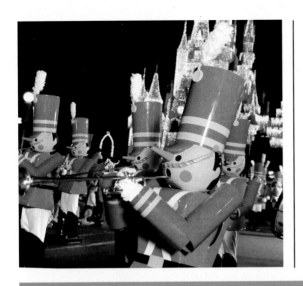

cookies, and snow flurries on Main Street, include a running (or two) of Mickey's Once Upon a Christmastime Parade and holiday shows, plus a special Wishes fireworks show. Disney characters are on hand, too.

The Christmas party is a very popular (and enjoyable) event. Purchase tickets way ahead of time. And don't forget to wear red and green; *www.disneyworld.com/christmasparty*.

NEW YEAR'S EVE: It has always been true that on December 31 the throngs here are body to body. Expect a dazzling, super-size fireworks display and oodles of happy holiday decorations. There's plenty of nip in the air as the evening goes on, so dress accordingly.

The Main Street Electrical Parade

BIRNBAUM'S ★BEST★ FP+ Whether you are experiencing the Main Street Electrical Parade for the first time or for the first time in 20 years, we guarantee you'll be back for more. This enchanting classic, which made its Walt Disney World debut in 1977, is back after a lengthy hiatus. Cue applause!

A mesmerizing mix of shimmering lights (nearly half a million of them) and merry music, the parade features 23 illuminated floats (some of the originals have been retired and a few new floats have been added), plus 80 performers. As visually stunning as this processional is, it's the infectious score that makes it a truly unforgettable show. The "electro-syntho-magnetic" musical sound of Baroque Hoedown brings a smile to all faces, young and old.

The parade follows the Magic Kingdom's traditional parade route (heading from Main Street, U.S.A., to Frontierland and vice versa).

PHOTO BY JILL SAFRO

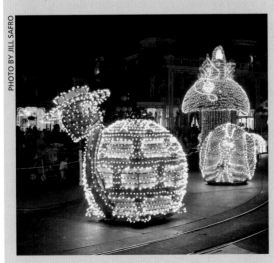

PHOTO BY JILL SAFRO

There are excellent viewing locations throughout the route, with many along the curbs of Main Street. It gets quite crowded there, so you must plan to claim your foot of curb about 45 to 90 minutes ahead of time (particularly for the earlier running). We enjoy the view from Frontierland (near the Country Bears).

The parade is presented during peak seasons and select evenings throughout the year.

Timing Tip: When the parade runs twice a night, the earlier presentation is always more crowded than the later one. So, if your party hasn't run out of steam, stick around for the late show. You'll be glad you did.

Note: Some performances may be canceled due to inclement weather.

- Start at a Fastpass+ kiosk to book Fast-passes for as many attractions as possible (if you haven't reserved in advance).

- For the best fireworks view, stand on Main Street between Town Square and Casey's Corner. (If you stand too close to the castle, some of the show may be obstructed.)

- If there are two performances of the nighttime parade, the later one tends to draw smaller crowds.

- If you're driving to the park, start out very early. Most people arrive between 9:30 A.M. and 11:30 A.M., and the roads and parking lots are jammed. Plan to be at the gates to the Magic Kingdom before they open, and then be at the end of Main Street when the rest of the park opens.

- Table-service restaurants are in high demand in this park. Book yours as early as possible. And don't forget to confirm.

- Eager to meet Mickey Mouse? Head for the Town Square Theater on Main Street (near the train station). He greets guests there all day. Get a Fastpass+ if you can.

- You can get in line for an attraction right up until the minute the park closes.

- Avoid the mealtime rush hours by eating early or late: before 11:30 A.M. or after 2 P.M., and before 5 P.M. or after 8 P.M.

- At busy times, take in these less-packed attractions: WDW Railroad, Liberty Belle Riverboat, Hall of Presidents, and Tomorrowland Transit Authority PeopleMover.

- Check the Tip Board for information on the wait times for popular attractions.

- Break up your day. Consider heading back to your hotel (if it's not too far) for some swimming. Be sure to hold on to your admission pass, stroller and/or wheelchair receipt(s), and your parking stub, so that you can reenter the Magic Kingdom.

- There are picnic facilities at the Transportation and Ticket Center (TTC).

- If your party decides to split up, set a meeting place and time. Avoid meeting in front of Cinderella Castle, since this area can become quite congested.

- If a quick-service eatery has several lines, those on the left are usually shorter.

- For a full-service meal, be sure to make reservations in advance by calling 407-WDW-DINE (939-3463).

- Park guests have the right to chicken out at any time while waiting in line. In other words, should you or a member of your party have second thoughts about soaring on Space Mountain, visiting with the grinning ghosts of the Haunted Mansion, or braving another attraction, simply inform an attendant and you'll be discreetly whisked out a special exit.

- If you've rented a stroller, consider returning it just before the night's fireworks presentation. That way, after the show, you'll be able to make a beeline for your bed rather than stand in a line to return your stroller.

- Some merchandise found in shops at Walt Disney World may be purchased through Guest Services. Call 877-560-6477 for info.

- Travel light. The fewer bags you have, the faster you'll pass through security.

- Allow extra time to get through the turnstiles on the way into the park—security and the "ticket tag" system can make for big delays—especially during peak times and on Extra Magic Hours days.

Hidden Mickeys

Disney Imagineers have hidden Mickey's image all over Walt Disney World. Some are easier to track down than others. Here are some of the most popular "Hidden Mickeys" at the Magic Kingdom. How many can you find? Check the box when you spot each one!

❤ Pirates of the Caribbean: As you enter the main building and jump on the standby line (the queue on the left), keep your eyes peeled for four large gun cabinets hanging on both sides of the wall (you'll pass a set of smaller ones on the right before reaching these). The locks on the cabinets form Hidden Mickeys. ■

❤ Splash Mountain: About halfway through the ride and in the room with jumping water, look quickly to your right and find a turtle floating on its back on a small geyser. Now look just above and behind the turtle for one of the most creative Hidden Mickeys in the park: It's a bobber attached to a fishing line. There is a more obvious one in the clouds beside the riverboat in the "Zip-a-dee-doo-dah" room, after the big splash. ■

❤ Big Thunder Mountain Railroad: At the very end of the ride and after the train slows, look to your right to find two sets of gear shifts laying on the ground. The second set forms a Hidden Mickey, although you may notice that the dimensions are not quite proportional (Mickey's "ears" are significantly smaller than his "head"). ■

❤ The Haunted Mansion: In the ghostly party scene, look at the bottom left corner of the banquet table for a Hidden Mickey made of two saucers and a plate. ■

❤ Carousel of Progress: In the Christmas scene, look to the far left for four nutcrackers lined up on top of the fireplace. The nutcracker farthest to the left is a Mickey nutcracker. Also in this scene, look for a Mickey plush toy in a box under the Christmas tree and a special pepper grinder on the kitchen counter (it's best seen from seats on the right side of the theater). ■

❤ Buzz Lightyear's Space Ranger Spin: Once you enter the interior queue, look for a poster on the right called "Planets of the Galactic Alliance" and find the planet "Pollost Prime." One of the continents forms a Mickey profile. Keep your eyes open during the attraction's space video scene (about halfway through) and you'll see this same planet fly by on the right. ■

❤ The Hall of Presidents: While you're waiting to enter the theater, take a moment to inspect the portrait of George Washington—it's hanging on the right side of the entrance to the show. There is a gilded Mickey on the tip of the first President's sword. ■

❤ It's a Small World: Don't rush into the queue, because the wait time sign forms a Hidden Mickey if you tilt your head to the left. Once on the ride, pay close attention to the Africa room and search for purple leaves hanging from the ceiling that form several Hidden Mickeys. (Hint: They're by the giraffes.) ■

❤ The Magic Carpets of Aladdin: You'll feel like a pro once you find this small but very cool Hidden Mickey. First find the Agrabah Bazaar shop (across from the Magic Carpets of Aladdin exit) and find the pole with a thick blue stripe at the bottom. Take three steps toward the attraction and look down to find a charm in the cement with a Mickey in the center. ■

❤ Tomorrowland Transit Authority People-Mover: Toward the end of the ride, you will glide past a futuristic lady getting her hair done. That lady has a Hidden Mickey on her belt buckle! (Hint: She's on the right side of the ride vehicle's forward motion.) ■

❤ Swiss Family Treehouse: As you make the trek up (and down) the treehouse stairs, take a good look at the giant tree trunk. Cleverly camouflaged by moss and bark? A subtle-but-familiar silhouette. ■

Specifics may change during 2015.

Where in the World?

All of the photos on this page were taken at the Magic Kingdom. Do you know where? We challenge you to find all the spots where these images were shot and snap a photo for yourself as you discover each one. Happy hunting! (For locations, turn to page 356.)

MAGIC KINGDOM

1

NOW SHOWING
THE ART OF DISNEY

2

3

4

6

"it's a small"

5

7

8

PHOTOS 1–7 BY JILL SAFRO; PHOTO 8 BY MIKE CARROLL

Epcot

143 **Getting Oriented**

144 **Park Primer**

145 **Future World**

155 **World Showcase**

169 **Entertainment**

170 **Hot Tips**

I magine a place whose entertainment inventory includes both a rich sampling of world cultures and a fun, enlightening journey to the technological frontier. You now have an inkling of the eye-opening and mind-broadening potential of Epcot—a place that's evolved most imaginatively in each of the 33 years it's been open.

Walt Disney suggested the idea back in 1966: "Epcot will be an experimental prototype community of tomorrow that will take its cue from the new ideas and technologies that are emerging from the creative center of American industry." It would never be completed, he said, but would "always be introducing and testing and demonstrating new materials and systems." On October 1, 1982, Walt Disney's dream became a reality. Test Track puts guests on the thrilling inside track of the fast and perilous world of automobile testing. Soarin' delivers the breathtaking sensation of flight. And favorites like The Seas with Nemo & Friends and Imagination! continue to ignite the creative forces within us all.

The park consists of two distinct areas of exploration: Future World and World Showcase. The former examines ideas in science and technology in ways that make them seem not only comprehensible but downright irresistible. The latter celebrates the diversity of the world's peoples, portraying a stunning array of nations, with extraordinary devotion to detail.

Think of Epcot as Disney's playground for the curious and the thoughtful. The experiences it delivers—all of them wonders of the real world—continue to amaze, educate, inspire, and (of course) entertain.

EPCOT

WORLD SHOWCASE

FUTURE WORLD

N

WORLD SHOWCASE LAGOON

MOROCCO

FRANCE

INTERNATIONAL GATEWAY

JAPAN

THE AMERICAN EXPERIENCE

UNITED KINGDOM

ITALY

CANADA

GERMANY

IMAGINATION!

THE LAND

CHINA

NORWAY

SHOWCASE PLAZA

MEXICO

INNOVENTIONS WEST

TEST TRACK

INNOVENTIONS EAST

THE SEAS

MISSION: SPACE

SPACESHIP EARTH

To Buses

UNIVERSE OF ENERGY

Entrance Plaza

Getting Oriented

Triple the Magic Kingdom park and you have an idea of the size of Epcot. As for layout, the park is shaped something like a giant hourglass. The pavilions of Future World fill the northern bulb, while the international potpourri called World Showcase occupies the southern bulb. Future World is anchored on the north by the imposing silver "geosphere," dubbed Spaceship Earth.

As you pass through Epcot's main Entrance Plaza, Spaceship Earth looms straight ahead. Pathways curve around the 180-foot-tall geosphere, winding up at Innoventions Plaza. Here, in addition to a show fountain, you'll see signs for Innoventions, whose two buildings cradle the east and west sides of the plaza. Beyond this central area, there are two roughly symmetrical north-south avenues; these are dotted with the seven pavilions that form the outer perimeter of Future World. Mission: SPACE, Test Track, and Universe of Energy flank Spaceship Earth on the east, while Imagination!, The Land, and The Seas with Nemo & Friends lie to the west.

In World Showcase, the international pavilions are arranged around the edge of sparkling World Showcase Lagoon, with The American Adventure directly south of Spaceship Earth on the lake's southernmost shore. A walkway from Future World leads to World Showcase Promenade, a 1.2-mile thoroughfare that wraps around the lagoon, winding past each World Showcase pavilion in the process.

HOW TO GET THERE

Take Exit 67 off I-4. Continue along to the Epcot Auto Plaza; if you park in a distant lot, take a tram to the park's main entrance.

By WDW Transportation: From the Grand Floridian, Contemporary, and Polynesian Village: hotel monorail to the Transportation and Ticket Center (TTC), then switch to the TTC-Epcot monorail. From Magic Kingdom: express monorail to the TTC, then switch to the TTC-Epcot monorail. From Downtown Disney: bus to any resort, then transfer to an Epcot bus or boat. From Disney's Hollywood Studios, Disney's Animal Kingdom, all other Walt Disney World resorts, Four Seasons resort, and the resorts on Hotel Plaza Boulevard: buses.

Note: A second Epcot park entrance, called International Gateway, provides entry directly to World Showcase. It may be reached via walkways and the FriendShip water launches from Disney's Hollywood Studios, plus the Swan, Dolphin, Yacht and Beach Club, and BoardWalk resorts. The boat deposits guests between the France and United Kingdom pavilions. It is possible to purchase theme park admission here, at Epcot's "back door."

PARKING

All-day parking at Epcot is $17 for day visitors (free to Disney resort guests with a resort ID or MagicBand, as well as annual passholders). Attendants will direct you to park in one of several lots named for steps in the creative process, such as Discover and Imagine. Trams circulate regularly, providing transportation between the distant lots and the main entrance. Be sure to note the section and aisle in which you park. Parking tickets allow for re-entry to the area (and other theme parks) throughout the day.

HOURS

Future World is usually open from about 9 A.M. to 9 P.M. (though some attractions may close at 7 P.M.). World Showcase hours are about 11 A.M. to 9 P.M. During certain holiday periods and the summer months, hours are extended. It's best to arrive a bit before the posted opening time, particularly during these busy seasons. On select days, the park opens one hour early or stays open two hours late for Disney resort guests only. Call 407-824-4321 for current schedules, or visit *www.disneyworld.com*.

GETTING AROUND

Water taxis, called FriendShip launches, ferry guests across the World Showcase Lagoon. Docks are located near Mexico, Canada, Germany, and Morocco. (The only other way to traverse the vast area is on foot.)

Admission Prices

ONE-DAY BASE TICKET
(Restricted to use only in Epcot. Prices do not include sales tax and are likely to rise in 2015.)

Adult	$95
Child*	$89

*3 through 9 years of age; children under age 3 free

Park Primer

BABY FACILITIES

There are changing tables and facilities for nursing mothers at the Baby Care Center in the Odyssey Center, between Test Track and Mexico. Disposable diapers are kept behind the counter at many Epcot shops; just ask.

CAMERA NEEDS

The Camera Center in Entrance Plaza and World Traveler at International Gateway stock memory cards, batteries, and disposable cameras, as well as camera straps and cases, frames, photo albums, and other accessories.

DISABILITY INFORMATION

Nearly all attractions, shops, and restaurants are accessible to guests using wheelchairs. Parking for guests with disabilities is available. Additional services are available for guests with visual and hearing disabilities. The complimentary *Guide for Guests with Disabilities* is available at the park entrances and at Guest Relations. It provides a detailed overview of all services. For more information, turn to the *Getting Ready to Go* chapter of this book.

FIRST AID

Minor medical problems can be handled at the First Aid Center, in the Odyssey Center, between Test Track and Mexico. Keep in mind that many guests could avoid a trip to First Aid simply by staying well hydrated. If you have an emergency, notify an employee and call 911.

INFORMATION

Guest Relations, which has one location to the right of the main entrance plaza and another next to Spaceship Earth, is equipped with guidemaps, Times Guides, and a helpful staff.

LOCKERS

Lockers are found immediately west of Spaceship Earth. Cost is $7–$9, plus a $5 refundable deposit for unlimited use all day.

LOST & FOUND

Lost and Found is located at Guest Relations in Innoventions East. To inquire about lost items after your WDW visit, call 407-824-4245. If you find an item, present it to a cast member (aka park employee).

LOST CHILDREN

Alert an employee and report lost children at Guest Relations or the Baby Care Center.

MONEY MATTERS

There are ATMs at the main entrance, on the path between Future World and World Showcase, at International Gateway (near United Kingdom) and at The American Adventure. Some foreign currency may be exchanged at Guest Relations. Credit cards (American Express, JCB, Discover, Diner's Club, Visa, MasterCard, the Disney Visa card), traveler's checks, Disney Dollars, Disney gift cards, MagicBand bracelets, and WDW resort IDs are accepted at most park locations (if backed up with a major credit card).

PACKAGE PICKUP

Epcot shops can arrange for most purchases to be transported (for free) to the Gift Stop in Entrance Plaza or International Gateway in World Showcase for later pickup.

SAME-DAY RE-ENTRY

Be sure to wear your MagicBand bracelet (if you used it for admission) or retain your ticket if you plan to return later the same day.

SECURITY CHECK

Guests entering Disney theme parks will be subject to a security check. Backpacks, parcels, purses, etc., will be searched by security personnel before guests are permitted to enter.

STROLLERS & WHEELCHAIRS

Strollers, wheelchairs, and Electric Conveyance Vehicles (ECVs) may be rented from venues at both park entrances. Wheelchairs are also available at the Gift Stop. Cost is $15 for single strollers, $31 for double strollers, and $12 for wheelchairs. A Length-of-Stay rental yields a $2-per-day discount. It's $50 a day for an ECV, plus a $20 refundable deposit. Quantities are limited. ECVs tend to sell out early. Keep your rental receipt; it can be used that same day to get a replacement at Epcot or another theme park.

TIP BOARDS

Check a digital board in Innoventions Plaza, near The Land, or by Mission: SPACE to learn current waiting times for popular attractions.

Future World

PHOTO BY JILL SAFRO

HOT TIP!

If you've got small children in your party, be sure to visit The Seas with Nemo & Friends and the Imagination! pavilions in Epcot's Future World, and the Kidcot Fun Stop craft areas in World Showcase.

A mere listing of the basic themes covered by the pavilions at Future World—agriculture, communication, car design, the ocean, the land, energy, imagination, technology, and space—tends to sound a tad academic. But when these serious topics are presented with a special flair, they become part of an experience that ranks among Disney's most entertaining.

Some of these subjects are explored in the course of lively and unusual "adventures," involving a whole arsenal of motion pictures, special effects, and Audio-Animatronics figures so lifelike that it is hard to remain unmoved. The basic elements are also appealing in their own right, from the palm-tree-dotted Entrance Plaza to the dramatic fountain just past Spaceship Earth, the many-faceted "geosphere" that has become the universal symbol of Epcot.

The park is so vast that it's hard to know what to do first. Many guests stop at Spaceship Earth on their way into Future World. As a result, they end up spending more time waiting in line than they need to. A wise alternative is to save Spaceship Earth for later in the day (when the lines inevitably thin out), and head for Soarin', the "less intense, non-spinning" Mission: SPACE, The Seas with Nemo & Friends, and Test Track (if motion sickness isn't an issue for

you) as soon as the park opens (the lines tend to stay long throughout the day). Take in as many Future World attractions as time allows, making sure to see the ImageWorks playground in the Imagination! pavilion, and save World Showcase for the evening hours. This strategy works well for families. (Refer to page 35 for a detailed version of this plan of attack.)

Another alternative—one that requires quite a bit of extra walking, but can help skirt a long line or two—is to explore Future World until World Showcase opens at 11 A.M. Then, in the afternoon, when many guests have shifted over to World Showcase, return to the Future World area. Innoventions is not only an interesting spot to pass the busy hours after lunch, but also a cool refuge when high temperatures prevail outdoors. And although queues can be found during peak seasons at Soarin', Mission: SPACE, Test Track, Imagination!, The Seas with Nemo & Friends, and Living with the Land throughout most of the late morning and afternoon, the period from late afternoon until park closing is usually less hectic. But don't forget to make it back to World Showcase in time to see the nighttime spectacular, IllumiNations—Reflections of Earth.

Left a Legacy?

Epcot has invited guests to "Leave a Legacy" near its front gate since its big Millennium Celebration. And? More than 550,000 have done so! They left their mark, in the form of a one-inch-square tile affixed on massive stone walls. While the program has officially come to a close, the cluster of monoliths continues to stand near the base of Spaceship Earth.

To locate a tile, inquire at the Leave a Legacy locating station inside the Camera Center by Spaceship Earth.

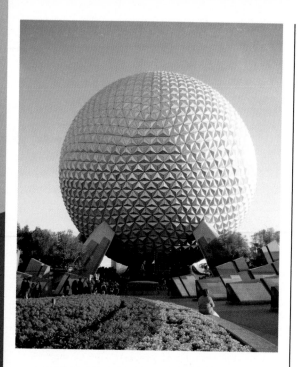

SPACESHIP EARTH FP+

As it looms impressively just above the Earth, this great, faceted silver structure looks a little bit like a spaceship ready to blast off. It appears large from a distance, and it seems even more immense when viewed from directly underneath. It's no surprise that some visitors simply stop beneath it and gawk.

The show inside, which explores the continuing quest by human beings to create the future, remains one of Epcot's compelling—if slower moving—attractions. It's an intriguing, narrated journey through time. It's also got a new interactive element that's a real hoot.

A common misconception about Spaceship Earth is that it is a geodesic dome. Not so. It is a geosphere. A geodesic dome is only half a sphere, while Spaceship Earth is almost completely round. Affectionately known to many simply as "the Ball," Spaceship Earth is a sight to behold.

Noted science-fiction writer Ray Bradbury, together with consultants from the Smithsonian Institution, the Los Angeles area's prestigious Huntington Library, the University of Southern California, and (among others) the University of Chicago, collaborated with Disney in developing this memorable 14-minute journey. It begins in an inky-black time tunnel, complete with a musty smell that suggests the dust of ages, and continues through history from the days of Cro-Magnon man (30,000 or 40,000 years ago) to the future.

Every scene is executed in exquisite detail. The symbols on the wall of that Egyptian temple really are hieroglyphics, and the content of the letter being dictated by the pharaoh was excerpted from a missive actually received by an agent of a ruler of the period.

Epcot veterans will notice two cool new scenes: a 1970s mainframe computer room and a garage scene depicting the creation of the personal computer.

All of these sights are enough to keep heads turning as the "time machines" wend their way upward. The most dazzling scene is saved for the ride's finale, when the audience is placed in outer space—with a prime view of our beautiful, blue planet, also known as Spaceship Earth. The journey winds down with a clever, custom look at your own future, courtesy of a touch screen in the ride vehicle.

The post-show area—Project Tomorrow—features several interactive areas, all emphasizing technology and its influence on daily life. Themes include medicine, power, and accident avoidance. You can also take a peek at a photo of yourself (snapped while you were experiencing the Spaceship Earth attraction). Expect to spend up to an hour in this high-tech playground.

INNOVENTIONS

Creativity abounds at Innoventions as guests celebrate the ingenuity and wonders of modern life. This imaginative zone is filled with interactive, hands-on exhibits. A highlight for daredevils is the Sum of All Thrills—an exhibit that explains the importance of science and math in roller coaster design. Oh, yeah—it also lets guests design and ride their own roller coaster! This experience is one of the most popular additions to Epcot in recent years.

Another stop here presents a new twist on the old adage "a penny saved is a penny earned." The Great Piggy Bank Adventure challenges guests of all ages to learn the importance of sound financial planning. Over at Where's the Fire?, guests learn about fire safety and get their photo snapped at a 30-foot pumper truck. Little ones love it.

HOT TIP!

The line for Spaceship Earth is usually quite long during the early morning hours and relatively short in the late afternoon and evening.

One of Walt Disney's dreams for Epcot was for the exhibits to change periodically. And indeed they do. Innoventions covers two buildings, referred to as East and West. The area between the pavilions is filled with color, light, spinning mobiles, and sidewalks glistening with fiber-optic lighting effects.

Above all, count on spending time exploring the exhibit areas (at least an hour). There's so much to see and do that curiosity will often get the better of any schedule here.

MOUSE GEAR: This enormous shop continues to offer a seemingly infinite and top-notch selection of Disney merchandise. Mouse Gear stocks character memorabilia, key chains, T-shirts, hats, books, candy (including a wall of jelly beans and various gummy treats), Vinylmation collectibles, mugs, photo albums, jewelry, towels, footwear, toys, and much more—making this the best source for character merchandise in Epcot. There are also items related to the park itself, along with Disney-themed apparel and children's clothing. It is one of the best shops at Disney, and it stays open at least a half hour longer than the park does. It's a nice place to browse as the crowds exit the park after IllumiNations.

THE ART OF DISNEY: This is Epcot's spot for a special assortment of Disney collectibles. The store showcases a wide variety of art inspired by Disney animation and theme parks. There is a collection of unique pieces by acclaimed artists, including prints, sculptures, figurines, and more.

THE SEAS WITH NEMO & FRIENDS

Welcome to one of the largest facilities ever dedicated to humanity's relationship with the ocean. It was designed by Disney Imagineers, in cooperation with distinguished oceanographic experts and scientists.

Though it enjoys the distinction of being one of Future World's original pavilions, what used to be known as The Living Seas is as fresh as ever—thanks to a little clownfish called Nemo and some of his fishy friends.

Once inside, guests can find the animated critters' real-life counterparts, including clownfish, blue tangs, sharks, and puffer fish.

The pavilion also features a Nemo–themed ride, an interactive encounter with an animated turtle, and an engaging post-show area. Little ones enjoy frolicking in Bruce's Shark World—a hands-on play area that celebrates the ocean's toothiest residents. From there, take a look at a simulated Caribbean coral reef environment. For the record, the crowning jewel of the pavilion is the simple-but-spectacular Turtle Talk with Crush.

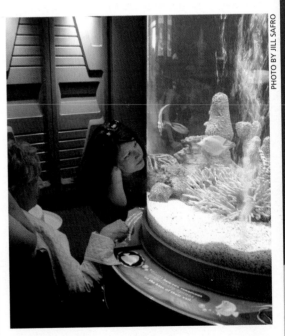

PHOTO BY JILL SAFRO

BIRNBAUM'S ★BEST **TURTLE TALK WITH CRUSH:** FP+ If ever there was an attraction that left guests smiling and asking, "How do they do that?!"—this is it. The concept is simple enough—a 10-minute, animated show featuring the surfer-dude sea turtle from *Finding Nemo*. The amazing part?

Under the Sea

Three behind-the-scenes tours offer guests a closer look at life in The Seas with Nemo & Friends underwater environs: DiveQuest gives certified scuba divers the opportunity to explore one of the world's largest aquariums. Epcot Seas Aqua Tour lets guests snorkel The Seas. And Dolphins in Depth offers guests the chance to learn about dolphin behavior as they closely observe researchers and trainers interacting with dolphins. Reservations for any tour can be made by calling 407-WDW-TOUR (939-8687). For more information on all of these programs, turn to pages 232–234 of the *Everything Else in the World* chapter.

The cartoon critter interacts with the audience. In doing so, he imparts turtle-y wisdom, answers questions, and cracks more than a few jokes. You have to see it to believe it. To do that, you'll have to wait in line—it's extremely popular with guests of all ages. It's totally awesome, dude.

THE SEAS WITH NEMO & FRIENDS ATTRACTION: FP+ Imagineered in the style of classic family attractions, this undersea adventure is fun for everyone. In it, guests climb aboard a "clam-mobile" and enter a colorful coral reef. It seems Nemo has wandered off again, and his teacher, Mr. Ray, needs help finding him. So keep your eyes peeled! There's

a bit of suspense involved—including moments of darkness and a stressful jellyfish encounter—but rest assured, it all ends happily.

CARIBBEAN CORAL REEF: The man-made reef exists in an enormous tank that holds about six million gallons of salt-water and more than 60 species of sea life. Among the 2,000 or so inhabitants are turtles, angelfish, sharks, dolphins, and diamond rays. It's worth it to stop by as the park opens—that's usually when breakfast is served to the fish.

Guests sometimes get to see scuba divers testing and demonstrating diving gear and underwater monitoring equipment as they carry on training programs with dolphins.

THE LAND

Occupying six acres, this enormous skylighted pavilion examines the nature of one of everybody's favorite topics—food. It also gives guests a chance to soar above the clouds in a celebration

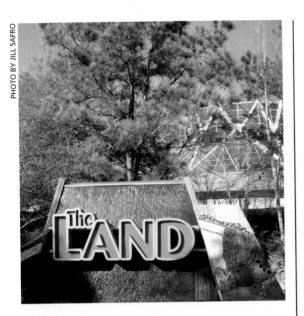

PHOTO BY JILL SAFRO

of flight. A film, *The Circle of Life*, uses characters from *The Lion King* to deliver an entertaining yet inspirational message about humanity and the environment. A boat ride explores farming in the past and future. Narration gives visitors the chance to learn about the experimental agricultural techniques practiced in the pavilion.

Timing Tip: This pavilion's Soarin' is a wildly popular attraction. So much so that Fastpass+ assignments may all be gone early. It's best to visit first thing in the morning and get a Fastpass+ while the gettin's good!

HOT TIP!

Got a rumbly in your tumbly? Head for Sunshine Seasons in The Land pavilion. There's a variety of counter-service choices—apt to please even the pickiest of eaters.

LIVING WITH THE LAND: FP+ This pavilion's 13½-minute boat ride through meticulously re-created natural locales opens with a dramatic storm scene. Guests sail through tropical rainforests, prairie grain fields, and a family farm. As the boat passes through each realistic setting, recorded narration offers commentary on humanity's ongoing struggle to cultivate and live in harmony with the land. Note the details that make each setting so convincing, such as sand blowing over the desert and light flickering from the television in the farmhouse window.

In the next segment, guests enter a plant research laboratory and solarium. Here, our planet's major food crops are being grown in research projects, along with rare new crops that may someday help meet Earth's ever-growing dietary needs.

Also of interest are the experiments being conducted to explore the practice of farming fish, and a desert farm area, where plants get nutrients through a drip irrigation system that delivers just the right amount of water—important in a dry climate.

As unreal as they appear, all the plants on view in the experimental greenhouses are living. In contrast, those in the biomes (the ecological communities viewed from the boat ride) were made in Disney studios out of lightweight plastic that simulates the cellulose found in real trees. The trunks and branches were molded from live specimens; the sycamore in the farmhouse's front yard, for example, duplicates one that stands outside a Burbank, California, car wash. Thousands of polyethylene leaves were snapped on.

Note that all of the greeenhouse flora is quite real—please resist the urge to touch plants or the sand in which they live.

Club Cool

Future World's Club Cool is a great place to beat the heat. Located near Innoventions, it is Coca-Cola's complimentary International Tasting Station. Here, you can sample eight different soft drinks from around the world, some tastier than others.

After you've quenched your thirst, courtesy of the Coca-Cola Company, you may have a desire to do some shopping. Not coincidentally, there's plenty of Coke merchandise to choose from (at this point, you will have to open your wallet or wave that MagicBand if you'd like a souvenir).

At press time, Club Cool was open for business during Future World's regular operating hours.

EPCOT

BIRNBAUM'S ★BEST★ **SOARIN':** FP+ Up, up, and away! On this high-flying Epcot attraction (it's one of the most popular attractions at Walt Disney World), you'll be suspended in a hang glider 45 feet in the air, above a giant IMAX projection dome, and treated to an aerial tour of some of the most awe-inspiring landscapes the state of California has to offer.

With the wind in your hair and your legs dangling in the breeze, the multi-passenger hang glider feels so convincingly real that you may even be tempted to pull up your feet for

Character Connection

Where do Disney characters hang out when they aren't marching in parades or dancing in shows? The Epcot Character Spot! FP+ This brilliantly hued, Zip-a-Dee-Doo-Dah zone is the place to go to meet Disney faves such as Mickey and Minnie Mouse, Chip 'n' Dale, Pluto, and Goofy. The gang's here all day long, but it's best to arrive early in the morning—as the line gets downright beastly in the afternoon. The entrance to the Character Spot is next to Fountain View (near Innoventions West). Check a park Times Guide for the character appearance schedule during your visit to Epcot. Get a Fastpass+ assignment if you can.

Mad About the Mouse?

Can't get enough of all things Disney? Then D23 is the place to be. It's the official community for Disney fans. To join, you'll need nothing more than a computer or smartphone and an unebbing enthusiasm for the House that Walt built. Upgrade to Silver-level membership ($35 annual dues) to net access to special events, an official membership card and certificate, a collectible gift (plus the chance to purchase exclusive merchandise), and more. Gold level ($75) includes a subscription to the D23 magazine. For details or to join the club, visit *www.disney.com/D23*. FYI: Walt Disney founded what would become the Disney Studios in 1923. Hence, the name D23.

fear of tripping over a treetop as you dip down toward the ground. During the gentle, rather peaceful journey, flyers glide toward the Upper Yosemite Falls of Yosemite Valley, past an active naval aircraft carrier in San Diego Bay, by San Francisco's Golden Gate Bridge, and then down over the vast desert of Death Valley and the lush wine country of Napa Valley. In all, the airborne trip takes about five minutes and employs synchronized wind currents, scent machines, and a moving musical score set to a film that wraps 180 degrees around you, making this a thoroughly enveloping experience.

Note: You must be 40 inches tall and free of back problems, heart conditions, motion sickness, and other physical limitations to ride. It's calmer than traditional "thrill" rides, but the sensation of flight is quite realistic. If you're afraid of heights, sit this one out.

Timing Tip: This is one of the most popular attractions in Walt Disney World. Get a Fastpass+ assignment in advance or get there immediately as the park opens to avoid a *minimum* wait of about 50 to 90 minutes.

THE CIRCLE OF LIFE: This 20-minute film uses animation and live action to illustrate some of the dangers to our environment, as well as potential solutions. Presented as a fable featuring *The Lion King* favorites Simba, Timon, and Pumbaa, the film takes an optimistic approach to a serious subject. It is shown in the Harvest Theater, just inside the entrance to The Land. Soon after the film begins, Simba's startled by the exuberant shout of "Timber!" and is drenched by the splash of a fallen tree in the water. The culprits are none other than his friends Timon and Pumbaa, who are clearing the savanna for the development of the Hakuna Matata Lakeside Village. Simba seizes the opportunity to tell them a tale about creatures who sometimes forget that everything is connected in the circle of life: humans.

Simba demonstrates to Timon and Pumbaa the consequences of progress, as his lessons are driven home by visual evidence of humans' mistreatment of the air, water, and land. (Timon: "And everybody was *okay* with this?") The effect is a mix of entertainment and a message about responsibility.

IMAGINATION!

The oddly shaped pyramids that house the Imagination! pavilion are quite a striking sight to behold. They certainly set the stage for the atypical experiences inside. One of the main attractions here is a classic 3-D movie called *Captain EO*. Guests are also invited behind the scenes of the Imagination Institute in a slow-moving attraction known as Journey Into Imagination with Figment.

Another pavilion highlight is the pair of quirky fountains outside—the Jellyfish Fountains, which spurt streams of water that spread out at the top, looking for an instant like their namesake sea creature, and the Leap Frog Fountains, which send out smooth streams of water that arc from one garden plot to another in the most astonishing fashion. Kids just can't get enough of them.

CAPTAIN EO: FP+ This Future World show is actually a blast from the past—a classic musical spectacular known as *Captain EO*, starring Michael Jackson. Back by popular demand, this crowd-pleasing film originally ran from 1986 through 1994 in this very theater.

Produced by George Lucas and directed by legendary Hollywood helmsman Francis Ford Coppola, *EO* is a thrilling, musical, space-fantasy adventure. Better yet, it's in 3-D! It's fun for all ages, but some youngsters may be frightened when EO and his crew encounter a dark planet and its villainous Supreme Leader. Of course, good prevails when the gang magically—and musically—transforms the darkness into a happy and colorful world.

In addition to the King of Pop, the 17-minute *Captain EO* film features a cast of mythical space critters such as Hooter (a little green elephant-like fellow who sneezes musical notes), Fuzzball (an orange-haired monkey with butterfly wings), the golden-haired, two-headed Geex, and many more.

Note: *Captain EO* has returned for a limited engagement and is presented in the theater formerly occupied by Honey, I Shrunk the Audience attraction.

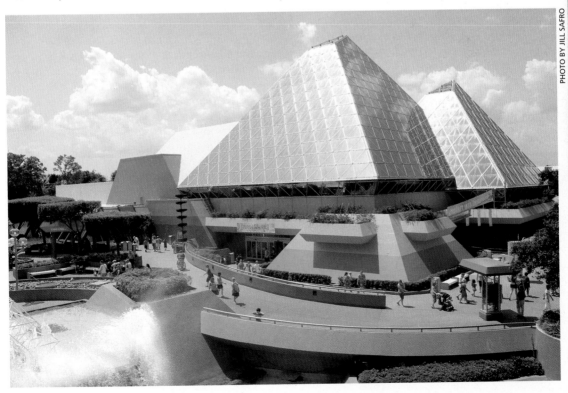

PHOTO BY JILL SAFRO

JOURNEY INTO IMAGINATION WITH
FIGMENT: [FP]+ He's back! Figment, the tiny purple dragon with the orange wings and yellow eyes, is on hand to guide guests on an imaginative quest. The goal? To figure out, once and for all, the best way to capture your imagination.

The journey takes place at Imagination Institute, where guests are invited to tour the institute's various labs, such as the Sight Lab, the Sound Lab, and the Smell Lab. All in all, it's a tame experience, save for the occasional blast of air or flashing lights.

Nostalgia buffs, take note: The classic song "One Little Spark," which made its debut with the original incarnation of this attraction, underscores the show once more.

IMAGEWORKS LABS: It's a rare Image-Works visitor who doesn't experience at least some of the emotion felt by the little kid who cried when her parents tried to tear her away. That's not surprising, because the area has activities that give visitors the chance to have some fun while stretching the imagination. Plan to spend up to 20 minutes exploring these entertaining labs—especially if you have very young children.

> ## HOT TIP!
> At press time, new activities were in the works for ImageWorks Labs. Be sure to stop by in 2015 to check them out!

Test Track [FP]+

BIRNBAUM'S ★BEST★ Fasten your safety belt! This newly refreshed pavilion puts guests through the creative and frenetic motions of automobile design and testing. The experience starts with guests designing a vehicle in the attraction's high-tech pre-show area. What is important to you in a car: efficiency, power, responsiveness, or capability? Use a touch screen to design your car with your

PHOTO BY MIKE CARROLL

priorities in mind, then take your virtual "SimCar" over to the Sim Track and give her a test drive. (Yes, they easily could have renamed this attraction Sim Track—a Test Track by any other name would be just as cool.)

> ## HOT TIP!
> If you don't mind splitting up your party, head for the "single rider" line at Test Track. It generally moves faster than the standby line.

The 4-minute ride is similar to the old version of Test Track—there's lots of zigging and zagging on the front end followed by a dramatic near-miss with a big noisy truck. Along the way, you'll learn how well your car did in each of the categories featured in the design stage. Finally, a long straightaway feeds into a series of banked turns and another straight shot that sends vehicles rocketing around the pavilion at top speed (up to 65 mph!). The computer-controlled, six-seater vehicles are equipped with video and audio, but no steering wheels or brake pedals. After all is said and done, guests may create a 15-second commercial for their new car and send the video to a friend via e-mail.

Note: Kids under 7 must be accompanied by an adult; guests under 40 inches cannot ride; passengers must be free of back problems, heart conditions, motion sickness, and other physical limitations. Pregnant women are advised to sit this one out.

MISSION: SPACE FP+

Think you've got "the right stuff"? Well, this is your chance to prove it. Epcot's out-of-this-world attraction has a bold mission—to give you a chance to feel the excitement and extreme intensity of space travel without ever leaving the planet.

There are actually two ways to travel to Mars at this attraction: the "highly intense" way (aka Orange Team) and the "less intense" experience (Green Team). The original Mission: SPACE attraction provides a galaxy of thrills for many brave and sturdy theme park guests. The adventure begins with a white-knuckle blast-off of a spacecraft (which has snug seating for four) on an important mission to Mars. The sustained G-force during the launch is intended to be most realistic. Once en route, expect a rather strange, spectacular sensation. It's not quite weightlessness, but according to astronauts who've felt the real thing, it's pretty darn close. (So much so that it also tends to duplicate the not-so-spectacular sensation of space sickness. In fact, Mission: SPACE has the dubious distinction of being the first attraction in theme park history to be equipped with motion-sickness bags.)

Throughout the journey, you're expected to work with your fellow crew members (assuming the roles of navigator, captain, engineer, and pilot) to accomplish the mission. For the "highly intense" version, we recommend ignoring this call to duty and keeping your eyes glued to the screen. This will allow you to sit back and enjoy the ride and decidedly downsize the dizziness factor.

The original attraction can wreak havoc on the equilibrium. To cut the chances of losing

HOT TIP!

Epcot is bigger than it seems, so allow lots of time to get from place to place. (It can take a half hour to walk from Spaceship Earth to The American Adventure in World Showcase.) Keep this in mind if you have restaurant reservations or hope to snag a nice IllumiNations viewing location on the World Showcase promenade.

your lunch, keep your eyes open at all times and fixed on the screen in front of you. You may be tempted to tilt your head or shut your eyes. Don't. (We promise you will arrive on Mars whether you fulfill your astronaut duty or not.)

Bottom line? Most guests who don't get queasy on the "highly intense" Orange Team version tend to rave about Mission: SPACE. For us, well, we admit we prefer the ride's gentler version—aka the Green Team. It's intended for those who would rather not spin. The experience is a bit different on "Mission: SPACE-lite," but it gives everyone a chance to ride without getting queasy. The effects may be toned down, but they are quite extraordinary. We completely enjoy the "less intense," non-spinning mission to Mars.

All guests must be at least 44 inches tall and free of back and heart problems, motion sickness, and other physical limitations. Pregnant women should skip the trip, as should anyone with claustrophobic tendencies. In fact, if you have any health issues whatsoever, sit this out. And don't eat before riding!

EPCOT

PHOTO BY JILL SAFRO

UNIVERSE OF ENERGY

BIRNBAUM'S ★BEST★ In the mood for a chuckle? Set a course for this attraction. You'll get a few giggles and learn something to boot.

Although it's easy to spot this pavilion's mirrored pyramid, the facade does not provide any clue at all to the 45 minutes of surprises in store. One of the most technologically complex experiences at Epcot, a show called Ellen's Energy Adventure consists of several movies and a ride-through segment. None of these is exactly what Epcot guests might expect.

The show begins with a film (featuring a few familiar faces). In it, Ellen DeGeneres is watching *Jeopardy!* One of the contestants is Ellen's annoying college roommate, Judy.

Ellen plays along but keeps striking out, particularly in the energy category. As she watches, her neighbor Bill Nye the Science Guy pops in and is aghast at Ellen's ignorance. Shortly thereafter, Ellen dozes off.

Ellen dreams she is a contestant on the show, competing against Albert Einstein and her nemesis Judy. This time, all of the questions are about energy. As Einstein ponders and Ellen fumbles, Judy is racking up points. Ellen, who has a negative score ("this nightmare game is a lot harder than the home version"), decides to freeze her dream and ask Bill Nye the Science Guy for some help.

The second segment leads guests into a theater, where Bill vows to educate Ellen about the importance of energy. He persuades her to

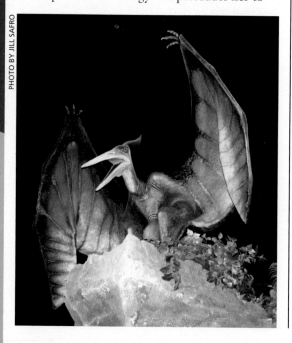

travel back in time to see where some of our energy sources came from. Suddenly (but very slowly), the whole seating area rotates, then breaks up into six sections that inch forward. The vehicles embark with Ellen upon an odyssey through the primeval world. Gigantic prehistoric trees crowd the forest. Apatosauruses wallow in the lagoon out front. A lofty allosaurus battles with an armored stegosaurus, and an elasmosaurus bursts out of a tide pool with frightening suddenness—all under the watchful gaze of winged pteranodons. (This zone spooks tots.)

Next, guests move out of the forest and view a montage of pictures capturing the history of civilization, from cave dwellers to the present. The issue of alternative-energy sources is raised, and the message is that there is no save-all source, but rather there are many possibilities with promise.

The attraction winds up with Ellen returning to the game show of her dreams. This time, she's beating her friend Judy, who is not at all happy about how much Ellen has learned during the commercial break. To win, she must name the one energy source that will never be depleted. (We won't reveal the answer, but we got it right!)

Almost as intriguing as the attraction is the technology behind it. The vehicles weigh about 30,000 pounds when fully loaded with passengers, yet are guided along the floor by a wire that is only one-eighth inch thick.

World Showcase

PHOTO BY JILL SAFRO

Noble sentiments about humanity and the fellowship of nations, which have motivated so many World's Fairs in the past, also inhabit World Showcase. But make no mistake about it: This area of Epcot is unlike any previous international exposition.

The group of pavilions that encircles World Showcase Lagoon (a body of water that is the size of several football fields, with a perimeter of about 1.2 miles) demonstrates Disney conceptions about participating countries in remarkably realistic, consistently entertaining styles. You won't find the real Germany here—rather, the country's essence, much as a traveler returning from a visit might remember what he or she saw.

Shops, restaurants, and attractions are housed in a group of structures that is an artful pastiche of all the elements that give that nation's countryside and towns their distinctive flavor. Although occasional liberties have been taken when scale and proportion required them, careful research governed the design of every nook and cranny.

Equally impressive is the cuisine. With no fewer than 14 upscale eateries to choose from, it's no wonder some guests here do nothing but nosh. (That is especially true during Epcot's popular International Food & Wine Festival, a time when dozens more nations contribute to an already fortified international menu. See page 11 for additional information.)

In the shops, many of the wares represent the country in whose pavilion they are sold. Craftspeople are occasionally on hand to demonstrate their arts. Thanks to special cultural-exchange programs and recruiting efforts, many World Showcase staffers hail from the countries the pavilions represent.

A diverse lineup of entertainment ensures that all visitors experience more than a little culture, foreign or otherwise. The entertainment is as authentic as the Disney casting directors can make it, with native performers commonly featured and new festivities always in the works.

HOT TIP!

World Showcase pavilions may open at 11 A.M. or later. However, guests may use the International Gateway entrance as much as a half hour prior to Future World's official opening time.

Phineas and Ferb: Agent P's World Showcase Adventure

Calling all secret agent wannabes! How would you like to help Perry the Platypus save the world from the evil Dr. Heinz Doofenshmirtz? Here's your chance. The interactive game is based on the Disney Channel show *Phineas and Ferb*. Of course, one need not be familiar with the show to get a kick out of the Epcot version. Once you borrow a F.O.N.E. (Field Operative Notification Equipment) from a special kiosk (near Italy, Norway, or the United Kingdom), you are ready to start the scavenger hunt.

If you and your team follow instructions and find the clues, you will complete your very important mission: to save the world! There is no extra charge to play this game, but guests do have to return the F.O.N.E.s after they declare "mission accomplished."

Pavilions are described in the order in which they are encountered while moving counterclockwise around the World Showcase Lagoon after crossing the bridge from Future World.

CANADA

Celebrating the many beauties of the U.S.A.'s neighbor to the north, the area devoted to the Western Hemisphere's largest nation is complete with its own mountain, waterfall, rushing stream,

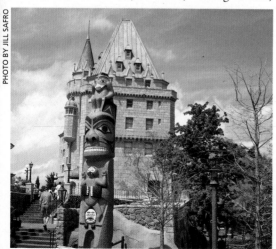

PHOTO BY JILL SAFRO

rocky canyon, mine, and splendid garden massed with flowers. There's even a totem pole, a trading post, and an elaborate, mansard-roofed hotel similar to ones built by Canadian railroad companies as they pushed west around the turn of the twentieth century. All this is imaginatively arranged somewhat like a split-level house, with the section representing French Canada on top, and another devoted to the mountains alongside it and below. From a distance, the Hôtel du Canada, the main building here, looks like little more than a bump on the landscape—as does Epcot's single Canadian Rocky Mountain. But up close, they both seem to tower as high as the genuine article.

The gardens were inspired by the Butchart Gardens, on Vancouver Island, British Columbia, a famous park created on the site of a limestone quarry. The hotel is modeled, in part, after Ottawa's Victorian-style Château Laurier. Entertainment is provided by a troupe of Celtic rock musicians called Off-Kilter. They perform on a stage facing the promenade.

O CANADA!: Step into the Circle-Vision 360 film, *O Canada!*, and find yourself surrounded by the breathtaking sights and sounds of this northern nation. Of course, you won't be alone—Canadian actor Martin Short stars as your guide, taking guests through prairies, plains, snowfields, rivers, rocky mountainsides, and beyond. Humor and hockey are included. The motion picture provides a you-are-there feeling that makes all of this spectacular scenery still more memorable. Note that there are no seats in this theater.

NORTHWEST MERCANTILE: Found to the left upon entering the pavilion's plaza, this spot features NHL T-shirts (Canadian teams, of course), plush toys (moose, owls, otters, etc.), and maple-flavored snacks, tiny totem poles, plus other Canada-themed collectibles. Skeins of rope, tin scoops, lanterns, and antique ice skates hanging from the long beams overhead set the mood, together with the structure itself.

UNITED KINGDOM

In the space of only a few hundred feet, visitors to this pavilion stroll from an elegant London square to the edge of a canal in the rural countryside—via a bustling urban English street framed by buildings that constitute a veritable rhapsody of historic architectural styles. But one scene leads to the next so smoothly that nothing ever seems amiss. Here again, note the attention to detail: the half-timbered High Street structure that leans a bit, and the hand-painted "smoke" stains that make the chimneys look as if they have been there for centuries. When a thatched roof is required, it's right where it should be—though the roof may be made of plastic broom bristles because fire regulations prohibit the real thing. Off to the side is a pair of scarlet phone booths identical to those that used to be found around the U.K. And there are eight architectural styles characteristic of the streetscapes, from English Tudor to Georgian and Victorian.

There is no major attraction in this pavilion; instead, it features half a dozen shops and a pub that serves a selection of beers and ales that would be the toast of any "local" in London itself. There's lots of entertainment, including a group of comedians called the World Showcase Players, who, when not engaged in general clowning on the World Showcase Promenade, coax audience members into participating in their farcical playlets. In the pub, a pianist has been known to play late into the evening. A band known as British Revolution plays classic rock favorites in the garden courtyard. They're a true crowd-pleaser. (Entertainment is subject to change.)

THE CROWN & CREST: This shop looks like a backdrop for a child's fantasy of the days of King Arthur, with its high rafters decked out with bright banners, a fireplace (and crossed swords above), and wrought-iron chandelier. Souvenirs featuring the Union Jack flag and the Rose & Crown Pub (the U.K. pavilion's watering hole) are the stock-in-trade at this emporium adjoining the Sportsman Shoppe. Name histories and family crests are also available, as are swords, shields, and knights in shining armor. There's also a line of Guinness Stout merchandise (think glasses, shirts, bottle openers, etc.).

HOT TIP!

A great place to watch IllumiNations is from the Rose & Crown Pub in the United Kingdom pavilion. Try to snag a lagoonside table—whether within the pub's boundaries or in the self-serve sitting area nearby—about 30 minutes before the show is set to begin. (Note that on nights when the wind is blowing directly toward the Rose & Crown, it might be better to grab a bite and watch the show from Mexico's Cantina, on the other side of the lagoon.)

EPCOT

SPORTSMAN'S SHOPPE: Head here for clothing and accessories centered on uniquely British locales and sports. You can expect to find a large selection of football (soccer) team gear. Don't miss the tartan map on the wall opposite The Crown & Crest; it identifies plaids from Glen Burn and Gordon to Langtree and St. Lawrence. Outside, the shop resembles a stone manor built during the last half of the sixteenth century. TV fans will appreciate the selection of merchandise featuring their favorite British programs (*Dr. Who*, *Downton Abbey*, etc.).

THE TEA CADDY: Fitted out with heavy wooden beams and a broad fireplace to resemble the Stratford-upon-Avon cottage of William Shakespeare's wife, Anne Hathaway, this shop stocks English teas, both loose and in bags, in a wide variety of flavors. Other items include teapots, china, biscuits, and assorted candies.

THE TOY SOLDIER: This shop presents a nice selection of rock-'n'-roll-themed items, highlighting well-known British bands, as well as merchandise featuring the gang from the Hundred Acre Wood: Pooh, Piglet, Eeyore, and Tigger, too. Also found here? Toy swords and shields, books, and candy.

THE QUEEN'S TABLE: This shop (opposite the Sportsman's Shoppe) may be one of the loveliest in all of Epcot. That is particularly true of the store's elegant Adams Room, embellished with elaborate moldings and a crystal chandelier. The setting is a lovely background for the handbags, jewelry, soaps, and other fragrant items that are available.

Don't neglect to inspect small, serene Britannia Square outside the shop farthest from the promenade. But for its small size and the Florida climate, it feels like London itself.

INTERNATIONAL GATEWAY

Informally known as Epcot's back door, the International Gateway is between the United Kingdom and France pavilions. There's a ticket window just outside the gate. (Yes, it's possible to enter and exit the park here.) In addition to restrooms and an ATM, you'll also find:

FRIENDSHIP LANDING: Disney's water taxis, known as FriendShip boats, ferry guests to the Yacht and Beach Club, BoardWalk, and the Swan and Dolphin resorts, and finally to Disney's Hollywood Studios (the last stop before the boat returns to the resorts and back to Epcot). The dock is located outside the International Gateway turnstiles. It's possible to walk to all of the aforementioned destinations, too.

Where to Eat in Epcot

A complete listing of all eateries—full-service restaurants, fast-food emporiums, and snack shops—can be found in the *Good Meals, Great Times* chapter. See the Epcot section, beginning on page 251.

STROLLER AND WHEELCHAIR RENTAL:
Strollers and wheelchairs are available for rent at this location. Remember to keep your rental receipt; it can be used on the same day in the Magic Kingdom, Disney's Hollywood Studios, Animal Kingdom, or again in Epcot, should you leave and return later on. It is also possible to get a replacement stroller here.

WORLD TRAVELER: Candy, soft drinks, books, kitchen items, convenience items, strollers (for purchase), and a package pickup depot are located at this spot near the United Kingdom pavilion. Disney fashions, home items, character merchandise, and Epcot souvenirs are also for sale here.

FRANCE

The buildings here have mansard roofs and casement windows so Gallic in appearance that you may expect to see a Bohemian poet looking down from above. A canal-like offshoot of the lagoon seems like the Seine itself; the footbridge that spans it recalls the old Pont des Arts. There's a kiosk like those that punctuate the streets of Paris and a bakery whose heavenly rich aromas announce its presence long before it's visible.

Shops sell perfumes and other items. Their roofs are of real copper or slate, and the cabinetry is finely crafted. Galerie des Halles—the iron-and-glass-ceilinged market that Paris once counted as one of its most beloved institutions—lives again. But perhaps most special of all are the people. Hosts and hostesses who hail from Paris and the French provinces answer questions in French-accented English. Keep an eye out for Serveur Amusant, the comedic waiter who does one heck of a balancing act.

An interesting background note: the main entrance to the pavilion recalls the architecture of Paris, most of which was built during the Belle Epoque ("beautiful age"), the last decades of the nineteenth century.

Don't miss the garden on the opposite side of this pavilion. It is one of the most peaceful spots in World Showcase.

BIRNBAUM'S ★BEST★ IMPRESSIONS DE FRANCE: Shown in the Palais du Cinéma, a little theater that's not unlike the one at Fontainebleau, this enchanting 18-minute film takes viewers on a trip through France.

The film shows off a beautiful tree-dotted estate, fields and vineyards at harvest time, a flower market and a pastry shop, a glacier, and a harbor full of squawking gulls. Viewers visit the Eiffel Tower; Versailles and its gilt Hall of Mirrors (just outside Paris); Mont Saint Michel; the French Alps; and Cannes, the star-studded resort city on the Mediterranean coast. All this is even more appealing thanks to a superb soundtrack, consisting almost entirely of the music of French-classical composers.

The exceptionally wide screen adds yet another dimension. This is not a Circle-Vision 360 film like the movies shown at China and Canada. The France film used only five cameras, and it is shown on five large projection surfaces—200 degrees around. It's a beautiful film, one of the park's best. We recommend stopping for a French pastry break after the show.

PLUME ET PALETTE: One of the loveliest shops in World Showcase, this Art Nouveau–inspired location is home to the Givenchy Shop—the only location in the world that carries the complete line of Givenchy fragrances, skin care products, and cosmetics.

LA SIGNATURE: Another beautiful spot, this boutique features a selection of Guerlain cosmetics and fragrances.

L'ESPRIT DE LA PROVENCE: This little shop stocks a selection of textiles, ceramics, and kitchen accessories from the Provence region of Southern France. They offer loose chocolates and children's books, too.

LES HALLES BOUTIQUE DE CADEUX: Everything from Eiffel Tower statues to Impressionist-style prints is offered at this location near the exit of the cinema. Mugs, tote bags, T-shirts, berets, flags, and picture frames are among the offerings available. The area is based on Paris's now-demolished Les Halles, the city's old fruit and vegetable market. This space is also the new

PHOTO BY JILL SAFRO

location of the ever-popular bakeshop known as Boulangerie Patisserie des Halles.

LES VINS DE FRANCE: Selections in this wine shop range from the inexpensive to the pricey, from *vin ordinaire* going for several dollars to upward of $99 for a rare vintage. Wine tastings are held here to sample the offerings (note that a charge is levied for each taste). Other wares include wine glasses with a World Showcase theme, books about wine, bottle openers and toppers, aprons, candy, kitchenware, and soaps. There's a big barrel of ice cold beer, too. Dig in for a sudsy treat.

HOT TIP!

Don't try to fit all of the World Showcase movies into one day, especially if you are traveling with kids.

MOROCCO

Nine tons of tile were handmade, hand cut, and shipped from Morocco to Epcot to create this World Showcase pavilion. To capture the unique quality of this North African nation's architecture, Moroccan artisans came to Epcot to practice the mosaic art that has been a part of their homeland for thousands of years. Koutoubia Minaret, a detailed replica of the famous prayer tower in Marrakesh, stands guard at the entrance. A courtyard with a fountain at the center leads to the medina (Old City). Between the traditional alleyways and the more modern sections are the pointed arches and swirling patterns of the Bab Boujeloud gate, a replica of the one that stands in the city of Fez. An ancient working waterwheel irrigates the gardens, and the motifs repeated throughout the buildings include carved plaster and wood, tile, and brass. Mo'Rockin takes over the courtyard, with musicians playing lively Western music with an Arabic twist. (Entertainment varies.)

THE BRASS BAZAAR: Interspersed among the decorative brass plates in this store are ceramic pitchers, planters, pots, ornate bottles of rosewater, serving sets, colorful maps, wooden collectibles, books, framed prints, baskets, tiles, couscous, hummus, and tabbouleh mixes, lamps, spices, and other Moroccan selections.

PHOTO BY JILL SAFRO

EPCOT

THE ART OF HENNA: In the market for a temporary henna body decoration? Look no farther than this cozy corner of the Morocco pavilion. Henna "tattoos" are available—for a fee—in various sizes and designs between 1 P.M. and 9 P.M. daily (hours may vary).

CASABLANCA CARPETS: In addition to handmade carpets, this store features an intriguing and eclectic selection of merchandise. Look for lamps, fez hats, jewelry, books, and more.

MARKETPLACE IN THE MEDINA: Hand-woven baskets, sheepskin wallets and bags, assorted straw hats, drums, sandals, postcards, scarves, jewelry, clothing, and small carpets are among the available wares.

SOUK AL MAGREB: This waterside enclave located on the World Showcase promenade spills over with hand-crafted keepsakes. Look for Moroccan lamps, baskets, and leather goods. One can also find rosewater and coffee products.

TANGIER TRADERS: This is the place to shop if you're in the market for a fez, woven belts, leather sandals and purses, and other traditional Moroccan clothing and accessories.

JAPAN

Serenity rules in Japan. Except, of course, when the pavilion resounds with traditional music performed by a drum-playing duo or group.

The landscaping, designed in accordance with traditional symbolic and aesthetic values, contributes to the pavilion's peaceful mood. Rocks, which in Japan represent the enduring nature of the Earth, were brought from North Carolina and Georgia (since boulders are scarce in the Sunshine State). Water, symbolizing the sea (which the Japanese consider a life source), is abundant; the Japan pavilion garden has a stream and pools inhabited by koi (fish). Evergreen trees, which in Japan are symbols of eternal life, are here in force.

Disney horticulturists created this very Japanese landscape using few plants native to that country because the climate there is so

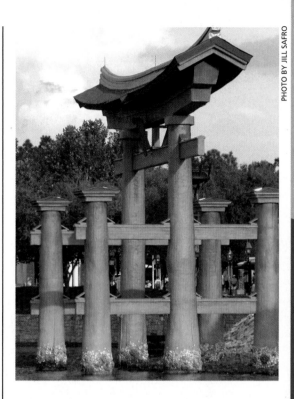

PHOTO BY JILL SAFRO

different from that of Florida. Among the few trees here native to Japan are the sago, near the courtyard entrance to the Katsura Grill; the two Japanese maple trees, identifiable by their small leaves, not far away (near the first stairway from the promenade on the left side of the courtyard as you face it); and the prickly monkey-puzzle trees, near the walkway to the promenade, on The American Adventure side of the pagoda. Needle-sharp thorns make the latter the only species of tree that monkeys cannot climb.

The pagoda was modeled after an eighth-century structure located in the Horyuji Temple, in Nara, Japan. The striking torii gate on the shore of World Showcase Lagoon derives from the design of the one at the Itsukushima shrine in Hiroshima Bay.

BIJUTSU-KAN GALLERY: Housing a changing cultural display, this small museum has offered, among other exhibitions, the Kitahara Collection of Tin Toys, featuring toys produced between 1880 and 1970. Recently, the exhibit "Spirited Beasts—From Ancient Stories to Anime Stars" was featured here.

MITSUKOSHI MERCHANDISE STORE: There are kimonos, T-shirts bearing Japanese characters, fine jewelry, and a selection of bowls and vases meant for flower arranging for sale at this spacious store set up by Mitsukoshi— a four-centuries-old retail firm.

DID YOU KNOW?

The five stories of the Japanese pagoda symbolize earth, water, fire, wind, and sky.

The shop features a wall of sake selections, plus chopsticks, bonsai, jewelry, china, paper fans, and origami products. There is also a bounty of snacks, candies, and teas. You can even get an oyster and hope to find a pearl! The pleasant atmosphere and variety of merchandise make this establishment a most rewarding experience for both the casual browser and the serious shopper. The building's design was inspired by the Gosho Imperial Palace, which was constructed in Kyoto in 794 A.D.

THE AMERICAN ADVENTURE

BIRNBAUM'S ★BEST★ When it came to creating The American Adventure, the centerpiece of World Showcase, Disney Imagineers were given relatively free rein. So the 110,000 bricks of the imposing Colonial-style structure that houses a stirring show, fast-food restaurant, and shop are the real thing —patiently crafted by hand from soft Georgia clay.

The show inside stands out because of its wonderfully evocative settings, its detailed sets, and the 35 superb Audio-Animatronics players, some of the most lifelike ever created by the Disney organization. A stellar a cappella vocal group called Voices of Liberty periodically serenades guests in the building's foyer. By all means, catch a performance.

THE AMERICAN ADVENTURE SHOW: One of the most ambitious Epcot attractions, this 26-minute presentation celebrates the American spirit from the nation's birth. Beginning with the arrival of the pilgrims at Plymouth Rock and their harsh first winter on the western shore of the Atlantic, the Audio-Animatronics narrators— a lifelike Ben Franklin and a thoroughly convincing Mark Twain—recall key people and events in American history: the Boston Tea Party, George Washington and the grueling winter at Valley Forge, the influential abolitionist Frederick Douglass, the celebrated nineteenth-century Nez Perce chief Joseph, and many more. The Philadelphia Centennial Exposition is remembered, along with women's rights campaigner Susan B. Anthony, telephone inventor Alexander Graham Bell, and the steel giant and philanthropist Andrew Carnegie. Naturalist John Muir converses onstage with Teddy Roosevelt. Charles Lindbergh, Rosie the Riveter, Jackie Robinson, and Walt Disney are represented. So are John Wayne, Lucille Ball, Margaret Mead, John F. Kennedy, Martin Luther King Jr., and Billie Jean King.

The idea is to recall episodes in history, both negative and positive, that contributed to the growth of the spirit of America, by engendering "a new burst of creativity" (in the designers' words) "or a better understanding of ourselves as partners in the American experience."

PHOTO BY JILL SAFRO

For information about how each of the many featured historical figures spoke during his or her lifetime, researchers contacted historians and cultural institutions—the Philadelphia Historical Commission, the State Historical Society of Missouri, the Department of the Navy's Ships Historical Branch, and others. When recordings were not available, educated guesses were made: Alexander Graham Bell's voice was created on the basis of contemporary comments about his voice's clarity, expressiveness, and crisp articulation, combined with the fact that his father taught elocution. A highlight of the show is the majestic music played by the Philadelphia Symphony Orchestra.

Seats toward the front of the house afford the best view of the Audio-Animatronics figures. If you have some extra time before the show, be sure to read the inspirational quotes that line the walls—Jane Addams, Charles Lindbergh, Herman Melville, and Ayn Rand are among the prominent Americans who are quoted.

AMERICAN HERITAGE

GALLERY: Inside the pavilion (on the right side of the grand lobby), the addition of this art gallery brought Epcot's grand total to six. Its current exhibition is from the The Kinsey Collection. The exhibit features more than 40 pieces of art, artifacts, books, and sculptures that, together, tell an inspirational story of African-American history.

HOT TIP!

While all of the seats in the American Adventure theater provide good views, the sound quality is best in the middle and toward the front.

HERITAGE MANOR GIFTS: Visit this shop to find Americana in all of its red-white-and-blue glory. Gifts include T-shirts, tote bags, pillows, tri-corner hats, flags, and books about U.S. history. "Made in America" merchandise includes wine, fragrances, barbecue sauce, pasta sauce, and jam.

THE AMERICA GARDENS THEATRE: An ever-changing slate of live entertainment is presented throughout the year in this lakeside amphitheater in front of the American Adventure pavilion. Showtimes are posted at the theatre and in the park Times Guide. Be sure to note the pruning of the western sycamores overhead: The old-fashioned pollarding method used, which involves trimming the treetops flat and allowing the lower branches to interlock, produces a thick canopy. The flower beds are planted appropriately with fragrant red, white, and blue blossoms. How patriotic!

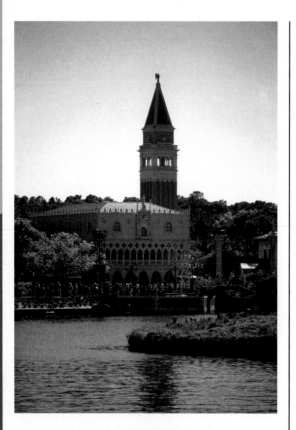

ITALY

The arches and cutout motifs that adorn the World Showcase reproduction of the Doge's Palace in Venice are just the more obvious examples of the attention to detail lavished on the individual structures in this relatively small pavilion. The angel perched atop the scaled-down campanile was sculpted on the model of the original, right down to the curls on the back of its head. It was then covered with real gold leaf, despite the fact that it was destined to be set almost 100 feet in the air.

The other statues in the complex, including the sea god Neptune presiding over the fountain in the rear of the piazza, are similarly exact. And the pavilion even has an island like Venice's own, its seawall appropriately stained with age, plus moorings that look like barber poles, with several distinctively Venetian gondolas tied to them. St. Mark the Evangelist is also remembered, together with the lion that is the saint's companion and Venice's guardian. These can be seen atop the two massive columns that flank the small arched footbridge that connects the island to the mainland. The only deviation from Venetian reality is the alteration of the site of the Doge's Palace in reference to the real St. Mark's Square.

The quaint pavilion is equally interesting from a horticultural point of view. The island boasts kumquat trees, citrus plants typical of the Mediterranean, and a couple of olive trees that can be seen on the sidewalls of the Enoteca Castello shop. Originally located in a Sacramento, California, grove, the olive trees arrived in Florida via flatbed truck a bit slimmer than when they started out. (Arizona border inspectors decreed that the trees be trimmed to the ten-foot width required by state law; therefore, the ancient olives were shorn en route. The hardy trees survived, leaving only their scars to remind visitors of the ordeal; the darker bark is what remains of the original, while the lighter areas are new growth.) The tall, narrow trees that stand like dark columns are Italian cypresses, which are common in their native country.

ENOTECA CASTELLO: This shop on the edge of the piazza features a selection of red and white Italian wines. Items such as cappuccino makers, wine glasses, olive oil, spices, chocolate, cookies, espresso, cookbooks, and decorative bottle toppers are also on hand. It's also possible to purchase an ice cold Italian beer.

IL BEL CRISTALLO: There is an abundance of sports-themed apparel and accessories, plus purses, wallets, and bags, inside this shop (just off the promenade on the Germany side of the piazza). Other featured wares include scarves, ties, fragrances, and jewelry. This shop also boasts a large assortment of exquisite, hand-crafted Venetian masks (which range in price from about $30 to $500).

GERMANY

There are no villages in Germany quite like this one. Inspired by various towns in the Rhine region, Bavaria, and the German north, it boasts structures reminiscent of those found in urban enclaves as diverse as Frankfurt, Freiburg, and Rothenburg. There are stair-stepped rooflines and towers, balconies and arcaded walkways, and so much overall charm that the scene seems to come straight out of a fairy tale. The beer hall to the rear is almost as lively as the one at Munich's famed Oktoberfest, especially late in the evening. The shops, which offer a range of merchandise from wine and sweets to ceramics and cuckoo clocks, toys, and books—and even art—are so tempting that it's difficult to leave the area empty-handed.

The elements that constitute the Germany pavilion are described here as they would be encountered while walking counterclockwise around the cobblestone-paved central plaza. (The plaza is known as the St. Georgsplatz, after the statue at its center.) St. George, the patron saint of soldiers, is depicted with a dragon that legend says he slew during a pilgrimage to the Middle East.

Try to time your World Showcase peregrinations to take you to the Germany pavilion on the hour, when the handsome, specially designed glockenspiel at the plaza's rear can be heard chiming in a melody composed specifically for the pavilion.

DAS KAUFHAUS: This two-story structure, whose exterior is patterned after a merchants' hall known as the Kaufhaus (located in the German town of Freiburg im Breisgau), stocks athletic apparel and footwear. Film and sundries are also available.

DER TEDDYBAR: Located adjacent to the Volkskunst clock shop, this is a toy store with a bit of flair. It's home to one of Walt Disney World's best selections of toys, including an assortment of stuffed keepsakes. Duffy the Disney Bear is among the plush items sold here.

KARAMELL-KÜCHE: This caramel kitchen tempts with housemade sweet treats made from buttery caramel. Many items are made fresh in an on-stage kitchen. Favorites include fresh strawberries hand-dipped in chocolate and drizzled with gooey caramel, caramel-filled chocolate chip cookies, crunchy apples enveloped in caramel, chocolate or vanilla cupcakes

topped with rich vanilla icing with a dab of caramel on top, packaged Werther's candies, and much more. Don't come here on an empty stomach—you could go bankrupt! It took over the space formerly occupied by Glas und Porzellan in late 2010.

KUNSTARBEIT IN KRISTALL: This shop to the left of the Biergarten features Austrian and crystal jewelry (including tiaras), beer mugs, wine glasses in traditional German tints of green and amber, and crystal decanters. Glassware may be etched on the spot.

STEIN HAUS: The "house" is really a tiny shop that sells German steins and collectibles.

VOLKSKUNST: Small and appealing, this establishment is filled with a burgher's bounty of German timepieces, plus a smattering of other items made by hand in the rural corners of the nation. As for cuckoo clocks, some are small and unobtrusive, while others are so immense that they'd look appropriate only in some cathedral-ceilinged hunting lodge. This is also one place to pick up a traditional German beer stein, wine accessories, bells, books, crafts, and music.

WEINKELLER: Germany's wine shop, situated between the cookie shop and the crystal shop toward the rear of St. Georgsplatz, offers about 50 varieties of German wine. Wine tastings are held here daily (for a fee). The selection includes vintages meant for everyday consumption, plus a few fine estate wines. These are white (with a few exceptions), because white wine constitutes the bulk of Germany's vinicultural output. (Only 20 percent of German bottlings are red.) The setting itself is quite attractive—low-ceilinged and cozy, and full of cabinets embellished with carvings of vines and bunches of grapes.

DIE WEIHNACHTS ECKE: A shop like this can set a visitor's mind to thoughts of Christmas —even on the hottest dog days of summer. Ornaments, decorations, and gifts manufactured by various German companies line the shelves of this store.

One item of note is the pickle ornament. Pickle ornaments are considered a special Christmas tree decoration by many families in Germany. Historically, it is always the last ornament hung on the tree, with a parent hiding it among the other ornaments. Kids gleefully search for it—and the one who finds it gets a special little present from St. Nicholas, left for the most observant child.

CHINA

Dominated by the Disney equivalent of Beijing's Temple of Heaven and announced by a pair of banners that proclaim good wishes to passersby (the Chinese characters translate to: "May good fortune follow you on your path through life" and "May virtue be your neighbor"), this pavilion conveys a level of serenity that offers an appealing contrast to the hearty merriment of the bordering Germany and the gaiety of nearby Mexico. Part of this quiet environment is the by-product of the soothing, traditional Chinese music. The gardens also make a major contribution. They are full of rosebushes native to China, and there is a century-old mulberry tree (to the left of the main walkway into the pavilion), with a pomegranate tree and a wiggly-looking Florida native known as a water oak nearby.

Village Traders

Located between the Germany and China pavilions, this open-air shop sports a selection of hand-crafted gift items from Africa, India, Spain, and Australia. Browse through such souvenirs as wind chimes, handbags, hats, and, of course, T-shirts.

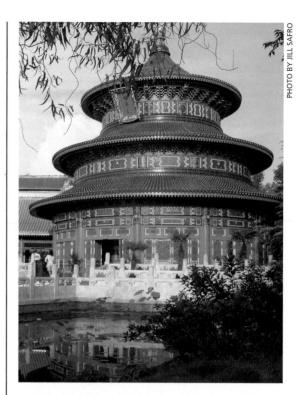

PHOTO BY JILL SAFRO

The number of stones in the floor of the pavilion's main structure is not random; the center stone is surrounded by nine stones because nine is considered a lucky number in China. Around the edge of the outer room rise 12 columns—because 12 is the number of months in the year and the number of years in a full cycle of the Chinese calendar. Be sure to stand on the round stone in the center: Every whisper is amplified.

A spacious emporium is devoted to Chinese wares, and two restaurants add to the overall atmosphere. However, all this is secondary to the motion picture shown inside the Temple of Heaven—a Circle-Vision 360 film that is one of the most diverting World Showcase attractions. Keep in mind that this is a standing-room-only viewing experience.

REFLECTIONS OF CHINA: This cinematic presentation shows the beauties of a land that few Epcot visitors have seen firsthand—and does it so vividly that it's possible to see the film twice and still not fully absorb all the wonderful sights.

The film replaced *Wonders of China*, the Circle-Vision 360 movie that played at Epcot's China pavilion since 1982. Just as with the original, filmmakers used nine cameras to capture cultural and scenic images that wrap completely around viewers. The majestic tour includes some rural stops, plus visits to cities such as Hong Kong, Macau, Beijing, and Shanghai.

The film includes footage of many landmarks, such as the 2,400-year-old Great Wall and Tiananmen Square, as well as some newer cultural developments. Overall, it showcases the majesty of this ancient country and highlights some of the more dramatic changes that have taken place over the past 20 or so years. Note that the theater has no seats.

HOUSE OF WHISPERING WILLOWS: When exiting, pass by the House of Whispering Willows, an exhibit of ancient Chinese art and artifacts. Changed periodically, it invariably includes fine pieces from well-known collections.

HOUSE OF GOOD FORTUNE: This vast emporium, located off the narrow, charming Street of Good Fortune, offers a huge assortment of merchandise—lanterns, hats, wine, beer, fine jewelry, silk robes, shoes (including a variety of sandals and flip-flops), prints, porcelain items, tea sets, candles, neckties, Buddah statues, chess sets, reading glasses, and much more. Kids adore the huge variety of panda-themed plush toys. Handheld fans may be personalized on the spot.

NORWAY

Set between Mexico and China is Norway, a pavilion added to the World Showcase mix in 1988. Built in conjunction with many Norwegian companies, the pavilion celebrates the rich history, folklore, and culture of one of the Western world's oldest countries.

The cobblestone town square is an architectural showcase of the styles of such Norwegian towns as Bergen, Alesund, and Oslo. There's also a Norwegian castle fashioned after Akershus, a 14th-century fortress still standing in Oslo's harbor; the castle here houses the Akershus restaurant. Few can resist walking into the bakery for a taste of its treats. In a show of modernity, a statue of Norway's legendary marathoner Grete Waitz stands behind the bakery. Shops stock handicrafts and folk items: hand-knit woolens, wood carvings, and glass and metal artwork.

For a free tour of the pavilion in addition to a crash course in Norwegian culture and architecture, stop by the Norway Tourism desk.

MAELSTROM: FP+ Visitors tour Norway by boat—16-passenger, dragon-headed longboats inspired by those Eric the Red and other Vikings used a thousand years ago. The five-minute voyage begins in a tenth-century Viking village, where a ship is being readied to head out to sea.

Seafarers then find themselves in a mythical Norwegian forest, populated by trolls who cause the boats to plummet backward, through a maelstrom, to the grandeur of the Geiranger fjord, where the vessel nearly spills over a waterfall. After a plunge through a rocky passage, the boats wind up in the stormy North Sea. As the boats pass the legs of an oil rig, the storm calms and a coastal village appears on the horizon. Note that this attraction features an appearance by a three-headed troll and has some moments of darkness that tend to frighten tots.

Survivors disembark and enter a movie theater, where the journey continues on-screen for five more minutes. If you wish to skip the flick, walk straight through the theater to exit before the movie begins.

STAVE CHURCH GALLERY: Inside the wooden stave church, there is a small exhibit that explores Norwegian culture. It's interesting (and sad) to note that only about 30 stave churches remain in Norway today.

THE PUFFIN'S ROOST: Norwegian gifts—sweaters, activewear, Viking helmets, trolls, toys, fragrances, jewelry, candy—are the wares for sale here. Want to pose for a photo with a giant troll? You've come to the right place!

PHOTO BY JILL SAFRO

MEXICO

The tangle of tropical vegetation surrounding the great pyramid that encloses this pavilion and the Mexican restaurant at the lagoon's edge on the promenade provides only the barest suggestion of the charming area inside.

Dominated by a re-creation of a quaint plaza at dusk, the pyramid's interior is rimmed by balconied, tile-roofed, colonial-style structures. Crowding a fountain area is a quartet of stands selling Mexican handicrafts, and to the left is a shop stocked with other handsome wares. A Mariachi Cobre band keeps things lively—as does the tequila bar. To the rear, the San Angel Inn serves authentic fare. Behind it, a waterborne attraction features a whirlwind Mexican tour.

Take a look at the cultural exhibit inside the pyramid entrance on the way in. Note that the building itself was inspired by Meso-American structures dating from the third century A.D.

GRAN FIESTA TOUR STARRING THE THREE CABALLEROS: Big news! The Three Caballeros (that would be Donald Duck, Panchito, and José Carioca) are reuniting for a big show in Mexico City! Unfortunately, the ever mischievous Donald has gone missing in Mexico—and guests join Panchito and José in the quest to find him. In doing so, you will be treated to a whirlwind (if slow-moving) boat tour of the country. The cheery montage of film, props, and Audio-Animatronics figures is reminiscent of It's a Small World, though on a smaller scale.

LA PRINCESSA DE CRISTAL: Presented by Arribas Brothers and located next to the entrance to the Gran Fiesta Tour Starring the Three Caballeros attraction, this alcove offers crystal tiaras, character figurines, rings, bracelets, necklaces, and glass slippers. If you're lucky, you'll get to watch glass blown by an in-house artisan.

PLAZA DE LOS AMIGOS: Even if you're not in a buying mood, make a point of stopping by this bustling marketplace. Brightly colored paper flowers, sombreros, malachite, baskets, mariachi music (available on CD), and pottery make this mercado (market) at the plaza's center as bright and almost as lively as one in Mexico itself. The brilliantly hued papier-mâché piñatas that figure strongly in the scenery here are quite popular. Authentic pre-Columbian figures are on display. Also available for purchase are spices, salsa, liquors (mostly tequila), cocktail accessories, candy, and musical instruments.

EL RANCHITO DEL NORTE: Located on the lagoon side of World Showcase Promenade, this spot features gifts and souvenirs.

LA TIENDA ENCONTATA: Visit this store inside the pyramid and you'll discover jewelry, bags, and women's fashions.

SHOWCASE PLAZA

DISNEY TRADERS: Merchandise combining the charm of classic Disney characters and Epcot themes is the primary stock-in-trade. Sundries are also sold. This is also the park's "Duffy Central." Stop here for all things related to Duffy the Disney Bear.

PORT OF ENTRY: A shop carrying toddlers' and kids' clothing, girls' character dresses, plush dolls, and toys. There are a few clothing options for grown-ups, too.

Entertainment

Epcot presents an intriguing array of live performances each day, making it very important to consult a park Times Guide when you arrive. For updates, call 407-824-4321.

AMERICA GARDENS THEATRE: The lagoonside venue at The American Adventure pavilion hosts an ever-changing program of live entertainment, such as the popular Flower Power concert series presented during the annual Flower and Garden Festival. Check an Epcot Times Guide for specifics.

ILLUMINATIONS—REFLECTIONS OF EARTH: FP+ This nighttime spectacular presents the entire history of our planet in 13 minutes—from its creation to the present and a look toward the future. A dazzling mix of lasers, fireworks, fountains, and music, this show is a highlight of any Epcot visit.

The extravaganza, visible from anywhere on the World Showcase promenade, takes place nightly at closing time. There are excellent viewing locations all around the World Showcase Lagoon. Note that additional viewing areas have been added to the stretch between the Germany and China pavilions.

KIDCOT FUN STOPS: There is an activity area in each of the countries of World Showcase. These spots invite kids to play games and make colorful cut-outs of Duffy the Disney Bear.

WORLD SHOWCASE PERFORMERS: It's all but impossible to complete a circuit of World Showcase without catching performances en route. Keep an eye on the schedule and be sure to take in entertainment at each pavilion, often performed by natives of the country represented. Among the possibilities: worldly comedians, a Mexican mariachi band, an American a cappella group and a Fife & Drum corps, Moroccan belly dancers, a Canadian rock band, and more.

Holiday Happenings

During certain holidays, such as Easter Week, the Fourth of July, Thanksgiving, Christmas week, and New Year's Eve, Epcot usually offers extended hours and presents additional entertainment to celebrate the respective occasion.

Call 407-824-4321, or visit *www.disneyworld.com*, for schedules and details.

CHRISTMAS: Epcot is exceptionally festive throughout holiday season. The park celebrates Christmas with a gigantic tree and its popular candlelight choral processional.

The Candlelight Processional, a stirring presentation of traditional holiday songs, features a reading of the Christmas story by a celebrity narrator. This is a very popular event—and one of our favorites. See page 12 of the *Getting Ready to Go* chapter for details.

HOT TIPS!

- Start at a Fastpass+ kiosk to book Fastpasses for as many attractions as possible (if you haven't reserved Fastpass+ in advance).

- On your way into the park, pick up a free guidemap and a Times Guide. Consult the entertainment schedule first thing.

- Lines throughout Epcot are longest at midday and shortest in the early evening.

- During peak seasons, preferred reservation times at Epcot's table-service restaurants book quickly—make reservations as far in advance as possible. However, some tables may be available on a first-come, first-served basis (with a bit of a wait). Arrive a few minutes ahead of your reservation time.

- Most World Showcase restaurants seat guests until park closing. To make advance plans, call 407-WDW-DINE (939-3463).

- Check the Tip Boards in Innoventions Plaza and on both sides of Future World for wait times at the most popular attractions, and adjust your plans accordingly. And use Fastpass+ whenever possible.

- Interactive fountain areas at Epcot provide guests of all ages with an opportunity to cool off. Be sure to pack swimsuits (and water-proof diapers) for little ones who'll undoubtedly spend time splashing in the water.

- If you plan to play at ImageWorks, the interactive play area inside Imagination, take along the e-mail address of a friend. It may come in handy.

- Allow plenty of time to explore the hands-on exhibits at Innoventions East and West, and at ImageWorks in the Imagination pavilion.

- When it comes to park-hopping, Epcot is an ideal park to hop to. It's usually open late.

- FriendShip water taxis are unlikely to transport you across World Showcase Lagoon any faster than a brisk walk, but they are a peaceful, foot-friendly way to make the half-mile-plus journey.

Where to Find the Characters

Epcot Character Spot is a fantastic place to meet classic Disney characters. (It's located in Innoventions West in Future World.) Characters such as Mickey Mouse, Chip, and Dale host dinner at the Garden Grill restaurant in The Land pavilion in Future World. Disney princesses invite you to join them for a meal at Norway's Akershus Royal Banquet Hall. Snow White mingles at the Germany pavilion. Belle and Marie (from *The Aristocats*) visit France, Aladdin and Jasmine (Morocco), Mulan (China), Duffy, and others have been known to greet guests at World Showcase. Check an Epcot Times Guide for schedules and greeting locations.

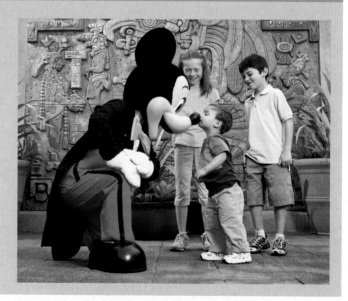

EPCOT

Hidden Mickeys

These are some of the most popular "Hidden Mickeys" at Epcot. How many can you find? Check the box when you spot each one!

❤ **Soarin':** Pay attention and you'll be rewarded with two Hidden Mickey sightings here. As you "fly" over the golf course, keep an eye on the golf ball as it hurtles toward you. Yep, Mickey's on the ball! ■

At the end of the ride, as you soar over Disneyland, the second burst of fireworks forms a Mickey. ■

❤ **Mission: SPACE:** When your ship lands on Mars, you may spy a Mickey on a rooftop to the right of the landing strip. (It's made of satellite dishes.) ■

After you exit the ride and enter the gift shop, look up in the center of the room to find a side profile of Mickey painted on the ceiling. ■

❤ **Mexico:** Toward the end of the Gran Fiesta Tour boat ride, you'll see a barge on your left. On that barge is a Hidden Mickey made of strategically arranged bongo drums. ■

❤ **Living with the Land:** As you walk through the queue, try to find the three bubbles on the large mural that come together to form a Hidden Mickey. (Hint: It's near the middle of the mural.) ■

About halfway through the ride, you may notice a water hose coiled into the shape of Mickey Mouse's noggin'. ■

❤ **American Adventure pavilion:** Look for a painting of early American settlers crossing a river with covered wagons. One of the wagon-pulling oxen has a Mickey near its left front leg. ■

❤ **Norway:** In the stave church's Vikings exhibit, find King Olaf II and examine his tunic for a blue Hidden Mickey close to his right thigh. ■

❤ **France:** Check out the meticulously pruned bushes on the canal side of the France pavilion— one of them is shaped like a classic Mickey. As you walk through the queue, try to find the three bubbles on the large mural that come together to form a Hidden Mickey. (**Hint**: It's near the middle of the mural.) ■

Be sure to eyeball the grates surrounding the trees near the entrance to Les Chefs de France. There are several HMs in the intricate grillwork. ■

While in France, pay close attention to the wedding party scene in the *Impressions de France* movie—there is a Hidden Mickey on a second-floor window! ■

❤ **Canada:** If you take a peek at the top of the totem pole, you'll spot a tiny, blue mouse. ■

❤ **The Seas with Nemo & Friends:** In Bruce's Shark World, look for two large posters—one titled "Did You Know?" and the other titled "Bruce's Shark World" (they are on opposite sides of the room). Each has an oyster in the lower right-hand corner that contains Mickey-shaped pearls. ■

❤ **Journey Into Imagination with Figment:** About halfway through the ride and as you move through Figment's house, look up in the bathroom. Figment's commode forms a Hidden Mickey with two red circles on the ground next to it. ■

❤ **Spaceship Earth:** In the Renaissance scene, look quickly to your left to find the first painter standing in front of a table (his back is to you). On the top left of the table, three white-paint circles form a Hidden Mickey. ■

Later in the ride, keep your eyes open for a Hidden "WDI" (the abbreviation for Walt Disney Imagineering) on the microphone of the radio broadcaster (on your left). ■

❤ **Germany:** Look up to spot three armor-wearing fellows festooning a facade to the right of the clock in St. Georgsplatz. The suit closest to the glockenspiel sports an H.M. ■

❤ **Canada:** It's easy to find the totem poles in this pavilion—but it's a bit more challenging to find the Hidden Mickey on the left one. ■

Specifics may change during 2015.

Where in the World?

All of the photos on this page were taken at Epcot. Do you know where? We challenge you to find all the spots where these images were shot and snap a photo for yourself as you discover each one. Happy hunting!

(For locations, turn to page 356.)

EPCOT

172

PHOTOS BY JILL SAFRO

Disney's Hollywood Studios

175 **Getting Oriented**

176 **Park Primer**

177 **Attractions**

185 **Shopping**

187 **Entertainment**

188 **Hot Tips**

D isney's Hollywood Studios—formerly (and famously) known as Disney-MGM Studios—has been described as "the Hollywood that never was and always will be." A bit hokey, perhaps—but also true. Enter the gates and the mosaic of flashy neon, chromed Art Deco, streamlined architecture, and star-gazing street characters immediately plunges you into the Hollywood of the 1940s. A nostalgic view of the movie-making capital has been combined with a variety of current TV- and movie-themed attractions and a delightful selection of eateries to create this Walt Disney World enclave. Throw in a character-laden nighttime spectacular, and the result is an entertainment wallop worthy of a rave review.

The Studios' water tower, known to punsters (for obvious reasons) as the "Earful Tower," is reminiscent of the structures looming over Hollywood studios of the Golden Age. Here, however, it gets that special Disney touch—it's capped by a Mouseketeer-style hat. In true Hollywood style, this established star has been somewhat upstaged by the most unlikely of attention grabbers: a haunted hotel stationed at the far end of Sunset Boulevard.

Since opening in 1989, the park continues to expand and evolve. Its eclectic lineup of classic attractions is joined by such thrillers as an enhanced (and scarier) Tower of Terror, the rollicking Rock 'n' Roller Coaster, a dynamic vehicle stunt show, and an explosive struggle between good and evil in Fantasmic! Each adds a whole new dimension to the Hollywood term "action."

- **A** Beauty and the Beast— Live on Stage
- **B** Fantasmic!
- **C** The Twilight Zone™ Tower of Terror
- **D** Rock 'n' Roller Coaster
- **E** The Magic of Disney Animation
- **F** Disney Jr.—Live on Stage!
- **G** Walt Disney: One Man's Dream
- **H** Voyage of The Little Mermaid
- **I** Toy Story Mania!
- **J** Studio Backlot Tour
- **K** American Film Institute Showcase
- **L** Honey, I Shrunk the Kids Movie Set Adventure
- **M** Muppet★Vision 3-D
- **N** Star Tours—The Adventures Continue
- **O** Indiana Jones™ Epic Stunt Spectacular
- **P** The Great Movie Ride
- **Q** Lights, Motors, Action! Extreme Stunt Show

Sunset Blvd.

Pixar Place

Hollywood Blvd.

Streets of America

▲Bus Transportation

Walt Disney World Resort Guest Boat Transportation ▲

Getting Oriented

Disney's Hollywood Studios, though festive, has a sprawling layout with no distinctive shape or main thoroughfare. As such, the Studios can be a bit of a challenge to navigate. Be sure to study a guidemap as you enter.

The park entrance is at Hollywood Boulevard. This shop-lined avenue leads straight to Hollywood Plaza, address of the Studios' Chinese Theater, a replica of Grauman's Theatre that doubles as the site of The Great Movie Ride. Walking along Hollywood Boulevard, toward the plaza, you will come to Hollywood Junction. Here, a wide, palm-fringed street known as Sunset Boulevard branches off to the right.

Stroll down Sunset Boulevard and you'll come across The Hollywood Hills Amphitheater, home of Fantasmic! and Rock 'n' Roller Coaster. At the street's far end is The Hollywood Tower Hotel, home of The Twilight Zone™ Tower of Terror. The strip is also graced with shops, the Sunset Ranch Market, and the Theater of the Stars amphitheater, where Beauty and the Beast —Live on Stage is performed daily.

Stand in Hollywood Plaza, facing the Great Movie Ride, and you'll notice an archway just off to your right. This leads to Animation Courtyard. Pixar Place, the area on the street veering off to the left of Animation Courtyard, leads to Toy Story Mania! and the Studio Backlot Tour. If you turn left off Hollywood Boulevard and go past Echo Lake, you're on course for such attractions as Indiana Jones Epic Stunt Spectacular and Star Tours—The Adventures Continue. Just beyond Star Tours there is another entertainment zone, near the Streets of America (in the backlot area). The biggies to see here: Muppet★Vision 3-D; Lights, Motors,

Action!—Extreme Stunt Show; and the Honey, I Shrunk the Kids Movie Set Adventure.

HOW TO GET THERE

Take Exit 64B off I-4. Continue about half a mile to reach the parking area. Take a tram to the park entrance.

By WDW Transportation: From the Swan, Dolphin, Yacht & Beach Club, and BoardWalk: boat, or walkway. From Fort Wilderness: bus from the Outpost stop. From Epcot: boat or bus. (Fitness-minded folks may hoof it from Epcot's International Gateway exit to the Studios. The walk takes about 30 minutes.) From Magic Kingdom, Animal Kingdom, all other Walt Disney World resorts and the resorts on Hotel Plaza Boulevard: bus only. From Downtown Disney: bus to any WDW resort and transfer to a Studios bus or boat.

PARKING

All-day parking at the Studios is $17 for day visitors (free to WDW resort guests and annual passholders). Trams circulate regularly, providing transportation from the parking area to the park entrance. Be sure to note the section and the aisle in which you park. The parking ticket you receive allows for re-entry to the parking area throughout the day.

HOURS

Disney's Hollywood Studios is usually open from about 9 A.M. until about one hour after sunset. During certain holiday periods and summer months, hours are extended. It's best to arrive about 20 minutes before the posted opening time—guests are often let in early. Depending on the season, some stage shows do not open until late in the morning.

Admission Prices

ONE-DAY BASE TICKET
(Restricted to use only in Disney's Hollywood Studios. Prices do not include sales tax and are expected to rise in 2015.)

Adult $95
Child* $89

* 3 through 9 years of age; children under age 3 free

Park Primer

BABY FACILITIES

Changing tables and facilities for nursing mothers can be found at the Baby Care Center at Guest Relations near the park entrance.

CAMERA NEEDS

The Darkroom on Hollywood Boulevard stocks a variety of camera supplies, including memory cards, batteries, camera cases and straps, disposable cameras, and more.

DISABILITY INFORMATION

Most Walt Disney World attractions, restaurants, shops, and shows are accessible to guests using wheelchairs. Additional services are available for guests with visual or hearing disabilities. Stop by the park's Guest Relations window when you arrive. For a detailed overview of the services offered, including transportation, parking, attraction access, and more, pick up a free copy of the *Guide for Guests with Disabilities*. For more information, refer to the *Getting Ready to Go* chapter of this book.

FIRST AID

Minor medical problems can be handled at the First Aid Center, located next to Guest Relations at the park entrance.

INFORMATION

Guest Relations, located just inside the park entrance, has free guidemaps, Times Guides, and an ever-resourceful staff. To make same-day dining arrangements for certain Studios eateries, head over to the booth at the junction of Hollywood and Sunset boulevards.

LOCKERS

Lockers, found by Oscar's Super Service, just inside the park entrance, cost $9 per day for large lockers, $7 a day for small ones (plus a $5 refundable deposit) for unlimited use. They may be rented from the Crossroads of the World kiosk, directly across from Oscar's classic pickup truck. Your receipt entitles you to a locker at any other WDW theme park on the same day (not including the deposit).

LOST CHILDREN

Report lost children at Guest Relations and alert a Disney employee to the problem.

LOST & FOUND

Located at Guest Relations, near the park entrance. To report lost items after your visit, call 407-824-4245.

MONEY MATTERS

There is an ATM just outside the park entrance, near Keystone Clothiers, by Min and Bill's Dockside Diner, and inside the Pizza Planet Arcade. In addition to U.S. currency, credit cards (American Express, Visa, Discover, JCB, Diner's Club, and MasterCard), traveler's checks, Disney gift cards, MagicBand bracelets (backed up with a major credit card), and WDW resort IDs are accepted at most park locations.

PACKAGE PICKUP

Shops can arrange for purchases to be transported to Package Pickup, next to Oscar's Super Service (by the park entrance), where they can be picked up later. The service is free.

SAME-DAY RE-ENTRY

Be sure to wear your MagicBand (if you used it for admission) or retain your ticket if you plan to return later the same day.

SECURITY CHECK

Guests entering Disney theme parks will be subject to a security check. Bags will be searched by Disney security personnel before guests are permitted to enter the park.

STROLLERS & WHEELCHAIRS

Strollers, wheelchairs, and Electric Conveyance Vehicles (ECVs) may be rented from Oscar's Super Service, inside the park entrance on the right. Cost for strollers is about $15; about $12 for wheelchairs. A double stroller costs $31. A Length of Stay rental ticket saves wheelchair and stroller renters $2 a day. Cost for ECVs is $50, plus a $20 refundable deposit. Keep the receipt—it can be used on the same day for a replacement at any theme park. Quantities are limited (especially for ECVs).

TIP BOARDS

Check the Tip Boards at the junction of Hollywood and Sunset boulevards and on the Streets of America to learn the waiting times for the most popular attractions in the park.

The Main Attractions

Disney's Hollywood Studios has a brand of attractions altogether unique. Some offer guests behind-the-scenes looks at the creative and technical processes that generate television, movies, and animation. Others go so far as to allow guests to gain a bit of showbiz experience along with the insight. Still others present popular characters and stories in new forms—from stage shows to thrill rides.

Many shows and attractions are presented at scheduled times, or keep shorter hours than the park itself—consult a Times Guide or the park's Tip Board for starting times.

The Twilight Zone™ Tower of Terror FP+

BIRNBAUM'S ★BEST★ The Hollywood Tower Hotel is the creepy home of a spectacular thrill ride. On the facade of the 199-foot-tall building hangs a sparking electric sign. As the legend goes, lightning struck the building on Halloween night in 1939. An entire guest wing disappeared, along with an elevator carrying five people.

The line for the ride runs through the lobby, where dusty furniture, cobwebs, and old newspapers add to the eerie atmosphere. As guests enter the library, they see a TV brought to life by a bolt of lightning. Rod Serling invites them to enter The Twilight Zone.

Guests are led toward the boiler room to enter the ride elevator. (This is your chance to change your mind about riding—ask an attendant to point you toward the "chicken exit.") Once you take a seat in the elevator, the doors close and the room begins its ascent. At the first stop, the doors open and guests peek down a corridor. Among the effects is a ghostly visit by the hotel guests who vanished. The doors close and you continue the trip skyward.

At the next stop, you enter another dimension, a combination of sights and sounds reminiscent of *The Twilight Zone* TV series. In fact, Disney Imagineers watched each of the 156 original *Twilight Zone* episodes at least twice for inspiration. This part of the ride is a somewhat disorienting experience, in part because the elevator moves horizontally.

What happens next depends upon the whim of Disney Imagineers, who have programmed the ride so that the drop sequence is chillingly random. At the top (about 157 feet up), passengers can look out at the Studios below. Once the doors shut, you plummet 13 stories. The drop lasts about two seconds, but it seems a whole lot longer.

Just when you think it's over, the elevator launches skyward, barely stopping before it plunges again. And again. As you exit, Rod Serling claims this is the kind of thing "they don't tell you about in any guidebook." It's been our privilege to prove him wrong.

From the time you are seated, the trip takes about five minutes. Note that you must be at least 40 inches tall to ride. It is not recommended for pregnant women, people with heart conditions, or with back or neck problems. Though thrilling (and scary), the drops are surprisingly smooth. Still, if you'd rather not experience the sensation of being a human yo-yo, sit this one out.

PHOTO BY JILL SAFRO

DISNEY'S HOLLYWOOD STUDIOS

Rock 'n' Roller Coaster Starring Aerosmith FP+

BIRNBAUM'S ★BEST The fastest roller coaster in Walt Disney World history is guaranteed to rock your world. Rock 'n' Roller Coaster is ideally suited for those who consider the Tower of Terror just a little on the tame side.

The indoor attraction reaches a speed of nearly 60 miles per hour—in 2.8 seconds flat. Other twists include two loops and a corkscrew—marking the first time Disney has turned guests upside down on American soil.

HOT TIP!

You'll need to stop at a locker (near the park entrance) before riding Rock 'n' Roller Coaster—there's no place to store loose articles in the ride vehicles.

The ride's premise is this: The rock band Aerosmith has invited you to a backstage party. The only thing standing between you and the big bash is a classically chaotic Los Angeles freeway.

To get to the party on time, you'll have to zip through the nighttime L.A. streets in a stretch limo. The ride vehicles (designed to resemble limousines) are equipped with a high-tech sound system (five speakers per seat make for a mega-decibel ride), and the remainder of the journey features rockin' synchronized sound—adding a very dramatic dimension to the roller coaster experience most daredevils have come to expect.

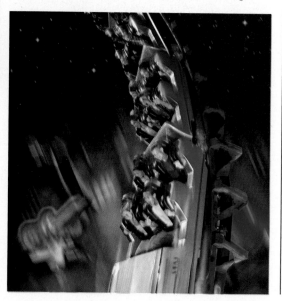

You must be free of back, neck, and heart problems to experience this topsy-turvy tour. Expectant mothers should sit this one out. Guests must be at least 48 inches tall to ride.

Beauty and the Beast– Live on Stage FP+

BIRNBAUM'S ★BEST Here's the show that inspired the Broadway musical. Several times each day, Belle, Gaston, Mrs. Potts, and the rest of the cast of the Disney film *Beauty and the Beast* come to life at the 1,500-seat Theater of the Stars, near the Tower of Terror, on Sunset Boulevard.

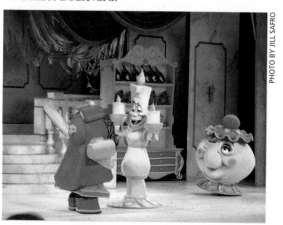

PHOTO BY JILL SAFRO

The 30-minute show is as entertaining as they come. The staging's just right and the music's simply addictive as it traces the classic tale—from Belle's dissatisfaction with her life in a small French town to the climactic battle between the staff of the Beast's castle and Gaston and the townspeople. Lumiere and friends perform the song "Be Our Guest" with a delightful display of dancing flatware. Check a park Times Guide for performance schedule.

The Magic of Disney Animation

This attraction gives guests an insider look at the creative process behind Disney's many animated blockbusters.

The majority of the action takes place in a theater. Here, you'll be greeted by a jovial, knowledgeable host and treated to a whimsical explanation of how Disney animators bring characters to life. This segment of the tour is cohosted by Mushu, the wisecracking little dragon from the film *Mulan*. After breezing past desks once used by animators, you'll be invited to take part in a group animation lesson. The capacity for this part of the tour is smaller than the rest, so you may have to wait a bit to get in. If you don't want to stick around, there's an area where you can lend your voice to an animated character in a movie clip, stations where you can paint characters using a computer, and a personality test to determine which Disney character you are most like.

There's a little treat at the end of the tour: Copies of some of the Academy Awards won by the Disney animation team are on display, along with drawings from famous films. Note that the working animation facility has been shuttered, so there are no actual animators to spy on anymore.

Before moving on, spend some time browsing at the Animation Gallery, where Disney animation cels, exclusive limited-edition reproductions, books, figurines, and many other Disney-themed collectibles are for sale.

Voyage of The Little Mermaid FP+

One of Disney's Hollywood Studios' most popular attractions, this is a 17-minute live musical production, adapted from the Disney animated classic. The show is presented in a theater with an underwater feel. In it, many of the film's beloved animated characters, such as Flounder and Sebastian, are brought to life by puppeteers. The show opens with a lively rendition of "Under the Sea," then animated clips from the movie are shown as performers join the puppets onstage.

Ariel is the star and performs songs from the film. Prince Eric makes an appearance, and an enormous Ursula glides across the stage to steal

PHOTO BY JILL SAFRO

Ariel's voice. Of course, as in the movie, the happy ending prevails. The story line is a little bit disjointed, hopping from scene to scene, and some of the signature songs are missing. However, most viewers are familiar with the film, so this choppiness doesn't detract much from the show.

There are many special effects, including cascading water, lasers, and a lightning storm that may be a bit frightening for very young children. Note that many of the effects are best enjoyed from the middle to the rear of the theater. Keep in mind that, although this is a Fastpass+ attraction, performances are still presented at scheduled times throughout the day. Current showtimes are always listed on the Times Guide (available at many locations throughout the park).

HOT TIP!

Don't miss the special tribute to the man who started it all: Walt Disney himself. The exhibit, entitled Walt Disney: One Man's Dream, is housed in a theater near the Pixar Place area of the park.

Disney Junior– Live on Stage! FP+

Fans of Disney Junior shows should enjoy this live, audience-participation production. It features several audience favorites—*Mickey Mouse Clubhouse, Doc McStuffins, Sofia the First,* and *Jake and the Never Land Pirates* (all the popular Disney Junior TV series). Familiar characters engage guests with stories, song, and dance as they visit each of the aforementioned Disney Junior realms. The fun culminates with a birthday party for Minnie Mouse. Very young guests tend to be the most enthusiastic members of the audience.

The performance space holds large crowds (of mostly tiny people) at a time. There are just a handful of seats, but there's plenty of room to sprawl out on the carpeted floor. This show is presented in the Animation Courtyard area of the theme park. The park Times Guide lists performance times.

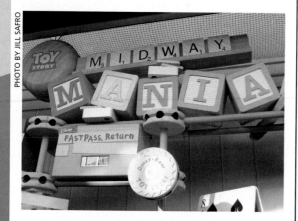

PHOTO BY JILL SAFRO

Toy Story Mania! FP+

BIRNBAUM'S ★BEST★ This engaging experience is an energetic, interactive toy box tour with a twist: Guests wear 3-D glasses as they take aim at animated targets with toy cannons. The adventure is about as high-tech as they come, yet rooted in classic midway games of skill. As points are scored, expect effusive encouragement from a cast of cheerleaders— *Toy Story*'s Woody, Buzz, Hamm, Rex, Trixie, and, of course, the Green Army Men.

Fans of the Magic Kingdom's Buzz Light-year's Space Ranger Spin will no doubt delight in this adventure, which takes the experience of the interactive attraction into a whole new dimension. As far as skill level goes, there's something for everyone at Toy Story Mania!— from beginners to seasoned gamers alike.

Note: This is a wildly popular attraction with guests of all ages. Get there as early in the morning as possible and try to snag a Fastpass+ assignment as soon as you can.

Studio Backlot Tour

Guests board a tram to learn about aspects of TV and movie production on this 30-minute tour. The first stop is a large, outdoor special-effects area. This zone features a water tank, and teaches guests how special effects can be created on a set.

Guests then travel to the backlot, where they get a look at the vast wardrobe department. More than 100 designers create costumes for Disney's movie, television, and other entertainment projects—and with 2.5 million garments for its workers, Disney World has the planet's largest working wardrobe. Famous costumes are on display.

Where in Central Florida can you find an active oil field in the middle of a dry, rocky, barren desert canyon prone to flash floods? In Catastrophe Canyon. As the guide will tell you, crews are filming a movie in which a backstage tram gets stuck in the canyon during a flash flood. But supposedly it's safe to go in because they're not filming today.

In a series of special effects, a rainstorm begins. Then there's an explosion, complete with flames that are so hot, even riders on the right side of the tram feel them, followed by a flash flood that is so convincing, it forces everyone to lean the other way. The road underneath the tram shifts and dips, lending even more reality to the adventure.

HOT TIP!

Guests on the left side of the tram may get wet at Catastrophe Canyon, while those on the right stay dry. Choose accordingly. And be sure to cover your cameras and other electronics.

From Catastrophe Canyon, the tram rides by the Streets of America, where reproduced building facades line urban streets. Though the brickwork looks authentic, these backless facades are constructed mostly of fiberglass and Styrofoam. The skyscrapers, including the Empire State Building and the Chrysler

PHOTO BY JILL SAFRO

Building, are actually painted flats. Forced perspective (the same technique that makes Cinderella Castle appear taller than it is) makes the four-story Empire State Building appear as if it were the actual 102-story structure. (The tram also passes near the Lights, Motors, Action!—Extreme Stunt Show theater. If there is a show in progress, warn little ones to cover their ears—it can be extremely noisy.)

The Backlot Tour has merits, but because there is no longer a working studio here, this attraction's heyday, like the Golden Age of Hollywood, lies predominantly in the past.

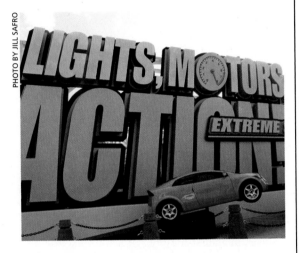

Lights, Motors, Action! Extreme Stunt Show

When it comes to action, this attraction takes the phrase "cut to the chase" quite seriously. Here, tires squeal and flames burst as cars hurtle over trucks and Jet Skis rocket from a canal. The overall guest experience is twofold: On the one hand, it is a thrilling display of seemingly death-defying feats; and on the other, it's an inside, backstage peek at how some of the movie magic happens.

Taking place in a huge theater beyond the Streets of America (on a site once occupied by Residential Street), the show is presented several times a day. Check a Times Guide for showtimes and arrive early (at least 15 minutes). This lavish show was originally presented at Disneyland Paris, where it is known as Moteurs . . . Action! Parts may be too loud or intense for some small children (for example, a stuntperson is [safely-but-dramatically] set on fire). Though most youngsters are truly thrilled by the brief appearances by Mater and Lightning McQueen, the four-wheeled stars of the Disney•Pixar film Cars.

American Film Institute Showcase

Though it is the final stop on the Backlot Tour, it is possible to visit this treasure chest of Hollywood memorabilia without taking the tour itself. Costumes, props, and set pieces used in recent, as well as classic, movies and television programs are on display in this ever-changing exhibit.

Although showcased items will be different when you visit the Studios, previous displays here have included Barbara Stanwyck's costume from *Sorry, Wrong Number*, the police car from *Dick Tracy*, an Academy Award won by the film *My Fair Lady*, concept artwork from *Toy Story*, and live-action sets and stop-motion puppets from *James and the Giant Peach*.

The Great Movie Ride FP+

Housed in a full-scale reproduction of historic Grauman's Chinese Theatre, this 19-minute attraction captivates guests' imaginations from the get-go. The queue area winds through a lobby and into the heart of filmmaking, where movie scenes are shown on a large screen.

The guided tour begins in an area reminiscent of the hills of Hollywood (which, as the

HOT TIP!

Parts of the Great Movie Ride are a more than little scary for young children, e.g., the dramatic guest appearance by a very lifelike Wicked Witch of the West.

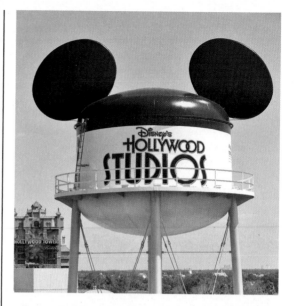

famous, now abbreviated, sign indicates, was once known as Hollywoodland) in its heyday. As a ride vehicle whisks guests under a vibrant marquee, they are transported to the celluloid world of yesteryear. About 60 dancing mannequins atop a cake greet guests in a replay of the "By a Waterfall" scene from the Busby Berkeley musical *Footlight Parade*.

Gene Kelly's memorable performance from *Singin' in the Rain* is the next scene, in which rain seems to drench the soundstage but does not dampen the spirits of the Audio-Animatronics representation of Mr. Kelly. (Gene Kelly personally inspected his likeness.) Then Mary Poppins and Bert the chimney sweep entertain (Julie Andrews and Dick Van Dyke, respectively), as Mary floats from above via her magical umbrella and Bert sings "Chim Chim Cher-ee" from a rooftop.

From the world of musical entertainment, guests segue to adventure. James Cagney re-creates his role from *Public Enemy* as the ride proceeds along Gangster Alley. A mob shoot-out begins and puts guests in the midst of an ambush. An alternate route leads to a Western town, where John Wayne can be seen on horseback eyeing some would-be bank robbers. When the thieves blow up the safe and flames pour from the building, heat can be felt from the trams.

As the ride vehicle glides into the spaceship from *Alien*, Officer Ripley guards the corridor while a slimy monster threatens riders from

overhead. (Note that this and other scenes may upset young children.)

The legendary farewell from *Casablanca* is also depicted, complete with a lifelike Rick and Ilsa. (Ingrid Bergman's daughter Isabella Rossellini once brought her kids here to "see Grandma.") Guests are moved from the airfield to the swirling winds of Munchkinland, where a house has just fallen on the Wicked Witch of the East. Her sister, as portrayed by Margaret Hamilton, appears in a burst of smoke. This Audio-Animatronics figure is impressively realistic (and scary). But happy endings prevail, and guests follow Dorothy and company along the Yellow Brick Road to the Emerald City of Oz. As the ride draws to a close, guests view a montage of memorable moments from classic films.

Timing Tip: If the queue extends outside the building, you're in for a long wait. It takes about 25 minutes to reach the ride vehicles once you've entered the theater.

HOT TIP!

The American Idol™ Experience attraction packed up its microphones and closed its doors in late 2014.

Walt Disney— One Man's Dream

Follow Walt Disney from "Mickey Mouse to the Magic Kingdoms" in this multi-media exhibit next to Voyage of The Little Mermaid attraction. Among the treasures included in this tribute to the man behind the mouse are Walt's second-grade school desk, the original Audio-Animatronics Abraham Lincoln from the 1964 New York World's Fair, *Mickey Mouse Club* props, Jungle Cruise and Spaceship Earth models, costumes from *Mary Poppins*, and more.

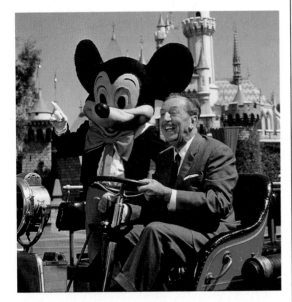

Cap off your trip down memory lane with a screening of *In Walt's Words*. The 15-minute film, presented in a theater in the back of the gallery, is hosted by Julie Andrews. Seating is on a first-come, first served basis.

Indiana Jones™ Epic Stunt Spectacular FP+

Earthquakes, fiery explosions, and assorted other dramatic events give guests some insight into the science of movie stunts and special effects at this 2,000-seat amphitheater. Stunt people re-create scenes from Indiana Jones films to demonstrate the skill required to keep audiences on the edge of their seats. Show director Glenn Randall, who served as stunt coordinator of *Raiders of the Lost Ark, E.T.,* and *Jewel of the Nile,* calls the show "big visual excitement." But the 30-minute show isn't all flying leaps. Guests also see how the elaborate stunts are pulled off—safely—while the crew and an assistant director explain what goes on both in front of and behind the camera.

In one segment, a dramatic scene from *Raiders of the Lost Ark* is staged. A 12-foot-tall rolling ball chases a Harrison Ford look-alike out of the temple. The steam and flames are so intense that the audience can feel the heat. The crew then dismantles the set, revealing the

remarkable lightness of movie props, as assistants roll the ball uphill for the next show.

In a scene at a busy "Cairo" street market, "extras" chosen from the audience play the famous scene in which Indiana Jones pulls a gun while others are fighting with swords. The explosive action continues and leads to a desert finale in which the hero and his sweetheart make a death-defying escape.

There are moments during this show when audience members might wonder if something has actually gone wrong. But by revealing tricks of the trade, the directors and stars show that what appears to be dangerous is actually a safe, controlled bit of movie magic.

Star Tours—The Adventures Continue FP+

BIRNBAUM'S ★BEST★ Inspired by George Lucas's blockbuster series of Star Wars films, this beloved attraction—which originally opened in 1989—just got even better! A new Star Tours experience touched down in 2011, complete with a new story line and eye-popping technology. The 3-D experience offers guests the opportunity to ride on StarSpeeders, the exact same type of flight simulator used by military and commercial airlines to train pilots.

The action takes place in the time period between the two sets of Star Wars trilogies. A galaxy of trouble awaits Jedi wannabes, but fear not—the Force will be with you. The best part? There are more than 50 different adventures, so you never know where the Force will take you.

This is a turbulent trip—seat belts are definitely required. Passengers must be free of back problems, heart conditions, motion sickness, and other physical limitations to ride. Guests under 40 inches tall and kids younger than 3 may not ride. Pregnant women must skip this one.

Muppet★Vision 3-D FP+

BIRNBAUM'S ★BEST★ One of the most entertaining attractions at the Studios, this 3-D movie is quite remarkable. As with so many other Disney theme park attractions, much of the appeal is in the details. A funny 12-minute pre-show gives clues about what's to come. Once inside the theater, many will notice that it looks just like the one from Jim Henson's classic TV series *The Muppet Show*.

Even the two curmudgeonly fellows, Statler and Waldorf, are sitting in the balcony, bantering with each other and offering their typically critical commentary on the show.

The production comes directly from Muppet Labs, presided over by Dr. Bunsen Honeydew —and his long-suffering assistant, Beaker—and introduces a new character, Waldo, the "Spirit of 3-D." Among the highlights is Miss Piggy's solo, which Bean Bunny turns into quite a fiasco. Sam Eagle's grand finale leads to trouble as a veritable war breaks out, culminating with a cannon blast to the screen from the rear balcony, courtesy of everyone's favorite Swedish Chef.

The 3-D effects, spectacular as they may be, are only part of the show: There are appearances by live Muppet characters, fireworks, and lots of funny details built into the walls of the huge theater. Including the pre-show, expect to spend about 29 minutes with Kermit and company. Shows run continuously throughout the day. Note that guests must wear 3-D glasses to enjoy this show. If your child is too young to keep the glasses on, skip this Muppet encounter.

PHOTO BY JILL SAFRO

Honey, I Shrunk the Kids Movie Set Adventure

The set for the backyard scenes of the classic Disney movie has been re-created as an oversize, soft-surface playground. Enter it and experience the world from an insect's (or shrunken kid's) point-of-view.

Blades of grass soar 30 feet high, paper clips are as tall as trees, and LEGO bricks are practically big enough to live in. There are caves to explore and many climbing opportunities (tremendous tree stumps and sprawling spiderwebs are among the better ones). A giant squirt

toy also provides entertainment as it sprays water on unsuspecting guests, as does a super-sized puppy snout. The props make everyone look and feel as though they were, indeed, shrunk by *Honey, I Shrunk the Kids*' Professor Wayne Szalinski. This "adventure" holds the most appeal for younger guests (the experience can be a little intimidating for grown-ups). Strollers must be parked outside the play zone. (The quarters can get a bit cramped here as it is!)

HOT TIP!

Even if you plan to skip Fantasmic!, it's good to know when it's being presented. Plan to hit the exit about 15 minutes after the 26-minute show is scheduled to begin. That way you'll beat the potential post-show bottleneck at the park exit. Showtimes are listed in the Times Guide. Pick one up at the park entrance or in any of a number of shops.

Shopping

Hollywood Boulevard

CELEBRITY 5 & 10: Modeled after a 1940s Woolworth's, this large shop carries housewares such as pillows, towels, teapots, aprons, and Mickey ice-cube trays, plus items that can be personalized—including Mouse ears.

COVER STORY: A small area located just through The Darkroom, this is the place to pick up your picture if you've had it taken by any of the park photographers.

CROSSROADS OF THE WORLD: In the middle of the entrance plaza, Mickey Mouse keeps watch from atop this Hollywood Boulevard landmark. The kiosk deals mostly in pins, but has some souvenirs and sundries. This is also the place to stop if you'd like to rent a locker.

THE DARKROOM: The Art Deco facade of this shop features a giant camera, so it's easy to find. Cameras (including the disposable kind) and photography accessories are sold here.

PHOTO BY JILL SAFRO

KEYSTONE CLOTHIERS: Women's and men's fashions and accessories are Keystone Clothiers' specialties of the house.

L.A. CINEMA STORAGE: A great source for kids' clothing and toys for infants, toddlers, and small children. Many items, such as watches and candy, feature classic Disney characters.

MICKEY'S OF HOLLYWOOD: The place to find character shirts, hats, plush toys, watches, socks, bags, books, and sunglasses, plus items emblazoned with the Studios park logo.

MOVIELAND MEMORABILIA: This kiosk, located just to the left of the Studios' main entrance, stocks shoes, bags, stuffed toys, hats, sunglasses, key chains, and other souvenirs.

OSCAR'S SUPER SERVICE: In addition to renting strollers and wheelchairs, Oscar stocks diapers, strollers (to buy), snacks, sundries, soft drinks, and souvenirs.

PHOTO BY JILL SAFRO

Sunset Boulevard

LEGENDS OF HOLLYWOOD: Modeled after the Academy Theater, which was built in Inglewood, California, in 1939, this store offers items featuring classic Disney characters, plus MagicBand accessories.

MOUSE ABOUT TOWN: The best source for clothing (for the whole family) featuring the famed mouse subtly embroidered onto apparel. Expect to find hats, ties, shirts, jackets, pajamas, accessories, and more.

ONCE UPON A TIME: This shop's exterior replicates the Carthay Circle Theatre in Hollywood, where *Snow White and the Seven Dwarfs* premiered in 1937. The cheery store specializes in children's apparel, plush toys, and souvenirs with Disney touches.

PLANET HOLLYWOOD SUPERSTORE: This shop sells items branded with the P.H. logo. Look for T-shirts, hats, mugs, bottle openers, rain gear, and more.

ROCK AROUND THE SHOP: Survive the Rock 'n' Roller Coaster and earn the right to shop here. Look for music-related items, such as drumsticks and rock star Mickey Mouse toys.

SUNSET CLUB COUTURE: A sophisticated selection of fashion accessories (including limited-edition watches), plus apparel with a Mickey theme.

SUNSET RANCH: This open-air shop carries Disney character hats, totes, and apparel, plus sunscreen, disposable cameras, memory cards, and assorted sundries.

SWEET SPELLS: This shop, which is within the Beverly Sunset building, has a super selection of candy, cookies, and other ooey, gooey snack items. The caramel apples are to die for.

TOWER GIFTS: Inside the Hollywood Tower Hotel, near the ride exit, this spot specializes in Hollywood Tower Hotel merchandise.

VILLAINS IN VOGUE: Look for souvenirs featuring your favorite Disney bad boys and girls—with an emphasis on characters from Tim Burton's *The Nightmare Before Christmas*. The shop also sells Disney's Vinylmation collectibles, cookies, candy, and other snacks.

Beyond the Boulevards

AMERICAN FILM INSTITUTE SHOWCASE: This shop, at the exit of the Studios Backlot Tour, features gifts themed to classic movies and Disney's Hollywood Studios. Fans of the old Sid Cahuenga's One-of-a-Kind Shop should enjoy perusing merchandise once proffered by Mr. Cahuenga: autographed photos of sports and matinee idols and an assortment of Hollywood mementos.

ANIMATION GALLERY: Don't overlook this pleasant shop in the Animation Building, where limited-edition figurines, Disney animation cels, books, statues, Vinylmation figurines, and other

collectibles ensure great browsing, even if buying isn't on your mind.

THE DISNEY STUDIO STORE: Expect to find T-shirts, hats, and accessories inspired by Disney films at this Animation Courtyard shop.

IN CHARACTER: In front of the Voyage of The Little Mermaid, this costume shop has everything a child needs to dress like a Disney princess—plus dolls, pillows, and plush toys.

INDIANA JONES ADVENTURE OUTPOST: Next to the Indiana Jones attraction, you'll discover adventure clothing, as well as memorabilia emblazoned with the Indy insignia.

SPECIAL FX MAKE-UP: Wanna get your face painted like a cat, puppy, princess, superhero or something equally festive? Head here. Most paint jobs cost about $15.

STAGE 1 COMPANY STORE: Situated near the exit of Muppet★Vision 3-D, guests can find toys, shirts, and other merchandise with the likenesses of Kermit the Frog, Miss Piggy, Fozzie Bear, and other Muppet characters, as well as items featuring Mickey and pals.

TATOOINE TRADERS: A shop near the Star Tours exit, Tatooine Traders offers intergalactic souvenirs themed to *Star Wars*, as well as the Star Tours attraction.

THE WRITER'S STOP: This nook next to Sci-Fi Dine-In Theater has specialty coffees, souvenirs, and reading material—plus fresh-baked cookies.

Where to Eat in the Studios

A complete listing of eateries at the Studios—full-service restaurants, fast-food emporiums, and snack shops—can be found in the *Good Meals, Great Times* chapter. See the Disney's Hollywood Studios section, beginning on page 260.

Entertainment

In these parts, it's always showtime. The following list is a good indication of the Studios' stage presence. As always, we advise that you check a park Times Guide for schedules.

CITIZENS OF HOLLYWOOD: This troupe of enthusiastic performers infuses Hollywood Boulevard with old-time, Tinseltown ambience. Would-be starlets searching for their big break, fans seeking guests' autographs, and gossip columnists chasing leads entertain daily.

JEDI TRAINING ACADEMY: *Star Wars* fans and Jedi-wannabes can learn the ways of the Force right here in Disney World. A Jedi Master is on hand to teach guests dos and don'ts of using a light saber, as well as helping them fend off an unexpected march of Stormtroopers. Expect a special appearance by one notable Dark Lord who'll attempt to lure you to the dark side. "Younglings" ages 4 through 12 may participate.

Holiday Happenings

The park usually stays open extra late to mark holidays such as New Year's Eve, the Fourth of July, and Christmas. During these times, lots of special entertainment is often in store. Call 407-824-4321 for up-to-the-minute schedules.

BIRNBAUM'S BEST **CHRISTMAS:** The Osborne Family Spectacle of Dancing Lights is the Studios' twinkling homage to the season. The display featuring millions of lights is a perennial favorite. It's usually presented on the Streets of America. For 2015 status updates, visit *www.disneyworld.com*.

Trip the Light Fantasmic!

BIRNBAUM'S BEST FP+ Fantasmic!, a lavish musical production, plays on select nights at The Hollywood Hills Amphitheater on Sunset Boulevard. A dramatic mix of fireworks, fountains, lasers, and Disney characters, it invites guests to take a peek into the dream world of Mickey Mouse.

Though similar to its Disneyland counterpart, half of this 26-minute production is original. The action follows Mickey through a series of dreams. In the first dream, he appears on a mountain, shoots fireworks from his fingertips, and conducts an orchestra of colorful fountains. (Guests seated up front get spritzed.) Soon, Mickey is plagued by nightmares as Disney villains take over his dreams. (This has been known to scare small children.) In the end, the Mouse and his pals prevail (of course!).

Seating begins about 90 minutes before showtime—though some guests line up even earlier. Check a Times Guide for the schedule. We recommend sitting toward the back—the view is good and it's easier to get out after the show. There is standing room, too. After the finale, plan to sit for a bit. It can take 20 minutes for the crowd to exit the theater.

Timing Tip: The show is presented on select nights. Check a Times Guide for the schedule during your visit. On nights when Fantasmic is presented twice, see the later show. Afterward, as the masses exit the park, take some time to browse the shops that keep their doors open after hours.

HOT TIPS!

- Unless you actually enjoy waiting in line, get Fastpass+ assignments whenever you can.

- The line for The Great Movie Ride is generally the longest early in the morning. It thins a bit later in the day.

- Some attractions keep shorter hours than the park itself. Check a Times Guide when you arrive. It lists current hours and schedules.

- Check the Studios' Tip Board often to get an idea of showtimes and crowds.

- Visit Rock 'n' Roller Coaster, Tower of Terror, and Toy Story Mania! early in the day, before crowds build up.

- Hoping to meet Doc McStuffins and Sofia the First? Know that this is the only WDW park in which they appear.

- For a table-service meal, make a reservation before you arrive at the park, or by visiting Hollywood Junction or these park eateries: 50's Prime Time Cafe, Mama Melrose's Ristorante Italiano, Hollywood Brown Derby, Sci-Fi Dine-In Theater, or Hollywood & Vine. For reservations, call 407-WDW-DINE (939-3463) up to 180 days ahead of your preferred dining date.

- The shops on Hollywood Boulevard are open about half an hour past park closing.

- Tower of Terror is a popular attraction with long lines. Use Fastpass+ whenever possible. And never ride immediately after a meal.

- Your tot may love the Muppets, but if he or she won't wear the glasses necessary to enjoy Muppet★Vision 3-D, skip the attraction.

- Park hoppers take note: There is a water taxi link between Disney's Hollywood Studios and Epcot. The boat docks to the left as you exit the Studios. You may also reach Epcot, as well as all other parks, by bus. Ambitious athletes may choose to walk. (It'll take you about 20 to 30 minutes to make the trip on foot.)

- Fantasmic! is now offered on most nights. Check a Times Guide to see when it will be offered during your visit. Know that it may be canceled due to inclement weather.

- Many attractions and shows stop admitting guests prior to the park's closing time (and some don't open until a few hours after the park does). Check a Times Guide for schedules. Attractions that you may enter up until the last minute include The Twilight Zone™ Tower of Terror, The Great Movie Ride, Rock 'n' Roller Coaster, Muppet★Vision 3-D, and Star Tours—The Adventures Continue.

- If you choose to skip Fantasmic!, plan to exit the park before the show ends. This way, you'll avoid the inevitable bottleneck at the exit. If you're watching the show, consider making your exit before the big finale.

- Toy Story Mania! is a tremendously popular attraction. If you hope to experience it without sacrificing 60 to 120 minutes waiting in the standby line, get a Fastpass+ assignment as soon as possible. Good luck!

Where to Find the Characters

You'll find Disney Channel characters in Animation Courtyard. Woody, Jessie, Bullseye, and other *Toy Story* friends may be spotted on Pixar Place. *Cars* and *Monsters, Inc.* characters greet guests on the Streets of America—as do Phineas and Ferb. Mickey mingles with park-goers in several locations, including Animation Courtyard. He often appears at the park entrance when the park opens, too. Chip, Dale, and Donald Duck have been known to join him. Characters sometimes mingle with guests in the area in front of the Studios' Arch, too.

Hidden Mickeys

These are some of the most popular "Hidden Mickeys" at Disney's Hollywood Studios. How many can you find? Check the box when you spot each one.

❤ **Front Entrance Gates:** This is an easy one. Simply look for Mr. Mouse in the grillwork of the gates at the entrance. ■

An even easier one? Look up to spot the water tower that's become a symbol of the park. It's capped with a gigantic pair of Mouse Ears! (Hence the name Earful Tower.) ■

❤ **Rock 'n' Roller Coaster:** In the pre-show room, look on the floor on the right side of the room just in front of the guitar stand to see some wire coiled into a Hidden Mickey. ■

❤ **Star Tours—the Adventures Continue:** Keep an eye on the folks walking past the "window" in the second room you enter while waiting for the attraction. One of the droids sports mouse ears. ■

There's a Hidden Mickey in the shop at the ride's exit, too—on the front panel of a counter. ■

❤ **Twilight Zone™ Tower of Terror:** Take a peek at the balcony in the lobby, and you may spot a row of Mickeys. ■

Then, as you watch the pre-show, pay close attention to the "disappearing guests." The little girl is clutching a plush Mickey Mouse. ■

❤ **Mama Melrose's Ristorante Italiano:** As you enter, look for the Dalmatian in the waiting area. One of its spots is Mickey-shaped. ■

❤ **Stage 1 Company Store:** Inside the store, locate a tall bureau with paint cans on the top (the shelves are covered with Disney hats for sale). On the desk area, you'll find a green Hidden Mickey. ■

❤ **The Hollywood Brown Derby:** Look for two Hidden Mickeys in the cloud mural outside the restaurant. One is on the left side, above the red Stage 5 sign. ■

The other can be found on the far upper right-hand side. ■

❤ **Cover Story:** There is a sign in the window of this Hollywood Boulevard shop that says "Melrose." Find it, then look below it for a pattern that creates many Hidden Mickeys in the store's structure. ■

❤ **The Great Movie Ride:** Pay attention to the posters on the left as you enter the gangster area of the ride. When you see a poster for the film *The Public Enemy*, look in the lower left corner to find Mickey's shoes (they are brown) and his tail poking out from under the poster. ■

You can also spot Mickey Mouse in the Indiana Jones room (aka The Well of Souls). He's hiding in the hieroglyphics on the wall to the left of the ride vehicle. ■

❤ **Studio Backlot Tour:** After the stunt demonstration, as you enter the prop shop, pay attention to a yellow refrigerator on the right side in the first aisle to find a silver Hidden Mickey. ■

During the tour, check out Walt Disney's plane. One Mickey is rather obvious, the other is a bit more subtle. ■

❤ **Muppet★Vision 3-D:** Mickey first appears in a test pattern in the lobby. ■

Next you'll notice him in balloon form during the show's finale. ■

As you exit, you'll see a poster detailing Five Reasons to Return Your 3-D Glasses. Take a close look at the artwork beside number 2. It has a Hidden Mickey! ■

Outside of the attraction, "Director" Gonzo is balancing on a Hidden Mickey raft in the Miss Piggy fountain. Can you spot him? ■

❤ **Pizza Planet:** First, find the mural inside this arcade/restaurant near Muppet★Vision 3-D. (It's in the arcade area.) Then locate the moon in the mural. Can you spot Mickey's profile? (Hint: He's just to the left of an alien hanging from the ceiling.) ■

Specifics may change during 2015.

Where in the World?

All of the photos on this page were taken at Disney's Hollywood Studios. Do you know where? We challenge you to find all the spots where these images were shot and snap a photo for yourself as you discover each one. Happy hunting! (For locations, turn to page 356.)

(For locations, turn to page 356.)

DISNEY'S HOLLYWOOD STUDIOS

190

PHOTOS BY JILL SAFRO

Disney's Animal Kingdom

193 Getting Oriented

194 Park Primer

195 Attractions

205 Shopping

206 Entertainment

206 Hot Tips

With a mix of lush landscapes, thrilling attractions, and close encounters with exotic animals, this is clearly a theme park raised to a different level of excitement. Here, guests do more than just watch the action—they live it. They become paleontologists, explorers, and students of nature. And if, by doing so, they leave with nothing more than a great big smile, Disney will have accomplished one of its major goals. But many guests come away with a little bit more: a renewed sense of respect for our planet and for the life-forms we share it with (not to mention a few boffo souvenirs).

The shows and attractions at Disney's Animal Kingdom are meant to engage, entertain, and inspire. They immerse guests in a tropical landscape and introduce them to creatures from the past and present—as well as a few that exist only in our collective imagination.

The park, which is accredited by the Association of Zoos and Aquariums, is home to more than 1,700 animals representing 250 different species. Most of the creatures are of the animate variety, as opposed to the Audio-Animatronics kind. Despite that, you won't see many beasts behind bars here. Instead, you'll go on safari and see a menagerie of wild critters living in spacious habitats, with remarkably few separations visible to the naked eye.

The following pages will help you get the most out of your visit to Disney's Animal Kingdom. It is, after all, a jungle out there.

AFRICA

A Kilimanjaro Safaris

B Pangani Forest
Exploration Trail

C Wildlife Express
to Rafiki's Planet Watch

D Rafiki's Planet Watch

E Festival of the Lion King

DISCOVERY ISLAND

F The Tree of Life

G Discovery Island Trails

H It's Tough to be a Bug!

ASIA

I Flights of Wonder at Caravan Stage

J Maharajah Jungle Trek

K Kali River Rapids

L Expedition Everest

DINOLAND U.S.A.

M Dinosaur

N The Boneyard playground

O Finding Nemo—The Musical

P Chester & Hester's Dino-Rama!

Getting Oriented

Though Disney's Animal Kingdom encompasses about five times the area of its Magic counterpart, one need not be in training for the Olympics to tackle it. (Most of the land is reserved for non-homo-sapien critters.) By all estimates, pedestrians rack up about the same amount of mileage in one day here as they do in a day at Epcot.

The park's layout is relatively simple: a series of sections, or "lands," connected to a central hub. In this case, the hub is Discovery Island (formerly known as Safari Village), an island surrounded by a river, and home to the Tree of Life, the park's icon. A set of bridges connect Discovery Island with other lands: the Oasis, DinoLand U.S.A., Asia, and Africa.

As you pass through Animal Kingdom's entrance plaza, you approach the Oasis. Feel free to meander at a leisurely pace, absorbing the soothing ambience of a thick, elaborate jungle, or you can proceed more quickly and plan to revisit this relaxing region later on. Each of several pathways deposits you at the foot of a bridge leading to Discovery Island. As you emerge from the Oasis, you'll see the awe-inspiring Tree of Life, a 14-story Disney-made tree, looming ahead. The massive tree, which stands near the middle of the island, is surrounded by Discovery Island Trails.

To the southeast lies DinoLand U.S.A., home of countless prehistoric animals, a fossil dig, a high-spirited stage show called Finding Nemo—The Musical, and an attraction that's sure to induce a mammoth adrenaline surge: Dinosaur. Behind Discovery Island and to the northwest is Africa, where guests may go on an African safari, explore a nature trail, and take the Wildlife Express train to Rafiki's Planet Watch, the park's research and education center.

Asia is northeast of Discovery Island. Here, guests come face-to-face with the Yeti (aka Abominable Snowman) on the Expedition Everest thrill ride, encounter real tigers on the exotic Maharajah Jungle Trek, and take a daring journey through the rainforest on a raft at the splashy Kali River Rapids.

HOW TO GET THERE

Take Exit 65 off I-4. Then follow the signs to Disney's Animal Kingdom. Trams run between the parking lot and the main entrance.

By WDW Transportation: From all Walt Disney World resorts: buses. From Downtown Disney: bus to any resort or the TTC, then transfer to an Animal Kingdom bus. From the Magic Kingdom: ferry or monorail to the TTC, then bus to Animal Kingdom. From Epcot, Disney's Hollywood Studios, and the resorts on Hotel Plaza Boulevard: buses.

PARKING

All-day parking at Animal Kingdom is $17 for day visitors (free to Walt Disney World resort guests with presentation of resort ID, MagicBand, or Annual Pass). Trams circulate regularly, providing transportation from the parking area to the park entrance. Be sure to note the section and aisle in which you park. Also, be aware that the parking ticket allows for re-entry to the parking area throughout the day.

HOURS

Although hours are subject to change, the gates are generally open daily from about 9 A.M. until about 5 P.M. During certain holiday periods and the summer months, hours may change. It's best to arrive up to a half hour before the official opening time. For current schedules, call 407-824-4321, or visit *www.disneyworld.com*.

Admission Prices

ONE-DAY BASE TICKET
(Restricted to use only in Disney's Animal Kingdom. Prices do not include sales tax and are likely to rise in 2015.)

Adult	$95
Child*	$89

* 3 through 9 years of age; children under age 3 free

Park Primer

BABY FACILITIES

Changing tables and facilities for nursing mothers can be found at the Baby Care Center on Discovery Island, near Creature Comforts. It's also possible to purchase certain necessities, such as formula and diapers, at this facility.

CAMERA NEEDS

Basic supplies such as memory cards, batteries, camera straps and cases, and disposable cameras can be purchased at Animal Kingdom shops such as Garden Gate Gifts, Disney Outfitters, Duka La Filimu, Mombasa Marketplace, and Chester and Hester's Dinosaur Treasures.

DISABILITY INFORMATION

Nearly all of the Animal Kingdom attractions, shops, and restaurants are accessible to guests using wheelchairs. Additional services are available for guests with visual or hearing disabilities. The *Guide for Guests with Disabilities* provides a detailed overview of the services available, including transportation, parking, and attraction access. (For more information, refer to the *Getting Ready to Go* chapter of this book.)

FIRST AID

Minor medical problems can be handled at the First Aid Center, located on Discovery Island on the northwest side of the Tree of Life, near Creature Comforts.

INFORMATION

Guest Relations, located just inside the park entrance, is equipped with guidemaps, Times Guides, and a helpful staff. Free guidemaps are also available in many shops.

LOCKERS

Lockers are located just inside the main entrance area, near Guest Relations. Cost is $9 for large lockers, $7 for small ones (plus a $5 refundable deposit) for unlimited use all day.

LOST & FOUND

The department is located at Guest Relations, just inside the park entrance. To report lost items after your visit, call 407-824-4245. We recommend affixing contact information to valuables. That'll make them easier to track.

LOST CHILDREN

Report lost children at the park's Baby Care Center, on Discovery Island, or alert the closest Disney employee to the matter.

MONEY MATTERS

There is an ATM at the park entrance and another in DinoLand. Currency exchange is done at Guest Relations. Disney Dollars, in $1, $5, and $10 denominations, are also available at Guest Relations. In addition to cash, credit cards (Disney Visa, American Express, Diner's Club, Discover Card, JCB, MasterCard, and Visa), Disney gift cards, traveler's checks, and Disney resort IDs and MagicBands (backed up with a credit card) are accepted for admission and merchandise, and meals at most restaurants.

PACKAGE PICKUP

Shops can arrange for purchases to be sent to Garden Gate Gifts for later pickup or directly to a Walt Disney World resort (packages should be ready for pickup about three hours after purchase). The service is free.

SAME-DAY RE-ENTRY

Be sure to wear your MagicBand or retain your ticket if you plan to return later the same day. A hand-stamp is no longer necessary.

SECURITY CHECK

Guests entering Disney theme parks will be subject to a security check. Expect backpacks, parcels, purses, etc., to be searched.

STROLLERS & WHEELCHAIRS

Strollers, wheelchairs, and Electric Conveyance Vehicles (ECVs) may be rented at Garden Gate Gifts. The cost is $15 for strollers and $12 for wheelchairs (double strollers cost $31 a day). Length of Stay rentals yield a $2-per-day discount. It's $50 for ECVs, plus a $20 refundable deposit. Quantities are limited (and they run out early in the day). Keep your receipt; it may be used the same day to get a replacement here or at the other theme parks.

TIP BOARD

There is a Tip Board on Discovery Island, near Wilderness Explorer Headquarters. Check it to learn the wait times for popular park attractions.

The Oasis

Traditionally, one has to travel across a long, sunbaked stretch of desert in order to experience the soothing atmosphere of a tropical oasis. With that in mind, think of the Animal Kingdom parking lot as a concrete version of the Sahara. Once you've trekked across it, your journey takes you through the park's front gate and entrance plaza. What's that up ahead? Could it be a towering African tree? Here in Central Florida? It must be a mirage.

But, no. Within seconds you arrive at the Oasis, a thriving tropical garden filled with waterfalls, running streams, and lush vegetation. The transition is by no means a subtle one. Guests are immediately enveloped in a world of nature. The peaceful setting is most idyllic.

Though not a full-fledged "land" per se, this small jungle simply oozes atmosphere. It is thick and elaborate, and comes complete with critters. (Some are more difficult to spot than others. When searching for the naturally camouflaged creatures, remember to look up occasionally.) As park visitors walk along the pathways, they may catch glimpses of different kinds of animals, from deer and iguanas to anteaters and birds. As in the rest of Disney's Animal Kingdom park, there is the illusion that guests are walking among the wildlife.

The Oasis is at once an exciting and calming experience. It sets the stage for what's to come. Guests have several options once they've entered the Oasis. They can continue on a northerly path, making tracks toward the Tree of Life and across a bridge to Discovery Island. They can proceed at a more snail-friendly pace, keeping a tally of the various life-forms that slither by. Or they can simply take time to stop and smell the flowers.

> "I have learned from the animal world. And what everyone will learn who studies it is a renewed sense of kinship with the Earth and all of its inhabitants."
>
> — WALT DISNEY

Timing Tip: Making a trip through the Oasis is the only way to get in (and out of) Animal Kingdom. Some paths can become congested during the hours closest to opening and closing times. To beat the crowds, use a path to the left when you enter and exit the park.

Discovery Island

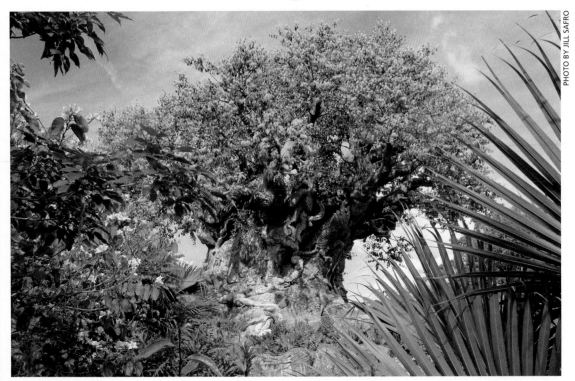

Once you've passed through the Oasis, you will come to a bridge spanning a peaceful river. The bridge leads to Discovery Island, an area at the center of Disney's Animal Kingdom and the hub from which all other realms of the park may be reached.

Discovery Island is defined by the brilliant colors, tropical surroundings, and equatorial architecture of Africa and the South Pacific. The facades of the buildings are all carved and painted based on the art of nations from around the world. Don't fail to notice all the bright, whimsical folk-art images representing various members of the animal kingdom.

This island is the shopping and dining center of Animal Kingdom. Many of the park's fast-food restaurants can be found here, including Pizzafari and Flame Tree Barbecue.

By far the most striking element standing on Discovery Island is the Tree of Life. It is on the map, but chances are you'll have no trouble finding it. Rising from the middle of the island and as tall as a 14-story building, the Tree of Life is hard to miss.

The Tree of Life

The Tree of Life is the dramatic 145-foot icon of Disney's Animal Kingdom. The imposing tree, with its swaying limbs and gnarled trunk, looks an awful lot like the real thing—from a distance. Up close, it's apparent that this is a most unusual bit of greenery. Covered with more than 325 animal images, it is a swirling tapestry of carved figures, painstakingly assembled by a team of artisans. The tree, though inorganic, stands as a symbol of the connected nature of life on Earth. We think Joyce Kilmer would have approved.

DISCOVERY ISLAND TRAILS: Walkways that snake around the Tree of Life allow guests to get a close-up view of the trunk and even play a game of "spot the animals." (The spiraling

---

HOT TIP!

Take a minute to study a guidemap as you enter Animal Kingdom. It will give you a sense of the layout. The park Times Guide provides information about showtimes for Festival of the Lion King, Finding Nemo— The Musical, and other attractions.

Wilderness Explorers

In the movie *Up*, Russell is a very dedicated—and decorated—Wilderness Explorer. He is on a constant quest to add to his merit badge collection. Now Animal Kingdom guests can be Wilderness Explorers, too. Start by heading to the W.E. Headquarters at the Oasis bridge. After taking the official pledge, guests receive field guides describing a variety of challenges. Complete a challenge and earn a badge! There are about 30 different badges to collect. There is no extra charge to become a Wilderness Explorer, and the badges are free. While targeted to the 7- to 10-year-old set, the challenges are fun for the whole family.

animal images go all the way to the top of the tree. You'll need binoculars if you hope to see them all.) Scattered about the tree's base is a variety of animal habitats. Animals can be seen in a very open, somewhat traditional park-like setting, with lush grass, trees, and other vegetation. Among the creatures you may recognize are kangaroos, deer, porcupines, tortoises, flamingos, otters, and exotic birds. Others to which you may be introduced for the very first time as you meander through the exhibits include ring-tailed lemurs (not quite monkeys' uncles, more like cousins). The trails are accessible from several points around the tree. *Note that this section of the park may not be open in all of 2015.*

BIRNBAUM'S ★BEST★ **IT'S TOUGH TO BE A BUG!:** FP+ Inside the trunk of the Tree of Life is a 430-seat auditorium featuring an eight-minute, animated 3-D film augmented by some surprising "4-D" effects. The stars of the show are the world's most abundant inhabitants—insects. They creep, crawl, and demonstrate why, someday, they just might inherit the Earth. It's a bug's-eye view of the trials and tribulations of their multi-legged world.

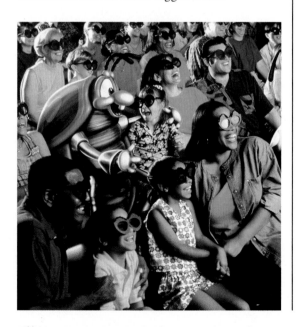

As guests enter The Tree of Life Repertory Theater, the orchestra can be heard warming up amid the sounds of chirping crickets. When Flik, the emcee (and star of *A Bug's Life*), appears, he dubs audience members honorary bugs and instructs them to don their bug eyes (3-D glasses). Then the mild-mannered ant introduces some of his not-so-mild-mannered cronies, including a Chilean tarantula, dung beetles, and "the silent but deadly member of the bug world"—the stink bug. What follows is a manic, often humorous, revue.

Note: The combination of intense effects and frequent darkness tends to terrify tots and young kids. And anyone at all leery of spiders, roaches, and their ilk is advised to skip the performance, or risk being seriously bugged.

WINGED ENCOUNTERS—THE KINGDOM TAKES FLIGHT: This show, which got off the ground in mid-2014, features flocks of colorful macaws. Because of their claws? No, because their macaws! (Sorry, we just couldn't resist a quote from the Enchanted Tiki Room.) Six types of the beautiful bird, some with wingspans of up to 60 inches, are included: hyacinth, green-winged, blue and gold, scarlet, blue-throated, and military. Expect them to swoop and soar overhead and over Discovery Island.

After the show, guests may interact with avian experts and learn how Disney is working to help conserve the endangered species' native habitats in South and Central America. Check a park Times Guide for performance times. Note that the open-air show may be canceled due to inclement weather.

Africa

The largest section of Animal Kingdom, Africa, is bigger than the Magic Kingdom all by itself. This 110-acre, truer-than-life replica of an African savanna is packed with pachyderms, giraffes, hippos, and other wild beasts. All guests enter Africa through Harambe, a village based on a modern East African coastal town. It is the dining and shopping center of Animal Kingdom's Africa.

The instant you walk across the bridge to Harambe, you are transported to Africa. Everything here is authentic, from the architecture to the landscaping to the merchandise in the marketplace. The result was achieved after Disney Imagineers made countless trips to the continent. After seven years of observing, filming, and photographing the real thing, they re-created it here in North America. It even feels a bit warmer here than it does at the other theme parks!

The animals that live here, however, are not re-creations. They are quite real, most varied, and extremely abundant. In fact, this chunk of land puts the animal in Animal Kingdom.

Kilimanjaro Safaris FP+

BIRNBAUM'S ★BEST★ The Kilimanjaro Safaris have something for everyone: lovely landscapes, majestic, free-roaming animals, and a thrilling adventure. It is everything you may expect from an actual trip to Africa, and (hopefully) more.

The 20-minute safari begins with a brief introduction from a guide who does double duty as your driver.

HOT TIP!
There's no need to stampede toward the Kilimanjaro Safaris ride first thing in the morning—the animals are out and active throughout the day. That said, if you do ride early, consider coming back later in the day. The beauty of this attraction is that you tend to see something new each time you ride.

Once you climb aboard the ride vehicle, look at the plates above the seat in front of you. They will help you identify the animals you see. And have those cameras ready.

PHOTO BY JILL SAFRO

As the vehicle travels along dirt roads, you'll spot free-roaming wild animals: zebras, antelope, hippos, elephants, warthogs, rhinos, lions, and more. Some animals wander near your vehicle, and others cross its path. (Relax. Only the harmless critters will approach. Others, such as lions and cheetahs, only appear to invade your safe, personal space.)

The majesty of the Serengeti may lull you into a state of serenity, but it's merely the calm before the storm. You'll soon be jostled and jolted as the vehicle crosses pothole-filled terrain and rickety bridges—one of which puts you close to a horde of sunbathing crocodiles.

If you're prone to motion sickness, back trouble, or have other physical limitations, you may want to sit this one out. The ride is a rather bumpy one.

Festival of the Lion King FP+

BIRNBAUM'S ★BEST★ In addition to rustling up grubs in their new neighborhood, the talented cast of *The Lion King* performs a 30-minute stage show in the new Harambe Theater.

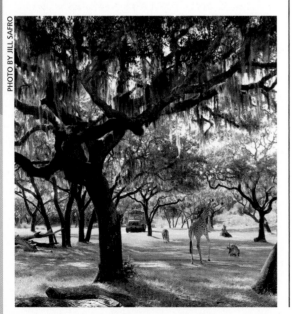

PHOTO BY JILL SAFRO

Presented in the round, this lavish musical revue is as bright and boisterous as they come. The dramatic opening features a parade of performers in colorful costumes. What follows is an intriguing, energetic interpretation of the

film, including songs, dances, and acrobatics. With the exception of Timon, who plays himself, lead characters are portrayed by humans draped in bold African costumes.

Songs include Scar's nasty version of "Be Prepared," as well as "The Circle of Life," and a rousing rendition of "The Lion Sleeps Tonight."

Timing Tip: Although this theater accommodates nearly 1,400 guests at a time, plan to arrive at least 45 minutes before a performance time.

Pangani Forest Exploration Trail

This self-guided walking trail winds past communities of gorillas and other rare African animals. Access it at the end of the Kilimanjaro Safaris or by the entrance in Harambe.

PHOTO BY JILL SAFRO

The first major stop on Pangani trail (the name of which translates to "place of enchantment" in Swahili) is the Research Station. The station contains exhibits, including naked mole rats. Just outside are a free-flight aviary and an aquarium teeming with fish. Not far away is the hippo exhibit, which provides close-up views of hippopotamuses both in and out of water.

Farther along the trail there is a scenic overlook point, where you can get an unobstructed view of the African savanna. This is also known

as the "Timon" exhibit, featuring a family of perky meerkats. Afterward, you may catch an up-close glimpse (through a glass wall) of a cavorting gorilla or two.

As you come to the end of the suspension bridge, you'll find yourself in a beautiful green valley. Congratulations! You've finally reached the gorilla area—an experience well worth the wait. (Note that you may have to wait a little bit longer for that first gorilla sighting. Our evolutionary cousins have been known to play hide-and-seek in the lush vegetation.)

Rafiki's Planet Watch

On the east side of the village of Harambe is the Harambe Train Station. That's where you board the Wildlife Express and experience a behind-the-scenes look at a Disney park while en route to Rafiki's Planet Watch.

As part of the 5½-minute, narrated trip, you'll glide past the buildings where animals sleep. All guests disembark at the Rafiki's Planet Watch station and cover the remaining distance on foot. (It's about a 5-minute walk.) Note that you'll have to reboard the train to return to Harambe.

While Animal Kingdom's stories often carry a conservation theme, this part really brings the message home. This is the park's conservation headquarters. It's also a veterinary lab, as well as the research and education hub. Exhibits are geared to spark curiosity about wildlife and conservation efforts around the world. Here are a few highlights:

Habitat Habit!: An outdoor discovery trail that yields glimpses of cotton-top tamarins, and helpful hints on how to share our world with all members of the animal kingdom.

Affection Section: An animal encounter area with critters (mostly goats) to see and touch. This is an enjoyable experience for young guests. Be sure to stop at the hand-washing station before leaving this area.

Conservation Station: The center of Disney's effort to promote wildlife conservation awareness. Inside, you'll find:

Animal Cams: Use these guest-operated video cameras to spy on gorillas, hippos, bats, and other critters throughout the park.

Animal Health & Care: A tour of veterinary labs and research facilities.

Rafiki's Planet Watch Video: An interactive video that provides guests information about endangered animals.

Song of the Rainforest: A thoroughly entertaining "3-D" audio show that surrounds guests with sounds of the rainforest.

Asia

HOT TIP!

Everyone and everything gets wet on Kali River Rapids. Items that simply must stay dry should be stored in a locker (across the pathway at the attraction's entrance) or with a non-riding member of your party.

On the far side of a Himalayan-style bridge, beyond an ancient temple, lies the tranquil village of Anandapur (Sanskrit for "place of delight"). The buildings' design was inspired by structures in Thailand, Indonesia, and other Asian countries known for their rich architectural history.

A product of Disney Imagineering, the village epitomizes the complex, enduring relationship between the animals and ecosystems of the Asian continent. The tiny village borders an elaborate re-creation of a Southeast Asian rainforest. As such, Disney's Asia is an ideal location for trekking through the lush jungle, shooting the rapids on a raging river, and gazing upon the multi-hued inhabitants of this treasured terrain.

Kali River Rapids FP+

BIRNBAUM'S ★BEST Before guests board rafts at Kali (pronounced KAH-lee) River Rapids, a wise voice admonishes that "the river is like life itself, full of mysterious twists and turns." What the voice doesn't say is that this particular river is also full of splashing water and a blazing inferno. This may be business as usual for some daring souls, but for most of us, these elements make for one dramatic, drenching adventure.

All guests begin the journey in the offices of Kali River Rapids Expeditions, a river rafting company. A slide show offers a look at the sometimes unscrupulous business of logging—how it has ravaged the rainforest and deprived

animals of habitats. But, thanks to ecotourism (among other things), there is hope. Peaceful voyages give people a new appreciation and sense of responsibility for this endangered land.

A 12-seater raft whisks "ecotourists" up a watery ramp and through an arching tunnel of bamboo. It proceeds onward, through a hazy mist and past remnants of an ancient shrine. As the raft moves along curves of the river, guests enjoy views of undisturbed rainforest.

The tranquility is shattered by a startling sight. A huge chunk of forest has been gutted by loggers. On both sides of the river, the forest has vanished. As guests absorb the image, they are besieged by more disturbing sights and sounds. Straight ahead, the river is choked with a tangled arch of burning logs—and the raft is headed straight for it. Suddenly, the rainforest isn't the only thing endangered.

Kali River Rapids is an especially soggy experience. It is the rare guest who leaves the ride without a thorough soaking. Should you wish to repel as much precipitation as possible, pack a plastic poncho. Stash valuables in a nearby locker while you ride (no charge).

Note: This is a bumpy adventure. In order to experience it, you must be at least 38 inches tall. It is not recommended for pregnant women, guests with heart conditions, people with back or neck problems, or anyone who wishes to stay dry.

Maharajah Jungle Trek

BIRNBAUM'S ★BEST Welcome to the jungle! The Maharajah Jungle Trek is a self-guided walking tour of a tropical paradise, complete with roaming tigers and dense greenery. Throughout the expedition, trekkers encounter a deluge of flora and fauna typically found in the rainforests of Southeast Asia. Komodo dragons, fruit bats, and a conglomeration of colorful birds call this corner of

Animal Kingdom home. Majestic Asian tigers can be spotted stalking ancient ruins, strategically separated from would-be prey. Deer and antelope graze and frolic nearby, blissfully oblivious of their fearsome neighbors' proximity.

Approximately midway through the thicket stands a rustic, tin-roofed assembly hall. Step inside to witness the breathtaking sight of giant fruit bats showing off their six-foot wingspans. As you look through the windows, thinking that the crystal clear glass was cleaned by a super-diligent window washer, think again. There is no

glass in some of the windows—and, therefore, nothing separating you from the giant creatures fluttering about on the other side. What keeps the big bats from getting up close and personal with guests? They're a lot less interested in humans than humans are in them. (Can't say that we blame them.) Note that some viewing areas are adorned with wire or glass—for guests who are more comfortable with a bat buffer.

Flights of Wonder

A 1,000-seat, open-air theater, the Caravan Stage features performances by actors wearing nothing but feathers and the occasional crown. Members of more than 20 different bird species have starring roles in Flights of Wonder, a high-flying celebration of the winged wonders of the world. Hawks, owls, falcons, and even chickens have been known to awe spectators as they swoop, soar, and strut their stuff in each 20-minute performance. Some demonstrate how they hunt. Others display their grape-grabbing or money-grubbing talents. Check a park Times Guide for the schedule. This show has morphed quite a bit from its original incarnation. It's a hoot!

Expedition Everest FP+

BIRNBAUM'S ★BEST★ Walt Disney World's mountain range is a bit more intense these days, as the world's tallest mountain—Everest—has risen from the peaceful village of Serka Zong in Animal Kingdom's Asia. Like its sister peaks, Space, Splash, and Big Thunder, this E-ticket precipice promises to deliver "coaster thrills, spills, and chills." Does it deliver on that promise? Boy, does it ever.

The attraction features an old tea train chugging and churning as it climbs up and around snowcapped peaks. Suddenly, the track comes to an end in a gnarled mess of twisted metal. Lurching forward and backward, the train hurtles through caverns and icy canyons before depositing guests in the presence of the legendary Yeti (aka the Abominable Snowman)—who's not too happy that you've scaled the mountain he so fiercely protects.

Feeling up to the challenge of a dramatic, high-speed train ride? If you are free of heart, back, and neck problems, are not pregnant, have no fear of heights (or abominable snowpeople), and are at least 44 inches tall, go for it. As always, never eat right before experiencing a ride as topsy-turvy as this one.

HOT TIP!
Fastpass+ assignments for Expedition Everest tend to be gone quickly. Get yours as early as possible.

PHOTO BY JILL SAFRO

DinoLand U.S.A.

If the look and feel of DinoLand U.S.A. seems familiar, there's a reason: It was designed to capture the flavor of roadside America. It is a mixture of culture and kitsch—the likes of which you might stumble upon during a cross-country road trip. Here, you may ride a flying Triceratop, jump into gigantic footprints, and browse through a typically tacky roadside souvenir stand, where you can pick up some dinosaur mementos for the folks back home.

This corner of Animal Kingdom comes complete with its own dramatic entrance: a 50-foot skeleton of a brachiosaurus. As guests stroll beneath the bones, they find themselves smack in the middle of a paleontological dig. Here, guests of all ages (especially little ones) have the chance to play paleontologist as they dig through a fossil-packed pocket of dino discovery.

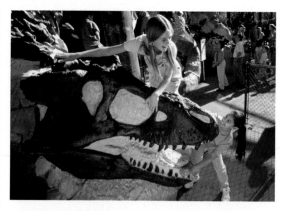

bang out a primitive tune on a bony xylophone (it's located near the car; to make a sound, firmly press on a rib), zip down prehistoric slides, and work your way through a fossil-filled maze. While exploring, watch your step: If you accidentally wander into a giant dinosaur footprint, you might be greeted with a some-what ominous roar.

While in DinoLand, be sure to check out the OldenGate Bridge. It's a gateway structure made from a dinosaur skeleton. The bridge links one end of The Boneyard with the other. This is a good place to take young children while other members of your party ride Dinosaur.

DID YOU KNOW?

Many of the benches in Disney's Animal Kingdom are made of recycled plastic milk jugs. It takes roughly 1,350 jugs to make a single bench!

The dinosaurs that dwell here, though often quite animated, are all of the inanimate variety. But do keep your eyes peeled for the prehistoric life-forms that actually live in this land—that is, for real creatures that exist in the here and now, but whose ancestors kept company with the likes of the carnotaurus and its cousins from the Cretaceous era.

The Boneyard

The Boneyard gives guests—especially the very young ones—an opportunity to dig for fossils in a discovery-oriented playground. They will excavate the ancient bones of a mammoth in this re-creation of a paleontological dig (think huge sandbox). They will also unearth clues that may help them solve the mystery of how and when the creature met its untimely demise.

For serious "boneheads" who just aren't satisfied with simple digging, there are plenty of other bone-related activities here. Youngsters can

Chester & Hester's Dino-Rama!

A colorful land-within-a-land, Chester and Hester's is an area ideally suited for roadside carnival fans. Located just beyond The Boneyard playground, this wild-and-woolly zone features old-fashioned midway games and two rides: Primeval Whirl and TriceraTop Spin.

PRIMEVAL WHIRL: FP+ A small roller coaster (with spinning cars) that seems to have been plucked from a traveling fair, this ride may have a familiar feel to it. By all means, give it a whirl—it's a truly wild ride. You must be at least 48 inches tall to spin. Skip it if you are pregnant or susceptible to motion sickness or think the jarring bumps will cause you discomfort.

PHOTO BY JILL SAFRO

TRICERATOP SPIN: The ride is apt to please fans of the Magic Kingdom's Dumbo the Flying Elephant and the Magic Carpets of Aladdin. Guests ride in one of the 16 flying dinos, each of which resembles an oversize tin toy. It's rather tame when compared to its Dinosaur attraction neighbor, but certainly worth checking out—especially for young dinosaur groupies.

FOSSIL FUN GAMES: Chester and Hester's Dino-Rama is home to several silly games of skill, including Whac-A-Packycephalosaur

Get Involved

When it comes to conservation efforts, the folks at the Walt Disney Company want you to do as they say—and as they do: The Disney Worldwide Conservation Fund helps nonprofit groups protect and study endangered and threatened animals and habitats. Among those groups are the Dian Fossey Gorilla Fund, Conservation International, the Wildlife Conservation Society, and Jane Goodall Institute. And guests who "Add a Dollar" while making purchases at Animal Kingdom shops and restaurants help, too.

Of course, as a trip to Animal Kingdom makes clear, there are many ways to help our planet's wild inhabitants. Stop by Rafiki's Planet Watch during your visit. There, you can get information about conservation efforts in your neck of the woods. Don't leave your enthusiasm behind when you leave the park!

HOT TIP!

For a slightly less turbulent experience on the Dinosaur attraction, request an inside seat near the front of the ride vehicle.

(smack mischievous dinos with a mallet), Mammoth Marathon (roll balls into holes to move your wooly mammoth in a race to the finish line), Bronto-Score (basketball toss), Comet Crasher (toss "comets" into a moving cups), and Fossil Fueler (a gas-station-themed squirt game). Just like the midway games after which they are modeled, these games come with a fee. Game coupons may be purchased at the souvenir stand in the games area and at Chester and Hester's Dinosaur Treasures. Each game costs about $3 per person. Dino-themed prizes are awarded to winners.

If you'd rather stick to included-with-the-price-of-admission diversions, we highly recommend checking out the fun-house mirror for some simple, silly fun.

Dinosaur FP+

BIRNBAUM'S ★BEST★ This dizzying adventure begins with guests being strapped into vehicles and catapulted back in time to complete a dangerous, albeit noble, mission: to rescue the last iguanodon—a 16-foot plant-eating dinosaur—and bring him back to the present. The iguanodon, which lived more than 65 million years ago (during the Cretaceous period), just might hold the answer to the mysterious disappearance of his dino brethren.

Throughout the frenetic quest to locate the elusive iguanodon, you cling to an out-of-control vehicle while dodging blazing meteors and a mix

DISNEY'S ANIMAL KINGDOM

Finding Nemo—
The Musical FP+

BIRNBAUM'S ★BEST★ DinoLand is just about as far off Broadway as one could be. Yet, this show's got the ingredients of a Broadway smash: beloved characters (e.g., Marlin, the overprotective clownfish dad; Nemo, his curious son; and Dory, the endearing royal blue tang with the short-term memory loss); original songs by a Tony-winning composer (Robert Lopez); and dancers, acrobats, and the theatrical puppetry of Michael Curry (who designed the richly detailed puppets seen in the Broadway version of Disney's *The Lion King*). You can catch this 40-minute performance at the enclosed and air-conditioned Theater in the Wild. Check a Times Guide for showtimes—and get there early.

This show has appeal for guests of all ages, but the 40-minute run time is a tad too long for some kids (especially the wee ones).

of friendly and ferocious dinosaurs. Soon you encounter the carnotaurus—a fearsome, carnivorous dinosaur. The carnotaurus, which has horns like a bull and a face like a toad, is a remarkable unsightly specimen. In fact, all of the dinos move as though they were alive. Even their nostrils move as they "breathe."

This 3½-minute attraction offers more than a thrill a minute. You rocket through time, are practically pelted by meteors, and narrowly escape becoming a dino dinner as the carnotaurus suddenly turns the tables and chases you!

Guests reach the attraction through the Dino Institute, a museum-like building deep in the heart of DinoLand. Here, you'll be treated to a pre-show by Bill Nye the Science Guy (audio only) and see a dinosaur skeleton, and an assortment of fossils and other artifacts.

This is an extremely rough (and dark) attraction. You must be at least 40 inches tall to experience it. It should be skipped by pregnant women, or people with heart conditions, back or neck problems, or any other physical limitations. Small kids will most definitely be frightened.

HOT TIP!

Animal Kingdom veterans will note that Camp Minnie-Mickey is no more. So what is happening in the space it once occupied? Disney Imagineers are hard at work, constructing attractions themed to the blockbuster film *Avatar*. The dust is expected to settle by the end of 2017.

Where to Find the Characters

You'll discover Mickey and Minnie at the Adventurers Outpost on Discovery Island. Pluto and Goofy mingle with guests in DinoLand, by the entrance to Chester & Hester's Dino-Rama. Donald can usually be found nearby, on the Cretaceous Trail. Russel and Dug have a clubhouse on Discovery Island, near It's Tough to be a Bug. Rafiki, Chip, and Dale hang out at Rafiki's Planet Watch. Baloo and King Louie greet folks at Asia's Upcountry Landing (near Flights of Wonder). Characters such as Daisy, Goofy, and Mickey join Donald for his Safari Breakfast at Tusker House in Harambe (near the Kilimanjaro Safaris). Reservations are required for Donald's Safari Breakfast.

DISNEY'S ANIMAL KINGDOM

Shopping

Entrance Area

GARDEN GATE GIFTS: Stop here for park souvenirs, snacks, sundries, and camera supplies. ECVs may be rented here. (Wheelchairs and strollers are available at a nearby counter.) This is also the park's package pickup and PhotoPass viewing location.

OUTPOST: A small shop located just outside the park's entrance, Outpost offers character merchandise, snacks, and more.

Discovery Island

DISNEY OUTFITTERS: Nature-themed gifts and apparel are the stock-in-trade here. There's an abundance of clothing (for the whole family), plus various items with an animal theme and Disney souvenirs. Make a point of checking out the authentic carved animal totem poles in the center room—they are rather impressive.

ISLAND MERCANTILE: This sprawling shop is themed as a shipping company that celebrates working animals—camels, elephants, beavers, and others. Here, you'll find character merchandise, clothing, candy, and Disney paraphernalia. Note that this shop stays open about a half hour after Animal Kingdom closes for the day.

Africa

DUKA LA FILIMU: Situated near the entrance to Kilimanjaro Safaris, this is an ideal place to load up on photo supplies for your trip.

MOMBASA MARKETPLACE & ZIWANI TRADERS: An African marketplace and trading company, these connected shops feature animal toys, safari clothing, T-shirts, books, wine, and Africa-themed gifts such as pottery, masks, and musical instruments.

OUT OF THE WILD: Located just outside the exit of Rafiki's Planet Watch, this open-air shop stocks a variety of souvenirs, including shirts, hats, notebooks, and toys.

Asia

BHAKTAPUR MARKET: A small shop with a big Asian influence, Bhaktapur sells summer shoes, bags, robes, shirts, teapots and teas, toy dragons and plush animals, chopsticks, and items with a Yak & Yeti theme.

MANDALA GIFTS: Just a stone's throw from Royal Anandapur Tea Company, this spot offers Asian-inspired clothing, scarves, and handbags, plus souvenirs featuring the Animal Kingdom park logo.

SERKA ZONG BAZAAR: Located at the exit of Expedition Everest (it can be accessed from the outside for those who skip the ride), this bustling bazaar sells souvenirs with a Yeti theme, plus a slew of shirts, hats, books, frames, etc., that celebrate the Expedition Everest attraction.

DinoLand U.S.A.

CHESTER & HESTER'S DINOSAUR TREASURES: Themed as an American roadside souvenir stand, this shop pays homage to all reptiles and prehistoric animals. Its focus is reflected in an assortment of wacky items strewn about the shop.

THE DINO INSTITUTE SHOP: It should come as no surprise that you'll find dino-themed items and other souvenirs here. It's also the spot to view (and buy) that photo of you looking terrified while riding Dinosaur.

DID YOU KNOW?

Many of the costumes worn by Animal Kingdom cast members are made of wood—actually, a natural fabric called lyocell, made from wood pulp. The pulp is harvested from trees grown specifically for this fabric.

Entertainment

AFRICAN ENTERTAINMENT: Sounds of Africa often fill the air as drummers serenade guests passing through Harambe. Entertainers perform around the park throughout the day.

ANIMAL ENCOUNTERS: Enjoy up-close encounters with some of the smaller members of the animal kingdom as they wander the park with their human keepers.

HOT TIPS!

- If you plan to park hop, Animal Kingdom is a good park at which to begin the day.

- Most of Animal Kingdom's attractions take place outdoors. Don't become overheated! Make a point of slipping into an air-conditioned shop or restaurant from time to time to cool off.

- Narrow, winding paths, grooved pavement, and hilly terrain make this the most challenging Disney theme park in which to navigate a wheelchair or heavy stroller.

- Check the Animal Kingdom Tip Board often to get an idea of showtimes and crowds.

- When the weather gets steamy, keep a reusable water bottle with you at all times.

- Rainforest Cafe generally keeps longer hours than the park does. (Buses run until one hour after park closing time.)

- The line for Kilimanjaro Safaris tends to dwindle a bit by midday. See it then (the experience is enjoyable at any time of day).

- Get a Fastpass+ for Expedition Everest as soon as you possibly can—they run out quickly. It is a wildly popular ride!

- Bumpy rides aren't for everyone—or for every camera. When it comes to thrill (or wet) rides, it's smart to stash your camera in a locker or with a non-riding member of your party.

- Island Mercantile on Discovery Island stays open a half hour after the park closes.

Where to Eat in Animal Kingdom

A complete listing of eateries at Disney's Animal Kingdom—table-service restaurants, fast-food spots, and snack stands—can be found in the *Good Meals, Great Times* chapter. See the Animal Kingdom section, beginning on page 264.

Hidden Mickeys

These are some of the most popular "Hidden Mickeys" at Animal Kingdom. How many can you find? Check the box when you spot each one!

❤ Tree of Life: A Hidden Mickey made of moss is on the front of the Tree of Life just to the right of the tiger and to the left of the buffalo. Although you may be able to spot it from several vantage points, the best place is right when you enter Discovery Island and before the path splits to Africa and DinoLand. ■

❤ Kilimanjaro Safaris: Pay close attention to the flamingo pond on your left just after you enter elephant country. The center island is shaped like a Hidden Mickey (sit toward the left side of the ride vehicle for the best view). ■

❤ Maharajah Jungle Trek: There are more than 10 Hidden Mickeys throughout this jungle trek, but we suggest hunting for these two to start: Inside the first archway near the tiger exhibit, pay attention to the mural on the left and look for three leaves that form a Hidden Mickey underneath the extended arm of a king. Now walk to the second arch and look at the mural on the right to find a Hidden Mickey in the clouds. ■

❤ Pangani Forest Exploration Trail: Okay, while not a Hidden Mickey, the Hidden Jafar found in this trail is well worth searching for. Just past the gorilla viewing area, you'll reach a suspension bridge. Look directly to your right and you'll see a huge 3-D head of Jafar carved out of the rock that's covered in moss. ■

❤ Rafiki's Planet Watch: Conservation Station is a Hidden Mickey paradise with more than 20 Mickeys in the entrance mural alone. Two favorites: Just inside the building on the right ■. Find a possum with a Hidden Mickey in its eye ■. Then look above it to find a butterfly with two Hidden Mickeys (one on each wing). For good measure, here's a third: Find a frog just to the right of an alligator on the left wall, then find Mickey's smiling face under the frog's right eye. ■

❤ Expedition Everest: To find this Hidden Mickey, you'll need a Fastpass+ assignment for Expedition Everest. As you travel through the Fastpass+ queue, pay close attention to the Yeti Museum room. In the second display of expedition artifacts and supplies, look for a lantern on a shelf—three dents in the metal form a sideways Hidden Mickey. ■

❤ It's Tough to be a Bug!: This is one of the more challenging Hidden Mickeys to locate at Disney's Animal Kingdom, but cast members are happy to help you spot it if you need them to. ■ After you enter the "underground" room with all the silly musical posters (but before entering the main theater), find the other entrance to the far side of the room. Now look at the far left wall. This well-concealed (but very cool) Hidden Mickey is hiding in the shadows. ■

❤ DinoLand U.S.A.: First, find the two large dinosaurs holding up a "Chester & Hester's Dino-Rama" sign near the TriceraTop Spin ride. Stand directly underneath the sign and close to the blue dinosaur. Check out the dino's wrist—there's a Hidden Mickey on it! ■ Then head to the dig site area of The Boneyard playground. Can you spot where two hard hats and a fan combine to form another H.M.? ■

❤ Dinosaur: Before you travel back in time, your ride vehicle passes a laboratory scene on the left (the vehicle actually stops here for a second to give you plenty of time to look). Search carefully to find a blue Hidden Mickey drawn on the lower left corner of a whiteboard. ■

❤ Cretaceous Trail: At the end of this short DinoLand trail sits a proud dino. We think he's proud of the Hidden Mickey on his back! ■

Specifics may change during 2015.

Where in the World?

All of the photos on this page were taken at Disney's Animal Kingdom. Do you know where? We challenge you to find all the spots where these images were shot and snap a photo for yourself as you discover each one. Happy hunting! (For locations, turn to page 356.)

(For locations, turn to page 356.)

1

2

3

4

5

6

7

8

Everything Else in the World

210 **Downtown Disney**

219 **BoardWalk**

220 **Water Parks**

224 **Daredevil Disney**

225 **Fort Wilderness**

228 **WDW Spas**

230 **Just for Kids**

231 **Specialty Cruises**

232 **Tours and Programs**

EVERYTHING ELSE IN THE WORLD

While the total turf of the World encompasses about 40 square miles, the theme parks cover a mere fraction of the property. Much of the remaining Walt Disney World terrain is crammed with irresistible activities of a variety and quality seldom found anywhere else.

There's superb golf and tennis, beaches for sunbathing, lakes for motorboating, fishing, and sailing, canoes to rent and winding streams to paddle along, bicycles for hire, campfire sites, horseback riding, race-car driving, nature trails, and picnic grounds. The recreation options continue with Typhoon Lagoon, a lushly landscaped, state-of-the-art water park complete with surfing lagoon; and Blizzard Beach, a thrilling, watery wonderland that translates the hallmarks of a ski resort to the realm of swimming.

A lineup of lavish spas provide guests with ample opportunity to pamper themselves silly. Intriguing "backstage" programs invite the curious to slip behind the scenes and learn about the workings of Walt Disney World. Add to all that, Downtown Disney—an evolving dining, shopping, and entertainment district currently including the Marketplace, a colorful assortment of shops and restaurants; the West Side, a cluster of themed eateries, shops, and entertainment experiences, and the waterfront region in between the two (previously known as Pleasure Island). It seems this really is a World without end.

Downtown Disney

Sprinkled across 120 waterfront acres are the shops, lounges, restaurants, and entertainment sites that collectively make up Downtown Disney. Like the downtown area of any thriving metropolis, Walt Disney World's Downtown consists of distinct neighborhoods. At press time, they were known as the Marketplace and the West Side. The whole area is undergoing a metamorphosis and a name change. (For more details, refer to the Disney Springs sidebar on page 213.) Unlike a typical downtown, the Disney depiction dispenses with the downside. You won't see litter on the streets, unsightly storefronts, or weary workers rushing home at five o'clock. What you will see is a series of spirited spots designed solely for your dining, shopping, and playing pleasure.

That said, it can get a tad congested—especially on the roads leading here. However you're traveling, allow plenty of extra time to get to and from this fun zone. For information, visit *www.disneyworld.com*, or call 407-934-7639.

Downtown Disney Essentials

GUEST RELATIONS: Between Marketplace Co-op and Ghirardelli Soda Fountain and Chocolate Shop in the Marketplace, and near DisneyQuest on the West Side, these information centers are also the places to go for help making dining reservations, Lost and Found, tickets, and more. Note that stroller and wheelchair rentals are available at DisneyQuest and at a location between Tren-D and Once Upon a Toy. There are several ATMs scattered throughout the Downtown Disney district.

HOW TO GET THERE: Downtown Disney is accessible from exits 67 and 68 off I-4.

By WDW Transportation: From Old Key West, Port Orleans French Quarter and Riverside, and Saratoga Springs: boats or buses. From all other WDW resorts: bus. There is no direct transportation from Disney theme parks to Downtown Disney. The Marketplace is within walking distance of several resorts on Hotel Plaza Boulevard. For more information, turn to *Transportation & Accommodations*.

By Taxi: Authorized cabs service the Downtown Disney area. The cost to most WDW resorts is usually $15 to $25.

Note: Stick with authorized taxis such as Mears Taxi and avoid independent drivers. Their fees aren't regulated and are often outrageous. And pay attention to the route the driver takes to be sure it is as direct as possible.

WEST SIDE

PLEASURE ISLAND

amc

Marketplace

Located on the shores of Village Lake, the Marketplace is a relaxing setting for shopping, dining, and much more. The waterside enclave is sprinkled with gardens featuring whimsical topiaries. Little kids are fond of the Downtown Disney Marketplace carousel (see Marketplace Rides, page 212). While many guests opt to eat in a restaurant, others grab a bite from the Earl of Sandwich and sit at waterfront tables. (Refer to *Good Meals, Great Times* for restaurant information.) Afterward, some gravitate toward the marina for a nightcap.

Shopping

The descriptions that follow suggest the types of wares each store offers. Most shops in the Downtown Disney Marketplace are typically open daily from about 9:30 A.M. to 11 P.M.

ARRIBAS BROS.: This shop sells hand-crafted items from Spanish artisans and designers. Large, cut-glass bowls and vases are available, along with mugs, sculptures, and other wares, many of which can be personalized. Aspiring Cinderellas will appreciate the selection of tiaras and glass slippers. It is located between Basin and Marketplace Co-op.

THE ART OF DISNEY: Original Disney art, porcelain figures, ceramics, posters, and other collectibles are available at this engaging gallery.

BASIN: Products designed to clean you up and calm you down are the stock-in-trade at this soothing establishment. Candles, soaps, and bath crystals are some of the wares on hand. A sampling area allows shoppers to try before they buy. The bath bombs are the best!

MARKETPLACE

PHOTO BY JILL SAFRO

Touch here to Design-A-Tee!

DESIGN-A-TEE: This shop is T-shirt central. Aspiring fashion designer? Simply step up to one of eight computer kiosks and design away. Your first step is to select a size and color for the shirt (there are samples shirts to help you gauge proper sizes). Next, choose art from a set of categories such as Characters, Pirates, Princesses (which includes Princes), or Celebrations. Finally, personalize your creation with text of your own choosing. When you're finished, a ticket will be printed for you. Present it to the cashier to pay for your shirt and plan to come back in a half hour or so to pick it up.

DISNEY'S DAYS OF CHRISTMAS: Here is the best place to deck the halls Disney style—it's the largest Christmas shop on Disney property. In addition to character items, the shop boasts a large assortment of hand-crafted ornaments. Other items to look for: Mickey Mouse nutcrackers, Santa hats with mouse ears, stockings, and books. Some ornaments can be personalized. This store is so thoroughly themed, it actually smells like a candy cane.

PHOTO BY JILL SAFRO

DISNEY'S PIN TRADERS: This shop boasts a tremendous assortment of collector pins and various pin-collecting accessories.

DISNEY'S WONDERFUL WORLD OF MEMORIES: Preserve the memories of your Disney adventure with the scrap-booking supplies, journals, frames, photo albums for sale at this shop across from Disney's Days of Christmas. Camera supplies (memory cards, batteries, straps, cases, and chargers) are available, too. There's a make-your-own Disney charm bracelet station and a wall of mouse ear hats just waiting to be personalized.

PHOTO BY JILL SAFRO

GOOFY'S CANDY COMPANY: One-stop shopping to satisfy sugary cravings, this shop has a sumptuous selection of chocolates, a dipping kitchen, and much more. It also hosts birthday parties. Call 407-WDW-BDAY (939-2329) for information or to book a Princess- or Goofy-themed birthday party.

On warm days, we gravitate to the corner of this shop known as Goofy's Glaciers for a frozen slushie treat. Available in flavors with goofy names such as Rootin' Tootin' Red, Orange You Happy, and Pucker Purple. They also serve coffee, cookies, pastries, and ice cream.

Marketplace Rides

Downtown Disney Marketplace has two honest-to-goodness kiddie rides for tykes to enjoy: a carousel and a tiny train. The cost for each is $2 per child. Be sure to purchase a token before boarding (payment can be made with MasterCard, Visa, or cash). Parents can accompany small children on the train (no charge, provided they ride in the same car). The train can only accommodate two adults per trip (hey, we said it was tiny), and grown-ups are not allowed to ride in the engine car. For the carousel, kids under 42 inches tall must be accompanied by an adult (who rides for free). The rides are situated between Marketplace Fun Finds and The Earl of Sandwich.

LEGO IMAGINATION CENTER: World of Disney's neighbor, this newly renovated emporium is a showcase for larger-than-life LEGO models. It also invites guests to flaunt their creativity in an interactive outdoor play area. A new computer hub lets guests design LEGO structures and play games. The store sells a vast selection of LEGO products.

LEFTY'S: Step up to southpaw central for scissors, can openers, writing implements, notebooks, and more—all made especially for the differently handed. The open-air stand also sells shirts and hats lauding left-handedness.

HOT TIP!

Now you can get a taste of the Disney theme parks at Downtown Disney. Four food trucks (representing Magic Kingdom, Epcot, Disney's Hollywood Studios, and Animal Kingdom) serve fan favorites throughout the day. They tend to park in different places, so keep an eye out.

LITTLE MISSMATCHED™: The problem of mismatched sock syndrome has finally been solved: Nothing here matches! In addition to socks (which are sold in packs of three), the store sells colorful pajamas, pencil pouches, backpacks, and other miscellany.

MARKETPLACE FUN FINDS: Here's the place to find Disney merchandise at low prices. In fact, every item in the store is under $25. Hey, that *is* fun!

Disney Springs

The patch of land that was known as Pleasure Island continues to undergo a dramatic metamorphosis. What's in store for our old friend P.I.? Well, that's in the hands of Disney's Imagineers. In addition to a new name, the neighborhood is slated to welcome lots of new tenants. At press time, we were told to expect an "extraordinary mix of dining and shopping." While festive, this area and its neighbors to the east (the Marketplace) and west (West Side) will have less of a bustling marketplace vibe and feel more like a lush waterfront district. To reflect that shift, Downtown Disney is earmarked for a modified moniker, too. When the dust settles, this entertaining zone will have a few new neighborhoods and be known as Disney Springs. The multi-year transformation—which is under way—should be complete by 2016.

MICKEY'S PANTRY: Stop here for Disney-themed glasses, cookbooks, mugs, and cooking utensils, plus spices, teas, and coffees. Many of the designs are subtle, others not so much: Mickey pasta, anyone? Note that the Spice & Tea Exchange is located inside Mickey's Pantry (see page 214 for details).

MARKETPLACE CO-OP: A cavernous retail zone, the Co-op is home to six specialty shops: **Beautifully Disney** is a beauty destination featuring makeup, fragrances, and accessories; **Cherry Tree Lane** appeals to "the sophisticated woman with a passion for scarves, shoes, bags, and jewelry"; **D-Tech on Demand** is a place to personalize and customize your electronic accessories; **The Trophy Room** offers sports apparel and collectibles; **The Centerpiece** showcases home products for folks who dig a dash of Disney in their furnishings, textiles, and everyday ware; and **Zoey and Pickles** proffers the latest trends in fashion for budding fashionistas. This shop has replaced Team Mickey.

THE PEARL FACTORY: Pick an oyster, any oyster. Then pry it open (with some assistance), and *voila*—a pearl! The cost is about $16 per oyster and you are guaranteed at least one genuine pearl. The open-air shop, "Hawaii's Original Pearl-in-the-Oyster," proffers pearl earrings and necklaces, too.

Festival of the Masters

November is for art lovers. At least that's the case at Downtown Disney, as it hosts an annual open-air art show dubbed Festival of the Masters. Approximately 150 award-winning artists showcase their unique creations (most available for purchase) at the fest: painting, sculpture, photography, jewelry, and more. Admission and parking are free. The same goes for the live entertainment and multitude of hands-on activities. Growing in scope and popularity every year, the Festival of the Masters has become one of the nation's most acclaimed art festivals. For the 2015 schedule, visit *www.disneyworld.com/art*.

ONCE UPON A TOY: A sprawling toy box of a store, this site features plush toys, action figures, Duffy merchandise, a Mr. Potato Head play zone, and a Build Your Own Light Saber station. Oodles of brand names are represented. Be sure to look up—there's a model train set suspended from the ceiling.

PHOTO BY JILL SAFRO

SILHOUETTE PORTRAITS: A classic, Disney "lasting memory," single silhouettes cost $14, doubles $20, triples $24, and quads $27 (plus tax). You will receive three copies. Black oval frames go for about $12 a piece.

THE SPICE & TEA EXCHANGE: Neatly nestled into a corner of Mickey's Pantry, this fragrant destination offers the opportunity to purchase gourmet spices, salts, sugars, teas, and more. It's a rather unique shopping experience thanks, in part, to a large selection of sample jars in which you are encouraged to stick your nose.

TREN-D: The Mouse is quite a trendsetter. Need proof? Swing by this boutique. It is bursting with quirky Disney merchandise, from loungewear to jeweled sunglasses and other trendy accessories.

WORLD OF DISNEY: A gigantic space stuffed with a huge selection of Disney merchandise, this is the place for one-stop shopping. Colorful rooms provide the backdrop for the array of goods. Characters are available on everything from watches to luggage. (If you're an annual passholder, you may receive a discount when you present it at the register. It depends on the type of pass, and the discount is subject to change.)

Cinderella's Fairy Godmother has set up shop here in the Princess Room. Her Bibbidi Bobbidi Boutique, which is run by "Fairy Godmothers in training," caters to royal-wan-nabes ages 3 to 12. Here, kids can get their faces painted with glitter makeup, do their nails and hair, and even don tiaras. The boutique is open daily. Kids are transformed into princesses and princely royal knights. Reservations are encouraged; call 407-WDW-STYLE (939-7895) for reservations and pricing (cheap it is not!).

World of Disney is also a good place to buy Disney Dollars. It is a dollar-for-dollar exchange and purchases are limited to $50 per person, per day. (They tend to run low on Disney Dollars by the afternoon, so be sure to get there early.)

HOT TIP!

Dinosaur fans make their own Cretaceous creatures at Downtown Disney's Build-a-Dino (it's similar to Build-a-Bear). The shop is inside the T-Rex Cafe, near the LEGO store. Prehistoric plush pets range in price from about $15 to $20.

WETZEL'S PRETZELS: Head to the Wetzel's stand for fresh, hand-rolled soft pretzels in multiple varieties, such as Sinful Cinnamon, Cheese Meltdown, and Almond Crunch. Plain pretzels can be purchased, too. Dip selections include cheddar cheese, jalapeño cheese, pizza sauce, and sweet caramel. Pretzels may be ordered with or without butter. Wetzel's also serves hot dogs wrapped in pretzel rolls and fresh-squeezed lemonade.

West Side

When Disney's shopping and entertainment district underwent its latest growth spurt, it did so in true American style: It went west. The West Side boasts a wide (and growing) variety of restaurants, shops, movies, and clubs.

AMC DOWNTOWN DISNEY 24: The most popular multi-screen movie theater complex in Florida is also one of the largest. The many screens show a wide selection of current movie releases. The seats are roomy and comfortable—and some of the theaters offer seat-side food and beverage service (see page 266 for details). For current movie schedules, call 407-298-4488.

BONGOS CUBAN CAFE: Situated across from the AMC Theatres on the edge of Village Lake, Bongos echoes the style of clubs in Miami's South Beach. Created in part by Gloria Estefan, it features the flavors and rhythms of Cuba and other Latin American countries. The bold design is dramatic yet whimsical. Guests dine and, if the mood strikes, even dance amid the colorful, tropical decor (and one remarkably oversized pineapple, which houses a multi-level cocktail lounge).

The food at Bongos moves to a Latin beat as well, with a slate of traditional and nouvelle Cuban dishes. There is entertainment on Friday and Saturday nights.

CIRQUE DU SOLEIL: The big, white building that towers over all the others at Downtown Disney West Side closely resembles a tent—a circus tent. It's the home of a most extraordinary

Where to Eat at Downtown Disney

A complete listing of restaurants, bars, and snack spots can be found in the *Good Meals, Great Times* chapter. See the Downtown Disney restaurant listing, beginning on page 266. Most restaurants here are open from about 11:00 A.M. to 10 P.M. Planet Hollywood serves until midnight. West Side spots may serve as late as 2 A.M. See page 266.

PHOTO BY JILL SAFRO

CIRQUE DU SOLEIL

entertainment experience: Cirque du Soleil. This original show, titled La Nouba, is a Walt Disney World exclusive.

Known for their high energy and artistic performances, Cirque du Soleil performances feature a mix of acrobatics and modern dance combined with colorful costumes and live, dramatic original music. A cast of more than 60 international performers showcase their physical talents twice a day, five days a week (Tuesday through Saturday).

Tickets for the show may be purchased up to six months in advance. Call 407-939-7328, or visit *www.disneyworld.com/lanouba*, for information or to order tickets. If you have not already purchased tickets to La Nouba, consider stopping by the Cirque du Soleil box office at Downtown Disney West Side—some seats may be available at the last minute. Note that the show is quite popular.

DISNEYQUEST: This imaginative entertainment complex features high-tech activities that engage kids and grown-ups alike. Sometimes

described as a self-contained, interactive theme park, the five floors under the DisneyQuest roof are packed with games—plus some treasured blasts from the past.

Each floor features rides and games from the simple (classic video games such as Tetris) to some of the more technologically advanced (e.g., CyberSpace Mountain, in which guests not only design gravity-defying roller coasters but get to ride their creations in a simulator).

Expect to be engaged for two to three hours (or until sensory overload sets in). DisneyQuest is open daily from late morning till late evening. Admission covers most games. It's included with a Premium Annual Pass and the Water Park Fun & More add-on for a Magic Your Way base ticket. If admission isn't included with your pass, pay at the box office near the entrance. It's a nice place to escape the rain or extreme heat, but those conditions make for bigger crowds.

HOUSE OF BLUES: A combination restaurant-music hall with standing room for 2,000, House of Blues was inspired by one of America's most celebrated musical traditions. There is a lively dose of jazz and country, plus a little bit of R&B and some rock 'n' roll thrown into the music mix. The Southern-inspired cooking lures diners here—especially on Sunday mornings, when the chefs prepare an all-you-care-to-eat buffet feast, complemented by live gospel music. Tickets can be purchased in advance through Ticketmaster (call 407-839-3900, or visit *www.ticketmaster.com*) or the House of Blues box office (407-934-2583).

PHOTO BY JILL SAFRO

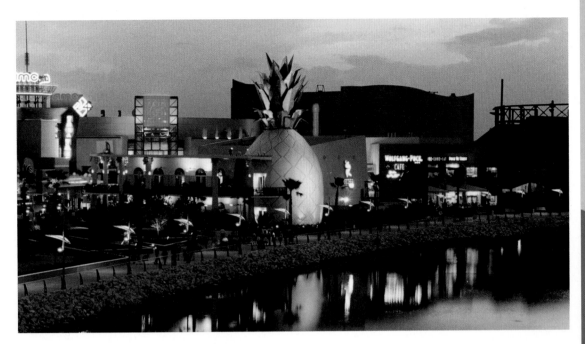

The H.O.B restaurant features a mélange of cuisine, including jambalaya, slow-smoked pulled pork, shrimp with grits, and bread pudding.

WOLFGANG PUCK CAFE: There are three dining areas in this two-story restaurant—an express counter, a cafe, and a formal dining room on the second floor—plus a sushi bar. All feature the celebrated chef's signature pizzas, rotisserie chicken, and other specialties. The sushi bar is a good go-to should you find yourself famished and without reservations.

Shopping

BLINK BY WET SEAL: Bringing fresh fashion to Downtown Disney, this BLINK store from Wet Seal features apparel, denim, and accessories for women.

PHOTO BY JILL SAFRO

CANDY CAULDRON: Stop here for some homemade sweets in an open candy kitchen. Among the biggest crowd-pleasers here are the made-to-order specialty apples—fresh, crunchy apples slathered in the candy coating of your choice. Yum!

CURL BY SAMMY DUVALL: You have to figure that anybody who spent not one but 17 years as a champion water-skier has to know quite a bit about trends in beachwear and water-sport equipment. See for yourself at this high-end surf shop. Among the wares you will find sunglasses, watches, jewelry, activewear, earphones, and shoes. The shop can be found next door to Splitsville. It's usually open from 10:30 A.M. until 11 P.M.

D STREET: This industrial space showcases a mix of Disney-inspired merchandise and Vinyl-mation collectibles (guests are invited to trade and/or create their own). Also available are pop culture novelties, apparel, and more.

FIT2RUN—THE RUNNER'S SUPERSTORE: A super stop for guests on the run, this shop sells footwear, apparel, performance sunglasses, and more. Need help selecting the perfect shoe for you? Take advantage of this shop's high-tech video gait analysis. Ready, set, run!

HOYPOLOI: The glass, ceramics, sculpture, jewelry, and other eclectic, decorative items on display here make this shop seem more like an art gallery. It's worth a peek. Note that photography is not permitted in this shop.

ORLANDO HARLEY-DAVIDSON: No motorcycles for sale here (though any employee will happily tell you how to buy one), but the custom Harleys on display are definitely ogle-worthy. Hog fans can browse Harley-Davidson T-shirts, gifts, and other collectibles, and even customize their own biker vests (using Harley-Davidson patches and pins).

POP GALLERY: This gallery features artist-signed limited-edition sculptures and paintings, as well as high-end gift items. There's a champagne bar, too. Hence the "pop." The shop is located next to the AMC Theatres and across from Splitsville.

SOMETHING SILVER: The AMC Theatres next-door neighbor, Something Silver sells fashionable jewelry (rings, earrings, bracelets, and charms) and a collection of timeless classics for men, women, and children.

SOSA FAMILY CIGAR COMPANY: For adults only, this shop specializes in premium cigars. Feel free to puff away here—the shop's a rare smoking zone. In addition to the art of hand-rolling, Sosa Family Cigars features an authentic solid cedar humidor room to keep the wares as fresh as possible.

PHOTO BY JILL SAFRO

SPLITSVILLE LUXURY LANES™: Come for some casual bowling, stay for some fab food and live entertainment. The West Side's newest venue features 30 bowling lanes, two high-end kitchens, a full bar, live music—and billiards, to boot. Housed in what was once the Virgin Megastore, this massive 'ville (50,000 square feet) is fun for all ages. However, some areas are restricted to guests over the age of 21 (with legal ID to prove it). It's generally open until about 2 A.M. daily; the restricted "21 and up" area is open on Fridays and Saturdays after 10:30 P.M.

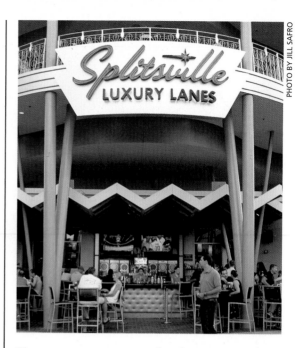

PHOTO BY JILL SAFRO

Shoppers can peruse merchandise at Memory Lanes, a shop tucked into a corner on the first floor of Splitsville. Expect to find items such as shirt, pants, hats, glasses, jewelry, and more. For more information, visit *www.splitsvillelanes.com* and refer to page 268.

STARBUCKS: That ubiquitous mermaid icon can be spotted on the shore of Village Lake. Expect to find all of Starbucks' specialties—from fresh-brewed, free-trade cups of joe to sweet and chilly Frappuccinos. Treats include cupcakes, brownies, muffins, and cake pops. Smoothies, teas, fresh fruit, crunchy veggies, juice, milk, soda, and water are also offered. (There are several Disney Dining Plan snack options to choose from.)

SUNGLASS ICON: Looking for some super-cool shades? This snazzy shop is full of high-end brands to protect your peepers.

HOT TIP!

In 2014, soccer fans stocked up on gear and caught World Cup fever at a new shop called United World Soccer. At press time, it was possible that this emporium would extend its stay into 2015. Check *www.disneyworld.com* for updates on U.W.S. and other new shops in the area.

BoardWalk

A stroll at Disney's BoardWalk is a journey back in time. Inspired by the Middle Atlantic seaside attractions of the early 1900s, BoardWalk recaptures the carefree atmosphere of that bygone era. The resort is surrounded by restaurants, clubs, and amusements similar to those enjoyed by beachgoers of yesteryear. It's bordered by a wood-planked walkway that hugs the shore of Crescent Lake. By day, BoardWalk is a peaceful place to soak up sun, enjoy lunch, or simply walk the boards. After dark, the place turns into a twinkling center of nighttime activity—some of it elegant, some of it downright raucous.

WildWood Landing challenges onlookers to test their luck and skill at a collection of classic carnival games, while strolling performers enchant passersby of all ages with magic shows, balloon tricks, or other antics.

BoardWalk is open to everyone. Although there is no admission price, individual venues may charge a cover. There is a $12 charge for valet parking (even for guests staying at a WDW resort). Self-parking is free. For dining details, refer to this book's *Good Meals, Great Times* chapter.

Clubs

ATLANTIC DANCE: This is a lovely atmosphere in which to dance the night away. A deejay cranks up tunes, tempting guests to twist and shout on the spacious dance floor. Request your favorite music videos and bust a move while they play on the big screen.

In addition to traditional cocktails, the club serves specialty drinks. Sample one in the "big room" or on the waterfront balcony.

Guests must be 21 or older, with a legal photo ID, to enter. There was a $5 cover charge at press time, but that could change. Hours are generally 9 P.M. until 2 A.M., Tuesday through Saturday.

This club is known for reinventing itself: specifics may be different during your visit.

ESPN CLUB: This club aims to please sports enthusiasts of all kinds, from the casual armchair quarterback to the most rabid fanatic. It has a broadcast facility, table-service eatery, and a bar.

Nearly 100 TVs broadcast sports events, so guests always know the score. (Need to make a pit stop at a crucial moment of the game? Don't sweat it . . . there are even TVs in the bathrooms.)

As you enter the club, you're at The Sidelines area. You can catch a game on a TV above the "penalty box" bar or sit at a nearby table. Beer, wine, and soft drinks are available, as is the usual pub fare.

Sports Central, the main dining area, has a big screen showing—what else?—the big game. The kitchen is open until 11:30 P.M. for meals, 12 A.M. for appetizers and desserts.

Though the restaurant doesn't typically take reservations, there is a "VIP Seating" option for select sporting events. Call 407-939-3463 to reserve a banquette-style seat on the second tier of the Sports Central dining room. Note that there is a minimum of $50 per adult and $25 per kid. Prices do not include tax or gratuity and are subject to change.

JELLYROLLS: You might want to warm up your vocal cords before crossing the threshold. They don't call it a sing-along bar for nothing: Guests are expected to sing, clap, and join in the fun at this warehouse home of dueling pianos. You'll hear everything from Gershwin to *Grease*. The piano players take requests, so plan ahead. Write the request—a cocktail napkin will do—and slip it onto the piano. (Although it's not required, we recommend slipping a tip along, too. It will increase the odds of you hearing the request and help the musicians pay their rent.)

Jellyrolls is open from 7 P.M. until 2 A.M. nightly. There is usually a $12 cover charge to enter. (Note that the cover charge may vary.) To get in, you must be at least 21 years old and willing to prove it. It's often quite chilly in this venue (year-round). Bring a sweater.

Water Parks
Typhoon Lagoon

This watery playground was inspired by an imagined legend: A typhoon hit a tiny resort village many years ago, and the storm—plus an ensuing earthquake and volcanic eruption—left the village in ruins. The locals, however, were resourceful and rebuilt their town as this "wateropolis."

The centerpiece of Typhoon Lagoon is a huge watershed mountain known as Mount Mayday. Perched atop its peak is the *Miss Tilly*, a marooned shrimp boat originally from Safen Sound, Florida. *Miss Tilly*'s smokestack erupts every half hour, shooting a 50-foot flume of water into the air.

The surf lagoon is huge: Giant slides snake through caves, tamer ones offer twisting journeys, and tiny slides delight small kids. Guests under age 10 must be accompanied by an adult.

PHOTO BY JILL SAFRO

SURF POOL: The main swimming area contains nearly three million gallons of water, making it one of the world's largest wave pools. The Caribbean-blue lagoon is surrounded by a white-sand beach, and its main attraction is the waves that come crashing to the shore every 90 seconds. The less adventurous can loll about in two relatively calm tide pools, Whitecap Cove and Blustery Bay.

CASTAWAY CREEK: The "creek" is really a 2,100-foot circular river that winds through the park and offers a lazy, relaxing orientation to Typhoon Lagoon. Tubes may be borrowed and are the most enjoyable way to make the trip along the three-foot-deep waterway. The ride takes guests through a rainforest, where they are cooled by mists and spray; through caves and grottoes that provide welcome shade on hot summer days; and through an area where "broken" pipes from a water tower unleash showers on helpless passersby. There are exits along the way, where guests can hop out for a while and do something else. It takes 20 to 35 minutes to ride around the whole park.

CRUSH 'N' GUSHER: This "water coaster" thrill ride is one of a kind. In it, daredevils are whisked along a series of flumes and tossed and

turned as they weave through an abandoned tropical fruit factory. There are three spillways to choose from: Banana Blaster, Coconut Crusher, and Pineapple Plunger.

GANGPLANK FALLS, KEELHAUL FALLS, AND MAYDAY FALLS: These white-water rides offer guests a variety of slippery trips, two of them in inner tubes. All of the slides course through caves and waterfalls, and past rockwork, making the scenery an attraction in itself. Gangplank Falls gives families a chance to ride together in a three- to five-passenger craft.

HUMUNGA KOWABUNGA: These three speed slides, reported to have been carved into the landscape by the historic earthquake, will send guests zooming through caverns at speeds of 30 miles per hour. The 214-foot slides each offer a 51-foot drop, and the view from the top is a little scary. But it's over before you know it, and once-wary guests hurry back for another try. Guests must be at least 4 feet tall, and free of back trouble, heart conditions, and other physical limitations to take the trip. Pregnant women are not permitted to ride.

KETCHAKIDDEE CREEK: Open only to those children 4 feet tall or under (and their adult guardians), this area has small rides for pint-size visitors. All children must be accompanied by an adult. There are slides, fountains, waterfalls, squirting whales and seals, a mini-rapids ride, an interactive tugboat, and a grotto with a veil of water that kids love to run through.

SHARK REEF: Guests borrow snorkel equipment for a swim through a coral reef, where they come face-to-face with sharks and fish. The reef is built around a sunken tanker. The sharks, by the way, leopard and bonnethead, are passive members of the species. Everyone must shower before entering. Guests must be older than age 5 to experience Shark Reef. Kids under 10 must be accompanied by an adult.

STORM SLIDES: The Jib Jammer, Rudder Buster, and Stern Burner body slides send guests off at about 20 miles per hour down winding fiberglass slides, in and out of rock formations and caves, and through waterfalls. It's a somewhat tamer ride than Humunga Kowabunga, but still offers a speedy descent. The slides run about 300 feet, and each offers a different view and experience.

SURFING: Surf clinics are offered on select mornings before the park opens. For information, call 407-WDW-SURF (939-7873).

Essentials

WHEN TO GO: Typhoon Lagoon gets very crowded early in the day. Hours vary seasonally, but the park is generally open from 10 A.M. to 5 P.M., with extended hours in the summer months. All of the pools are heated in the winter. Note that this park is usually closed for refurbishment during certain winter months. The park may also close due to bad weather. Call 407-824-4321 for updates.

HOW TO GET THERE: Bus service begins from all resorts approximately one hour before Typhoon Lagoon opens for the day. The buses stop at the water park and then at the Downtown Disney Marketplace before 10 A.M. After 10 A.M., resort buses stop at the Marketplace and then Typhoon Lagoon. Buses stop running from the water park about one hour after it closes. Parking is free.

LOCKER ROOMS: Restrooms with showers and lockers are located close to the entrance. Other restrooms are available farther into the park. Small lockers cost $8 (plus a $5 deposit) to rent for the day, while large lockers cost $10, plus a $5 deposit. Towels rent for $2; life jackets and tubes are available free of charge.

WHERE TO EAT: Both of Typhoon Lagoon's eateries offer similar fare and outdoor seating. Leaning Palms has burgers, pizza, salads, and snacks. Typhoon Tilly's (open seasonally) serves fish & chips, chicken tenders, wraps, BBQ pork sandwiches, and ice cream. Let's Go Slurpin' has frozen drinks and spirits. Guests may bring their own food to enjoy in designated picnic areas. Alcoholic beverages and glass containers may not be brought into the park. Coolers are allowed.

FIRST AID: A first aid station capable of handling minor medical problems is located just to the left of Leaning Palms.

BEACH SHOP: Singapore Sal's, located near the park's main entrance, is set in a ramshackle building left a bit battered by the typhoon. Swimsuits, sunglasses, hats, towels, sunscreen, souvenirs, water shoes, and Typhoon Lagoon logo products are available.

Admission Prices

Prices do not include sales tax and are subject to change. **Note:** Admission is an option with a Magic Your Way ticket that includes a Water Park Fun & More add-on and is also included with a Premium Annual Pass.

	ADULTS	CHILDREN*
One-Day Ticket	$53	$45
Annual Pass	$104	$85

* 3 through 9 years of age; children under age 3 free

Blizzard Beach

A wintry, watery wonderland, Blizzard Beach is said to be the result of a freak storm that dropped a mountain of snow onto Walt Disney World, prompting the quick construction of Florida's first ski resort. When temperatures soared and the snow began to melt, designers prepared to close the resort. But when they spotted an alligator sliding down the slopes, they realized that they had created an exhilarating water adventure park. The slalom and bobsled runs became downhill waterslides. The ski jump is one of the world's tallest (120 feet) and fastest (60 miles per hour) free-fall speed slides.

The centerpiece of Blizzard Beach is the snowcapped Mount Gushmore and its Summit Plummet. Most of the more thrilling runs are found on the slopes of this mountain, which tops out at 90 feet. At the summit, swimmers have a choice of speed slides, flumes, a white-water raft ride, and an inner-tube run. Guests may reach the top of Mount Gushmore via chairlift. The lift has a gondola for guests with disabilities. There are stairs, too.

This is the most action-packed Disney water park yet, with enough activities for the entire family to fill at least a day. Note that kids under 10 must be accompanied by an adult. One-piece bathing suits are highly recommended.

CROSS COUNTRY CREEK: This meandering 3,000-foot waterway circles the entire park. A slow current keeps visitors moving merrily along. Inner tubes, which are free, are the most pleasant way to travel. The ride includes a trip through a bone-chilling ice cave, where guests are splashed with the "melting ice" from overhead.

DOWNHILL DOUBLE DIPPER: Guests travel down these two parallel 230-foot-long racing slides at speeds of up to 25 miles per hour. The partially enclosed water runs feature ski-racing graphics, flags, and time clocks. You must be 48 inches tall to ride.

HOT TIP!

Early birds get the lounge chairs around these parts. If you want to snag a chair at either of Disney's water parks, arrive as close to park opening as possible.

MELT-AWAY BAY: A one-acre pool at the base of Mount Gushmore, the "bay" has its own wave machine. There are no tsunamis here, however—just a pleasant, bobbing wave.

RUNOFF RAPIDS: On this inner-tube run, guests careen down three twisting, turning flumes in a single or double tube.

SKI PATROL TRAINING CAMP: An area designed specifically for preteens, Frozen Pipe Springs looks like an old pipe and drops sliders into eight feet of water. The Thin Ice Training Course tests agility as kids try to walk along broken "icebergs" without falling into the water. Snow Falls's "wide" slides allow a parent and child to ride together. At the Ski Patrol Shelter, guests grab on to a T-bar for an airborne trip. At any point in the ride they can drop into the water below. Ski patrol participants also experience Cool Runners, where riders can count on hurtling and whirling over lots of moguls on twin inner-tube slides. No bunny slopes for these brave daredevils.

SLUSH GUSHER: This relatively tame, double-humped waterslide offers a brisk journey through a snowbanked mountain gully. Topping out at 90 feet, Slush Gusher is the tallest slide of its kind. You'll find it on Mount Gushmore, next to Summit Plummet. Guests must be at least 48 inches tall to ride.

SNOW STORMERS: A trio of flumes descends from the top of the mountain. Guests race down on a switchback course that includes ski-type slalom gates.

SUMMIT PLUMMET: This thrilling ride begins 120 feet in the air on a platform 30 feet above the top of Mount Gushmore. Brave souls travel about 60 miles per hour down a 350-foot slide. You must be at least 48 inches tall to take the plunge.

TEAMBOAT SPRINGS: The longest family white-water raft ride in the world takes six-passenger rafts down a twisting, 1,400-foot series of rushing waterfalls.

HOT TIP!

Premium cabana-like spaces known as Polar Patios are available for daily rental. They include an attendant, refreshments, towels, and more. Each patio accommodates up to six guests and costs about $250 per day. Premium beach spaces are available, too. For details or to make a reservation, call 407-WDW-PLAY (939-7529).

TIKE'S PEAK: A kid-size variation of Blizzard Beach, this attraction features miniature versions of Mount Gushmore's slides and a snow-castle fountain play area. Adults must be accompanied by a child to enter this zone.

TOBOGGAN RACERS: An eight-lane water-slide sends guests racing over a number of dips. They lie on their stomachs on a mat and travel headfirst down the 250-foot route.

Essentials

WHEN TO GO: As a guest favorite, Blizzard Beach tends to get very crowded early in the day. Hours vary seasonally, but the park is generally open from 10 A.M. to 5 P.M., with extended hours in summer. On select "peak" days, Blizzard Beach may offer an Extra Magic Hour to guests staying in a WDW-owned-and-operated resort and at the Hilton on Hotel Plaza Boulevard.

All pools are heated in winter. The park is often closed for refurbishment during certain winter months. It may also close due to inclement weather. For schedules, call 407-WDW-PLAY (939-7529).

HOW TO GET THERE: Blizzard Beach is served by the buses that go to and from Animal Kingdom. There is service to and from Epcot and Disney's Hollywood Studios, as well. Parking is free.

LOCKER ROOMS: There are restrooms with showers near the main entrance. Other restrooms and dressing rooms are located around the park. Small lockers cost $8, plus a $5 deposit for the day, while large lockers cost $10, plus a $5 deposit. Towels rent for $2, and life jackets and tubes may be used for free.

WHERE TO EAT: Burgers, hot dogs, pizza, salads, and drinks are sold at Lottawatta Lodge in the main village area. Two snack stands with limited offerings are located in more remote areas: Avalunch and The Warming Hut (both open seasonally). Polar Pub offers drink specialties and spirits. Those in need of a java fix can get one at Frosty the Joe Man Coffee Shack, while those looking for frozen lemonade or fresh fruit can find it at Frostbite Freddy's. There are picnic areas for those who pack their own food. Alcoholic beverages and glass containers may not be brought into the park. Coolers are allowed.

FIRST AID: Minor medical problems are handled at this station near the main entrance.

BEACH SHOP: The Beach Haus shop stocks bathing suits, T-shirts, shorts, sunglasses, hats, sunscreen, beach towels, and more.

Admission Prices

Prices do not include sales tax and are likely to change in 2015. **Note:** Admission is an option with a Magic Your Way ticket that includes a Water Park Fun & More add-on and is included with a Premium Annual Pass.

	ADULTS	CHILDREN*
One-Day Ticket	$53	$45
Annual Pass	$104	$85

* 3 through 9 years of age; children under age 3 free

Daredevil Disney

You've catapulted through the galaxy on Space Mountain, braved an encounter with an angry Yeti at Expedition Everest, and become something of a human yo-yo on the Tower of Terror. Now what? Believe it or not, there are plenty of thrills awaiting you outside the theme park gates. Some of them, such as the wedgie-inducing slides at the water parks, are well known. Others may be lower key, but they're definitely high octane. Here's a rundown of our favorite theme-park-alternative thrill rides.

BALLOONING: Going up! A huge, tethered, helium balloon known as "Characters in Flight" lifts guests 400 feet high into the sky. Moored to a landing at Downtown Disney West Side, the balloon can accommodate up to 29 guests at a time—treating all to sweeping panoramic views of Walt Disney World and beyond. It operates on a first-come, first-served basis Sunday through Thursday from 8:30 A.M. until 11 P.M. and from 10:30 A.M. until midnight on Friday and Saturday. Adults pay about $18 per flight, while kids (ages 3 through 9) pay about $12. Expect to be airborne for about 8 to 10 minutes. This attraction does not operate during windy or inclement weather.

MOTORBOATING: If you've been to Walt Disney World before, you've no doubt seen folks tooling about in zippy little motorboats. But have you ever actually given one a try? It's an experience we highly recommend.

For starters, the watercraft known as Sea Raycers are indeed speedy. And it's an experience everyone can enjoy (though guests need to be at least 12 years old and at least 5 feet tall to drive). Expect to pay about $35 for a half hour. Be sure to wear a watch, as you're apt to lose track of time. For more info, turn to page 238.

PARASAILING: Even if you've never had the urge to be a human kite, consider giving this a whirl. After a simple liftoff from the back of a boat, you and your parachute gradually climb skyward. Before you know it, you're eye level with the roof of the Contemporary resort hotel. A few peaceful minutes later, the hotel and the nearby Magic Kingdom appear to have shrunk considerably. It's not unlike the illusion of flying over London in Peter Pan's Flight. Only this

flight's no illusion: You're really 450 or so feet above it all. And don't worry about the landing. It's as smooth as the trip itself. The attendants simply reel you in for a soft touchdown on the back of the boat.

For information on prices and reservations, turn to page 238.

STOCK CAR RACING: Few people can say they've ridden shotgun in a race car, let alone driven one. And this is the real deal. Whether you do it as a driver or a passenger, the Richard Petty Driving Experience is guaranteed to deliver the adrenaline surge of a lifetime. The track is a bit off the beaten path (though it is close to the Magic Kingdom parking lot), so some Walt Disney World guests fail to notice it. Those who do tend to come back for more.

For the ride-along experience, you'll don a helmet and climb through the window into the passenger seat. Buckle up and . . . you're off! The big challenges here: (1) not obsessing over the speedometer (it may reach 145 mph) and (2) keeping your head straight (the force from the velocity tends to push noggins to the right).

The expert driver will take you inches from the wall and zip in and out of traffic. (Yes, there are other cars on the track at the same time.) If you're in the driver's seat, you'll have an expert driver to follow.

For details on pricing, reservations, and the scoop on the new kids' program, see page 242.

SURFING: When the sun comes up, so does the surf at Disney's Typhoon Lagoon. On select days, guests can take part in a surf clinic taught by competitive surfers. Instructors control the height of the waves—and they give Mother Nature a run for her money.

If you've never hung ten before, know this: It ain't easy. But once you've managed to get up on a board, it's a blast.

For more information, call 407-939-7873.

WATERSKIING: Florida weather being what it is (hot!), waterskiing (as well as wakeboarding and tubing) never really goes out of season. It's a refreshing way to see the sights of Bay Lake—and a serious workout to boot. Sammy Duvall instructors are on hand to assist. For additional information, see page 239.

EVERYTHING ELSE IN THE WORLD

Fort Wilderness

In a part of the state where campgrounds tend to look like dried pastures—barren and very hot—the Fort Wilderness Resort and Campground, located almost due east of the Contemporary resort, is an anomaly—a forested, 750-acre wonder of tall slash pines, white-flowering bay trees, and ancient cypresses hung with Spanish moss. Seminole Indians once hunted and fished here.

There are nearly 800 campsites arranged in several campground loops (including sites that are big-rig ready). There are more than 400 Wilderness Cabins (which fall into Disney's "moderate" resort category) available for rent, completely furnished and fitted with all the comforts of home. For additional information, refer to the *Transportation & Accommodations* chapter of this book.

Scattered throughout the campground loops are sporting facilities, including two tennis courts and many small playgrounds, basketball, tetherball, and volleyball courts. Fort Wilderness has riding stables (with rather mellow horses), two swimming pools, a marina full of boats, a canoe livery, a beach, bikes and golf carts for rent, and a nature trail. Some facilities are available to Fort Wilderness guests only; some are open to all.

There's a pony farm (which offers rides to young guests) and a barn that's home to the horses that pull the Magic Kingdom's Main Street trolleys. The barn houses a small museum that celebrates horses and the cherished role they've played in Disney history.

Two stores—the Settlement Trading Post and the Meadow Trading Post—stock campers' necessities, a limited supply of groceries, and souvenirs. And then there's Pioneer Hall, the home of the Hoop-Dee-Doo Musical Revue dinner show (described in the *Good Meals, Great Times* chapter). This rustic structure (made of white pine shipped from Montana) also houses a popular (and reasonably priced) buffet restaurant and a small lounge area. Mickey's Backyard Barbecue is offered here during busy times of the year (when the weather's nice).

ARCHERY: It takes a steady hand to hit the bull's-eye at the Fort Wilderness Archery Experience. After a brief training session led by a skilled guide, participants (age 6 and up) get to shoot for that coveted bull's-eye. Cost is about $25. To book the Fort Wilderness Archery experience, call 407-WDW-PLAY (939-7529).

BEACHES AND SWIMMING: The beach on the shore of Bay Lake is a good spot for sunning or snoozing in a hammock. There are also two pools for campers' use. The Meadows Pool complex has a new slide and water play area. Note that the beaches and pools are open to Fort Wilderness guests only. Swimming and wading are not allowed at the beach (due to a naturally occurring bacteria found in many Florida lakes).

BIKE RENTALS: Bicycles may be rented at the Bike Barn for trips along the paths of Fort Wilderness— or just for getting around. Bikes cost about $9 per half hour or $22 per day. Helmets are included at no extra charge.

BLACKSMITH SHOP: The pleasant fellow who shoes the draft horses that pull trolleys in the Magic Kingdom park is on hand most mornings to answer questions and talk about his job; occasionally, guests may even watch him at work, fitting the big, friendly animals with the special polyurethane-covered, steel-cored horseshoes that are used to protect the animals' hooves. This shop is located at the Tri-Circle-D Ranch.

BOATING: Fort Wilderness is ribboned with tranquil canals that make for delightful canoe trips of one to three hours—or longer if you take fishing gear and elect to wet your line. Canoe rentals are available at the Bike Barn for about $8 per half hour or $12 per hour. For a trip around Bay Lake, zippy little Sea Raycer motorboats, Boston Whaler Montauks, and pontoon boats are available for rent at the marina, at the north end of the campground. (Refer to the *Sports* chapter for details.)

CAMPFIRE SING-ALONG: Held nightly (weather permitting) near the Meadow Trading Post at the center of the campground, this evening program features Disney movies, a sing-along, and a marshmallow roast. Chip and Dale often put in an appearance. It's open to WDW resort guests only. There is no charge to attend, but marshmallows come with a small fee.

CARRIAGE RIDES: Guests may enjoy a relaxing and intimate carriage ride through the picturesque grounds of Fort Wilderness. The rate for each 25-minute ride is $45.

Small carriages can hold up to 2 adults and a small child. Larger carriages fit 4 adults, or 2 adults and up to 3 small kids. Reservations are a must. Rides are offered nightly. Call 407-WDW-PLAY (939-7529) for information or to make a reservation. Walk-up reservations are sometimes possible. (Ask the driver about buying tickets. If they're available, expect to pay with cash or a Disney Resort ID card. Credit cards are not accepted.) Rides may be canceled due to inclement weather. Cancellations must be made at least 24 hours ahead to avoid paying full price.

Note that guests are picked up in front of Crockett's Tavern at Pioneer Hall. Feel free to bring your own liquid refreshments.

ELECTRIC CART RENTALS: Available at Reception Outpost (about $50 for 24 hours) for sightseeing or transportation. Renters must be at least 18 years old and have a valid driver's license. Reservations are necessary; call 407-824-2742 for reservations and information.

FISHING EXCURSIONS ON BAY LAKE: Walt Disney World's restrictive fishing policy means plenty of angling action—largemouth bass weighing two to eight pounds, mainly—for those who sign up for fishing excursions.

The fee ranges from approximately $225 to $250 for up to five people for a two-hour excursion (one additional hour is about $100) and includes gear, a guide, and soft drinks; no license is required. The price varies based on time of day, with the early morning trips commanding the highest rate.

Note that all fishing is strictly catch-and-release. Call 407-WDW-BASS (939-2277) for exact times and to make reservations.

FISHING IN THE CANALS: In addition to largemouth bass, catfish and panfish can be caught here as well. Those without their own fishing gear will find cane poles and lures for sale at the trading posts; equipment is also available for rent at the Bike Barn. No license is required. Fort Wilderness resort guests may toss their lines in right from the shore. All WDW fishing is strictly catch-and-release. For pricing and more info, visit *www.disneyworldfishing.com*. Fort Wilderness is the only place on Walt Disney World property where canal fishing is allowed.

LAWN MOWER TREE: The remnants of a tree that mysteriously grew around a lawn mower is a Fort Wilderness point of interest worth seeking out. It's just off the path leading to the marina, across the way from the Meadow Trading Post.

PLAYGROUNDS, VOLLEYBALL, TETHER-BALL, AND BASKETBALL COURTS: These are scattered throughout the camping loops. There is no charge to use the courts.

ELECTRICAL WATER PAGEANT: Originally presented for the dedication of the Polynesian Luau dinner show in 1971, this cavalcade of lights is presented nightly on the waters of Bay Lake and the Seven Seas Lagoon. The simple pageant consists of two strings of seven barges, each carrying a 25-foot-tall screen of lights featuring King Neptune and creatures of the sea.

And it's all set to music. The show can be seen from the beach at Fort Wilderness, as well as from the Contemporary, Polynesian Village, and Grand Floridian resorts. (We've caught it while waiting for the monorail at the Magic Kingdom, too.) Ask for the schedule at your resort's lobby concierge desk.

PONY RIDES: This enclave behind Pioneer Hall is home to some friendly ponies. Pony rides, offered seasonally, are available between 10 A.M. and 5 P.M. for $5. (The pony-ride weight limit is 80 pounds.) The farm is a good place to visit before the Hoop-Dee-Doo Musical Revue.

TENNIS: Two tennis courts are available; play is on a first-come, first-served basis.

TRAIL RIDES: Guided horseback trips depart four times daily from the Trail Blaze Corral and take riders on a leisurely, meandering ride through the Florida wilderness, where it is not uncommon to see birds, deer, and even an occasional alligator. Galloping is not part of the experience, so you don't need riding know-how to sign up. Cost is about $46 per person. Children under age 9 are not allowed to ride. Parents must sign consent forms for kids under age 18. There is a weight limit of 250 pounds. Sturdy shoes with defined heels are recommended; open-toed shoes are not permitted. Reservations are necessary; call 407-WDW-PLAY (939-7529) up to 180 days in advance.

TRI-CIRCLE-D RANCH: This corner of Fort Wilderness is the place that the world champion Percherons and the draft horses that pull trolleys down Main Street in the Magic Kingdom call home. You may watch them chomping on their food and occasionally see young colts and fillies as well. The Tri-Circle-D insignia above the barn door—two small circles atop a large one with the letter D inside—is the WDW brand. The barn is also the site of a museum that pays tribute to horses and their role in Disney history.

WAGON RIDES: The wagon departs from Pioneer Hall at 7 P.M. and 9:30 P.M. and carries guests on a trip through wooded areas near Bay Lake. Each ride lasts about 45 minutes and concludes at Pioneer Hall. Purchase tickets from the wagon ride host: $8 for adults, $5 for kids ages 3 through 9. Children under age 12 must be accompanied by an adult.

On nights when the Magic Kingdom offers a fireworks presentation, Fort Wilderness offers "fireworks wagon rides." These excursions are in addition to those regularly scheduled. Expect fireworks wagon rides to depart at 8:30 P.M. for a 9 P.M. fireworks show. The Wishes fireworks show is viewed from a distance, but the experience is made special by plugging into the show's audio soundtrack.

Group wagon rides are available by calling 407-824-2734 (at least 24 hours in advance). The price is about $300 per hour.

WILDERNESS BACK TRAIL ADVENTURE: A 2-hour "off-road" Segway tour of Fort Wilderness, this experience costs about $85 per person. For details, refer to page 234 or call 407-WDW-TOUR (939-8687).

Essentials

HOW TO GET THERE: From outside the World, take Magic Kingdom Exit 64B off I-4 onto U.S. 192, go through the Magic Kingdom Auto Plaza, and, bearing to your right, follow the Fort Wilderness signs. This is the most expeditious way to go, even for Walt Disney World resort guests.

By WDW Transportation: Buses or boats. Buses can get you just about anywhere, but allow yourself plenty of time—the transportation system, while efficient, is time-consuming.

Boats are also available from Magic Kingdom marinas (about a 30-minute ride) and from the Contemporary and Wilderness Lodge resorts (about a 25-minute ride).

WHERE TO EAT: For a description of the Trail's End restaurant at Fort Wilderness, refer to the *Good Meals, Great Times* chapter.

The Settlement Trading Post, located not far from the beach at the north end of the campground, and the Meadow Trading Post, located near the center of Fort Wilderness, offer a limited supply of food staples. For serious grocery shopping, head to a nearby supermarket. Ask the lobby concierge for directions.

HOT TIP!

Festive, horse-drawn "sleigh rides" may be offered at Ft. Wilderness from Thanksgiving week through December. For details or reservations, call 407-WDW-PLAY.

WDW Spas

Spa Tips

- Reserve treatments far in advance and be sure to confirm all appointments.

- If you'll feel more comfortable with either a male or a female spa therapist, let your preferences be known when you make your reservation. The spas will accommodate such requests whenever possible.

- Plan to arrive 30 minutes prior to your appointment. That'll give you time to change and relax. (Arriving late will reduce your treatment time.)

- Guests under age 18 must be accompanied by an adult doing a spa treatment.

- If you're scheduled for a body treatment, leave all clothes in a locker. Robes (and slippers) are provided.

- Leave valuables in the safe in your resort room. (If you forget, you can store it in a locker at the spa.)

- Before you stash your mobile phone in a locker, be sure to turn it off.

- It's always a good idea to take a quick shower before a treatment—especially if you've been at the beach or running around theme parks beforehand.

- Drink plenty of water after your spa visit. It will counter any dehydrating effects you may experience as the result of a treatment.

- Build time into your schedule to enjoy post-treatment relaxation time at the spa. You'll want to hold on to that glow as long as possible!

- Most spas include a 20 percent gratuity with each spa service. Additional gratuities may be added at your discretion.

For many guests, a day at the theme parks is an exciting test of physical endurance—complete with sprinting (say, from Dumbo to Splash Mountain before that Fastpass+ time expires), weight lifting (toting tired toddlers), and long-distance hiking (covering more than a mile to reach the American Adventure pavilion from Epcot's front gate—and back again!). Fortunately, there are many ways to rest and rejuvenate weary bones, throbbing feet, and noise-addled noggins. Chief among them is a visit to a soothing spa (aah). There are four such spots on Disney property, open to WDW resort guests and day visitors alike.

SENSES, A SPA AT DISNEY'S GRAND FLORIDIAN RESORT: You don't need a magic wand to make your stress disappear—not if you can pay a visit to the elegant pampering palace called Senses. In addition to the treatments offered at its sister spa at the Saratoga Springs resort (see page 229), this spot also offers a selection of soothing packages. Among them: the bridal package (de-stress bath, massage, facial and pedicure), express package (featuring an abbreviated massage, facial, and manicure), and the couples' escape package (back sugar scrub and massage).

Signature treatments include revitalizing aromatherapy baths, coconut age-reducing facial, and a citrus-and-mint hydrating body wrap. Massage options: Swedish, warm stones, and one specially designed for expectant mothers. Manicures, pedicures, and other hand and foot treatments are also available. There are manicures for kids, too.

Treatment hours are usually 8 A.M. to 8 P.M. daily. Prices start at about $135 for a 50-minute massage and about $145 for a facial, plus tax.

To book an appointment at the spa, call 407-WDW-SPAS (939-7727). For details, visit *https://disneyworld.disney.go.com/spas/*.

MANDARA SPA AT THE DOLPHIN: As exotic as it is peaceful, this retreat officially pampered its first visitors in 2006. Guests have been stepping up to swap their stress for smiles ever since.

Mandara, which has locations throughout the world, specializes in treatments that are meant to reflect the "beauty, spirit, and traditions of both Eastern and Western cultures." The spa menu showcases Balinese massage, a variation of Swedish massage. It incorporates stretching, "vigorous yet relaxing" movements, and elements of acupressure. Of course, that's just one of many services offered here—all of which emphasize physical wellness and spiritual well-being. Other treatments include the Mandara Four Hand massage, Elemis Aroma Stone Therapy, and Elemis Deep Tissue Muscle massage. The Elemis Visible Brilliance Facial ($160) is perfect for those dark circles under the eyes while smoothing wrinkles. And the exotic Frangipani Body Nourish Wrap ($220, plus gratuity, for 75 minutes) includes 50 minutes of massage and incorporates a special oil from the rare and fragrant Balinese Frangipani flower.

In addition to Balinese-inspired architecture, two interior gardens provide retreats before guests begin the spa ritual. The goal here is to provide a place for guests to rejuvenate their minds as well as those aching "I can't believe I covered four theme parks in two days!" muscles. For more information, call 800-227-1500 or 407-934-4772, or visit *www.swandolphin.com.*

SENSES, A SPA AT DISNEY'S SARATOGA SPRINGS RESORT: Along with its new name, the Saratoga spa has a new look. This soothing space is something of a sibling to the spa over at Disney's Grand Floridian resort. Signature services include those offered at the Grand Floridian location (see page 228), plus a Sweet Red Rose Body treatment (50 minutes), custom bath treatment (25 minutes), and the "Revitalizing Blueberry Facial" (80 minutes). Also on tap: aromatherapy, Swedish massage, warm-stone massage, rejuvenation treatments focused on the hands and feet, plus body wraps and scrubs. Manicures, pedicures, and organic facials are options, too.

Located on the shore of Village Lake, the spa is near the Fitness Center at the Saratoga Springs resort. The hours are generally from 8 A.M. to 8 P.M. A 50-minute massage starts at about $135, with facials going for about $145 (plus gratuity). A variety of packages is available. For more information and to make reservations, call 407-WDW-SPAS (939-7727).

THE SPA AT BUENA VISTA PALACE: A plush, peaceful place, this spa is as well equipped as they come. High-tech chairs with whirlpool footbaths make getting a pedicure a real event. And a cool-mud Theme Park Leg Relief Wrap can put the spring back in the step of even the most labored lower limbs. Landscaped, outdoor whirlpools, plus locker room saunas and steam rooms, are there to aid the relaxation process.

Among the more than 75 soothing treatments from which to choose are aromatherapy and massage, including shiatsu, Swedish, deep-tissue, and reflexology. A variety of special facials (including one for sun-stressed skin), scrubs, and wraps are available. The spa also offers massages for kids, as well as Little Princess facials, manicures, and pedicures. A salon offers the usual lineup of services.

The Spa at the Buena Vista Palace hotel is across from the Downtown Disney Marketplace, on Buena Vista Drive. Hours are usually 8 A.M. to 8 P.M., but vary seasonally. A 25-minute massage costs about $70, and facials are about $70. Full- and half-day packages are available, as are custom packages. For information, call 407-827-3200. Reservations are recommended and are accepted up to one year in advance.

Internet Access at WDW

We'll resist the urge to chastise you for insisting on checking your office e-mail while on vacation (since we're similarly obsessed) and instead happily report that all Walt Disney World resorts offer free in-room, high-speed Internet access. Of course, you'll need to supply the hardware. Complimentary Wi-Fi (wireless fidelity) is offered at all Walt Disney World-owned-and-operated resorts, plus the four theme parks and Downtown Disney. Naturally, your computer, tablet, or phone must be Wi-Fi ready. Note that in-room, high-speed Internet service (Wi-Fi or with a connection cable) is also available at the Four Seasons and the Swan and Dolphin resorts.

If you'd like to access the Internet but didn't pack your own equipment, ask your lobby concierge to direct you to the nearest resort business center. There you can check your e-mail, peruse the news, manage your fantasy sports teams, and more. Fees vary— be sure to inquire before you start surfing.

Just for Kids

Walt Disney World may appeal to the kid in all of us, but some activities are meant for the actual young—not just the young at heart. With the exception of the Princess Tea Party, the following programs are specifically for guests who can't remember life before the Internet. (Grown-ups can relax while their kids are entertained.) The programs are popular and accommodate a limited number of guests—so book early (up to 180 days ahead): 407-WDW-PLAY (939-7529). Note that the adventures listed are not offered every day.

ALBATROSS TREASURE CRUISE: Thar be treasure in Crescent Lake! Kids are invited to follow clues and join in the hunt. The 2-hour quest takes young adventurers to several stops and includes a reading of the "The Legend of the Albatross." The ship weighs anchor at the Yacht Club marina on select mornings at about 9:30 A.M. Cost per child is about $40. It's open to potty-trained guests ages 4–12. Participants should wear socks and sneakers.

BAYOU PIRATE ADVENTURE: Young adventurers sporting bandannas board a pirate vessel at Port Orleans Riverside and learn all about Captain John Lafitte as they follow his map on a quest for booty. Cost per child is about $34. It's open to potty-trained guests ages 4–12 on select mornings. Participants should wear socks and sneakers.

ISLANDS OF THE CARIBBEAN PIRATE CRUISE: Young buccaneers board a battered pirate ship at Caribbean Beach resort and set sail with a seasoned scallywag at the helm. The captain tells tall tales and leads his crew through treacherous waters (okay, so they're not really treacherous) on a hunt for treasure. Cost per child is about $34. It's open to potty-trained guests ages 4–12. Participants should wear socks and sneakers.

MY DISNEY GIRL'S PERFECTLY PRINCESS TEA PARTY: Young regals (and their grown-up guardians) are encouraged to dress like their favorite princess for this festive tea party, offered daily from 10:30 A.M. to noon (except Tuesdays and Saturdays) in the Garden View Lounge at Walt Disney World's Grand Floridian resort. The tea party is hosted by Miss Rose Petal, a magical rose from Aurora's garden that has come to life to lead storytelling, sing-alongs, and a princess parade. Guests may take a break from sipping tea and eating cake to visit with Princess Aurora, aka Sleeping Beauty.

All guests between the ages of 4 and 12 get a My Disney Girl doll, dressed as Princess Aurora, plus accessories. The cost for one adult and child (ages 3–12) is $275, including gratuity (tax is extra). Each extra child is about $182 (plus tax), while an extra adult pays about $94 (plus tax). If you'd like a child under age 3 to receive the merchandise, they should be listed as a 3-year-old. Reservations are required and may be made up to 180 days ahead.

PIRATE ADVENTURE: Ahoy there, mateys! In this adventure, young pirates don red bandannas and hit the high seas in search of treasure. The ship shoves off at the Grand Floridian marina on select mornings. From there, it visits exotic ports of call (other resort marinas), where guests collect valuable treasures and enjoy a light snack. It's available to potty-trained kids ages 4–12 on select mornings. Cost per child is about $34. Reservations are required and are available up to 180 days ahead. Note that participants should wear socks and sneakers.

WONDERLAND TEA PARTY: Fans of Alice and her Wonderland friends will have a blast at this party presented at 1900 Park Fare at Disney's Grand Floridian resort. During the hour-long event, kids make and eat cupcakes. They'll also be treated to a story and have tea with the characters. The cost is about $50 per child, ages 4–12 (potty-trained). The tea party is offered Monday through Friday at 2 P.M. Reservations are required and are available 180 days in advance.

Specialty Cruises

At Walt Disney World, every evening ends with a bang—which comes in the form of pyrotechnic spectaculars. Two such presentations, the Magic Kingdom's Wishes fireworks and Epcot's IllumiNations: Reflections of Earth, are seen by thousands of park-goers on a nightly basis. However, these displays are also enjoyed by a privileged few, far removed from the hubbub of theme park crowds, yet close enough to marvel at the subtleties of each brilliant burst. These are the guests who chose to book a specialty cruise. This vintage vantage point is available to everyone, provided that the rates don't break the budget and that reservations are made in advance. Of course, there is the other extreme: a peaceful, moonlit cruise on the quiet waterways of the World. This option is also available to guests who book a specialty cruise.

Reservations are accepted up to 24 hours ahead; advance reservations, accepted up to 180 days ahead, are strongly recommended. While specifics may change, the following is an indication of what was available at press time.

THE GRAND I: This striking 52-foot Sea Ray Sedan Bridge yacht escorts up to 17 guests at a time. A 3-hour tour of the Seven Seas Lagoon and Bay Lake culminates with a front-row seat for the Magic Kingdom's fireworks, when

possible. (The vessel has an audio feed that allows guests to hear the show's soundtrack.)

The *Grand I* yacht departs from the Grand Floridian, but can stop at the Polynesian Village, Contemporary, Wilderness Lodge, or Fort Wilderness on request. It starts at about $700 per hour to rent, with the per-boatload fee covering up to 17 guests, plus a driver and a deckhand. Butler and private dining service is available (for an additional fee). This is the most luxurious watercraft experience at Walt Disney World. Call 407-824-2682 for more *Grand I* yacht pricing information or to make a reservation.

PONTOON BOATS: More practical than luxurious, Disney's fleet of pontoon boats still deliver a crowd-pleasing cruise experience. The boats, which accommodate up to 10, take guests on tours of the Seven Seas Lagoon and Bay Lake, near the Magic Kingdom, as well as Crescent Lake, near Epcot's World Showcase. Those in the Magic Kingdom area are treated to VIP viewing of the Wishes fireworks show (as well as the audio), while Epcot-area cruisers take in IllumiNations: Reflections of Earth, when available. Larger "premium" pontoon boats offer the Wishes soundtrack—a special treat!

Pontoon cruises last about one hour. Magic Kingdom fireworks excursions depart from the Grand Floridian, Polynesian Village, Contemporary, Wilderness Lodge, and Fort Wilderness marinas. IllumiNations cruises leave from the Yacht Club marina. The cost for cruises (which includes a driver) starts at about $225 to $375 per boatload (higher for fireworks cruises). Call 407-WDW-PLAY (939-7529) for additional details or to make reservations.

VIP Tour? Sure!

You may have seen them in the theme parks—those cheery folks in the plaid vests. They are VIP guides, leading guests on customized trips through Walt Disney World.

The point is to minimize the hassle factor, while maximizing the overall magic component. Though participating in a VIP tour won't necessarily let you cut the line, it may yield some special seating for stage shows and parades. One tour guide can host up to 10 guests at a cost of about $175–$315 per hour. There is a 6-hour minimum per trip. Parties larger than 10 will require a second guide. Make your needs known when you book the tour. Cancellations must be made at least 48 hours in advance to avoid a fee. Call 407-560-4033 for additional VIP tour information or to make a reservation.

Tours and Programs

Here's your chance to experience Walt Disney World from the inside out. Adult guests may be required to carry a photo ID when attending backstage programs. Tours and prices are subject to change in 2015; for information or to make reservations, call 407-WDW-TOUR (939-8687) between 8 A.M. and 8 P.M. (daily) and have your credit card handy. Photography is not permitted while in "backstage" areas of Walt Disney World. **Note:** Tours marked with an asterisk (∗) may be included with the Magic Your Way Premium Package, though restrictions may apply. Prices quoted do not include tax.

BACKSTAGE MAGIC (Monday through Friday; 9 A.M.): This is one of Disney World's best programs. Highlighting the nearly 8-hour exploration of the Magic Kingdom, Disney's Hollywood Studios, and Epcot may be an underground tour of the Magic Kingdom's Utilidors—Disney's tunnel system. Lunch is included, as are a few surprises. Cost is $250, plus tax. Park admission is not required or included. This is one of the most popular WDW experiences—book it as early as possible.

BACKSTAGE SAFARI∗
(Monday, Wednesday, Thursday, Friday; 8:30 A.M. and 1 P.M.): This 3-hour tour offers guests a look at conservation, animal care, behavioral studies, and the Animal Nutrition Center and Veterinary Hospital, plus a special ride on Kilimanjaro Safaris. The cost is about $72, and theme park admission is required, but not included. Guests must be at least 16 years old to participate in the tour.

BEHIND THE SEEDS∗ (daily; every hour between 10:30 A.M. and 4:30 P.M.): An opportunity for guests of all ages to get a closer look at the four greenhouses and fish farm that are part of The Land pavilion at Epcot. During the encounter, guests will have close encounters with insects and plants. A guide shares knowledge of hydroponics growing systems and interesting crops from around the globe. You may have a chance to release some ladybugs or feed the fish. Expect to be on your feet for the full hour of this experience. Cost is $20 per adult, $16 per child (ages 3–9). This tour is best enjoyed by sturdy adults and older kids. Reservations may be made in advance or at the tour desk on the lower level of The Land (near the entrance to Soarin').

DISNEY'S FAMILY MAGIC TOUR∗ (daily; 10 A.M.): Families and friends may join in this 2-hour "scavenger-hunt-style" quest to save the Magic Kingdom. Cost is $34 (it's available to everyone, but recommended for parties with kids between the ages of 4 and 12). Magic Kingdom admission is required but is not included.

DIVEQUEST (Tuesday–Thursday; 4:30 and 5:30 P.M.; Friday and Saturday; 4:30 and 5:30 P.M.): The highlight of the 2½-hour program is a 40-minute underwater adventure—complete with sharks, turtles, rays, and other fish—in The Seas with Nemo & Friends aquarium. Participants must show proof of current scuba certification. Cost is about $175. Guests ages 10–12 must dive with a parent or guardian. Gear is provided. Epcot park admission isn't required or included.

DOLPHINS IN DEPTH (Tuesday–Saturday; 9:45 A.M.): This 3-hour Epcot program (about 30 minutes takes place in the water) teaches guests about dolphin behavior as they interact with the animals and observe researchers and trainers working with them. Cost is about $199. Minimum age is 13. Guests 13–17 must be accompanied by a paying adult. Park admission is not required or included. Wet suits are provided; wear your own swimsuit.

EPCOT SEAS AQUA TOUR (Tuesday–Saturday; 12:30 P.M.): A 2½-hour program (about 30 minutes of which is in the water) that lets guests learn about and interact with ocean life in The Seas with Nemo & Friends pavilion. First, guests watch a video about sea creatures, then they join them in their habitat using a Supplied-Air Snorkel system. Cost is about $140. Gear is included, as are refreshments, a T-shirt, and a group photo. Guests must wear a bathing suit. Age 8 and up. Epcot admission is not required or included.

KEYS TO THE KINGDOM* (daily; 8:30, 9, and 9:30 A.M.): A 5-hour tour that offers an on-site orientation to the history and workings of Walt Disney World's original theme park, the Magic Kingdom. Guests visit an attraction (waiting in the regular attraction line) and take a peek at the Utilidors (the legendary tunnels underneath the park). Cost is about $80, plus theme park admission. Lunch is included. Guests must be at least 16 years old to participate.

PHOTO BY JILL SAFRO

THE MAGIC BEHIND OUR STEAM TRAINS* (Monday–Saturday; 7:30 A.M.): A 3-hour tour that gives guests an inside look at the Walt Disney World Railroad. In addition to an exploration of Walt Disney's passion for steam trains, guests visit the backstage "roundhouse" where the steam trains are stored and join the opening crew as they prepare for the daily railroad operation in the Magic Kingdom. Guests must be at least 10 to take the tour. Cost

is about $54 per person. Theme park admission is required but not included.

WALT DISNEY: MARCELINE TO MAGIC KINGDOM (Monday, Wednesday, Friday; 8:15 A.M.): Explore how events in Walt Disney's life helped shape the Walt Disney World Resort and the attractions within it in this 2½- to 3-hour walking tour. As one of Walt's final visions, the Magic Kingdom shares many similarities with the story of his life. By using the park as a walking timeline, guests discover how Walt's life inspired him to create some of the most cherished stories and attractions the parks have to offer. Guests also get an insider look at several of those aforementioned attractions. Tours cost $30 per person (plus park admission). Guests should arrive 15 minutes early and wear their most comfortable walking shoes (expect to cover a lot of ground). It's available to guests age 12 and up.

THE UNDISCOVERED FUTURE WORLD* (Monday—Friday; 9 A.M.): Walt Disney dreamed about making the world a better place. In this 4-hour tour, guests are taken back to the creation of Epcot and learn about Walt's lofty ambitions and his legacy.

Guests walk to Future World pavilions and learn how each area celebrates humanity's accomplishments and challenges. The goal is to share the vision behind the park.

Cost is about $64 per person, plus tax. Guests must be at least 16 years old to attend this walking program. Park admission is required but is not included.

WANYAMA SAFARI (daily; 3:45 P.M.): A 3-hour experience that includes a private tour of the animal savannas surrounding Disney's Animal Kingdom Lodge. Following the tour, guests have dinner at Jiko—The Cooking Place. (It's a family-style meal.) Guests must be at least

HOT TIP!

Are you a Walt Disney World Annual Passholder? Perhaps you are a member of Disney Vacation Club (DVC) or the Automobile Association of America (AAA), or hold a Disney Visa card? If so, you may be able to save a chunk of change on some of the tours described on these pages! Be sure to inquire about potential discounts when you call 407-WDW-TOUR (939-8687).

Wild Africa Trek

A thrilling, 3-hour adventure, the Wild Africa Trek is not for the faint of heart or those with any trepidation about teetering on a rickety rope bridge a mere 10 feet above a congregation of crocodiles—who have been known to leap as much as 8 feet at a time!

The guided tour, which is offered daily at Disney's Animal Kingdom park, is a VIP safari adventure for groups of 12 or less. It includes hiking through jungle, near the edge of a cliff, and over the savanna—plus many up-close encounters of the animal kind.

Available to guests age 8 and above, the rain-or-shine trek costs vary, depending on the season, and includes snacks (you can't bring your own) and a PhotoPass CD. Park admission is required but not included. This is an active experience—be sure to wear comfortable shoes and attire. Note that there are no "chicken exits" here. For pricing and information, visit *www.disneyworld.com*. To make a reservation, call 407-939-8687.

Guests who wish to participate in a less physical journey or a wheelchair accessible trek may call 407-938-1373 to request an alternative offering.

scenes. As guests explore various lands, a guide offers insight into the complexities of caring for wild animals and their habitats.

A light continental breakfast is served at the tour's halfway point. Cost is about $60 per person (plus tax). Theme park admission is required, but not included. Guests must be at least 14 years old to participate.

WILDERNESS BACK TRAIL ADVENTURE (Tuesday through Saturday): A 2-hour experience, this adventure lets guests explore the Fort Wilderness area while aboard a Segway personal transporter. (It's a special model with "off-road" type tires.) The first hour is devoted to training (it's not as easy as it looks!), with the second spent exploring with an experienced storytelling guide. Guests must be at least 16 and in good health. (You'll be on your feet the whole time, and operating the Segway requires more muscle than one might expect.) The cost is approximately $90, plus tax.

YULETIDE FANTASY (seasonal): A festive 3½-hour experience, this program showcases the way Disney weaves stories and folklore into decorations found in the theme parks and resorts. It offers a unique perspective on how colors, textures, architecture, and illusions help all of Walt Disney World deck the halls for the holidays.

The cost is about $95, plus tax per person. Theme park admission is not included or required for this experience. Guests must be at least 16 years old to participate. All guests must present a photo ID.

8 years old and staying at Animal Kingdom Lodge. Cost is about $191 per person. (Price includes tax and gratuity.) The Wanyama Safari may be booked up to 180 days in advance. Call 407-938-4755 for more information or to make a reservation.

PHOTO BY MIKE CARROLL

WILD BY DESIGN* (Monday, Wednesday–Friday; 8:30 A.M.): A 3-hour experience that invites guests to learn how art, architecture, historical artifacts, and storytelling were combined to create Disney's Animal Kingdom. The tour takes place in the park, not behind the

Sports

236 WDW Golf

237 Tennis

238 Waters of the World

240 ESPN Wide World of Sports Complex

241 More Sporting Fun

SPORTS

First-time visitors don't always realize that Disney provides a plethora of sporting opportunities. Within WDW's 40 or so square miles, there are more tennis courts than at most tennis resorts and more holes of championship-caliber golf than at most golf centers, plus so many other diversions—from fishing and biking to boating, swimming, parasailing, and horseback riding—that the quantity and variety are matched by few other vacation destinations.

So while the family golfers are pursuing a perfect swing on one of three first-rate, 18-hole courses, tennis buffs can be wearing themselves out on the courts, sailors can be sailing, water-skiers can be skimming back and forth across powerboat wakes, and anglers can be casting away in hopes of hooking a big bass. Those who prefer to spectate rather than participate can visit a virtual sports mecca at the ESPN Wide World of Sports complex, an enormous, state-of-the-art facility that hosts a staggering array of sporting events, both amateur and professional. And those who prefer the sedate can treat themselves to a soothing spa treatment.

Instruction, as well as guides, drivers, and assorted supervisors, makes every sport as much fun for beginners as for hard-core aficionados. Moreover, the ready accessibility of WDW sporting activities—via an extensive system of public transportation (see *Transportation & Accommodations*)—means that no family member need curtail playtime to chauffeur others around.

WDW Golf

Most people don't immediately think of Disney World for a golf outing. Yet there are four superb 18-hole courses here: The Magnolia and the Palm are across from the Polynesian Village resort. Nearby is the Lake Buena Vista course. Its fairways are framed by Saratoga Springs and Old Key West resorts. And the Four Seasons resort boasts a stellar course, too. While the WDW courses won't set anyone's knees to knocking, they're demanding enough to have merited the status of a stop on the PGA Tour tournament trail.

PALM & MAGNOLIA: The wide-open, tree-dotted Magnolia measures 5,232 yards from the front tees, 6,642 from the middle, and 7,073 from the back. The Palm (which was recently redesigned by Arnold Palmer Course Design) is tighter, with more wooded fairways and nine water hazards; it measures 5,311 yards from the front, 6,461 from the middle, and 7,010 from the back. Both courses have received a four-star ("outstanding") rating from *Golf Digest* magazine. The Magnolia and Palm share two driving ranges and putting greens.

HOT TIP!

Single-rider, adaptive golf carts and clubhouse accommodations are available for guests with disabilities at all Walt Disney World resort golf courses. Call 407-WDW-GOLF (939-4653) for information.

Oak Trail: This nine-hole, 2,913-yard layout, a walking course tucked into a corner within the Magnolia, was designed for beginners and junior golfers, but it has some tough holes, including two par 5s. Many moderate and accomplished golfers enjoy the opportunity to tune up or play a quick 9.

LAKE BUENA VISTA COURSE: Joe Lee's design measures 5,194 yards from the front tees, 6,264 from the middle, and 6,749 from the rearmost markers. Among the shortest of the 18-hole, par-72 courses, it has a fair amount of water, and its tree-lined fairways are Walt Disney World's narrowest. The course is well suited for beginners but challenges experienced players. A driving range and putting green are also available.

Essentials

WHEN TO GO: January through April is peak golfing season. To beat the crowds, play on a Monday or Tuesday, and tee off in the late afternoons (mornings are very busy when the mercury rises). Summer discounts may apply. From June through late September, guests pay as little as $49 after 10 A.M. at Lake Buena Vista and Palm; and $59 at Magnolia after 10 A.M. After 3 P.M., the price drops to $39. Midmorning and midafternoon discounts, as well as Florida resident and Disney Vacation Club member specials, may be offered. Annual golf memberships are also a possibility.

RESERVATIONS: Call 407-WDW-GOLF (939-4653), or visit *www.disneygolf.com* to confirm rates and to secure tee times. From January through April, morning and early afternoon tee times should be reserved well in advance; starting times after 3 P.M. are often available at the last minute. Guests with confirmed reservations at a WDW-owned-and-operated resort, Swan, Dolphin, or at a resort on Hotel Plaza Boulevard may reserve 90 days ahead and save up to $25 per round. Others may book tee times 60 days ahead. Reservations must be made with a major credit card. Cancellations must be made at least 48 hours ahead to avoid penalties.

FEES: At the 18-hole courses, greens fees (including a required cart) vary with the course and season. Rates range from about $100 to $165 for day visitors (not staying at a Walt Disney World resort). Rates are usually discounted for guests staying at any resort on WDW property (including Swan, Dolphin, and the resorts on Hotel Plaza Boulevard).

Midafternoon rates, known as "twilight rates," may yield discounts. Available throughout the year, twilight rates run about $35 to $70.

Cost for adults to play Oak Trail is $38 for 9 holes; juniors (17 and under) pay $20 for 9 holes. Prices don't include tax and are subject to change.

INSTRUCTION: At the WDW Golf Studio at the Palm and Magnolia, private 45-minute lessons cost $75 for adults and $50 for juniors (up to age 17). Lessons are customized to all levels of experience. Video analysis may be used.

Reservations may be made up to 120 days in advance; call 407-WDW-GOLF (939-4653).

DRESS: Proper golf attire is required. Collared shirts or golf-style collarless shirts are necessary, and any shorts must be Bermuda length.

EQUIPMENT RENTAL: Equipment can be rented at all courses; club rentals start at about $55, plus tax. Photo ID is required for rentals. Range balls (about $7 per basket) are among available items. Guests staying at most WDW resorts receive complimentary club rental when they purchase a non-discounted round of golf at Disney's Palm, Magnolia, or Lake Buena Vista courses. Also included are range balls and transportation to and from the WDW resort via taxi (paid with vouchers). Swan, Dolphin, Four Seasons, and resorts on Hotel Plaza Boulevard are not included in transportation.

Tennis

Saratoga Springs Resort & Spa has two clay courts. All other Walt Disney World tennis is played on hard courts. Yacht and Beach Club share one court; Fort Wilderness, Saratoga Springs, Contemporary's Bay Lake Tower, Animal Kingdom's Kidani Village, and BoardWalk each have two; Old Key West has three; and the Swan and Dolphin share a four-court facility. Courts are free to guests staying at a WDW resort. For details or to make lesson reservations, call 321-228-1146.

Essentials

WHEN TO GO: Courts are often open from about 8 A.M. to 7 P.M. daily; courts at the Swan and Dolphin are open 24 hours a day (lighted courts are available). Weather-wise, January, October, and November are prime months for playing tennis. All courts are available on a first-come, first-served basis. During very busy periods, the length of time a single group of players can occupy a court is restricted to two hours on any morning, afternoon, or evening.

Equipment rental is limited at Walt Disney World (Swan and Dolphin only). Guests should bring their own tennis racquets and balls.

DRESS: Tennis whites are appropriate, but not required, for play on Disney's courts. Tennis shoes are a must.

Waters of the World

Boating

Disney World is the home of the country's largest fleet of pleasure boats. Cruising on Bay Lake and the Seven Seas Lagoon can be excellent sport, and a variety of boats are available for rent at WDW resort marinas. Bay Lake excursions originate from the Contemporary, Wilderness Lodge, and Fort Wilderness. The Polynesian Village and Grand Floridian send boaters out from their marinas on the shore of Seven Seas Lagoon. The Caribbean Beach resort rents watercraft for use on its own 45-acre Barefoot Bay. The Yacht and Beach Club, BoardWalk, Swan, and Dolphin share a boating haven in 25-acre Crescent Lake.

To rent, guests must show a valid driver's license or passport. Rental of certain craft may carry other requirements. No privately owned boats are permitted on WDW waters. All prices and times are subject to change.

BOSTON WHALER MONTAUK BOATS: These 17-foot motorboats are a good choice for relaxing cruises. They accommodate up to six passengers, and may be rented for about $45 per half hour at the Polynesian Village, Contemporary, Grand Floridian, Wilderness Lodge, Yacht and Beach Club, and Fort Wilderness marinas.

CANOEING: A long paddle down the Fort Wilderness canals is such a tranquil way to pass a misty morning that it's hard to remember that the bustle of the Magic Kingdom is not far away. Canoes may be rented at the Bike Barn at Fort Wilderness (about $8 per half hour, $12 per hour). Canoes may also be rented at the Caribbean Beach marina. Ocean kayaks (open-top kayaks) may be rented at La Marina at Coronado Springs (seasonally), Fort Wilderness Bike Barn, and at Port Orleans Riverside (about $8 per half hour, $12 per hour).

MOTORBOATING: It seems there are always dozens of small boats zipping back and forth across Bay Lake, Seven Seas Lagoon, Lake Buena Vista, Crescent Lake, and Barefoot Bay. These are called Sea Raycers, and they're just as much fun as they look. The boats are quick enough so that a lot of watery terrain can be covered in a half hour (for about $35).

Sea Raycers can be rented year-round at the Grand Floridian, Polynesian Village, Wilderness Lodge, Contemporary, Yacht & Beach Club, and Fort Wilderness marinas. At Coronado Springs, they are available seasonally. Guests must be at least 12 years old and 5 feet tall to rent Sea Raycer boats. Kids under the minimum age and height may ride as passengers, but they're not allowed to drive. We suggest that drivers wear a waterproof watch—it's amazing how the time flies!

PARASAILING: Excursions are offered at the Contemporary resort marina. Each 8- to 10-minute flight costs about $95 for one person to soar to 450 feet and $130 to rise to 600 feet, $170 for two to ride tandem at 450 feet and $195 for two to hit a height of 600 feet. Flights are offered 7 days a week, weather-permitting. (They will be canceled due to lightning, high wind, or other inclement weather—in which case a full refund will be issued.) Reservations must be made at least 24 hours in advance (and made up to a year ahead); visit *www.sammyduvall.com*, or call 407-939-0754. Walk-ups are accepted on a first-come, first-served basis. Wear loose-fitting clothing, but don't bother with a swimsuit—guests take off from and land on the back of the boat without getting wet.

The minimum age to parasail is 6. Guests younger than 18 must have an adult present. The minimum weight requirement is 130 pounds (guests under 130 pounds may fly tandem with another guest in order to reach the minimum weight allowance). The maximum weight per flight is 330 pounds.

PEDAL BOATS: These craft rent for about $7 per half hour or $11 per hour at Old Key West, and Swan and Dolphin marinas. Hydro Bikes (boats resembling bicycles affixed to pontoons) may be rented at the Swan and Dolphin marina when it isn't too windy; single-bike units cost about $8 per half hour; doubles, about $16 per half hour.

SPORTS

PERSONAL WATERCRAFT AND GUIDED EXCURSIONS: Three-seat personal Jet Ski–style watercraft are available for rent at Sammy Duvall's Watersports Centre at the Contemporary resort. Hours to rent are 9 A.M. to 5 P.M. The cost is about $80 (plus tax) for a half hour, $135 (plus tax) for an hour for up to three passengers (of any age). The maximum weight total per vehicle is 400 pounds. Participants must be at least 16 years old to drive. Guests under age 18 must have an adult sign a waiver prior to the trip.

It's also possible to start the day with a guided excursion aboard a 3-seat personal watercraft. Departing daily at 9 A.M. from the Contemporary resort marina, a guide will call attention to points of interest on and around Bay Lake and the Seven Seas Lagoon. At the end of the tour, guests have time to ride on their own, under the guide's supervision. A maximum of four rental units operate during each excursion. Cost is about $135 (plus tax) for up to 3 people. For additional information or to make reservations, visit *www.sammyduvall.com*; 407-939-0754.

PONTOON BOATS: Motorized, canopied platforms on pontoons are perfect for families, inexperienced boaters, and visitors more interested in serenity than in thrills. Available at most resort marinas, the 21-foot craft hold up to ten passengers and cost about $48 per half hour. Guests must be at least 18 years old (with a valid driver's license) to drive a pontoon boat.

SAILBOATS: The running room and usually reliable winds of Bay Lake and Seven Seas Lagoon make for good sailing, and the Polynesian Village resort marina rents a variety of craft so that guests might get a little wind in their sails on the 600-acre expanse. Various types of sailboats are available; models accommodate two to six people and may be rented by the hour. Prices start at about $25.

WATERSKIING, WAKEBOARDING, AND TUBING: Ski boats with Sammy Duvall instructors and equipment are available at the Contemporary resort marina. Watercraft may be reserved here, too. Reservations must be made at least 24 hours in advance and may be made up to a year ahead. Same-day walk-ups are accepted on a first-come, first-served basis; call 407-939-0754, or visit *www.sammyduvall.com* for pricing and to make reservations. Minors under 18 must have a legal guardian sign a waiver prior to departure. Note that activities may be canceled due to inclement weather (such as lightning, wind, etc).

Fishing

The 70,000 bass with which Bay Lake was stocked in the mid-1960s have grown and multiplied as a result of WDW's restrictive fishing policy. (It's strictly catch-and-release.) No angling is permitted on Bay Lake or the Seven Seas Lagoon, except on the guided fishing expeditions. Largemouth bass weighing two to eight pounds are the most common catch.

Fishing excursions are presented by BASS, the world's largest fishing organization. Guests who participate in a WDW excursion receive a one-year BASS membership, which includes 11 issues of *Bassmaster* magazine, a membership pack, decal, handbook, eligibility to compete in national events, discounts, and other benefits.

Bay Lake excursions depart daily (call 407-939-2277, or visit *www.disneyworldfishing.com* for details). Trips last two or four hours and includes guide, gear, and refreshments (soft drinks). Guides will pick up guests at the Contemporary, Grand Floridian, Polynesian Village, Fort Wilderness, and Wilderness Lodge.

Guides will pick up guests at Old Key West, Saratoga Springs, and Port Orleans Riverside and French Quarter, too. Two- and four-hour excursions accommodate up to five anglers and include guide, gear, and drinks. Kids under 16 must be accompanied by an adult.

Anglers might also consider two-hour tours that depart from the Yacht and Beach Club at 7 A.M., 10 A.M., and 1:30 P.M. All trips accommodate up to five people. Two-hour trips depart the BoardWalk dock at 7 A.M., 10 A.M., and 1:30 P.M. daily. A guide, gear, and drinks are included.

The Magic Kingdom resorts, Coronado Springs, and Caribbean Beach resorts also offer two-hour excursions on Nitro bass boats that accommodate one or two guests. They depart from the resort marinas at 7 A.M., 10 A.M., and 1:30 P.M. daily. The $235 to $270 price includes equipment and a guide.

Reservations must be made at least 24 hours in advance and may be made up to 180 days ahead; call 407-WDW-BASS (939-2277). Note that excursions may be canceled or cut short if the weather is stormy or there is lightning in the WDW vicinity.

Fishing on your own—again, strictly catch-and-release—is permitted in the canals at Fort Wilderness. Fort Wilderness guests may toss in lines from any campground canal shore. Fishing licenses are not required. Rods and reels, and cane poles are available for rent at the Fort Wilderness Bike Barn. Bait may be purchased.

ESPN Wide World of Sports Complex

Variety is the name of the game at the ESPN Wide World of Sports complex. The multi-million-dollar complex invites athletes and spectators alike to dive into more than 60 types of sporting experiences. It's a grand slam for die-hard sports fans.

The 255-acre facility—which recently teamed up with ESPN—hosts amateur and professional events in everything from archery to wrestling. The home of the Pop Warner Super Bowl and National Cheer & Dance championships is also the spring training site for Major League Baseball's Atlanta Braves.

Designed as a modern vision of old-time Floridian building styles, the architecture harks back to the days when sports facilities were extensions of their neighborhoods; to that end, there is even a town commons (which serves as a welcome center).

The complex includes a baseball stadium; a field house that accommodates basketball, wrestling, and volleyball; a track-and-field complex; tennis courts; and multipurpose fields fit for football, soccer, and more.

A general-admission ticket costs about $15 for adults and $10 for kids ages 3 through 9. Tickets may be purchased at the front gate and allow guests to watch all "nonpremium" events. Guests are only admitted on days when events are scheduled. Tickets to premium events, such as Atlanta Braves spring training games (beginning in late February or early March), may be purchased through Ticketmaster (800-745-3000; or *www.ticketmaster.com*) and include general admission to the complex.

Premium-event tickets may also be purchased at the Wide World of Sports complex box office on the day of an event, depending on availability. Prices vary from event to event. Note that in addition to traditional seats, the baseball stadium has lawn seating. If you purchase lawn tickets, bring something to sit on and get there as early as possible. Prime locations go fast!

Another sports complex crowd-pleaser is the interactive Playstation Pavilion, adjacent to the ESPN World Wide of Sports Grill. The cost is $5 for 30 minutes of playtime (all ages).

Essentials

HOW TO GET THERE: Direct bus transportation is available at All-Star, Pop Century, and Caribbean Beach resorts. Other WDW resort guests must take a bus (plan to transfer at a park or Downtown Disney) to one of these resorts. Allow at least an hour for the commute (more if you're attending a premium event). Buses run Thursday through Monday from 5 P.M. until about 11 P.M. Resort buses also run when events are taking place, starting one hour prior to complex opening time, until 11 P.M. or the time the complex closes (whichever is later).

If you are driving, take Exit 65 off I-4 to Victory Way. The complex is between U.S. 192 and Osceola Parkway. Parking is free but limited. If you plan to attend a premium event, arrive as early as possible—or risk scrambling for a spot in an unpaved, auxiliary lot.

WHERE TO EAT: The big-ticket eatery here is ESPN Wide World of Sports Grill. (This venue operates on event days only.)

There are more than 30 concessions for those seeking a somewhat lighter bite. They offer hot dogs, popcorn, soft drinks, and beer, as well as a few more substantial, yet just as portable, snacks.

Touch Base

Get the scoop on all the scheduled action at the ESPN Wide World of Sports complex by calling 407-939-4263 or visiting the Website *www.disneysports.com*.

More Sporting Fun

ARCHERY: Channel your inner Robin Hood at the Fort Wilderness program known as the Archery Experience. The 90-minute experience includes a quick but thorough lesson and lots of shooting time. It takes place every Thursday through Saturday at 2:45 P.M. Available to guests age 6 and older, the Archery Experience costs about $39 per person (plus tax). Book it up to 90 days in advance by calling 407-WDW-7529.

BIKING: Pedaling along the rustic pathways and lightly trafficked roads at Fort Wilderness can be a pleasant way to spend a couple of hours. Both areas are spread out, so bicycles are a practical way to get around. Bikes are also available for rent year-round at Old Key West, Wilderness Lodge, Port Orleans, Caribbean Beach, BoardWalk, Yacht and Beach Club, and Saratoga Springs. They are available on a seasonal basis at Coronado Springs. The cost is about $10 an hour or $20 per day. Bikes with training wheels or baby seats are available. Helmets are mandatory for guests up to the age of 16 and may be borrowed for free.

RUNNING: Except from late fall to early spring, the weather is usually much too steamy in Central Florida for jogging. If you run very early in the morning in warm seasons, the heat is somewhat less daunting. The 1.4-mile promenade around the lake at the Caribbean Beach resort is ideal for running, as is the three-quarter-mile promenade that surrounds Crescent Lake (a waterway that's bordered by the Swan and Dolphin, Yacht and Beach Club, and BoardWalk resorts), and the nearly mile-long path circling Coronado Springs' Lago Dorado. Fort Wilderness and the Wilderness Lodge share a three-quarter-mile path with exercise stations. Old Key West also has scenic routes. Courses are all about one mile in length.

MINIATURE GOLF: The Fantasia Gardens Miniature Golf complex, located near the Swan, Dolphin, and BoardWalk resorts, offers players two 18-hole courses themed to the Disney film *Fantasia*. The Fantasia Fairways course offers a difficult layout sure to tantalize serious golfers. It features traditional golf obstacles, such as water hazards, doglegs, and roughs. Don't be fooled by the small size of Fantasia Fairways—the challenges are big. (The record for the par-61 course is 47.)

Fantasia Gardens, on the other hand, is all in fun, with clever things (a dancing hippo, xylophone stairs, brooms dumping buckets of water) at every hole. The degree of difficulty varies from hole to hole, but overall this is an easy course to conquer. There are several challenges out there, however. Hole 15, for example, is one of the trickier ones. Here, golfers aim through mini-geysers that randomly squirt water into the air.

Disney's Winter Summerland miniature golf course is a mere stone's throw from the Blizzard Beach water park (they share a bus stop during Blizzard Beach hours). Designed as a vacation retreat for Santa and his elves, the two 18-hole courses boast a festive atmosphere, complete with Christmas carol soundtracks. The sandy-surface course is a bit more challenging than its snowy-surface counterpart.

A round on any course costs about $14 for adults, $12 for kids ages 3 through 9. The second round is half price. Typical playing time is about an hour. Hours are generally 10 A.M. to 11 P.M., but vary seasonally. For information, call 407-WDW-PLAY (939-7529).

SPAS AND HEALTH CLUBS: Health clubs include the Contemporary's Olympiad Fitness Center, Sturdy Branches at Wilderness Lodge, Zahanati at Animal Kingdom Lodge, La Vida at Coronado Springs, Saratoga Springs Fitness Center, Muscles and Bustles at BoardWalk, the Health Club at the Grand Floridian, Resort Fitness Center at Old Key West, Ship Shape at the Yacht and Beach Club, and the fitness center at the Swan. Registered guests may use their respective resort's facility for free. Guests not registered in a resort with a health club can use the facilities for a fee.

In addition to fitness centers, full-service spas are located at the Grand Floridian, Saratoga Springs, the Dolphin, and Buena Vista Palace. There are special spa packages available at each of these resorts. (See pages 228–229 for details on WDW resort spas.)

STOCK CAR RACING: The Richard Petty Driving Experience (RPDE) takes motorsports fans out of the grandstands and into a scene that most can only dream about: behind the wheel of a stock car. The RPDE, located at the Walt Disney World Speedway, near the Magic Kingdom guest parking lot, is a training ground for racer wannabes.

For the less "driven" daredevils, there is the Riding Experience, which sends guests zooming around the track at blazing speeds while still maintaining their passenger status. No reservations are required for the Riding Experience. Rides begin at 9 A.M. daily. The cost is about $116, plus tax.

The Rookie Experience includes instruction and eight high-speed (up to 145 miles per hour) laps around the one-mile oval track, as well as a warm-up and a cool-down lap. The three-hour program costs about $479, plus tax. Reservations are required.

The King's Experience is a total of 18 laps behind the wheel. Cost is about $904, plus tax. Reservations are required.

The Experience of a Lifetime is a 30-lap program completed over three sessions. Participants work on building speed and establishing a comfortable driving line. The cost is about $1,385, plus tax. Reservations are a must.

The Exotic Driving Experience puts you behind the wheel of supercars made by Ferrari, Lamborghini, Audi, and Porsche. This "exotic" experience starts at 6 laps with a pro. Extra laps may be added. Packages start at about $169 to $419, depending on the vehicle. (The coupon at the back of this book can net you a discount on a 3-lap ride-along experience.)

The new Piston Cup Junior Ride-Along program is open to kids ages 6 to 13 (and at least 48 inches tall). Riders experience real-life racing excitement as they ride shotgun with a professional driver in Aiken Axler or Sage Vanderspin—character cars created by *Cars* creative director Jay Ward. The 3-lap adventure costs $59. Reservations are not necessary. Piston Cup cars have special seats to ensure youngsters' safety.

The RPDE operates daily year-round. Shuttle transportation is provided from the Transportation and Ticket Center (TTC). Call 800-237-3889, or visit *www.drivepetty.com* for information and to make reservations. To drive, guests must have a valid license. Prices are subject to change.

TRAIL RIDES: Guided horseback rides into pine woods and palmetto country set off from the front of Fort Wilderness four times daily. This trip is not meant for seasoned gallopers—you can't wander off on your own. The horses have been culled for gentleness, so trips are suitable for novices. Cost is about $46 per person for a 45-minute tour. Kids under the age of 9 are not allowed to ride, and there's a weight limit of 250 pounds. (Younger kids can saddle up on ponies at the Fort Wilderness Pony Farm for about $5.) Reservations are necessary and may be made up to 180 days in advance by calling 407-WDW-PLAY (939-7529).

VOLLEYBALL & BASKETBALL: Resort volleyball courts are reserved for Walt Disney World resort guests. The Grand Floridian, Yacht and Beach Club, Fort Wilderness, Swan and Dolphin, Coronado Springs, and Old Key West have volleyball courts. Contemporary, Fort Wilderness, Saratoga Springs, Animal Kingdom Lodge (Kidani Village), and Old Key West have basketball hoops.

SPORTS

Good Meals, Great Times

244   In the Theme Parks

266   In Downtown Disney

270   In the WDW Resorts

282   Character Dining

299   Reservations Explained

300   Dinner Shows

301   Bars & Lounges of WDW

GOOD MEALS, GREAT TIMES

Although fast food is in great supply, it is hardly the entire Walt Disney World dining story. Epcot adds international flavors to the WDW menu. Tempting options at the other theme parks, BoardWalk, and Downtown Disney— not to mention new dining frontiers in the ever-growing brood of WDW resorts— make deciding where to eat a mouth-watering dilemma. Disney's ongoing effort to expand its culinary horizons has certainly been successful, producing prominent palate-pleasers such as Le Cellier Steakhouse and Flying Fish Cafe, plus family favorites such as Chef Mickey's and 50's Prime Time Cafe.

Because there's such a large number and variety of eateries around the World, this chapter presents dining information in two formats. First, we've included an area-by-area rundown—a comprehensive section with descriptions of food purveyors, including sample menu options, that will prove most helpful when you get hungry in a particular part of the World. Second, we've compiled a collection of what we consider to be the best restaurants in a particular category. To select these standouts, we looked at the menu, theme, and overall enjoyability of each restaurant. And, of course, we sampled the food.

Finally, in the chapter's last section, we offer a guide to the varied lounges of the World, along with a briefing on Disney's reservations system and dinner show options—and assurance that great times are destined to follow.

The Restaurants of WDW In the Magic Kingdom

A lot has changed since Walt Disney World's original theme park opened in 1971. Back then, when it came to quelling hunger pangs, it was pretty much burger or bust. Nowadays, the options are a lot more diverse—with everything from egg rolls to cinnamon rolls, smoked turkey legs to lamb stew, and clam chowder to seafood fra diavolo. And yes, you can still sink your teeth into a juicy burger. Regardless of your tastes or budget, the six "lands" in the Magic Kingdom boast a bounty of palate-pleasers for the whole family.

First Things First

The letters at the end of each entry refer to the meals served there: breakfast (B), lunch (L), dinner (D), or snacks (S).

• When you see a not-so-hidden Mickey (🐭) at the end of an entry, it means that eatery was a Basic Disney Dining Plan* participant at press time (see page 20).

• Eateries in this chapter have been designated inexpensive (under $15), moderate ($15 to $36), expensive ($36 to $60), and very expensive ($60 and up). Prices are based on an adult-sized meal consisting of a beverage, entrée, and either one appetizer, side order, or dessert (not including tax and tip). These classifications are reflected by dollar symbols at the end of each entry (all symbols are defined by the key at the bottom of each page). Note that breakfast and lunch generally cost less.

• All Walt Disney World restaurants and fast-food spots (except some with outside seating or at the Swan and Dolphin resorts) are nonsmoking only. Some restaurants at BoardWalk and Downtown Disney may set aside outdoor sections for smokers.

• Reservations for table-service restaurants (and dinner shows) should be made 180 days in advance; call 407-WDW-DINE (939-3463) or visit *www.disneyworld.com/dining/*.

We recommend calling 407-WDW-DINE to confirm all WDW restaurant information.

*Disney Dining Plan locations are subject to change without notice.

Adventureland
FAST FOOD & SNACKS

ALOHA ISLE: Switzerland meets Hawaii (hey, this is the Magic Kingdom!) at this snack stand across from the Swiss Family Treehouse. Stop here for all things pineapple—juice, spears, floats, and the ever-popular Dole Whip frozen pineapple soft-serve dessert. Also on the menu are cola and root beer floats. This spot has been around forever—they are definitely doing something right. S·$·🐭

SUNSHINE TREE TERRACE: After you sing with the birdies in the Enchanted Tiki Room or fly on a magic carpet, you can take a break with one of the chilliest snacks in the park—a refreshing Citrus Swirl (vanilla soft-serve swirled with orange slush). Ice cream floats (made with soda or coffee), espresso, and coffee drinks round out the menu. It's possible to get soft-serve ice cream in a cone or cup, too. A park staple, Sunshine Tree has been dishing out treats for as long as we can remember. S·$·🐭

TORTUGA TAVERN: The shady spot, located across from the Pirates of the Caribbean, offers selections such as a chicken, vegetable, or beef burrito (more of a wrap than a typical burrito) and taco salad. Kids enjoy the pint-sized quesadilla that's made just for them. There is a toppings bar. This venue operates seasonally, so it may not be open during your visit to the park. LS·$–$$·🐭

HOT TIP!

It's now possible to reserve most Disney restaurants via the Internet. Simply visit *www.disneyworld.com/dining/* up to 180 days ahead and book away. Of course, dining reservations may still be made via telephone (407-939-3463).

Fantasyland

TABLE SERVICE

BE OUR GUEST: Nestled under Beast's Castle, this massive eatery transports guests into the realm of Disney's *Beauty and the Beast*. Guests can enjoy one of three themed dining rooms—the cavernous Ballroom, West Wing, or Rose Gallery—and enjoy a quick-service lunch or table-service dinner.

Lunch guests enter the Beast's parlor to place orders at touch terminals. Quick-service meals are delivered via a clever bit of technology involving an "enchanted" rose. The menu includes items such as *croque monsieur* (ham and Gruyère cheese sandwich), carved turkey on a baguette, tuna niçoise salad, grilled steak sandwich, and vegetable quiche. The portions are a bit smaller and the prices a bit steeper here than at other M.K. quick-service eateries. The kids' lunch menu includes whole-grain macaroni, carved-turkey sandwiches, and Mickey meatloaf. While many lunch guests gravitate toward the stately Ballroom, we head right for the West Wing—just don't tell the Beast!

Dinner is a more elegant affair, with starters such as mussels steamed in white wine, French onion soup, and salad with a champagne vinaigrette. Entrées pay homage to a castle feast from the 1400s with chicken breast Provinçal, thyme-scented pork chop, and pan-seared salmon with leek fondue and saffron potatoes. Heavenly cupcakes and mousse-filled cream puffs are served tableside. Beer and wine are offered with the evening meal. Reservations are required for dinner. Book as early as possible. L D S · $–$$$ · ❤

CINDERELLA'S ROYAL TABLE: You don't have to be a royal to eat like one. At least, not in the Magic Kingdom. This regal eatery, tucked inside Cinderella Castle, is a high-ceilinged, majestic mead hall. It's tiny as Disney spots go, but there's no feeling cramped —thanks to a small number of tables and towering windows. Hosts and hostesses wear Renaissance-inspired garb and address guests as "my lady," or "my lord."

Cinderella welcomes "Fairytale Dining" guests into her home all day and greets them in the Castle lobby, while her princess friends mingle in the dining room. Breakfast favorites include lobster and crab crepes, and cream-cheese-stuffed French toast, along with traditional fare. Lunch and dinner showcase seasonal ingredients, featuring items such as pork loin, beef tenderloin, and fish of the day.

The all-inclusive cost for breakfast is about $58 for adults and $36 for kids (ages 3–9); lunch is about $60 for adults, $38 for kids; dinner is about $73 for adults, $43 for kids. Prices include sales tax, gratuity, and a photo package (all parties may pose [as a group] with Cinderella in the lobby). Prices may be higher during peak times of year. Reservations are an absolute must. **A 180-day advance booking is almost always necessary for all meals. Full payment is required at time of booking.** Guests staying

Toughest Ticket in Town

Cinderella's Royal Table is—hands down—the most difficult restaurant reservation to secure at Walt Disney World. Why? For starters, Cinderella is one popular princess. And there's the allure of dining in the castle—the most famous landmark in the world's most popular theme park.

Potential guests may make a reservation by visiting www.mydisneyexperience.com (starting at 6 A.M., 180 days ahead) or by calling 407-WDW-DINE (939-3643) at exactly 7 A.M. Eastern Standard Time, 180 days in advance. The meal must be paid for at the same time the reservation is made. There's no charge for infants, but they must be included in the reservation. *Note that Cinderella's Royal Table will be closed for refurbishment in early 2015.*

Expect your credit card to be charged immediately upon making the reservation. Cancellations or changes to the reservation must be made at least 24 hours ahead to receive a full refund. The only one who can change or cancel a reservation is the one whose name is on the credit card. Reservations cannot be transferred. Guests using the Disney Dining Plan must also book the table with a credit card, but it will not be charged. However, two table-service credits are required for all meals here, as it is a "Signature" restaurant.

Whew! That's a lot of work for one dining experience. Is it worth it? Judging by the smiles we see day in and day out, we have to say yes.

GOOD MEALS, GREAT TIMES

at a Walt Disney World-owned-and-operated resort should note our Hot Tip on page 248. *Note that Cinderella's Royal Table will be closed for refurbishment in early 2015. Call 407-939-3463 for details and re-opening date.*

Cancellations must be made at least 24 hours in advance to avoid the $10-per-person surcharge. Cinderella recommends that you arrive a few minutes early. This is an extremely difficult table to reserve (see page 245)—so don't get little ones' hopes up until you actually book it. **B L D · $$$ · 🐭**

FAST FOOD & SNACKS

CHESHIRE CAFE: A small stand that's a good spot to cool off with a lemonade, raspberry and lemonade slush, orange juice, or coffee, the cafe serves muffins, cereals with milk, and whole fruit, too. If the Gourmet Cake Cups are offered during your visit, try one. The parfait-style treats make us smile like the Cheshire Cat. **S · $ · 🐭**

THE FRIAR'S NOOK: A walk-up window next to Storybook Treats, this place sells hot dogs, three types of mac and cheese, veggies and chips with hummus, plus carrot cake, and apple and caramel dippers. Open seasonally. **L S · $ · 🐭**

GASTON'S TAVERN: A cozy little lodge nestled in Fantasyland's Enchanted Forest, Gaston's serves roasted pork shank, hummus and chips, mixed vegetables with dip, fruit cups, sliced apples with caramel sauce, chocolate croissants, warm cinnamon rolls, and soft drinks. The specialty of this teetotaling tavern? LeFou's Brew—a not-too-sweet concoction made from frozen apple juice with a hint of toasted marshmallow and topped with all-natural passion fruit-mango foam. And, yes, Gaston really does use antlers in all of his decorating. **L D S · $ · 🐭**

PINOCCHIO VILLAGE HAUS: One of the better spots to target with kids in tow, Pinocchio Village Haus, is also a good place to take picky adult eaters. It may seem small from the outside, but there are many dining rooms through that door. One room boasts picture windows that overlook the It's a Small World loading area. It's fun to watch the boats bob by as you munch on lunch. Pinocchio offers pizza (aka flatbread), meatball subs, Italian wedding soup, tomato basil soup, chicken nuggets, salads (Mediterranean and Caesar), fries, and soft drinks. Kids' picks include mac and cheese, PB&J, and cheese or pepperoni pizza. This is a popular destination—try to go a bit before or after the mealtime rush. **L D S · $ – $$ · 🐭**

PRINCE ERIC'S VILLAGE MARKET:

Appropriately anchored across from The Little Mermaid attraction, this alfresco snack spot specializes in healthier-than-usual snack fare. Fresh fruit, crunchy veggies, hummus, and Greek yogurt are served along with fruit juices and all-natural lemonade. Frozen lemonade and shaved ice (blue raspberry, cherry, grape, orange, or watermelon) are also available. **S · $ · 🐭**

STORYBOOK TREATS: Ice cream fans appreciate this window next to the Many Adventures of Winnie the Pooh. It offers soft-serve cones and cups, hot fudge sundaes and brownie sundaes, plus milk shakes and floats. Chocolate chunk cookies are also served. **S · $ · 🐭**

Frontierland
FAST FOOD & SNACKS

GOLDEN OAK OUTPOST: In the mood for chicken? Head here. This little wagon offers chicken nuggets or fried spicy chicken breast sandwiches (served with choice of french fries or apple slices). Also on the menu? Carrot cake, chocolate cake, chocolate chip cookies, coffee, tea, and soft drinks. The Outpost operates seasonally. **L D S · $ · 🐭**

Healthier Options

Health-conscious folks need not abandon all restraint for want of suitable sustenance. Walt Disney World recently phased out added trans fats and partially hydrogenated oils from food served in parks and resorts. Most restaurants offer low-fat, low-cholesterol, low-salt, low-carb, and vegetarian entrées. Even fast-food stands feature healthier fare such as salads, grilled chicken sandwiches, fresh fruit, and turkey burgers. The WDW trend toward healthier dining extends to kids' meals, too. They come with a beverage choice of low-fat milk, 100 percent fruit juice, or water, and a side dish such as unsweetened applesauce, baby carrots, or fresh fruit. These healthy selections are easy to find on menus throughout Walt Disney World— keep an eye out for the Mickey Check symbol!

GOOD MEALS, GREAT TIMES

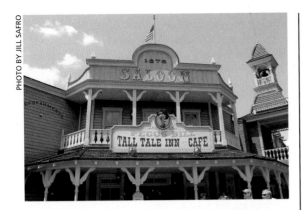

PECOS BILL TALL TALE INN & CAFE:

Pecos Bill—a classic "oldie but goodie"— has been feeding hungry cowpokes for more than 40 years. The look has changed a bit over time, but the reliable quality of the vittles remains. Cheeseburgers, BBQ pork sandwiches, and salads (Southwest chicken or taco) are the staples. If you'd rather not get fries, let them know when you place your order—you can swap them for apple slices or corn on the cob. Other sides include chili cheese fries, sweet potato fries, and onion rings. Kids can choose from burgers, turkey sandwiches, or PB&J sandwiches—all come with grapes and carrot sticks with a choice of low-fat milk or water.

What sets this spot apart from other burger establishments? Two words: fixin's bar. It's full of items with which to garnish your meal. Among them: lettuce and tomato, and freshly sautéed mushrooms and onions. Pecos Bill Cafe is one of the most popular eateries in the Magic Kingdom.
LDS·$–$$·❤

HOT TIP!
The hours from 11 A.M. to 2 P.M., and again from about 5 P.M. to 7 P.M., are mealtime rush hours in the Magic Kingdom. Try to eat earlier or later whenever possible.

Liberty Square
TABLE SERVICE

LIBERTY TREE TAVERN: Step back in time at this Early American tavern where the decor has a tendency to outdazzle the fare. Here, wallpaper looks as if it might have come from Colonial Williamsburg, the curtains hang from cloth loops, and the rooms are filled with mementos that might have been found in the homes of Thomas Jefferson, George Washington, and Ben Franklin. The restaurant is aptly located across from the Hall of Presidents attraction.

The à la carte lunch menu includes pot roast, turkey, seasonal fresh catch, and New England clam chowder. Dinner is an all-you-can-eat feast—salad, roast turkey breast, sliced pork, carved beef, mac and cheese, and more— all served family style. Dinner costs about $34 for adults and $17 for children ages 3 through 9. Note that some beverages cost extra and no alcohol is served. Reservations are recommended (arrive about 20 minutes early). Disney characters do not visit here. LD·$$–$$$·❤

Magic Kingdom Mealtime Tips

- The hours from 11:30 A.M. to 2 P.M., and again from about 5 P.M. to 7 P.M., are the mealtime rush hours in Magic Kingdom restaurants. Try to eat earlier or later whenever possible.

- When a fast-food restaurant has more than one service window, don't just amble into the nearest queue. Instead, inspect them all, because occasionally, the one farthest from an entrance will be wait-free (or nearly so).

- Table-service restaurants offering full-scale meals are usually less crowded at lunchtime than they are during traditional dinner hours.

- To avoid queues, eat at a restaurant that offers reservations—Tony's Town Square, Crystal Palace, or the Plaza Restaurant on Main Street; Liberty Tree Tavern in Liberty Square; Fantasyland's Be Our Guest (reservations at dinner only) or Cinderella's Royal Table. Reservations may be made in advance by calling 407-WDW-DINE (939-3463), via *www.disneyworld.com*, or the My Disney Experience app. Check for same-day seating at the individual restaurant or City Hall (as early in the day as possible).

- Consider taking the monorail to the Contemporary, Polynesian, or Grand Floridian to have lunch or dinner in a resort restaurant, and then return to the Magic Kingdom after you eat. (Remember to keep your ticket or MagicBand handy for re-entry to the park.)

FAST FOOD & SNACKS

COLUMBIA HARBOUR HOUSE: This lively spot adds some interesting (and healthy!) options to the quick-service lineup, including broccoli peppercorn salad served with chicken, grilled salmon with couscous and steamed broccoli, and the popular Lighthouse sandwich (with hummus, tomato, and broccoli slaw). You can still find fried shrimp, chicken nuggets, and clam chowder, too. For dessert there's strawberry yogurt and chocolate cake. Disney has done up this fast-food emporium with style—complete with antiques, model ships, harpoons, nautical instruments, and even lace tieback curtains. In addition to the chowder, we savor the salmon and love that Lighthouse sandwich. The upstairs dining rooms are quite charming (and usually less crowded). **L D S · $ – $ $ ·** 🏰

SLEEPY HOLLOW: Often missed by guests rushing toward the Haunted Mansion or other park hot spots, this window has a lot to offer: waffles with various toppings, waffle sandwiches (sweet and spicy chicken or ham and cheese), fruit, ice cream cookie sandwiches, ice cream cups, funnel cakes (dusted with powdered sugar and cinnamon or strawberries and cream), and more. Sleepy Hollow is near the Liberty Square bridge. Eat on the patio and get a stunning view of Cinderella Castle at no extra charge. **S · $ ·** 🏰

Main Street
TABLE SERVICE

CRYSTAL PALACE: What's the big draw here? Winnie the Pooh and his pals host meals all day. One of the Magic Kingdom's cherished landmarks, this spot takes its architectural cues from a similar structure that once stood in New York, and from San Francisco's Conservatory of Flowers, which still graces that city's Golden Gate Park. The place is spacious, with tables scattered amid a Victorian-style indoor garden, complete with fresh flowers and hanging greenery. Tables in the front look out on flower beds, while those at the east end have views of a courtyard. The restaurant is on a pathway at the end of Main Street, U.S.A.

Four topiaries—Winnie the Pooh, Tigger, Eeyore, and Piglet—greet guests at the entrance, a sign of the character presence here. (Their furry counterparts mingle inside.)

Offerings vary according to season and available produce. The all-you-can-eat buffet features a variety of breakfast items every morning; a salad bar, deli bar, pasta, chicken, and fish for lunch; and spit-roasted carved meats,

B breakfast   **L** lunch   **D** dinner   **S** snacks / **$** under $15   **$$** $15–$36   **$$$** $36–$60   **$$$$** $60 and up

GOOD MEALS, GREAT TIMES

chicken, pastas, fish, and inventive sides for dinner. The evening salad bar, with its grilled veggies, peel-and-eat shrimp, cold pasta salads, and variety of greens and grains, is first-rate. The cost for breakfast is about $26 for adults and $15 for kids ages 3 through 9; lunch is about $30 for adults and $16 for children; dinner is about $40 for adults and $20 for children. Reservations are recommended. B L D · $ $ – $ $ $ · ❤

PLAZA RESTAURANT: This windowed establishment, next to the Plaza Ice Cream Parlor, is done up in mirrors with sinuous Art Nouveau frames. The menu has salads, burgers, and hot and cold sandwiches—plus ice cream, shakes, malts, floats, and sundaes. Our favorite sundae presentation has to be Mickey's Kitchen Sink, served in a sink shaped like Mickey's pants and big enough for two. Reservations are recommended. Arrive early—there is usually a wait (even with a reservation). They are not known for speedy service. L D · $ $ · ❤

TONY'S TOWN SQUARE: Tony's decor was inspired by Walt Disney's classic feature *Lady and the Tramp* (which can be viewed in the restaurant's waiting area). The terrazzo-style patio offers a fine view of Town Square (though tables there are in limited supply). The lunch menu offers Italian specialties, including paninis (sandwiches). Pizzas with selected toppings are good bets. Other staples include Caesar salads and pasta dishes.

At dinner, select from chicken parmigiana, steak, pork tenderloin, and spaghetti, along with daily specials. If you require gluten-free pasta, just ask—Tony is happy to accommodate. Top it off with an Italian sweet or foamy cappuccino. If you time it right, you can fold your napkin, settle the bill, and wander onto Main Street to enjoy the fireworks from one of the best vantage points in the Magic Kingdom. Reservations are highly recommended. L D · $ $ $ · ❤

HOT TIP!

Tomorrowland Terrace's dessert party offers snacks and a view of Wishes, the Magic Kingdom's nightly fireworks presentation. Prices vary, but expect to pay about $25 per adult and $13 per child. For details and to make reservations up to 180 days in advance, call 407-WDW-DINE (939-3463).

Magic Kingdom Resorts

Is the Magic Kingdom open late when you plan to visit? If so, consider heading over to the Contemporary, Polynesian, Grand Floridian, or Wilderness Lodge to have an early dinner, and then return to finish the day at the park. Each of the aforementioned resorts is reachable by monorail and/or water taxi. Remember to keep sporting that MagicBand bracelet if you used it for admission or keep your ticket handy for re-entry into the Magic Kingdom. Transportation generally runs for one hour after the park's posted closing time for the day (this does not include Extra Magic Hours). Note that, as with most WDW eateries, reservations are necessary at resort restaurants. Don't forget to book that table!

FAST FOOD & SNACKS

CASEY'S CORNER: Casey's is a grand slam for baseball fans—and those who just happen to love the food associated with "America's pastime," big old hot dogs and salty fries. This old-fashioned stop is on the west side of Main Street (near the Crystal Palace). Tables line the sidewalk, where a ragtime pianist often tickles the ivories. There's a back room with indoor seating (Casey recently added a bunch of new tables) and screenings of sports-themed animated shorts. The bill of fare retains the mood—hot dogs, corn dog nuggets, nachos, fries, brownies, cotton candy, and soft drinks. You have to love a place that supplies free cheese sauce and malt vinegar for your fries. It's a popular spot for a late-night snack, and a Magic Kingdom classic. L D S · $ · ❤

MAIN STREET BAKERY: After an extensive refurbishment, this Main Street classic has reopened as a turn-of-the-twentieth-century bakery and coffee shop. If the sight of this old-fashioned storefront doesn't lure you in, the aroma most certainly will. The Main Street Bakery is a nice choice for a light breakfast, coffee break, or midafternoon rest stop. The vast array of tea and coffee concoctions come courtesy of Starbucks. Assorted pastries, fresh-baked cookies, fresh fruit and veggies, and other snacks are also served. B S · $ · ❤

PLAZA ICE CREAM PARLOR: This happy place for ice cream lovers boasts the Kingdom's largest variety of hand-scooped ice cream flavors.

It's great for a before-the-parade or an on-the-way-out-of-the-park nosh. Children enjoy the Mickey Mouse kids' cone. To keep things moving, choose flavors and desired number of scoops before jumping in line. They have floats and sundaes—including the Mickey's Kitchen Sink for two. It's busiest before and after parades and nightly fireworks presentations. S·$·🐭

Tomorrowland
FAST FOOD & SNACKS

AUNTIE GRAVITY'S GALACTIC GOODIES: Ice cream may not seem futuristic, but chances are it'll be around at least another billion years, give or take. Located across from the Tomorrowland Speedway, Auntie G's offers up chilly smoothies made from non-fat yogurt (strawberry-banana, orange-pineapple, and more), soft-serve ice cream, sundaes, and floats. Soft drinks are available, too. There's virtually no atmosphere in this corner of the galaxy, but we still gravitate toward the goodies. S·$·🐭

COSMIC RAY'S STARLIGHT CAFE: This is across from the Tomorrowland Speedway, it's like several quick-service counters in one. There are separate stations, with a slightly different menu offered at each.

You must wait in more than one line if you want food from different sections. Choose Bay 1 for rotisserie chicken, barbecue pork sandwiches, grilled chicken sandwiches, chicken breast nuggets, barbecue ribs, and salads; Bay 2 for cheeseburgers, veggie burgers, and hot dogs; and Bay 3 for burgers, salads, yogurt, and sandwiches (including a vegetarian option). A kosher selection is available. An Audio-Animatronics lounge lizard known as Sunny Eclipse entertains in the dining area. L D S·$–$$·🐭

LUNCHING PAD AT ROCKETTOWER PLAZA: If it's a snack or simple meal you're after, stop at the base of the Astro Orbiter located in the center of Tomorrowland's concrete plaza. This window offers "gourmet" hot dogs on oversize buns, cream-cheese-stuffed-pretzels, assorted chips, soda slushies, milk (regular and soy), and soft drinks. S·$·🐭

TOMORROWLAND TERRACE: This sleek spot serves simple fare such as cheeseburgers, pastas, and salads. Tables on the lower terrace afford nice views of Cinderella Castle. It operates on a seasonal basis. L D S·$·🐭

Baby Needs

Babies. They're a needy lot. Fortunately, most of the requisite supplies can be found somewhere at Disney World—if you know where to look. Formula and jarred food can be purchased at the Baby Care Center in each of the theme parks and at every WDW resort. Most restaurants have kids' menus with toddler-friendly food (mac and cheese, chicken nuggets, and the like).

If your baby is partial to a specific formula or brand of food, consider shipping a box of it to your hotel before you leave home. Keep in mind that there are several grocery stores near Walt Disney World. If you'll have a car, it is worth the trip (a guest relations clerk can offer directions). The selections are more varied, as are the prices. Stash perishables in an in-room refrigerator—they are standard in all Disney-owned-and-operated resorts. Some other points of interest regarding baby diners at Walt Disney World:

- Most eateries have high chairs and booster seats. Request one when you make your restaurant reservation.

- Stroller use inside restaurants is discouraged. Park it outside.

- WDW restaurants are often chilly. Be sure to pack a sweater or blanket.

- Be it a fast-food or table-service restaurant, bring toys to keep little ones busy.

- The following resorts have 24-hour snack bars: Grand Floridian, Dolphin, Polynesian Village, Wyndham, and Buena Vista Palace (on Hotel Plaza Boulevard). The middle-of-the-night pickings may be slim, but milk and cereal are served around the clock.

- If you'd like a spot to nurse an infant, head to a Baby Care Center in any of the theme parks. They all have rooms with rocking chairs.

- If you're headed for a long day in a theme or water park, pack simple, healthy snacks for hungry toddlers. And look for the Mickey check symbol on menus (see page 246 for details).

- To make your dining experience less harried, consider feeding your baby before you get to the restaurant.

- If you prefer organic milk (and more) for your children, consider ordering from *gardengrocer.com* or swinging by a local grocery store (for details, see Baby Food on page 47).

GOOD MEALS, GREAT TIMES

In Epcot

The eclectic, international lineup of fare offered here threatens to overshadow the attractions themselves. With no fewer than 11 different countries represented in the World Showcase section of the park, Epcot provides guests with the opportunity to eat their way around the world without leaving Central Florida. Less ambitious diners will likely have their taste needs met, too—there's a bountiful food court in Epcot's Future World, as well as a smattering of simple yet satiating snack spots and quick-service locations. Reservations are an important factor the Epcot dining equation; call 407-WDW-DINE (939-3463) up to 180 days in advance.

DID YOU KNOW?

More than 30 tons of fruits and vegetables have been grown at The Land pavilion in Epcot and served to guests dining in Walt Disney World restaurants.

Future World
TABLE SERVICE

CORAL REEF (The Seas with Nemo and Friends): This water-themed restaurant is all about nibbling on creatively prepared fish under the watchful eyes of their brethren. The place is decorated in cool greens and blues to complement its surroundings, and every table has a panoramic view of a living coral reef; some are right up against the glass. (Don't worry: You are not actually eating Epcot residents—most of Disney's catches come fresh from fishing boats

each day.) Menu items run the gamut from a bounty of fresh fish and shellfish, including shrimp, mahi mahi, and salmon—prepared in a number of ways —to grilled New York strip steak and pan-seared chicken breast for those who are satisfied by simply spying on the fish. The menu tends to vary seasonally. Reservations are recommended. **L D · $ $ $ · ❤**

GARDEN GRILL (The Land): Guests are often so distracted by the sights and the jovial hosts (Chip, Dale, and friends) that they don't realize the restaurant is actually moving. As the eatery revolves, and it does so quite slowly, it moves past scenery featured in the Living with the Land boat ride. The view was designed with diners in mind, and provides them with a peek into a farmhouse window that's out of viewing range of the waterborne passengers.

Chip and Dale (who may be joined by Pluto and Mickey Mouse) host the nightly character dinner. The menu features rotisserie meats, sustainable fish of the day, fresh vegetables (some of which are grown inside The Land Pavilion), and a small selection of desserts. Cost is about $40 for adults, $19 for kids. (Prices may be a bit higher during peak times of year.) Beverages and dessert are included. Meals are served family-style (communal platters for the table). There is a special "little gardeners" menu with kid-friendly selections. Note that lunch is no longer served here. Reservations are recommended.

The restaurant moves in a circle. It's imperceptible to most, but if you are highly sensitive to motion, it may be best to dine in a more stationary environment. **D · $ $ – $ $ $ · ❤**

FAST FOOD & SNACKS

ELECTRIC UMBRELLA (Innoventions Plaza): This large establishment is a good bet when the weather is temperate enough to allow dining at the tables on the terrace outside—or when bound for the World Showcase with finicky eaters in tow. (There are indoor tables, too.) Offerings include chicken Caesar salad, flatbread (topped with sun-dried tomato pesto, mushroom, and feta), meatball sub, mac & cheese burger, fries, and soft drinks. Dessert options include fruit cups, strawberry cheesecake, chocolate chip cookies, and no-sugar-added brownies. It's possible to get grapes or carrots instead of fries with some menu selections. **L D S · $ – $ $ · ❤**

FOUNTAIN VIEW (Innoventions Plaza): Set beside that drama queen of a water fountain known as Fountain of Nations, this new Epcot destination is actually a futuristically themed Starbucks. As such, it is an ideal spot for a satisfying java jolt, a light meal, or a sweet snack. Sandwiches, pastries, cookies, and crunchy veggies are available—as are teas, Frappuccino drinks, and more. **BLS·$·❤**

SUNSHINE SEASONS (The Land): It's the closest thing to a mall food court you'll find in a WDW park, but a bit more upscale. Located near the entrance to Soarin' on the pavilion's lower level, Sunshine Seasons is an ideal destination for parties who can't quite agree on any one type of fare—there's bound to be something for everyone. Tables are scattered in several seating areas, beneath colorful hot-air balloons. Snagging a table can be a challenge during peak mealtimes. (There can be a bit of pedestrian congestion, too, thanks to the enormous popularity of the adjacent Soarin' attraction.)

Sandwich Shop is home of the oak-grilled vegetable flatbread, steak and blue cheese sandwich, and more. The **Soup and Salad Shop**'s creative salads include roasted beet and goat cheese, and seared tuna with sesame rice wine dressing. Soups are made fresh daily. **The Grill Shop** features rotisserie chicken and slow-roasted pork. Sustainable catch of the day is also offered. **Wok Shop** serves Mongolian beef with jasmine rice, and noodle bowls such as cashew chicken. The **Bakery** offers freshly made desserts. In addition to the house specialty—Soarin' Crème Brûlée—expect to find brownies, ice cream bars, and other sweet treats. There is a "grab and go" area with items such as sushi, fruit and cheese plates, hard-cooked eggs, salads, ice cream, and other snacks.

A word of advice: It's often a good idea to split up your party and stand in several lines at the same time. That'll increase your chances of actually eating together. Before doing so, select a table. That way, everyone in the group will know where to meet after they forage for their meals. It's also a nice spot to take a load off your feet while waiting for your Soarin' Fastpass+ window to kick in. **BLDS·$–$$·❤**

World Showcase
TABLE SERVICE

AKERSHUS ROYAL BANQUET HALL (Norway): The Norwegian castle of Akershus dominates Oslo's harbor, and is considered the most impressive of all Norway's medieval fortresses. It is actually half fortress and half palace, and many of its grand halls continue to be used for elaborate state banquets. At Epcot's castle-like Akershus, guests are treated to authentic royal Norwegian cuisine. They also get to dine with royalty—as Disney princesses interact with guests during all meals.

If you can't snag a reservation at Cinderella Castle, Akershus' Princess Storybook meals are a good alternative (Cinderella won't be there, but her royal friends will). An all-inclusive price

PHOTO BY JILL SAFRO

Let 'em Eat Cake!

What could possibly make celebrating a special occasion at Walt Disney World even more special? How about a custom-made, personalized cake? You can have one delivered to just about any table-service eatery on Disney property. Simply call the Cake Hotline (407-827-2253) at least 48 hours in advance to place an order.

If you miss the ordering deadline, don't despair—no one has to go cake-less at Disney World (perish the thought!). Spontaneous cake delivery is possible, provided you request one at the podium when you check in at a restaurant. At meal's end, you will receive a 6-inch non-personalized cake. It will add about $23, plus tax (and a few more calories), to the total.

entitles hungry Epcot guests to enjoy dishes that don't often leave Scandinavia. Included in the family-style sampling of the Norwegian *koldbord* is smoked salmon and seafood, Norwegian cheese, and chilled salads. Norwegian-inspired entrées include seafood, beef, and poultry selections. A kids' menu is available. Dessert and soft drinks are included.

For breakfast, guests enjoy the all-you-care-to-eat fare (bacon, eggs, potatoes, and sausage are brought to your table), as Disney characters mingle with diners. Belle, Jasmine, Snow White, Sleeping Beauty, and even Mary Poppins have made appearances. The character appearance schedule varies. Reservations are necessary. Cancellations must be made at least 24 hours in advance to avoid paying the $10-per-person surcharge. Breakfast costs about $45 for adults (ages 10 and up) and $27 for kids (ages 3–9); lunch is about $46 (adults) and $28 (kids); dinner costs about $51 (adults) and $28 (kids). Prices may be higher during peak seasons. BLD·$$–$$$·❣

BIERGARTEN (Germany): Located in the back of the St. Georgsplatz in the Germany pavilion, this huge, tiered eatery is a jolly stop on the Epcot world tour. This is partly because of the long tables that encourage togetherness among guests. But equal credit for the gemütlich atmosphere goes to the spot's lively entertainment.

There are scheduled appearances by Bavarian musicians—each clad in lederhosen or dirndl—who play accordions, cowbells, a musical saw, and a harp-like stringed instrument known as the "wooden laughter." The entertaining shows take place at scheduled times in the dining room. The schedule is usually posted at the door. Diners are usually invited to join the fun on the dance floor.

The food is hearty and presented as an all-you-can-eat buffet, featuring all sorts of sausages (such as bratwurst, Debrizinger, Bauernwurst), frankfurters, rotisserie chicken, spaetzle, assorted cold dishes, potato salad, cucumber salad, and many more German specialties. Because entertainment is intermittent, there's plenty of time to enjoy the pleasant setting. Reservations are highly recommended, particularly during peak seasons (book as early as possible). LD·$$–$$$·❣

CHEFS DE FRANCE (France): "Bright lights, big dining room" describes this airy Parisian brasserie. With some of France's best chefs responsible for this kitchen, the results are usually rewarding. The menu features fresh ingredients readily available from Florida purveyors, though the restaurant imports as many key ingredients from France as possible.

The offerings are in the nouvelle French cuisine style, which involves lighter sauces using less cream and butter than in classic French cooking. Menu items include broiled salmon, beef short ribs, and roasted chicken. Soups and appetizers such as onion soup, lobster bisque, and escargot are all-day staples. Chocolate tarts and crème brûlée are dessert specialties of note.

Chefs de France is one of the most popular World Showcase eateries, year in and year out. Reservations are recommended (book as early as possible). LD·$$$–$$$$·❣

LE CELLIER STEAKHOUSE (Canada): This wine-cellar-like spot is a favorite place for a memorable meal. The restaurant has low ceilings, stone walls, and candlelight, all of which contribute to the atmosphere.

There's a full menu of tempting items, starting with a (complimentary) bread basket that includes fresh-baked pretzel roll, plus sourdough, and whole-grain creations. Considered a "Signature" restaurant for both lunch and dinner (translation: It costs more to eat here than at most other WDW places and requires two Dining Plan credits per meal), the steakhouse specializes in high-quality beef. The filet mignon with white truffle-butter sauce is a real crowd-pleaser. Many choose to start with a longtime favorite cheddar cheese soup made with Moosehead beer, but the *poutine* (fries with cheddar, truffle salt, and a red wine reduction) are a popular starter, too.

Canadian beers and wines make for memorable pairings. Reservations are a must—this is an extremely popular and relatively tiny restaurant. L D · $$–$$$ · ❤

LA HACIENDA DE SAN ANGEL (Mexico): Open for dinner (starting at 4 P.M.), this festive newcomer sits on the shore of World Showcase Lagoon. The menu features starters such as *queso fundido* (warm cheese with poblano pepper and chorizo); a taco trio with rib eye, and *crema de elote* (creamy corn soup). Entrées include a mixed grill for two, roasted shrimp in pepper garlic broth, and grilled tilapia. We are particularly fond of the *paradilla del mar* (seafood platter for two). For dessert, there's chocolate mousse, corn ice cream, and fruit empanadas.

If you book a table for about 8:30 P.M., you may be treated to prime seats for IllumiNations (Epcot's nightly pyrotechnic extravaganza). While windowside tables cannot be guaranteed, there's always standing room. As an added bonus, the show's soundtrack is pumped into the eatery. It's quite impressive. D · $$$ · ❤

MARRAKESH (Morocco): It's not every day that you can slip into an exquisitely tiled Moroccan palace and be entertained by belly dancers and musicians as you polish off a plate of Moroccan cuisine. Want to know how authentic this place is? The king of Morocco sent craftspeople to Epcot to make sure they were creating a real Moroccan atmosphere. (Unfortunately, he didn't send his chef.) The menu includes roast lamb, chicken brochette, beef shish kebab, and couscous. Sampler platters are available. Reservations are recommended, but it is often possible to get in without too much of a wait. L D · $$$ · ❤

MONSIEUR PAUL (France): One flight above Chefs de France, this new eatery is filled with mementos of Chef Paul Bocuse's extraordinary culinary honors. It is an elegant bistro, but a bit less formal than its predecessor, Bistro de Paris.

The menu was crafted by Chef Francesco Santin, who worked with Chef Bocuse in his restaurant in Lyon, France, for 15 years. It features starters such as a ravioli d'escargots appetizer and mussel soup with saffron and light fennel cream. Main course selections include grilled beef tenderloin with mushroom crust, roasted free-range chicken, and seared scallops with vegetables. The wine list is *tres* French. You might want to stroll around the World Showcase promenade to walk off your meal—and your warm Grand Marnier dessert soufflé. Note that this can be one of the most expensive Disney World restaurants. Be aware that there is no kids' menu. The dress code is "resort casual"—no tank tops or tattered clothing, please. Reservations are recommended. D · $$$$ · ❤

NINE DRAGONS (China): This stop on Epcot's varied international restaurant tour transports guests to modern China when in the palatial dining room. À la carte and buffet selections allow guests to sample provincial cuisines. The menu includes starters such as walnut shrimp toast spring rolls, dumplings, and pot stickers. Entrée selections range from sweet-and-sour pork to Kung Pao chicken, veggie stir-fry, five-spiced fish, and Chinese barbecue. (No MSG is used in any dish.)

A selection of Chinese teas, beers, and wines is available. Desserts include banana cheesecake egg roll, strawberry red bean ice cream, caramel-ginger ice cream, and ginger cake. Reservations are recommended. L D · $$–$$$ · ❤

ROSE & CROWN PUB AND DINING ROOM (United Kingdom): Don't let the word "pub" throw you. While this place serves up some of the best brews on Disney property, its dining area is also known for such crowd-pleasing dishes as traditional fish and chips, steak, fish, shepherd's pie, and bangers and mash (sausages with mashed potatoes). Appetizer-wise, we recommend the Rose & Crown cheese plate. One of the side dishes that makes us happy? Mushy peas! (Sort of a lumpy-but-flavorful pea

Special Requests

All WDW table-service eateries that accept reservations strive to accommodate food allergies and intolerances such as gluten, wheat, shellfish, lactose, peanuts, etc., if requested at least 72 hours in advance. Kosher meals may be requested up to 24 hours in advance at most eateries. Note that 48 hours' notice is needed for eateries at the Swan and Dolphin, Yak & Yeti restaurant, and Rainforest Cafe. (Kosher meals are not available at Garden View Afternoon Tea [Grand Floridian], and Epcot's Teppan Edo and Tokyo Dining.) Make your request when booking your table by calling 407-WDW-DINE (939-3463). Note that kosher requests require a credit card guarantee and must be canceled within 24 hours of the reservation to avoid a penalty.

GOOD MEALS, GREAT TIMES

PHOTO BY JILL SAFRO

porridge.) For dessert, there are jaffa tarts, sticky toffee pudding, and bakewell tarts. Bass Ale from England, and Harp lager and Guinness stout from Ireland, and more are on tap. (They're served cold, not at room temperature, as some British guests may prefer.)

The decor is pretty—mainly polished woods, etched glass, and brass accents. In fine weather, it's pleasant to lunch under a canopy on the terrace outside and watch the FriendShip water taxis cruising across World Showcase Lagoon.

As for the pub's architecture, it incorporates three distinct styles. The wall facing the World Showcase promenade is reminiscent of urban establishments popular in Britain since the 1890s, while that on the south side evokes London's seventeenth-century Ye Olde Cheshire Cheese pub, with its brick-walled flagstone terrace, slate roof, and half-timbered exterior. The canal facade, with its stone wall and clay-tile

Food & Wine Festival

Once a year, Epcot's hopping dining scene expands exponentially in what's known as the International Food & Wine Festival. The event, which usually runs from late September through early November, is a celebration of the flavors of dozens of nations. Those countries without permanent stations at World Show-case set up temporary displays from which authentic samples of food, wine, and other spirits are sold. The samples range in price from about $3 to $8. It's possible to eat and drink your way around the world for about the same price as some table-service restaurants.

The festival also features demonstrations from top chefs, as well as wine and cooking seminars. For details, call 407-824-4321, or visit *www.disneyworld.com* or. Make reservations as early as you can—this is one popular festival.

roof, reminds visitors of the charming pubs so common in the English countryside.

The pub section of the Rose & Crown serves such snacks as fresh fruit and cheese plates, and fish and chips—along with all the brews noted earlier and traditional British mixed drinks, such as shandies (Bass Ale and Sprite), and black and tans (Bass Ale and Guinness stout). The pub is quite popular, so it's often necessary to queue up at the door. Note that the pub section also spills out onto the World Showcase promenade—where the first-come, first-served waterside tables make for a nice spot to sip a drink and, possibly, enjoy some fish and chips from a nearby snack stand. Reservations are not available in the pub areas, but recommended for the adjacent dining room.

If you're lucky, you'll catch a performance by the pub's artist-in-residence, aka the "Hat Lady." Feel free to sing along as she bangs out familiar tunes on her modest upright piano. She is quite a crowd-pleaser, so expect lots of company at the bar as you sip your pint. L D S · $ $ $ · 💛

SAN ANGEL INN (Mexico): The food at this establishment located to the rear of the plaza inside the Mexico pyramid (a corporate cousin of the famous Mexico City restaurant of the same name) may come as a surprise to most visitors. Although the tacos and tortillas and other specialties that usually fall under the broad umbrella of Mexican food are available, the menu also offers a wide variety of more subtly flavored fish, poultry, and meat dishes.

To start, there's *tostadas de tinga* (pulled chicken on fried corn tortillas with black refried beans, green tomatillo sauce, queso fresco, and sour cream) and duck tacos; plus much more. Entrées include *carne asada* (New York strip steak served with cheese enchilada), *peto an salsa poblana* (grilled wahoo fish served over roasted potatoes with vegetables and poblano sauce), and grilled fish tacos. The dinner menu is a bit more

PHOTO BY JILL SAFRO

GOOD MEALS, GREAT TIMES

💛 Disney Dining Plan participant at press time

elaborate than at lunch. Mexican desserts are largely unfamiliar to many diners, with the possible exception of the custard known as flan, but are well worth trying. *Bebidas* (drinks) such as Dos Equis, Sol, and Tecate beer, and margaritas make good accompaniments. Note that some of the dishes here have a bit of a kick. Oddly enough, this eatery does not offer hot sauce as a condiment. (Though you can buy it just outside the eatery, should you have a hankerin' for heat.) Reservations are recommended. **L D · $ $ $ ·** 🐭

SPICE ROAD TABLE (Morocco): Built on the shores of World Showcase Lagoon, this eatery's style was inspired by outdoor cafes along the shores of the Mediterranean. Popular for its stunning views of IllumiNations and its freshly prepared, palate-pleasing fare, Spice Road Table has made its way on to Epcot diners' must-do list. The eatery's whitewashed facade is accented in icy shades of blue from the famous "Blue City of Chefchaouen" in Morocco's Rif Mountains.

The menu features Moroccan small plates: zesty harissa chicken drumettes; lamb sliders; salted cod croquettes; mussels with preserved lemons and tomato sauce baked in an earthenware tagine pot; Moroccan merguez sausage with a fresh tomato salad; garlicky jumbo shrimp in a spicy chile pepper sauce; fried calamari, and more. Dessert selections include a chocolate pyramid with almond ice cream, saffron and lemon custard, and almond and rosewater cake. Soft drinks, beer, wine, and organic sangria are served. No reservations necessary. **L D S · $ $ – $ $ $ ·** 🐭

TEPPAN EDO (Japan): Tokyo Dining's lively neighbor, Teppan Edo offers a dinner-as-show experience. Guests sit around a large teppan grill and watch as a nimble chef demonstrates just how quickly enough chicken, beef, seafood, and vegetables can be chopped, seasoned, and stir-fried. Teppan Edo entrées are sizzling and

satisfying. Soups, salads, sushi, desserts, and cocktails (including Japanese beer and sake) are also on the menu. Don't wear your finest attire: There's always the potential for a little splattering. Reservations are recommended. **L D · $ $ – $ $ $ ·** 🐭

TOKYO DINING (Japan): A nice escape for lunch or dinner, this restaurant features freshly prepared sushi, sashimi, edamame, tempura, grilled items, bento boxes, and prix-fixe lunch specials. Other choices: garden salad, seaweed salad, miso soup, grilled chicken, and grilled New York strip steak. Finish with something sweet, such as chocolate ginger cake, fruit tart, green tea pudding, or soft-serve ice cream. Beer, wine, and a full sake list are available. There are a few windowside tables that offer a great view of IllumiNations. If you get there early, you may get lucky and snag one! Reservations are recommended. **L D · $ $ – $ $ $ ·** 🐭

TUTTO GUSTO (Italy): A welcome retreat for grown-ups, Tutto Gusto is a wine bar that transports guests to an ancient Italian wine cellar. Tutto Italia's next-door neighbor offers more than 200 wines, including grappa; Italian beers and specialty drinks; coffee concoctions; and a marvelous small-plate menu. Nibble on imported Italian cheeses, Sicilian eggplant salad, marinated olives, seafood salad, white asparagus, cured sliced meats, paninis (pressed sandwiches on ciabatta baguette), pastas, and more. For dessert, there is biscottini (assorted cookies), cannoli, and mocha tiramisu. Reservations are not accepted—come in the afternoon for the smallest crowds. *Salute!* **L D S · $ $ – $ $ $**

TUTTO ITALIA (Italy): There's an impressive menu at one of the most popular (and expensive) World Showcase destinations, and the addition of outdoor tables makes it one of the more appealing spots for an Epcot meal. Traditional starters such as fried calamari, fresh mozzarella

One-Stop Sweet Shop

A yummy addition to the World Showcase landscape, the Germany pavilion's Karamell Küche is sure to satisfy your sweet tooth—provided that you're a fan of fresh, gooey caramel draped or drizzled over chocolate, cookies, crunchy apples, and much more.

with tomatoes and basil, and Caesar salad can actually make a meal in and of themselves. Entrées extend toward fresh pastas—spaghetti, ravioli, fettuccine, and lasagna. The menu includes fish, steak, and chicken. Paninis are offered at lunch. For dessert, choose from items such as gelato, sorbet, cannoli, tiramisu, and cheesecake. Wine, beer, and specialty teas, coffees, and cocktails are served. Reservations are recommended. **L D · $ $ $ – $ $ $ $ · ❤**

VIA NAPOLI (Italy): It was a long time coming (roughly 30 years!), but Epcot's Italy finally has a pizza place. Tucked into the back of the pavilion, this welcome addition has a casual atmosphere and seating for 300. How serious are they about the pizza? They import the flour from Italy and select water so the crust tastes as authentically Neapolitan as possible. In addition to pizza, specialties include pastas, salads, sandwiches, soft drinks, and Italian wine. The Aqua Fresca is quite refreshing (signature seasonal fruit cooler). Dessert offerings include *zeppole di catarina* (ricotta cheese fritters), gelato, sorbet, and tiramasu. Reservations are recommended. **L D · $ $ · ❤**

FAST FOOD & SNACKS

LES HALLES BOULANGERIE PATISSERIE (France): The pastry shop in the France pavilion is not hard to find: Just follow the wonderful aroma, then watch the crowds lining up to consume the fresh baguettes (standard and mini), croissants, quiches, cheese plates, ham and cheese or turkey sandwiches, cheese tartines, soups, salads, éclairs, fruit tarts, chocolate mousse, and more. Beer, wine, lemonade, smoothies, coffee, and other soft drinks are served. Hint for those who hate to wait: This is a favorite snack spot among Epcot veterans; your best bet is to head here as soon as World Showcase opens or while other guests are watching IllumiNations. *Note that this shop, located toward the back of the pavilion, opens at 9 A.M.* **B L D S · $ – $ $ · ❤**

LA CANTINA DE SAN ANGEL (Mexico): Located just outside the entrance to Mexico's pyramid, this newly refurbished eatery serves hearty chicken and beef tacos (on fresh corn tortillas); nachos topped with cheese, ground beef, black beans, jalapeños, tomatoes, and sour cream; cheese empanadas; handmade guacamole with corn tortilla chips; hot dogs; and *churros con cajeta* (churros with caramel) and *paletas* (fruit ice pops). Beer, frozen margaritas, and soft drinks (including Mexican apple soda) are available. Kids' picks include cheese empanadas and chicken tenders, both served with tortilla chips and fruit. **L D S · $ – $ $ · ❤**

LA CAVA DEL TEQUILA (Mexico): Mexico's national drink is the star of this show—there are more than a hundred varieties to choose from. Also on the cocktail menu are sangria, mezcal, beer, wine, and specialty drinks. Snack on *queso blanco* (warm, white nacho cheese with pico de gallo sauce and tortilla chips), chips with guacamole or salsa, and Acapulco-style shrimp cocktail (served with spicy marinated tomato sauce and fried corn tortillas). **S · $ – $ $ · ❤**

Check, Please!

Paying for a meal at Disney World is a piece of cake—especially if you have a MagicBand or Disney resort ID (and load it with your Disney Dining Plan or back it up with a credit card). Both are accepted by most restaurants on Walt Disney World property. Notable exceptions: eateries at the Swan and Dolphin resorts, Four Seasons, and the resorts on Hotel Plaza Boulevard, and some snack carts. Simply scan your MagicBand bracelet or resort ID when the bill arrives (don't forget to add a tip where appropriate), and the charge will appear on your hotel statement when you check out. (If you are not staying at a WDW-owned-and-operated resort, visit *www.disneyworld.com* for details on how you can get the most from the MagicBand service.)

Of course, there are many alternative ways to pay the piper. In addition to United States currency, traveler's checks and most major credit cards are accepted in most locations. Foreign currency is a no-no. Disney currency (aka Disney Dollars) works like cash in all Disney-owned-and-operated venues. Disney Gift Cards are accepted at most of the aforementioned locations, too. (If you plan to pay with a gift card, tell your server when you place your order.)

COOL POST (between Germany and China): This is a perfect spot for a refreshing cold drink (soft drinks and beer are served). Frozen beverages, and soft-serve ice cream are also available. Ice cream comes in a waffle cone, as a sundae, or in a float. They have hot dogs, too. S·$·☙

FIFE & DRUM TAVERN (The American Adventure): Located in front of the Liberty Inn, this small brick edifice proffers American favorites. Among the options: turkey legs, pretzels, popcorn, ice cream, frozen lemonade, soft drinks, and Sam Adams beer. LDS·$–$$·☙

KABUKI CAFE (Japan): Step up to cool down at this quick-service kiosk: the specialty of the house is Kakigori, aka shaved ice. Flavors include cherry, tangerine, sweet strawberry, and more. Other chilly treats include green tea or ginger ice cream and strawberry smoothies (be sure to ask about the smoothie flavor of the day). Kabuki also offers edamame, miso soup, wafu (ginger-braised) pork ribs, California and spicy tuna rolls, beer, wine, sake, and soft drinks. LDS·$–$$·☙

KATSURA GRILL (Japan): Located to the left of the plaza, the exterior of the restaurant was inspired by the historic sixteenth-century Katsura Imperial Villa near Kyoto, Japan.

Among the fare here is Japanese chicken cutlet curry (a peppery sauce over rice with a panko-breaded chicken breast). That, along with teriyaki chicken, salmon, or beef (basted with soy sauce and sesame oil as it broils), sushi, miso soup, and udon noodles typify the offerings here. The beverage selection includes hot and cold sake, plum wine, green tea, beer, and soft drinks. The garden serves as a respite for those who want a break from the hustle and bustle of a busy Epcot day. And kids dig the koi pond—the fish are enormous! LDS·$–$$·☙

KRINGLA BAKERI OG KAFE (Norway): Tucked between the Norway pavilion's wooden church and a cluster of shops, this popular eating spot serves kringlas, sweet pretzels reserved for special occasions in Norway; cloudberry horns (flaky pastry filled with cream and tart cloudberries); and smørbrøds, sandwiches such as open-faced smoked salmon and eggs; ham and apple; Norwegian club; or roast beef, and vegetable tortes. There are excellent soups, as well as tossed salads, berry tarts, cheesecake, Norwegian school bread, fruit cups, pear almond tarts, rice pudding, and no-sugar-added chocolate mousse. Wine and beer are served. There is a shaded outdoor eating area directly under the grass-thatched roof. LDS·$–$$·☙

L'ARTISAN DES GLACES (France): An artisanal ice cream and sorbet shop, this spot fills cones and cups with 10 flavors of ice cream and 6 sorbets—all crafted in-house. The ingredients are all simple and fresh: milk, sugar, cream, eggs, and fruit. How cool is that?! Adults over age 21 may top their order off with a liqueur. S·$·☙

LIBERTY INN (The American Adventure): To many visitors from other countries, American food means hot dogs, burgers, chicken breast nuggets, grapes, and fries—and these are the staples at the Liberty Inn, located to the left of The American Adventure show on the far side of the lagoon. Caesar salad, Southwest chicken salad, barbecue pork sandwiches, apple blossoms, and brownies round out the selections. For those in search of a meat-free meal, the vegetarian plate will do in a pinch. Liberty Inn is a good destination for kids and unadventurous eaters. There is a kosher option, too. LDS·$–$$·☙

LOTUS BLOSSOM CAFE (China): Adjacent to the House of Good Fortune shopping gallery in the China pavilion, this fast-food counter recently underwent an extensive refurbishment. The menu offers orange chicken with steamed rice, beef noodle soup, Hong Kong–style vegetable curry (with or without chicken), shrimp fried rice, sesame chicken salad, and sesame chicken salad, plus pot stickers, egg rolls, and kid-friendly selections. Unlike most traditional Chinese cooking, the food here is prepared on a flat grill, as opposed to stir-fried. There is a covered outdoor seating area. **L D · $ – $ $ · 🐭**

REFRESHMENT PORT (Canada): Another good spot for a thirst quencher or a quick snack (croissant doughnuts!). Located on the World Showcase promenade, near Canada. **S · $ · 🐭**

SOMMERFEST (Germany): Bratwurst or frankfurter on a roll with sauerkraut, currywurst, Leberkäse Reuben (a German meatloaf), Nudel Gratin (baked macaroni with cheese custard—a new fan favorite), cold potato salad, housemade paprika potato chips, Black Forest cake, apple strudel with vanilla sauce, soft drinks, shots of Schnapps and Jägermeister, steins of German beer, and red and white wines are offered at this small, covered spot located toward the rear of the pavilion; seating is nearby. (Did you know that Spätburgunder means "pinot noir"?) **L D S · $ – $ $ · 🐭**

TANGIERINE CAFE (Morocco): Named for the Moroccan city of Tangier, this casual spot serves lentil salad, hummus, tangierine couscous salad, marinated olives, and tabbouleh, as well as meatball platters, rotisserie chicken, beef, and lamb combination platters, and veggie platters. For dessert, there are pastries such as baklava. Specialty coffees, frozen drinks, and beer are available, too. **L D S · $ – $ $ · 🐭**

YORKSHIRE COUNTY FISH SHOP (United Kingdom): A perfect choice for a simple meal, this stand offers classic fish and chips. (Don't forget the malt vinegar.) Soda, iced tea, light lemonade, Bass ale, and Harp lager are also available. English sugar cookies are also sold. **L D S · $ – $ $ · 🐭**

Epcot Mealtime Tips

- The international restaurants of World Showcase offer some of the best dining on the property. Since many of them are very popular, it's a good idea to arrange advance reservations for all table-service restaurants by calling 407-WDW-DINE (939-3463) long before arriving. However, it's important to note that some tables may be available for same-day seating. To make arrangements, head to Guest Relations first thing in the morning or to the kiosk located by the Tip Board in Innoventions Plaza. Meals may also be booked at the individual restaurants.

- Don't dismiss the idea of an early seating if you can get it: A 5 P.M. dinner may not only be welcome, but may provide an opportunity to spend time enjoying the pleasant, more temperate evening hours at Epcot's World Showcase.

- Lunch provides guests with another chance to enjoy the most popular Epcot restaurants. It also has an additional appeal: With reservations for 1 P.M., it's possible to spend some of the busiest hours in the park consuming a pleasant meal while less fortunate visitors are waiting in some of the longest lines of the day.

- If you aren't able to secure reservations for a meal, don't despair. There are satisfying alternatives to a traditional sit-down restaurant. Tutto Gusto (Italian wine bar) and Spice Road Table (in Morocco) both offer small plates and full service. Japan has Katsura Grill, good for sushi and chicken curry. Sample Mexican lunch specialties at La Cantina. Try the smoked salmon sandwiches at Kringla Bakeri og Kafe in Norway, the fish and chips in the United Kingdom, or Germany's bratwurst sandwiches and soft pretzels.

- Cravings for conventional fast foods will be satisfied at the Electric Umbrella in Innoventions and at the Liberty Inn in the American Adventure. Sunshine Seasons, in the Land pavilion, offers a bit of everything. However, it can get extremely congested at mealtime rush hours.

- The most unadventurous eaters can still find something pleasing—even in the more exotic restaurants of World Showcase. If you're undecided, ask at Guest Relations to see a booklet describing the menus. Keep in mind that most restaurants have menus for kids.

In Disney's Hollywood Studios

Lights, camera, lunch! This theme park, which was designed to resemble a working Hollywood backlot circa the 1940s, tackles the role of feeding guests with style and whimsy. Here you can sit in a classic car and enjoy a meal at a drive-in, rub elbows with the beautiful people at a reproduction of the Hollywood Brown Derby, and play the part of sitcom kid as you're served by "Mom" or "Dad" at the 50's Prime Time Cafe (no elbows on the table, please!). While the attention to theming is obvious, it doesn't upstage the fare. The eateries at Disney's Hollywood Studios are a breed apart. Some feature decor that returns guests to a bygone era; others recapture memorable moments from the big or small screen. All reprise a beloved part of Hollywood's star-studded heritage. The Studios has five full-service restaurants, whose atmospheres and menus are so distinct they satisfy altogether different moods and whims. Reservations are available for these dining rooms; call 407-WDW-DINE (939-3463). So grab a napkin, and get ready for your close-up.

TABLE SERVICE

50'S PRIME TIME CAFE: This retreat to the era of *I Love Lucy* is an amusing amalgam of comfort food, kitschy 1950s-style kitchen nooks, and attentive servers of the "No talking with your mouth full" ilk. Nostalgia abounds, with more cookie jars than you could shake an Oreo at, all meant to bring you back to the childhood of yesteryear; even the dessert menu is read on a View-Master, and TVs broadcast black-and-white clips from favorite fifties comedies (all related to food). Guests are waited on by "Mom" (and other family members) with considerable enthusiasm: They encourage everyone to keep

HOT TIP!

If you can stand to miss the evening's performance of Fantasmic! (The Studios' nighttime spectacular), consider dining in one of the park's popular table-service eateries during the show.

their elbows off the table, eat their vegetables, and clean their plates (or no dessert!). Misbehave and you may have to stand in the corner (the 1950s version of the "time out").

Adding to the appeal is the menu, which is packed with comfort foods. For openers, there's a choice of house-made chicken noodle soup or onion rings. Specialties of the house include magnificent meatloaf, served with mashed potatoes and vegetables; fried chicken; and old-fashioned pot roast. There are Caesar salad and chicken pot pie, too. Milk shakes, ice cream sodas, and root beer floats are filling accompaniments. And when you've finished everything on your plate, you may order dessert. Standouts include s'mores—graham crackers topped with chocolate and toasted marshmallows—sundaes, apple crisp, and no-sugar-added cheesecake topped with whipped cream and strawberry sauce. A full bar is available. Guests of all ages love this place. Reservations are recommended. **LD·$$–$$$·**🐭

HOLLYWOOD & VINE: The distinctive Art Deco facade ushers guests into a contemporary version of a 1950s diner—all stainless steel with pink accents. An elaborate 42-by-8-foot wall mural depicts notable Hollywood landmarks, including the Disney Studios, Columbia Ranch, and Warner Brothers (back when they were the only film studios in the San Fernando Valley). At the center of the mural is the Carthay Circle Theatre, where *Snow White and the Seven Dwarfs* premiered in 1937.

The buffet breakfast and lunch, known as Disney Junior Play 'N Dine, are character affairs featuring Sofia the First, Doc McStuffins, Jake the Never Land pirate, and Handy Manny. The morning meal includes Mickey waffles, frittatas, fresh fruit, and house-made pastries, and a create-your-own omelet station. Lunch may offer items such as salmon with maple mustard glaze, salads, and a create-your-own pasta

GOOD MEALS, GREAT TIMES

station. Dinner, which is character-free, features carved meats, peel-and-eat shrimp, and mussels. The dessert buffet boasts a chocolate fountain. Soft drinks are included. Beer and wine are served at an extra cost.

The dinner buffet costs about $43 for adults and $17 for kids, lunch is $34 (adults) and $18 (kids), while breakfast runs about $26 for adults and $15 for kids. Reservations are recommended. **BLD·$$–$$$·♥**

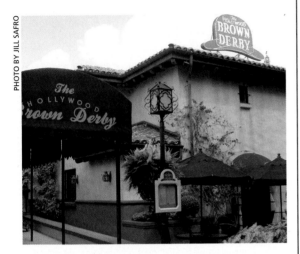

PHOTO BY JILL SAFRO

HOLLYWOOD BROWN DERBY: The home of the famous Cobb salad is alive and well. This re-creation of the former Vine Street mainstay is quite faithful, right down to the caricatures (reproduced from the original Derby collection) that cover the walls. Arch gossip queen rivals Louella Parsons and Hedda Hopper (portrayed by convincing actresses) may still be spotted dining here, just as they did in the heyday of the real Brown Derby. The place is decorated predominantly in teak and mahogany, and the elegant chandeliers and perimeter lamps (shaped like miniature derbies) are reminiscent of those in the original eatery.

The menu features the famed Cobb salad, created by owner Bob Cobb in the 1930s. It's a mixture of ever-so-finely chopped fresh salad greens, tomato, bacon, turkey, egg, blue cheese, and avocado, served with French dressing.

Desserts are tempting—particularly double vanilla crème brûlée and the legendary grapefruit cake, a Brown Derby institution. Some of the selections are a bit highbrow (and high-priced) for the theme park crowd, but if you're up for a splurge, this spot will likely rise to the occasion. We recommend the seafood cioppino; the filet mignon gets good marks, too.

The slightly formal atmosphere is not likely to enchant most children, but youngster-friendly fare is available. The New World wine list is excellent. There are some outdoor tables, though the menu may be limited there. Reservations are recommended. **LD·$$$·♥**

MAMA MELROSE'S RISTORANTE ITALIANO: This pleasant Italian restaurant (with a California twist) is located in a warehouse that has been converted into a dining room. Flatbreads are prepared in a wood-burning oven. The menu also features house-made pasta, grilled fish, and vegetarian options. Favorite dishes include seafood arrabbiata, charred strip steak, and oven-baked chicken parmesan. They serve whole wheat fettuccini with sautéed vegetables and goat cheese, too. Reservations are recommended. **LD·$$–$$$·♥**

SCI-FI DINE-IN THEATER: A convincing re-creation of a drive-in theater, the atmosphere here is completely absorbing. The tables are actually flashy, 1950s-era cars, complete with fins and whitewalls. Stars twinkle overhead in the "night sky," and drive-in theater speakers are mounted beside each car. Most seats are within cars, with most featuring front- and backseat counters facing front. Not terribly conducive to

HOT TIP!

While the Sci-Fi Dine-In Theater has tables that can accommodate guests who use wheelchairs, there aren't many. Be sure to request such a table when you make your reservations—and confirm it before you go: 407-WDW-DINE (939-3463).

Water Park Dining

Disney's duo of water parks, Typhoon Lagoon and Blizzard Beach, provides plenty of chances to defy Mom's plea to wait an hour to splash after you nosh. The fare is limited to the quick-service kind (who wants a sit-down meal in a soggy swimsuit?), and the quality of the offerings has been stepped up a bit of late. Typhoon Lagoon offers hot Italian sandwiches, fresh fruit bowls, meatball subs, and more.

At Blizzard Beach, you can order mozzarella sandwiches and hot dogs wrapped in a soft pretzel. Snacks are sold at spots with names like Typhoon Tilly's (❤), Leaning Palms (❤), and Avalunch (❤). Frozen drink specialties flow at Let's Go Slurpin' (Typhoon Lagoon) and at Blizzard Beach's Polar Bear Pool Bar.

Some folks prefer to pack a picnic lunch. Coolers may be brought into both of Disney's water parks, but alcoholic beverages and glass containers may not.

meaningful table talk, but ideal for viewing the large movie screen, where a 45-minute compilation of the best (and worst) science-fiction trailers and cartoons plays in a continuous loop. There are a couple of traditional tables within oversize cars—if this is your preference, make that known when you book the table and expect to wait a bit when you arrive.

Selections include Reuben sandwiches, pork ribs, burgers, and shrimp pasta. Kids enjoy the mac and cheese. Desserts include cheesecake, milk shakes, and ice cream sundaes. Reservations are recommended. Note that some of the movie trailers feature monsters and may frighten your little ones. **L D · $$–$$$ · ❤**

FAST FOOD & SNACKS

ABC COMMISSARY: Located near the Chinese Theater, this spot has shaken up the menu a few times of late. Most recently, it featured fish and chips, fried shrimp, cheeseburgers, couscous, quinoa and arugula salad with chicken or salmon, and an Asian-style salad. Desserts include chocolate mousse and no-sugar-added strawberry parfait. Beer, wine, and soft drinks are served. The restaurant is huge and does indeed resemble an actual studio commissary. We could do without the ads for ABC shows, which play on a continuous loop from TVs scattered throughout the dining area. Enough already! **L D S · $ · ❤**

BACKLOT EXPRESS: Designed to resemble the crafts shops on old studio backlot, this eatery is near the Star Tours attraction. The indoor seating areas carry out the prop-shop theme, with paint-speckled floors, car engines, and various other spare prop parts. Outdoor tables are situated amid plants and trees. Menu offerings include burgers, chicken nuggets, hot dogs, salads, grilled turkey sandwiches, and vegetable paninis (our favorite). For dessert, there's chocolate mousse and no-sugar-added strawberry parfait. Soft drinks, beer, and wine are available. **L D S · $ · ❤**

DINOSAUR GERTIE'S ICE CREAM OF EXTINCTION: Soft-serve ice cream is Gertie's go-to treat—vanilla, chocolate, or swirl, served in a cup or cone. Also on the menu? Mickey-shaped ice cream bars, and cookies and cream sandwiches. Gertie's operates seasonally. **S · $ · ❤**

HOLLYWOOD HILLS THEATER: If your stomach growls while waiting for Fantasmic! to begin, you can keep it quiet with a visit to this snack shack. Savory items include the chili-cheese bread cone, mac & cheese bread cone, nachos with cheese, hot dogs, popcorn, caramel corn, churros, and more. Sweet treats, such as ice cream bars, frozen bananas, fresh fruit, and glazed almonds, are also sold. Wash it all down with a soft drink, beer, or wine. **S · $–$$ · ❤**

ICE COLD: Need to cool off on a hot day? Swing by this stand near the park entrance. It sells ice cream, iced coffee, cool juices, and fizzy drinks. Other snack items include whole fruit, trail mix, pastries, and chips. **S · $ · ❤**

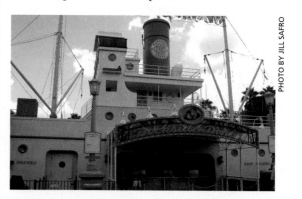

PHOTO BY JILL SAFRO

MIN AND BILL'S DOCKSIDE DINER: A waterside window offering thick chocolate shakes, as well as franks in pretzel rolls, pork shanks, turkey legs, Italian sausage sandwiches with pepper and onions, cookies, chips, coffee, frozen lemonade, soft drinks, and beer. **S · $ · ❤**

Hollywood Brown Derby, Mama Melrose's Ristorante Italiano, and Hollywood & Vine offer a "dinner and a show" combo (lunch is offered seasonally). General admission seating for Fantasmic! is included at no extra cost (though tax, gratuities, and alcoholic beverages carry an additional charge). For pricing information or to make arrangements, call 407-939-3463 and request the Fantasmic dinner package. Note that this package was recently tweaked and once again offers guaranteed seating for Fantasmic. Guests are advised to arrive at the theater 30 to 45 minutes before showtime to snag a seat.

OASIS CANTEEN: A tiny tin shack that sits beside the Indiana Jones Epic Stunt Spectacular, the Oasis Canteen dispenses funnel cakes topped with strawberries, vanilla ice cream, powdered sugar, or cinnamon; soft-serve ice cream in waffle cones or cups (chocolate, vanilla, or swirl); bottled water; and domestic draft beer. **S·$·❤**

PIZZA PLANET: Located inside a kid-magnate arcade, this is a counter-service spot with a limited but youngster-friendly menu. Select from simple individual pizzas (cheese, pepperoni, and veggie), meatball subs, salads, apple slices, chocolate chip cookies, cappuccino, and soft drinks (including chocolate milk and apple juice). There is seating upstairs and just outside the entrance. **LDS·$–$$·❤**

STARRING ROLLS CAFE: In a hurry? Head here to get the day off to a quick start, or take a nice break. Pastries, muffins, croissants, and no-sugar-added desserts are sold at this sweet-smelling shop. For lunch, there are ham sandwiches, turkey on focaccia bread, yogurt, and sushi (California, spicy tuna, and veggie rolls). Soft drinks and wine are served, too. Get there early if you really want sushi—they are always sold out by the time we arrive. This spot usually closes by 4 P.M. **BLS·$–$$·❤**

STUDIO CATERING CO.: Situated next to the Honey, I Shrunk the Kids Movie Set Adventure, the eatery offers Greek salad and a variety of sandwiches, including pressed Tuscan deli-style, pressed turkey club on multigrain bread, grilled veggie sandwich, and chicken

Caesar wrap. With a full-service bar attached, it's possible to order just about any refreshing libation under the sun. **S·$–$$·❤**

PHOTO BY JILL SAFRO

SUNSET RANCH MARKET: A celebration of California's outdoor lifestyle, this open-air cluster of snack stands has something for just about everyone. Rosie's All-American Cafe specializes in cheeseburgers, veggie black bean burgers, chicken nuggets, and soups; vanilla cake with chocolate custard, and banana parfait. Catalina Eddie's offers plain and pepperoni pizzas, plus sandwiches, salads, and chocolate cake. Fruit and vegetables, juice, and soft drinks are sold at Anaheim Produce. The nearby Toluca Legs Turkey Co. offers turkey legs and pork shank. Hollywood Scoops has a selection of creamy treats (including one of the no-sugar-added variety). And look no farther than Fairfax Fare for smoked specialties, including ribs and chicken, hot dogs, breakfast selections (pastries and sandwiches), plus salad. Umbrellas dot the outdoor seating area. **BLDS·$·❤**

Studios Mealtime Tips

- To avoid traffic jams at fast-food spots, consider eating at one of the restaurants that offer advance reservations—Hollywood Brown Derby, 50's Prime Time Cafe, Sci-Fi Dine-In Theater, Hollywood & Vine, or Mama Melrose's Ristorante Italiano.

- To arrange for reservations in advance, call 407-WDW-DINE (939-3463). To obtain same-day seating, go to the kiosk at Hollywood Junction (at the corner of Hollywood and Sunset boulevards) before 1 P.M. or to the restaurant itself.

- The many indoor and outdoor nooks within the Backlot Express seating area are nicely removed from the beaten path; relative quiet can frequently be enjoyed here even during prime mealtimes.

In Animal Kingdom

Whether you eat like a bird or more like a horse, you'll have no trouble finding something to sink your teeth into at one of Animal Kingdom's eateries. Walt Disney World's nature-oriented theme park is ideal for grazers; it may not be strong on table service (there are three such eateries), but it takes "quick service" quite seriously. When your stomach starts growling like the beasts at the Kilimanjaro Safaris attraction, consider a visit to Flame Tree Barbecue or Pizzafari. These quick-service options cater to carnivores and herbivores alike.

TABLE SERVICE

RAINFOREST CAFE: Like the Oasis, the Animal Kingdom region that it borders, this cafe is a lush, soothing tropical jungle. Unlike the Oasis, any quiet moment here is merely a calm before the storm—as brief thunderstorms occur throughout the day inside the restaurant. Gushing waterfalls, twisting tree trunks, and colorful fish add to the ambience. The environmentally conscious cuisine includes items like Planet Earth Pasta and the portobello mushroom sandwich. (The spinach-artichoke dip is an especially satisfying appetizer.) There is no net-caught fish on the menu, nor beef from countries that destroy rainforest land to raise cattle.

Note: Rainforest Cafe is accessible from inside and outside the park, so admission to the Animal Kingdom isn't necessary to enter, but parking fees apply. (It's on the left of the park's entrance plaza.) Buses stop running about one hour after the Animal Kingdom closes. Reservations are recommended. BLDS·$$–$$$

TUSKER HOUSE: Harambe village sets the stage for a dining adventure at this buffet restaurant. Seating inside is quite civilized, with cherrywood-colored tables and carved chair backs; there's also outdoor seating under the thatched roof for a pre- or post-meal cocktail. Breakfast and lunch are hosted by favorite Disney characters. At press time, the characters scheduled to attend were Donald, Daisy, Mickey, and Goofy (the latter three are subject to change). Note that Disney characters are not in attendance at dinner. Reservations are highly recommended for all meals. Book breakfast and lunch as early as possible. Tusker House opens at 8 A.M. BLDS·$$·❦

YAK & YETI: This place opens daily at 10 A.M. (though it doesn't serve breakfast). It specializes in Asian fusion cuisine. Menu items include maple tamarind chicken, crispy mahi mahi, baby back ribs, lo mein, seared miso salmon, and stir-fried beef and broccoli. Among the more tempting dessert options are fried (sweet) wontons and mango pie. The Yak & Yeti shop offers everything from sushi plates to fine teapots. You'll find Yak & Yeti in Asia, near Kali River Rapids. African beers and cocktails are available, too. LDS·$–$$$·❦

FAST FOOD & SNACKS

ANANDAPUR ICE CREAM TRUCK: Cool off with a soft-serve from Asia's local ice cream truck. The refreshing snack is available by the waffle cone, cup, or in a soda float. Bottled water and a variety of soft drinks (including root beer and light lemonade) are also served. S·$·❦

DINO-BITE SNACKS: Restaurantosaurus's neighbor, this snack shack proffers soft drinks and sweat treats. Order items such as hand-scooped ice cream, ice-cream cookie sandwiches, churros, and fresh-baked cookies. S·$·❦

FLAME TREE BARBECUE: If you can't find this eatery, just follow your nose. It serves a fragrant selection of BBQ sandwiches and platters, all wood roasted. Sample the mild, tomato-based Carolina-style sauce with your chicken, pulled pork, or hickory-smoked St. Louis ribs. The ovens produce 1,200 pounds at a time. Smoked turkey breast sandwiches, smoked chicken salads, turkey legs, fruit plates (served with honey yogurt), fries, onion rings, and chocolate or Key lime mousse round out the options. Platters come with baked beans and/or corn-on-the-cob. Fries and onion rings are offered. Beer, wine, and soft drinks are served. There's outdoor seating along the river (lovely when it's not 98 degrees). It's on Discovery Island, near DinoLand U.S.A. LDS·$–$$·❦

GARDENS: A Discovery Island kiosk, Gardens specializes in gluten-free and organic snacks. Folks with food sensitivities, take note: The savvy cast members here can steer you toward nibbles that will suit your diet to a tee. S·$·❦

GOOD MEALS, GREAT TIMES

HARAMBE FRUIT MARKET: Sometimes a crunchy apple is just what the doctor—or theme park guest—ordered. Apples, among other healthy snacks, are available at this stand near the entrance to Kilimanjaro Safaris. Stop here for pineapple spears, fruit cups, whole fruit, bottled water, and more. S · $ · 🐭

KUSAFIRI COFFEE SHOP & BAKERY: The bakery at Tusker House provides a steady stream of fresh-baked treats (such as colossal cinnamon buns), yogurt, fruit, cookies, brownies, cupcakes, and other desserts, plus cereal, soft drinks, low-fat milk, and specialty coffees. B S · $ · 🐭

PIZZAFARI: This big, colorful dining area has no-nonsense fare that tends to please young palates. Plain, pepperoni, and veggie pizzas; chicken and vegetable pasta salad; and hot Italian-style sandwiches are all on the menu. Little ones enjoy the bread sticks topped with cheese, served with marinara sauce. Animal murals decorate the walls of this restaurant, located on Discovery Island. B L D S · $ – $ $ · 🐭

ROYAL ANANDAPUR TEA COMPANY: After hiking through Africa to get to Asia, guests can build up quite a thirst. That's where this exotic tea stand comes in handy. Located near the Yak & Yeti in the villlage of Serka Zong, this hut dispenses a variety of iced and hot teas, fruit smoothies, specialty coffees, and sweet treats. S · $ · 🐭

RESTAURANTOSAURUS: Located deep in the heart of DinoLand U.S.A., this spot is a fishing lodge turned commissary for student paleontologists. It offers fast food at lunch and dinner: burgers, chicken nuggets, veggie subs, chicken BLT salad, and hot dogs (including a mac and cheese dog)—plus fries, apple slices, chocolate mousse, and cheesecake in a glass. It's filled with fossils, bones, and such; class notes line the walls. L D S · $ – $ $ · 🐭

TAMU TAMU REFRESHMENTS: Stop by this spot in Africa's Harambe (across from Tusker House) for a light meal or a quick snack. Here you can choose a slow-cooked chicken curry, vegetarian curry, or roasted chicken salad. Milk shakes and cheesecake are served, as is the frozen pineapple treat known as the Dole Whip (with or without rum). There's seating next door. Note that this spot usually opens around 10:30 A.M. L D S · $ · 🐭

TRILO-BITES: In DinoLand U.S.A., just inside the entrance (near the dinosaur skeleton bridge), this kiosk offers warm waffles with fresh strawberries and cream, bottled water, beer, and a variety of soft drinks throughout the day. During peak times of year, Trilo-Bites also offers a pulled buffalo chicken waffle sandwich. S · $ · 🐭

YAK & YETI LOCAL FOOD CAFES: Walk-up windows adjacent to the Yak & Yeti restaurant in Asia, the cafes specialize in items with pan-Asian influences. Entrées include sweet-and-sour pork, shrimp lo mein, crispy honey chicken or pork, orange beef, Asian chicken sandwich, chicken fried rice, and Mandarin chicken salad. Egg rolls, chocolate cake, and frozen lemonade are also served. Kids choose from chicken bites or a cheeseburger. There is ample outdoor seating nearby. L D S · $ – $ $ · 🐭

Animal Kingdom Mealtime Tips

- Tusker House and Rainforest Cafe are the only table-service places to offer breakfast; a handful of spots, including Pizzafari and Kusafiri Coffee Shop & Bakery, supply light breakfast options.

- At press time, the only restaurants that accepted reservations for all meals were Tusker House and Rainforest Cafe. (Yak & Yeti accepts lunch and dinner reservations.) To arrange for reservations in advance, available up to 180 days ahead for all meals, call 407-WDW-DINE (939-3463). To obtain same-day seating, go straight to the restaurant. We recommend making reservations. Rainforest Cafe may keep longer hours than the Animal Kingdom park.

- The many seating pavilions along the river near Flame Tree Barbecue provide waterside dining that's nicely removed from the hubbub of Discovery Island; it may be relatively calm here, even during prime mealtimes. Please resist the urge to feed any birds that come begging.

- A great place to meet Donald and pals such as Mickey, Daisy, and Goofy is at Tusker House at the daily character meals (breakfast and lunch only). The characters appearing here are subject to change—though Donald is always in attendance. Make reservations well in advance.

In Downtown Disney

The evolving region known as Downtown Disney encompasses the Marketplace, the West Side, and the space between them (formerly known as Pleasure Island). Restaurants usually operate from about 11 A.M. to midnight; most snack spots are open from 11 A.M. to late into the night. For the latest details, call 407-939-4636. It's worth noting that while the restaurants really hop at dinnertime, they are not always crowded at lunch (except, possibly, on the weekend).

AMC DINE-IN THEATRES (West Side): Popcorn and soda are upstaged by selections such as chicken Alfredo and mango margaritas in this in-theater dining experience known as Fork and Screen. Seat-side, table-top service (with a personal call button for the server) allows movie-goers to enjoy dinner and a movie simultaneously. The extensive menu includes appetizers, entrées, desserts, cocktails, and soft drinks—in addition to traditional movie munchies. Seating is reserved (and assigned when you purchase your movie ticket). Guests under age 18 must be accompanied by an adult (over the age of 18). **L D S · $ – $ $ · ♥**

BONGOS CUBAN CAFE (West Side): This Gloria Estefan creation spices up the Disney dining repertoire with a menu driven by Cuban and Latin American flavors. Its slate of traditional and nouvelle Cuban dishes includes black bean soup (or preferred dish), plantains, steak topped with onions, and flan. Indoors, the elaborate mosaic mural and palm-leaf railings set the scene; the patio for outdoor seating wraps around a two-story pineapple. A take-out window provides snacks on the go. Diners are sometimes treated to live music (feel free to sway in your seat). A small shop sells items such as shirts, hats, and glasses emblazoned with the Bongos logo. Reservations are recommended. **L D S · $ $ – $ $ $**

COOKE'S OF DUBLIN (Marketplace): Raglan Road's quick-service neighbor, this is the place to go for some of the freshest, most succulent fish and chips in the World. And don't ask for the recipe—it's a Cooke family secret! Other choices include battered scallops and shrimp, salads, beef and lamb pie, fisherman's pie, burgers, and chicken wings in whiskey and crushed pepper glaze. Save room for a fried candy bar dessert. **L D S · $ $ – $ $ $ · ♥**

EARL OF SANDWICH (Marketplace): This tip-top counter-service establishment is brimming with sweet and savory possibilities. Among the fare standing by is a variety of hot and cold sandwiches (freshly prepared on warm bread), wraps, tossed salads, and homemade desserts. A few more exotic selections such as Hawaiian BBQ (ham with fresh pineapple and Swiss cheese), The Original 1762 (warm roast beef sandwich with creamy horseradish sauce and cheddar cheese), and Caribbean Jerk Chicken are served, too. The Veggie sandwich is also an option. Breakfast items include sandwiches and baked goods. There are "grab and go" selections as well. Dessert can be cupcakes, cookies, muffin crowns, or English trifle. Beer, wine, and Kona coffee are on the menu, too. Seating is available inside and outside. It is not uncommon to see a very long line here, but it moves rather quickly. The Earl welcomes visitors daily from 8:30 A.M. until 11 P.M. **B L D S · $ – $ $ · ♥**

FOOD TRUCKS: Four new fancy food trucks —each themed to the "essence" of a Disney theme park—have parked at Downtown Disney. Enchanted Fare serves favorites from Disney Parks around the world. Look for items such as *croque monsieur* from Magic Kingdom, glass noodle salad from Hong Kong Disneyland, and hand-dipped corn dogs from Disney California Adventure. Namaste Café spices things up with dishes such as butter chicken, slow-cooked beef short ribs, and tandoori spice shrimp. Superstar Catering shines the spotlight on meatballs (the lamb

   B breakfast   **L** lunch   **D** dinner   **S** snacks   /   **$** under $15   **$$** $15–$36   **$$$** $36–$60   **$$$$** $60 and up meatball flatbread with tzatziki is one option). The World Showcase of Flavors features favorites from the Epcot International Food & Wine Festival. Possibilities include grass-fed beef sliders, perogies with kielbasa, and lobster rolls. **L D S · $$ – $$$ · 🐾**

FULTON'S CRAB HOUSE (Marketplace): This regal restaurant, originally known as the Empress Lilly (after Walt Disney's wife, Lillian Disney), occupies a three-deck riverboat. Though it looks as if it might set sail at any moment, the replica ship is permanently docked at the edge of Village Lake (near Portobello). Guests board the ship via gangway and are enveloped by polished woods, brass detailing, and nautical nostalgia.

The extensive (albeit pricey) menu changes with the day's arrivals. It's not unusual for Alaskan wild halibut to be seen next to Panama City (Florida) snapper. Signature seafood dishes include Dungeness crab legs; a San Francisco–style seafood stew with king crab, shrimp, scallops, mussels, and fish in a tomato broth; and crab and lobster platters. For landlubbers, bone-in rib-eye, filet mignon, and free-range chicken are all satisfying choices. Accompaniments extend to salt-crusted baked potatoes and grilled asparagus.

For a quicker fix, visit our top choice here: the ravishing raw bar at the adjoining Stone Crab Lounge. In fact, for a relatively reasonably priced lunch, it's lounge or bust. If the weather is pleasant, try for an outside table, on the bow of the ship. Reservations are highly recommended for lunch and dinner at Fulton's. Reservations are not available at the Stone Crab Lounge. **L D S · $$$ – $$$$**

GHIRARDELLI SODA FOUNTAIN & CHOCOLATE SHOP (Marketplace): What is it about an old-fashioned ice cream parlor that makes just about everybody giddy? Oh, yes, the ice cream. This spot does it one better and throws in its famous chocolate, to boot. Stop in for a chocolaty treat, root beer float, or a malt. We often duck in here for a quick cup of coffee and a chocolate chaser. And there is always the potential for a free candy sample. How sweet is that?! **S · $ – $$**

HOUSE OF BLUES (West Side): Thanks to the combination of its diverse menu and rustic, folk-art-studded design, House of Blues doesn't disappoint. Favorites include flatbreads (grilled, then finished in the pizza oven), lobster mac and cheese, tacos, corn bread, and jambalaya. At the far west of the West Side, House of Blues is a good choice for a satisfying meal or a late-night bite. Live music is presented in the restaurant and on the front porch on select days. There is a lively gospel brunch every Sunday. Reservations are recommended. To reserve a table at the House of Blues, call 407-934-BLUE (934-2583). **L D S · $$ – $$$**

HOUSE OF BLUES SMOKE-HOUSE (West Side): Tucked inside the former House of Blues Ticket booth, this new quick-service window offers a variety of BBQ selections (e.g., pulled pork or chicken sandwiches, smoked turkey legs, ribs, and baked beans), soft drinks, spirits, and more. **L D S · $ – $$**

PLANET HOLLYWOOD (West Side): Chances are, you will have no trouble finding this restaurant—just keep your eyes peeled for the giant globe. Built on three levels, this colossal sphere is jam-packed with classic movie and television memorabilia. The menu features salads, sandwiches, pasta dishes, burgers, appetizers, fajitas, and dessert specialties.

Consider sampling the chicken crunch appetizer, chicken Caesar salad, or lasagna. Cheesecake is among the dessert choices. Reservations are recommended. **L D S · $$ – $$$ · ❣**

PARADISO 37 (Marketplace): A lively, waterfront eatery (with indoor and outdoor seating), Paradiso 37 specializes in "mangled margaritas," stocks 37 different kinds of tequila, and offers the "coldest beer in the world." And they serve food, too!

The menu focuses on "street foods" of the Americas. Starters include the signature fire-roasted corn on the cob with a mild pepper sauce and cheese, mac and cheese bites, and potato pancakes. Entrées range from Argentinian skirt steak with chimichurri sauce to Chilean-style salmon and prickly pear shrimp salad. No reservations necessary. **L D S · $$ – $$$**

PHOTO BY JILL SAFRO

PORTOBELLO (Marketplace): This Italian trattoria is drenched in warm colors that match the rustic Italian cuisine. The best seats are on the waterfront porch (provided the weather is pleasant), and the wood-burning-oven pizzas are a top choice. Traditional Italian cuisine includes mix-and-match antipasti, hand-crafted sausage, pastas, and fish.

At lunchtime, the menu includes sandwiches (meatball, vegetarian, or Italian sub), pizza, and pasta. For dinner, try the Ravioli Gigante (filled with ricotta and spinach) with tomato, basil, and toasted garlic. The full-service bar offers a solid wine list of Italian favorites, specialty cocktails, and beer. For dessert it is tough to resist the house-made tiramisu. **L D S · $$$**

RAGLAN ROAD (between Marketplace and West Side): As authentically Irish as you can get on this side of the Atlantic, this warm and lively establishment blends fresh ingredients to create traditional Irish fare with a modern flair. The menu comes courtesy of Kevin Dundon, one of Ireland's best-known chefs. His selections are

PHOTO BY JILL SAFRO

perfectly complemented by the welcoming atmosphere, complete with antiques and bric-a-brac, free-flowing spirits, and live entertainment. Reservations are accepted for lunch and dinner. **L D S · $$ – $$$ · ❣**

RAINFOREST CAFE (Marketplace): There's no mistaking the environmental orientation of this Amazon-emulating eatery. The atmospheric dining environs transport guests to a makeshift rainforest, complete with banyan trees, tropical fish, gushing waterfalls, and a friendly population of hand-raised parrots. A talking tree offers a constant stream of ecological insights, and animal experts are on hand to field questions.

Special effects envelop guests in tropical storms, complete with lightning and thunder. Menu items include Planet Earth Pasta, Paradise Pot Roast, and Rumble in the Jungle Turkey Wrap. A shop stocks logo clothing. Reservations may be made by calling 407-827-8500. Without them, expect quite a wait. **B L D S · $$ – $$$**

SPLITSVILLE (West Side): Some go expecting just to enjoy a little bowling, not realizing that Splitsville's two kitchens turn out impressive casual fare such as freshly rolled sushi, 3-pepper calamari, seared ahi tuna, and sliders with onion rings and horseradish cream. They've also got a

Ears to You!

As if Mickey Mouse weren't already a sweet character, the folks at Goofy's Candy Company have made him even sweeter. Here you can get Mickey-shaped cookies, lollipops, candy-coated pretzels, crispy treats, and more. Elsewhere you can snack on Mickey ice cream bars. They're easy to find and colossally popular. Guests gobble up more than three million of them each year.

GOOD MEALS, GREAT TIMES

selection of pizzas, burgers, sandwiches, and salads. Many of the menu items are gluten free. Enormous desserts (great for sharing) include sundaes, brownie à la mode, and chocolate cake with cocoa frosting. There is a full bar and a "mix-your-own" Coca-Cola machine. Food is served lane-side or at designated "non-bowling" tables. Visit *www.splitsvillelanes.com* for details. **LDS·$$–$$$**

STARBUCKS (West Side and Marketplace): The Downtown Disney links of the famous coffee chain serve up all the usual Starbucks specialties: fresh-brewed coffee (hot or iced), Frappuccino blended drinks, teas, and kids' drinks, plus sweet and savory snack items. **LDS·$$$·**🐭

T-REX CAFE: A PREHISTORIC FAMILY ADVENTURE (Marketplace): Dinosaurs throw one heck of a dinner party. See for yourself at this eye-popping dino-themed, interactive feasting facility. When you enter, you'll be greeted by hosts we were all led to believe were extinct. Okay, they're life-size mechanical dinosaurs, but they're still pretty cool. As are the waterfalls, bubbling geysers, and fossil dig site. It's all so distracting, you may forget why you came here in the first place. When your stomach starts growling, plan to appease it with anything from Jurassic Salad to Mammoth Mushroom Ravioli. With soup, sandwiches, pasta, seafood, and steaks, this place aims to please everyone. You'll find it near the LEGO store at the Marketplace. Reservations are recommended: 407-828-8739. Doors open at 11 A.M. daily and close at 11 P.M. Sunday through Thursday and at midnight on Friday and Saturday nights. **LD·$$–$$$·**🐭

WETZEL'S PRETZELS (Marketplace): Whether you prefer pretzels on the salty or sweet side, this kiosk has something to satisfy. Snackers enjoy the Pepperoni Twist, Jalapeño Cheese Melt, Sour Cream & Onion, and the

Sinful Cinnamon varieties. Also served: hot dogs wrapped in a soft pretzel, frozen lemonade, and ice cream (cones, cups, and sundaes). **S·$**

WOLFGANG PUCK CAFE (West Side): Among Wolfgang's specialties are gourmet pizzas, pumpkin ravioli, and macadamia-nut-crusted breast of chicken. The menu is equal parts sophisticated and straightforward—and ever so fresh. There's also an excellent sushi bar. Colorful mosaics decorate his restaurants. Reservations are recommended. **LDS·$$$·**🐭

WOLFGANG PUCK CAFE—THE DINING ROOM (West Side): Don't be confused by the name. The Dining Room refers to a separate restaurant that happens to be under the same roof as Wolfgang Puck Café and Express (we call it Puck's Deluxe). The formal upstairs Dining Room serves cuisine such lobster risotto, duo of duck, spicy beef goulash, and organic chicken. For dessert, there's chocolate lava cake, carrot cake, chocolate mud pie, and more. Reservations are recommended. **D·$$$–$$$$·**🐭

WOLFGANG PUCK EXPRESS (Marketplace and West Side): Chef Wolfgang Puck turned his talents to fast service and signature treats, including wood-fired pizzas, rotisserie chicken, soups, focaccia sandwiches, and fresh salads—among them, BBQ chicken salad. The organic coffee here gets a big thumbs-up. (The West Side location is inside the Wolfgang Puck Café building [to the left of the entrance], while the Marketplace spot is near the Disney Days of Christmas shop.) **LDS·$–$$·**🐭

Eat and Fun

DisneyQuest devotees tend to work up quite the appetite after hours of gaming. The good news is these folks can refuel without leaving the confines of the multi-story arcade. An eatery called FoodQuest (located on the 5th floor) serves pizza, sandwiches, salads, and more quick-service selections. It serves lunch, dinner, and snacks—and participates in the Disney Dining Plan.

For a sweet treat, visit DisneyQuest's 4th-floor Wonderland Cafe. Choose from items such as cupcakes, brownies, cake, ice cream novelties, smoothies, and strawberry parfait. Note that admission must be paid to enter DisneyQuest before you can eat at either of the aforementioned spots.

In WDW Resorts

Each of the nearly 30 resorts at Walt Disney World offers its own set of specially themed eateries. There are clambakes at the Beach Club, luaus at the Polynesian Village, wild game at the Wilderness Lodge, and beignets at Port Orleans French Quarter. Meals may be served buffet, family, or traditional table-service or fast-food style. Disney characters are often on hand (especially for breakfast), and some snack spots stay open 'round the clock. In fact, the resort dining scene has expanded and been upgraded so much of late that the (occasionally arduous) task of resort-hopping is a more worthwhile experience than ever before.

Reservations are an important part of the full-service dining circuit (call 407-WDW-DINE [939-3463]).

All-Star Resorts

Each of these resorts features a colorful, themed central food court. All-Star Sports has the End Zone food court in Stadium Hall. The Intermission food court is in Melody Hall at the All-Star Music resort. And All-Star Movies has the World Premiere food court in Cinema Hall. The food courts offer similar food stands—although Movies is a cut above. (It's bigger and more modern.) The selections include pasta, pizza, burgers, hot dogs, sandwiches, salads, ice cream, a variety of breakfast and baked goods, plus "grab and go" selections. Expect to find kid-pleasers, such as chicken nuggets and mac and cheese, too. B L D S · $–$$ · 🐭

Animal Kingdom Lodge

BOMA—FLAVORS OF AFRICA: Designed to resemble an African marketplace, Boma offers an impressively diverse selection—the fare served represents the 53 countries that make up Africa. Though the eatery may be described as "cafeteria style," this is not a negative. It's one big buffet with multiple stations, and the food is as good as what you'd expect in a fine dining place.

The all-you-care-to-eat affair provides an excellent bang for your Disney dining buck. Breakfast features omelets, cereals, brioche, fresh fruit, sausage, biscuits, ham, corned beef, and more. At dinner, expect to fill your plate with items such as salads (including watermelon rind salad and Tunisian couscous salad), authentic African breads, soups, and stews; grilled seafood,

roasted meats, couscous, and an array of vegetarian selections. For dessert, do try the decadent zebra domes—you'll regret it if you don't. It's tempting to overeat at a bounteous feast such as this, so consider taking tiny portions of everything. You can go back for seconds of your favorites. The wine list includes selections from various African vineyards. Even if you're not staying at the lodge, it's worth the trip. Reservations are required. B D · $$ · 🐭

JIKO—THE COOKING PLACE: Jiko offers one of the more unusual Walt Disney World dining experiences. Its cuisine is inspired by the tastes of Africa, with influences from around the globe. Start with one of the paper-thin flatbreads (like roasted chicken with lime chakalaka, lamb chopper cheese, and pickled sweet bell peppers), grilled wild boar tenderloin, artisanal cheeses, or seasonal salads. Pan-seared yellow snapper is a signature dish, and you may find curry-rubbed lamb loin, braised beef short ribs, seared duck breast, and oak-grilled filet mignon on the menu, too. End your meal with a fabulous cheese course and/or sweets such as banana bread pudding or coffee crème brûlée.

The impressive wine list is exclusively South African, one of the most extensive collections in the U.S. This is an excellent choice for a grown-up splurge. Though it's hardly a kid favorite—the international, sometimes exotic, cuisine may not appeal to timid palates—there are child-friendly options on the kids' menu. Reservations are recommended. Incidentally, the word *jiko* is Swahili for "the cooking place." The small lounge area offers the full menu, too. D·$$$–$$$$·❤

THE MARA: An enormous fast-food restaurant that has something for just about everyone— including a "grab and go" section for those in a hurry. There are a couple of stations at which hot entreés are freshly prepared. Among the pre-packaged options are sandwiches, salads, fruit, yogurt, and baked goods. BLDS·$–$$·❤

SANAA: Pronounced sa-NAH, the name of this eatery means "artwork" in Swahili. The Kidani Village spot has a family-friendly menu featuring Disney's take on African-Indian cuisine. Signature dishes include chicken or shrimp curry and beef short ribs slow-cooked in tandoor ovens. For lunch, try the salad sampler. Even the burgers have an Indian touch, wrapped in soft, warm naan (a round flatbread). Desserts introduce many tastes, from mango berry tapioca pudding to cardamom coffee cake. The quality of the fare here is nothing short of outstanding. Reservations are recommended. LD·$$–$$$·❤

PHOTO BY MIKE CARROLL

Art of Animation

LANDSCAPE OF FLAVORS: "Better for you" options is the theme of this vividly adorned food court, where everything is made fresh once it is ordered. Breakfast offerings include egg white frittata, challah French toast, and vegetarian breakfast sandwiches on naan bread, as well as more traditional selections. Four mini shops offer soups, salads, pizza, sandwiches, burgers, pasta, shrimp, chicken, beef stir-fry, grilled fish, and tandoori acorn squash. There is a selection of "grab and go" items, too. Made-to-order beverage options include smoothies, lemonade, and pomegranate limeade. Also available are organic teas, beers (including a gluten-free selection), wine, coffee, and juices. There is a gelato station, too. Yum. BLDS·$–$$·❤

BoardWalk

BELLE VUE LOUNGE: This cozy cocktail spot, located on the resort's second floor, offers continental breakfast each morning. Expect to find items such as bagels, cereal, yogurt, whole fruit, muffins, and croissants, plus juice, milk, coffee, and tea. B·$·❤

BIG RIVER GRILLE & BREWING WORKS: Guests may observe (and later sample) as the brewmaster creates three flagship ales and two seasonal brews at this working brew pub. The straightforward-but-satisfying menu generally includes burgers, steaks, and salads. Sandwiches are a cut above. Other menu favorites: flame-grilled meatloaf and Atlantic salmon. This restaurant tends to be more low-key than other BoardWalk eateries and makes for a relatively quiet retreat during the day. The interior has a nice, pubby feel—but we prefer to sit at outdoor tables on the boardwalk (especially in the evening). Seating is available on a first-come, first-served basis. LDS·$$–$$$·❤

BOARDWALK BAKERY: The aromas wafting from Seashore Sweets' next-door neighbor on the boardwalk reveal the fresh-baked goods therein. This popular stop also offers sandwiches, soups, salads, and specialty beverages. Featured sandwiches include roast beef with horseradish mayo and provolone, and smoked turkey on seven-grain bread. Sweet treats (the real specialty of this house) run from eclairs and Jersey crumb cake to apple tarts and cupcakes. This is also the place for guests to purchase and fill up their refillable mugs. BS·$·❤

PHOTO BY JILL SAFRO

ESPN CLUB: For sports fans, this joint is nothing less than a miracle. The spacious, welcoming, occasionally frenzied bar/family restaurant is a hard-core sports club. If there's a game being played, chances are it's on one of the million (okay, hundred) TVs. If not, a simple request to any cast member may result in a channel change.

The standard, reliable fare includes wings, burgers, sandwiches, grilled fish and salads. Both the dining room and the bar area serve cocktails and the full menu. Reservations are not usually accepted, so arrive early. We make an effort to get there at least an hour ahead to get a table or a spot at the bar on days when big games are scheduled. That said, there is an option called "VIP Seating" available during certain popular events. Call 407-WDW-DINE to reserve a banquette-style seat—with prime viewing of the

Dinner at Sea

For Disney's ultimate dinner-and-a-show splurge, consider reserving the elegant *Grand 1* yacht. You and up to 17 lucky invitees can enjoy a private tour of the lakes near the Magic Kingdom capped off with a viewing of Wishes, the park's fireworks show—all the while devouring delightful delicacies prepared by chefs at the Grand Floridian resort. The possibilities range from an intimate cruise for two, complete with dinner and champagne, to a swinging cocktail party for up to 18, with a boatload of shrimp, chips, wings, beer, wine, and soft drinks.

It costs about $520 (plus tax) per hour to rent the 5-room floating fantasyland. Driver and deckhand are included; refreshments are not. To book, call 407-WDW-PLAY at least 24 hours and up to 90 days ahead. The *Grand 1* docks at the Grand Floridian but can pick up passengers at the Contemporary, Polynesian Village, and Wilderness Lodge.

theater-sized screen— on the second tier of the dining room, aka "Sports Central." Note that there is a $50 per adult and $25 per child minimum (tax and tip not included) required. **L D S · $$ – $$$ · 🐭**

FLYING FISH CAFE: Whimsical, sophisticated decor elevate the appeal of this upscale dining destination. In fact, this restaurant could give most fine, big-city gourmet spots a run for their money. (Expect the tab to rival cosmopolitan hot spots, too.)

HOT TIP!

Kouzzina by Cat Cora closed in September of 2014. Details on its successor were not available at press time. However, we have been assured a new family-friendly eatery is coming to town. For details on the new kid on the BoardWalk block, visit *www.disneyworld.com* or call 407-WDW-DINE (939-3643).

Chef Tim Keating is a wonderfully inventive chef, and his menu changes often. But you'll always find the signature potato-wrapped snapper with a rich leek fondue and red wine and butter sauce, the crisp crab cakes, and a char-crusted New York strip steak. We are routinely impressed by the service and find the menu worthy of the price tag. Reservations are highly recommended. Diners without reservations may sit at the counter. As far as the Disney Dining Plan goes, this is a "Signature" restaurant. **D · $$$ – $$$$ · 🐭**

Caribbean Beach

OLD PORT ROYALE: The food court in Old Port Royale features a large dining area and the following fast-food counters: Grab N Go Market serves croissants, pastries, ice cream, and other snacks. Italian specialties are the order at the Royale Pizza and Pasta Shop. Soups, salads, and hot and cold sandwiches make up the selections at Montego's Deli. Burgers and chicken nuggets are among the offerings at Old Port Royale Hamburger Shop, while Bridgetown Broiler Shop serves omelets for breakfast and items such as carved turkey and pork loin for dinner. This food court gets high marks for variety, but barely a passing grade for its fare. Some kids' meals come in a sand bucket—which makes little diners very happy. **B L D S · $ – $$ · 🐭**

SHUTTERS AT OLD PORT ROYALE:
The dining room here is as kid-friendly as a table-service eatery can be. Some of the spruced-up menu highlights include chorizo-black bean soup, fish with yucca dumplings and curry-lemon butter sauce, and New York strip with plantain and potato gratin. The eatery is in the Old Port Royale building, across from the food court. In addition to soft drinks, beer, wine, and cocktails are served. Reservations are recommended. D·$$–$$$·🐭

Contemporary

CALIFORNIA GRILL: Delighting diners for decades, the World-famous California Grill boasts a bold new look and tantalizingly tweaked menu. The West Coast theme shines through in dishes prepared with the freshest seasonal and local produce available. Standouts include an old-time favorite entrée with a twist: pork two ways with grilled tenderloin, goat cheese polenta, mushrooms, and apple sauce; oak-fired filet of beef with heirloom tomato risotto, basil, and tomato butter; and short rib filet with olive oil potato puree. Sushi classics include dragon roll with spicy tataki tuna, shrimp tempura, bell pepper, avocado, and chili-soy glaze; and spicy kazan roll (crab, shrimps, and scallops in a spicy fireball sauce).

The wine list—which includes 250 selections, 80 of which are available by the glass—is a mix of greatest hits and good finds. There are ten varieties of saki and a selection of (mostly Californian) craft beer. House-made desserts provide the finishing touches, and there are sweeping views of the Magic Kingdom and the Seven Seas Lagoon (from select seats).

HOT TIP!

Would you like to watch Wishes, the Magic Kingdom's fireworks display, from the private perch outside California Grill? You'll need to dine in the eatery—but it doesn't have to be during the show itself. If you finish your meal pre-Wishes, simply return to the second-floor check-in desk later the same day, present the receipt for your meal, and you'll be escorted to the eatery via private elevator.

The restaurant is consistently crowded and the fare is first-rate. Reservations are necessary and must be booked with a credit card. Changes or cancellations must be made at least 24 hours ahead to avoid the $10-per-person fee. This is a Disney Dining Plan "Signature" restaurant (so it requires two table-service credits per diner).

An outdoor perch (exclusively available to California Grill patrons) affords bird's-eye views of the Magic Kingdom and its nightly fireworks presentation (complete with the show's music). Guests (including those planning to visit the lounge) check in on the hotel's second floor and are escorted to the restaurant's express elevator. Dinner starts at 5 P.M. D·$$$–$$$$·🐭

PHOTO BY MIKE CARROLL

CHEF MICKEY'S: Chef Mickey and his pals host this buffet-style feast, with dramatic views of the monorail passing above. Colorful, life-size illustrations of Disney characters decorate the area. The changing menu takes advantage of seasonal offerings; a sundae bar provides a sweet finish. At some point during the meal, Chef Mickey will stop by your table, as will several of his friends. Be prepared to drop your fork and twirl your napkin on a moment's notice. This is a very popular eatery with an extremely loyal following. Kids adore the experience. Reservations are an absolute must. BD·$$–$$$·🐭

CONTEMPO CAFE: After leaving its first-floor home of 35 years, the Contemporary resort snack bar has moved up in the World—all the way to the fourth floor, beside Chef Mickey's. This spot serves light fare until about midnight. Food is ordered from computer kiosks near the entrance. After doing so, proceed to the cashier. Here you'll receive cups for beverages and a beeper (which lights up when your food is ready to be picked up at the counter). Thin-crust pizzas (aka flatbreads), sandwiches, and soup are among the selections. A "grab and go" section has drinks, wraps, yogurt, fresh fruit, and more. BLDS·$–$$·🐭

PHOTO BY MIKE CARROLL

THE WAVE . . . OF AMERICAN FLAVORS:

A stellar full-service eatery, this modern establishment features healthy, creative American fusion cuisine. Think "bold cooking inspired by locally sourced ingredients." Starters of note: Wave Appetizer for Two (lump crab, Florida rock shrimp cakes, and fish tacos) and a seasonal salad. Main courses include grilled beef tenderloin, seasonal vegetable stew with multigrain rice, and a sustainable fish of the day. Tempting desserts include those of the no-sugar-added variety. And the New World wine list is out of this world. It's possible to try several via flight samplers. The Wave is located on the resort's first floor. We would eat breakfast, lunch, and dinner here without a moment's hesitation. The adjacent lounge is a perfect place for an aperitif or after-dinner drink. Reservations are recommended. **BLD·$$–$$$·**🐭

Coronado Springs

CAFE RIX: Stop here for freshly prepared breakfast sandwiches, hot paninis, flatbreads, grilled shrimp, and fruit. There is a "grab and go" area, too. It has items such as pre-packaged sandwiches, salads, pastries, gelato, beer, wine, soft drinks, and coffee. **BLDS·$–$$·**🐭

MAYA GRILL: Guests here dine inside a Mayan pyramid, beside a volcano (dormant, of course). The menu has a little bit of everything: seafood, meat, and poultry, with a touch of Latino spices added to some of the creations. The empanadas duo and tortilla are interesting starts to dinner. Entrées range from grilled sirloin or pork chop to pan-seared salmon or vegetarian enchiladas, with many dishes cooked over an open-pit wood-fire grill. Desserts include coconut flan and fried ice cream. Dinner is usually served from 6 P.M. until 9 P.M. Breakfast is presented as an all-you-can-eat buffet. Reservations are recommended. **BD·$$$·**🐭

Tables in Wonderland

Attention, Annual Pass-bearers and Florida residents: You are eligible for the Tables in Wonderland (T.I.W.) discount dining program. It affords members a 10- to 20-percent savings off food and beverages at many WDW table-service eateries. The discount is good for you and up to 9 members of your party. Simply present a valid photo ID and your T.I.W. card when you place an order with a server. To net the discount for the rest of the party, the check must be paid by the T.I.W. member. Membership is valid for one year and costs $75 for Annual Passholders and $100 for Florida residents. For details or to order your Tables in Wonderland card, call 407-566-5858. For a list of participating dining locations, go to: *http://disneyworld.disney.go.com/passholder program/dining-discounts/*.

PEPPER MARKET: This busy-but-bedraggled spot has a large seating area and many food stands to choose from. The selections range from roast beef (or pork or turkey) to paninis, pizza, pasta, salads, "build your own burrito," and other Mexican fare—all prepared from scratch. For breakfast, there's Mickey waffles, Mexican eggs Benedict burrito, Southwestern omelets, and more. Non-alcoholic drinks are included, and anything may be ordered "to go." Everything is paid for at meal's end, as guests file past the cashier at the exit. Note that a ten percent gratuity is automatically added when you eat in the dining area. Given this resort's popularity with the convention set, expect a proliferation of people during weekday breakfast and lunch times. Specifics may change in 2015—at press time a renovation was long overdue. **BLDS·$–$$·**🐭

PHOTO BY MIKE CARROLL

Disney's Old Key West

GOOD'S FOOD TO GO: A walk-up window with a simple-yet-satisfying menu: Hamburgers, cheeseburgers, deli sandwiches, salads, ice cream, snacks, and breakfast items are among the many offerings at Good's. **BLDS·$·❤**

OLIVIA'S CAFE: We thoroughly enjoy the Key West manner with which Olivia's approaches its theme. The laid-back setting and menu convey the spirit of the leisure-centric locale. Breakfast includes standards, but also some interesting combos like poached eggs served over sweet potato hash, topped with Key West hollandaise. The all-day menu for lunch and dinner offers salads, conch chowder, crab cakes, seared scallops, burgers, and sandwiches. End with a Key lime tart, chocolate cake, or a banana bread pudding sundae. The menu changes seasonally. Wine, beer, and specialty cocktails are served. Reservations are recommended for all meals. **BLD·$$–$$$·❤**

Fort Wilderness

Many people choose to cook their own meals here. Some supplies are available at the Meadow and Settlement Trading Posts (open from 8 A.M. to 10 P.M. in winter; to 11 P.M. in summer).

TRAIL'S END RESTAURANT: True, it's a bit out of the way for anyone but Fort Wilderness guests (and even for some of them!), but for many, this rustic and unassuming spot is well worth the trip.

The informal log-walled restaurant offers a hearty buffet breakfast. The fare is not exactly gourmet, but it is bountiful. Breakfast selections include grits, biscuits and gravy, and breakfast pizza. The à la carte lunch features fried chicken and waffles; sandwiches; salads; sautéed catfish; and fried green tomatoes. For dinner, expect the buffet to have smoked pork ribs, peel-n-eat shrimp, fried chicken, carved meats, a salad bar, plus a variety of side dishes and desserts. Pizza is served nightly from 4 P.M. until 10 P.M. daily. Beer and wine are served by the glass. Reservations are recommended. Breakfast costs about $17 for adults, $11 for kids; lunch is à la carte; dinner is about $25 for adults, $15 for kids. After the meal, you can relax in a rocking chair on the front porch. It just doesn't get any better than that. (If you plan to eat here, allow a little extra travel time, just in case.) **BLDS·$–$$·❤**

Grand Floridian

CITRICOS: From the aromas wafting from the open kitchen, it's clear that the chef has vowed to wow you with cuisine from the Americas and the Mediterranean, herb by fragrant herb. The fare varies seasonally but may include such items as sautéed shrimp with tomato, lemon, and feta cheese; or braised veal shank. Adventurous palates are most at home here. The menu's not extensive, but the wine list certainly is. Restaurant sommeliers are on hand to recommend wine pairings.

A private dining room is available for parties of up to 12. The lounge is ideal for solo diners or those without a reservation (ask the bartender for a menu). Reservations are necessary for the restaurant. **D·$$$–$$$$·❤**

GASPARILLA ISLAND GRILL: Breakfast items along the lines of scrambled eggs, waffles, bagels, and cereal are served daily until 11 A.M. After that, made-to-order selections such as sandwiches, burgers, pizza, and salads are available. "Grab and go" options such as salad, sushi, yogurt, fresh fruit, and snacks are on hand 24/7 in this quick-service spot near the marina (note that the middle of the night pickin's may be slim). There is indoor and outdoor seating. If you purchase a refillable mug, this is the place to fill it up. **BLDS·$–$$·❤**

GRAND FLORIDIAN CAFE: A pleasant spot any time of day, the cafe is a relatively reasonably priced, low-key way to check out the poshest Walt Disney World resort.

The à la carte breakfast extends a wee bit beyond the usual fare. Lunch and dinner menus

Tea for Two (or Ten)

Teatime with all the trimmings—scones, finger sandwiches, pastries, strawberries and cream, etc.—is from 2 P.M. until 5 P.M. in the Garden View Tea Room at the Grand Floridian resort. This elegant lounge overlooks the lovingly tended gardens surrounding the resort's main swimming pool.

The menu here includes custom-blended teas from around the world. Guests may also sip coffees and spirited drinks such as port or sparkling wine. Note that guests must be at least 21 years of age (with valid photo ID) to consume alcohol.

The Grand Floridian offers tea parties for kids, too. For information on these special events, turn to page 230.

For details or to make reservations (which are strongly recommended), call 407-WDW-DINE (939-3463).

vary seasonally but have traditional American dishes: onion soup, burgers, and the signature Grand Floridian sandwich. The wine selection is excellent. Reservations are recommended, but it may be possible to get a table without one if you're willing to wait. (The restaurant is closed between 11 A.M. and 11:30 A.M.) B L D · $ $ $ · ❤

NARCOOSSEE'S: Named for a nearby Central Florida town, Narcoossee's specializes in fresh sustainable seafood—with the occasional land-based entrée making surf-and-turf combinations a decadent possibility. Narcoossee's menu has upscale selections (and prices), but the atmosphere is casual and, more than occasionally, clamorous. The display kitchen presents dishes such as steamed mussels, grilled steak, and Maine lobster. The international wine selection is quite good—you might even enjoy a pre-dinner glass on the veranda. The view of the Seven Seas Lagoon and Cinderella Castle (in the distance) completes the experience. Reservations are recommended. The lounge here offers a full menu (and does not require a reservation) as well as a full bar and an abundance of stellar wines offered by the bottle or the glass. The dress code here is business casual. D · $ $ $ – $ $ $ $ · ❤

1900 PARK FARE: The atmosphere is reminiscent of an old-time amusement park, but the sophisticated buffet menu and subtle decor make this one of the most elegant character restaurants on the property. Mary Poppins and her friends

mingle with guests during the bountiful daily breakfast. Cinderella and members of her royal family visit the dining room during the dinner hours. Keep in mind that the lineup of characters does change from time to time.

Dinner features seafood, salads, pastas, vegetables, breads, carved meats, and house-made desserts. The offerings change seasonally. A salad bar and dessert bar stand nearby. There's a kids' buffet, too. It offers pizza, pasta, and vegetables. The restaurant's focal point is Big Bertha, a band organ build in Paris nearly a century ago. She sits in a proscenium and rises 15 feet above the floor. Reservations are recommended. B D · $ $ $ · ❤

VICTORIA & ALBERT'S: The dining room in the only AAA 5-Diamond restaurant in Central Florida seats just 60 guests (all of whom must have already celebrated their 10th birthday). It is indulgent without being too haute to handle (although the steep prices may curb some folks' enthusiasm) and is considered by many to be the grand dame of the Disney dining scene.

The seven-course prix fixe menu changes frequently, always offering a selection of farm-fresh fish, poultry, and beef as main courses. But the beauty of this high-end experience is all the little tastes as you make your way through the $144-per-person (plus gratuity) adventure. You might start with lobster or quail, then move on to seared wild turbot or pork tenderloin. The cheese course is worth every calorie. And, even with seven courses, you must reserve room for the indulgent desserts: a flurry of soufflés, chocolate, and more. Perfect portions keep it all surprisingly manageable. The strains of a harp or violin provide a romantic backdrop. The wine list is encyclopedic. Wine pairings are available for an additional $65 per person (do let your server know about any personal wine preferences).

For an extra-special (and super-splurgy) experience, book the Chef's Table (for up to 10 guests; $224 per person) or the Queen Victoria Room (also $224 per diner). With just four tables, the latter provides the restaurant's most exclusive, luxurious setting.

At the end of the meal, all guests are given a souvenir menu and ladies receive a red rose. In sum, though the experience is an extremely expensive one, for many it is also quite special. Jackets are required for men. Guests must be at least 10 years old to dine here. Reservations are a must; call 407-939-3862. Restaurant information, sample menus, and pricing are available at *www.victoria-alberts.com*. D · $ $ $ $

Polynesian Village

CAPT. COOK'S: The Captain dispenses snacks and light fare 24 hours a day. It's a good spot for made-to-order breakfast items such as the ever-popular fried, banana-stuffed Tonga Toast, burgers, flatbreads, salads, sandwiches and "grab and go" items such as sushi, yogurt, fruit, and snacks. Milk (plain and chocolate), beer, wine, and soft drinks are also available. Come here to buy and fill the Poly's refillable mug with soft drinks. B L D S · $–$$ · 🐾

KONA CAFE: Warm colors, soft lighting, and South Seas decor render the crisp, fluid design of this open dining space rather cozy and casual. The menu tends toward the exotic side as far as Disney restaurants go, but there's a nice variety of choices. Lunch and dinner menus feature Asian-influenced entrées. Possibilities include teriyaki beef, grilled Kona-coffee-rubbed pork chop, (sumptuous) sushi, and market-fresh sustainable fish. The morning meal offers Tonga Toast (banana-stuffed, fried sourdough bread coated with cinnamon sugar), plus traditional breakfast items. There is a solid wine list, and island-inspired cocktails are served. The pressed-pot coffee is a fan favorite. You'll find Kona Cafe on the second floor of the Great Ceremonial House, just around the corner from 'Ohana. Reservations are recommended for all meals. B L D S · $$–$$$ · 🐾

KONA ISLAND: A coffee bar until noon, this is a super spot for a quick sip on your way to the monorail. Light breakfast items are offered, too.

When five o'clock rolls around, so does the sushi. Roll selections include Volcano (spicy tuna, shrimp salad, and tempura crunch), California Luau (fresh jumbo lump crab, pineapple, and avocado), Tuna Poke (traditional Hawaiian ahi tuna salad), and a cucumber roll (for vegetarians).

Sashimi fans will enjoy the salmon and tuna, as well as the chef's selection of the day. Seating is limited, but it's possible to get items to go. Beer, wine, sake, and other cocktails are served. B D S · $–$$ · 🐾

'OHANA: On the second floor of the Great Ceremonial House, this restaurant is a meticulously themed, family-friendly eatery, complete with entertainment. An interesting twist of note: 'Ohana's family-style dinner experience—a South Pacific feast prepared in the restaurant's open-fire cooking pit—does not come with a menu, so no decisions have to be made. The oak-grilled skewers of pork and beef just keep coming. Spicy peel-and-eat shrimp, green salad, pineapple-coconut bread, pan-Asian noodles tossed in teriyaki sauce, and stir-fried veggies are among the accompaniments, and dessert is bread pudding served à la mode with warm caramel sauce. Soft drinks are included. Beer, wine, and cocktails are extra.

'Ohana's setting, which features wood carvings under a vast thatched roof, is rather festive. So much so that there are periodic, boisterous hula hoop, limbo, and coconut-rolling contests for the little ones. Polynesian singers croon from time to time.

Breakfast is also a family affair—make that extended family, as Lilo, Stitch, and their good friends Mickey and Pluto host the morning meal. Breakfast fare is basic and presented family style. Keep in mind that the character lineup does change from time to time. Reservations are strongly recommended for both meals. B D · $$$–$$$$ · 🐾

PINEAPPLE LANAI: This sweet stop offers WDW's classic Dole Whip frozen pineapple dessert and other tropical treats. It's located near the Volcano pool. S · $ · 🐾

TRADER SAM'S GROG GROTTO: It's hard to be grouchy at this grog grotto—Trader Sam will see to that. With a theme inspired by the Jungle Cruise and Enchanted Tiki Room attractions, Trader Sam's features drinks (tropical and otherwise) and small plates. It's a real crowd-pleaser. S · $–$$

Pop Century

EVERYTHING POP!: The selection at this colorful food court in Classic Hall has included pasta, pizza, chicken, roast turkey, Asian dishes, seafood, burgers, hot dogs, sandwiches, salads, pizza, breakfast items, a build-your-own burrito station, and baked goods (tie-dyed cheesecake!). Savory sides include hummus, olive tapenade, and hot black bean salad. Feel free to join the cast members as they dance the Twist at 8 A.M. and the Hustle at 6 P.M. B L D S · $ – $ $ · 🐭

Port Orleans French Quarter

SASSAGOULA FLOATWORKS & FOOD FACTORY: A food court with a Mardi Gras theme, this spot offers pizza, pasta, burgers, sandwiches, soups, salads, spit-roasted chicken, barbecued ribs, ice cream, and bakery products. The Big Easy is well represented here: New Orleans–inspired menu items include classic gumbo, Creole burgers, muffalettas, and jambalaya. B L D S · $ – $ $ · 🐭

HOT TIP!

Guests staying at Port Orleans French Quarter and Riverside may have pizza delivered to their rooms between 4 P.M. and midnight. Call Sassagoula Pizza Express from your resort room telephone to order whole pies, drinks, and sweet snacks. There is a $15 minimum per order and the Disney Dining Plan is accepted.

Port Orleans Riverside

BOATWRIGHT'S DINING HALL: Southern specialties and American comfort food are the big draw here—think prime rib and jambalaya. Beer, wine, and cocktails are available, as are soft drinks. The restaurant is quite popular, as it's the resort's only table-service eatery, so reservations are encouraged. Walk-up requests are typically admitted when the restaurant opens at 5 P.M. D · $ $ – $ $ $ · 🐭

RIVERSIDE MILL: This high-ceilinged food court styled in the image of a working cotton mill (complete with working waterwheel) offers half a dozen food counters. Collectively, the stands offer pizza; pasta; fried, grilled, and roast chicken; burgers; salads; sandwiches (including New Orleans–style muffalettas); ice cream; and fresh baked goods. They're big on "create your own" here, too. (You can customize an omelet, salad, and/or pasta dish.) There's ample seating, so it's usually possible to get a table. All items may be packaged "to go." B L D S · $ – $ $ · 🐭

Saratoga Springs

THE ARTIST'S PALETTE: Set in a converted artist's loft within Walt Disney World's sprawling resort, this spot offers breakfast, lunch, and dinner. Among the selections are fresh tossed salads, made-to-order sandwiches, pizza, baked goods, and more. There are some grocery items, as well as a variety of "grab and go" selections. B L D S · $ – $ $ · 🐭

THE PADDOCK GRILL: Head to this quick-service window for sandwiches (spice-crusted fish, roasted veggie, etc.), chicken chopped salad, bacon cheeseburgers, and house-made potato chips (which were actually invented in Saratoga). B L D S · $ – $ $ · 🐭

THE TURF CLUB BAR & GRILL: A restaurant with an old-fashioned horse racing theme (and a pool table), this sporty eatery serves pasta, prime rib, grilled meats, sustainable fish, burgers, BLTs, salads, crab cakes, steamed mussels, grilled salmon, steak, penne pasta with shrimp, mint-crusted lamb chops, roasted chicken breast, and more. D · $ – $ $ · 🐭

Swan & Dolphin

CABANA BAR & BEACH CLUB: An elegant poolside eatery, the Dolphin's Cabana serves a sophisticated selection of starters, salads, and entrées. Appetizer options include crab egg rolls, fish tacos, and jerk-chicken wings. The main bites menu offers Cuban sandwiches, cheese-steaks, wraps, grilled chicken BLT, seafood gyros, turkey sliders, and burgers made from farm-raised, grass-fed, organic beef. For a sweet finish, consider a dish of gelato. Among the many signature cocktails are the Millionaire Margarita, the Bomb Pop, and the Orange Crush. For kids, Cabana serves pizza, burgers, grilled cheese, hot dogs, and chicken fingers. LDS·$-$$

THE FOUNTAIN: A soda fountain with some grown-up appeal, this is an ideal spot for a sweet snack or a satisfying meal. Homemade soft-serve ice cream is the house specialty. Be it served in a simple cone or in an elaborate sundae (the caramel apple sundae is a standout), the chilly treat is sure to please. Among the entrées from which to choose are ahi tuna burgers, cheese-burgers, and a classic B.L.T. Soups and salads can augment the meal, as can fries, onion rings, or chips and salsa. Drinks-wise, this place has everything from freshly brewed iced tea and specialty coffees to impressively inventive shakes (including the chocolate raspberry torte, coco loco, and peppermint concoctions), plus beer and wine. The Fountain is located at the Dolphin. An adjacent walk-up window offers ice cream for hungry folks on the go. LDS·$-$$

FRESH MEDITERRANEAN MARKET:
The Dolphin's airy eatery offers salads, sand-wiches, and soups. The morning menu includes pastries, yogurt, fresh granola, hot cereals, eggs, pancakes, and more. It's also possible to have a light lunch here, provided that you are a salad fan. Fresh offers many wines by the glass, including several organic varietals. Reservations are recommended for breakfast and lunch. BL·$$-$$$

GARDEN GROVE: This Swan eatery means to transport guests to the peaceful gardens of New York's Central Park—and the 25-foot oak tree is a most realistic touch. The restaurant offers a full breakfast menu (with Disney characters in the house on Saturday and Sunday mornings), and salads, sandwiches, and more for lunch. What's the dinner "special"? It comes with a side of Disney characters. Different nights also bring different fare. At press time, Wednesday and Sunday were featuring barbecue; Saturday, Tuesday, and Thursday offered Mediterranean selections; and Monday and Friday served up

seafood. Disney characters are on hand for dinner every night and for breakfast on Saturday and Sunday. Reservations are recommended. Visit *www.swandolphin.com* for more information. BLD·$$-$$$

IL MULINO NEW YORK TRATTORIA:
A swank Swan destination, Il Mulino offers upscale Italian cuisine in a relaxed yet vibrant trattoria-like setting. Specializing in *Piatti per il Tavolo*, or family-style dining, the spot is ideal for groups. The seasonal menu is characterized by blends of fresh ingredients drawn from the Abruzzi region of Italy. Signature items include *Gamberi al Mulino* (jumbo shrimp with spicy cocktail sauce), *Gnocchi Bolognese* (potato dumplings with meat sauce), *Pollo Fra Diavolo* (chicken in a spicy red sauce with sausage), and salmone (sautéed salmon in garlic and olive oil with wild mushrooms and broccoli rabe). *Mangia!*

All dinners begin with an antipasti tasting, on the house (what a treat!). Enjoy it while perusing the wine list's 250 or so varietals. The children's menu has pizza, pasta, and chicken parmigiana. For reservations, call 407-939-3463 or 407-934-1199, or visit *swandolphin.com*. D·$$$-$$$$

KIMONOS: In the mood for sushi with a side of karaoke? You've come to the right place! This Swan lounge is an honest-to-goodness karaoke bar (the only one at Walt Disney World). Some guests come to sing, while others are drawn to the sushi, sashimi, and tempura. It's also possible to order miso soup, salad, edamame, tempura udon, gyoza, and Kobe beef satay, among other selections. There is a full bar featuring such specialty cocktails as the Lychee Mojito and the Oriental Grape. This spot opens around dinnertime, serving Japanese food and drinks. The singing generally gets started at about 9 P.M. or so. A good time (and meal) is generally had by all. DS·$-$$

PICABU: This Dolphin cafeteria is a bit above the norm. The food is usually freshly prepared—with excellent sandwiches and salads, plus a customize-your-own taco and burrito station. The convenience store offers snacks and sun-dries. The house coffee is Starbucks (free refills during your meal). Note that this spot is a tad pricier than the average Disney World quick-service eatery, but the quality is appreciated by most. And some of the portions are big enough to share. The eatery (and store) is open 24/7. BLDS·$-$$

PHOTO BY JILL SAFRO

Resort to Resort

If you're staying in one resort and dining in another, you need to plan ahead—even if the resorts are linked by monorail or water taxi. Why? The transportation may be operating before dinner, but if you're out late enough you'll have to get yourself home another way.

The good news is you will never be stranded. Bus transportation runs until about 2 A.M.—but it's not direct. If the theme parks are closed, you'll have to take a bus to Downtown Disney and transfer to a bus to your hotel. If the theme parks are open, you can take a bus to any park and transfer to one that's headed to your resort. Keep in mind that the trip can take up to 90 minutes in either direction. If that thought is unpleasant, do what we sometimes do: splurge on a cab. Authorized taxis should run between $10 and $30, depending on the destination and traffic. If you have more than three people in your party, request a van (the rate is the same). Ask about calling a cab at the resort's bell services desk.

SHULA'S: Like the original Shula's in Miami, this Dolphin spot specializes in generous portions of certified Angus beef, plus soups, salads, chicken and fresh fish dishes. For dessert, there's apple crisp, vanilla cheesecake, molten chocolate lava cake, and more. The upscale eatery pays tribute to the 1972 Miami Dolphins—the year coach Don Shula led his team to a perfect NFL season. The prices are steep, but the steaks are first-rate and lovingly prepared. Though the interior celebrates the game of football, this is not a casual sports bar. The dress code is business or resort casual. Reservations are recommended. Don't ask for a kids' menu—there isn't one. FYI: Shula's is a frequent winner of *Wine Spectator*'s Award of Excellence. D·$$$$

SPLASH GRILL & DELI: Just steps from the Swan lap pool, Splash serves sandwiches, pizza, and salads. Made-to-order sandwiches

—complete with brown paper bags—include the Uncle Lou (deli meats and cheese on a garlic baguette), Big Bird (rotisserie chicken on a poppy seed roll), and Rocky Balboa (sliced prime rib and provolone cheese on Italian bread). Organic and gluten-free snacks are sold. Cocktails, espresso, and soft drinks are served. L S·$

TODD ENGLISH'S BLUEZOO: A sophisticated member of the Walt Disney World dining scene, the menu at this sleek Dolphin spot features coastal cuisine, incorporating an innovative selection of fresh seafood with both international and New American culinary influences. The raw bar's stocked with juicy (and a tad pricey) oysters and middleneck clams. If you prefer your seafood cooked, try the chilled poached jumbo shrimp or chilled Maine lobster tail. A popular starter is the brothy clam chowder with salt-cured bacon and oyster crackers. All of the entrées are tempting: from miso-glazed mero to bluezoo's signature dancing fish (whole fish roasted on a rotating spit).

Not in the mood for a selection from the sea? Consider dry-aged beef or pan-roasted chicken breast. If you've got room when the dessert menu arrives, expect to be tempted by sweets such as warm chocolate cake with a liquid ganache center. Reservations are recommended. Note that it is possible to get food service at the bar, a plus for small groups or solo diners without a reservation. Closing time at the bar tends to vary nightly (depending on just how crowded the place is). It's a good idea to get there on the early side. D S·$$$–$$$$

Wilderness Lodge

ARTIST POINT: The Pacific Northwest theme of this eatery is announced in landscape murals while tall red-framed windows look out to Bay Lake. The cavernous dining room is by no means intimate, but it's not without charm.

Artist Point's hallmark is its knack for translating fresh, seasonal ingredients from the Pacific Northwest into flavorful creations. A good example is the freshly flown-in-salmon served on a smoking cedar plank. The menu may also include beef, pork, venison, and chicken selections. The extensive wine list features many vintages, including pinot noirs and syrahs from Oregon and Washington State. If it's offered, we highly recommend starting your meal with the heirloom tomato salad.

For dessert, many loyal visitors swear by the berry cobbler, which is made with seasonal berries and is far from traditional. Ask your server for a description. Reservations are recommended. The dress code is resort casual. D·$$$–$$$$·❤

ROARING FORK: Set in a stone-walled area (a bit dungeon like, but in a cool way), this snack bar serves salads, burgers, fries, pizza, sandwiches, chili, and snacks. Breakfast items such as cereal, yogurt, oatmeal, eggs, and waffles are available. Soft drinks, beer, and wine are also offered. This is the spot to top off refillable resort mugs. (Purchase the mug and refill it for free for the length of your stay here or at any Disney-owned-and-operated resort.) B L D S·$·❤

WHISPERING CANYON CAFE: The name is ironic, as there is nothing quiet about this place. A family favorite, Whispering Canyon is one of the most boisterous Disney restaurants. All meals are offered à la carte and "all you can eat" style. The latter means heaping plates keep coming to the table until you say "when."

Starting at the crack of dawn, the air is filled with aromas of bacon and potatoes and other traditional breakfast fare (omelets, waffles, etc.). Lunch offers pulled pork sandwiches, fish and chips, salads, and more. For supper, expect such items as baked chicken and smoked pork ribs. The smoothies, milk shakes, and homemade desserts are quite popular. Reservations are recommended. B L D·$$$·❤

Yacht & Beach Club

BEACH CLUB MARKETPLACE: The beachy setting extends to this snack bar/convenience store. There are baked goods, made-to-order sandwiches, and packaged "grab and go" items —small salads, hard-cooked eggs, fruit cups, and more. There is limited seating. If you purchase a refillable resort mug, head here to fill 'er up. B L D S·$–$$·❤

BEACHES & CREAM SODA SHOP: This small, classic soda fountain is poolside at Beach Club. It offers sundaes, cones, floats, shakes, and sodas. Cheeseburgers, chicken sandwiches, hot dogs, and fries are served, too. Many of the creamy treats are available to go. Grab-and-go selections include salads, fresh fruit, cereal, candies, and a small supply of grocery items. This is a Walt Disney World resort mug refilling station, too. Reservations are recommended (this pocket-sized place is very popular). B L D S·$–$$·❤

CAPE MAY CAFE: Goofy and his pals greet Beach Club visitors each morning at this whimsical dining area. The breakfast buffet includes all the standards, plus a few specialties. Breakfast doesn't disappoint, but dinner is the big event here. Dinner is an all-you-can-eat New England–style clambake buffet, and it's one of WDW's most popular meals and better values. The lineup includes crab legs, mussels, steamed clams, carved meats, salads, pastas, corn on the cob, potatoes, and desserts. Soft drinks are included, but cocktails cost extra. Reservations are recommended. B D·$$$·❤

CAPTAIN'S GRILLE: This American grill serves steak, seafood, and more. Breakfast features a buffet and an a la carte menu; lunch and dinner are à la carte. The hand-cut salt and vinegar fries pair nicely with the lump crab cake with fire-roasted corn succotash. The house-made potato cheese gnocchi, rosemary-brined pork tenderloin, and New England–style lobster rolls are all crowd-pleasers. The dessert menu features hazelnut gianduja chocolate cake with salted caramel sauce and gluten-free angel food cake with berry compote. Reservations are recommended. B L D·$$–$$$·❤

HURRICANE HANNA'S WATERSIDE BAR & GRILL: Hanna's serves hamburgers and cheeseburgers, lobster and shrimp rolls, chopped field green salad, grilled chicken breast sandwiches, and vegetarian quinoa wraps—plus cocktails and frozen concoctions. The kids' menu includes grilled chicken sandwiches, chicken nuggets, and burgers. This is also a refillable WDW resort mug station. L S·$·❤

YACHTSMAN STEAKHOUSE: You know you're in for a serious steak experience the moment you walk through the door. There's an actual butcher shop here. Yes, the Yachtsman delivers an experience to rival those of revered New York City steak houses.

Generous portions begin with house-made rolls and may continue with an appetizer such as lobster bisque. There's no skimping on the expertly prepared entrées, so good luck finding room for crème brûlée. In addition to the beef, the menu includes lamb, chicken, and seafood. It's possible to feast on side dishes alone, with sautéed mushroom caps, oven-roasted Brussels sprouts, rainbow carrots, and truffle mac and cheese all vying for your attention. Located at the Yacht Club. Reservations are recommended. D·$$$–$$$$·❤

WALT DISNEY WORLD

Name & Location	Meals	Style*	Price**	Characters	Theme
Akershus Norway Pavilion, Epcot (page 252)	Breakfast Lunch Dinner	Family style	B: $39/24 L: $38/23 D: $43/24	Belle, Jasmine, Snow White, and Aurora	Fourteenth-century Norwegian castle
Cape May Cafe Yacht and Beach Club resorts (page 281)	Breakfast	Buffet	B: $31/17	Goofy, Minnie, Donald Duck	Seaside picnic
Chef Mickey's Contemporary resort (page 273)	Breakfast Dinner	Buffet	B: $35/18 D: $43/22	Mickey, Minnie, Donald, Goofy, and Pluto	A family celebration
Cinderella's Royal Table Magic Kingdom (page 245)	Breakfast Lunch Dinner	B/L: Family style D: a la carte	B: $58/36 L: $60/38 D: $73/43	B, L, D: Princesses B, L, D: Cinderella greets guests in the Castle lobby	Medieval banquet
Crystal Palace Magic Kingdom (page 248)	Breakfast Lunch Dinner	à la carte	B: $27/15 L: $30/16 D: $40/19	Pooh, Eeyore, Tigger, and Piglet	Sunlit conservatory
Garden Grill Epcot (page 251)	Dinner	Family style	$40/19	Mickey, Pluto, Chip, and Dale	Home-style country cooking

* Family-style and buffet meals are all-you-can-eat dining experiences. Family-style features a set menu and table service; buffet-style meals usually present more dining options and are self-serve.

** Adult prices are followed by children's prices (diners ages 3 through 9). Prices may be higher during select "peak" times of year.

CHARACTER DINING

Featured Items	For Dessert	Tip	Wins for . . .
B: Scrambled eggs, potato casseroles, French toast sticks, bacon, sausage, fruit L/D: Norwegian fare and kid-friendly selections	Chocolate mousse cake, lingonberry cheesecake	This is the only table-service breakfast option at Epcot.	**It's not Cinderella's Castle, but it's still pretty cool.** (It's much easier to score reservations here, too.)
Eggs, breakfast pizza, Mickey waffles, sausage, fruit, cereal, grits	Doughnuts, Danish, fresh berries	For guests staying in the Epcot area, Cape May is one of the best breakfast options.	**Best Chance of Getting a Table Without Reservations** (But make the arrangements, anyway!)
B: Eggs, pancakes, Mickey waffles, fruit, cereal D: Carved meats, seafood, pasta, veggies, pizza, salads	Make-your-own sundaes, cheesecake, cookies, and other fresh housemade desserts	A celebration happens every 45 minutes. Be sure to stick around for at least one little party.	**Best All-Around Character Meal** (It has a fun and festive setting and a kid-pleasing menu.)
B: Frittata, lobster and crab crepes, eggs, French toast, bacon, pastries L/D: Catch of the day, pork shank, beef short ribs, and beef tenderloin	Seasonal cheesecake, flourless chocolate cake, and dessert trio	Payment in full is required at time of booking for all meals.	**Best Setting** (The restaurant is inside Cinderella Castle!)
B: French toast, eggs, cereal, frittatas, fruit L/D: Shrimp, carved meats, pasta, veggies, pizza, salad	B: Sticky buns L/D: Cakes, pies, make-your-own sundaes, cookies	Don't be put off by this restaurant's size—the characters make the rounds surprisingly quickly.	**Best Theme Park Buffet** (Lovely setting, convenient location, and an appetizing menu.)
Catfish, beef, chicken, veggies, potatoes (mac and cheese for kids)	Freshly made desserts	The room rotates very slowly throughout the meal. It's hardly noticeable to most, but may be disorienting to those highly sensitive to motion.	**Best for Vegetarians** (Be sure to ask for the vegetarian meal—it's usually a tasty seasonal selection.)

All characters, menu items, and prices are subject to change. Prices are rounded to the nearest dollar. Call 407-WDW-DINE (939-3463) for details or to make reservations. This listing is not comprehensive. Character meals are also presented at the Hilton (Sunday breakfast at Covington Mill) and Buena Vista Palace (Sunday breakfast at Watercress Cafe). See pages 108 and 110 for details.

Name & Location	Meals	Style*	Price**	Characters	Theme
Garden Grove Swan resort (page 279)	Breakfast (week-ends) Dinner (daily)	Buffet	B: $21/13 D: $30/14	B: Goofy & Pluto (Sat.); Goofy, Pluto, Chip, & Dale (Sun.) D: Goofy & Pluto (Tues.–Thurs., Sat.); Goofy, Pluto, Chip, & Dale (Fri., Mon., Sun.)	Picnic in the park
Hollywood & Vine Disney's Holly-wood Studios (page 260)	Breakfast Lunch	Family style	B: $27/15 L: $34/18	Doc McStuffins, Sofia the First, Handy Manny, and Jake the Never Land pirate	A celebration of (and with!) Playhouse Disney
Wonderland Tea Party Grand Floridian resort (page 230)	Lunch	Tea-party style	$49 (per child, ages 4–12)	Alice and the Mad Hatter	Pint-size, interactive tea party
Mickey's Backyard Barbecue Dinner show at Fort Wilderness (page 300)	Dinner	Buffet	$55/32	Mickey and friends such as Goofy, Minnie, Chip, and Dale	Backyard barbecue/ hoedown
'Ohana Polynesian Village resort (page 277)	Breakfast	Family style	$27/15	Lilo, Stitch, and others, such as Pluto and Mickey	Tropical hut
1900 Park Fare Grand Floridian resort (page 276)	Breakfast Dinner	Buffet	B: $26/15 D: $40/19	B: Stars like Mary Poppins and Alice D: Cinderella and friends	Turn-of-the-century circus
Tusker House Donald's Safari Breakfast at Animal Kingdom (page 264)	Breakfast Lunch	Buffet	B: $33/18 L: $35/19	Donald, Daisy, Goofy, and Mickey	Safari feast

* Family-style and buffet meals are all-you-can-eat dining experiences. Family-style features a set menu and table service; buffet-style meals usually present more dining options and are self-serve.

** Adult prices are followed by children's prices (diners ages 3 through 9). Prices will be higher during select "peak" times of year.

Featured Items	For Dessert	Tip	Wins for ...
B: Omelets, eggs, bacon, fruit D: Varies by day	Fresh pastries	For dinner, Sunday and Wednesday are barbecue; Monday and Friday, seafood; Tuesday, Thursday, and Saturday are Mediterranean.	**Best Variety** (You can have four dinners in one week and have a different type of cuisine each time.)
B: Mickey waffles, scrambled eggs, yogurt L: Salads, pasta dishes, fish, and chicken	Pineapple upside-down cake, Key lime tart	Ask for Play 'N Dine at Hollywood & Vine when you call to reserve (that's the official name!).	**Tot-Pleasing** (Little ones love to dine along with Doc McStuffins.)
PB&J sandwiches, chicken nuggets, fruit, and kid-friendly "tea" (apple juice)	Cupcakes, crispy treats	Parents can stick around for the party, but kids are well supervised. Many adults choose to snooze by the pool or relax in a Grand Floridian lounge.	**Most Fun with Food** (What's cooler to a kid than eating a cupcake? Decorating it first!)
Chicken, ribs, hot dogs, corn on the cob, baked beans	Watermelon and marble cake	Available on Tuesdays and Thursdays from March through December.	**Country Music Fans** (There is a live country band and line dancing.)
Mickey waffles, eggs, biscuits, fruit, bacon	Sweet baked goods	Don't forget your autograph book and camera. The characters spend a good amount of quality time at each table.	**Speediest Service** (Servers keep those family-style platters coming fast and frequently.)
B: Pancakes, eggs, waffles D: Prime rib, pasta, seafood	B: Sticky buns, muffins, Danish D: Key lime pie, cheesecake, bread pudding	Breakfast here is a nice way to start a Magic Kingdom day. The park is just one monorail stop away.	**Fanciest Foods** (The quality is superior to many buffets, and there's plenty to please the kids.)
B: Mickey waffles, quiche, eggs, fruit L: Spit-roasted chicken and beef, roasted pork loin, vegetarian offerings, salmon, salads, bread	B: Danish, muffins L: warm cinnamon bread, pudding with vanilla sauce, chocolate cake	This spot is just steps from Kilimanjaro Safaris, making it an ideal location for a pre-safari breakfast or post-safari lunch.	**Best Place to Find Donald Duck** (As the host, he greets guests at breakfast and lunch.)

All characters, menu items, and prices are subject to change. Prices are rounded to the nearest dollar. Call 407-WDW-DINE (939-3463), or visit *www.disneyworld.com/dining/* for updates or to make reservations. This listing is not comprehensive.

BIRNBAUM'S BEST
RESTAURANT ROUNDUP

Dining Disney-style is one of the most enjoyable aspects of the vacation for many visitors. But with so many different restaurants to choose from, it can be difficult to select the spots that will best suit your family. Regulars to WDW are quick to recommend their favorites to newcomers. We, of course, are no exception to the rule. What follows is a rundown of the restaurants that we always try to include in our trips to the World and wholeheartedly recommend to those who are planning a visit. To pick these Birnbaum's Bests, we considered such factors as food quality, restaurant atmosphere, location, and overall value.

TOP WDW RESTAURANTS FOR FAMILIES WITH KIDS

TABLE SERVICE

Boma—Flavors of Africa .... Animal Kingdom Lodge resort (p. 270)
Cape May Cafe .... Beach Club resort (p. 281)
Chef Mickey's .... Contemporary resort (p. 273)
Cinderella's Royal Table .... Magic Kingdom (p. 245)
Crystal Palace .... Magic Kingdom (p. 248)
50's Prime Time Cafe.. Disney's Hollywood Studios (p. 260)
Garden Grill .... Epcot (p. 251)
1900 Park Fare .... Grand Floridian resort (p. 276)
Rainforest Cafe .... Animal Kingdom and Downtown Disney (pp. 264, 268)
Sci-Fi Dine-In Theater .... Disney's Hollywood Studios (p. 261)
T-Rex Cafe...Downtown Disney (p. 269)
Tusker House .... Animal Kingdom (p. 264)
Via Napoli.. Epcot (p. 257)
The Wave . . . of American Flavors .... Contemporary resort (p. 274)

QUICK SERVICE

Columbia Harbour House .... Magic Kingdom (p. 248)
Cooke's of Dublin .... Downtown Disney (p. 266)
Earl of Sandwich .... Downtown Disney (p. 266)
Everything Pop! .... Pop Century resort (p. 278)
Flame Tree Barbecue .... Animal Kingdom (p. 264)
Liberty Inn .... Epcot (p. 258)
Pecos Bill Cafe.. Magic Kingdom (p. 247)
Pinocchio Village Haus .... Magic Kingdom (p. 246)
Sunset Ranch Market .... Disney's Hollywood Studios (p. 263)
Sunshine Seasons .... Epcot (p. 252)

BEST KIDS' MEAL PRESENTATION

Old Port Royale .... Caribbean Beach resort (p. 272)
(The meal comes in a sand bucket with a shovel.)

BEST PLACE TO CELEBRATE A CHILD'S BIRTHDAY

Chef Mickey's .... Contemporary resort (p. 273)

RUNNER-UP

Mickey's Backyard Barbecue .... Fort Wilderness (p. 300)

BEST FIREWORKS VIEW

California Grill .... Contemporary resort (p. 273)

BEST VEGETARIAN MEALS

Jiko—The Cooking Place
Animal Kingdom Lodge resort (p. 270)

BEST SPLURGE FOR GROWN-UPS

Victoria & Albert's .... Grand Floridian resort (p. 276)

RUNNERS-UP

California Grill .... Contemporary resort (p. 273)
Citricos .... Grand Floridian resort (p. 275)
Flying Fish Cafe .... BoardWalk resort (p. 272)
Fulton's Crab House .... Downtown Disney, Marketplace (p. 267)
Il Mulino New York Trattoria .... Swan resort (p. 279)
Jiko—The Cooking Place .... Animal Kingdom Lodge resort (p. 270)
Monsieur Paul .... Epcot (p. 254)
Yachtsman Steakhouse .... Yacht Club resort (p. 281)

BEST DINNER SHOW

Hoop-Dee-Doo Musical Revue: This crowd-pleasing saloon hall show has been going like gangbusters since 1974. Kids enjoy the silly humor, while adults eat up the bottomless buckets of ribs, fried chicken, and other simple dishes. Presented at Fort Wilderness (p. 300).

RUNNER-UP

Mickey's Backyard Barbecue: It's more of a big, informal party than a show, complete with a kickin' country band, games for the kids, and line dancing with Disney characters. The self-serve, all-you-can-eat barbecue fare is plentiful. Presented at Fort Wilderness (p. 300).

BEST PIZZA FOR GROWN-UPS

Portobello .... Downtown Disney, Marketplace (p. 268)
Via Napoli .... Epcot (p. 257)

BEST PIZZA FOR KIDS

Pizzafari .... Animal Kingdom (p. 265)
Pizza Planet .... Disney's Hollywood Studios (p. 263)

BEST FIXIN'S BAR

Pecos Bill Cafe
Magic Kingdom (p. 247)

BEST ROOM SERVICE

Yacht and Beach Club resorts
(p. 281)

BEST BUYS

Trail's End Restaurant .... Pioneer Hall, Fort Wilderness (p. 275)
Boma—Flavors of Africa .... Animal Kingdom Lodge (p. 270)

BEST ITALIAN FARE

Via Napoli .... Epcot (p. 257)

RUNNERS-UP
Il Mulino New York Trattoria .... Swan resort (p. 279)
Portobello .... Downtown Disney, Marketplace (p. 268)
Tutto Italia .... Epcot (p. 256)

BEST THEME

50's Prime Time Cafe ....Disney's Hollywood Studios (p. 260)

RUNNERS-UP
Sci-Fi Dine-In Theater .... Disney's Hollywood Studios (p. 261)
T-Rex Cafe .... Downtown Disney, Marketplace (p. 269)

BEST OUTDOOR DINING

Tutto Italia ....Epcot (p. 256)

RUNNER-UP
Big River Grille & Brewing Works .... BoardWalk resort (p. 271)

GOOD MEALS, GREAT TIMES

BEST SEAFOOD

Flying Fish Cafe .... BoardWalk resort (p. 272)

RUNNERS-UP

Coral Reef .... Epcot (p. 251)
Fulton's Crab House .... Downtown Disney, Marketplace (p. 267)
Narcoossee's .... Grand Floridian resort (p. 276)
Todd English's bluezoo .... Dolphin resort (p. 280)

BEST CRAB CAKES

Stone Crab Lounge .... Fulton's Crab House, Downtown Disney, Marketplace (p. 267)
The Wave . . . of American Flavors .... Contemporary resort (p. 274)

BEST BLOODY MARY

Stone Crab Lounge .... Fulton's Crab House, Downtown Disney, Marketplace (p. 267)

BEST ALL-AROUND WDW RESTAURANT

The Wave . . . of American Flavors .... Contemporary resort (p. 274)

BEST VEGGIE BURGER

Cosmic Ray's Starlight Cafe .... Magic Kingdom (p. 250)

BEST STEAK

Yachtsman Steakhouse ....Yacht Club resort (p. 281)

RUNNERS-UP

Le Cellier Steakhouse .... Epcot (p. 253)
Flying Fish Cafe .... BoardWalk resort (p. 272)

BEST SUSHI

Kimonos .... Swan resort (p. 279)

RUNNERS-UP

California Grill .... Contemporary resort (p. 273)
Kona Cafe.................................. Polynesian Village resort (p. 277)

GOOD MEALS, GREAT TIMES

289

BEST ICE CREAM

Beaches & Cream Soda Shop .... Beach Club resort (p. 281)
L'Artisan des Glaces .... Epcot (p. 258)
Plaza Restaurant .... Magic Kingdom (p. 249)

BEST SPORTS BAR

ESPN Club
BoardWalk resort (p. 272)

BEST COFFEE

Flying Fish Cafe .... BoardWalk resort (p. 272)

RUNNERS-UP

Kona Cafe .... Polynesian Village resort (p. 277)
Boma—Flavors of Africa .... Animal Kingdom Lodge resort (p. 270)
Starbucks.. (multiple locations; see Index)
Ghirardelli Soda Fountain .... Downtown Disney, Marketplace (p. 267)

BEST MILK SHAKE

Beaches & Cream Soda Shop .... Beach Club resort (p. 281)
Min and Bill's Dockside Diner .... Disney's Hollywood Studios (p. 262)

BEST FRESH-BAKED COOKIES

The Writer's Stop .... Disney's Hollywood Studios (p. 186)
Main Street Bakery .... Magic Kingdom (p. 249)

BEST CHARACTER MEAL

Cinderella's Royal Table .... Magic Kingdom (p. 245)

RUNNERS-UP

Akershus Royal Banquet Hall ....Epcot (p. 252)
Chef Mickey's .... Contemporary resort (p. 273)
Garden Grill ....Epcot (p. 251)
1900 Park Fare ....Grand Floridian resort (p. 276)

BEST RESORT SNACK BAR

Picabu .... Dolphin resort (p. 279)

RUNNERS-UP

Capt. Cook's .... Polynesian Village resort (p. 277)
Contempo Cafe............................ Contemporary resort (p. 273)

Where to Find ...

From french fries to filet mignon, fried chicken to seared scallops with black truffle spaghettini, Disney dishes truly run the gamut. To help you zero in on the eateries that best fit your needs, we've created a handy index of specialized lists:

PHOTO BY JILL SAFRO

BAKERIES/PASTRY SHOPS
Beach Club Marketplace (Beach Club resort)
BoardWalk Bakery (BoardWalk resort)
Kringla Bakeri og Kafe (Epcot, World Showcase)
Goofy's Candy Co. (Downtown Disney, Marketplace)
Kusafiri Coffee Shop & Bakery (Animal Kingdom, Harambe)
Les Halles Boulangerie Patisserie (Epcot, World Showcase)
Main Street Bakery (Magic Kingdom, Main Street, U.S.A.)
Starring Rolls Cafe (Disney's Hollywood Studios)
Sunshine Seasons (Epcot, The Land)

BARBECUE
Flame Tree Barbecue (Animal Kingdom, Discovery Island)
House of Blues Smokehouse (Downtown Disney, West Side)
Mickey's Backyard Barbecue (see Dinner Shows, page 300)

BEST BANG FOR THE BUFFET BUCK
(all-you-can-eat)
Biergarten (Epcot, World Showcase)
Boma—Flavors of Africa (Animal Kingdom Lodge)

Cape May Cafe (Beach Club resort)
Chef Mickey's (Contemporary resort)
Hollywood & Vine (Disney's Hollywood Studios)
1900 Park Fare (Grand Floridian resort)
Trail's End Restaurant (Fort Wilderness resort)
Tusker House (Animal Kingdom, Harambe)

BEST WITH BABIES (table service)
Akershus Royal Banquet Hall (Epcot, World Showcase)
Biergarten (Epcot, World Showcase)
Chef Mickey's (Contemporary resort)
Crystal Palace (Magic Kingdom, Main Street, U.S.A.)
Donald's Safari Breakfast at Tusker House (Animal Kingdom, Harambe)
Garden Grill (Epcot, Future World)
Hollywood & Vine (Disney's Hollywood Studios)
'Ohana (Polynesian Village resort)
Olivia's Cafe (Disney's Old Key West resort)
Rainforest Cafe (Animal Kingdom and Downtown Disney)
Shutters at Old Port Royale (Caribbean Beach resort)
Tony's Town Square (Magic Kingdom, Main Street, U.S.A.)
Trail's End Restaurant (Fort Wilderness resort)

BRUNCH
House of Blues (Downtown Disney, West Side)

BUFFET (all-you-can-eat)
Akershus Royal Banquet Hall (Epcot, World Showcase—*appetizers only*)
Biergarten (Epcot, World Showcase)
Boma—Flavors of Africa (Animal Kingdom Lodge)
Cape May Cafe (Beach Club resort)
Captain's Grille (breakfast; Yacht Club resort)
Chef Mickey's (Contemporary resort)
Crystal Palace (Magic Kingdom, Main Street, U.S.A.)

Garden Grove (Swan resort)
Hollywood & Vine (Disney's Hollywood Studios)
1900 Park Fare (Grand Floridian resort)
Trail's End Restaurant (breakfast and dinner; Fort Wilderness)
Tusker House (Animal Kingdom, Harambe)
Wave . . . of American Flavors, The (Contemporary resort, breakfast only)

BURGERS
Backlot Express (Disney's Hollywood Studios)
Cabana Bar & Grill (Dolphin resort)
Capt. Cook's (Polynesian Village resort)
Cosmic Ray's Starlight Cafe (Magic Kingdom, Tomorrowland)

PHOTO BY JILL SAFRO

Electric Umbrella (Epcot, Future World)
ESPN Club (BoardWalk resort)
Everything Pop! (Pop Century resort)
Food Courts (All-Star resorts)
Fountain, The (Dolphin resort)
Liberty Inn (Epcot, World Showcase)
Old Port Royale (Caribbean Beach resort)
Pecos Bill Cafe (Magic Kingdom, Frontierland)
Planet Hollywood (Downtown Disney, West Side)
Restaurantosaurus (Animal Kingdom, DinoLand)
Riverside Mill (Port Orleans Riverside resort)
Sassagoula Floatworks & Food Factory (Port Orleans French Quarter resort)
Sci-Fi Dine-In Theater (Disney's Hollywood Studios)
Sunset Ranch Market (Disney's Hollywood Studios)

CHEAP EATS—FAST FOOD
Backlot Express (Disney's Hollywood Studios)
Columbia Harbour House (Magic Kingdom, Liberty Square)
Everything Pop! (Pop Century resort)

Flame Tree Barbecue (Animal Kingdom, Discovery Island)
Katsura Grill (Epcot, World Showcase)
Landscape of Flavors (Disney's Art of Animation resort)
Pinocchio Village Haus (Magic Kingdom, Fantasyland)
Pizzafari (Animal Kingdom, Discovery Island)
Restaurantosaurus (Animal Kingdom, DinoLand)
Sommerfest (Epcot, World Showcase)
Starring Rolls Cafe (Disney's Hollywood Studios)
Sunshine Seasons (Epcot, Future World)
Wolfgang Puck Express (Downtown Disney, Marketplace and West Side)
Yorkshire County Fish Shop (Epcot, World Showcase)

CHEAP EATS (relatively speaking)— Table Service
Beaches & Cream Soda Shop (Beach Club resort)
Cape May Cafe (Beach Club resort)
ESPN Club (BoardWalk resort)
Olivia's Cafe (Disney's Old Key West resort)
Planet Hollywood (Downtown Disney, West Side)
Plaza Restaurant (Magic Kingdom, Main Street, U.S.A.)
Rainforest Cafe (Animal Kingdom and Downtown Disney, Marketplace)
Spice Road Table (Epcot, World Showcase)
Trail's End Restaurant (Fort Wilderness resort)
Tusker House (Animal Kingdom, Harambe)
Via Napoli (Epcot, World Showcase)

DISNEY CHARACTERS (dining with)
(see pages 282–285)

ETHNIC EATERIES
African
Boma—Flavors of Africa (Animal Kingdom Lodge)
Jiko—The Cooking Place (Animal Kingdom Lodge)
Marrakesh (Epcot, World Showcase)
Sanaa (Animal Kingdom Lodge, Kidani Village)
Spice Road Table (Epcot, World Showcase)
Tangierine Cafe (Epcot, World Showcase)
Tusker House (Animal Kingdom, Harambe)

American

Artist Point (Wilderness Lodge)
Big River Grille & Brewing Works
(BoardWalk resort)
Boatwright's Dining Hall (Port Orleans
Riverside resort)
California Grill (Contemporary resort)
ESPN Club (BoardWalk resort)
50's Prime Time Cafe (Disney's Hollywood
Studios)
Flying Fish Cafe (BoardWalk resort)
Garden Grill (Epcot, Future World)
Grand Floridian Cafe (Grand Floridian resort)
Hollywood Brown Derby (Disney's Hollywood
Studios)
House of Blues (Downtown Disney, West Side)
Liberty Inn (Epcot, World Showcase)
Liberty Tree Tavern (Magic Kingdom,
Liberty Square)
Narcoossee's (Grand Floridian resort)

PHOTO BY JILL SAFRO

1900 Park Fare (Grand Floridian resort)
Olivia's Cafe (Old Key West resort)
Sci-Fi Dine-In Theater (Disney's Hollywood
Studios)
Trail's End Restaurant (Fort Wilderness resort)
Wave . . . of American Flavors, The
(Contemporary resort)

British

Earl of Sandwich (Downtown Disney,
Marketplace)
Rose & Crown Pub & Dining Room (Epcot,
World Showcase)
Yorkshire County Fish Shop (Epcot,
World Showcase)

Canadian

Le Cellier Steakhouse (Epcot, World
Showcase)

Chinese and Southeast Asian

Lotus Blossom Cafe (Epcot, World Showcase)
Nine Dragons (Epcot, World Showcase)
Yak & Yeti (Animal Kingdom, Asia)

Cuban

Bongos Cuban Cafe (Downtown Disney,
West Side)

French

Be Our Guest Restaurant (Magic Kingdom,
Fantasyland)
Chefs de France (Epcot, World Showcase)
Les Halles Boulangerie Patisserie (Epcot,
World Showcase)
Monsieur Paul (Epcot, World Showcase)

German

Biergarten (Epcot, World Showcase)
Sommerfest (Epcot, World Showcase)

Italian/Mediterranean

Il Mulino New York Trattoria (Swan resort)
Mama Melrose's Ristorante Italiano (Disney's
Hollywood Studios)
Portobello (Downtown Disney, Marketplace)
Tony's Town Square (Magic Kingdom, Main
Street, U.S.A.)
Tutto Gusto (Epcot, World Showcase)
Via Napoli (Epcot, World Showcase)

Japanese

Kabuki Cafe (Epcot, World Showcase)
Katsura Grill (Epcot, World Showcase)
Kimonos (Swan resort)
Teppan Edo (Epcot, World Showcase)
Tokyo Dining (Epcot, World Showcase)

Mexican/Latin American

La Cantina de San Angel (Epcot,
World Showcase)
La Hacienda de San Angel (Epcot,
World Showcase)
Maya Grill (Coronado Springs resort)
San Angel Inn (Epcot, World Showcase)
Tortuga Tavern (Magic Kingdom, Adventureland)

Norwegian

Akershus Royal Banquet Hall (Epcot,
World Showcase)
Kringla Bakeri og Kafe (Epcot, World
Showcase)

FAMILY-STYLE (all-you-can-eat)

Akershus Royal Banquet Hall (Epcot, World Showcase)
Cape May Cafe (Beach Club resort)
Garden Grill (Epcot, Future World)
Garden Grove (Swan resort)
Hoop-Dee-Doo Musical Revue (see page 300)
Liberty Tree Tavern (Magic Kingdom, Liberty Square)
Mickey's Backyard Barbecue (see page 300)
'Ohana (Polynesian Village resort)
Spirit of Aloha (see page 300)
Whispering Canyon Cafe (Wilderness Lodge)

FRUIT

Aloha Isle (Magic Kingdom, Adventureland)
Harambe Fruit Market (Animal Kingdom, Harambe)
Liberty Square Market (Magic Kingdom, Liberty Square)
Prince Eric's Village Market (Magic Kingdom, Fantasyland)
Sunset Ranch Market (Disney's Hollywood Studios)
Sunshine Seasons (Epcot, Future World)

GOOD FOR GROUPS

Biergarten (Epcot, World Showcase)
Boma—Flavors of Africa (Animal Kingdom Lodge)
California Grill (Contemporary resort)
Cape May Cafe (Beach Club resort)
Captain's Grille (Yacht Club resort)
Crystal Palace (Magic Kingdom, Main Street, U.S.A.)
Flame Tree Barbecue (Animal Kingdom, Discovery Island)
Flying Fish Cafe (BoardWalk resort)
Hollywood & Vine (Disney's Hollywood Studios)
House of Blues (Downtown Disney, West Side)
Mickey's Backyard Barbecue (see page 300)
'Ohana (Polynesian Village resort)
Raglan Road (Downtown Disney, between Marketplace and West Side)
Sunshine Seasons (Epcot, Future World)
Teppan Edo (Epcot, World Showcase)
Todd English's bluezoo (Dolphin resort)
Tusker House (Animal Kingdom, Harambe)
Via Napoli (Epcot, World Showcase)
Wave . . . of American Flavors, The (Contemporary resort)

HOT DOGS

Backlot Express (Disney's Hollywood Studios)
Casey's Corner (Magic Kingdom, Main Street, U.S.A.)
Liberty Inn (Epcot, World Showcase)
Lunching Pad, The (Magic Kingdom, Tomorrowland)
Min and Bill's Dockside Diner (Disney's Hollywood Studios)
Restaurantosaurus (Animal Kingdom, Dinoland)
Sunset Ranch Market (Disney's Hollywood Studios)
Wetzel's Pretzels (Downtown Disney, Marketplace)

ICE CREAM AND FROZEN TREATS

Aloha Isle (Magic Kingdom, Adventureland)
Anandapur Ice Cream Truck (Animal Kingdom, Asia)
Beaches & Cream Soda Shop (Beach Club resort)
Cheshire Cafe (Magic Kingdom, Fantasyland)
Cool Post (Epcot, World Showcase)
Dino-Bite Snacks (Animal Kingdom, DinoLand)
Fountain View (Epcot, Future World)

PHOTO BY JILL SAFRO

Gaston's Tavern (Magic Kingdom, Fantasyland)
Ghirardelli Ice Cream & Chocolate Shop (Downtown Disney, Marketplace)
Hollywood Scoops (Disney's Hollywood Studios)
Min & Bill's Dockside Diner (Disney's Hollywood Studios)
Plaza Ice Cream Parlor (Magic Kingdom, Main Street, U.S.A.)
Plaza Restaurant (Magic Kingdom, Main Street, U.S.A.)
Seashore Sweets' (BoardWalk resort)

Storybook Treats (Magic Kingdom, Fantasyland)
Sunshine Tree Terrace (Magic Kingdom, Adventureland)

KIDS' FAVORITES
Akershus Royal Banquet Hall (Epcot, World Showcase)
Cape May Cafe breakfast (Beach Club resort)
Casey's Corner (Magic Kingdom, Main Street)
Chef Mickey's (Contemporary resort)
Cinderella's Royal Table (Magic Kingdom, Fantasyland)
Crystal Palace (Magic Kingdom, Main Street,)
50's Prime Time Cafe (Disney's Hollywood Studios)
Garden Grill (Epcot, Future World)
Hoop-Dee-Doo Musical Revue (see page 300)
Liberty Inn (Epcot, World Showcase)
1900 Park Fare (Grand Floridian resort)
'Ohana (Polynesian Village resort)
Pecos Bill Cafe (Magic Kingdom, Frontierland)
Pinocchio Village Haus (Magic Kingdom, Fantasyland)
Pizzafari (Animal Kingdom, Discovery Island)
Pizza Planet (Disney's Hollywood Studios)
Planet Hollywood (Downtown Disney, West Side)
Rainforest Cafe (Animal Kingdom and Downtown Disney, Marketplace)
Sci-Fi Dine-In Theater (Disney's Hollywood Studios)
Sunset Ranch Market (Disney's Hollywood Studios)
Sunshine Seasons (Epcot, Future World)
Tusker House (Animal Kingdom, Harambe)
T-Rex Cafe: A Prehistoric Family Adventure (Downtown Disney, Marketplace)
Whispering Canyon Cafe (Wilderness Lodge)

KNOCKOUT VIEWS
Big River Grille & Brewing Works (outdoor seating; BoardWalk)
California Grill (Contemporary resort)
Coral Reef (Epcot, Future World)
La Hacienda de San Angel (Epcot, World Showcase)
Rose & Crown Pub & Dining Room (Epcot, World Showcase)
Sanaa (Animal Kingdom Lodge)
Tomorrowland Terrace (Magic Kingdom, Tomorrowland)

KOSHER (fast-food selections)
ABC Commissary (Disney's Hollywood Studios)
Artist's Palette, The (Saratoga Springs resort)
Cosmic Ray's Starlight Cafe (Magic Kingdom, Tomorrowland)
Electric Umbrella (Epcot, Future World)
Everything Pop! (Pop Century resort)
Food Courts (All-Star and Port Orleans Riverside resorts)
Gasparilla Island Grill (Grand Floridian resort)
Landscape of Flavors (Art of Animation resort)
Liberty Inn (Epcot, World Showcase)
Mara, The (Animal Kingdom Lodge)
Old Port Royale (Caribbean Beach resort)
Pizzafari (Animal Kingdom, Discovery Island)
Roaring Fork (Wilderness Lodge)

LOUNGES AND BARS (with food)
Big River Grille & Brewing Works (BoardWalk resort)
Cabana Bar & Grill (Dolphin resort)
California Grill Lounge (Contemporary resort)
Cítricos Lounge (Grand Floridian resort)

PHOTO BY JILL SAFRO

Crew's Cup (Yacht Club resort)
Crockett's Tavern (Fort Wilderness resort)
ESPN Club (BoardWalk resort)
Garden View (Grand Floridian resort)
Hurricane Hanna's (Yacht & Beach Club resorts)
Il Mulino New York Trattoria Lounge (Swan resort)
Kimonos (Swan resort)
La Cava de Tequila (Epcot, World Showcase)
Leaping Horse Libations (BoardWalk resort)
Mardi Grogs (Port Orleans French Quarter resort)
Martha's Vineyard (Beach Club resort)
Mizner's (Grand Floridian resort)
Muddy Rivers (Port Orleans Riverside resort)

Narcoossee's (Grand Floridian resort)
Outer Rim (Contemporary resort)
Paradiso 37 (Downtown Disney, between Marketplace and West Side)
Portobello (Downtown Disney, Marketplace)
Raglan Road (Downtown Disney, between Marketplace and West Side)
Rainforest Cafe (Magic Mushroom bar; Animal Kingdom and Downtown Disney, Marketplace)
River Roost (Port Orleans Riverside resort)
Rix Lounge (Coronado Springs resort)
Rose & Crown Pub (Epcot, World Showcase)
Sanaa lounge (Animal Kingdom Lodge)
Sand Bar (Contemporary resort)
Shark Bar at T-Rex Cafe (Downtown Disney, Marketplace)
Siestas (Coronado Springs resort)
Sommerfest (inside Germany; Epcot, World Showcase)

Splash Terrace (Swan resort)
Stone Crab Lounge (inside Fulton's Crab House; Downtown Disney, Marketplace)
Tambu Lounge (Polynesian Village resort)
Territory Lounge (Wilderness Lodge)
Trader Sam's Grog Grotto (Polynesian resort)
Tune-In Lounge (Disney's Hollywood Studios)
Turf Club Bar & Grill, The (Saratoga Springs resort)
Turtle Shack (Disney's Old Key West resort)
Tutto Gusto (Epcot, World Showcase)
Uzima Springs (Animal Kingdom Lodge)
Yak & Yeti Lounge (Disney's Animal Kingdom)

OPEN 24 HOURS

Capt. Cook's (Polynesian Village resort)
Gasparilla Island Grill (Grand Floridian resort)
Picabu (Dolphin resort)
Sundial Cafe 24-7 (Wyndham hotel)

PIZZA

Capt. Cook's (Polynesian Village resort)
Everything Pop (Pop Century resort)
Food Courts (All-Star resorts)
Gasparilla Island Grill (Grand Floridian resort)
Mama Melrose's Ristorante Italiano (Disney's Hollywood Studios)
Pinocchio Village Haus (Magic Kingdom, Fantasyland)
Pizza Planet (Disney's Hollywood Studios)
Pizzafari (Animal Kingdom, Discovery Island)
Planet Hollywood (Downtown Disney, West Side)
Riverside Mill (Port Orleans Riverside resort)
Roaring Fork (Wilderness Lodge)
Royale Pizza Shop (Caribbean Beach resort)
Sassagoula Floatworks & Food Factory (Port Orleans French Quarter resort)
Sunset Ranch Market (Disney's Hollywood Studios)
Trail's End Restaurant (Fort Wilderness resort)
Via Napoli (Epcot, World Showcase)
Wolfgang Puck Café (Downtown Disney, West Side)
Wolfgang Puck Express (Downtown Disney, Marketplace and West Side)

SALADS

Artist's Palette, The (Saratoga Springs resort)
Big River Grille & Brewing Works (BoardWalk resort)
Boma—Flavors of Africa (Animal Kingdom Lodge)
Cape May Cafe (Beach Club resort)
Columbia Harbour House (Magic Kingdom, Liberty Square)
Flame Tree Barbecue (Animal Kingdom, Discovery Island)
Gasparilla Island Grill (Grand Floridian resort)
Hollywood Brown Derby (Disney's Hollywood Studios)
Il Mulino New York Trattoria (Swan resort)
Pecos Bill Cafe (Magic Kingdom, Frontierland)
Pepper Market (Coronado Springs resort)
Picabu (Dolphin resort)
Pinocchio Village Haus (Magic Kingdom, Fantasyland)
Plaza Restaurant (Magic Kingdom, Main Street, U.S.A.)
Rainforest Cafe (Animal Kingdom and Downtown Disney, Marketplace)
Sunshine Seasons (Epcot, Future World)

Wave . . . of American Flavors, The (Contemporary resort)

Wolfgang Puck Café (Downtown Disney, West Side)

SEAFOOD

Artist Point (Wilderness Lodge)

California Grill (Contemporary resort)

Cape May Cafe (Beach Club resort)

Columbia Harbour House (Magic Kingdom, Liberty Square)

Coral Reef (Epcot, Future World)

Flying Fish Cafe (BoardWalk resort)

Fulton's Crab House (Downtown Disney, Marketplace)

Kimonos (Swan resort)

Kona Cafe (Polynesian Village resort)

Narcoossee's (Grand Floridian resort)

Todd English's bluezoo (Dolphin resort)

Wave . . . of American Flavors, The (Contemporary resort)

SNACK BARS (at the resorts)

Beach Club Marketplace (Beach Club resort)

Cabana Bar & Grill (Dolphin resort)

Capt. Cook's (Polynesian Village resort)

Contempo Café (Contemporary resort)

Gasparilla Island Grill (Grand Floridian resort)

Mara, The (Animal Kingdom Lodge)

Picabu (Dolphin resort)

Roaring Fork (Wilderness Lodge)

SOLO DINERS

California Grill (Contemporary resort)

Cítricos lounge (Grand Floridian resort)

Crew's Cup (lounge, Yacht Club resort)

ESPN Club (BoardWalk resort)

Flying Fish Cafe (BoardWalk resort)

Il Mulino New York Trattoria (Swan resort)

Jiko—The Cooking Place lounge (Animal Kingdom Lodge)

Narcoossee's lounge (Grand Floridian resort)

Stone Crab Lounge (inside Fulton's Crab House, Downtown Disney, Marketplace)

Tune-In Lounge (Disney's Hollywood Studios)

Wave . . . of American Flavors Lounge (Contemporary resort)

Wolfgang Puck Café Bar (Downtown Disney, West Side)

STEAK

Be Our Guest Restaurant (Magic Kingdom, Fantasyland)

La Hacienda de San Angel (Epcot, World Showcase)

Le Cellier Steakhouse (Epcot, World Showcase)

Shula's Steak House (Dolphin resort)

Wave . . . of Amercian Flavors, The (Contemporary resort)

Yachtsman Steakhouse (Yacht Club resort)

SUPER SPLURGES (for grown-ups)

Artist Point (Wilderness Lodge)

California Grill (Contemporary resort)

Chefs de France (Epcot, World Showcase)

Flying Fish Cafe (BoardWalk resort)

Hollywood Brown Derby (Disney's Hollywood Studios)

Il Mulino (Swan resort)

Jiko—The Cooking Place (Animal Kingdom Lodge)

Le Cellier Steakhouse (Epcot, World Showcase)

Monsieur Paul (Epcot, World Showcase)

Sanaa (Animal Kingdom Lodge)

Shula's Steak House (Dolphin resort)

Victoria & Albert's (Grand Floridian resort)

Yachtsman Steakhouse (Yacht Club resort)

SUSHI

California Grill (Contemporary resort)

Capt. Cook's (Polynesian Village resort)

Kabuki Cafe (Epcot, World Showcase)

Katsura Grill (Epcot, World Showcase)

Kimonos (lounge; Swan resort)

Kona Cafe (Polynesian Village resort)

Kona Island (after 5 P.M.; Polynesian Village resort)

Mitsukoshi's Tokyo Dining (Epcot, World Showcase)

Splitsville (Downtown Disney, West Side)

Wolfgang Puck Café (Downtown Disney, West Side)

TERRIFIC THEMING

Akershus Royal Banquet Hall (Epcot, World Showcase)

Be Our Guest Restaurant (Magic Kingdom, Fantasyland)

PHOTO BY MIKE CARROLL

Biergarten (Epcot, World Showcase)

Cinderella's Royal Table (Magic Kingdom, Fantasyland)

50's Prime Time Cafe (Disney's Hollywood Studios)

Liberty Tree Tavern (Magic Kingdom, Liberty Square)

'Ohana (Polynesian Village resort)

Rainforest Cafe (Animal Kingdom and Downtown Disney, Marketplace)

Sanaa (Animal Kingdom Lodge)

Sci-Fi Dine-In Theater (Disney's Hollywood Studios)

T-Rex Cafe: A Prehistoric Family Adventure (Downtown Disney, Marketplace)

Tusker House (Discovery Island, Animal Kingdom)

VEGETARIAN SELECTIONS

Backlot Express (Disney's Hollywood Studios)

Boma—Flavors of Africa (Animal Kingdom Lodge)

Columbia Harbour House (Magic Kingdom, Liberty Square)

Cosmic Ray's Starlight Cafe (Magic Kingdom, Tomorrowland)

Everything Pop (Pop Century resort)

Food Courts (All-Star resorts)

Jiko—The Cooking Place (Animal Kingdom Lodge)

Mama Melrose's Ristorante Italiano (Disney's Hollywood Studios)

Pecos Bill Cafe (Magic Kingdom, Frontierland)

Pizzafari (Animal Kingdom, Discovery Island)

Pinocchio Village Haus (Magic Kingdom, Fantasyland)

Rainforest Cafe (Animal Kingdom and Downtown Disney, Marketplace)

Sanaa (Animal Kingdom Lodge)

Sunset Ranch Market (Disney's Hollywood Studios)

Sunshine Seasons (Epcot, Future World)

Tony's Town Square (Magic Kingdom, Main Street, U.S.A.)

Tusker House (Animal Kingdom, Harambe)

Via Napoli (Epcot, World Showcase)

PHOTO BY JILL SAFRO

Wolfgang Puck Express (Downtown Disney, West Side and Marketplace)

WINE AND DINE (great wine lists)

Artist Point (Wilderness Lodge)

Be Our Guest Restaurant ([dinner] Magic Kingdom, Fantasyland)

Boma—Flavors of Africa (Animal Kingdom Lodge)

California Grill (Contemporary resort)

Chefs de France (Epcot, World Showcase)

Cítricos (Grand Floridian resort)

Flying Fish Cafe (BoardWalk resort)

Hollywood Brown Derby (Disney's Hollywood Studios)

Il Mulino New York Trattoria (Swan resort)

Jiko—The Cooking Place (Animal Kingdom Lodge)

Monsieur Paul (Epcot, World Showcase)

Narcoossee's (Grand Floridian resort)

Portobello (Downtown Disney, Marketplace)

Sanaa (Animal Kingdom Lodge)

Shula's Steak House (Dolphin resort)

Victoria & Albert's (Grand Floridian resort)

Wave . . . of American Flavors, The (Contemporary resort)

Wolfgang Puck Café—The Dining Room (Downtown Disney, West Side)

Yachtsman Steakhouse (Yacht Club resort)

Reservations Explained

Disney's reservation system, formerly known as "priority seating," covers most full-service restaurants on WDW property. The name may have changed, but the procedure is the same. It was designed to provide the assurance of a reservation without delays caused by no-shows and latecomers. Here's how it works: You call ahead to request a seating time; you arrive five minutes before the assigned time and check in at the podium; you receive the next available table that can accommodate your party. The system works like traditional reservations in that you will be seated before any walk-ins.

We recommend making advance arrangements. Seating times can be secured up to 180 days ahead (see box below) for most Walt Disney World eateries by calling 407-WDW-DINE (939-3463), or by visiting *www.disneyworld.com/dining/*. The dining hotline is open daily from 7 A.M. to 10 P.M. The number of tables available in advance varies. If you are unable to book ahead of time, try to make same-day arrangements.

Most Walt Disney World resorts have at least one phone in the main lobby that provides direct contact with the Dine Line. Simply touch 55 —the call is free. From other locations, dial 407-WDW-DINE (939-3463). Once at the theme parks, dining reservations can be made at the eatery itself; at City Hall in the Magic Kingdom; in Epcot at Guest Relations by Spaceship Earth; by Hollywood Junction in Disney's Hollywood Studios; and at Guest Relations in Animal Kingdom. Bookings can also be made at Guest Relations in Downtown Disney Marketplace and at the West Side.

For Disney Resort Guests Only

Do you have a confirmed reservation at a Disney-owned-and-operated resort? If so, you are entitled to a special perk: Call 180 days prior to the first day of your hotel reservation and you can make dining reservations for up to 10 days of your stay. That's like getting a 1- to 10-day jump on everyone else! (Stays longer than 10 days will require a second call. Inquire when you make your first set of dining reservations.) Have your confirmation number handy when you call 407-WDW-DINE.

Advance Planning

While some WDW restaurants always seem to have an open table (like Marrakesh in Epcot's World Showcase), most are booked far in advance. The restaurants for which careful planning is essential include Be Our Guest and Cinderella's Royal Table in the Magic Kingdom (call 180 days ahead and keep your fingers crossed!); Le Cellier Steakhouse and Chefs de France in Epcot; Tusker House breakfast and lunch in Disney's Animal Kingdom; and California Grill in the Contemporary resort.

While the Walt Disney World reservation system is often successful, there are times when the wait for a table can be unexpectedly long. This is most likely to occur during peak mealtimes at restaurants that offer buffets or family-style meals, where patrons will often opt for seconds (or thirds). For this reason, be sure to check in at the restaurant particularly early for all character-hosted meals.

Reservations are necessary for all dinner shows—the Hoop-Dee-Doo Musical Revue,

HOT TIP!

At most WDW restaurants, reservations are scheduled in five- or ten-minute intervals. If they don't have a 6 P.M. availability, ask about a 6:05 P.M.

Mickey's Backyard Barbecue, and the Polynesian Village resort's Spirit of Aloha; they can be made by calling 407-WDW-DINE (939-3463). Reservations can be booked up to 180 days in advance. If you can't get a table for an early performance, consider a later one (they are usually less heavily booked).

Keep in mind that, with the exception of dinner shows, a WDW seating time does vary from a traditional reservation—you may have to wait a bit when you arrive at your assigned time. Rest assured, however, that your party will be given the first table that opens up.

Note: Because the dining scene at Walt Disney World is ever-evolving, we advise calling 407-WDW-DINE (939-3463) to confirm current reservation policies.

Dinner Shows

The fact that Disney is expert in family entertainment is nowhere more readily apparent than amid the whooping and hollering troupe of singers and dancers who race toward the stage at Fort Wilderness resort's Pioneer Hall. As guests plow through filling barbecue fare (ribs, fried chicken, strawberry shortcake, beer, wine, and soft drinks), these enthusiastic performers sing, dance, and joke up a storm.

The gags are groaners, but the audience eats 'em up. It's all in the course of an evening at the *Hoop-Dee-Doo Musical Revue*, presented nightly at 4 P.M., 6:15 P.M., and 8:30 P.M. Cost is about $59 per adult and $30 for children (ages 3 through 9) for Category 3 seating; about $63 for adults, $31 for kids in Category 2; and about $70 and $36 for Category 1. (The best views are in Category 1—seating is on the main floor.)

Note that the dining room in Pioneer Hall can be chilly year-round. Bring a sweater to combat the sometimes intense air-conditioning.

HOT TIP!

The Hoop-Dee-Doo Musical Revue is a very popular show. Make your reservations as far in advance as possible.

Also presented at Fort Wilderness is *Mickey's Backyard Barbecue*. A country band gets guests out on the floor to kick up their heels, and Disney characters join in the fun.

Dinner consists of plenty of basic picnic favorites: barbecued ribs and chicken, corn on the cob, and baked beans. The seasonal dinner show costs about $57 per adult and $33 for kids. Tickets are required, so book ahead.

Disney's Polynesian luau show is called *Spirit of Aloha*. Set in the beachfront backyard of a Hawaiian house (at the Polynesian Village resort), the show invites guests to join in a musical celebration.

The luau experience combines traditional music as well as more contemporary ditties from the animated Disney film *Lilo & Stitch*. The performers' dancing is some of the most authentic this side of Hawaii. The Spirit of Aloha is presented in an open-air dining theater in Luau Cove, adjacent to the Seven Seas Lagoon.

The all-you-can-eat feast is influenced by the

PHOTO BY JILL SAFRO

flavors of Polynesia and includes draft beer, wine, soft drinks, and dessert. Menu items include roasted chicken, barbecued pork ribs, fresh pineapple, Polynesian-style rice, and vegetables. The kids' menu features PB&J sandwiches, mac and cheese, chicken nuggets, and hot dogs. The cost is about $61 for adults and $31 for kids in Category 3; about $64 and $34 for Category 2; and about $72 and $39 for Category 1 (again, the best views are from Category 1 seats).

Plan to arrive at least 30 minutes before showtime, and allow extra time for transportation and parking. (Note that all prices are subject to change.) The show may be canceled due to inclement weather (though tables are sheltered).

Reservations: Arrangements for dinner shows may be made up to 180 days in advance by calling 407-WDW-DINE (939-3463). Groups of eight or more should call 407-939-7707. *Prices include tax and gratuity and may be higher during peak seasons.*

A credit card number is required for all dinner show reservations. Full payment is required upon booking. It's also possible to redeem Disney Dining Plan credits for dinner shows. At press time, all Disney dinner shows were participating in the dining plan. They are considered "Signature" meals and cost two table-service meals per person. *Note that cancellations for dinner shows must be made at least 48 hours prior to showtime to avoid paying full price.*

Bars & Lounges of WDW

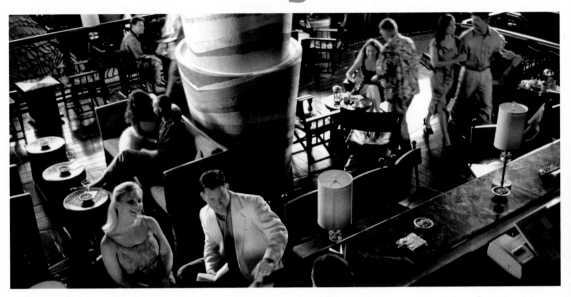

What distinguishes Walt Disney World pubs and lounges from many bars in the real world? Well, in addition to over-the-top theming, you can almost always get a savory nibble to accompany that cocktail. Most Disney lounges serve food, be it from their own menu, or from that of a neighboring restaurant.

Hours vary, but theme park watering holes (at Epcot, Disney's Hollywood Studios, and Animal Kingdom) shut their doors at park closing time. Pool bars at the resorts keep daytime pool hours. Last call at resort lounges is anywhere from about 10 P.M. to midnight. Downtown Disney Marketplace spots stay open till the shops close, usually 11 P.M. Other lounges may keep things going until about 1 A.M.

All-Star Movies, All-Star Music, & All-Star Sports

POOL BARS: There are small poolside oases in All-Star Movies, All-Star Music, and All-Star Sports: Silver Screen Spirits, Singing Spirits, and Grandstand Spirits, respectively. Each serves a selection of beer, wine, traditional cocktails, and specialty drinks.

Animal Kingdom

DAWA BAR: An oversized, open-air hut, Dawa is a pleasant place to take a load off weary feet and sip Safari Amber beer and other cocktails.

It's next to Tusker House. There is occasional live music, too.

RAINFOREST CAFE: The colorful Magic Mushroom bar serves, among other things, fruit blends and specialty drinks. Bar stools resemble animal legs (hooves and all). The bar is inside the Rainforest Cafe. Admission to Animal Kingdom is not necessary to enter. It's possible to order off the restaurant's menu from here, too.

YAK & YETI LOUNGE: A small-but-escapist space inside one of the restaurant's themed dining areas, the Yak & Yeti lounge has a fully stocked bar and seating for six. (There's standing room, too.) House specialties include the Yak Attack, Bonsai Blast, Big Bamboo, and Everest Avalanche. Beer, wine, and sake are also served.

Animal Kingdom Lodge

CAPE TOWN LOUNGE AND WINE BAR: Sip African wines at this intimate spot adjacent to Jiko—The Cooking Place. In addition to a full menu, it has the largest selection of African wines in the United States.

MAJI: A poolside bar (*maji* means "water" in Swahili) serves beverages when the Samawati Springs pool is open (in Kidani Village).

SANAA: Located in the resort's Kidani Village, this lounge is within the restaurant of the same name. South African beers and wines are the specialties of the house.

UZIMA SPRINGS: The bar near the resort's main pool serves beer, wine, and specialty cocktails during pool hours. The (liquor-free) Espresso Freeze—espresso blended with frozen cappuccino and ice cream—is a delightful way to counter the Florida heat.

VICTORIA FALLS: On the mezzanine level overlooking Boma—Flavors of Africa, this lounge offers coffee and spirits, plus the soothing sounds of the falls. (The actual Victoria Falls are located in Africa, between Zambia and Zimbabwe, and are nearly a mile wide.)

Art of Animation

DROP OFF BAR: Open from noon until midnight, this poolside lounge offers specialty cocktails (with and without alcohol), soft drinks, and smoothies—plus sushi, sandwiches, and fresh fruit.

BoardWalk

ATLANTIC DANCE: This nightclub has music, videos, and a deejay. The design is Art Deco, but the tunes are from the '80s through today. The club is open Tuesday–Saturday night, and guests must be at least 21 years old (and show government-issued photo ID) to enter.

BELLE VUE LOUNGE: A full bar accompanies old-time tunes from antique radios in this lobby cocktail lounge. Continental breakfast may be offered (from 6 A.M. until 11 A.M.). Board games are usually available for on-site use (free of charge). There's limited seating at the bar, but there are plenty of tables and comfy couches to lounge on. The lounge starts serving cocktails at about 5 P.M. 🐭

Got I.D.?

The legal drinking age in the state of Florida is 21. However, just being 21 isn't enough to get served—you have to prove it. To do so, present a government-issued photo ID. If your driver's license doesn't have a photo, bring it and an official photo ID (a passport is ideal). Otherwise, you'll have to stick to soft drinks. (Some lounges won't even admit you without ID.)

BIG RIVER GRILLE & BREWING WORKS: A working microbrewery, Big River patrons may order appetizers at the bar and sample the brewmaster's flagship ales and specialty beers. They may even get to watch as a new batch is brewed. In addition to the fresh-brewed beer, beverage selections include fresh-squeezed lemonade, strawberry lemonade, and pomegranate lemonade, and more. Note that Big River does not accept reservations, so the bar can get crowded during mealtimes (and right after Epcot closes at night). 🐭

ESPN CLUB: The ultimate sports bar provides live radio and television broadcasts along with a menu of ballpark favorites (including, of course, hot dogs). With nearly 100 screens, chances are you'll find the game you're looking for. The place fills up quickly on big game days—plan to arrive at least an hour early on such occasions. Note that on NFL Sundays, the match-ups scheduled for screening are usually noted right on the TVs. If not, ask the bartender or inquire at the podium near the front entrance. 🐭

JELLYROLLS: Dueling pianos and lively sing-alongs are the draw at this club, serving beer, wine, and other drinks. There is usually a cover in the neighborhood of $12, and guests must be at least 21 years old to enter. (Proper government-issued, photo ID is required.) Requests are encouraged. And don't forget to tip the piano players before you leave. Note that it can be exceptionally chilly here: Bring a sweater.

PHOTO BY JILL SAFRO

LEAPING HORSE LIBATIONS: The pool bar—designed to resemble a carousel (hence, the leaping horses)—offers cocktails, sandwiches, soft drinks, and simple snacks during pool hours.

Caribbean Beach

BANANA CABANA: Refreshing drinks and snack items are served at this poolside bar near Old Port Royale.

Contemporary

CALIFORNIA GRILL LOUNGE: Perched atop the Contemporary resort, this revitalized space tops many a "must-visit" list. Tucked within the acclaimed restaurant, the lounge offers the full menu and shares access to California Grill's exquisite wine list that boasts about 250 vintages (about 80 offered by the glass), featuring California's finest. If you need help navigating the wine list, fear not: One of the Grill's 20 sommeliers will be happy to help you make a selection.

In addition to wine, the lounge features sake, craft beers and ciders, mixed drinks, alcohol-free signature drinks, and more. Guests of the lounge may order anything off the restaurant menu (including the spectacular sushi). Just as with the restaurant itself, all guests hoping to visit the California Grill Lounge must check in at the desk on the Contemporary's second floor. From there they are escorted to an express elevator. The lounge does not accept reservations and opens at 4:30 P.M. daily. 🐭

COVE BAR: Set beside the pool in the resort's Bay Lake Tower, Cove Bar serves sweets (apple slices with caramel dipping sauce, fruit, and frozen desserts) and lunch items (chicken Caesar salad, turkey BLT sandwich, veggie wrap, Asian chicken salad, hot dog, and sushi). Wash it all down with one of their specialty drinks, such as the Banana Cabana or Poolside Plunge. 🐭

OUTER RIM: Located on the resort's fourth floor across from Contempo Cafe, this modern lounge has about seven bar stools and an abundance of tables with cocktail service. The main draw here is not the view of the large-screen TV, but rather the sweeping views of Bay Lake and Fort Wilderness (on the lake's far shore). Parts of this lounge host guests waiting

HOT TIP!

At some Walt Disney World lounges, you may order food from a neighboring or nearby restaurant's menu. Just ask.

for a table at the ever-popular Chef Mickey's restaurant, so it can be congested here at mealtimes. Beer, wine, sangria, specialty drinks, and alcohol-free kiddie cocktails are served from about 4:30 P.M. till 10 P.M.

SAND BAR: A full bar is offered poolside, weather permitting. Fast food, hummus dip, salads, and sandwiches are available at the adjacent counter area. 🐭

THE WAVE . . . OF AMERICAN FLAVORS LOUNGE: On the first floor of the resort, this spacious bar boasts a wine list that is mostly screw cap (yes, that's a good thing)—a quaffable selection of quality vintages. About 50 are available by the glass; tasting flights are a great choice for those who wish to sample several selections. Also poured: organic beers, ports, and specialty drinks. It's possible to order from The Wave's outstanding menu. Our humble opinion? The Wave is one of the very best Disney World lounges. It's also an excellent place for groups to gather.

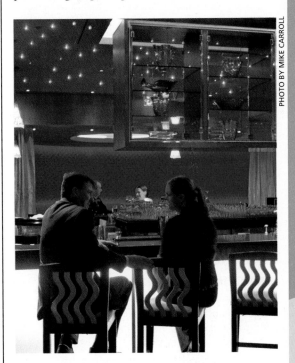

PHOTO BY MIKE CARROLL

Coronado Springs

RIX LOUNGE: Located in the resort's main building, this upscale, eye-and-palate-pleasing lounge serves specialty drinks, beer, wine, soft drinks, and tapas-style appetizers. Cappuccino is an option. The 300-seat venue features house music and a Mediterranean-inspired atmosphere.

SIESTAS: Swimmers can take time out for burgers, sandwiches, tacos, and cocktails at this spot near the pool in the Dig Site area. ❤

Disney's Hollywood Studios

PHOTO BY MIKE CARROLL

TUNE-IN LOUNGE: A sitcom living-room setting, with comfy stools and couches, characterizes this lounge next to the 50's Prime Time Cafe. Old TV sets play scenes from beloved sitcoms (all of which feature food). Appetizers, cocktails, beer, and wine are served.

Disney's Old Key West

GURGLING SUITCASE: This pocket-size lounge on the Turtle Krawl boardwalk serves an assortment of Key West specialties along with traditional cocktails, beer, and wine.

TURTLE SHACK: Refreshments at this poolside spot include cocktails and a small selection of fast-food items.

Downtown Disney

BONGOS: Home to two bars, Bongos' "lobby" bar has a dozen or so bongo drum stools. Mojitos are the specialty of the house, but martinis and other mixed drinks, wine, sangria, and beer are also served. This is a pleasant spot, but we prefer to relax in the big pineapple. Bongos' two-story pineapple bar has indoor and outdoor seating and offers a full bar, plus appetizers. This is one of the more atmospheric spots at Downtown Disney, West Side.

HOLE IN THE WALL: Blink and you miss it, this tiny establishment is bookended (and dwarfed) by Raglan Road on the left and Cooke's of Dublin on the right. A full bar is available, but the Irish stout stands out. In addition to the outstanding nibbles (whipped up over at Raglan Road), this diminutive spot boasts something that is beyond rare at Walt Disney World: Happy Hour specials (from 3 to 7 P.M.).

HOUSE OF BLUES: Set in the back of the eatery section of H.O.B., this bar serves drinks that are as cool as the atmosphere. It's also possible to have drinks in the enclosed Voodoo Garden (table-service only). Guests may order from the restaurant menu.

PHOTO BY MIKE CARROLL

LAVA LOUNGE: The newest addition to Rainforest Cafe is a lively waterside watering hall set beside a lava-spewing volcano. Cocktails, specialty drinks, soft drinks, and snacks are served. The view is quite lovely in the evening.

MAGIC MUSHROOM BAR: When the Rainforest Cafe restaurant is mobbed, we recommend taking in the thunderstorms and waterfalls from this central, mushroom-capped bar. Simply saddle a stool (all of which are shaped like animal legs) and enjoy the festive "natural" ambience. You can sip a cocktail and order a snack from the restaurant's menu. There is another Magic Mushroom Bar inside the Rainforest Cafe at Disney's Animal Kingdom.

PARADISO 37: The bar at Paradiso 37 features an international wine list, an extensive selection of tequilas, frozen margaritas, and the "coldest beer in the world." It is possible to order items from the restaurant's menu, too.

PLANET HOLLYWOOD: Though far from the most atmospheric Walt Disney World bar, this tiny enclave within the Planet Hollywood eatery has a lot to offer a thirsty visitor. In addition to beer, wine, and champagne, the resident mixologists routinely whip up "shooter" creations known as Banana Pudding, Bubble Gum, and Grape Crush. Frozen specialties include Mama Mia!-ritas and Die Harder Daiquiris. Soft drinks are served, too.

PORTOBELLO: In the heart of Portobello Country Italian Trattoria, the bountiful bar has an alluring atmosphere and ample seating. An oenophile's dream come true, the international wine list has something for just about everyone. Italy is well represented, and other offerings come from Sonoma, South Africa, Colombia, New York, and other locales. Many wines are available by the glass, bottle, and half bottle. The cordial menu boasts brandy, cognac, port, sherry, grappa, and dessert wines. There's a full bar and a selection of locally brewed, organic beers.

RAGLAN ROAD: Top 'o the evening to you! This jovial joint is an authentic Irish pub and simply oozes Irish charm. The polished interior is a meticulously decorated Emerald Isle oasis—complete with freshly prepared Irish cuisine and live entertainment (the latter starting at about 9 P.M.). Oh, and of course, pints of stout and other spirited beverages. This place is popular and can get quite crowded on weekend evenings.

SHARK BAR: This space, inside the T-Rex Cafe, puts the water in watering hole. Anchored under the belly of a Technicolor squid, the aqueous area serves all kinds of cocktails, plus items from the restaurant's menu. (One of our favorite things to order here is the tomato soup.) Guests must be at least 21 to sit at the bar.

STONE CRAB LOUNGE: Inside Fulton's Crab House, Stone Crab is an excellent raw bar with prime water views and a honey-wheat house brew. The Bloody Marys are made from scratch and garnished with shrimp. And the bartenders here are among the friendliest at Walt Disney World. What's not to love? Hours generally run from about 11:30 A.M. till about 11:30 P.M.

Epcot

All eateries, including some fast-food spots, serve alcoholic beverages. A few other Epcot locales specialize in liquid refreshments.

LA CAVA DEL TEQUILA: A warm glow envelopes all guests who visit this little lounge in the big pyramid at the Mexico pavilion—and that's before they sample any of the 70-plus tequilas on the menu. In addition to blended margaritas (many made with fresh fruit and spices), guests may sip Mexican beer, wine, cocktails, and soft drinks. Tapas-style snack selections include fresh guacamole, ceviche, and mahi mahi tostadas. This 30-seat escape is open from about noon until Epcot closing time.

HOT TIP!

At Epcot's Rose & Crown Pub (located in the United Kingdom pavilion at World Showcase), a specially designed ale warmer can heat your Guinness to 55 degrees—the temperature favored by some patrons at authentic British pubs.

ROSE & CROWN PUB: This classic pub—a veritable symphony of polished woods, brass, and etched glass—adjoins the Rose & Crown Dining Room in the United Kingdom pavilion. English, Scottish, and Irish beers are available, along with a score of specialty drinks and appetizing snacks imported from the other side of the Atlantic. If you're lucky, there will be live (and lively) piano music during your visit. Feel free to sing along. Seating indoors and out is limited and available on a first-come, first-served basis. ❤

SOMMERFEST: Just outside the Biergarten in Germany, there's a shaded space where soft pretzels, bratwurst, frankfurters, apple strudel, and other treats may be washed down with a stein of cold German beer. They also serve German wines (red and white), Jägermeister, Goldschlager, and soft drinks. ❤

TUTTO GUSTO: A happy addition to the Italy pavilion, Tutto Gusto offers 200 different wines (including grappa), beers imported from Italy, Italian specialty drinks, coffee drinks, and a small plate menu. The best time to visit is in the afternoon (that's when crowds are usually lightest). Reservations are not available.

Fort Wilderness

CROCKETT'S TAVERN: You needn't brandish a coonskin cap to belly up to the bar in this rustic saloon, merely a government-issued photo ID to prove you're not a young'un (all guests must be at least 21 years of age to drink spirits of any kind). Tucked into a corner of the Trail's End restaurant, this spot is small but cozy, and the barkeeps are as amiable as they come. Last we

visited, there were a couple of domestic beers on tap, plus a full bar. Pizza, chicken wings, and nachos are served, too. The TV is usually tuned to the big game of the moment. ❤

Grand Floridian

CITRICOS LOUNGE: As inviting as any lounge on Disney property, this place has one stellar wine list. Old World, New World, red, white, sparkling . . . you name it, they got it. Also on tap are beer, port, sherry, specialty coffees, and creative cocktails (think along the lines of a Citropolitan or Pomegranate Splash).

Soup, salad, and appetizers may be ordered until about 10 P.M. (If it's busy, the bar may continue to serve drinks until the crowd dwindles.) Menu selections have included sautéed shrimp, spiced and slow-cooked beef and pork in crisp phyllo with tamarind sauce, seared tofu, and the exquisitely crispy arancini risotto (fried balls of rice with cremini mushrooms, Asiago cheese, and white truffle aioli). There are a handful of seats at the bar and roughly ten tables in the lounge. If you sit at a table, be sure to place your order with the bartender before grabbing a seat at a table.

MIZNER'S: Named after the eccentric architect who defined much of the flavor of Florida's Gold Coast, this handsome retreat serves beer, wine, cocktails, ports, brandies, and appetizers. Cigars may be purchased here, too (although they must be puffed elsewhere, as this, like most WDW bars, is a nonsmoking venue).

If you're in the mood for a nibble, consider the veal bolognese, PEI mussels (pan-seared with garlic and olive oil), artisanal cheese plate, or sautéed shrimp. Sweet temptations include lemon cheesecake, chocolate banana torte, and seasonal berry gratin. Food is served usually from about 5:30 P.M. until about 10 P.M., while the spirits usually flow until about midnight.

HOT TIP!

Grand Floridian visitors take note: The resort's grand lobby is a divine setting in which to savor a fine wine or a frosty brew. While there's no in-lobby service, guests may buy a drink at Mizner's (see above) and sip it while relaxing on an overstuffed lobby chair or comfy couch. If you time it right, you'll be serenaded by the lobby pianist or a live band.

❤ Disney Dining Plan participant at press time

NARCOOSSEE'S LOUNGE: This upscale bar-within-a-restaurant offers a little bit of everything: appetizers, entrées, desserts, and cocktails (including dessert drinks). There is an extensive list of international wines, 40 of which are available by the glass. How serious are they about wine here? Our last bartender was a certified sommelier. Note that the dress code for this lounge is "business casual." 🐭

POOL BAR: This Grand Floridian pool/beach bar stands by with beer, wine, frozen specialty drinks, soft drinks, and snacks.

Polynesian Village

BAREFOOT BAR: An oasis near the volcano pool, this bar serves beer, wine, frozen tropical drinks (with and without alcohol), and soft drinks. Items of note: frozen strawberry daiquiri and piña colada. (We like 'em mixed together, aka The Lava Flow.) This bar may get a name change in 2015.

TAMBU: Adjoining 'Ohana, this small tiki bar offers appetizers, cocktails, and specialty drinks in a tropical setting. There is seating at the bar and at tables. Note that the table section serves as the waiting area for guests dining at 'Ohana, so it tends to get very busy at mealtimes.

TRADER SAM'S GROTTO GROG: The festive first-floor lounge (expected to open by early 2015) is next to Captain Cook's snack bar. Sam's is a welcome addition to the Disney bar scene, offering tropical drinks and small plates in a richly themed locale.

Pop Century

PETALS: This poolside watering hole serves beer, wine, and cocktails.

Port Orleans French Quarter

MARDI GROGS: Beer, specialty drinks, and snacks are among the offerings at this pool spot.

SCAT CAT'S CLUB: Next to the Sassagoula Floatworks & Food Factory, this large, informal lounge pays tribute to the uniquely American music that is jazz. In fact, live jazz music is presented four nights a week (Wednesday through Saturday, from 8 P.M. till about

midnight). In addition to the usual brews and blends, this spot specializes in Southern drinks—including Hurricanes. There is an appetizer menu, too.

Port Orleans Riverside

MUDDY RIVERS: The poolside bar serves beer, specialty concoctions, and snack items.

RIVER ROOST: Situated in a room designed as a cotton exchange, this spacious lounge features specialty drinks, as well as light hors d'oeuvres. Sink into a comfy chair, beside the glow of the fireplace, and sip cocktails with a Southern flair. There are stools at the bar and tables, too. Live entertainment is presented on select evenings (usually Wednesday through Saturday, from 8 P.M. until about midnight).

Saratoga Springs

THE TURF CLUB: This charming corner of the resort serves all manner of spirits. There's a pool table, too.

Swan & Dolphin

CABANA BAR & BEACH CLUB: Come for the food, stay for drinks. This Dolphin spot's sophisticated air and edgy design is a definite draw for the grown-up set, yet the place doesn't take itself so seriously that it fails to please little ones (think pizza, ice cream, and raspberry lemonade). Grown-up pleasers include the seafood gyro, Cuban sandwich, and veggie wrap.

Classic cocktails such as the Mai Tai, Beachcomber, and Singapore Sling share the stage with creative, original concoctions. Frozen libations abound, as do beer (micro- and macrobrews), rum, and tequila. Wine, scotch, cognac, and cigars are offered, too.

Soft thirst-quenchers include iced teas, lemonade, soda, chocolate milk, and coffees.

IL MULINO NEW YORK TRATTORIA

LOUNGE: A lovely spot (at the Swan) to sip wines and cocktails and/or enjoy the bar menu, this lounge features live music on Friday and Saturday evenings. There are lots of seats at the bar, plus tables and comfy couches. It's usually open for business starting in the late afternoon.

KIMONOS: This Swan lounge, attractively decorated in Japanese style, has a full bar, as well as sushi and other culinary treats. It opens in late afternoon/early evening, and last call is usually between 10:30 P.M. and 1 A.M. The karaoke starts cranking at about 9:30 P.M.

LOBBY LOUNGE: The Dolphin lobby bar serves beer, wine, cocktails, and soft drinks, sometimes accompanied by live piano music. Lobby Lounge hours are generally 4 P.M. until about 11 P.M.

SHULA'S LOUNGE: This small, austere Dolphin saloon within Shula's Steak House features rich wood tones and plush seating— the perfect place to sip a cocktail while playing armchair quarterback.

SPLASH TERRACE: A poolside oasis near the Swan, Splash shares the menu with its Dolphin neighbor, Cabana Bar & Beach Club (see page 307 of this chapter).

TODD ENGLISH'S BLUEZOO BAR: The underwater mojo of Todd's bluezoo restaurant extends to the sizable bar/lounge area (booths and tables augment the bar seating, easily accommodating large parties). In addition to the liquid refreshments, this is a genuine raw bar—many guests order a cocktail with a side of something fishy.

Last call varies, depending on how crowded the place is at any given moment. Figure on getting the boot between 9 P.M. and 11 P.M.

Wilderness Lodge

TERRITORY LOUNGE: Located between Artist Point and Whispering Canyon Cafe, this rustic homage to the explorers of the Great West is a nice spot for a pre-dinner treat. Appetizers, soft drinks, beer, wine, and cocktails are served. The Pomegranate Sparkler is a no-alcohol treat.

TROUT PASS: This poolside bar serves beer, wine, and frozen drinks.

Yacht & Beach Club

ALE AND COMPASS: The nautically themed Yacht Club lobby lounge offers a full drink menu with premium spirits and light appetizers. Coffee (sans liquor) and light breakfast items are served each morning. The lounge is usually open until about midnight. ❤

CREW'S CUP: Styled after a traditional New England waterfront pub, this lounge has a seafaring feel to it. It's next door to the Yachtsman Steakhouse and has well over 25 beers. There is also a tempting menu. This is one of our favorite places to relax after a long day in the parks. Food is usually served from noon until midnight.

HURRICANE HANNA'S WATERSIDE BAR & GRILL: This poolside oasis is a sophisticated yet casual place to sip a beverage and enjoy a savory snack. The menu includes items such as sea salt fries, pulled pork sliders, seared tuna, Hanna's one-third-of-a-pound bacon cheeseburger, and more. Kids' meals come in a small sand bucket, complete with attached shovel. ❤

MARTHA'S VINEYARD: While a full bar is available, a small but satisfying selection of wines from Martha's Vineyard (and other areas) is this Beach Club bar's specialty. Light appetizers are served, too.

Disney Cruise Line

A BIRNBAUM BONUS

310   **Land & Sea Vacations**

312   **Sample Itineraries**

314   **Before You Sail**

324   **All Aboard!**

Walt Disney World, which boasts one of the largest fleets of pleasure craft on the planet, has an inimitable nautical neighbor: Disney Cruise Line. And three of its majestic ocean liners—the award-winning *Magic*, *Dream*, and *Fantasy*—call Central Florida's Port Canaveral home. That's a mere 50 miles from Walt Disney World, making the prospect of pairing a visit to WDW with a Disney Cruise a convenient temptation for many a World traveler.

A voyage with Disney Cruise Line, however, is atypical in a number of ways. First, there's the simultaneous catering to families with kids, and grown-ups *sans* offspring. In fact, each ship has programming designed to draw young and old, and those in between, to entirely different recreational areas. Then there's the innovative "rotational dining system," a lineup of lavish musical productions, deck-shaking dance parties, and, of course, the possibility of a unique grand finale: a full day at Castaway Cay—Disney's private, tropical island.

Like swaying in a hammock in the aforementioned paradise, the process of selecting a cruise package and combining it with a stay at Walt Disney World should be as carefree as possible. Within this Birnbaum bonus chapter, you'll find detailed information meant to ensure that planning a "land and sea" holiday is smooth sailing. *Bon voyage!*

Land & Sea Vacations
Pairing a Disney Cruise with a Walt Disney World Vacation

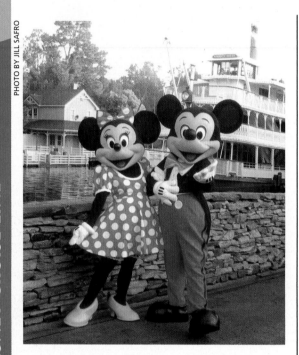

PHOTO BY JILL SAFRO

It's the ultimate surf-and-turf experience for Disney fans—a Walt Disney World vacation that's paired with a Disney Cruise. (What better way to chase the Pirates of the Caribbean attraction than by visiting the Caribbean?! Minus real pirates, of course.) And, with the addition of the *Dream* and the *Fantasy* to the fleet, "land and sea" opportunities are limitless. The pages that follow describe how Land and Sea vacations work and give a brief overview of the Disney Cruise Line fleet.

If you've been to Disney's world before (or read the first 300 or so pages of this book), you know that it is not a small one. In fact, it covers 40 square miles—and with about as many attractions, restaurants, and places to stay as one might expect from an area that size. There are four theme parks, two water parks, two dozen hotels, a dining, shopping, and entertainment district, championship golf courses, boating, fishing, tennis, and more. Add a cruise to the mix, and even seasoned Disney veterans run the risk of becoming overwhelmed.

The good news is that a customized vacation package can include just about everything you'd ever want. That frees you up to focus on an important goal: having fun.

HOT TIP!

Disney Cruise Vacations offers a day-before option at a non-Disney resort with some packages. For information, contact a travel agent or call 800-951-3532.

Surf & Turf

Though "Land and Sea" packages are occasionally offered via *www.disneycruise.com*, most guests build their own vacations (with a little help from DCL or a travel agent). In addition to settling on a travel budget, there are a certain decisions to be made: 1. Do you want to cruise before of after you visit WDW?; 2. How long do you wish to play on land and on sea? 3. Where do you want to stay on Land? 4. Which Disney Cruise Line itinerary is best for you? (See page 312 for a selection of popular itineraries that depart from Central Florida's Port Canaveral.)

Disney Cruise Line Air Program

If you plan to fly to the port, consider allowing the Disney Cruise Vacations Air Program to help you make the arrangements. In addition to lining up round-trip airfare for your whole party, they will secure motor coach ground transportation and baggage transfers.

The service is available in more than 150 cities in the United States, United Kingdom, and Canada. At press time, this service was not included in the price of any Disney Cruise Line vacation packages. For details and pricing call 877-566-0967.

HOT TIP!

While many folks enjoy "Sea and Land" vacations (starting with a cruise), we prefer to begin with a visit to Walt Disney World. That way we are already in the vicinity of the port on sail-away day, thus alleviating any anxiety about flight delays or late arrivals.

To pair a visit to Walt Disney World with a Disney cruise, contact a travel agent or call 800-951-3532. (That's the number to call if you'd like help finding a hotel near Disney Cruise Line's other home ports, too.)

PHOTO BY JILL SAFRO

Combination Vacation

Walt Disney World/Disney Cruise Line combination vacations can include accommodations on land (at a WDW resort) and a stateroom on a Disney ship. In addition to accommodations, shipboard meals, snacks, soft drinks, and entertainment are included with all Disney Cruise Line packages.

What's not included in a "Land and Sea" combination vacation? Meals and beverages at Walt Disney World (unless the WDW Dining Plan is purchased in advance), transfers to Port Canaveral (these may also be purchased in advance), airfare, excursions, meals ashore in ports of call—with the exception of Castaway Cay, where food and soft drinks are included (see page 343), extra gratuities, laundry or valet services, parking at the port, or any other items not specifically included.

What can be added? Just about everything. Options include tickets to Disney World theme and water parks, dinner shows, and more. For details, visit *www.disneycruise.com*, or call 800-951-3532.

Walt Disney World Resort Options

The following is a comprehensive list of Walt Disney World-owned-and-operated resort hotels. For details on these resorts, turn to our *Transportation & Accommodations* chapter. The information was correct at press time but is subject to change. In addition to Walt Disney World, it's possible to book vacations that pair a cruise with a hotel stay in Barcelona, Miami, Vancouver, or other destinations. For additional information, visit *www.disneycruise.com*, or call 800-951-3532.

DELUXE:
Animal Kingdom Lodge (see page 99)
BoardWalk* (see page 91)
Contemporary Resort* (see page 76)
Dolphin* (see page 89)
Grand Floridian Resort & Spa* (see page 80)
Old Key West Resort (see page 97)
Polynesian Village Resort (see page 78)
Saratoga Springs Resort & Spa (see page 96)
Swan* (see page 89)
Wilderness Lodge (see page 82)
Yacht & Beach Club (see page 86)

MODERATE:
Caribbean Beach Resort* (see page 85)
Coronado Springs Resort (see page 101)
Port Orleans French Quarter* (see page 94)
Port Orleans Riverside* (see page 95)

VALUE:
All-Star Movies (see page 98)
All-Star Music (see page 98)
All-Star Sports (see page 98)
Art of Animation (see page 103)
Pop Century (see page 102)

* Direct transportation to Port Canaveral is available from this resort.

Sample Itineraries

Three of the four Disney ships—the *Magic*, *Dream*, and *Fantasy*—are scheduled to cruise out of Port Canaveral, Florida, throughout 2015. (The *Wonder* is sailing from Miami and Vancouver.) What follows is a sampling of the itineraries offered from Port Canaveral, the port closest to Walt Disney World—and most logically paired with a WDW vacation. Note that most include a stop at Disney's private island, Castaway Cay (see page 343). For a complete list of ports and itineraries, visit *www.disneycruise.com*.

3-Night Bahamian Cruise — *Disney Magic*
Itinerary A

DAY	ITINERARY
DAY 1	Check in at Port Canaveral Terminal. Aboard by 4 P.M.
DAY 2	Ashore at Nassau at 9:30 A.M. Aboard by 5:45 P.M.
DAY 3	Ashore at Castaway Cay at 8:30 A.M. Aboard by 4:45 P.M.
DAY 4	Ship at Port Canaveral beginning at 7:30 A.M.

4-Night Bahamian Cruise — *Disney Dream*
Itinerary A

DAY	ITINERARY
DAY 1	Check in at Port Canaveral Terminal. Aboard by 4 P.M.
DAY 2	Ashore at Nassau at 9:30 A.M. Aboard by 5:45 P.M.
DAY 3	Ashore at Castaway Cay at 8:30 A.M. Aboard by 4:45 P.M.
DAY 4	Full day at sea.
DAY 5	Ship at Port Canaveral beginning at 7:30 A.M.

5-Night Bahamian Cruise — *Disney Magic*
Itinerary B

DAY	ITINERARY
DAY 1	Check in at Port Canaveral Terminal. Aboard by 4 P.M.
DAY 2	Ashore at Key West, Florida, at 12:30 P.M. Aboard by 7:30 P.M.
DAY 3	Full day at sea.
DAY 4	Ashore at Nassau at 7 A.M. Aboard by 5:45 P.M.
DAY 5	Ashore at Castaway Cay at 8:30 A.M. Aboard by 4:45 P.M.
DAY 6	Ship at Port Canaveral beginning at 7:30 A.M.

7-Night Eastern Caribbean Cruise — *Disney Fantasy*
Itinerary A

DAY	ITINERARY
DAY 1	Check in at Port Canaveral Terminal. Aboard by 3:45 P.M.
DAY 2	Full day at sea.
DAY 3	Full day at sea.
DAY 4	Ashore at St. Maarten at 8 A.M. Aboard by 6:45 P.M.
DAY 5	Ashore at St. Thomas/St. John U.S. Virgin Islands at 8 A.M. Aboard by 7:30 P.M.
DAY 6	Full day at sea.
DAY 7	Ashore at Castaway Cay at 9:45 A.M. Aboard by 4:45 P.M.
DAY 8	Ship at Port Canaveral beginning at 7:30 A.M.

7-Night Western Caribbean Cruise — *Disney Fantasy*
Itinerary B

DAY	ITINERARY
DAY 1	Check in at Port Canaveral Terminal. Aboard by 3:45 P.M.
DAY 2	Full day at sea.
DAY 3	Ashore at Grand Cayman, Cayman Islands at 1 P.M. Aboard by 5:45 P.M. (This port requires tendering.)
DAY 4	Ashore at Costa Maya, Mexico, at 1 p.m. Aboard by 5:45 P.M.
DAY 5	Ashore at Cozumel, Mexico, at 8:30 A.M. Aboard by 5:45 P.M.
DAY 6	Full day at sea.
DAY 7	Ashore at Castaway Cay at 9:30 A.M. Aboard by 4:45 P.M.
DAY 8	Ship at Port Canaveral beginning at 7:30 A.M.

Before You Sail

What to do, what to do. There are many factors to consider when pairing a cruise package with a stay at Walt Disney World. Among the most important are destination, budget, time available, stateroom needs, and preferred itinerary.

If you want to take the most inexpensive cruise possible, then a shorter cruise in a standard inside stateroom is probably a good choice. If money is no object, consider a 7-night adventure in the super-deluxe Walt Disney Suite. Of course, there are plenty of things in between.

Check Your Calendar

Determining the length of your cruise depends on several things—the first, how much time do you have in your busy schedule to devote to leisure? If your answer is only four days, don't despair: Disney has short cruises to the Bahamas (most of which include a stop at Disney's own private island, Castaway Cay). If you have at least a week to sail, you may choose a 7-night-or-longer cruise to the Caribbean. For details, call 800-910-3659 or visit *www.disneycruise.com*.

www.disneycruise.com

We've done our best to provide accurate, current information regarding all things Disney Cruise Line. That said, rates, itineraries, excursions, and other specifics are subject to change. For additional information or to book a cruise, shore excursion, and more, visit the interactive Website: *www.disneycruise.com*. It's one of the most user-friendly Websites we have ever seen.

Check Your Checkbook

The cost of your cruise is the next issue on the planning board. Budget constraints can be eased in several ways: by taking one of the shorter cruises, choosing a less-expensive stateroom class, and by limiting the number of land tours and excursions you take at the various ports of call. (We often forgo pricey excursions because the ships themselves have so much to offer.) Plan to eat aboard the ship, too—meals and snacks are included in the vacation package, as are many extras, including stage shows, movies, tours, lectures, games, bands, deck parties with Disney characters, and more.

Selecting a Stateroom

Sure, you'd like the largest suite on the ship. No question, you want the biggest verandah. And, of course, you absolutely must have a great view. But if these don't fit your budget, there are other appealing options. Consider this: Every stateroom boasts nautical decor, has ample closet space, a television, and a small safe. Inside staterooms can be a bit less expensive and not much smaller than their outside counterparts; on the *Dream* and the *Fantasy* they have virtual portholes (aka "magical" portholes, these high-tech wonders have HD digital screens). On the other hand, should you decide to splurge, know that there are concierge rooms and larger suites with private verandahs where you can savor a refreshing beverage and read the newest page-turner, periodically taking a moment to gaze out at the sea.

Of course, there are other factors to think about when selecting a stateroom. How many people are in your party? Are you traveling with young children? Perhaps a Deluxe Stateroom would suit your family's needs. These accommodations have queen-size beds, bunk beds for the kids, and a split bath (one room with a sink and a toilet and another with a sink and a shower/tub). A curtained divider provides a bit of privacy.

Of course, there's always the Walt Disney Suite and the Roy O. Disney Suite—so if money is no object, treat your crew to one of these thousand-plus-square-foot homes away from home. No matter what your requirements, chances are good that Disney Cruise Line can meet them.

What's Not Included with a Cruise?

Rest assured that all of your basic vacation needs are covered by the "all-inclusive" price of the cruise. However, there are always "extras" for which you may want to ante up a little cash. Here's a list of items and services that carry an extra charge while aboard Disney ships:

- Child care for tots ages 3 months to 3 years (see pages 320 and 340)
- Port Adventures (aka shore excursions)
- Expenses incurred while on land in ports of call (with the exception of food and most soft drinks at Castaway Cay)
- Alcoholic beverages
- Palo and Remy (These optional, reservations-necessary, adults-only restaurants carry an extra charge: about $25 per person for dinner and brunch at Palo; about $50 per person for champagne brunch and $75 for dinner at Remy.)

- Refreshments at Cove Cafe, Vibe, and any bar or lounge
- Spa treatments
- Arcade games and sports simulators
- Photographs snapped by the ship's photographers
- Internet usage (see page 321)
- Cell phone usage (see page 322)
- Ship-to-shore telephone calls (There is a sizable fee for all calls, incoming and outgoing. Calls within the ship are free.)

With the exception of non-Disney ports of call, all "incidental" charges will be billed to your stateroom, provided that you leave a credit card number upon check-in. It's a good idea to have some cash on hand (we bring about $300, just in case), but there are few chances to use it. Except for tips, cash isn't accepted on the ships. Same goes for Castaway Cay, with the exception of the post office—stamps must be purchased with cash. Most of the non-Disney port shops accept major credit cards, and most accept U.S. currency.

How to Book a Cruise

In addition to using *www.disneycruise.com* or calling Disney Cruise Line (800-910-3659), many guests book through travel agents.

PAYMENT METHODS: Cruise packages, as well as incidentals, gratuities, hotel bills, and deposits, may be paid by credit card (Visa, MasterCard, JCB Card, American Express, Diners Club, Disney Visa, etc.), traveler's check, cashier's check, money order, or personal check. Personal checks must bear the guest's name and address, be drawn on a U.S. bank, and be accompanied by proper identification (a valid driver's license with photo or government-issued photo ID). The reservation number should be written on the face of the check. Checks will not be accepted within 21 days prior to vacation commencement date. Keep in mind that the final payment for a cruise package must be made between 75 and 150 days prior to the cruise, depending on the itinerary and category. Final payment due date varies for special itineraries.

Payments sent via mail should be addressed to: Disney Cruise Line, P.O. Box 277763, Atlanta, GA 30384-7763.

Payments sent via courier service (e.g., FedEx or UPS) should be sent to: Disney Cruise Line, Bank of America, Lockbox Services, Lockbox 277763, 6000 Feldwood Road, College Park, GA 30349 (407-566-3500).

DEPOSIT REQUIREMENTS: When you book a cruise, you'll get a "due date" for a deposit. The deposit is 20 percent of the total fare. Reservations will be canceled if a deposit is not received by the deadline. (Packages that are booked within the final payment due date or in categories IGT, OGT, and VGT get special instructions.)

CANCELLATION POLICY: Cancellations may be made by phone or mail (we prefer the phone). To avoid the sad fate of paying for a canceled cruise, we recommend insuring your trip.

Fees paid for canceling depend on when that call is made. For cruises of less than 10 days

Ground Transfers

Disney Cruise Line provides reliable, friendly service aboard its motor coaches (aka: buses). Getting to the buses is easy. Upon arrival at Orlando International Airport, take a shuttle to the Main Terminal. Once there, proceed to Disney's Magical Express Welcome Center. It's on Level One, Side B. The real bonus here is the baggage handling: For flights before 10 P.M., Disney reps will pull your tagged luggage and make sure it gets delivered to your room. (Guests arriving after 10 P.M. may collect their luggage and proceed to the Magical Express Welcome Center.) From the airport, a bus will take you to Port Canaveral or a WDW hotel. (For guests with transfers included in their cruise package, your bus departure location and information is included in your cruise documentation.) What if you're staying at a resort that's not designated as a departure location or at an off-property hotel? You'll have to get yourself to one of the WDW departure spots to catch a bus to the ship! Here's the pricing for Orlando ground transfers:

TRANSFER TRIP	PRICE*
Airport to select WDW resort (one-way)	Free**
Select WDW resort to Port Canaveral	$35
Round-trip from Orlando International Airport (MCO) to Port Canaveral	$70
Land and Sea vacation (Orlando airport to select WDW resort; WDW resort to Port Canaveral; Port Canaveral to airport)	$70

*Prices are per person, were correct at press time, and are subject to change.
**Disney's Magical Express transportation is a free service for WDW resort guests. For pricing details about transfers to and from other locations, call 800-951-3532.

where embark or debark is a U.S. port, cancellation fees are as follows:

- For all suites and concierge rooms, the deposit is nonrefundable regardless of when the reservation is canceled.
- For each non-suite/concierge stateroom guest, canceling 74 to 45 days before sailing costs the deposit.
- For all rooms, a cancellation within 44 to 30 days costs 50 percent of the vacation price.
- For all staterooms, a cancellation within 29 to 15 days costs 75 percent per guest.
- Should a cruise be canceled less than 14 days ahead, you'll pay for the whole package.

For cruises 10 days or more or less than 10 days where embark and debark is a non-U.S. port, the fees are as follows (this does not apply to cruises out of Port Canaveral, Florida):

- For all suites and concierge rooms, the deposit is non-refundable regardless of when the reservation was canceled.
- For all non-suite/concierge staterooms, canceling within 119 to 56 days before the sailing costs the deposit per guest.
- Canceling within 55 to 30 days costs 50 percent of the vacation cost per guest.
- Canceling within 29 to 15 days costs 75 percent of the vacation package per guest.
- Canceling less than 14 days ahead means you'll pay for the whole package.

What to Pack

"Cruise Casual" is the operative phrase with Disney. Shorts, T-shirts, sundresses, and the like are fine daytime wear. At dinnertime, casual takes on a more formal meaning: Set aside the flip-flops and plan on nice slacks (jeans are okay, except at Palo and Remy) and a collared shirt for men, with real shoes, as opposed to those of the tennis variety. The same goes for women, while dresses are suitable, too. On 7-night-or-longer cruises,

HOT TIP!

Guests who plan to arrive at Port Canaveral the night before setting sail might consider staying at one of these resorts on nearby Astronaut Boulevard:

Country Inns & Suites by Carlson. Rates range from about $89–$129, and there is a shuttle to the cruise terminal; 321-784-8500 or 888-201-1746.

Residence Inn by Marriott. Rates range from about $169–$220; 321-323-1100 or 800-331-3131.

Identification Papers

Unlike a visit to Disney's Epcot, where it only feels as if you're leaving the country, in the case of a Disney Cruise Line vacation, you really do. Given that, you'll need to provide proper proof of citizenship when passing through Customs. U.S. government regulations related to passport requirements are subject to change. Therefore, all guests must have a valid passport for all cruises. Visit *http://travel.state.gov*, or call 877-487-2778 for current requirements.

there is a semi-formal and a formal night. While some folks don black tie and sequins, it's fine to sport a less formal look. On these occasions, the *Personal Navigator* (see page 330) will tip you off as to the appropriate attire. Many guests pack pirate garb, too, in anticipation of "Pirates IN the Caribbean" party night—don't forget to pack your puffy shirt and eye patch. (The Pirate party takes place on most sailings.)

Bathing suits are a must, as are beach shoes, wraps, sunscreen, sunglasses, and hats. Some sundries, such as shampoo, conditioner, and body lotion, are provided in your stateroom. Others are available for purchase, but the prices are steep, and the shops aren't always open (U.S. Customs limits the operating hours).

PACK A DAY BAG: Guests may check in at the port and board the ship as early as 1 P.M., but your checked luggage may not arrive until 6 P.M. (though usually earlier). Keep in mind that you will have access to your stateroom beginning at 1:30 P.M., along with most shipboard amenities, including all pools, so pack your swimsuit in a day bag. This should serve as, or fit in, a carry-on, as checked bags will be out of your hands once you surrender them. (Day bags can't be larger than 9 inches by 14 inches by 22 inches and do not count as part of the two-bag-per-passenger quota.) The bag should also include your passports, valuables, breakable items, and

HOT TIP!

You will always have to show your "Key to the World" card (Disney-issued stateroom key and ID) when disembarking or boarding the ship. Adults also need a government-issued photo ID (a passport is ideal). Note that your WDW MagicBand or hotel key won't work on the ship.

What's in a Name?

A whole lot, when it comes to Disney Cruise Line accommodations. Here's a listing of the types of rooms available on each of the ships. Note that it is possible to request side-by-side staterooms, but it can't be guaranteed. For specifics on staterooms, see page 328.

- Standard Inside Stateroom
- Deluxe Inside Stateroom
- Deluxe Ocean-view Stateroom
- Deluxe Family Ocean-view Stateroom (*Dream* and *Fantasy*)
- Deluxe Ocean-view Stateroom with Navigator's Verandah (*Magic* and *Wonder*)
- Deluxe Ocean-view Stateroom with Verandah
- Deluxe Family Ocean-view Stateroom with Verandah
- Concierge Family Ocean-view Stateroom with Verandah (*Dream* and *Fantasy*)
- Concierge 1-Bedroom Suite with Verandah
- Concierge 2-Bedroom Suite with Verandah (*Magic* and *Wonder*)
- Concierge Royal Suite with Verandah

anything else you might need during those first hours on board. Note that most airlines require that carried-on liquids be in 3.4-ounce-or-smaller containers and fit into one quart-size, clear, plastic zip-top bag.

Booking Shore Excursions

Shore Excursions, aka Port Adventures, are quite popular and fill up early. To book yours, visit *www.disneycruise.com*. To make last-minute arrangements, visit your ship's Port Adventures desk. Note that Port Adventures are not operated by the Walt Disney Company—not even those on Disney's private island, Castaway Cay (see page 343).

For descriptions of all excursions offered in more than 30 worldwide destinations, including Castaway Cay, visit *www.disneycruise.com*. (We considered including all of them here, but that would have added about 600 pages to this book!)

Cancellations or changes to excursion reservations may be made up to 3 days before the start of a cruise to net a full refund. After that, you pay whether you play or not.

How to Get to Port Canaveral

BY PLANE: Fly to Orlando International Airport. We prefer to arrive the night before or take a flight that is scheduled to arrive in the early morning hours. (That helps avoid potential travel delays.) If you get there on the early side, you can make a day of it. And, if your flight is delayed, you'll still have a shot at making it to the port before the ship sails. (When you book your cruise, ask about the check-in cut-off time. Don't be late!)

FROM THE AIRPORT: As you get off the shuttle and enter the main terminal, proceed directly to the Disney Magical Express Welcome Center. It's on Level 1, Side B of the terminal. After your party has checked in, a Disney rep will direct you toward a motor coach. Don't worry about checked luggage. For guests with transfers, all bags bearing appropriate tags will be claimed by Disney and delivered to your stateroom. (If you are driving to the ship, see information to the right.)

The following details apply specifically to cruises departing from Port Canaveral, Florida. For details for other departure ports (such as Miami, Vancouver, or Barcelona), call 800-910-3659 or visit *www.disneycruise.com*.

DISNEY MOTOR COACH: The bus trip from Orlando International Airport or a Disney World resort to Port Canaveral takes about 90 minutes (without traffic). While onboard, you can fill out paperwork (though it is best to do this ahead of time). There's a restroom onboard. Motor coach transportation may be purchased with a cruise package.

CAR SERVICE: Noris Limousine and Florida Towncar offer friendly, reliable service between Orlando International Airport (MCO) and Port Canaveral. For rates, information, or to make a reservation with Noris Limousine, call 407-240-4533, or visit *www.norislimousine.com*. For Florida Towncar, go to *www.floridatowncar.com*, or call 800-525-7246 or 407-277-5466. Reservations are necessary, and cancellations must be made at least 48 hours in advance. Disney Cruise Line's reservations department can take your car service request, too.

AUTOMOBILE: Disney Cruise Line's Port Canaveral Terminal is located on the north side of "A" Cruise Terminals; 9155 Charles M. Rowland Drive, Port Canaveral, Florida, 32920. It's about a 90-minute drive from Orlando International Airport and from Disney World. The parking facility, which is operated by the Canaveral Port Authority, accepts cash (U.S. currency), Visa, MasterCard, and traveler's checks only. Personal checks are not accepted. Parking costs about $15 per day. Rates are subject to change. Guests may also make a reservation for a parking space prior to arrival. To do so, have a credit card handy and visit *http://portcanaveral.com/cruising/parking.php*.

From Orlando International Airport, take State Road (S.R.) 528 East (Beachline

Expressway). Continue over the Indian River and the Banana River. Turn right onto S.R. 401, which will loop and head north over the channel locks. Stay in the right-hand lane and follow signs to the "A" Cruise Terminals. S.R. 528 is a toll road.

If you are driving from Walt Disney World, take State Road 536 East to 417 (the GreeneWay). Follow 417 to S.R. 528 East (Beachline Expressway). At the fork in the road, veer right to stay on S.R. 528. Continue over the Indian and Banana rivers. Turn right onto S.R. 401. Stay in the right lane and follow signs leading to the "A" Cruise Terminals. Note that 417 and 528 are toll roads.

Guests who are driving from North Florida should take I-95 South exit #205 for S.R. 528 East (Beachline Expressway). Continue over the Indian and Banana rivers. Turn right onto S.R. 401. Stay in the right lane and follow signs to "A" Cruise Terminals.

Drivers originating in South Florida should take I-95 North. Exit at #205 for S.R. 528 East (The Beachline). Take S.R. 528 to S.R. 401. Keep to the right and follow the signs to "A" Cruise Terminals.

GETTING TO PORT CANAVERAL FROM WALT DISNEY WORLD WITHOUT A CAR:

Disney Cruise Line has buses to take guests directly from Walt Disney World resorts. One-way transfers cost $35 per person, while $70 will cover the round-trip. Guests with transfers will get a letter in their resort room with departure details. Bell services will automatically pick up luggage when transfers have been prearranged. (Car services make the trip to and from Port Canaveral, too. See page 318 for details.)

Customized Travel Tips

TRAVELING WITH BABIES

Cribs: If you are traveling with a baby, it is possible to have a playpen-like, foldaway crib sent to your stateroom. (The cribs are 39.8 inches long, 28.25 inches wide, and 31.25 inches high.) Request one when you make a reservation, and confirm it before leaving home. (If you booked your cruise package through a travel agent, call said agent with requests such as this.) Supplies are limited. Bring a blanket, as the cribs come with fitted sheets only.

Diaper Service: It is possible to have a disposable diaper system sent to your stateroom. You can request it when you make a reservation, or speak with your Stateroom Host or Hostess upon arrival.

Tag Your Bags

Flying to Orlando International Airport for a cruise out of Port Canaveral? After you book your cruise and purchase ground transfers, you'll get a personalized info packet in the mail. Included in this valuable envelope will be colorful luggage tags. We cannot overemphasize the importance of affixing these tags to all checked luggage. Why? Once you say good-bye to your bags at the airport, you won't see them again until they arrive at your stateroom. Disney reps collect bags and deliver them to your stateroom by 6 P.M.

If you arrive by car or bus, drop your bags with porters at the terminal. They will be delivered to your stateroom for you. Guests who arrive from Walt Disney World via Disney motor coach need to tag their bags, too. (Tags come with cruise documents.) The driver will see to it that tagged bags are removed from the bus and loaded on the ship.

If you'd rather not haul your bags off the ship, expect to use a similar color-coding method at the end of your cruise (this applies to all cruises). A set of tags will be left in your stateroom. Slap them on your bags, make a note of the color, and place them in the hall on the last night of the cruise. (Be sure to keep items such as pajamas, sundries, and clothes for the morning in a day bag.) Look for them in the designated section of the terminal once you debark. Guests participating in onboard airline check-in don't have to claim their bags until their plane lands at their home airport. Restrictions apply. Note that it is not mandatory that guests surrender their bags on the last night of a cruise—but they are responsible for removing all of their luggage from the ship in the morning.

Food: Staterooms on the *Wonder* have a small "beverage cooler," which maintains a temperature of approximately 55 degrees. Formula and food can be stored safely within the unit. (*Magic*, *Dream*, and *Fantasy* staterooms have small refrigerators.) At least one shop on board sells diapers, formula, and a limited selection of food. (The shop isn't always open, as U.S. Customs limits its hours.) If you'd like to save money, pack as many baby rations as possible. Round-the-clock room service means you will never get caught with a screaming, hungry little one and no means of quelling the hunger pangs. Note that homemade baby food is not permitted on board any Disney ship.

Cold and Flu Advisory

Disney Cruise Line follows extraordinary sanitation efforts to ensure the safety and comfort of guests. Even so, people can get sick. If you or a member of your party experience any symptom of illness (cold, flu, etc.) within 72 hours of sailing, you may be evaluated by a medical team. (If necessary, Cruise Line representatives will direct you to someone to help your party make alternate plans.) Fees apply at the Medical Center.

Once on board, all guests are asked to wash their hands frequently and thoroughly, as this is a highly effective barrier to spreading germs. If you or someone in your party does become ill during your trip, head directly to the Health Center. You'll be taken care of there, and immediate treatment will help limit the potential impact to others.

Babysitting: Onboard babysitting is available for tots age 12 weeks to 3 years. The cost is $9 an hour for the first child, with a one-hour minimum. Each additional child (who must be the first child's sibling) is $8 per hour. The service is offered in the ship's nursery. Reservations can be made at *www.disneycruise.com* or on board (based on availability). In-room babysitting is not offered on any ship.

Other Supplies: Diapers, pacifiers, pool toys, and more can be purchased on board. The ships' shops aren't always open, so take inventory and plan ahead to avoid being caught short. If it's an emergency, inquire at Guest Services. They can help with just about any onboard crisis.

Bottle sterilizers and warmers are available at the Guest Services desk. You can order supplies

in advance through Babies Travel Lite (see Lighten Your Luggage, on page 321, for details).

TRAVELERS WITH DISABILITIES: Measures have been taken to make your stay as comfortable and effortless as possible. Disney Cruise Line offers special equipment and facilities for guests with disabilities. Each ship has staterooms that are equipped for guests using wheelchairs. They have ramped bathroom thresholds, open bed frames, bathroom and shower handrails, fold-down shower seats, handheld showerheads, and lowered towel and closet bars. Open-captioning is available for stateroom televisions and for some onboard video monitors. Stateroom communication kits may be reserved upon request. They include door-knock and phone alerts, phone amplifier, bed shaker notification, a strobe light smoke detector, and a text typewriter (aka TTY). There is no charge for the kit, but supplies are limited. Make your needs known when you make your reservation and confirm them prior to sailing. Wheelchair-accessible restrooms are available in several common areas on board. There are accessible pool lifts on the *Magic*, *Dream*, and *Fantasy*. A small number of sand wheelchairs are available on Castaway Cay. American Sign Language interpretation is available for live performances on various cruise dates. (The service is not available on every cruise, so be sure to start planning your trip as far in advance as possible.) For additional information or to make special requests, ask your reservationist. For more information via TTY (text typewriter), please call 407-566-7455.

TRAVELERS WITHOUT CHILDREN: This being a Disney cruise, one could argue that you—the footloose, fancy-free folks—are on their turf. And, as such, you might expect to have youngsters underfoot at all times. This is simply not the case. The Disney ships were designed with three specific types of vacationers in mind: families, kids, and grown-ups without kids. On board, there is an adults-only deck area, complete with its own pool (not to mention music and games). There's a gourmet restaurant (two on the *Dream* and *Fantasy*) and a cozy coffee bar. It goes without saying that those spots, as well as several lounges, are strictly for the grown-up set (as in adults with legal proof of age). Plus, there are countless other ways to enjoy a grown-up getaway in the various ports of call. With that in mind, Castaway Cay (Disney's private island) guarantees you and your ilk a piece of prime beachfront real estate where you can bask in the sun or read a novel in the shade without the fear of sand being kicked in your face. You can even have a massage in a cabana overlooking the ocean. Can you manage to spend days on end without encountering the wee ones of our species? No way. But who'd want to?

MEDICAL MATTERS: The Health Center, located forward on Deck 1, is open daily to assist with any medical emergencies or health concerns. Regular hours are from 9:30 A.M. to 11 A.M. and from 4:30 P.M. to 7 P.M. All Disney ships have a physician and nurse on call 24 hours a day (even while in port) for conditions that require immediate attention. Health services are provided by a company independent of Disney Cruise Line, and standard prevailing fees will be charged for all services. Fees will be charged to your stateroom account.

In extreme cases, Disney Cruise Line will arrange to have a passenger taken to the nearest port to receive medical care.

The cost of this varies with the location of the ship and the nearest port. Because all health care provided qualifies as "care outside the United States," you will be responsible for paying any charges incurred while on board prior to debarkation and submitting the request for

Medicine Storage

All staterooms on the *Magic*, *Dream*, and *Fantasy* have a mini fridge (perfectly suitable for storing medicine), but staterooms on the *Wonder* have a "beverage cooler." They are fine for storing food, but not necessarily medication (especially if it requires a stable temperature). Guests who need to store medicine should visit the ship's Medical Center or Guest Services, or request a small refrigerator. Availability is limited, so ask for one at the same time you reserve your cruise package. Call to confirm it before you leave.

coverage to your insurance carrier (all paperwork will be provided).

If you get sick while on shore, your guide should direct you to your ship's tour director at the dock, who will help you get back to the ship.

Regarding younger passengers, know that any child exhibiting symptoms of illness will not be allowed to participate in the youth activities or be cared for in the ship's nursery. No exceptions.

Fingertip Reference Guide

BUSINESS SERVICES: Wait a minute, aren't you here to relax? For those of you who must get a little work done while at sea, there are some business services available for an additional charge. Among them are fax transmission, copies, and AV equipment. Wireless Internet service is available throughout the ships (including staterooms) for a fee. Guests access the Web via cell phone and various personal computing devices. Computer stations are available at the Internet Café on the *Magic* and *Wonder*, and computer devices are available for rental on the *Dream* and *Fantasy* (inquire about computer rentals at the ships' Guest Services desk). Note that the Wi-Fi service at sea can best be described as "low speed." Very low. Expect lots of buffering time and dropped connections. All staterooms have phones (ship-to-shore rates apply), and electrical outlets are laptop friendly. Note that the ships' computers don't accept uploads and do not run any Microsoft Office applications (so any attachments from associated e-mail accounts cannot be opened). There is, however, a handy printer at the ready. Are you planning on holding meetings during your cruise? For details on business services, visit *www.disneymeetings.com*.

Lighten Your Luggage

Traveling with an infant or toddler? Life just got easier for you! It's now possible to order baby supplies online and have them delivered directly to your stateroom. This Disney Cruise Line exclusive is provided by a company called Babies Travel Lite and offers more than 1,000 brand-name products (diapers, baby food, formula, etc.). Access the service by visiting *www.disneycruise.com*.

Getting Around It

Disabled travelers already know that travel requires a lot of advance planning. Disney has equipped all of its ships with a variety of amenities geared toward those guests with special needs.

Wheelchair-accessible staterooms are equipped with ramp entrances to bathrooms, fold-down shower seats, handheld shower-heads, lowered towel and closet racks, a bathroom phone, and emergency call buttons.

There is a limited number of sand wheelchairs available on Castaway Cay (first come, first served). **Note:** If you will need a wheelchair throughout the cruise, you are encouraged to bring your own.

Throughout the ship, there are wheelchair-accessible restrooms.

Pool lifts are available on the *Magic*, *Dream*, and *Fantasy*.

Guests with hearing disabilities need not miss any of the fun on board. In-cabin TVs can be equipped with open-captioning, and assisted-listening devices are available at most theaters and show rooms. Also available are communication kits equipped with alarm clock, door-knock, and telephone alerts with bed shaker notification. Make your needs known when you book your cruise.

CAMERA NEEDS: By all means, bring a camera. Memory cards and accessories are sold on board. There are also roving photographers capturing moments throughout the day. You'll find shots taken at "static locations" (e.g., character sets in the lobby) are available for viewing at photo kiosks at Shutters (the photo store on all Disney ships). Unlike the PhotoPass system at Walt Disney World, these photos may only be viewed and purchased during the cruise. Pictures taken by roaming photographers (e.g., in the dining rooms, by the pool, on Castaway Cay, etc.) may be viewed, printed, and purchased at Shutters on all four ships. Photos can be purchased on a single CD—one-stop shopping. The photos are very high in quality (and in price).

DRINKING LAWS: The drinking age on the ships is 21 and is strictly enforced. Valid government-issued photo ID is required. Disney Cruise Line reserves the right to refuse alcohol sales to anyone. On cruises departing from European countries where the legal age is lower than 21, a legal guardian who is sailing with a passenger

between the ages of 18 and 20 may sign a waiver allowing their charge to imbibe.

MAIL: Letters and postcards may be mailed from the post office at Castaway Cay. Stamps are the only things available for purchase here (cash only). It is also possible to mail items from other ports—it's just less convenient. If you plan to buy stamps from the Castaway Cay post office, do so early. The office is operated by Bahamian authorities and may not be open late in the day. Even if it's closed, you can still mail letters from the post office, and items will be delivered with a Castaway Cay postmark. Note that postcards and stamps may be purchased on the ship.

MONEY MATTERS: There is no need for cash on the ship. You can apply a credit card to your account during the check-in process. (Most major credit cards, including MasterCard, JCB, Visa, and American Express, are accepted.) From then on, all you'll need to do is sign for extras you want (including excursions booked on the ship), and these amounts will be charged to that card.

Cash or credit cards will be necessary for meals, taxis, and other purchases made in all ports but Castaway Cay (where a stateroom key is accepted in all cases except for stamps, which must be bought with cash). A few hundred dollars should suffice. Standard gratuities are automatically attached to your cruise folio. Extra gratuities may be charged to a stateroom or paid in cash. Special envelopes will be delivered to

HOT TIP!

If you plan to use your cell phone during your cruise, be sure to check with your wireless provider before leaving home. Ask if you will be able to get service through them while on board and how much voice, data, and text service costs—including roaming rates.

your stateroom. They may be used to present extra gratuities and/or receipts for prepaid tips.

Automated teller machines may be available in ports of call, but there are none on the ship. Be sure the machine dispenses U.S. currency before you use it.

SMOKING: All Disney ships are, for the most part, smoke-free zones. Smoking (including e-cigarettes) is prohibited in all staterooms and verandahs. (Guests who violate this policy are subject to a $250 deep-cleaning fee.) There are designated smoking areas on each ship.

TELEPHONE CALLS: All staterooms have phones with ship-to-shore capability. Rates range from about $7–$9.50 per minute (rates are subject to change). Toll-free and collect calls can't be placed from ship phones. Wireless service is available in staterooms (fees apply). Be sure to check with your mobile carrier (before you leave home) for talk and text rates and roaming fees. Note that text rates are usually lower than talk rates. Some ports have pay phones (you will need an international calling card to use them).

TIPPING: Some servers, such as bartenders, get an automatic 15 percent gratuity each time you call upon their services. That said, folks such as your dining room servers and stateroom host or hostess rely on guests to tip them appropriately. Suggested gratuity amounts will be posted to your account during the cruise (it's okay to leave more if you deem the service to be outstanding). If you prefer to pay in cash, inform Guest Services at the beginning of the cruise. For those guests dining at Palo, the gratuity amount is at your discretion.

WEDDINGS: Whether you are saying your "I do's" for the first time, committing yourselves to each other, or renewing your vows, Disney Cruise Line has the means to make the occasion exceptionally memorable. Ceremonies may be performed on the ship or at Castaway Cay. Some happy couples invite family members along for the trip, while others prefer to have this time to themselves. For details, call 321-939-4610, or contact your travel agent. Call as far in advance as possible and before you book your cruise.

All Good Things

How time flies when you're having fun. You blink and it's time to go home! Here are a few tips about the debarkation process.

The day before your return to the debarkation terminal, you'll receive an information packet that includes a set of colored luggage tags. The color coding designates the area of the terminal in which you can pick them up. Be sure to remove the original tags from the inbound trip before you put new tags on all bags. (Guest Services has extra tags.) You'll also get a U.S. Customs form when applicable. Hand this form in as you leave the terminal (one form per family).

On the night before debarkation, you'll place luggage outside your stateroom. (Bags will be collected and delivered to a color-coded area at the terminal.) Keep valuables, clothing for debarkation, medications, tickets, passports, and other key documents with you. (You have the option of "express walk off" if you're able to take your own bags off the ship in the morning.) Your waitstaff will tell you about last-morning breakfast options. After breakfast, it's time to leave the ship, taking all your happy memories and, quite possibly, the promise to return again soon. Of course, guests participating in onboard airline check-in don't have to claim bags until their plane lands at their home airport. Certain restrictions apply.

About to begin the "land" part of your vacation? Fetch your bags in the terminal and make a beeline for the bus depot. Flash your Key to the World card (to show you purchased the transfer) and climb aboard. You're going to Disney World!

All Aboard!

The moment you cross the gangway, you'll realize this vessel is no ordinary home away from home. Step into the grand, multistory atrium, and, amidst the happy hubbub, your presence is made known in dramatic fashion—with a heartfelt announcement for all to hear. And so begins your high-seas adventure.

The *Disney Magic, Wonder, Dream,* and *Fantasy* rank among the world's finest ocean-going vessels. The ships are casually elegant and designed to capture the majesty of early ocean liners. They're equipped to satisfy most cruisers, with a mix of traditional seafaring diversions and classic Disney touches. Though some theming and entertainment vary from ship to ship, the accommodations and amenities are similar. As is the service, which is expertly provided by a cast of thousands (representing dozens of countries). All staterooms aboard the quartet of ships are a cut above normal cruising quarters—with an average of 25 percent more space than industry standard. The ships were designed to lure families and grown-ups without offspring to entirely different recreational areas. So, cast aside any preconceived notions you may have about cruising, and expect the unexpected.

Checking In

No matter where it is they call home—be it Bangkok or Boca—all Disney Cruise Line guests begin their respective journeys by checking in at a port terminal. Most Bahamas- and Caribbean-bound guests leaving from Port Canaveral check in at the "A" Terminal. Guests may choose from several different queues at check-in: concierge,

Castaway Club (for repeat guests), and general check-in. For details on other ports the ships may visit throughout 2015, go to *www.disneycruise.com* or call 800-910-3659.

Though no one may board the ship until 1 P.M., guests are welcome to arrive earlier—and guests who check in online choose assigned times in advance. (All guests must board the ship by 3:45 P.M.) The terminal has restrooms and ample seating to relax in while waiting to board. (At Port Canaveral, Florida, there's also a nifty model of the ship to give you a preview of the real thing.) And, if little ones get antsy, there's lots of room for them to roam around, plus a TV that runs a loop of Disney cartoons. Mickey Mouse and his friends occasionally greet guests in the terminal, too.

Okay, we may have gotten ahead of ourselves. Before you can enter the main part of the terminal, all members of your party must go through a security checkpoint. It's a lot like airport security, so save the holey socks for the second day of your trip (you may be asked to remove your shoes, along with jackets, glasses, belts, etc.). Since kids must go through the security check, too, we recommend having snacks and games to entertain them while you wait (in case the line is more than a few minutes long). Once you've cleared security, your whole party needs to go to the check-in counter so ID photos may be taken.

At the counter, you will be asked to present a valid passport for yourself and each member of your party (see page 317). This is also where you'll be asked for all of your completed cruise paperwork (which can also be completed via the

Internet at *www.disneycruise.com* under the "My Online Check-in" section; be sure to select your port arrival time, print and sign the forms, and remember to bring them with you) and a major credit card. This card will be the one to which all of your extra cruise expenses are charged. If you'd like to split expenses with another guest staying in your room, it is possible to register two credit cards. Once the cruise begins, you'll use your stateroom key—aka Key to the World—card to make purchases and to open your stateroom door. The card also serves as ID for debarking and reboarding purposes (though all ports of call also require a photo ID such as a driver's license for guests over age 18). If you'd prefer that any member of your party not have charging privileges, advise a representative at check-in (or indicate your preference when you check in online).

Once the check-in process is complete, take a peek at your watch. Is it before 1 P.M.? If so, sit back, relax, and wait for the boarding process to begin. You could also use the extra time to register kids for shipboard youth activities. If it's after 1 P.M., wait for your boarding number to be called (every party receives one when they check in). When your number's called, grab the kids and your day bags and head for the gangway. All aboard!

The Boarding Experience

After you slip through the entry portal, you'll enter a subdued hallway. This is where you may have your "pre-cruise" photo taken by a Cruise Line photographer. Try to look as stressed out as possible. That'll make the "post-cruise" shots that much more enjoyable. (You can buy the photo on the ship later that day or soon after. Just stop by Shutters, the ship's photo shop.)

On the far side of the photo-op area, there's a door leading to a gangway. Cross it and you'll be deposited in the ship's grand lobby—a dramatic backdrop for a dramatic entrance.

Depending on the time (staterooms are usually ready by 1:30 P.M.) and your level of starvation, you may want to make a quick stop, change, and head out for lunch. Pools are usually open all afternoon. After that, a visit to the stateroom is imperative, as the mandatory safety drill takes place at 4 P.M. on all Disney ships. Once the safety drill is complete, you may head back to your

room to prepare for the sailaway deck celebration known as Adventures Away (*Magic* and *Wonder*) and Sailing Away (*Dream* and *Fantasy*). If you've got an early dinner seating, this is the ideal time to change into your evening attire.

Finally, we simply cannot overemphasize the importance of making reservations for spa treatments and for Palo and Remy (adults-only eateries) as early as possible. (It's best to book before the trip begins, via *www.disneycruise.com*.) Make last-minute spa appointments at the spa itself. For Palo, which begins accepting reservations at about 1 P.M. on day one of the cruise, head for Fathoms (*Magic*), WaveBands (*Wonder*), or D Lounge (*Dream* and *Fantasy*). Reservations for Remy (upscale dining for grown-ups on the *Dream* and *Fantasy*) may be made here, too. Plan to register children for youth activities in the terminal or soon after boarding.

The Disney Ships

The Disney ships are equipped to satisfy even the most savvy of cruisers, with a mix of traditional seafaring diversions and Disney touches. The ships' classic exteriors recall the majesty of early ocean liners. Guests enter a three-story atrium, where traditional definitions of elegance expand to include bronze character statues and subtle cutout character silhouettes along a grand staircase. Recreation areas are designed to draw families and kid-free adults to different parts of the ship. By day, fun in the sun alternates with touring, lunch, indoor distractions, and perhaps even a little bingo action. Evenings give way to sunset sail-away celebrations, themed dining experiences, and theatrical extravaganzas.

Decked Out

Here's the deck-by-deck rundown, from top to bottom (the first section of this deck-specific data refers to the *Magic* and *Wonder*; the section that follows covers the *Dream* and *Fantasy*):

MAGIC AND WONDER

DECK 11: On the *Magic* and *Wonder*, you'll find the teen club Vibe (though access to the club is on Deck 10). This venue is exclusively available to teenage guests (see page 340).

DECK 10: Known as the Wide World of Sports Deck (*Magic* and *Wonder*), we find it a perfect late-night place to watch the moon and stars. There's also a basketball court. And this is one of the best places to be during the sail-away party. Palo is here, too (see page 333). For adults only, this dining spot offers fine cuisine and panoramic views. The Disney *Wonder* has the Outlook Café, too.

DECK 9: Pampering, Disney style, can be enjoyed in the soothing Spa & Salon (Vista on the *Wonder*, Senses on the *Magic*). At the spa, guests may experience treatments in the spa villas, as well as a little Rest & Relaxation on the outdoor verandah. Fitness-minded folk can get a one-on-one fitness consultation. There's lots of exercise equipment, saunas, a steam room, and spa treatments. Personal training is offered too. (For details, see page 343.)

Deck 9 is where you'll find the ships' pools: Quiet Cove (for adults); Mickey's Pool (*Wonder* kids' pool), Twist 'n' Spout splash zone (*Magic*) and AquaDunk and AquaLab (waterslide and kids' water zone on the *Magic*), plus a kids' slide and a splash zone for little ones; and Goofy's

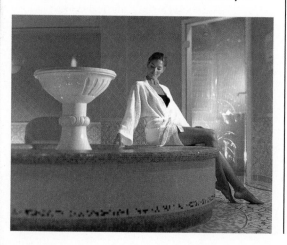

Pool (for families). This deck is also home to Cove Cafe (a coffee bar/lounge for adults only), Quarter Masters (arcade), Goofy's Galley, Pinocchio's Pizzeria, Pluto's Dog House, Topsider (*Wonder*), and Cabanas, Daisy's De-Lites, Pete's Boiler Bites, Frozone Treats, and Eye Scream (*Magic*).

DECK 5: Kids have the run of more than half of this deck. It's one of the largest dedicated areas of children's space afloat, with comprehensive, interest-specific activities.

The Buena Vista Theatre is also located here on all ships. A full-screen cinema with Dolby Sound and 3-D technology, it offers films every day, featuring Disney classics and first-run releases. It hosts guest speakers on occasion, too.

DECK 4: Here you'll find the Walt Disney Theatre, Shutters (photo shop), and Animator's Palate (restaurant). The *Magic* has D Lounge, and the *Wonder* offers Studio Sea. This is also a lovely deck on which to enjoy a leisurely stroll, a jog, or a nice nap.

The Walt Disney Theatre is a grand venue that features one of the most sophisticated show settings at sea or on land. The formal theater boasts extraordinary lighting and technical facilities, and showcases up to three distinct Broadway-style musical productions (each with a decidedly Disney touch) during each cruise.

Animator's Palate is a cheerful restaurant that offers creatively prepared cuisine in a room that features a colorful masterpiece of synchronized light and sound. Deck 4 on the *Magic* and *Wonder* is also the place where you can find a duo of shops selling Disney Cruise Line–themed clothing for the family, character merchandise, collectibles, specialty items, jewelry, and sundries (see pages 341–342 for more details).

DECK 3: This is the place for dining and dancing on the *Magic* and *Wonder*; After Hours (*Magic*) and Route 66 (*Wonder*) are adult-oriented evening entertainment districts that offer themed clubs (see pages 336–337 for details). Fathoms (*Magic*) and WaveBands (*Wonder*) often have themed parties—and don't forget the room's biggest attraction . . . bingo! There is a sports bar (Diversions on the *Wonder*, O'Gill's on the *Magic*); Radar Trap (*Wonder*) and Sea Treasures (*Magic*) are duty-free shops; Keys (on the *Magic*) and Cadillac Lounge (on the *Wonder*) are casual yet sophisticated places to relax and listen to live piano music; and Promenade Lounge is a place to enjoy a drink and hear music (on the *Magic* and *Wonder*). Adjacent to the Promenade Lounge is the Internet Cafe. Also here are Parrot Cay (*Wonder*), an island-inspired restaurant; Carioca's (*Magic*), an eatery inspired by Rio de Janeiro; and Lumière's, serving continental cuisine (on the *Magic*). Lumière's has a French flair and a beautiful mural of Disney's *Beauty and the Beast*. Its counterpart on the *Wonder*, Triton's, has an underwater-like setting of blues, greens, and purples. Guest Services is also on this deck and is open 24 hours a day. The Port Adventures (aka shore excursions) desk is nearby.

DECK 2: All Disney ships have staterooms on this deck. Mid-ship is where you'll find Edge, the tween-only hangout for 11- to 14-year-olds. The interactive play area has a lab with child-friendly computers, video game consoles, arts and crafts tables, TVs, and comfy couches. Kids can also sing karaoke, go on scavanger hunts, and more.

DECK 1: This is where you will find the ship's Health Center. There are some staterooms located here, too.

DECKS 1, 2, 5, 6, 7, AND 8: Shipboard accommodations are spread over these decks.

DREAM AND FANTASY

DECK 14: The pinnacle of these sister ships, Deck 14 is the site of Outlook, a lounge that offers sweeping ocean vistas in addition to adult beverages.

DECK 13: Here you'll find Edge (tweens hangout), Currents (open-air bar), and Goofy's Sports Deck. This is also where concierge guests may enjoy a private sundeck. On the *Fantasy*, there's Satellite Falls—a waterfall-endowed wading pool for guests age 18 and older.

DECK 12: This is the home of the luxurious Senses Spa & Salon (which extends to Deck 11), Meridian (lounge), Palo, and Remy (both are upscale eateries for grown-ups; Remy is trés indulgent). Grown-up guests may sip spirits and soft drinks at Waves Bar (*Dream*). Deck 12 is also the site of AquaLab (*Fantasy*) and mini-golf and the AquaDuck water coaster (*Dream* and *Fantasy*).

DECK 11: On the *Dream* and *Fantasy*, this a destination deck for hungry guests: Cove Cafe (coffee bar for adults); Cabanas (buffet); and Flo's Cafe, a quick-service eatery composed of three stations (Luigi's Pizza, Tow Mater's Grill, and Fillmore's Favorites). Also on this deck are Eye Scream and Frozone Treats. Deck 11 is home to Mickey's Pool, Quiet Cove Pool, Donald's Pool, Nemo's Reef (splash zone), and Arr-cade.

DECK 10, 9, 8, 7, 6, AND 2: On the *Dream* and *Fantasy*, these decks are devoted primarily to staterooms.

DECK 5: Deck 5 is kid-central—and they wouldn't want it any other way! In addition to the It's a Small World Nursery (see page 340), this is the site of the kids' programming areas known as Disney's Oceaneer Club and Lab (page 340), as well as Vibe (teen club). It's also the site of the Buena Vista (movie) Theatre's balcony. Bibbidi Bobbidi Boutique (*Fantasy*) and Pirate's League (princess and pirate makeovers) are here, too (*Dream* and *Fantasy*).

DECK 4: Here you'll find the Buena Vista Theatre (movies), Vista Gallery (art), and Shutters (photo shop). The Walt Disney Theatre is a grand venue that showcases Broadway-style productions (with a distinct Disney flair) during each cruise. This venue extends to Deck 5.

Also found on Deck 4 of the *Dream* and *Fantasy*: D Lounge (family lounge and nightclub) and the ships' respective adults-only entertainment zones. Among the offerings in The District on the Dream: Skyline (lounge with panoramic views of various city skylines), District Lounge, Evolution (dance club), a sports bar called 687, and Pink (a champagne lounge). On the *Fantasy*, expect to find these spots in the Europa entertainment district: La Piazza (a lounge that celebrates Italian plazas), Skyline (bar with panoramic views of famous cities), O'Gill's (sports pub), Ooh La La (an elegant champagne bar inspired by a French boudoir), and The Tube (a dance club with a London Underground motif).

DECK 3: This deck is home to the Art Deco–inspired lobby, the Walt Disney Theatre (stage shows), a bar, shops, and restaurants. Bon Voyage lounge is on the port side of the grand lobby. Beyond this imbibing zone are the ship's shops: Mickey's Mainsail, Whitecaps, and Sea Treasures.

Animator's Palate is a cheerful restaurant that offers creatively prepared cuisine in an impeccably designed dining room (for additional information on the restaurant, see page 331).

Other Deck 3 dining options include Royal Palace (*Dream*) and Royal Court (*Fantasy*).

Guest Services, which is open around the clock, is also located on Deck 3.

DECK 2: The Enchanted Garden eatery.

DECKS 2, AND 5–12: Shipboard accommodations are spread over these decks.

DECK 1: The Health Center is on Deck 1.

Staterooms

The accommodations on Disney's ships range from standard inside rooms to suites with verandahs. All staterooms are a cut above the standard cruising cabin. On average, Disney's staterooms offer more space, most have a split bath (one room with a sink and toilet and another with a sink and a shower/tub), and the majority of them are outside rooms with ocean vistas—many with verandahs.

Staterooms are decorated in a nautical theme with natural woods and imported tiles. Universal amenities include a TV, Wave phones that allow

you to call or text another member of your party while on board (two phones are included per stateroom—extras may be rented), telephone with voice mail (and ship-to-shore capability), an in-room safe, a room service menu (in the Directory of Services book), and lots of drawer space. The *Magic*, *Dream* and *Fantasy* also come equipped with small refrigerators. (On the *Wonder*, there's a "cooling box" instead of a fridge. It's chilly enough to store most perishables, but not medication.) Note that the queen bed cannot be split into 2 twin beds on the *Magic*. After that, different types of accommodations—which are labeled by category—offer different amenities (verandahs are included in the square footage):

MAGIC AND *WONDER*

CATEGORIES 11A–11C: Standard inside staterooms. They have a queen bed or two twin beds, a single convertible sofa, a privacy divider, and a bath. Each room measures 184 square feet and sleeps up to 3 or 4.

CATEGORY 10A–10C: Deluxe inside staterooms. These accommodations are similar to those found in categories 11A–11C but have 214 square feet of space and a split bath.

CATEGORIES 9A–9D: Deluxe ocean-view staterooms. These come with a queen or two twin beds, a single convertible sofa, a privacy divider, and split bath. Rooms on Deck 1 have two small windows, while those on Deck 2 and above feature one large window. Each room is 214 square feet. It sleeps up to 3 or 4 guests.

Laundry Facilities

Laundry and dry cleaning services are available for a fee. Items will be picked up and delivered to your stateroom. If you'd rather go the self-service laundry route, you can do so in one of several Guest Laundry Rooms. Here you'll find washers, dryers, and ironing equipment. (Due to safety concerns, the laundry room is the only place in which iron use is permitted.) There is no fee to use an iron. Machines run about two bucks a load. Laundry detergent may be purchased here, too. At press time, a small box cost about $1. Simply wave your Key to the World card and charge it to your stateroom account.

Guest Services Desk

If you have any questions or concerns while on board, head to the Guest Services Desk (Deck 3, midship). This is also the spot to go to secure copies of the *Personal Navigator*, color-coded luggage tags (for use on the last day of the cruise), and postage stamps. Should you have any type of problem while on board, bring it to their attention. More often than not, they will resolve the issue in a matter of minutes.

CATEGORIES 5A–5C, 6A, AND 7A: Deluxe ocean-view staterooms with verandahs. Each has one queen or two twin-size beds, a single convertible sofa, a privacy divider, split bath, and a verandah. These rooms are 268 square feet (including the verandah) and sleep up to 4. Category 7A has an enclosed "Navigator's Verandah," a private balcony with nautical touches. Verandahs in 5A–5C are open, while those in 6A feature a solid whitewall verandah. Accommodations are otherwise the same.

CATEGORY 4A, 4B, AND 4E: Deluxe ocean-view family staterooms with verandah. This room type has a queen or two twin beds, a single convertible sofa, and a bed that pulls down from the wall. There is a privacy divider, split bath, and open verandah (verandahs in the aft area are not open). It covers 304 square feet (including verandah) and sleeps up to 5.

CATEGORY 00T: Concierge one-bedroom suites with verandah. These have a queen bed, an area with a double convertible sofa, and a pull-down bed, two full baths, walk-in closet, wet bar, DVD player, open verandah (except for the aft-area staterooms), and concierge service. The suite is 614 square feet (including the verandah) and sleeps up to 4 or 5 guests.

CATEGORY 00S: Concierge two-bedroom suites with verandahs. These suites come with a queen bed, a sleeper-sofa, and a pull-down bed. There are 2.5 baths, a whirlpool tub, walk-in

HOT TIP!

The midship elevators are the most crowded throughout the day—especially at mealtimes. Try to use the forward and aft elevators whenever possible.

closets, a DVD player, unstocked wet bar, verandah, and concierge service. The suite measures 945 square feet (including the verandah) and sleeps up to 7 guests.

CATEGORY 00R: Concierge royal suite with verandah. Comes with a queen bed in one bedroom, two twin beds in a second bedroom, and two ceiling pull-down upper berths. There are 2.5 baths, a whirlpool tub in the master bedroom, a living room, media library (with a pull-down bed), dining salon, pantry, unstocked wet bar, walk-in closets, DVD player, private verandah, and concierge service. The suite measures 1,029 square feet (including the verandah) and sleeps up to 7.

DREAM AND FANTASY

CATEGORIES 11A–11C: Standard inside staterooms. They have a queen, a single convertible sofa, upper berth pull-down bed (in some), and a bath with a tub and shower. Each room measures 169 square feet and sleeps up to 3 (category 11C) or 4 (categories 11A and 11B). They also have "magical portholes" (see Category 10A).

CATEGORY 10A: Deluxe inside staterooms. These accommodations are similar to those found in categories 11A–11C, but have 204 square feet and sleep up to 3 to 4 guests. They also have split baths, plus a bit of technological and artistic wizardry known as "magical portholes." These beauties have a real-time digital view that could be seen from a real porthole at any given time of day or night, and they feature visits from animated Disney characters. Most folks say they forget they are in an inside stateroom—the effect is that convincing.

CATEGORIES 9A–9D: Deluxe ocean-view staterooms. These come with a queen bed, a single convertible sofa, upper berth pull-down bed (in some), split bath, and porthole. Each room is 204 square feet and sleeps up to 3 or 4 guests.

CATEGORIES 8A–8D: Deluxe family ocean-view staterooms. These come with a queen bed, a single convertible sofa, wall pull-down bed (in most) or upper berth pulldown bed, and a split bath with a round tub (in most). Each stateroom features a large porthole window with built-in seating, measures 241 square feet, and sleeps up to 3 or 5. The 8A stateroom has two large porthole windows but does not have a split bath.

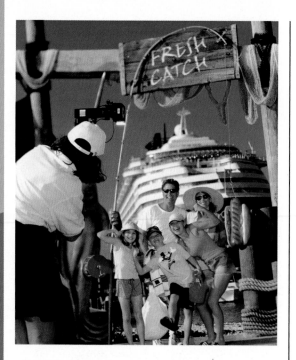

CATEGORIES 5A–5E, 6A–6B, 7A: Deluxe ocean-view staterooms with verandahs. Each has one queen bed, a single convertible sofa, pull-down bed if sleeping 4, a split bath, and a verandah. These rooms are 246 square feet (including the verandah) and sleep up to 3 or 4. The verandahs in 5A and the aft rooms of 6A and 6B feature whitewall verandahs. 7A rooms either have a smaller verandah or an obstructed view. 5E staterooms have larger verandahs and are all aft. Accommodations are otherwise the same.

CATEGORY 4A–4E: Deluxe ocean-view family staterooms with verandah. This room type has a queen bed, a single convertible sofa, upper berth pull-down bed (in most), a split bath with a round tub (in most) and a shower, and a verandah. Each stateroom is 299 square feet (including verandah) and sleeps up to 5. The verandahs in 4E rooms are twice the size of the verandahs in other Category 4 staterooms.

CATEGORY 00V: Concierge Deluxe family ocean-view staterooms with verandah. This room type has a queen bed, a double convertible sofa, upper berth pull-down bed, full bath (with a vanity, sink, round tub, and shower), half bath (vanity, sink, and toilet), a verandah, and concierge service. Each stateroom covers 306 square feet (including verandah) and sleeps up to 5.

CATEGORY 00T: Concierge one-bedroom suites with verandah. The suites have a bedroom with a queen bed, a living area with a double convertible sofa, and a single pull-down bed in the living room, walk-in closet, two full bathrooms (with a whirlpool in the master bath), verandah, and concierge service. The suite is 622 square feet (including verandah) and sleeps up to 5.

CATEGORY 00R: Concierge royal suite with verandah. Comes with a queen bed in the master bedroom, 1 wall pull-down double bed and 1 wall pull-down single bed in the living room. There are 2 full bathrooms, including a master bath with double sinks, rain shower, and whirlpool tub (there is also a whirlpool tub on the verandah), plus living room, media library, open dining salon, pantry, wet bar, walk-in closet, verandah, and concierge service. The suite measures 1,781 square feet and sleeps up to 5.

The Personal Navigator

An in-house publication called the *Personal Navigator* will help you make the most of every day. Updated daily and delivered to all staterooms (also available via smartphone app), the publication is a comprehensive listing of a day's onboard activities, events, and entertainment.

The *Personal Navigator* is an indispensable tool. When you get your hands on it (the first one should be waiting for you in your stateroom), read it cover to cover. In addition to listing the lineup of activities scheduled for the rest of the day, it'll provide handy bits of information such as the suggested evening attire for that day. It changes from day to day, so be sure to note it. It also gives the time and location of character appearances, any points of interest the ship may have scheduled, a notification of any time zone changes, as well as any special offers at shops or lounges. Keep an eye out for discounts on Internet use, too.

Disney Cruise Line Gifts

Whether you'll be celebrating a special occasion or simply consider the cruise a special occasion unto itself, you may want to have a gift item delivered to your stateroom as an added surprise. Among the items that can be pre-ordered by calling 800-601-8455 or visiting *disneycruise.com* are flower arrangements, food and beverage packages, wine selections, cakes, and Disney Cruise Line merchandise. Orders must be placed at least 72 business hours before sail date.

Dining

A Disney cruise is not the place to count calories—although most special dietary needs can be accommodated upon request. There's no shortage of rations on these ships. If your tastes are simple (say, a hot dog poolside) or sublime (how does a juicy filet mignon, prepared at Palo, sound?), rest assured you'll never be hungry. Or understimulated, for that matter, as many of the restaurants are downright entertaining. And, thanks to a system called "rotational dining," you will get to experience three restaurants, all the while being made to feel like a VIP by your serving staff. That means you'll eat at a different one of the three main restaurants each evening,

often with the same table guests, and enjoy the services of the same waitstaff. Your serving team gets to know you, as well as your likes and dislikes, very well. The system, which is unique to Disney Cruise Line, tends to get the thumbs-up from cruise veterans and newcomers alike. The only exceptions are Palo and Remy, the adults-only, reservations-necessary restaurants.

How do you know where to go on which night? Easy. A ticket with details will be placed in your stateroom. Check the *Personal Navigator* to note the style of attire for the evening.

TABLE SERVICE

ANIMATOR'S PALATE: The pièce de résistance—as far as Disney creativity goes—is without a doubt Animator's Palate, a place where diners not only have to decide what to eat, but also what to watch! Simple surprises abound at each stage of the evening meal. There is an Animator's Palate eatery on each of the four ships, but the dining experience varies depending on which ship you are sailing on. The Animator's Palate experience on the *Magic* and *Wonder* is a culinary journey—from black-and-white to full

color: Upon entering the monochromatic room, note the soft background music and the black-and-white sketches along the wall. While you're doing so, drinks and appetizers will be served. If you ignore this distraction and keep your gaze fixed on the walls, you may notice a bit of color creeping into that sketch of Cinderella. By the time the entrées make their entrance, the room is ablaze in living color.

If you are sailing on the *Dream* or the *Fantasy*, your Animator's Palate experience will be somewhat different. Like its siblings on the *Magic* and *Wonder*, the decor was inspired by the magic of Disney and Pixar animation. It's teeming with everything you'd expect to find inside an actual animator's studio: character sketches, paintbrushes, colored pencils, computer workstations, and other tools of the animation trade. Scenes and characters from Disney films adorn the walls, and that totally awesome, animated turtle called Crush actually interacts with diners on the *Dream* and *Fantasy*.

The *Fantasy* one-ups it sister ships with a dinner show called Animation Magic. Hosted by Sorcerer Mickey, the interactive experience encourages guests to express themselves with a drawing—and over the course of dinner, they'll witness their drawings being brought to life through the magic of Disney animation. Every show is a smash hit with artists of all ages. Crush the turtle appear here on some nights, too.

Dining rooms details vary, but the menu is the same on all four ships. It's featured starters such as smoked salmon tartare, sesame-flavored rock shrimp, and wild mushroom risotto and porcini twist. Entrée have included grilled Pacific black cod, lemon-thyme marinated all-natural chicken breast, black bean chipotle cakes, ginger-teriyaki dusted beef tenderloin and the Animator's trio of veal. If they're available, we recommend starting with the butternut squash soup and ending with a slice of white chocolate fudge cheesecake or the crunchy walnut cake.

ENCHANTED GARDEN: This picturesque spot, which is located on the *Dream* and *Fantasy*, seems to be truly enchanted, as the immersive, outdoorsy environment transforms from day to night over the course of your dinner.

Breakfast, served buffet style, is offered on select days of each cruise. Ditto for lunch. The daily dinner is a four-course affair of seasonal selections. For an extra charge (plus gratuity), guests may enjoy bar drinks, bottled water, and specialty coffee. Soft drinks (coffee, soda, fruit juice, milk, and tea) carry no charge.

LUMIÈRE'S: Located on the *Magic* only, this elegant spot provides fine dining in a setting inspired by Disney's *Beauty and the Beast*. The sprawling dining room is elegant and softly lit, though a bit more raucous than its cosmopolitan contemporaries. Note that the later seating is usually a bit more sedate (fewer small kids).

Menu selections at dinner have included crispy roasted duck breast with braised napa cabbage, and aged Angus beef tenderloin. Vegetarians can opt for the mushroom-stuffed pasta in a vegetable broth. And vegetarians won't feel at all cheated by the grilled marinated tofu. For dessert, consider the crème brûlée or soufflé.

TRITON'S: Passengers aboard the *Wonder* may dine in the elegant Triton's, where the specialty of the house is seafood. The ocean theme is enhanced by subtly changing lighting with every course, the room getting more under-the-sea-like as the meal progresses. Menu items have included French onion soup, Gruyère and cheddar cheese lobster macaroni; smoked oven-baked salmon royale crowned with king smoked salmon; and roasted rack of lamb. For dessert, there's chocolate mousse, Grand Marnier soufflé, sundaes, and more.

PARROT CAY: This tropical spot, which is located on the *Wonder* and is pronounced Parrot *KEY*, is certainly one of the most colorful spaces you'll ever dine in. Done up in vibrant shades of orange, green, blue, and yellow, it boasts a rainbow of cleverly formed napkin displays at each table. The island-like feel has been complemented by such dinner dishes as shrimp and avocado salad, braised jerk-seasoned pork, Caribbean roasted chicken, and mixed grill. Dessert-wise, expect the likes of lemon meringue pie with kumquat sauce, chocolate s'more vanilla cake, and French toast banana bread. This is exclusive to the *Wonder*.

CARIOCA'S: A vibrant restaurant (on the *Magic*), Carioca's is a tribute to the city of Rio de Janeiro (the second-largest city in Brazil). The name of the eatery, however, honors José Carioca—one of the stars of *The Three Caballeros*. The menu has featured items with Latin-infused flavors such as adobo-rubbed rack of lamb; lobster *croquetas* with banana and lentil salad; and lobster, shrimp, and salmon kebabs with black bean rice and *pico de gallo*. Finish the meal with cream cheese flan with caramel bananas.

ROYAL PALACE/ROYAL COURT: This regal restaurant (Royal Palace on the *Dream* and Royal Court on the *Fantasy*) got its inspiration from classic Disney animated features such as *Sleeping Beauty*, *Beauty and the Beast*, and *Cinderella*. You will find the eatery on Deck 3, midship.

French-inspired, continental cuisine is offered for breakfast, lunch, and dinner. Breakfast is offered on select mornings of each cruise, as is a full-service lunch. A four-course dinner takes place nightly. One of the favorite appetizers at dinner is the *escargots gratinés* (herb-marinated snails). Grilled beef tenderloin and shrimp is a featured entrée. Vegetarian selections such as mushroom-filled pasta are served, too. And do save room for the "sweet temptations" dessert offering: a trio of peanut butter mousse, mango cheesecake, and vanilla crème brûlée. Yum!

Seating Times and Situations: There are normally two seating sessions for dinner; however, the times vary depending on what itinerary the ship is sailing at the time. The most common times are 5:45 P.M. and 8:15 P.M. If you have a preference, tell your travel agent or reservationist the moment you book your cruise. Requests for any seating cannot be guaranteed. If you get closed out of a preferred seating time, check with Guest Services after boarding. Seating times may open up after boarding. Most seating at table-service restaurants is communal, except at Palo and Remy. If you are traveling as a family with kids, expect to be seated with similar travelers. Adults without children will be seated together if possible.

Parents of young kids, listen up! There is a dining convenience designed just for you. Dine and Play lets parents with late dinner seatings check their kids (ages 3–11) into the Youth Activities programs starting about 45 minutes after dinner seating has begun. In other words, after the kids have eaten, they can go play while you finish your meal in a leisurely manner. Neat, huh? If you wish to partake of the complimentary Dine and Play service, simply inform your servers upon arrival in the dining room. They will make sure kids get their meals quickly, while serving the grown-ups at a more relaxed pace.

Youth activities counselors arrive in the restaurant 45 minutes after the seating begins, and assign children to groups right there in the dining room. No need for parents to escort junior to Deck 5. (Though they will eventually have to pick the kids up!) Remember, this service is for guests with late dinner seatings only.

PALO: For adults only (age 18 and up), Palo is an ideal spot for special celebrations or just a quiet, romantic evening. Offering brunch and dinner, Palo is worth the small surcharge (at press time, prices were $25 for brunch and dinner) to indulge in a five-star dining experience that includes an ocean view.

True to its roots (palo means "pole" in Italian), the restaurant has echoes of Venice, Italy. Masks from that city's Carnevale line the walls, and the menu reflects some of the best continental fare you'll find on either side of the Atlantic. Dinner appetizers include *fritto di calamari* and tuna carpaccio—thin slices of tuna brushed with the chef's special lemon olive oil. The entrée menu tempts with selections such as oregano-and-parmesan-crusted rack of lamb and lobster mascarpone ravioli.

A warning: Save room for dessert or you will never forgive yourself. The chocolate soufflé (with hot chocolate and vanilla sauces) is beyond amazing. (The sweet soufflé must be ordered in advance.) The pineapple-and-almond ravioli and Palo's homemade tiramisu yield raves, too.

Brunch at Palo is a special event. (It's offered on cruises of 4 nights or more.) The buffet is so vast that it requires a guided tour. Expect fruit, salads, seafood, heavenly flatbreads, pastries, made-to-order omelets, fish, and chicken entrées, and more.

Palo is for diners ages 18 years and older. Make reservations at *www.disneycruise.com*; at Fathoms (*Magic*), WaveBands (*Wonder*), or D Lounge (*Dream* and *Fantasy*); or at the restaurant itself starting at approximately 1 P.M. on the first day of a cruise.

REMY: For adults (guests age 18 and older) on the *Dream* and *Fantasy*, Remy is a ritzy, palate-pleasing delight. Considered the most upscale dining experience available on the ship, Remy serves fine French-inspired cuisine for dinner (all cruises) and brunch (on cruises of 4 nights or more). The luxurious dining room has Art Nouveau touches and a rich color scheme. Tables are set with Frette linens, Riedel glassware, Christofle silverware, and custom-created Bernadaud china.

Once the meal is booked and guests are aboard the ship, they can meet with a sommelier in Remy's wine room to pick out wines for their pending feast (for an additional price).

The evening meal begins with a champagne cocktail and continues with 8 to 9 small (and delectable) courses. There's nothing more thrilling than a table-side visit from the trolley of international cheeses—except, perhaps, for the wine decanting stations and after-dinner coffee service.

A Tender Subject

Some ports require a process called "tendering." This means, rather than pulling right up to a dock, the ship will pull close to port and drop anchor. Ferries take guests back and forth to shore. It's an efficient system, but it could knock you for a loop if you're not expecting it—especially if you've got an early excursion booked. In this case, you may have to leave a bit earlier than you originally anticipated. That is accounted for in the "meet time" for all excursions.

HOT TIP!

To avoid being charged for canceling a Palo or Remy reservation, you must cancel by 2 P.M. on the day of the reservation.

The private Chef's Table experience takes place in a special 8-seat dining room and features *Ratatouille*-inspired decor.

Oenophiles appreciate the lovely Wine Room, which accommodates up to 8 guests. Here, guests dine in a glass-walled room with marble flooring amid 900 bottles of wine.

Reservations are required to dine at Remy, and meals come with a $75-per-person surcharge for dinner and $50 per person for brunch. Reservations may be made online (75 days ahead for first-time cruisers, 90 for Silver Castaway Club members, 105 days ahead for Gold members, and 120 days in advance for concierge guests and Platinum members).

Like its neighbor, Palo, Remy also has a dress code. Dinner is more formal here than at Palo: jackets, dress pants, and dress shoes for men (ties are optional); dresses, suits, blouses, and dress pants for women. Leave the jeans, shorts, tank tops, yoga pants, sandals, flip-flops, and sneakers in your room. Jackets are optional for brunch.

What to Wear for Dinner: Generally speaking, "cruise casual" is the way to go in all spots except for Palo and Remy: collared shirts, blouses, cotton pants, jeans, and sundresses are generally acceptable for evenings in all other restaurants—swimsuits, T-shirts, and tank tops are not. On select nights, there will be a theme: tropical, pirate attire, semi-formal, etc. On such days, the desired style of dress will be noted in the *Personal Navigator*. (While parents are the best judges of what attire is appropriate for their children, most guests over the age of 13 are usually comfortable wearing attire that is similar to what is recommended for all passengers.) Note that Palo and Remy, grown-ups-only destinations, are considered more formal and guests are asked to dress accordingly: pants and shirt are required for men

(jacket optional at Palo, required for Remy), and a dress or pants and shirt combo for women. No jeans, shorts, flip-flops, or sneakers, please. Likewise, the indoor area of Meridian Bar, located between Palo and Remy, has the same formal dress code as Palo. However, the outdoor patio of Meridian Bar has a slightly more relaxed vibe (think business casual).

Wine and Dine: Most of the table-service restaurants offer many vintages by the glass or by the bottle. If you order a bottle and fail to finish it by meal's end, ask your server to store it for you. (You'll get it with the next evening's meal.) Disney offers two wine packages (both red and white selections).

Special Dietary Needs: Certain special dietary needs may be met aboard Disney cruise ships. All requests should be made well in advance, preferably at the time of booking the cruise package. It's always a good idea to confirm the request prior to setting sail.

SELF-SERVE, FAST FOOD, AND SNACKS

VIBE: This teens-only spot—which can be found on all ships—serves up fruit smoothies and other soft drinks. There are lots of games and magazines, and some refreshments are free of charge. However, there is an extra charge for smoothies. This area is hopping all day—and often past midnight. FYI: The teen spots on the *Magic* and *Wonder* used to be known as Aloft and The Stack, respectively.

BEVERAGE STATION: There is a self-serve station on every ship. On the *Magic* and *Wonder*, you'll find it on Deck 9, aft (port side). On the *Dream* and *Fantasy*, look for the beverage station on Deck 11, midship (there is a station on each side of the Mickey pool). Help yourself to water, juice, soda, iced tea, lemonade, coffee, hot chocolate, and hot tea. There is an ice machine, too. The station is open 24/7, though not all selections are available at all times. Soft drinks are free here and with meals, but not at bars or through room service.

BEACH BLANKET BUFFET: Located on the Disney *Wonder*, this self-service buffet offers breakfast and lunch. The morning meal brings selections such as fresh fruit, cereal, eggs, sausage, and oatmeal. Lunch fare usually has a theme: Italian, Chinese, seafood, etc. (Check a

HOT TIP!

At table-service restaurants, a gratuity of 15 percent is automatically added to the bill for alcoholic beverages. At bars and lounges, a gratuity is added for all drinks (including soft drinks).

Personal Navigator, or at the eatery itself, to learn if there's a theme for the meal.) In addition to the buffet (which you will encounter as you enter), there is a serving station by the seating area. This area usually serves omelets in the morning and something special for lunch. There are indoor tables and others out on the deck. Beach Blanket offers table service and casual dining for dinner on most evenings.

CABANAS: Located on the *Dream*, *Fantasy*, and *Magic*, this casual indoor eatery serves three meals a day. This spot recalls a breezy boardwalk along the coast, with a dash of Disney (e.g., colorful *Finding Nemo*–themed mosaics). Made-to-order breakfast and lunch selections are offered "on the boardwalk" on most days (check your *Personal Navigator* for times and specifics). In other words, a variety of food stations proffer freshly prepared edibles. Dinner is a table-service affair. Cocktails may be ordered from the Clam Bar. Cabanas is located on Deck 11, aft on the *Dream* and *Fantasy*; Deck 9 aft on the *Magic*.

COVE CAFE: A cozy, adults-only lounge, Cove Cafe can be found on all ships. It features espresso and specialty coffees and a full bar (fees apply). Complimentary cakes and cookies are available. Books and magazines are on hand for on-site perusing, as is a TV (often showing a big game or the news). Board games may be borrowed, too. Wireless Internet access is available (for a fee). The cafe is located near the Quiet Cove pool.

DAISY'S DE-LITES: *Magic*: Visit Daisy's for bagels, fresh fruit, salads, wraps, sandwiches, cookies, and more. Hours are usually from 11 A.M. till 7 P.M. daily.

EYE SCREAM AND FROZONE TREATS: *Magic*, *Dream*, and *Fantasy*: Guests craving a chilly treat can find satisfaction at adjoining snack stations. Eye Scream (with theming inspired by famous eyeball Mike Wazowski) doles out soft-serve ice cream. Mike's neighbor, a spot that pays tribute to Frozone from *The Incredibles*, serves made-to-order mixed fruit smoothies and cocktails (for a fee).

FLO'S CAFE: *Dream* and *Fantasy*: Flo's Cafe, located on Deck 11 near the Donald pool, is actually a trio of side-by-side walk-up windows, all themed to characters from the animated feature *Cars*. Here you'll find Luigi's Pizza, Tow Mater's Grill, and Fillmore's Favorites. Menu options at these filling stations include pizza (often featuring a special pizza of the day), chicken tenders, salads, sandwich wraps, fruit, burgers, and more. Luigi's tends to stay open the latest of the three.

PETE'S BOILER BITES: *Magic*: Looking for a tasty treat without the formality of a table-service eatery? Or perhaps a nibble between meals? Head here! Pete serves chicken tenders, burgers, hot dogs, veggie burgers, and tacos.

PINOCCHIO'S PIZZERIA: *Magic* and *Wonder*: This counter-service spot serves spirits and soft drinks (for a fee), and cheese and pepperoni pizzas (no charge for food). There is often a special pizza of the day. Be sure to ask.

PLUTO'S DOG HOUSE: *Wonder*: Located on Deck 9, aft, this counter spot serves hot dogs, bratwurst, burgers, veggie burgers, fish burgers, grilled chicken sandwiches, and tacos.

GOOFY'S GALLEY: *Wonder*: A popular spot for a snack or a light meal, this counter features self-serve soft-serve ice cream. It also offers salads, wraps, pressed panini sandwiches, cookies, and fresh fruit.

ROOM SERVICE

Stateroom dining service delivers 24 hours a day (except on the final night of a cruise, when service stops promptly at 1:30 A.M.)—handy if you're traveling with kids or if you have a snack craving in between meals. Most menu items are included with your cruise package. At press time, selections included soups, salads, sandwiches, burgers, pizza, cookies, and selections for kids. There is a charge for some beverages and snack selections (such as candy, popcorn, wine, beer, soda, and bottled water). Note that a gratuity is not always included.

SPECIAL DINING EXPERIENCES

PIRATES IN THE CARIBBEAN PARTY: If there's one thing Disney really knows how to do right, it's throw a party. On one night during most cruises, guests enjoy a buccaneering soirée. If you own any pirate attire or regalia, wear it to the big event. (You may purchase some from a ship shop, too.) It takes place on the upper decks, where pirate villains set their sights on taking over the ship. An epic battle ensues as the good guys take on the villains. The greatest spectacle of all is the show's grand finale—fireworks (offered on most itineraries). A feast fit for a pirate king is served post pyrotechnics (in Beach Blanket Buffet on the *Wonder*, and in Cabanas on the *Magic*, *Dream*, and *Fantasy*).

CHARACTER BREAKFAST: An up-close-and-personal morning starring furry favorites is a very Disney way to start the day. (This is available for most of the 7-night-or-longer itineraries on the *Magic* and *Wonder*.) Everyone may attend one character-hosted breakfast per cruise. Check your Dining Ticket for assigned morning and location (characters vary). Disney characters have even been known to dance with guests. Don't forget to bring your camera!

Many of the character breakfast selections remain staples—eggs, bacon, cereal, fruit, yogurt, and French toast, for example.

CAPTAIN'S GALA DINNER: Even on this, one of the planet's most casual of cruises, there is a chance to don your finery and join the sparkle and glitter of this black-tie (optional) affair. If you'd rather not get completely decked out, go with a business casual look (but not too casual). The French-continental menu is offered in each of the main dining rooms on all ships. A menu favorite is the baked lobster tail served in the shell with lemon butter and rice. The Captain's Gala is offered on most cruises of 7 nights or longer.

FAREWELL DINNER: Presented on the final evening of cruises 7 nights or longer, this evening meal is a chance to enjoy favorite dishes, celebrate new friends, and perhaps start planning (or at least dreaming about) your next cruise.

FAMILY TEA: A tea party with one of Disney's beloved characters is a true kid-pleaser. During this break in the day's activities, the party's host will tell stories, sign autographs, and pose for pictures. The tea is offered on most cruises of 7 nights or longer on the *Magic* and *Wonder*. Reservations may be made at Guest Services. (There is no extra charge for Family Tea, but a reservation is necessary.)

Bars and Lounges

From elegant spots with live piano music to rousing sports bars, Disney ships have a bounty of bars and lounges in which to wet your whistle or simply unwind and watch the waves or the sunset. (Most beverages offered in these spots come with an extra charge.)

BON VOYAGE: A casual lounge located on Deck 3, midship (*Dream* and *Fantasy*). Beverages are available all day.

CADILLAC LOUNGE: Unique to the Route 66 entertainment zone (*Wonder*), this sophisticated spot celebrates classic cars with soothing music, wine, martinis, and other drinks.

COVE CAFE: This cozy adults-only lounge can be found aboard all of the ships in Disney's fleet. It offers specialty coffees and a full bar (charges apply). Complimentary snacks are available, too. Magazines are on hand for on-site perusing, as is a TV. Board games may be borrowed for on-site use. Wireless Internet is available (for a fee).

CURRENTS: A breezy spot with stellar ocean views, Currents is on Deck 13, forward (*Dream* and *Fantasy*).

DISTRICT LOUNGE: This intimate bar is located in the *Dream*'s adults-only District entertainment zone.

HOT TIP!

If your mobile phone, laptop, or tablet is equipped for wireless Internet access, bring it along. All areas on the Disney ships offer Wi-Fi service known as Connect@Sea. Rates may vary, but expect to pay 25 cents per megabite (mb) of data or buy a package of 100 mb for $19, 300 minutes for $39, or 1,000 mb for $89. Prices are per stateroom, and packages may be shared. For additional information, visit *www.disneycruise.com*.

DANCE CLUB: A butterfly-themed hot spot, Evolution celebrates all styles of music on the *Dream*. On the *Fantasy*, it's The Tube, a dance spot that pays tribute to the city of London. The venues feature various activities and dance parties. (Guests must be at least 18 years old to come here at night, 21 to imbibe.)

FATHOMS: This After Hours joint (*Magic*) fancies itself a celebration of the sea. It uses special effects, lighting, and sound to create different festive atmospheres. There's a dance floor, plus tables and bar seating. Themed parties are thrown here on select evenings.

KEYS: The *Magic*'s version of an intimate piano bar, this lounge serves cocktails and wines by the glass. Keys provides a refined retreat.

LA PIAZZA: The *Fantasy*'s celebration of Italian cities features a festive carousel bar. Venetian masks and glasswork add to the fun.

MERIDIAN BAR: Found on the *Dream* and *Fantasy*, Meridian is located on Deck 12, aft, and has indoor and outdoor seating. The dress code for the indoor area: Dress pants and shirt are required for men and a dress or dress pants for women. On the outside deck, the dress code is cruise casual (jeans and shorts are okay, swimsuits and tank tops are not).

OOH LA LA: A *Fantasy* champagne bar, this space was inspired by a French boudoir.

OUTLOOK CAFÉ: Overlooking the Quiet Cove Pool on the *Wonder* (above Cove Cafe), this lounge serves cocktails and coffee drinks.

PINK: An elegant nightspot designed to look like the inside of a champagne bottle, this lounge is in the *Dream*'s District entertainment zone.

PROMENADE LOUNGE: This lounge serves cocktails and soft drinks on the *Magic* and *Wonder*. At night, it offers live music.

SIGNALS: On Deck 9 of the *Magic* and *Wonder*, this poolside spot serves cocktails and soft drinks.

SKYLINE: The *Dream*'s District area and the *Fantasy*'s Europa boast Skyline, a cosmopolitan bar with majestic views of famous cities from around the world. The cityscapes change over the course of the evening.

SPORTS BAR: A sports fan's dream come true, this lounge has a satellite feed, plus suds and wings, hot dogs, or other munchies. It's Diversions on the *Wonder*, 687 on the *Dream*, and O'Gill's on the *Fantasy* and *Magic*.

THE TUBE: Housed in the *Fantasy*'s Europa district, The Tube is a metropolitan dance club themed to the London Underground (aka the tube).

VISTA CAFÉ: *Dream* and *Fantasy* guests in need of a java jolt can head to this cheery destination on Deck 4, midship. Snacks and cocktails are served, too.

WAVEBANDS: Vintage radios and album covers line the walls and set the stage for a lively dance club. A deejay keeps the place grooving till the wee hours. All manner of drinks are available at this Route 66 club (*Wonder*).

WAVES: An open-air bar on the *Dream* and *Magic*, this spot serves beverages all day.

Entertainment

For some, a deck chair, a good book, and a steady stream of sunshine are all the entertainment required. Others may delight in an evening of dancing or a bingo-filled afternoon. And some are satisfied with nothing short of an all-out Broadway-style stage show. Fortunately, Disney Cruise Line has all of the above, plus guest lecturers, tours, and more. Note that all shows are not presented every day or on every cruise. The entertainment lineup is tweaked from time to time, so details may differ during your cruise.

THE GOLDEN MICKEYS—A TIMELESS TRIBUTE: A dynamic production that pays tribute to the musical legacy of Walt Disney

Studios. It's got all the glitz and glamour of a Hollywood celebration, paying homage to the comedy, romance, and heroes (plus a few key villains) of classic Disney animated films. This show is presented on the *Wonder* and *Dream*. It's a crowd-pleaser worthy of a Golden Mickey!

WELCOME ABOARD SHOW: This sweet presentation is a nice way to "meet" your ship's crew. The captain, cruise director, and many of their comrades introduce themselves and welcome guests aboard. Musical numbers and vaudeville-like variety acts round out the bill. This show is presented on most cruises of 7 nights and longer.

DISNEY'S ALADDIN—A MUSICAL SPECTACULAR: This musical showcases a variety of classic (and new) songs and characters from the animated feature and regales guests with theatrical treats. It's a *Fantasy* exclusive.

DISNEY'S BELIEVE: Who doesn't believe in the power of pixie dust? A little girl named Sophia certainly does. But her serious-minded father, Mr. Greenaway, is a much tougher sell. Follow his journey from skeptic to believer in this rousing musical show. In addition to classic Disney tunes, this crowd-pleaser features the lovely original song "What Makes a Garden Grow." It is presented on the *Dream* and *Fantasy*.

DISNEY DREAMS—AN ENCHANTED CLASSIC: This bedtime story features a galaxy of familiar Disney stars, including the Blue Fairy, Peter Pan, Belle, Beast, Aladdin, Cinderella, and Ariel. Together and through the power of song and dance, the characters teach a skeptical girl about the power of dreams. It takes place on the *Magic* and *Wonder*.

TOY STORY—THE MUSICAL: The story isn't entirely new—but much of the music in this stage show is. The tunes help tell the story of Buzz, Woody, and the toys from Andy's room in an ambitious way. This show is presented exclusively on the *Wonder*.

TWICE CHARMED—AN ORIGINAL TWIST ON THE CINDERELLA STORY: A Broadway-style extravaganza (*Magic* only), this musical production begins with the wedding of Cinderella and Prince Charming. Things take a sudden turn when the wicked Fairy Godfather makes his presence known and, after granting a wish to one evil stepmother, sends the family back in time, where—*gasp*—the glass slipper gets

broken! Does this turn of events destroy Cinderella's chances of living happily ever after? You'll just have to catch the show to find out.

VILLAINS TONIGHT!: It seems old Hades is losing his evil edge and, with it, his status as "Lord of the Underworld." Perish the thought! In an effort to regain his meanie mojo, he enlists some of Disney's most dastardly villains in what turns out to be an enjoyable comic/musical revue. The hour-long show can be seen on the *Magic* and *Dream*.

DISNEY'S WISHES: As high school kids face graduation day, they discover that the secret to becoming a grown-up is to stay connected to your inner child. And what's a wonderful way to do that? By making a wish and spending a fun-filled, musical—and magical—day at Disneyland. This show is presented exclusively on the *Fantasy*.

REMEMBER THE MAGIC—FAREWELL SHOW: This show wraps up the trip as performers celebrate a week of shipboard activities and island-hopping. This particular production is presented on the *Magic* and *Wonder*, but the *Fantasy* and *Dream* have a special good-bye show known as An Unforgettable Journey.

DECK PARTIES

When it comes to on-deck celebrations, the area by the family pool is party central. Starting with a Sailing Away Celebration and continuing with daily dance fests with Disney characters, live bands, and fireworks (except on Alaska cruises), it seems like there is always a reason to party. Check the daily *Personal Navigator* for celebration specifics.

FAMILY ENTERTAINMENT

D LOUNGE: This family-friendly lounge and nightclub is on the *Magic, Dream,* and *Fantasy* (Deck 4, midship). Head here for dance parties, character greetings, karaoke, games, and more.

STUDIO SEA: A colorful "television studio" environment (on the *Wonder*) is the setting for audience-participation family game shows. Mickey Mania lets you put your knowledge of Disney trivia to the test, while Karaoke Night encourages families to take the stage and sing together. Finally, the Family Dance Party gives everyone a chance to kick up their heels (or sneakers) and enjoy a party for guests of all ages. Keep in mind that the entertainment lineup, though always dynamic, is subject to change from time to time.

CHARACTER BREAKFAST: On most cruises that are 7 nights or longer (on the *Magic* and *Wonder*), a bountiful breakfast is hosted by Disney friends.

FAMILY TEA: Guests of all ages, but especially younger ones (on most 7-night-or-longer cruises on the *Magic* and *Wonder*), are invited to enjoy afternoon tea with some of their favorite Disney pals. The event takes place at Studio Sea (*Wonder*) and D Lounge (*Magic*). In addition to learning the proper way to serve tea and cookies, guests are treated to stories about their host's or hostess's adventures. Tickets are necessary and are available at Guest Services (they're free). For details, turn to page 336.

FOR GROWN-UPS ONLY

The 18-and-over set on the *Magic* and *Wonder* can attend demonstrations (e.g., Disney's Art of Entertaining), lectures and conversations with guest speakers, tours, and specially tailored nighttime events (such as Match Your Mate, a game show in which you and your mate will find out how much you know about each other), as well as theme nights, cabaret shows, and more.

On the *Dream* and *Fantasy*, adults have the chance to participate in interactive cooking demonstrations as part of the Anyone Can Cook! series; learn the secrets of Disney animation in the Illusion of Life series; and attend a presentation about the making of the ship.

JUST FOR KIDS

The wildly popular kids' programs and activities tend to elicit raves from participants and parents alike. For starters, adults who leave their kids at supervised facilities can be assured that the watchword here is safety. There are plenty of counselors on hand, and the secured programming ensures that they know where every child is at any given time. Kids are checked in with Youth Activities when entering and signed out when exiting with an authorized guardian. Upon check-in, each child is given an electronic wristband. (The band assists with the check-in and check-out process and adds an additional level of security to youth venues.) Records of a child's allergies or other particular needs are entered into their file.

Every child is required to wear a wristband that identifies him or her as a participant in the program. Parents have Wave Phones (which can be found in all staterooms) and can be contacted immediately if their child has a problem or just wants to see them.

Cleanliness is a priority, too. In fact, kids entering the Oceaneer Club and Lab are promptly asked to wash their hands. Play areas are cleaned three times a day, with a deep-down cleansing done at the end of each day.

The kids' programs are concentrated on Deck 5, and kids registered into the secured programming always remain in either the Lab or Club. The specially tailored programming is open to kids who are completely potty-trained, able to interact comfortably within the counselor-to-child ratio groups, and able to mix well with peers.

Kids between age 3 and 12 can choose to play in the Oceaneer Club or Oceaneer Lab based on whatever interests them. Siblings and friends between the age of 3 and 12 can play together regardless, as kids are not segregated by age group. And don't worry about little ones ever being dominated by bigger kids—participants are closely monitored at all times.

Kids who exhibit any symptoms of illness—even if it's just a runny nose—will not be allowed to participate. If a child becomes disruptive, he or she will be asked to play with a parent or guardian during open house hours.

Except for the nursery, there is no fee for youth activities on any Disney ship. The following descriptions of the youth activities were accurate at press time, but specifics are subject to change from time to time.

OCEANEER CLUB: A wonderfully detailed adventure zone, this club has several distinctly themed areas on the *Magic, Dream,* and *Fantasy* and a pirate theme on the Wonder. In addition to computer games, costumes, and other games, there are many organized activities. It's open to all kids age 3–12 (potty-trained) on all ships (provided the kids show no sign of illness).

At the Oceaneer Club, kids find a combination of free play and structured activities featuring interactive, playful experiences with some of their favorite Disney characters. These may include reading a story with Belle, learning how to be a pirate from Captain Hook, and even playing games with Mickey Mouse. Lunch and dinner are served (at no extra charge). It's usually open from 9 A.M. till midnight.

OCEANEER LAB: The Oceaneer Lab is open to (potty-trained) kids age 3–12 on all Disney ships. It is located on Deck 5, midship. The entertaining space is filled with wacky inventions and opportunities for exploration. There are games, books, toys, child-friendly computers, video games, drawing materials, and more. As with the Oceaneer Club, there are also several imaginative organized activities. It is usually open from 9 A.M. till midnight.

Programs here allow kids to be very hands-on while learning the skills of Disney animators, becoming a sleuth to solve mysteries with Disney characters, and joining a chef for a *Ratatouille*-inspired cooking experience. Check a *Personal Navigator* for specific dates and times for various activities while on board. Lunch and dinner are served (at no additional charge).

Reminder: Kids ages 8–12 may check themselves in and out of the Oceaneer Lab with their parents' permission.

HOT TIP!

Children's menus are available in all shipboard restaurants (with the obvious exceptions of Palo and Remy). Buffets all stock kid-friendly vittles such as mac and cheese and chicken tenders.

EDGE: There are video games, arts and crafts, and movie screenings in this tween hangout. There are evening activities such as scavenger hunts and karaoke, too. Edge can be found on Deck 2 on the *Magic* and *Wonder*.

Also a tween space on the *Dream* and *Fantasy*, Edge is located on Deck 13 inside the forward funnel. Its high-tech features include an illuminated dance floor, a video wall, and notebook computers for game-playing.

FLOUNDER'S REEF NURSERY AND IT'S A SMALL WORLD NURSERY: Open to kids ages 12 weeks through 3 years, these colorful spaces are the ships' babysitting centers. (Flounder's Reef is on the *Wonder*, while It's a Small World is on the *Magic, Dream,* and *Fantasy*.) For an hourly fee, the nursery offers activities and a quiet area, complete with cribs.

No food is available at the nursery, but if parents provide prepared bottles or jarred food that is clearly labeled with a child's name, staffers will happily feed their hungry tyke. Space is limited and gets booked early. In fact, reservations are accepted via *www.disneycruise.com* and on embarkation day on a first-come, first-served basis. Due to the high demand, multiple requests might not be honored —so don't count on securing several sessions, though it can't hurt to try. The fee for the babysitting service is $9 per hour for the first child, $8 per each additional child with a one-hour minimum (only siblings net the discount). Nurseries are generally open from 9 A.M. until 11 P.M. Stateroom babysitting is not available on any ship.

TEENS ONLY

Teens can enjoy their own special hangout and activities while aboard Disney ships. Vibe is their exclusive place to hang out. (If you're old enough to vote, KEEP OUT!) It's got popular music, games, dance parties, big-screen TVs, and more. The activities and sodas are free, but smoothies cost extra. Other teen-oriented programs include karaoke, organized sports activities, a pool party, and more. Vibe is open from 11 A.M. till 2 A.M.

FUN AND GAMES

ARCADE: Located on Deck 9 of the *Magic* and *Wonder* by Goofy's Family Pool, Quarter Masters Arcade is replete with electronic games and an air hockey table. On the *Dream* and *Fantasy*, the pirate-themed—and appropriately named— Arr-cade is on Deck 11. You will have to purchase credits to play in any of the ships' arcades.

BINGO: Perhaps it's something in the ocean air, but nothing brings out the bingo fanatic in you like a few days at sea. The closest thing to gambling that you'll find on a Disney vessel, the daily bingo sessions are extremely popular. You have to be at least 18 to play, but kids can watch over a grown-up's shoulder and cheer them on.

GAMES: Ping-pong, foosball, shuffleboard, basketball . . . they're all here. Equipment can usually be found by the tables or courts. (Don't monopolize it—it's for everyone to share.) Kooky competitions are sometimes held poolside. The *Dream* and *Fantasy* offer mini-golf and sports simulators (there is a charge to use the simulators). See a *Personal Navigator* for details.

MOVIES: The Buena Vista Theatre shows new film releases—some in 3-D (courtesy of Disney's patented technology). This is the perfect place to head when the weather is less than ideal. Get there early, as the seats fill up quickly.

If you prefer your flicks alfresco, make a beeline for the Goofy or Donald pool. A jumbo screen (on the forward funnel and known as Funnel Vision) broadcasts Disney features, sports, and more throughout the cruise.

Shopping

While on board Disney's cruise ships, you can enjoy tax-free (on all items) and duty-free (select items) shopping.

The shops have limited hours due to U.S. Customs regulations and can't operate during any time when the ship is in port. Use your stateroom key (Key to the World) to buy items in the ship's shops and on Castaway Cay. Purchases will be charged to your stateroom account. (Note that the Castaway Cay post office does not honor Key to the World cards. It accepts cash only.) Shops in all other ports of call generally accept major credit cards, and many accept cash.

ONBOARD SHOPS

PRELUDES (All ships): There is a snack bar/ concessions window on either side of the Walt Disney Theatre. It closes at about 10 P.M. but opens at different times. Among the items for sale are cookies, candies, nuts, and drinks (spirits and soft drinks are served for a fee, too).

MICKEY'S MAINSAIL (*Magic*, *Dream*, and *Fantasy*): Located on Deck 3, midship, Mickey stocks all manner of Disney and Disney Cruise Line merchandise.

MICKEY'S MATES (*Wonder*): Located on Deck 4, forward, this shop offers Disney Cruise Line logo merchandise, including souvenirs, clothing, beach towels, swimwear, mugs, costumes, postcards, snack items, and plush toys.

QUACKS (*Magic*): Located on Deck 9, midship, Quacks sells swimming essentials, plus merchandise celebrating the ship's waterslide, the AquaDunk.

SEA TREASURES (*Magic*, *Dream*, and *Fantasy*): Located on Deck 3, midship, the treasures here include collectibles, sportswear, swimwear, purses, watches, fragrances, and accessories.

TREASURE KETCH (*Wonder*): Directly across the hall from Mickey's Mates on Deck 4, this shop sells jewelry, loose gemstones, and limited-edition Disney collectibles. There's a selection of clothing, including shirts, sweatshirts, hats, jackets, and other Disney Cruise Line logo items. The store also stocks batteries, postcards, disposable cameras, books, magazines, sun-care products, and a limited selection of sundries (including aspirin and Dramamine). Be sure to check out the nightly promotions.

RADAR TRAP (*Wonder*): Located on Deck 3, forward, this counter-service spot offers tax- and duty-free liquor, snacks, and more. Note that any liquor purchased here may not be consumed while on board. It will be delivered to your room on the last evening of your cruise.

WHITE CAPS (*Magic, Dream,* and *Fantasy*):

This is the place for duty-free items such as perfume, watches, liquor, and tobacco products (which will be delivered to your room on the last night of your cruise).

WHOZITS & WHATZITS (*Dream* and *Fantasy*):

A tiny shop located on Deck 11, near the Donald pool, Whozits & Whatzits sells deckwear, magazines, sunscreen, towels, and other poolside necessities.

SPORTS AND RECREATION

FITNESS CENTER: The fitness center is located within the Vista Spa & Salon on the *Wonder* and within the Senses Spa & Salon on the *Magic, Dream,* and *Fantasy.* There is no fee to use the equipment, which includes treadmills, bikes, stair-climbing machines, free weights, and more. (Some of the machines sport TVs—bring headphones or borrow a pair at the front desk.) Fitness consultations are offered. The fitness center is open from about 6 A.M. to 10 P.M., while the spa is open from 8 A.M. to 8 P.M.

WIDE WORLD OF SPORTS DECK (*Magic* and *Wonder*):

Deck 10 is home to the Wide World of Sports deck. Though open to everyone, it's a huge kid and teen magnet. The basketball hoops are hopping day and night. Basketballs and other equipment are on-site (no charge). This deck is also popular with casual strollers, though jogging on the *Magic* and *Wonder* is relegated to Deck 4 (where one lap is about one-third of a mile). Deck 4 is where you'll find the shuffleboard court, too.

GOOFY'S SPORTS DECK (*Dream* and *Fantasy*):

Located on Deck 13, aft, the always bustling Goofy's Sports Deck is an all-ages, open-air activity center. The basketball court can easily be converted to a volleyball court or a

small soccer arena. The zone also has a sports simulator (soccer, golf, tennis, and basketball; fees apply) and an honest-to-goodness (or is that Goof-ness?) mini golf course.

SWIMMING (*Magic* and *Wonder*): There are three guest swimming areas on board, all located on Deck 9: Mickey's Pool (*Wonder* kids' pool), Mickey's Splash Zone (*Wonder*), Nephews' Splash Zone (*Magic*), and AquaLab (*Magic*) are located toward the back, or aft; Goofy's Family Pool is midship; and the Quiet Cove Adult Pool is on Deck 9, forward. Though the names are self-explanatory, we'll state the obvious: Mickey's pool is for the young'uns and their friends. The Quiet Cove pool is earmarked for splashers age 18 and up. Don't let the name fool you; Quiet Cove may be for grown-ups, but it isn't always the picture of serenity. Organized games engage giddy adults from time to time. Finally, Goofy's pool is for everyone, but kids under age 10 must be accompanied by an adult, and swimmers must be potty-trained. Goofy's pool and Quiet Cove have two whirlpools each. Mickey's pool, which is in the shape of the Big Cheese's head, has a special element: Mickey's Splash Zone. The soft-surface spray area is reserved for tots in swim diapers.

SWIMMING (*Dream* and *Fantasy*): Deck 11 is pool central on these ships. Donald's Pool is the family pool and can be found midship. Mickey's Pool is strictly for kids and their guardians, and the Quiet Cove pool is a grown-ups-only splash zone. Nemo's Reef is a soft-surface spray zone for the toddler set (swim diapers are required).

Tired of all that poolside relaxation? Head for Deck 12 and the ship's ultimate adrenaline-inducer: the AquaDuck. This 765-foot-long "water coaster" propels guests through a clear tube on a journey that includes a trip over the ocean and through the forward funnel, and a

4-deck drop. Check a *Personal Navigator* for operating hours. Guests must be at least 42 inches tall to ride the AquaDuck and 54 inches tall to ride alone. Kids under age 7 must be accompanied by someone 14 years of age or older. It's a hoot—and not as scary as it looks.

AQUADUNK (*Magic*): Step into the 3-story, translucent tube, the trapdoor opens and . . . *kerplunk!* The ride is quick and splashy. Guests must be at least 48 inches tall to take the plunge.

AQUALAB (*Fantasy* and *Magic*): Found on Deck 12, aft, on the *Fantasy* and Deck 9, aft on the *Magic*, Aqualab is a colorful family splash zone. This interactive playground is open to guests age 3 and up. Families may frolic among pop jets, bubblers, and geysers, and slip along the "Twist and Spout" waterslide. (Guests must be between 38 and 84 inches tall to ride.)

NEPHEWS SPLASH ZONE (*Magic*): Deck 9, aft, is home to the *Magic*'s "splashtacular" zone. Designed for guests age 3 and under, the 500-square-foot play area features geysers and bubble jets and a soft deck surface.

SATELLITE FALLS (*Fantasy*): A watery haven for grown-ups, this Deck 13, forward, spot has a circular splash pool with benches and a cascading curtain of water.

SPA & SALON (All ships): Pampering, Disney style, can be enjoyed at the ships' ocean-view spas and salons—Vista Spa & Salon on the *Wonder* and Senses Spa & Salon on the *Magic*, *Dream*, and *Fantasy*. Here, fitness-minded folk can work with a trainer, take a class, or work out solo. As for the pampering, well, that can come by way of any number of treatments.

Book appointments ahead of time by visiting *www.disneycruise.com*, or go to the spa when you board the ship. The spa and salon are open to guests age 18 and older.

The spa is open from 8 A.M. to 8 P.M. every day, except on days when the ship is docked at its home port. Prices are posted in the spa. If you miss a reserved treatment, your stateroom will be charged. Note that Cabana Massages (located at Serenity Bay on Castaway Cay) and the Vista Spa Villas (indoor-outdoor treatment villas for one or two at Vista Spa) may be booked here, too.

Spa amenities include sandals and robes for use during treatments, steam room, sauna, locker room, showers, and more. A selection of beauty products is available for purchase.

CHILL SPA (*Magic*, *Dream*, and *Fantasy*): A spa within a spa, Chill is a place reserved exclusively for teen guests. It offers a variety of spa services and treatments, including facials, massages, and manicures.

Reservations for Chill Spa may be made by phone or on-site any time after 1 P.M. on the first day of your cruise. Appointments book fast—book as soon as you board.

Castaway Cay

If you've ever dreamed of getting away to a private, tropical island, the folks at Disney Cruise Line have made it easy to fulfill that fantasy. Almost every Disney Cruise Line trip that departs from Port Canaveral, Florida, wraps up with a visit to Castaway Cay (pronounced *key*), a tiny island in the Albacos, one in the string of Bahamian isles. This little patch of paradise was secured for the sole use of passengers cruising on Disney ships. It's small—only 3.1 miles long by 2.2 miles wide—and most of it was intentionally left undeveloped so that nature lovers may enjoy the still-unspoiled terrain.

Here you can take a ride in a glass-bottom boat, go back to nature on a kayak adventure, try your wings at parasailing, or go snorkeling offshore—and then return to a barbecue feast. Of course if you'd prefer to loll about in a palm-tree-shaded, beach-side hammock, refreshing beverage in hand, well, that can be arranged.

Other island amenities include biking, beach games, organized activities for kids and teens; a shaded pavilion complete with billiards, ping-pong, basketball, shuffleboard, and more; Disney character greetings; plus a secluded grown-ups-only beach.

Returning guests (they always come back!) will be pleased to see that this happy place has gotten even happier—new additions include an expansion of the family beach, two water play areas known as Pelican Plunge and Spring-a-Leak, and nearly two dozen furnished beach cabanas.

For details or to book Castaway Cay port adventures, visit *www.disneycruise.com*.

WE'RE GOING TO DISNEY WORLD!

DAY 1

DATE

FLIGHT INFORMATION

RESORT & CONFIRMATION NO.

PARK WE PLAN TO VISIT TODAY

FASTPASS+ ASSIGNMENTS:

1. Attraction: _____
   Time: _____

2. Attraction: _____
   Time: _____

3. Attraction: _____
   Time: _____

DINING RESERVATIONS

NOTES

DAY 2

DATE

PARK WE PLAN TO VISIT
in the morning

PARK WE PLAN TO VISIT
in the afternoon/evening

FASTPASS+ ASSIGNMENTS:

1. Attraction: _____
   Time: _____

2. Attraction: _____
   Time: _____

3. Attraction: _____
   Time: _____

DINING RESERVATIONS

NOTES

A DAY-BY-DAY TRIP TRACKER

DAY 3

_____
DATE

PARK WE PLAN TO VISIT
in the morning

PARK WE PLAN TO VISIT
in the afternoon/evening

FASTPASS+ ASSIGNMENTS:

1. Attraction: _____
   Time: _____

2. Attraction: _____
   Time: _____

3. Attraction: _____
   Time: _____

DINING RESERVATIONS

NOTES

DAY 4

_____
DATE

PARK WE PLAN TO VISIT
in the morning

PARK WE PLAN TO VISIT
in the afternoon/evening

FASTPASS+ ASSIGNMENTS:

1. Attraction: _____
   Time: _____

2. Attraction: _____
   Time: _____

3. Attraction: _____
   Time: _____

DINING RESERVATIONS

NOTES

WE'RE GOING TO DISNEY WORLD!

DAY 5

_____
DATE

PARK WE PLAN TO VISIT
in the morning

PARK WE PLAN TO VISIT
in the afternoon/evening

FASTPASS+ ASSIGNMENTS:

1. Attraction: _____
   Time: _____

2. Attraction: _____
   Time: _____

3. Attraction: _____
   Time: _____

DINING RESERVATIONS

NOTES

DAY 6

_____
DATE

PARK WE PLAN TO VISIT
in the morning

PARK WE PLAN TO VISIT
in the afternoon/evening

FASTPASS+ ASSIGNMENTS:

1. Attraction: _____
   Time: _____

2. Attraction: _____
   Time: _____

3. Attraction: _____
   Time: _____

DINING RESERVATIONS

NOTES

A DAY-BY-DAY TRIP TRACKER

DAY 7

_____
DATE

PARK WE PLAN TO VISIT
in the morning

PARK WE PLAN TO VISIT
in the afternoon/evening

FASTPASS+ ASSIGNMENTS:

1. **Attraction:** _____
   Time: _____

2. **Attraction:** _____
   Time: _____

3. **Attraction:** _____
   Time: _____

DINING RESERVATIONS

NOTES

Last Day

_____
DATE

CHECK-OUT TIME

FLIGHT INFORMATION

NOTES

Index

A

accommodations, 61–110
  All-Star resorts, 70, 74, 98–99, 301
  Animal Kingdom Lodge, 68, 72–73, 99–100, 301
  Art of Animation resort, 70, 92, 103, 271, 302
  Bay Lake Tower, 73, 76, 89
  Beach Club resort & villas, 69, 72, 86–88, 92
  BoardWalk resort, 68, 72, 91–93
  cancellation policy, 66
  Caribbean Beach resort, 70, 74, 85–86, 92
  check-in and check-out times, 67
  Contemporary resort, 68, 72, 76–77, 92
  Coronado Springs resort, 70, 101–102
  deposit requirements, 66
  Disney Cruise Line, 328–330
  Disney Vacation Club, 93
  Dolphin resort, 68, 72, 89–90
  Fort Wilderness resort and campground, 70, 74, 83–84
  Four Seasons Orlando, 104–105
  Grand Floridian Resort & Spa, 68, 72, 80–81
  for guests with disabilities, 53–54
  Hotel Plaza Boulevard, resorts on, 106–110
  ID cards, 67
  money-saving tips, 28
  Old Key West resort, 70, 96
  online check-in, 66
  payment methods, 66
  Polynesian Village resort, 68, 72, 78–79, 92
  Polynesian Village Villas & Bungalows, 79
  Pop Century, 70, 74, 92, 102
  Port Orleans French Quarter, 70, 74, 94
  Port Orleans Riverside, 29, 70, 74, 92, 95–96
  rates, 72–75
  reservation guide, 24, 31, 75
  resort finder (rating system), 72–74
  Saratoga Springs Resort & Spa, 70, 73, 96
  Shades of Green, 110
  special room requests, 87
  Swan resort, 68, 72, 89–90
  tipping, 60
  Wilderness Lodge & Villas, 68, 72, 82–83
  Yacht Club resort, 68, 72, 86–88, 92
admission prices, 21–27
  Blizzard Beach, 223
  Disney's Animal Kingdom, 193
  Disney's Hollywood Studios, 175
  Epcot, 143
  Magic Kingdom, 115
  Magic Your Way tickets, 21–24
  Typhoon Lagoon, 221
Adventureland, 118–119, 133, 244
Africa, 198–199, 195, 264–265
African entertainment, 206
air travel, 15
  shuttle service from Orlando International Airport to WDW, 14, 16
All-Star resorts, 70, 98–99
  lounges, 98, 301
  restaurants, 98, 270
AMC Theatres, 45, 215, 266
America Gardens Theatre, The, 163, 169
American Adventure, The, 162–163, 247, 258
American Film Institute Show-case, 181, 186
American Idol Experience, The, 182
Art of Animation resort, 70, 92, 103, 271, 302
Asia, 200–201, 205, 264–265
Astro Orbiter, 129–130
ATMs, 58
  Disney's Animal Kingdom, 194
  Disney's Hollywood Studios, 176
  Downtown Disney, 210
  Epcot, 144, 158
  Magic Kingdom, 115
automobile clubs, 15, 56

B

Baby Care Centers, 64
  Disney's Animal Kingdom, 194
  Disney's Hollywood Studios, 176
  Epcot, 144
  Magic Kingdom, 114
Backstage Magic, 232
Backstage Safari, 232
banking. See ATMs; money matters
barbers, 56, 132
Basin, 211
basketball, 26, 242
Bay Lake Tower, 73, 76, 89
Beach Club resort, 68, 72, 86–88, 92
  lounges, 87, 308
  restaurants, 88, 281
beaches, 68, 70, 76, 78, 83, 85
Beauty and the Beast—Live on Stage, 178
beauty salons, 56, 81, 88, 90, 102, 110, 343
behind-the-scenes tours, 148, 232–234
Behind the Seeds, 232
Be Our Guest restaurant, 245
Best Western Lake Buena Vista, 107
Big Thunder Mountain Railroad, 122
biking, 83, 84, 86, 92, 94, 95, 96, 97, 101, 224, 241
B in the Walt Disney World Resort, 109
Birnbaum's Walt Disney World for Kids, 17, 46

Blizzard Beach, 222–223
BoardWalk Inn & Villas resort, 68, 91–93
  entertainment district, 219
  lounges, 92, 302
  restaurants, 91–92, 271–272
boating, 77, 79,81, 83, 84, 86, 88, 90, 94, 95, 96, 97, 101, 224, 238–239
Boneyard, The, 202
Bongos Cuban Café, 215, 266, 304
Buena Vista Palace Hotel & Spa, 110
  spa, 110, 229
bus travel, 16
  in WDW, 63–64, 113, 143, 175, 193, 210
business services, 56
Buzz Lightyear's Space Ranger Spin, 129

C

cameras and film, 56
  Disney Cruise Line, 322
  Disney's Animal Kingdom, 194
  Disney's Hollywood Studios, 176
  Epcot, 144
  Magic Kingdom, 114
campfire program, 80, 84, 226
Camp Minnie-Mickey, 214
campsites at Fort Wilderness, 67, 70, 84
Canada, 156, 253, 259
Captain EO, 151
Captain Jack Sparrow's Pirate Tutorial, 135
Caribbean Beach resort, 70, 74 85–86, 92
  lounges, 86, 303
  restaurants, 85–86, 272–272
Caribbean Coral Reef Ride, 148
car travel, 14–16
  automobile clubs, 15, 56
  parking, 62 113, 143, 175, 193
  rentals, 63
  road maps, 14–15
  service and maintenance, 56
Casey Jr. Splash 'N' Soak Station, 127

cash machines. See ATMs
Castaway Cay, 311, 312, 314, 317, 343
cell phones, 52, 60
Characters In Flight, 216
check-in and check-out times, 67
Chester & Hester's Dino-Rama!, 202–203
children, traveling with, 46–48
  Birnbaum's Walt Disney World for Kids, 17, 46
  child care, 46, 88
  Disney Cruise Line, 319–320
  lost children, 56–47, 114, 144, 176, 194
  restaurant dining suggestions, 250
  "rider switch" policy at theme parks, 46
  schedules with young children, 34, 36, 38, 40, 41
  special programs for, 82, 88, 230
  stroller rentals, 48, 67, 115, 144, 159, 176, 194, 210
  See also Baby Care Centers
China, 166–167, 254, 259
Christmas festivities, 8, 12, 136–137, 169, 187, 252
Cinderella Castle, 125, 135
Cinderella's Royal Table, 31, 125, 245
Cinderella Wishing Well, 125
Circle of Life, The (film), 150–151
Cirque du Soleil, 12, 20, 24, 45, 215–216
climate. See weather
clothing suggestions, 17
Club Cool, 149
clubs. See BoardWalk; Downtown Disney West Side
Contemporary resort, 68, 76–77
  lounges, 77, 303
  restaurants, 76–77, 273
convention and meeting facilities, 88
Coronado Springs resort, 70, 101–102
  lounges, 101, 303–304
  restaurants, 101, 274
Country Bear Jamboree, 120
credit cards, 58, 115, 144, 176,

194, 226, 257
crowd patterns, 8–9
cruises
  specialty cruises, 231
  See also Disney Cruise Line
Curl by Sammy Duvall, 217

D

Daredevil Disney (theme-park alternative thrill rides), 224
dining. See restaurants
dinner shows, 31, 300
DinoLand U.S.A., 202–204, 205, 264–265
Dinosaur, 203–204
disabilities, hints for travelers with, 50, 53–54, 114, 144, 176, 194, 320, 322
  transportation, 53
  wheelchair rental, 53, 115, 132–133, 144, 159, 176, 194, 210
Discovery Island, 196–197, 205
Disney characters (where to find)
  at Disney's Animal Kingdom, 44, 204, 284–285
  at Disney's Hollywood Studios, 38, 43, 188, 284–285
  at Epcot, 11, 42, 150, 170, 252, 282–283
  at Magic Kingdom, 125, 126, 282–283
  meals with, 104, 282–286, 336
Disney Cruise Line, 309–343
  business services on board, 321
  booking shore excursions, 317
  cancellation policy, 315–316
  checking in, 324–325
  children's programs, 339–340
  deck-by-deck rundown, 325–328
  deposit requirements, 315
  drinking laws, 322
  entertainment, 337–341
    adults only, 339
    children, 339–340
  ground transfers, 316
  Guest Services, 329
  how to book a cruise, 315

identification papers, 317
Internet access, 336
Key to the World, 317
land and sea packages,
    310–311
    Walt Disney World resort
    options, 311
    what's included, 311
laundry facilities, 328
lounges, 336–337
medical matters, 320, 321
packing, 316–317
payment methods, 315
Personal Navigator, 330
pets policy, 323
planning, 314–317
restaurants, 331–336
    meals with Disney
    characters, 336
    reservations, 333, 334
room service, 335
sample itineraries, 312–313
shopping, 341–342
sports, 342–343
staterooms, 317–319
swimming, 342–343
tipping, 323
transportation to, 318
travelers with disabilities, 320,
    322
traveling with children,
    319–320
weddings, 323
Disney Cruise Vacations Air
    Program, 310
Disney Dining Plan, 20, 225
Disney Dollars, 58, 115, 144,
    194
Disney Florist, 11
Disney *Dream* (Disney Cruise
    Line ship), 312
Disney *Fantasy* (Disney Cruise
    Line ship), 312
Disney *Magic* (Disney Cruise
    Line ship), 312
Disney Information Center, 17
Disney Junior—Live on Stage!,
    179–180
DisneyQuest, 45, 216, 269
Disney Vacation Club, 73, 79, 93
Disney *Wonder* (Disney Cruise
    Line ship), 312
Disney World monorail system,
    63–64

Disney Worldwide Conservation
    Fund, The, 203
Disney's Animal Kingdom,
    191–208
    admission prices, 193
    Africa, 198–199, 205
    Asia, 200–201, 205
    best times to visit, 8–9
    camera needs, 194
    Camp Minnie-Mickey, 204
    crowd patterns, 195
    DinoLand U.S.A., 202–205
    disability information, 194
    Discovery Island, 196–197
    Disney characters, where to
    find, 44, 204, 285–285
    entertainment, 206
    first aid, 194
    getting oriented, 194
    Guest Relations, 194
    hours, 12, 193
    information, 194
    Kilimanjaro Safaris, 198, 206
    lockers, 194
    Lost and Found, 194
    lounges, 301
    map, 192
    money matters, 194
    Oasis, The, 195
    parking, 193
    resorts, 98–103
    restaurants, 270–271
    reservations, 265, 299
    same-day re-entry, 194
    sample schedules, 39–40, 44
    security check, 194
    shopping, 205
    stroller and wheelchair
    rentals, 194
    Tip Board, 194, 206
    tips, 206
    transportation to, 193
    travelers with disabilities, 194
Disney's Animal Kingdom
    Lodge, 68–69, 99–100
    lounges, 100, 301
    restaurants, 100, 270–271
Disney's Family Magic Tour, 232
Disney's Fastpass+. *See* Fast-
    pass+
Disney's Hollywood Studios,
    173–190
    admission prices, 175
    attractions, 177–184

    best times to visit, 8–9
    camera needs, 176
    disability information, 176
    Disney characters, where to
    find, 188
    entertainment, 187
    first aid, 176
    getting oriented, 175
    Guest Relations, 176
    holiday happenings, 10–12,
    187
    Hollywood Boulevard, 185
    hours, 13, 175, 187
    lockers, 176
    Lost and Found, 176
    lounges, 304
    map, 174
    money matters, 176
    parking, 175
    restaurants, 175, 260–263
    reservations, 265, 299
    same-day re-entry, 176
    sample schedules, 37–38, 43
    security check, 176
    shopping, 185–186, 188
    stroller and wheelchair
    rentals, 176
    Sunset Boulevard, 185–186
    Tip Board, 176, 188
    tips, 188
    transportation to, 175
    travelers with disabilities, 194
Disney's Magical Express service,
    14, 16, 19, 60, 66, 110
Disney's Magical Holidays
    (December), 8, 12
Disney's Old Key West resort,
    70, 97
    lounges, 97, 304
    restaurants, 97, 275
Disney's PhotoPass, 133
Disney's Saratoga Springs
    Resort & Spa, 70, 96
    lounges, 96, 307
    restaurants, 96, 278
    spa, 96, 229
Disney's Vero Beach Resort, 93
Disney's Winter Summerland
    miniature golf course, 241
DiveQuest, 148, 232
Dixie Landings. *See* Port Orleans
    Riverside
Dolphin resort, 68, 89–90
    lounges, 87, 307–308

restaurants, 87, 278–280
spa, 229–229
Dolphins in Depth, 148, 232
DoubleTree Suites by Hilton, 107–108
Downtown Disney, 210–218
map, 210–211
resorts, 94–97
Downtown Disney Marketplace, 211–214
hours, 13
lounges, 304–305
restaurants, 266–267
shopping, 211–214
transportation to, 210
Downtown Disney West Side, 215–218
hours, 13
kiddie rides, 212
lounges, 304–305
resorts, 94–97
restaurants, 215–217, 266–267
shopping, 217–218
transportation to, 210
Dream Along with Mickey, 135
drinking laws, 56, 322
Dumbo the Flying Elephant, 126

E

Electrical Water Pageant, 226–227
electric cart rentals, 226
Electric Conveyance Vehicles (ECVs), 53, 54, 115, 132, 144, 176, 194, 210, 320
Enchanted Tales with Belle, 127
Enchanted Tiki Room, The, 119
Epcot, 35–36, 42, 141–172
admission prices, 143
best times to visit, 8, 170
camera needs, 144
crowd patterns, 8–9
disability information, 144
Disney characters, where to find, 42, 150, 170
entertainment, 169
first aid, 144
getting oriented, 143
Guest Relations, 144
holiday happenings, 10–12, 169
hours, 13, 143, 170

information, 144
lockers, 144
Lost and Found, 144
lounges, 305–306
map, 142
money matters, 144
parking, 143
resorts, 85–93
restaurants, 251–259
reservations, 31, 42, 153, 244, 299
same-day re-entry, 14
sample schedules, 35–36, 42
security check, 144
stroller and wheelchair rentals, 144
Tip Board, 144, 170
tips, 170
transportation to, 143
travelers with disabilities, 144
See also Future World; World Showcase
Epcot Character Spot, 150
Epcot International Food & Wine Festival, 11, 255
Epcot Seas Aqua Tour, 148, 233
ESPN Wide World of Sports complex, 51, 235, 240
Expedition Everest, 201
Extra Magic Hours, 13, 22, 65

F

Fairytale Garden, 125, 135
Fantasia Gardens Miniature Golf complex, 241
Fantasmic!, 37, 184, 187, 188, 260, 263
Fantasyland, 125–127, 134, 245–246
fast food and snack spots. See restaurants
Fastpass+, 24, 25, 30, 139
Festival of Fantasy Parade, 135
Festival of the Lion King, 198–199
Festival of the Masters art show, 214
Finding Nemo—The Musical, 204
fireworks displays, 8, 11, 135, 136, 137, 153, 169, 184, 226
IllumiNations: Reflections of Earth, 11, 35, 42, 157,

169, 252
first aid, 57–58, 114, 176, 194
fishing, 76, 79, 81, 83, 86, 94, 95, 101, 239
fitness centers. See health clubs
Flag Retreat, 135
Flights of Wonder, 201
florist, 11
foreign currency exchange, 52, 59, 115, 144, 176, 194
Fort Wilderness Resort & Campground, 72, 73, 83–84, 225–227
activities, 225–227
Archery experience, 225
campfire program, 226
family entertainment after dark, 84
lounge, 84, 306
restaurant, 84, 276
transportation to, 84, 227
Four Seasons Orlando, 104–105
France, 159–160, 253, 254
Frontierland, 120–122, 133–134, 246–247
Frontierland Shootin' Arcade, 120
Future World, 45, 145–154, 251–252
Caribbean Coral Reef, 148
Club Cool, 149
Imagination!, 151–152
Innoventions, 146–147
Land, The, 148–151
map, 142
Mission: SPACE, 153–154
restaurants, 251–252
Seas with Nemo & Friends, The, 145, 147, 148
Soarin', 159
Spaceship Earth, 146
Test Track, 152
Turtle Talk with Crush, 147–148
Universe of Energy, 154

G

Germany, 165–166, 253, 257, 306
Ghirardelli Soda Fountain & Chocolate Shop, 267
golf, 81, 96, 105, 236–237
miniature, 241

Gran Fiesta Tour Starring the Three Caballeros, 168
Grand Floridian Resort & Spa, 68–70, 80–81
  lounges, 81, 306–307
  restaurants, 80–81, 275–276
  spa, 81, 228
Grand I (boat for specialty cruises), 231, 272
Great Movie Ride, The, 181–182
Guest Relations, 18, 25, 27, 42, 46, 52, 54, 56, 57, 58, 60, 114, 144, 176, 194, 210, 250, 259, 299
  tips for international travelers, 52
guided tours
  behind-the-scenes tours, 148, 232–234

H

Hall of Presidents, The, 123
Halloween, 12, 136
Haunted Mansion, The, 124
health care. See medical matters
health clubs, 81, 83, 88, 90, 92, 96, 97, 100, 102, 107, 108
Hidden Mickeys, where to find, 139, 171, 189, 207
Hilton, 108–109
Holiday Inn (at the Walt Disney World Resort), 109
holiday happenings, 8, 10–12, 71, 136–137, 169, 187, 234, 252
Holidays Around the World celebration, 8, 12
Hollywood Boulevard, 185
Honey, I Shrunk the Kids Movie Set Adventure, 184
honeymoons, 55
Hoop-Dee-Doo Musical Revue, 20, 84, 225, 287, 299, 300
horseback riding, 227, 242, 299
Hotel Plaza Boulevard, resorts on, 106–110
hotels. See accommodations
hours, 13
  Disney's Animal Kingdom, 193, 206
  Disney's Hollywood Studios, 175, 188

Epcot, 143, 170
Magic Kingdom, 113, 138
House of Blues, 217–218, 267, 304

I

ID cards, 115
IllumiNations: Reflections of Earth, 11, 35, 42, 157, 169, 231, 252
ImageWorks, 152, 170
Imagination!, 145, 151–152
Impressions de France, 159
Indiana Jones Epic Stunt Spectacular, 183
information sources, 17–18, 114, 144, 176, 210
Innoventions, 146–147
insurance, vacation, 50
International Gateway, 154
international travelers, tips for, 52
Internet
  access at WDW, 229
  address for WDW, 8, 25
Italy, 154, 256, 257, 306
It's a Small World, 126
It's Tough to be a Bug!, 197

J

Japan, 161–162, 256, 258
Jedi Training Academy, 187
jogging, 79, 85, 103, 107
Journey Into Imagination With Figment, 152
Jungle Cruise, 118
Just for Kids (special programs), 230

K

Kali River Rapids, 200
Keys to the Kingdom tour (guided tour), 233
Kidcot Fun Stops, 36, 142, 145, 169
Kid's Nite Out, 46
Kilimanjaro Safaris, 198, 206
Kosher meals, 47, 250, 254, 258
Kouzzina by Cat Cora, 272

L

Lake Buena Vista golf course, 236
Land, The, 148–151
Leave a Legacy program, 145
Liberty Belle Riverboat, 123–124
Liberty Square, 123–124, 134, 247
Lights, Motors, Action!–Extreme Stunt Show, 180
Living with the Land, 149
lockers, 56–57, 67,114, 144, 176, 194, 221
lost adults, 60
Lost and Found, 51, 57, 114, 144, 176, 194, 210
lounges, 301–308, 336–337

M

Mad Tea Party, 127
Maelstrom, 167
MagicBands, 20, 24, 27, 31, 64, 67, 257
Magic Behind Our Steam Trains, The (guided tour), 233
Magic Carpets of Aladdin, The, 119
Magic Kingdom, 111–139
  admission prices, 115
  Adventureland, 118–119, 133, 244
  barber shop, 132
  best times to visit, 8–9, 138
  camera needs, 114
  Cinderella Castle, 125, 134–135
  crowd patterns, 8–9, 113, 117, 131, 137
  disability information, 114
  Disney characters, where to find, 136
  entertainment, 135–137
  Fantasyland, 125–127, 134, 245–246
  first aid, 114
  Frontierland, 120-122, 133–134
  getting oriented, 113
  Guest Relations, 114
  holiday happenings, 12, 136
  hours, 13, 113, 138
  information, 114

Liberty Square, 123–124, 134, 247
lockers, 114
Lost and Found, 114
Main Street, U.S.A., 116–117, 131–133, 248–250
Main Street Electrical Parade, The, 137
map, 112
money matters, 115
parking, 113
resorts, 76–84
restaurants, 131, 138, 244–248
    reservations, 244, 299
same-day re-entry, 115
sample schedules, 32–44
security check, 115
shopping, 116, 131–134
stroller and wheelchair rentals, 115, 132–133
Tip Boards, 115, 138
tips, 138
Tomorrowland, 128–130, 134
transportation to, 112
travelers with disabilities, 194
Magic of Disney Animation, The, 178–179
Magic Your Way packages (vacation package), 19, 24, 27
Magnolia golf course, 236
Maharajah Jungle Trek, 200–201
mail, 57, 322
Main Street, U.S.A., 116–117, 131–133, 248–250
Main Street Electrical Parade, 137
Mandara Spa at the Dolphin, 228–229
Many Adventures of Winnie the Pooh, The, 127
map(s)
    Disney's Animal Kingdom, 192
    Disney's Hollywood Studios, 174
    Downtown Disney, 210–211
    Epcot, 142
    Hotel Plaza Boulevard area, 106
    Magic Kingdom, 112
    road maps, 14–15
medical matters, 57–58, 320, 321

meetings and conventions, 88
Mexico, 168, 254, 255, 257, 305–306
Mickey's Backyard Barbecue, 84, 300
Mickey's Boo-to-You Halloween Parade, 12
Mickey's Not-So-Scary Halloween Party, 12
Mickey's Once Upon a Christmas-time Parade, 8, 12
Mickey's PhilharMagic, 125
Mickey's Very Merry Christmas Party, 8, 12, 136
miniature golf, 241
Mission: SPACE, 153
money matters, 58–59
    Coupons, 357
    Disney Cruise Line, 322–323
    Disney Dollars, 58, 115, 144, 194
    Disney's Animal Kingdom, 194
    Disney's Hollywood Studios, 176
    Epcot, 144
    foreign currency exchange, 52, 59, 115, 144, 176, 194
    Magic Kingdom, 115
    payment methods at WDW resorts, 66
    rates at WDW resorts, 72–75
    See also ATMs
money-saving tips, 28–29
    discounts, 29, 233
    making a budget, 30
monorail system. See Disney World monorail system
Monsieur Paul, 254
Monsters, Inc. Laugh Floor, 129
Morocco, 160–161, 254, 256, 259
motels. See accommodations
Mouse Gear, 147
Muppet★Vision 3-D, 183–184
My Disney Experience, 24, 55

N

New Year's Eve celebration, 12, 137, 187
nightlife
    BoardWalk, 219

dinner shows, 300
Downtown Disney West Side, 215–217
lounges, 300–308
specialty cruises, 231
Norway, 167, 252–253, 258

O

Oak Trail golf course, 236
Oasis, The, 195
O Canada!, 156
older travelers, hints for, 50
Orlando-area highways, 62
Orlando International Airport, 14–16
Osborne Family Spectacle of Dancing Lights, The, 12, 187

P

packages (package tours), 8, 18–19
    Magic Your Way package, 19–24, 27
packing suggestions, 17, 316–317
Palm golf course, 236
Pangani Forest Exploration Trail, 199
parades, 8, 12, 135, 137
Paradiso 37, 268
parasailing, 77, 224, 238
parking, 63, 113, 143, 175, 193
Personal Navigator, 330
Peter Pan's Flight, 126
pets, traveling with, 59
pharmacies, 58
Phineas and Ferb, 156
Photo Hunt, 140
physicians. See medical matters
picnicking, 28, 221, 223
pin trading, 35, 83, 133, 147
Pirates of the Caribbean, 119
Planet Hollywood, 267–268
planning the trip, 7–60
    admission prices, 20–24
    booking a cruise, 314
    crowd patterns, 8–9
    getting there, 14–16
    holiday happenings, 10–12
    hours, 13
        Extra Magic Hours, 22
    international travelers, 52

making a budget, 30
money-saving tips, 28–29
packages, 8, 18–19
  Magic Your Way package,
    19–24, 27
packing, 17
reference guide, 56–60
reservations guide, 31
sample schedules, 32–45
special events calendar,
  10–12
teens, tips for, 48
telephone calls, 52
theme park tickets, 21–27
travelers with disabilities,
  53–54
traveling with children, 46–48
traveling without children,
  49–50
weather, 13, 60
weddings and honeymoons,
  55
when to go, 8–12
Polynesian Village resort, 68–69,
  78–79
  lounges, 78, 307
  restaurants, 78–79, 277
Polynesian Village Villas and
  Bungalows, 79
pontoon boats, 231, 238
pony rides, 227
Pop Century, 70, 102
  lounges, 102, 307
  restaurants, 102, 278
Port Orleans French Quarter,
  70, 94
  lounges, 94, 307
  restaurants, 94, 278
Port Orleans Riverside, 70,
  95–96
  lounges, 95, 307
  restaurants, 95, 278
Portobello, 268, 305
post office, 57
prescriptions, 58
Primeval Whirl, 303
Prince Charming Regal
  Carrousel, 125
Princess Fairytale Hall, 126

R

Rafiki's Planet Watch, 199
rainy days, 45, 132

rating system for WDW resorts,
  72–74
refillable mugs, 270
Reflections of China (film),
  166–167
religious services, 59
rental cars, 63
reservations, 65, 244, 299
  for dinner shows, 30, 300
  Disney Dining Plan, 20
  for fishing excursions, 239
  for golf courses, 237
  special room requests, 87
  time line, 31
restaurants, 244–281
  advance planning, 20, 244, 299
  All-Star resorts, 98, 270
  Art of Animation, 271
  Beach Club resort, 87, 281
  Blizzard Beach, 262
  BoardWalk, 91–92, 271–272
  Caribbean Beach resort,
    85–86, 272–273
  Cinderella's Royal Table, 245
  Contemporary resort, 76–77,
    273–274
  Coronado Springs resort, 101,
    274
  dining with children, 250
  dining with Disney characters,
    282–285
  dinner shows, 300
  Disney Cruise Line, 331–335
  Disney Dining Plan, 20, 256
  Disney's Animal Kingdom,
    264–265
  Disney's Animal Kingdom
    Lodge, 100, 270–271
  Disney's Hollywood Studios,
    260–263
  Disney's Old Key West resort,
    97, 275
  Dolphin resort, 89–90,
    278–280
  Downtown Disney, 266–269
  Epcot, 251–259
  ESPN Wide World of Sports
    complex, 235
  Fort Wilderness, 83–84, 275
  Grand Floridian resort, 80–81,
    275–276
  Magic Kingdom, 244–250
  mealtime tips, 247, 259, 263,
    265

Polynesian Village resort,
  78–79, 277
Pop Century, 102, 278
Port Orleans French Quarter,
  94, 278
Port Orleans Riverside, 95, 278
reservations, 244, 299, 334
recommended restaurants,
  286–290
Saratoga Springs, 96, 278
special requests, 254
Swan resort, 89–90, 278
Typhoon Lagoon, 262
Wilderness Lodge, 82–83,
  280–281
Yacht Club resort, 86–87, 281
"rider switch" policy (in the
  theme parks), 46
Rock 'n' Roller Coaster Starring
  Aerosmith, 178

S

sailing, 238–239
salons. See beauty salons
sample schedules, 32–44
Sanaa, 100, 271
scuba diving, 148, 232
Seas with Nemo & Friends, The,
  145, 147–148
security check
  Disney's Animal Kingdom, 194
  Disney's Hollywood Studios, 176
  Epcot, 144
  Magic Kingdom, 115
Segway tours, 84, 227, 234
senior citizens. See older travelers,
  hints for
Senses (spa), 228, 229
Seven Dwarfs Mine Train, 127
Shades of Green, 110
shopping
  Disney Cruise Line, 341–342
  at Disney's Animal Kingdom,
    205
  at Disney's Hollywood
    Studios, 185–186, 188
  at Downtown Disney
    Marketplace, 211–214
  at Downtown Disney West
    Side, 201–204
  at Magic Kingdom,
    131–134
  for necessities, 59

package pickup, 57, 115, 132, 144, 159, 176, 194, 205

See also World Showcase

single travelers, hints for, 51

smoking policies, 60, 218, 244, 306, 323

Soarin', 150

solo travelers, hints for, 51

Sorcerer's of the Magic Kingdom, 122

Space Mountain, 130

Spaceship Earth, 146

spas, 81, 90, 96, 105, 110, 228–229, 242, 343

special events
calendar of, 10–12
weddings & honeymoons, 55
See also holiday happenings

specialty cruises, 231

Spectacle of Lights, The. See Osborne Family Spectacle of Dancing Lights

speedboating, 81

Spirit of Aloha, The, 300

Splash Mountain, 121

sports, 235–242
basketball, 226, 242
biking, 83, 84, 86, 92, 94, 95, 96, 97, 100, 224, 241
boating, 77, 79, 81, 83, 84, 86, 88, 90, 94, 95, 96, 97, 101, 224, 238–229
ESPN Wide World of Sports complex, 51, 235, 240
fishing, 76, 79, 81, 83, 86, 94, 95, 101, 239
golf, 81, 96, 236–237
health clubs, 77, 81, 83, 88, 90, 92, 96, 97, 100, 102, 107, 108
horseback riding, 227, 242
jogging, 79, 85, 103, 107
parasailing, 77, 224, 238
reservations guide, 237, 239, 241, 242
sailing, 238–239
scuba diving, 148, 232
speedboating, 81
stock car racing, 224, 242
surfing, 224
swimming, 77, 79, 81, 83, 86, 88, 90, 92, 94, 95, 96, 97, 98, 100, 102, 103,

225, 342–343
tennis, 77, 88, 90, 92, 96, 97, 100, 237
tubing, 77, 224, 239
volleyball, 77, 87, 90, 97, 101, 105, 108, 110, 225, 226, 240, 242
wakeboarding, 77, 239
waterskiing, 224, 239

stamps, 57, 322

Starbucks, 249, 252, 269

Star Tours—The Adventures Continue, 183

Stitch's Great Escape, 128

stock car racing, 224, 242

stroller rentals, 48, 67, 115, 144, 159, 176, 194, 210

Studio Backlot Tour, 180–181

Sunset Boulevard, 185–186

surfing, 224

Swan resort, 68, 89–90
lounges, 90, 307–308
restaurants, 89–90, 278–280

swimming, 77, 79, 81, 83, 86, 88, 90, 92, 94, 95, 96, 97, 98, 100, 102, 103, 105, 225, 342–343

Swiss Family Treehouse, 118

T

Tables In Wonderland, 274

taxi service, 14, 64, 210

teenagers, tips for, 48

telephone calls
cell phones, 52, 60, 323
dos and don'ts, 52
local, 60

temperature, year-round, 13

tennis, 77, 88, 90, 92, 96, 97, 100, 105, 237

Test Track, 152

tickets. See admission prices

tipping, 60, 323

Todd English's bluezoo, 90, 104, 280, 308

Tomorrowland, 128–130, 134

Tomorrowland Speedway, 130

Tomorrowland Transit Authority PeopleMover, 129

Tom Sawyer Island, 120–121

tours. See guided tours; packages

Toy Story Mania!, 180

trail rides, 227, 242

train travel, 16

transportation, 14–16, 63–64
from airport to WDW, 14
to Blizzard Beach, 223
to Disney Cruise Line, 318
Disney's Magical Express service, 14, 16, 19, 60, 66, 110
to Disney's Animal Kingdom, 193
to Disney's Hollywood Studios, 175
to Downtown Disney, 210
to Epcot, 143
to ESPN Wide World of Sports complex, 240
to Fort Wilderness, 84, 227
ID requirements, 67
to Magic Kingdom, 113
Orlando-area highways, 62
taxi service, 14, 64, 210
travelers with disabilities, 53
traveling arrangements, 17–18
to Typhoon Lagoon, 221
WDW transportation system, 63–64
See also air travel; bus travel; car travel; train travel

Transportation and Ticket Center (TTC), 27, 53, 57, 58, 63, 64, 77, 79, 81, 83, 84, 113, 114, 143, 193, 242

traveler's checks, 58–59

Tree of Life, The, 196–197

Triceratop Spin, 203

Tri-Circle-D Ranch, 225, 227

tubing, 77, 224, 239

Turtle Talk with Crush, 147–148

Twilight Zone™ Tower of Terror, The, 177

Typhoon Lagoon, 220–221, 262

U

Under the Sea—Journey of The Little Mermaid, 127

Undiscovered Future World, The (guided tour), 233

United Kingdom, 157–158, 254–255, 259, 306

Universe of Energy, 154

V

vacation insurance, 50
valet parking, 62
Village Traders, 166
VIP Tours, 231
visual disabilities, hints for
    guests with, 54
volleyball, 77, 87, 90, 97, 101,
    105, 108, 110, 225, 226,
    240, 242
Voyage of The Little Mermaid, 179

W

wagon rides, 12, 84, 227
wakeboarding, 77, 239
Walt Disney: One Man's Dream,
    182–183
Walt Disney's Carousel of
    Progress, 130
Walt Disney Travel Company,
    8, 18, 19, 51, 106
Walt Disney World Marathon
    Weekend, 10
Walt Disney World Railroad,
    34, 113, 117, 120, 122, 233
Wanyama Safari, 233–234
water parks, 13, 220–223
    Blizzard Beach, 222–223
    Typhoon Lagoon, 220–221
waterskiing, 224, 239
weather, 13, 60
    rainy days, 45, 132
Websites
    www.disneycruise.com, 310
    www.disneyhoneymoonregistry
        .com, 55
    www.disneysports.com, 240
    www.disneyvacationclub.com, 93
    www.disneyweddings.com,
        55
    www.disneyworld.com, 8
    www.disneyworld.com/dining/,
        66, 244
    www.swandolphin.com, 89
weddings and honeymoons, 53,
    105, 323
wheelchair rentals, 53, 115,
    132–133, 144, 159, 176,
    194, 210
Wild Africa Trek, 234
Wild by Design (guided tour),
    234

Wilderness Back Trail Adventure,
    234
Wilderness Cabins, 68, 83–84
Wilderness Explorers, 197
Wilderness Lodge & Villas, 68,
    82–83
    lounges, 82, 308
    restaurants, 280–281
Winged Encounters—The
    Kingdom Takes Flight, 197
Wishes Fireworks Show, 135,
    231, 249, 272, 273
Wolfgang Puck Cafe, 217,
    269
World Showcase, 155–168,
    252–259
    American Adventure, The,
        162–163, 258
    Canada, 156, 253, 259
    China, 166–167, 254, 259
    entertainment, 169
    France, 159–160, 253, 254,
        257, 258
    Germany, 165–166, 253,
        259
    International Gateway, 155,
        158–165
    Italy, 164, 256, 257
    Japan, 161–162, 256, 258
    map, 142
    Mexico, 168, 254, 255, 257
    Morocco, 160–161, 254, 256,
        259
    Norway, 161, 252, 258
    performers, 169
    restaurants, 158, 170,
        252–259
    shopping, 155–168
    Showcase Plaza, 168
    stroller and wheelchair
        rentals, 144
    United Kingdom, 157–158,
        254, 259
Wyndham Lake Buena Vista
    Resort, 108

Y

Yacht Club resort, 68, 72,
    86–88, 92
    lounges, 87, 308
    restaurants, 87, 281
Yuletide Fantasy (guided tour),
    234

Where in the World?
(photo locations)

Magic Kingdom:
1. Train station, inside front gate
2. Main Street Cinema
3. Tikis, near The Jungle Cruise
4. Pinocchio statue, in the Castle Hub area of Main Street, U.S.A.
5. Liberty Belle Riverboat
6. It's a Small World sign
7. Mickey's PhilharMagic sign
8. Under the Sea—Journey of The Little Mermaid

Epcot:
1. Canopy above the plaza in Future World
2. Torii gate in Japan
3. Universe of Energy pavilion
4. Sign in front of The American Adventure pavilion
5. Italy
6. Spaceship Earth entrance
7. Viking statue in Norway
8. Monorail in front of Test Track

Disney's Hollywood Studios:
1. Left side of Studios arch
2. Above Rock 'n' Roller Coaster entrance plaza
3. The Streets of America
4. Animation Courtyard statue
5. Dinosaur Gertie's Ice Cream of Extinction
6. Stage 1 Company Store entrance
7. Honey, I Shrunk the Kids Movie Set Adventure
8. The Darkroom shop

Animal Kingdom:
1. Chester & Hester's Dino-Rama sign
2. Park entrance
3. Bird above Discovery Island Bridge
4. Rain Forest Cafe outdoor space
5. The back of the Tree of Life (from the path between Asia and Harambe)
6. Expedition Everest
7. Anandapur Ice Cream (in Asia)
8. Inside Serka Zong Bazaar (by the exit of Expedition Everest)

Coupons

10% OFF
food and beverages

(discount excludes alcohol)

Call 407-939-3463 for reservations.

Subject to terms and conditions on reverse side

10% OFF
ANY PURCHASE
(valid on food & beverage only)

Subject to terms and conditions on reverse side

10% OFF

A chocolate purchase
or $1.00 off a specialty sundae

Subject to terms and conditions on reverse side

10% OFF

food and beverages

(discount excludes alcohol and tax)

Subject to terms and conditions on reverse side

20% OFF
food and beverages

Experience a world of magical flavors
at Joffrey's Coffee and Tea Co. kiosks
throughout Walt Disney World parks and resorts.

Subject to terms and conditions on reverse side

$5 OFF
child care services

AND/OR $5 OFF ANY BABY EQUIPMENT RENTAL
OF 4 DAYS OR MORE

Subject to terms and conditions on reverse side

Coupons

HOUSE OF BLUES

15% OFF

lunch or dinner for up to 8 guests in the HOB Restaurant (discount on food only)

Enjoy distinctive Southern-inspired cuisine in an enjoyable atmosphere filled with creative folk art. Opens daily at 11:30 A.M. For reservations, call 407-934-2623.

Subject to terms and conditions on reverse side

FULTON'S CRAB HOUSE

20% OFF

food and beverages for up to 4 guests

(discount excludes alcohol)

For reservations, call 407-934-2628.

Subject to terms and conditions on reverse side

WOLFGANG PUCK Grand Cafe

20% OFF
food and beverages

(discount excludes alcohol)

For reservations, call 407-938-9653.

Subject to terms and conditions on reverse side

Paradiso 37 — TASTE OF THE AMERICAS

10% OFF

food only at lunch and dinner

Subject to terms and conditions on reverse side

BONGOS CUBAN CAFE

15% OFF
food and beverages

(discount excludes alcohol)

Subject to terms and conditions on reverse side

PORTOBELLO
COUNTRY · ITALIAN · TRATTORIA

20% OFF

food and beverages for up to 4 guests

(discount excludes alcohol)

For reservations, call 407-934-8888.

Subject to terms and conditions on reverse side

TERMS AND CONDITIONS

Offer good at Fulton's Crab House.

Located at Downtown Disney.

Reproductions of coupon not accepted.

Coupon may not be redeemed for cash in whole or in part. Offer subject to change without notice. Coupon cannot be combined with any other offer or discount.

All minors must be accompanied by a paying adult.

www.fultonscrabhouse.com

Expires 12/31/15

TERMS AND CONDITIONS

Valid only in the HOB Restaurant at Downtown Disney® West Side.

Excludes alcohol, tax, and gratuity.

One offer per check for up to 8 guests.

Must present coupon to receive offer.

www.hob.com/orlando

Expires 12/20/15

TERMS AND CONDITIONS

Located at Downtown Disney.

Coupon cannot be combined with any offer.

This offer does not include beverages.

Reproductions of coupon not accepted in whole or in part.

Offer subject to change without notice.

Expires 12/31/15

TERMS AND CONDITIONS

Located at Downtown Disney.

Reproductions of coupon not accepted.

Coupon may not be redeemed for cash in whole or in part. Offer subject to change without notice.

All minors must be accompanied by a paying adult.

www.wolfgangpuckorlando.com

© Disney

Expires 12/31/15

TERMS AND CONDITIONS

Offer good at Portobello Country Italian Trattoria. Located at Downtown Disney.

Reproductions of coupon not accepted.

Coupon may not be redeemed for cash in whole or in part. Offer subject to change without notice. Coupon cannot be combined with any other offer or discount.

All minors must be accompanied by a paying adult.

www.portobellorestaurant.com

Expires 12/31/15

TERMS AND CONDITIONS

Located at Downtown Disney.

Coupon cannot be combined with any offer.

Reproductions of coupon not accepted in whole or in part.

Offer subject to change without notice.

Facebook.com/BongosCubanCafeOrlando

Expires 12/31/15

Coupons

10% OFF

Nine Dragons Restaurant, Lotus Blossom Café, and merchandise

(offer good for lunch and dinner; excludes alcohol)

Subject to terms and conditions on reverse side

10% OFF

Food, beverages, and merchandise

(offer good for lunch and dinner; excludes alcohol)

Subject to terms and conditions on reverse side

10% OFF LUNCH

Food and beverages for up to 4 Guests

(discount excludes alcohol)

Subject to terms and conditions on reverse side

10% OFF

Food, beverages, and merchandise

(offer good for lunch and dinner; excludes alcohol)

Subject to terms and conditions on reverse side

**Save on Accommodations
on select dates in 2015**

*For offer details and to check availability call 407-939-7652
and ask about the Birnbaum Offer.*

Subject to terms and conditions on reverse side

**Save on Accommodations
on select dates in 2015**

*For offer details and to check availability call 407-939-7652
and ask about the Birnbaum Offer.*

Subject to terms and conditions on reverse side

Coupons

Disney's Dolphins in Depth

10% OFF admission for up to 4 Guests

Disney's Dolphins in Depth is an educational dolphin interaction program open to all guests ages 13 and up.

Call 407-WDW-TOUR (407-939-8687)
for reservations.

Subject to terms and conditions on reverse side

15% OFF
admission to the Behind the Seeds Tour at The Land for up to 10 Guests

Bring the entire family backstage for a one-hour, interactive tour of the greenhouses and fish farm at The Land. For same-day reservations, present coupon at the Tour Desk next to the entrance of Soarin'. Or call ahead to 407-WDW-TOUR (407-939-8687) and mention the Birnbaum Offer. Admission to Epcot® is required.

Subject to terms and conditions on reverse side

10% OFF
Epcot® Dive Quest admission

Epcot® Dive Quest is a scuba-diving adventure open to all certified scuba divers ages 10 and up.

Call 407-WDW-TOUR (407-939-8687)
for reservations.

Subject to terms and conditions on reverse side

10% OFF
ADMISSION

This amazing aqua adventure takes you on a tour of the aquarium and into the water to explore The Seas with Nemo & Friends marine environment using a Scuba Assisted Snorkel unit.

Call 407-WDW-TOUR (407-939-8687)
for reservations.

Subject to terms and conditions on reverse side

20% OFF
2-Hour WALT DISNEY WORLD® Guided Fishing Excursion for you and up to 4 guests.

To make your reservation, call 407-WDW-BASS (407-939-2277) or visit *www.disneyworldfishing.com* and mention the coupon in the Additional Comments section of the request form. This coupon must be presented upon arrival.

Subject to terms and conditions on reverse side

COMPLIMENTARY
MICKEY MOUSE METAL BAG TAG &
SAME DAY REPLAY

Subject to terms and conditions on the reverse side

Book your tee time now by calling **407-WDW-GOLF** or go online at **www.disneygolf.com**

Operated By

TERMS AND CONDITIONS

Admission to Epcot® theme park is required.

Reproductions of coupons will not be accepted.

Coupon may not be redeemed for cash
in whole or in part.

Offer subject to change without notice.

All minors must be accompanied by a paying adult.

All tours and experiences are subject to availability.

© Disney

Expires 12/30/15

TERMS AND CONDITIONS

Reproductions of coupon not accepted. Coupon may
not be redeemed for cash in whole or in part.

Offer subject to change without notice.

All minors must be accompanied by a paying adult.

All tours and experiences are subject to availability.

© Disney

Expires 12/31/15

TERMS AND CONDITIONS

Epcot admission is not required.

Reservations recommended and are subject to
availability. Ages 8 years and above. All minors
must be accompanied by a paying adult.

Reproductions of coupon not accepted. Coupon
may not be redeemed for cash in whole or in part.

No jewelry allowed in the aquarium; no cameras
allowed in backstage areas. Forfeit entire price
of the tour if you fail to show or cancel within
2 days of your reservation.

Offer subject to change without notice.

© Disney

Expires 12/31/15

TERMS AND CONDITIONS

Reproductions of coupon not accepted.

Coupon may not be redeemed for cash
in whole or in part.

Offer subject to change without notice.

All minors must be accompanied by a paying adult.

All tours and experiences are subject to availability.

© Disney

Expires 12/31/15

TERMS AND CONDITIONS

Offer good on Disney's Palm, Disney's Magnolia, and
Disney's Lake Buena Vista Golf Courses. Must present
coupon at check-in to receive this offer. Photocopies
or other replications will not be accepted. Offer only
valid with non-discounted Day Guest and Resort Guest
rates. Complimentary replay round is on a same-day,
space-available basis. Offer does not apply to replay
rounds booked prior to the day of play. Complimentary
replay round must be played on the same course and
on the same day as the original round. This may not
be combined with any other offer and is not valid for
twilight, super twilight, or other discount offers. Offer
not valid for tournament, group, league, or any other
organized group play. May not be redeemed for cash.
Offer subject to change without notice.

© Disney

Expires 12/31/15

TERMS AND CONDITIONS

All excursions are subject to availability.

Prices and terms are subject to change without notice.

Offer not valid with any other discounted rate.

This coupon may not be redeemed for cash in whole
or in part, and may not be reproduced.

© Disney

Expires 12/31/15

Coupons

FREE UPGRADE

Book at *www.alamo.com*
or call 1-800-462-5266.

Reference Coupon Code AU5269DJK
at the time of reservation.

Subject to terms and conditions on reverse side

20% OFF
Any Exotic Driving Experience

Get behind the wheel of an exotic supercar and
make your driving dreams a reality.

1-855-822-0149

www.ExoticDriving.com

Subject to terms and conditions on reverse side

LOCATED AT DISNEY'S CONTEMPORARY RESORT

15% OFF ALL SAMMY DUVALL'S
WATERSPORTS CENTRE ACTIVITIES

- PARASAILING
- WATERSKIING, WAKEBOARDING, AND FAMILY TUBING
- PERSONAL WATERCRAFT

RESERVATIONS ARE SUGGESTED.
CALL 407-939-0754 FOR MORE INFORMATION.

Subject to terms and conditions on reverse side

CHARACTERS IN FLIGHT
operated by

$8 OFF adult tickets 8:30–10:30 A.M.
$2 OFF kid tickets 8:30–10:30 A.M.
20% OFF all tickets after 10:30 A.M.

Take flight in the world's largest tethered
helium balloon. (Weather permitting)

Subject to terms and conditions on reverse side

10% OFF
One single or double stroller rental

To make a reservation, go to
www.magicstrollers.com/Birnbaum

Subject to terms and conditions on reverse side

20% OFF
ONE-TIME MEMBERSHIP FEE

To sign up for "the purple place to store
your vacation stuff," go to
www.ownerslocker.com/Birnbaum

Subject to terms and conditions on reverse side

TERMS AND CONDITIONS

Reservations required. Driver release fee and applicable sales tax will be charged at the time of booking. Discount must be applied by calling 1-855-822-0149 and referencing promo code **Birnbaum 2015**.

Walt Disney World Speedway
(3450 N. World Drive, Lake Buena Vista, FL 32810)

Redeemable on any EDE operating day in 2015. For 2015 dates/times, visit *www.ExoticDriving.com* or call 1-855-822-0149. Offer valid at Walt Disney World Speedway only. Not valid on previous purchases, special or group events, or gift cards. Cannot be combined with any other offer. Driving Experience Age Restrictions: You must be at least 18 years old with a valid driver's license to participate in the Driving experience at Walt Disney World® Speedway.

Expires 12/31/15

Rent a compact through midsize vehicle, now through December 31, 2015. One coupon per Alamo rental and void once redeemed. Offer is subject to standard rental conditions. Blackout dates may apply. 24-hour advance reservation required. Not valid with any other discount or promotional rate. Subject to availability and valid only at these participating Orlando, FL, Alamo locations: Buena Vista Place Hotel, Orlando Walt Disney Car Care Center, Orlando International Airport, Shades of Green, Walt Disney World Dolphin. Taxes, other governmentally-authorized or imposed surcharges (including GST/VAT), license and concession recoupment fees, airport and airport facility fees, fuel, one-way rental charge and optional items (such as CDW up to US $30 per day) are extra. In the U.S. check your insurance and/or credit card for rental vehicle coverage. Renter and additional driver(s) must meet standard age, driver and credit requirements. 24-hour advance reservation required. Availability is limited. Subject to change without notice. Blackout dates may apply. Void where prohibited. Coupon VOID if bought, bartered or sold for cash. ©2014 Alamo Rent A Car. All rights reserved. In the U.S., offer valid for a one-car-class upgrade applied at the time of reservation. Must present original coupon at time of rental.

TERMS AND CONDITIONS

Located at Downtown Disney® West Side.

Coupon cannot be combined with any other offer.

Reproductions of coupon not accepted in whole or in part.

Minors must be accompanied by a paying adult.

Offer subject to change without notice.

Expires 12/31/15

TERMS AND CONDITIONS

Must present coupon at check-in to receive discount.
Discount does not apply to merchandise.
Call for activity restrictions.
All activities are subject to availability.

Sammy Duvall's reserves the right to cancel due to inclement weather.

Terms and conditions subject to change without notice. Coupon not valid with any other discount. Coupon cannot be copied or reproduced. Coupon cannot be redeemed for cash.

For more information, visit *www.sammyduvall.com* or call (407) 939-0754.

Expires 12/31/15

TERMS AND CONDITIONS

Limit one Owner's Locker Membership per unique coupon code. Owner's Locker reserves the right to require that this coupon be presented when the locker is picked up. Sign-up must be made online at: *www.OwnersLocker.com/Birnbaum*

The coupon code below must be entered to sign up. The unique coupon code can only be used once. Not valid with any other promotion.

Subject to change without notice

Coupon code:

936815715

Expires 12/31/15

TERMS AND CONDITIONS

Limit one stroller reservation per unique coupon code. Reservation must be made online at *www.magicstrollers.com/Birnbaum*

The coupon code below must be entered to make the reservation. The unique coupon code can only be used once. This coupon must be returned with the stroller at the end of the rental to receive the discount. Not valid with any other promotion. Subject to change without notice.

Coupon code:

849725815

Expires 12/31/15

Coupons

B BASIN
15% OFF Merchandise

Subject to terms and conditions on reverse side

SOMETHING SILVER®
www.somethingsilver.com

15% OFF
ENTIRE PURCHASE

OFFERING STYLISH, HIGH QUALITY
JEWELRY FROM TOP NATIONAL AND
INTERNATIONAL DESIGNER COLLECTIONS

Subject to terms and conditions on reverse side

Located at DOWNTOWN DISNEY® West Side

⊙ curl®
by sammyduvall

10% OFF
all Curl® merchandise

**Nixon • Roxy • Tom's • Billabong
Reef • Oakley • Maui Jim**

For information, call 407-842-1302.
Subject to terms and conditions on reverse side

OFFICIAL RUNNING RETAILER
run Disney

FREE
Videotaped Gait Analysis

to determine the most appropriate shoe for specific
foot types and styles of running or walking
(A $50 VALUE)

Subject to terms and conditions on reverse side

Pack more magic into your Disney vacation
with the *Disney Rewards*® Visa® Card and
get dreamy rewards and amazing perks.*

Plus, get a
$50 statement credit
after first purchase.

Apply today.

Visit **DisneyVisaOffer.com/Birnbaum**
or call 1-800-440-3733 and mention
key code 6DQC05.

*See back for details.

Let's create some magic.™